D1452498

HISTORICAL DICTIONARIES OF RELIGIONS, PHILOSOPHIES, AND MOVEMENTS
Edited by Jon Woronoff

1. *Buddhism,* by Charles S. Prebish, 1993
2. *Mormonism,* by Davis Bitton, 1994. *Out of print. See No. 32.*
3. *Ecumenical Christianity,* by Ans Joachim van der Bent, 1994
4. *Terrorism,* by Sean Anderson and Stephen Sloan, 1995. *Out of Print. See No. 41.*
5. *Sikhism,* by W. H. McLeod, 1995
6. *Feminism,* by Janet K. Boles and Diane Long Hoeveler, 1995
7. *Olympic Movement,* by Ian Buchanan and Bill Mallon, 1995. *Out of print. See No. 39.*
8. *Methodism,* by Charles Yrigoyen Jr. and Susan E. Warrick, 1996
9. *Orthodox Church,* by Michael Prokurat, Alexander Golitzin, and Michael D. Peterson, 1996
10. *Organized Labor,* by James C. Docherty, 1996
11. *Civil Rights Movement,* by Ralph E. Luker, 1997
12. *Catholicism,* by William J. Collinge, 1997
13. *Hinduism,* by Bruce M. Sullivan, 1997
14. *North American Environmentalism,* by Edward R. Wells and Alan M. Schwartz, 1997
15. *Welfare State,* by Bent Greve, 1998
16. *Socialism,* by James C. Docherty, 1997
17. *Bahá'í Faith,* by Hugh C. Adamson and Philip Hainsworth, 1998
18. *Taoism,* by Julian F. Pas in cooperation with Man Kam Leung, 1998
19. *Judaism,* by Norman Solomon, 1998
20. *Green Movement,* by Elim Papadakis, 1998
21. *Nietzscheanism,* by Carol Diethe, 1999
22. *Gay Liberation Movement,* by Ronald J. Hunt, 1999
23. *Islamic Fundamentalist Movements in the Arab World, Iran, and Turkey,* by Ahmad S. Moussalli, 1999
24. *Reformed Churches,* by Robert Benedetto, Darrell L. Guder, and Donald K. McKim, 1999
25. *Baptists,* by William H. Brackney, 1999
26. *Cooperative Movement,* by Jack Shaffer, 1999
27. *Reformation and Counter-Reformation,* by Hans J. Hillerbrand, 2000
28. *Shakers,* by Holley Gene Duffield, 2000

29. *United States Political Parties,* by Harold F. Bass Jr., 2000
30. *Heidegger's Philosophy,* by Alfred Denker, 2000
31. *Zionism,* by Rafael Medoff and Chaim I. Waxman, 2000
32. *Mormonism,* 2nd ed., by Davis Bitton, 2000
33. *Kierkegaard's Philosophy,* by Julia Watkin, 2001
34. *Hegelian Philosophy,* by John W. Burbidge, 2001
35. *Lutheranism,* by Günther Gassmann in cooperation with Duane H. Larson and Mark W. Oldenburg, 2001
36. *Holiness Movement,* by William Kostlevy, 2001
37. *Islam,* by Ludwig W. Adamec, 2001
38. *Shinto,* by Stuart D. B. Picken, 2002
39. *Olympic Movement,* 2nd ed., by Ian Buchanan and Bill Mallon, 2001
40. *Slavery and Abolition,* by Martin A. Klein, 2002
41. *Terrorism,* 2nd ed., by Sean Anderson and Stephen Sloan, 2002
42. *New Religious Movements,* by George D. Chryssides, 2001
43. *Prophets in Islam and Judaism,* by Scott B. Noegel and Brannon M. Wheeler, 2002
44. *The Friends (Quakers),* by Margery Post Abbott, Mary Ellen Chijioke, Pink Dandelion, and John William Oliver, Jr., 2003
45. *Lesbian Liberation Movement: Still the Rage,* JoAnne Myers, 2003
46. *Descartes and Cartesian Philosophy,* by Roger Ariew, Dennis Des Chene, Douglas M. Jesseph, Tad M. Schmaltz, and Theo Verbeek, 2003
47. *Witchcraft,* by Michael D. Bailey, 2003
48. *Unitarian Universalism*, by Mark W. Harris, 2004

Historical Dictionary of Unitarian Universalism

Mark W. Harris

Historical Dictionaries of Religions, Philosophies, and Movements, No. 48

The Scarecrow Press, Inc.
Lanham, Maryland, and Oxford
2004

SCARECROW PRESS, INC.

Published in the United States of America
by Scarecrow Press, Inc.
A wholly owned subsidiary of
The Rowman & Littlefield Publishing Group, Inc.
4501 Forbes Boulevard, Suite 200, Lanham, Maryland 20706
www.scarecrowpress.com

PO Box 317
Oxford
OX2 9RU, UK

British Library Cataloguing in Publication Information Available

Library of Congress Cataloging-in-Publication Data

Harris, Mark W.
Historical dictionary of Unitarian Universalism / Mark W. Harris.
p. cm. — (Historical dictionaries of religions, philosophies, and movements ; no. 48)
Includes bibliographical references.
ISBN 0-8108-4869-4 (alk. paper)
1. Unitarian Universalist churches—Dictionaries. 2. Unitarian Universalist Association—Dictionaries. 3. Unitarian Universalist Churches—History—Dictionaries. 4. Unitarian Universalist Association—History—Dictionaries. I. Title. II. Series.
BX9809 .H37 2003
289.1'03—dc21

2003011871

∞™ The paper used in this publication meets the minimum requirements of American National Standard for Information Sciences—Permanence of Paper for Printed Library Materials, ANSI/NISO Z39.48-1992.
Manufactured in the United States of America.

Contents

Editor's Foreword

Among the many religions included in this series, the Unitarian Universalist is certainly one of the smaller in numbers. But it is far from being small in its impact on the world around it. Rejecting the constraints of other Christian denominations, it sought tolerance for itself, and surprisingly, freely granted tolerance to others. Thus it has evolved in its principles and practices over a relatively short lifetime and shows every sign of developing further in the future, reaching beyond Christianity to embrace what is good in other, more diverse religions. It has also regularly been at the forefront in fighting for social causes, many and diverse, including abolition, temperance, women's suffrage, pacifism, educational reform, environmentalism, and more. This has not been without strain either, and it has not always been easy to keep its members together and also on happy terms with the rest of society. Yet, looking back, it is amazing not only how far the UUs have come, it is even more startling to see just how many outsiders they brought along with them.

This Historical Dictionary of Unitarian Universalism adopts the standard format of chronology, introduction, dictionary, and bibliography. In this case, the dictionary section is even more important than usual, and its person entries are particularly meaningful. For, despite its limited membership, this denomination has generated an incredible number of "famous" people, or perhaps numerous famous people have generated it. This includes not only persons of note within the religious community but also in countless other sectors. At times it reads like a who's who of literature, social work, education, politics, and even science. While entries may sometimes be long, they show how members were drawn to the church, adapted to and shaped it, attracted others and sometimes, in fact, left themselves. It is probably through these biographies that readers can best sense what the Unitarian Universalist experience is all about.

This volume was written by Mark W. Harris, who is presently minister of the First Parish of Watertown (Unitarian Universalist) in Massachusetts, the heartland of the denomination. Prior to that, he was student minister in Oakland and Davis, California, minister in Palmer and Milton, Massachusetts, as well as minister briefly in both Sheffield and London, England. So, he has a good overview of the broader situation. He also knows the administrative side, having been director of information at the Unitarian Universalist Association (UUA) for four years. But it takes a bit more than that to write a historical dictionary, so it is important to mention that he was once in a doctoral program in American history and is a former president of the Unitarian Universalist Historical Society. During his time with the UUA, he served as historian and archivist. Over the past two decades, Rev. Harris has written a number of pamphlets and publications, although clearly nothing of this impressive scope, which covers several centuries of history, on several continents, and shows where Unitarian Universalism has come from and where it is heading.

Jon Woronoff
Series Editor

Acknowledgments

This book has been at least eight years in the making. That period of time has given me a chance to assess some of the important recent studies of the Unitarian Universalist movement. For the last two years, I have been teaching history to lay leaders in the summertime and also teaching congregational polity to seminarians. I am grateful to all those people, including my student ministers in Watertown, who have in some way participated in stimulating discussions about our history. During the course of writing this book, I have been encouraged and helped by many people along the way. Both of my mentors in the ministry, Charles Slap and Arnold Crompton, are deceased, but I want to especially mention Dr. Crompton, who wrote fine works on Unitarianism in the West and Thomas Starr King and inspired me with his great stories. Although I was never his student, all Unitarian Universalist historians are forever indebted to the work of Conrad Wright, who always called us to task when I was on the board of the Unitarian Universalist Historical Society.

This work has been made possible by specific instances of assistance. Those people I would like to acknowledge are John Hurley and Jean Hartman of the Unitarian Universalist Association, Fran O'Donnell of the Andover Harvard Library, and especially her predecessor there, Alan Seaburg. Alan's brother Carl was my predecessor at the UUA. Until he died in 1998, he was a fine historian, good friend, and continuing inspiration. George "Hoppy" Robinson, now deceased, told me all about Lewis Latimer, and Leo Collins helped with information about ministers who served First or Second Church of Boston. Finally, Andrew Hill of Edinburgh, Scotland, was especially helpful in providing international updates. Special thanks to my colleague and summertime neighbor Peter Richardson, who read portions of the manuscript for accuracy. I am sure there are factual errors, and I take full responsibility for them. If any reader discovers such errors, please inform me. My wife, the Rev. Andrea Greenwood, has borne the consequences of having a missing husband sometimes during the past eight years while I wrote this tome. I am forever in her debt. I want to especially thank her for her encouragement to undertake this project. It happened because she said, "You can do it." Finally, I would like to dedicate this dictionary to my four boys, Joel, Levi, Dana, and Asher. They represent the future of my Unitarian Universalist faith.

List of Acronyms and Abbreviations

AUW	Alliance of Unitarian Women
AHA	American Humanist Association
AUA	American Unitarian Association
AUW	Association of Universalist Women
AYS	*About Your Sexuality* (*See also* Sexuality, About Your)
CUC	Canadian Unitarian Council
CLF	Church of the Larger Fellowship
CLC	Council of Liberal Churches
EUU	European Unitarian Universalists
FRH	Fellowship of Religious Humanists
FCF	Free Church Fellowship
FRA	Free Religious Association
GA	General Assembly
IARF	International Association for Religious Freedom
ICUU	International Council of Unitarians and Universalists
LREDA	Liberal Religious Educators Association
LRY	Liberal Religious Youth
MFC	Ministerial Fellowship Committee
UUA	Unitarian Universalist Association
UUHS	Unitarian Universalist Historical Society
UUMA	Unitarian Universalist Ministers Association
UUSC	Unitarian Universalist Service Committee
UUWF	Unitarian Universalist Women's Federation
UCA	Universalist Church of America
WUC	Western Unitarian Conference
YPCU	Young People's Christian Union
YPRU	Young People's Religious Union
YRUU	Young Religious Unitarian Universalists

Chronology

325 Nicene Creed adopted at Council of Nicea establishes dogma of the Trinity.

553 Emperor Justinian gets the Council of Constantinople to declare Origen's universalism a heresy.

1531 Michael Servetus publishes *On the Errors of the Trinity*.

1533 Michael Servetus is burned at the stake in Geneva.

1566 Francis David preaches against the doctrine of the Trinity.

1568 King John Sigismund (the Unitarian King of Transylvania) proclaims the earliest edict of complete religious toleration, the Edict of Torda.

1579 Francis David, condemned as a heretic, dies in prison.

1579 Faustus Socinus arrives in Poland.

1585 Founding of the Rakow Press in Poland (the first official Unitarian press).

1620 Plymouth colony founded, oldest parish in North America (later becomes Unitarian).

1629–1630 Massachusetts Bay Colony

1740s Great Awakening when Standing Order of Congregational Churches began to split along Evangelical and Rational lines.

1741 George de Bennevile emigrates to Pennsylvania and starts preaching a Universalist gospel.

1750 James Relly, an associate of the evangelist George Whitefield, withdraws from this connection and establishes himself as an independent preacher of Universalism.

1759 *Union* (a theological treatise of universal salvation) by James Relly published in London.

1770 John Murray lands in America. On September 30, Murry preaches his first sermon in America in the meeting house of Thomas Potter.

1774 Essex Street Chapel opened in London (marking the beginning of permanently organized Unitarianism in England).

1777 Caleb Rich organizes The General Society (Universalist) to ordain ministers and issue preaching licenses.

1779 First Universalist Church in America is founded in Gloucester, Massachusetts.

1785 The first Universalist convention with delegates from churches is held in Oxford, Massachusetts.

1785 Liturgy of King's Chapel, Boston, is revised, omitting references to the Trinity.

1786 Gloucester Universalists successfully contest the right of the state to raise taxes for the established church.

1787 Congregation of King's Chapel, disregarding Episcopal procedures, ordains lay reader James Freeman as its minister, thereby becoming the first independent church of Unitarian beliefs.

1791 Riots against Joseph Priestley and other Unitarians in Birmingham, England.

1793 Universalist General Convention

1794 Joseph Priestley brings Unitarianism to Philadelphia.

1803 Winchester Profession of Faith is adopted by Universalists at Winchester, New Hampshire.

1805 Henry Ware elected Hollis Professor of Divinity at Harvard; Unitarian controversy begins.

1805 Hosea Ballou publishes *A Treatise on Atonement*, a defense of universal salvation and also the first book published in America openly rejecting the doctrine of the Trinity.

1811 Maria Cook, considered the first woman to preach in Universalist pulpits, begins her work.

1811 Harvard Divinity School is established.

1819 The Universalists begin publishing a weekly paper, *The Universalist Magazine*, which became the *Christian Leader* and has been published continuously since, now part of the UU World.

1819 William Ellery Channing's Baltimore Sermon "Unitarian Christianity"

1820 Dedham Decision

1821 The *Christian Register* (Unitarian) begins publication.

1825 American Unitarian Association (AUA) is established.

1825 The British and Foreign Unitarian Association is founded.

1832 First recorded meeting of Unitarians in Montreal.

1833 Disestablishment of Congregational churches in Massachusetts.

1838 Ralph Waldo Emerson preaches *The Divinity School Address*.

1840 Brook Farm is founded by the Ripleys.

1841 Adin Ballou founds the utopian Hopedale Community in Hopedale, Massachusetts.

1841 Theodore Parker preaches "The Transient and Permanent in Christianity."

1842 First permanent Unitarian church is established in Montreal.

1843 A Universalist church is founded in Halifax, Nova Scotia.

1844 Meadville Theological School is established in Meadville, Pennsylvania.

1852 Tufts College (now University) is founded by Universalists at Medford, Massachusetts.

1856 Saint Lawrence University and Theological School is founded by Universalists at Canton, New York.

1856 Children's Sunday yearly observance is started by the Universalist Church in Chelsea, Massachusetts.

1862 The Universalist Publishing House is established.

1863 Olympia Brown becomes the first woman to be ordained by a denomination.

1865 The National Conference of Unitarian Churches is organized.

1867 The Free Religious Association is organized.

1869 Women's Centenary Association is formed. Later called the Association of Universalist Women, it unites in 1963 with the Alliance of Unitarian Women to become the UU Women's Federation.

1880 The General Alliance of Unitarian and other Liberal Christian Women (originally called Women's Auxiliary Conference) is organized.

1886 *Issue in the West*

1889 Joseph H. Jordan is fellowshipped as the first African American Universalist minister.

1889 Young People's Christian Union is formed (later called the Universalist Youth Fellowship).

1889 W. C. Gannett publishes "Things Most Commonly Believed Today among Us."

1890 Universalists begin a mission to Japan.

1893 World Parliament of Religions

1896 Unitarian Young People's Religious Union is organized.

1898 Isaac Morgan Atwood becomes the First General Superintendent of the Universalist Church.

1900 The International Congress of Free Christians and Other Religious Liberals (today the International Association for Religious Freedom), the oldest international interfaith body, is formed.

1904 Joseph Fletcher Jordan, third fellowshipped African American minister, heads the Suffolk (Virginia) Normal Training School for African Americans (later Jordan Neighborhood House).

1904 Starr King School for the Ministry is founded.

1919 The Unitarian Laymen's League is reorganized.

1933 Humanist Manifesto

1934 Commission of Appraisal is appointed by the AUA.

1935 Washington Profession of Faith is adopted by Universalist General Convention at Washington, D.C.

1936 AUA Commission of Appraisal publishes *Unitarians Face a New Age.*

1937 Frederick May Eliot is elected president of the AUA. Sophia Lyons Fahs is appointed children's editor.

1939 Unitarian Service Committee is organized.

1944 The Church of the Larger Fellowship is organized to serve Unitarians living in areas without Unitarian Churches.

1945 The Universalist Service Committee organizes and works in Hungary, Japan, and Phillipines, etc.

1953 Liberal Religious Youth (LRY) merges the Universalist and Unitarian youth organizations.

1953 The Council of Liberal Churches (Universalist-Unitarian), Inc., is organized for the federation of the departments of publication, education, and public relations.

1961 American Unitarian Association and the Universalist Church of America merge into the Unitarian Universalist Association (UUA).

1963 The Alliance of Unitarian Women and the Association of Universalist Women join to form the Unitarian Universalist Women's Federation (UUWF).

1963 The Unitarian Service Committee and the Department of World Service of the Unitarian Universalist Association unite to form the Unitarian Universalist Service Committee, Inc. (UUSC).

1963 First General Assembly resolution in support of abortion rights.

1964 First resolution against the Vietnam War is passed by a General Assembly.

1965 James Reeb killed in Selma, Alabama.

1967 Black Unitarian Universalist Caucus organized.

1970 First UUA Resolution affirming gay, lesbian, and bisexual rights.

1972 Beacon Press publishes *Pentagon Papers*, and the federal government investigates UUA bank records.

1977 Women and Religion Resolution

1983 Young Religious Unitarian Universalists (YRUU) succeeds LRY.

1984 UUA resolution affirming gay and lesbian services of union

1985 UUA Principles and Purposes

1985 Election of President William F. Schulz.

1987 Tabloid *Unitarian Universalist World* becomes the *World*, publishing in magazine format.

1989 Sister (later Partner) Church Program established between UUA and Transylvanian churches.

1992 World Summit of Unitarian Leaders in Budapest, Hungary

1993 Election of President John Buehrens

1994 *Journey toward Wholeness* report commits UUA to confront racism.

1995 International Council of Unitarians and Universalists (ICUU) is organized.

2001 Election of President William Sinkford

Introduction

Unitarians and Universalists have always been heretics. They are heretics because they want to choose their faith, not because they desire to be rebellious. Heresy in Greek means "choice," and during the first three centuries of the Christian church, believers could choose among a variety of beliefs about the man Jesus. Among these was a belief that Jesus was less than God, but sent by God on a divine mission. Those who denied the divinity of Jesus later came to be called Unitarian, which literally means the unity or oneness of God, rather than the belief in the trinity, God manifested in three persons. Another religious choice in the first three centuries of the Common Era (C.E.) was in universal salvation. This was the belief that no person would be condemned by God to eternal damnation in a fiery pit. Thus a Universalist believed that all people would be saved. Christianity lost its element of choice in 325 C.E. when the Nicene Creed established the Trinity as dogma. For centuries those who professed Unitarian or Universalist beliefs were persecuted.

This was true until the Protestant Reformation took hold in the remote mountainous country of Transylvania in Eastern Europe. Here the heritage of choice was extended to differing faith groups living in one political realm when the first edict of religious toleration in history was declared in 1568, during the reign of the first and only Unitarian king, John Sigismund. The court preacher, Francis David, was successively converted from Catholicism to Lutheranism to Calvinism and, finally, to Unitarianism because he could find no Biblical basis for the doctrine of the Trinity. Arguing that people should be allowed to choose among these faiths, he said, "We need not think alike to love alike." Here for the first time in history, congregations of Unitarians were established. These churches continue to preach the Unitarian message in present-day Romania. Like their heretic forbears from ancient times, these liberals could not see how the deification of a human being or simply reciting creeds helped them to live better lives, and so they said that they must follow Jesus, not worship him.

During the next two centuries, Unitarianism appeared briefly in scattered locations. A Unitarian community in Rakow, Poland, flourished for a time, and a book by a Spanish doctor, Michael Servetus, *On the Errors of the Trinity*, was circulated throughout Europe. But persecution frequently followed these believers. The Polish Unitarians were completely suppressed, and Servetus was burned at the stake. Even where the harassment was not so extreme, people still opposed the idea of choice in matters of religious faith. Joseph Priestley, the famed scientist and Unitarian minister had his laboratory burned in 1791 and he was hounded out of England. Nearly 20 years after he had helped establish the Unitarian church in England, he fled to America and founded some of the earliest Unitarian churches there in the Philadelphia area.

Despite all these European connections, Unitarianism as it is known in North America is not a foreign import. In fact, the origins of the faith begin with some of the most historic congregations in Puritan New England, where one can find churches called the First Parish, as they were the first church for the entire town. Each town was required to establish a congregationally independent church that followed Calvinist doctrines. Initially there were no religious choices, but over time the strict doctrines of original sin and predestination began to mellow. By the mid-1700s, a group of evangelicals was calling for the revival of Puritan orthodoxy. They asserted a belief in our eternal bondage to sin. Another group said that people have the ability to help save themselves because they are born as free moral agents. Those who opposed the revival, believing in free human will and the loving benevolence of God, became Unitarian. During the first four decades of the 19th century, hundreds of those original Congregational churches fought over ideas about sin and salvation, and especially over free will and how human Jesus was. Most of them split over these issues. A sermon called "Unitarian Christianity" delivered by William Ellery Channing in 1819 in Baltimore, Maryland, helped to give the Unitarians a strong platform. Six years later, the American Unitarian Association (AUA) was organized in Boston, Massachusetts.

The Universalist half of the liberal heritage developed independently of Congregationalism in at least three distinct geographical locations in America. Its European roots had a direct influence on its foundations in

North America in two of these instances. The earliest preachers of the gospel of universal salvation appeared in what were later the Middle Atlantic and Southern states, including European refugee George de Benneville. By 1781 Elhanan Winchester had organized a Philadelphia congregation of Universal Baptists. Among its members was Benjamin Rush, the famous physician and signer of the Declaration of Independence. The most well-known founder was John Murray, an English preacher, who arrived in 1770 and founded the first Universalist church in Gloucester, Massachusetts, which rose to a leadership role in the battle to separate church and state. The third strain was a completely indigenous movement. In the 1770s a small number of itinerant preachers in the rural, interior sections of New England led by Caleb Rich began to disbelieve in strict Calvinist doctrines of eternal punishment and discovered from their biblical studies the new revelation of God's loving redemption of all. From its beginnings, Universalism challenged its members to reach out and embrace people whom society often marginalized. The Gloucester church numbered a freed slave among its charter members, and the Universalists became the first denomination to ordain women to the ministry, beginning in 1863 with Olympia Brown.

Universalism was also a more evangelical faith than Unitarianism, as seen by the charismatic conversion style of many of its early leaders, including Caleb Rich, the mentor of Hosea Ballou. Ballou became the denomination's greatest leader during the 19th century. After officially organizing in 1793, the Universalists spread their faith across the eastern seaboard, with Ballou and his followers leading the way. Both Universalism and Unitarianism developed in Canada by the middle of the 19th century, beginning with a Universalist society in Stanstead, Quebec (1830), and a Unitarian congregation in Montreal (1842). Other preachers followed the advice of Universalist publisher Horace Greeley and went west. One such person was Thomas Starr King, who is credited with keeping California in the Union during the Civil War. In the 19th century Thomas Gold Appleton, brother-in-law of Henry Wadsworth Longfellow, defined the difference between Universalists and Unitarians. His witty statement accurately captured that one group relied on the goodness of the divine and the other on human ability and powers when he said that the humble small town Universalists "believed that God was too good to damn them," while the self-confident Unitarians believed that people like themselves "were too good to be damned." The

Universalists believed in a God who embraced everyone, and this later became central to their belief that lasting truth is found in all religions and that dignity and worth is innate to all people regardless of sex, color, race, class, or sexual orientation.

Growing out of this inclusive theology was a lasting impetus in both denominations to create a more just society. Both Unitarians and Universalists became active participants in many social justice movements in the 19th and 20th centuries. The great Unitarian preacher Theodore Parker was a prominent abolitionist, defending fugitive slaves and offering support to John Brown. Other reformers included Universalists such as Charles Spear, who called for prison reform, and Clara Barton, who went from Civil War "angel of the battlefield" to the founding of the Red Cross. Unitarians such as Dorothea Dix fought to "break the chains" of those incarcerated in mental hospitals, and Samuel Gridley Howe started schools for the blind. For the last two centuries, Unitarian Universalists have been at the forefront of movements for peace, abolition, suffrage, and women's rights, among others, working to free people from whatever bonds may oppress them.

Two thousand years ago, religious dissenters were persecuted for seeking the freedom to make religious choices, but such freedom has become central to both Unitarianism and Universalism. As early as the 1830s, both groups were studying and promulgating texts from world religions other than Christianity. By the beginning of the 20th century, humanists within both traditions advocated that people could be religious without believing in God. Unitarian Universalists believe that no one person, no one religion can embrace all religious truths. Freedom of choice is central to the faith.

By the middle of the 20th century it became clear that Unitarians and Universalists could have a stronger liberal religious voice if they merged their efforts, and they did so in 1961 by forming the Unitarian Universalist Association (UUA). Many Unitarian Universalists became active in the Civil Rights Movement, and this era is remembered for its struggles over "black power" and the martyrdom of James Reeb, a UU minister who was murdered in Selma after he and 20 percent of the denomination's ministers responded to Martin Luther King Jr.'s call to march for justice. Today the UUA is determined to continue to work for greater racial and cultural diversity. In 1977 a "Women and Religion" resolution was passed, and since then the denomination has responded to the feminist challenge to change sexist structures and language, especially with the publication of a new, inclusive hymnal. In 1999 the association announced that just over 50 percent of its active ministers were women. The denomination has been especially proactive in affirming gay and lesbian rights, including ordaining and settling gay and lesbian clergy in its congregations, and, in 1996, affirming same-sex marriage. All of these efforts reflect a modern understanding of "universal salvation." The history has carried the denomination from liberal Christian views about Jesus and human nature to a rich pluralism that includes theist and atheist, agnostic and humanist, Christian, Jew, and Buddhist. More recently they have affirmed earth-centered spirituality. God's love welcomes all to an expanding circle of understanding and choice in religious faith.

The last decades of the 20th century saw an increased emphasis on international contacts. Much of this was initiated during the presidency of William Schulz. In an effort to reestablish ties with the oldest Unitarian churches in the world in Transylvania, Schulz and UUA moderator Natalie Gulbrandsen planned a trip to Romania, which occurred in the wake of the fall of the Communist dictatorship. The UUA delegation that traveled there in 1989 sought guarantees of religious freedom for all. That same year a Sister Church program was established, eventually linking hundreds of American and Transylvania congregations with moral and financial support. Schulz also sought to bring international groups into UUA membership and succeeded when the Unitarian Universalist Church of the Philippines joined in 1988. Although Schulz's successor, John Buehrens, felt a primarily North American association could not provide adequate services to other cultures, Buehrens continued to advocate for more international cooperation, and the International Council of Unitarians and Universalists was established in 1995 after an organizational meeting in Essex, Massachusetts.

During the last 20 years the UUA has achieved slow, but steady, growth, unlike most mainline churches, which have declined. This is important for a denomination, which, despite its influence, is very small in numbers with only 1,055 congregations and 222,000 adults and children in North America. This growth has primarily taken place in the South and the west rather than in the traditional stronghold of New England. It continues to be a denomination of "come-outers," primarily peopled by individuals who reject the religion they were raised in and seek a nondogmatic, antiauthoritarian faith. Today Unitarian Universalists tend to be less rational and more interested in spirituality. Although the term is vague to some and overused by others, the trend toward supplementing reason with more worship rituals and personal religious disciplines has captured the hearts of many in the denomination. This has been fueled by the women's spirituality movement, Eastern traditions and practices, and a renewed appreciation for the interdependence of all creation. Young people are also seeking religious renewal within the Unitarian Universalist fold as the number of college-age groups has increased dramatically in recent years. Perhaps the denomination can change the trend where those who are raised in the faith tend to leave. As a result, the UUA has put an increased emphasis on Unitarian Universalist identity and community building, while deemphasizing individual freedom. Balancing radical religious individualism with strong institutional commitments will continue to be the great challenge for this liberal religion in the new millennium.

The Dictionary

– A –

ABBOT, FRANCIS ELLINGWOOD (1836–1903). One of the founders of the **Free Religious Association (FRA)** and the editor of its periodical, the *Index*. Abbot was born in Boston on November 6, 1836, attended **Harvard Divinity School**, and graduated from **Meadville Theological School** in 1863. Even as a student, Abbot became interested in debating the relationship between Unitarianism and Christianity. He was settled in the parish at Dover, New Hampshire, in 1864, but soon found himself increasingly dissatisfied with organized Unitarianism. He was especially disturbed that the preamble of the new National Conference professed "allegiance to the Lord Jesus Christ."

His inability to reconcile modern knowledge with Christianity led him to resign his pastorate in 1868. He was called back to the church under the condition that the Unitarian society dissolve itself and a separate Independent society be organized. The society split, and an injunction was sought forbidding Abbot's supporters from using the building. The Supreme Court in New Hampshire forbade Abbot, a non-Christian, from using the pulpit as long as any member objected. In 1867 the FRA was formed, with Abbot as one of the signers of the call to the meeting. He believed that faith in humanity was the great affirmation of free religion. Free religion transferred its loyalty from Christ to His principles: truth, righteousness, and love. This new faith made possible the reconciliation of science and religion.

In 1869 Abbot was called to the Unitarian Society in Toledo, Ohio, and he accepted contingent upon it dropping the sectarian connection and becoming an Independent society. After a series of sermons on free religion where the defects of Christianity were discussed, the society agreed to the change. Part of the plan was for Abbot to have sole editorship of a weekly journal, and this bore fruit when the first issue of the *Index* came out on January 1, 1870. The periodical carried Abbot's "Fifty Affirmations." This editorship continued until 1880. The latter stages of his career were devoted to writing, including *Scientific Theism* (1885), in which Abbot said that the pursuit of science and religion were essentially the same. He died by his own hand on October 23, 1903, after final years of personal sadness. Abbot was an uncompromising believer in intellectual freedom, and he was a leader of the revolt from a Christian basis for Unitarianism, saying, "If you want freedom, you must abandon Christianity."

ABOLITION OF SLAVERY. Unitarians and Universalists have often been portrayed as activists in the crusade to abolish slavery. George Willis Cooke in his *Unitarianism in America* (1902) wrote: "In proportion to its numbers no religious body in the country did so much to promote the antislavery reform as the Unitarian." In fact, the picture is mixed. **Conrad Wright** has categorized Unitarian ministers in three ways: Abolitionists who called for an immediate end to slavery; moderates, who were a majority, and strongly antislavery, but they preferred to contain it and see its gradual abolishment; and finally, an especially cautious group of moderates who believed that religious bodies should not take stands on political issues.

William Ellery Channing, the leader of the Unitarians, held moderate views on slavery. He believed, "A human being cannot rightfully be held and used as property. No legislation, not that of all countries or worlds, could make him so." The great scar of slavery on the individual soul was that it did not allow individuals the right to their own moral fulfillment. Although Channing became more outspoken on slavery prior to his death in 1842, he could not commit himself fully to abolitionism, partly because he was disturbed by radicals disrupting an orderly society and inviting conflict, and partly because he could not condemn all slaveholders as evil. His positive view of human nature made him believe that at least some slaveholders would recover their moral sense. Channing's conciliatory attitudes toward slaveholders derived from a brief period spent tutoring in Virginia when he was a young man. His greatest contribution may have come as an influence on others through his ability to link religion and abolition. In 1840 his friend **Charles Follen**, an active abolitionist, died, and the Massachusetts Antislavery Society requested the use of Channing's Federal Street Church for the service. The standing committee of the church initially agreed but then reversed itself. Channing was outraged that his friend's memory was insulted, and he proceeded to memorialize him at the church despite the vote of the leaders. After this, Channing's ministry at the church continued only in name, as he preached there but once during the last three years of his life.

There were other ministers who also experienced differences with their congregations over involvement in reform issues. John Pierpont was dismissed from his pulpit for "too busy interference" with reform. Outspoken pastors risked their jobs as many wealthy Unitarians were leaders in the textile industry. After the capture of fugitive slave Thomas Sims in 1851, William Lloyd Garrison's *Liberator* reported that the Universalist church bell and others in Waltham, Massachusetts, were tolled, but "the bell on the Unitarian Church being clogged with cotton would not sound." Some clergy were able to strike a balance. **Samuel J. May** was among the most eloquent and persuasive abolitionists without being too divisive. In 1845 the liberal clergy published *A Protest against American Slavery by One Hundred and Seventy-Three Unitarian Ministers*.

Other Unitarians used legislative means to combat slavery. **John Quincy Adams** spearheaded the battle in the U.S. House of Representatives over the "gag rule"—whether Congress could even discuss the subject of slavery. The leadership of Adams during this controversy (1835–1844) was exemplary. Adams's strategy was to subordinate the antislavery cause to the issue of civil liberty. Despite his advanced age and threats of censure and even assassination, Adams sponsored petition after petition to keep the issue open to debate. Adams's efforts resulted in a significant victory for freedom of speech with the defeat of the "gag rule" in 1844.

The truly radical Unitarian position was expressed by **Theodore Parker**, who labeled slavery "the great national sin." Parker made many enemies by attacking not only the slaveholders but also the Northern economic elite who profited from and perpetuated slavery through their banks, mills, and shipping interests. After the passage of the Fugitive Slave Law, Parker's views and actions became even more militant, "The man who attacks me to reduce me to slavery, in that moment of attack alienates his right to life, and if I were a fugitive, and could escape in no other way, I would kill him with as little compunction as I would drive a mosquito from my face." When Parker conducted a wedding ceremony for two fugitives, he said, "With this sword, I thee wed." After this, Parker wrote his sermons with a sword in the drawer under his ink stand and a loaded pistol in the flap of his desk. The arms were appropriate, as Parker soon enlisted others to the possible use of armed resistance. His vigilance committee evolved into a conspiratorial cabal of six prominent Northerners, who supplied the radical John Brown with money and weapons. The armed conflict they were materially and emotionally advocating became a reality the year after Parker died in 1860.

Although less well known, the Universalists also played a role in fighting the greatest social issue of the 19th century. In fact, the Universalists made the first official denominational challenge to slavery when they adopted the following resolution at their convention in Philadelphia in 1790. "*Of holding Slaves*—We believe it to be inconsistent with the union of the human race in a common Saviour, and the obligations to mutual and universal love, which flow from that union, to hold any part of our fellow creatures in bondage. We therefore recommend a total refraining from the African trade and the adoption of prudent measures for the gradual abolition of the slavery of the negroes in our country, and for the instruction and education of their children in English literature, and in the principles of the gospel." The eminent Dr. **Benjamin Rush** was responsible for this resolution and the foremost advocate of the antislavery impulse among Universalists. Rush had published two antislavery tracts in the 1770s and became president of an antislavery society in Philadelphia. **Elhanan Winchester** not only attacked slave traders and holders, but also preached directly to slaves in South Carolina and told them that "Jesus Christ loved them, and died for them as well as for white people." In New England this belief was reflected at the Universalist church in Gloucester, Massachusetts, where Gloster Dalton, an African brought to America as a slave, was one of the 85 signers of the Charter of Compact for the church in 1785.

Despite these early signs that Universalists would be especially prominent in efforts to condemn and abolish slavery, their record is as mixed as the Unitarians'. While a small number of Universalists made abolition the central goal of their lives, most opposed slavery but feared the divisive nature of the issue would destroy their denominational unity. As a group, Universalists usually argued against slavery on moral and religious grounds, rather than for political or economic reasons. Using their unique theology, they believed that humanity was "one great family" that would ultimately "share one common destiny." Like the Unitarians, most Universalists were against slavery, but they were more likely to refuse to be part of the mainstream antislavery movement for political and religious reasons (i.e., religion and politics do not mix, and refusal to be part of groups that included orthodox believers). Preferring to operate independently, their national influence was limited. Slowly the Universalists began to take an official position. The leader of the Universalists, **Hosea Ballou**, attended the third annual Universalist Anti-Slavery Convention in 1842 and declared himself "heartily opposed to slavery." Yet Ballou refused to sign the roll as a member on the ground that the discussion of slavery was not a proper denominational question. Increasingly a variety of state conventions found the courage to debate the question and risk disunity among themselves. It is fitting that Universalists in Maine were among the first to speak out. Like the Unitarians, they also had an ally in Congress in the person of **Israel Washburn**. Washburn, one of the founders of the Republican Party and the person responsible for choosing its name, made every effort to help curb the growth of slavery. Some Universalists who lived with slavery firsthand in the South became apologists for it. Others, like **Mary A. Livermore**, who witnessed slavery for three years when she taught in Virginia, became avowed abolitionists, supported Garrison's *Liberator*, and attended antislavery meetings at every opportunity. As the war approached, most Universalists believed that slavery was contrary to the basic teachings of the faith and it must be eradicated.

ABRAHAM LINCOLN CENTRE. Established in Chicago in 1905, the Abraham Lincoln Centre was initially an outreach project of **Jenkin Lloyd Jones**'s All Souls Church. For 10 years Jones and his congregation had been planning and raising funds for a cultural center for the community. On Easter Sunday 1905 a seven-story brick building was dedicated as "a proving place of worship unhampered by creed or dogma, or denominations, a place of study, and a platform for every honest message." The facility had a gymnasium, art gallery, guest rooms, chapel, and auditorium and offered every conceivable type of program to educate and uplift people. Jones became the first director and continued there until his death in 1918. This attempt to minister to the diverse types of human needs and longings has this stated purpose: "For the advancement of the physical, intellectual, social, civic, moral, cultural, and religious interests of the community without restrictions as to age, sex, race, creed, color, or economic circumstance."

During the 1930s the church collapsed, but then services were reinstated when a leading humanist, **Curtis Reese**, became dean of the center. Attendance dwindled as the surrounding neighborhood changed, and then services ended again when aid from the Community Fund required support of secular activities and not the maintenance of a church. In 1951 the Free Religious Fellowship, an intentional interracial church supported by the **American Unitarian Association (AUA)**, moved to the center. After this the fellowship lost a number of members, but its founder and minister, Lewis McGee, helped stabilize the congregation before he left in 1953. The church took on the original name All Souls and merged in 1971 with First Universalist Society. Jenkin Lloyd Jones's original dream of a community center that was interracial and provided education for the whole person continues today with day care programs, dance and drama classes, recreational events, and social and mental health services, among other programs at the Abraham Lincoln Centre.

ACADEMIES. The Universalists founded a number of academies and colleges in the 19th century. Although these were sustained by Universalists, they were nonsectarian so that all faiths were encouraged to attend, and no proselytizing was allowed. The schools were never under ecclesiastical control. One of the first such academies was Westbrook Seminary in Portland, Maine. Its charter was granted in 1830, and it opened in 1834 as a coeducational boarding and day school. Goddard Seminary was founded by the Universalist Convention of Vermont and Quebec in 1863. Located in Barre, Vermont, Goddard specialized in college preparation and music. Its president in the early 20th century was Orlando Hollister, who was also president of the convention.

The year after Goddard was founded, Oliver Dean of Franklin, Massachusetts, who was a Universalist benefactor, established Dean Academy. It also became the best endowed preparatory school and by 1905 had 150 boarders. All of these academies maintained a continuing history as Westbrook Junior College, Goddard College, and Dean Junior College and had no specific Universalist connections after 1922. There were several other academies founded by Universalists, of which the earliest was Clinton Liberal Institute in 1831, which was eventually absorbed by **St. Lawrence University** in Canton, New York. The broad level of Universalist support for education was a reflection of their aim to develop the mind to its fullest extent.

ADAMS, ABIGAIL (1744–1818). The daughter of a minister from Weymouth, Massachusetts, she was born Abigail Smith on November 11, 1744. She is revered by many as one of America's first advocates of women's rights. When her husband **John Adams** (whom she married in 1765) was working on the Declaration of Independence, she wrote in March 1776, "I desire you would remember the ladies and be more generous and favorable to them than your ancestors! Do not put such unlimited power into the hands of the husbands. Remember all men would be tyrants if they could. If particular care and attention is not paid to the ladies, we are determined to foment a rebellion." During her husband's frequent political forays, she effectively balanced motherhood and managing the family farm and business. They were partners and equals in their marriage.

Her independence of mind and spirit also applied to her religious beliefs. In 1815 and 1816 she wrote letters to her son **John Quincy Adams** saying: "There is not any reasoning which can convince me, contrary to my senses, that three, is one, and one three. . . . I acknowledge myself a Unitarian—believing that the Father alone is the supreme God, and that Jesus Christ, derived his Being, and all his powers and honours from the Father." In 1818 she wrote to her daughter-in-law, Louisa Catherine Adams: "True religion is from the heart, between Man and his creator, and not the imposition of Man or Creeds and tests." Adams died on October 28, 1818, and is buried in the crypt of the United First Parish in Quincy, Massachusetts, along with her husband, son, and daughter-in-law.

ADAMS, JAMES LUTHER (1901–1994). The son of a fundamentalist Baptist preacher, Adams became the outstanding Unitarian theologian of the 20th century. Born in Ritzville, Washington, on November 12, 1901, he graduated from the University of Minnesota in 1924 and **Harvard Divinity School** in 1927. That year he was ordained and installed as minister of the Second Church, Unitarian in Salem, Massachusetts. He was also married to Margaret Ann Young at that time, and eventually they had three daughters. Adams's lifelong interest in issues of social justice began with his pastorate in Salem, when he supported the striking workers of the Pequot Mills. He also briefly served the church in Wellesley Hills, Massachusetts. During the 1930s he made two trips to Nazi Germany and was detained by the Gestapo for a short time. In 1936 he joined the faculty of the **Meadville Theological School** (Chicago) first as professor of psychology and philosophy, and eventually he was a professor in Religious Ethics with the Federated Theology Faculty of the University of Chicago. Adams became an authority on Paul Tillich, and his doctoral dissertation at the University of Chicago was later published as Paul Tillich's Philosophy of Culture, Science, and Religion (1965).

In 1957 Adams returned to Harvard as professor of divinity. He went into active retirement in 1968 and held brief appointments at Andover Newton Theological School as professor of Social Ethics and at Meadville again. Many of his essays and other writings have been printed, most especially in *Taking Time Seriously* (1957), *On Being Human Religiously* (1976), and *The Prophethood of All Believers* (1986). Adams made the concept of the "voluntary association" central to his thinking. This was lived by Adams through his own affiliations with various denominational groups and professional societies. He was one of the leaders of the first Commission of Appraisal, a founder of Greenfield Group (a study group), and a leader in many other professional societies and voluntary associations. Adams was also a frequent editor of liberal religious journals.

During his long career Adams influenced countless students with his brilliant and lively lectures, sermons, and conversations. His theological perspective was that of a Unitarian Universalist Christian, but he challenged all perspectives with his belief that "religious liberalism affirms the moral obligation to direct one's effort toward the establishment of a just and loving community." He died on July 26, 1994. Adams received the Award for Distinguished Service to the Cause of Unitarian Universalism in 1973. His work is being carried on by the James Luther Adams Foundation.

ADAMS, JOHN (1735–1826). The second president of the United States was born in Braintree, Massachusetts, on October 19, 1735. Adams began reading books on religion when he was 12 and never stopped. As a young man he considered the ministry as a profession, but he believed that his unorthodox opinions might mean he would be denied fellowship, and so he became a lawyer instead. Even though he felt a minister could "do more good to his fellow-men, and make better provision for his own future happiness in this profession than in another," he was aware that there was a rumor that he was an Arminian, and with the spirit of dogmatism and bigotry abounding, he said that his life might involve "endless altercations." Like many liberals he later arose to a prominent place among the leaders of the American Revolution. Believing that every individual had the right to seek truth, Adams proclaimed: "Let the human mind loose. It will be loose. Superstition and Dogmatism cannot confine it." In 1815 he wrote to Jedediah Morse that the minister of the Quincy church (Lemuel Briant) 65 years before that date had been Unitarian, along with a number of other ministers. He chided Morse: "More than fifty years ago, I read Dr. Samuel Clark, Emlyn and Dr. Waterland. Do you expect, my dear Doctor, to teach me any thing new in favor of Athanasianism?" Adams asserted a strong link between religion and morality. In 1821 he wrote to his daughter-in-law: "I do not however attach much importance to creeds because I believe he cannot be wrong whose life is right."

After his retirement from public life, Adams began an extensive correspondence with **Thomas Jefferson** in 1812. Adams claimed to have been a Unitarian for 60 years, and with Jefferson affirming Unitarianism as well, they found common ground in their religious beliefs. The two former presidents both died on the same day, July 4, 1826. Adams' family had been members of the First Parish Church (then Unitarian) for two centuries, and he had provided a gift of land in 1822, the income from which was to be used to construct a new granite church (The Stone Temple) in Quincy, Massachusetts. It was completed in 1828. During that same year, Adams's remains, and those of his wife Abigail (d. 1818), were transferred from the Hancock Cemetery to their new tombs in the First Parish Church. On the wall of the church is a memorial tablet, where Adams is remembered for his pledge of "Life, Fortune and Sacred Honour" to the independence of his country and for affixing his seal to the treaty that redeemed the pledge. The tablet ends with these words: "This House will bear witness to his Piety: This Town, his Birth-Place, to his Munificence: History to his Patriotism: Posterity to the Depth and Compass of his Mind." His was a mind that always sought new truth, but it was the living out of those truths that became his essential faith. He once said of theological writings: "I have learned nothing of importance to me [from them] for they have made no change in my moral or religious creed, which has for fifty or sixty years been contained in four short words 'Be just and good.'"

ADAMS, JOHN QUINCY (1767–1848). The sixth president of the United States was born in Braintree (now Quincy), Massachusetts, on July 11, 1767. He was a child of the Revolution who stood with his mother and watched the Battle of Bunker Hill. Raised to be a statesman, after his graduation from Harvard, he became U.S. minister to the Netherlands at the age of 26 and never looked back. He was in turn a U.S. Senator, minister to Russia, secretary of state, president, and then made perhaps his greatest contribution as a U.S. Representative from 1831 to 1848, when he fought off the slave interests by not allowing the voices of freedom to be silenced. He has been called "one of the most accomplished persons ever to play a major role in American politics," but he also had a difficult time getting along with others, displaying what one Englishman called, "a vinegar aspect."

Like his father **John Adams**, John Quincy took his religion seriously, beginning every day by reading the Bible. But he seems to have had a harder time shaking orthodox beliefs than the elder Adams. In 1815 his father wrote to him expressing amazement that despite all that had been written by Samuel Clarke, Daniel Waterland, and **Joseph Priestley**, John Quincy still held to the Athanasian creed (i.e., Trinitarianism). The younger Adams wrote back in 1817 that he would not "cavil or quibble away" assertions about the divinity of Christ. "You see my orthodoxy grows upon me." Over the years Adams vacillated between doubt and belief with the miracle stories causing much of his questioning: "The miracles in the Bible furnish the most powerful of all the objections against its authenticity," and he wanted to strip it of all its "supernatural agency." He wrote in his *Memoirs*, "I believe in one God, but His nature is incomprehensible to me, and of the question between the Unitarians and Trinitarians I have no precise belief, because no definite understanding." Adams confessed that Jesus Christ was superhuman, "but whether he is God, or only the first of human beings, is not clearly revealed to me in the Scriptures." Adams publicly affirmed his membership in the Unitarian church in Quincy soon after his father died. The funeral was held in the church on July 7, 1826, and he decided that he wished to formally join, and did so on October 1. Despite his "smack of orthodox," Adams's devotion to the free mind led him to have anxious reflections about religious truth his entire life, but it also led him to fight against constraints on individual human freedom in society and helped make his one of the strongest voices in the battle against slavery. "Old Man Eloquent" died on the job in the Capitol building on February 23, 1848. Unitarian preacher and abolitionist Theodore Parker wrote: "The slave has lost a champion who gained new ardor and new strength the longer he fought; America has lost a man who loved her with his heart; religion has lost a supporter; Freedom an unfailing friend, and mankind a noble vindicator of our inalienable rights." Adams is memorialized on a tablet at the United First Parish in Quincy. Remembered for all his labors on behalf of his country as "A son, worthy of his Father, A Citizen, shedding glory on his Country, A scholar ambitious to advance mankind, This Christian sought to walk humbly In the sight of his God." His wife, Louisa Catherine (Johnson) Adams, died four year later on May 15, 1852, and they are both entombed in the church crypt with John Quincy's parents. *See also* ABOLITION OF SLAVERY.

ADDAMS, JANE (1860–1935). The founder of Hull House in Chicago, a settlement house that set the pattern for a generation of social work. Addams was born on September 6, 1860. Famous for her work with the poor, she was also a labor organizer and women's rights activist. She was awarded the Nobel Peace Prize in 1931, but ironically her pacifism prior to World War I led some detractors to call her a traitor. Early in life her religious affiliation was with the Presbyterians, but during her Hull House years, she attended both a Congregational Church and the Unitarian All Souls Church, where **Jenkin Lloyd Jones** was the minister. Jones came to Hull House to lecture, discuss the need for labor unions, and to help work in giving aid to the destitute. Addams in turn often supplied the pulpit for Jones and even performed weddings and funerals. Becoming a kind of teacher/pastor, Jones called her the "sage of Hull House." She wrote, "For many people without church affiliations the vague humanitarianism the settlement house represented was the nearest approach they could find to an expression of their religious sentiments." Although Hull House never had regular religious services, in the early years there were regular evening meetings with Bible readings and prayers. After the turn of the century, Addams increasingly turned toward agnosticism, and fewer traditional expressions of religious sentiment were seen at Hull House. Addams published many works, but is best known for *Twenty Years at Hull House*. She died on May 21, 1935.

AGNOSTICISM. Term coined by Thomas Huxley in 1870, agnosticism is a viewpoint that many Unitarian Universalists hold. In the 1989 Commission on Appraisal report, *The Quality of Religious Life in Unitarian Universalist Congregations*, 3 percent defined themselves as agnostic/skeptic in their religious position, but more telling was the response to a question in the survey asking how they would describe the divine. Two responses that indicate strong agnostic tendencies were 11 percent who said "don't know/uncertain" and another 11 percent who said "unknowable power." While the atheist states with final certainty that there is no God, the agnostic says that there is no way of absolutely knowing if God exists, and thus the agnostic will neither affirm nor deny the existence of God because they do not have the evidence to tell one way or the other. While similar to skepticism, the agnostic will not go to the extreme of saying that any true knowledge is impossible. The agnostic position is always open to discovery, willing to doubt, and is never complete. His father, Julian Huxley, also considered himself an agnostic and in *Religion without Revelation* wrote: "I hold that all our life we are oscillating between conviction and caution, faith and agnosticism, belief and suspension of belief." This exploring nature in matters of faith, led H. L. Mencken to say, "The most satisfying and ecstatic faith is almost purely agnostic."

ALCOTT, AMOS BRONSON (1799–1888). A brilliant and progressive, but misunderstood, educator, whose **Temple School** in Boston was among the most innovative education institutions of its times. Alcott was born in poverty near Wolcott, Connecticut, and had little formal schooling. His teaching career began in Cheshire, Connecticut, after a stint as an itinerant peddler. He called his school the Cheshire Pestalozzi School after the great Swiss educator of his day whose theories Alcott embraced. His educational innovations in this classroom included a large library, decorations for the room, and desks for each child. Every subject was taught in a different manner. For example, instead of studying maps for geography, the students made a map of their own schoolyard. Alcott's central concern was teaching children how to learn, but his progressive ideas alienated the parents, and after a couple of years the school was closed.

After a brief period in Boston, his next teaching experience was in Germantown, Pennsylvania, in a new private school, which again was closed when parents learned that Alcott wanted to treat the children with as much respect as the adults. This school was conducted (1831–34) with his new wife, Abigail May, whom he had married in 1830. During his life, Alcott tried many other projects that never seemed to come to fruition. His family was always in financial difficulty, especially after the failure of the Temple School (named for the Masonic Temple it was housed in on Tremont Street in Boston), which lasted from 1834 until 1839 when Alcott admitted an African American child, and all the white children except one were withdrawn by their parents. His philosophy and methods are seen in his *Record of Conversations on the Gospels* (1836). He assumed the spiritual integrity of young minds with an innate ability to embrace the divine in their own souls. Jesus was the great educator.

After the school's failure, the Alcotts moved to Concord in 1840, where "conversations" became one of the few means of income for the Alcotts. He took whatever work he could find, but mostly survived by being a woodchopper. The family followed the nutritional philosophy of Sylvester Graham, a vegetarian. Alcott was devoted to his four daughters, Anna, Louisa, Elizabeth, and May, to whom he taught the alphabet by acting out the shapes of the letters. He worked on the manuscript about their development, *Psyche*, for years. Alcott visited England in 1842 to see the Alcott School, which followed his imaginative ideas of education. **Ralph Waldo Emerson**, who often lent his friendly support to Alcott, wanted to learn the latest philosophical news from England and financed the trip to England. Alcott was a member of the **Transcendental Club**, and many of his writings were published in the ***Dial***, including his "Orphic Sayings" (1840). Here he encouraged youth to believe that "your heart is an oracle." In England, Charles Lane taught him some utopian notions. Alcott returned to America with three companions including Lane who made up a crowded household in Concord. Vowing to live simply off the land, Alcott started the utopian community **Fruitlands** in Harvard, Massachusetts, but it foundered after less than six months in 1843.

The family moved around a great deal and moved back to Boston where Alcott's wife Abigail became one of America's first social workers. Bronson made frequent appearances around the country as a lecturer. With Louisa's success as a writer, the family was finally able to settle in Concord permanently in 1857. After 1859 he was superintendent of the Concord public schools until 1865. In 1879 Alcott founded the Concord School of Philosophy, which remained a summer school of adult education until his death in 1888. Throughout his career he was befriended by the members of the Concord literary circle, and he left a great legacy as an educator and philosopher whose ideas were far in advance of his time.

ALCOTT, LOUISA MAY (1832–1888). The author of *Little Women* and numerous other books, Alcott is one of the most well-known writers in the American tradition. She was born in Germantown, Pennsylvania, on November 29, 1832. She was the second child of **A. Bronson Alcott**, the innovative Transcendentalist educator, and Abigail May Alcott, who was the sister of Unitarian minister **Samuel J. May**. Louisa learned at an early age that wealth and possessions could not matter to her, as the family struggled under the progressive idealism of her father, who had brilliant ideas about education for his time, but could never manage to earn a living. Two more girls were born in subsequent years (a boy died), making up the family who were later depicted in *Little Women*. After moving from Boston to Concord, Louisa began to write at the age of eight when she composed her first poem, "To the First Robin." Louisa's mother, known as Marmee, worked long hours to ensure the survival of her family. The family moved from place to place, including a time at the ill fated commune **Fruitlands** in Harvard, Massachusetts. During her teen years, Alcott's devotion to writing grew stronger. She kept a journal and wrote hundreds of poems, stories, and plays. She also helped support the family with sewing. Her first published piece of writing was a poem, "Sunlight." A collection of children's fables was published in 1854, *Flower Fables*. Her income as a writer eventually allowed her to help her parents purchase the Orchard House in Concord in 1857. This was the setting for *Little Women* (1868), whose characters were based on her family life. Her father is absent from the story, as a fictionalized chaplain away in the war. Louisa's experience in the Civil War as a field nurse was recounted in *Hospital Sketches* (1863), a major literary success. During the first year of the war she had sewn bandages, but she made an application to be a nurse in the fall of 1862, the month she turned 30. After a few months service, she fell ill and returned to Massachusetts. During her hospitalization she reflected on her friendship for **Henry David Thoreau**, who had recently died. The result was a poem published in the *Atlantic*, "Thoreau's Flute."

In 1864, Louisa published the novel *Moods*, which strays from her more familiar juvenile fiction to recount the complexities of relationships between men and women. After *Little Women*, the demand for her literary output was constant. *Little Men* was published in 1871. In 1873 she published *Work: A Story of Experience*, which offers a fictionalized account of women's work lives in factories and as domestics (she had worked as a servant in Dedham), as well as a portrayal of Unitarian minister **Theodore Parker**. She had been a frequent visitor at the Parker home in her twenties when she met **Frederic Henry Hedge** and **Julia Ward Howe**, among others. She said that Parker was her sort of Christian. He did not turn his back on any who needed help, she said, as some of the "pious" did. Alcott came to an abolitionist position early in life and wrote a poem to commemorate John

Brown's martyrdom, which was published in the *Liberator*. In her journal annotations, Alcott commented that she found religion as a girl when "mother Nature led her to God." She tried to maintain this "happy sense of nearness" all her life, even as she battled frequent depression. In 1881 she was a cofounder with her friend Ellen Emerson of the Women's Parish Association of the First Parish in Concord, the oldest church women's group in town. During the 1870s and 1880s she published numerous stories and sketches, which were collected in volumes for children. She continued to write in her attic room at the Orchard House in Concord with an output of several more works of fiction, including her last novel, *Jo's Boys* (1886). She died on March 6, 1888, only two days after her father.

ALGER, HORATIO JR. (1832–1899). The author of more than one hundred "rags to riches" stories for children, Alger had a brief career as a Unitarian minister before achieving fame as a writer. Alger was born on January 13, 1832, the child of the Unitarian minister of Chelsea, Massachusetts, Horatio Alger, and his wife, Olive Fenno Alger. Alger was small and asthmatic as a boy. One of five children, Horatio's family moved to a new parish in Marlborough, Massachusetts, in 1844. The elder Alger urged his son to become a minister, but the boy preferred writing and journalism. As a student at Harvard he was admonished for unexcused absences from prayers. In the early 1850s Alger wavered between which career to choose, as he enjoyed some success with publishing writings, and he was also a tutor. Even after he returned to divinity school, he continued to publish stories, including his first important tales for young people appearing in *Gleason's*. In the meantime, his father's political involvements, especially with a railroad controversy, led him to seek a new pastorate, and he moved to South Natick, Massachusetts, in 1860.

By 1864, several important adult magazines, including *Harper's Monthly*, had published Alger's stories, and a publisher had accepted his first book for boys, *Frank's Campaign*, a tale about a young boy who wanted to assist in the Union war effort. That fall Alger was called to be parish minister in Brewster, Massachusetts, but he only lasted for 15 months, when he was dismissed for "unnatural familiarity with boys." With this scandalous incident in his background, Alger abandoned the ministry forever and moved to New York City.

Writing became the sole focus of Alger's life, and some earlier stories about city life took their mature form in 1867 with the appearance of *Ragged Dick*. This young waif who struggled on the streets of New York to make a living captured the hearts of young American readers. Later Alger created a female street urchin, *Tattered Tom*. Publisher A. K. Loring wrote, "In his books he has captured the spirit of reborn America. . . . Above all you can hear the cry of triumph of the oppressed over the oppressor."

In his books Alger returned again and again to the same theme, but he was never known as a great American novelist, as was his dream when he first moved to New York. Despite his success with books, Alger continued to write stories and even composed a biography of James A. Garfield in 1881. Later in life Alger traveled some in both Europe and the western United States. Alger has been called the most popular boy's writer in American history, with sales in the hundreds of millions. Not known for its literary quality, the writing and its themes of poor young boys making a financial success of their lives through courage, honesty, character, and luck were enduring symbols for America. Alger became especially concerned about the treatment of children; he supported several during his lifetime and provided jobs for others. He frequented the Newsboy's Lodging House, drawing material for his stories and eventually became its chaplain. His writings on childhood exploitation helped to lead to the founding of the New York Society for the Prevention of Cruelty to Children. He died on July 18, 1899.

ALLEN, ETHAN (1737–1789). The famed leader of the Green Mountain Boys was also a radical religious thinker whose views especially influenced the Universalist leader **Hosea Ballou**. Allen was born in Litchfield, Connecticut, on January 10, 1737, and fell under the influence of the deist Thomas Young, an itinerant doctor. They both apparently worked on a manuscript that Allen later added to and published as *Reason the Only Oracle of Man, or a Compendious System of Natural Religion*. (1785). Known variously as "The Oracles of Reason" or "Allen's Bible," like many things in Allen's life, the book sparked a controversy. One biographer of Allen says, "Here for the first time in America was a full-length treatise aimed directly at the destruction of conventional Christianity, and, for that matter, all other forms of revealed religion." Ezra Stiles called Allen, "a profane & impious Deist." Allen acknowledged the truth in this label to even "being conscious I am no Christian, except mere infant baptism makes me one." Allen believed that the finite human mind could not apprehend the infinite God, but that aspects of God were revealed to human beings as they correctly interpreted the order of nature.

Allen's rebellious frontier spirit that questioned all forms of political and religious authority was evident in his suspicions of the "priestcraft" who had invented such falsehoods as original sin and total depravity to keep people in darkness and chains. The undemocratic principle that part of humanity received eternal damnation at the hands of God showed "a diabolical temper of mind in the elect." Allen was not sure about future rewards and punishments except "that they cannot be perpetual or eternal." His optimism that people would be "restored to virtue and happiness" was a Universalist statement that was becoming increasingly popular on the frontiers of New England. Allen believed that the Bible was neither infallible nor a miraculous revelation of God's will. Although "Allen's Bible" was poorly written and many copies were lost in a fire, it received a fairly wide readership and helped establish Allen's place in history along with his wartime seizure of Fort Ticonderoga. Allen's life was a continuing fight to reject all dogmas that inhibited the growth of human liberty. He died on February 12, 1789.

ALLIANCE OF UNITARIAN WOMEN (AUW). There were many organized women's groups on the local level prior to the Civil War. Among these was the Tuckerman Sewing Circle in Boston, organized in 1827 to assist **Joseph Tuckerman** in his work with the urban poor. During the war many women were instrumental in the work of the U.S. Sanitary Commission. The Alliance of Unitarian Women (AUW) was officially organized when a constitution was adopted on September 18, 1880, at Saratoga, New York, after two years of preparatory work. Known initially as the Women's Auxiliary Conference, its purposes were to provide a parent organization for local church women's groups, to promote the organization of such groups, to hold a biennial meeting in conjunction with the **National Conference**, and to assist in the work of raising money for denominational purposes. Within two years, 75 churches had auxiliary branches, with the aim that every church would have such a group. In 1881 a Women's Western Unitarian Conference was formed and in 1890 a Pacific Coast Conference.

Under its first president, Abby W. May, several important projects were undertaken by the AUW. The Post Office Mission was an effort to extend knowledge of Unitarianism by responding to inquiries that came through public relations efforts. This program sent thousands of sermons and pamphlets around the world, initially through the efforts of Sallie Ellis in Cincinnati, Ohio. Members also became involved in the **American Unitarian Association's (AUA)** Church Building and Loan Fund to help societies build churches. A second program was the publication of a monthly magazine, the *Cheerful Letter*. The program consisted of sending aid and comfort to isolated individuals, or those who were physically unable to participate in church life. Within a few years the Auxiliary began to consolidate with branches beyond the neighborhood of Boston, and a reorganization took place in 1890, when the alliance name was adopted and organizational independence from the AUA was established. Taking up permanent headquarters with the AUA in Boston, the alliance became a powerful force in the denomination. In 1902 a Junior Alliance program for young women was established and later a college committee. The alliance played a major role in extension efforts. In 1900 funds for circuit preachers, social service, and church building resulted in the first liberal congregation in North Carolina at Shelter Neck.

Emily Fifield, the recording secretary for the alliance from 1887 to 1913, is especially remembered for a westward campaign in 1900, and several churches from the Mississippi to the Pacific owe their existence to her. In 1926 the name was changed again to the General Alliance of Unitarian and Other Liberal Christian Women, in order to help local Alliance branches distinguish themselves from the central body. The early years of the 20th century saw the remarkable success of summer conferences on Star Island. International interest also began to grow and was especially useful during the relief efforts of World War II. Over the years the alliance had active program committees especially in the areas of education, service, and extension. By midcentury one of their objectives was to "put more fully into action the principles of free religion in their homes, their churches, their communities, and the world." This had always been true of their efforts. After consolidation with the Universalists in 1963, this organization became the **Unitarian Universalist Women's Federation**.

AMERICAN HUMANIST ASSOCIATION (AHA). The Humanist Press Association (HPA) (1935) was the first organized national association of humanism in the United States. It grew out of the Humanist Fellowship, which had begun gathering in Chicago in 1927. They were the publishers of *The New Humanist*. **Curtis Reese**, a leading humanist, was the inspiration for the reorganization and incorporation of the HPA in 1941 as the American Humanist Association (AHA). Ever since, this organization has been the major representative organization of humanism in the United States. For many years it was headquartered in Yellow Springs, Ohio, and later San Francisco, but since 1978 its offices have been located in Amherst, New York. Its publication is called *The Humanist*. In *The Philosophy of Humanism* (New York, 1969) Corliss Lamont wrote that "the purpose of the AHA is to educate the American people on the meaning of Humanism and to persuade as many of them as possible to adopt this way of life." The AHA is organized in local chapters. It was a major player with other humanist groups in an International Congress in 1952, which established the International Humanist and Ethical Union (IHEU). One of the key leaders of this effort was then executive director, the Rev. Edwin H. Wilson, who remained in that position for 14 years, was the first editor of *The Humanist*, and a founder of the Fellowship of Religious Humanists. The AHA has played an important role in the debate over issues such as prayer in the schools and the teaching of creationism. It has also been known for counseling services and rites of passage (weddings and funerals) for people who are uncomfortable with traditional religious ceremonies. The AHA states that humanism is free of supernaturalism and that it "derives the goals of life from human need and interest rather than from theological or ideological abstractions, and asserts that humanity must take responsibility for its own destiny."

AMERICAN UNITARIAN ASSOCIATION (AUA). The AUA was formed on May 25, 1825, at a special afternoon meeting following the annual meeting of the **Berry Street Conference** of ministers held that morning. The separation of the Unitarians from the Congregationalists had been years in the making but was formalized with the creation of this organization. Five years prior to this **William Ellery Channing** and others had formed the Berry Street Conference to organize the clergy into a group that was "a bond of union, a means of intercourse, and an opportunity of conference." Discussions concerning a general liberal religious organization were held on an informal basis at many other group meetings, and it seems the younger clergy especially desired a group that would unite the liberal Christians. The Anonymous Association, a club for the leading citizens of Boston, met at Josiah Quincy's home in the fall of 1824. After much discussion on the "practicality and expediency of forming a Unitarian convention or association," **Andrews Norton** made a motion that a committee of the club be formed to consider establishing an association that would express the principles of the liberal group in the Congregational churches, particularly through the publication of books and tracts. The committee, which included **Henry Ware Jr.**, called a meeting for January 27, 1825, in the Federal Street Church in Boston "in order to confer together . . . for the purpose of union, sympathy, and co-operation in the cause of Christian truth and Christian charity." Forty-four ministers and laymen attended the meeting, but there was a sharp division of opinion. Among those who favored such an organization was John Pierpont: "We have, and we must have, the name Unitarian. It is not for us to shrink from it. Organization is necessary in order to maintain it, and organization there must be. The general interests of Unitarians will be promoted by using the name, and organizing in harmony with it."

Another committee was appointed, but it never met due to the controversial nature of its intended purpose. Four months later some of the younger clergy, including Ware, James Walker, and **Ezra Stiles Gannett**, put their plan before the annual meeting of the Berry Street Conference. On May 25 the plan was presented: "It is proposed to form a new association, to be called the American Unitarian Society." They called for the uniting of all Unitarian Christians in the country with a purpose of the "publication and distribution of tracts, and the support of missionaries." Because members of the conference felt it was improper for them to act on such a subject, a meeting was held that afternoon, and all those who attended voted in favor of the proposal. The following morning a constitution (prepared by a committee consisting of Gannett, Walker, and Lewis Tappan) was presented that stated that the object of the new Association was to "diffuse the knowledge and promote the interests of pure Christianity." The group elected William Ellery Channing president, but he declined (Aaron Bancroft of Worcester was persuaded to take the office). Channing was opposed to an organization such as this for mere sectarian purposes. There were many who feared the loss of the pure democracy found in the Congregational church with authority being vested in a higher ecclesiastical entity.

With the organizational structure in place, a new institution had to be built. The work of the AUA largely fell to the Executive Committee, especially the secretary who was the chief executive officer (Gannett served in this capacity from 1825 to 1831). The AUA was formed as an association of individuals, not churches, and thus memberships had to be secured through the formation of auxiliaries in local congregations. In 1826 the association took on the responsibility of publishing the paper the *Christian Register*. The AUA was incorporated in 1847 during the administration of Charles Briggs. Initially the association did not have its own building, but used its publishing agent's offices for the conduct of business. After the Civil War the AUA owned two different buildings, and finally in 1886 the first 25 Beacon Street was built at the corner of Bowdoin Street next to the Massachusetts State House. The association moved into the "new" 25 Beacon Street (the same number was transferred to a nearby location) in 1927, where the merged **Unitarian Universalist Association (UUA)** remains today.

Until the Civil War, the AUA was primarily concerned with missionary activities and publications. The missionary activities mostly consisted of pulpit supply and grants for the building of new meetinghouses. Funds were also given to support Joseph Tuckerman's ministry to the poor. An essential part of the missionary effort was the publication of tracts, of which 10 or more were published each year. Although the AUA was not initially involved in the settlement of ministers, after 1860 ministers seeking settlements were listed in *The Monthly Journal*, and soon thereafter the secretary became directly involved with both candidates and congregations. The AUA was always a strong supporter of theological education, especially after **Meadville Theological School** was founded in 1844. Funds were eventually offered for the support of a principal, a professor, and for scholarships. During its formative years the AUA was hindered by lack of financial support. The Boston area churches had largely been fearful of bureaucratic control, but of greater concern were the theological differences. By 1853 Transcendentalists and other radicals threatened the Christian basis of the AUA, and in response the annual meeting passed a resolution affirming the "teachings of Christ . . . as infallible truth from God." They further declared that "the Divine authority of the Gospel, as founded on a special and miraculous imposition of God, is the basis of the Action of the Association."

In 1865 the **National Conference of Unitarian Churches** was organized, but the AUA remained an association of individuals until 1884, after which churches could become members. After 1900 administrative responsibilities changed, so that the president became the chief executive rather than the secretary. The first person in this position was **Samuel Atkins Eliot**, who served until 1927. By the end of his administration the annual budget was $170,000, and the AUA employed a staff of 27 (during the early years the AUA had a staff of one and a budget under $10,000). By 1900 there were 457 Unitarian churches in North America, but this fell to 377 active congregations in 1934 with 61,898 members. In 1912 a new Department of Religious Education was organized, and thereafter the prime responsibility for developing curriculum and training fell upon the AUA rather than the Sunday School Society. In the years leading up to merger with the Universalists, the AUA managed to reverse its decline during the presidency of **Frederick May Eliot**, 1937–58. The most significant event of this era was the development of the **fellowship movement**. At the time of merger, the AUA numbered 405 churches and 305 fellowships with a total membership of 117,000. Other significant events during this time included the establishment of a Department of Ministry, the founding of the Unitarian Service Committee, and on the controversial side, the removal of Stephen Fritchman as editor of the ***Christian Register*** after he was accused of being a communist. Over the years of its existence the AUA was hindered in its ability to function by local groups and individuals who feared centralized power and, especially, by theological and political controversies. The AUA ceased to exist when consolidation with the Universalists was finalized in May 1961.

AMES COVENANT. This covenant was composed by Charles Gordon Ames around 1880 for the Spring Garden Unitarian Society in Philadelphia, of which Ames was the founder. Ames was a Unitarian minister who was active in extension efforts in the west and also served the church in Germantown, Pennsylvania, and the Church of the Disciples in Boston. The original text read: "In the freedom of the truth, And the spirit of Jesus, We unite for the worship of God, And the service of Man." Many Unitarian churches adopted it as a spoken part of their worship services and continue to use it today. There have often been slight modifications of the text, especially the substitution of the word love for freedom, and most congregations have changed the word "man" to the more inclusive "all."

ANONYMOUS ASSOCIATION. The group that fomented the first organizational meeting of the **American Unitarian Association (AUA)**. The Anonymous Association was a conversation club consisting of approximately 35 liberals who were interested in promoting the liberal Christian viewpoint. David Reed, the editor of the ***Christian Register***, reported that this group met in private homes during 1824 to discuss religious and political issues. In one session held in the fall at Mayor Josiah Quincy's house, several members discussed promoting liberal Christianity through printed materials. A committee was formed consisting of **Henry Ware Jr.**, Alden Bradford, and Richard Sullivan. On December 29 they sent out an invitation to a meeting in January for all interested parties who wished to gather "for the purpose of union, sympathy, and co-operation in the cause of Christian truth and Christian charity." On May 25, 1825, the AUA held its first organizational meeting.

ANTHONY, SUSAN BROWNELL (1820–1906). One of the significant leaders of the woman's suffrage movement, Susan B. Anthony was born in Adams, Massachusetts, on February 15, 1820. Her family was fairly prosperous when she was young, as her father owned a cotton mill. A devout Quaker, Daniel Anthony believed in the education of both male and female children and was also an advocate for temperance. When she was 12, Susan joined the Society of Friends. She became a teacher and eventually moved to Rochester, New York, with her family after her father had suffered severe financial losses.

While in Rochester, she continued to teach. Her family began to become involved in antislavery activities and split with the Rochester Society of Friends over this issue. Susan, her father, and other liberal Quakers began to attend the First Unitarian Society around the time of the Women's Rights Convention in 1848, but she did not join the church until 1893. She remained an active participant in the life of the church, including teaching Sunday School. Both her parents and her sister Mary attended the second Women's Rights Convention at the Unitarian Church in 1848 and signed the Declaration of Sentiments.

In 1851 Susan met Elizabeth Cady Stanton, and soon a lifetime friendship and collaboration developed. Encouraged by her minister **William Henry Channing**, Anthony began to become active in the woman's rights movement. Before the Civil War, she organized a petition campaign that helped bring about the passage of a bill in the New York legislature that greatly extended the rights of married women. Realizing soon after the war that suffrage for women would not easily be won, Anthony and Stanton organized the National Woman's Suffrage Association in 1868, with Susan managing it with exceptional skill. She had been living in New York publishing a paper called *Revolution*. A more conventional group, the American Woman's Suffrage Association, was organized the following year. Twenty-one years later these groups merged, with Stanton and later Anthony serving as president. In 1876, the women gathered at the Centennial Exposition were denied the opportunity to present a "Woman's Declaration of 1876" by the Centennial Commission, but the First Unitarian Church in Philadelphia opened its doors for a meeting of this group. Anthony and Stanton joined efforts again in 1880 to write the *History of Woman Suffrage*.

Later Stanton published *The Woman's Bible* (1895), a series of commentaries on how the Bible had been used to subjugate women. Three Universalist clergy served on the committee to prepare the book. The National and American Woman's Suffrage Associations responded by voting to condemn their former president. Anthony fought against this: "The religious persecution of the ages had been carried on under what was claimed to be the command of God. I distrust those people who know so well what God wants them to do because I notice it always coincides with their own desires." From the early years in Rochester when she decided to defy the custom, vote and be arrested and fined, to her later years when she campaigned and spoke state by state, Anthony labored to convince both Republicans and Democrats alike that suffrage for women belonged in their party planks and in the Constitution. In her later years Anthony was friendly with her Rochester minister **William Channing Gannett** and his wife, Mary, who helped support her on one of her California campaigns. Anthony died on March 13, 1906, 14 years before the Nineteenth Amendment enfranchised women.

ANTI-TRINITARIANISM. A general term to characterize several theological viewpoints, all of which deny the full divinity of Jesus Christ. Anti-Trinitarianism encompasses **Arianism**, a fourth-century heresy that defines Christ as inferior to God the Father but having been created before the beginning of the world and being more than a mere mortal (a kind of demigod); **Socinianism**, a 16th-century heresy that defines Christ as strictly human (a humanitarian Christology) but called by God on a special mission; and Unitarianism, a word first used in 1569 in Transylvania to signify that God the Father is superior to the Son and the Holy Spirit—it is a position that may encompass either Arianism or Socinianism and perhaps even more radical positions such as the view held by many Unitarian Universalists in the 20th century that Jesus was merely a great teacher. Unitarian literally refers to the oneness of God as opposed to the Trinity. Other religious positions such as those held by deists (**Thomas Paine**, **Thomas Jefferson**, Benjamin Franklin) also rejected the doctrine of the Trinity. Before 1750 a public espousal of anti-Trinitarianism was rare in New England. In 1755 **Jonathan Mayhew** stressed the unity of God in his published book, *Sermons*. Arianism was the most common form of Unitarianism well into the 19th century. The more radical Socinian position was taken by **James Freeman** of King's Chapel. Socinianism was also associated with the Unitarianism of England. Because of this, liberals in New England were slow to accept the label "Unitarian"; their version of anti-Trinitarianism was predominately Arian. In 1812 Francis Parkman Sr. wrote that the liberals in Boston hold "high and exalted views of the person and mediation of Jesus Christ," and he said that Freeman was the only Unitarian minister. For the liberals Christ became less a source of atonement to God and more a source of revelation from

God who inspires humans by the purity of his character. Except for some early Universalists, including **John Murray**, most Unitarians and Universalists have held some variety of anti-trinitarianism. *See also* ARIANISM; SOCINIANISM.

✓**ARIANISM.** Arianism was a fourth-century heresy that denied both the divinity of the preexistent Christ, the Logos, and the divine nature in the born Christ, Jesus. It derives its name from Arius (c. 250–c. 336), a priest at Alexandria whose Christological viewpoints were condemned at the Council of Nicea in 325 and again at Constantinople in 381. Of utmost importance to Arius was the absolute unity of God. The eternal uniqueness of God made it impossible for God's being or essence to be shared, and thus the Trinity was rejected. Arius wrote: "We are persecuted because we say that the Son has a beginning, but God is without beginning." The absolute, unbegotten, eternal unity of God made the "begotten Son" subordinate and inferior. Despite his created nature, the Son was not like other creatures, but rather was "God's perfect creature," who became the "Source of all things." Thus the Son became a kind of exalted, intermediate being, who was neither fully divine nor fully human. After 381 Arianism was banished from the Roman Empire, but anti-Trinitarian viewpoints continued to appear from time to time. Arianism was adopted by most of the anti-Trinitarians in America in the late 18th and early 19th centuries. Only a few of those anti-Trinitarians who came to be called Unitarian held the Socinian view of the simple humanity of Jesus.

ARMINIANISM. Arminianism derives its name from Jacobus Arminius (1560–1609), a Dutch reformer whose views on Calvinist doctrines were condemned at the Synod of Dort in 1618. New England liberals were given this name because they also rejected the five traditional points of Calvinism (Predestination, Limited Atonement, Total Depravity, Irresistibility of Grace, and the Perseverance of the Saints), not because they were directly influenced by Arminius. The movement began at the time of the Great Awakening and especially flourished in greater Boston. Following a literal use of the Bible and human reason, the Arminians asserted the freedom of the will, rejected original sin, and declared that human beings are largely saved by their own efforts. Although God continued to determine the conditions for salvation within this scheme, individuals could make use of their opportunities, and moral striving and discipline would be rewarded. The concept of a totally corrupt and sinful human nature was replaced by the ability of every person to achieve goodness. In conjunction with this, a morally inscrutable God was replaced by a benevolent Father who desired the happiness of His children. By 1800 virtually all the Congregational ministers and churches in Boston were Arminian in orientation, and many of those were soon given the name Unitarian.

ASSOCIATION OF UNIVERSALIST WOMEN (AUW). The first general organization of Universalist women occurred in 1869 as a means to help raise funds for the General Convention's celebration of the 100th anniversary of John Murray's landing in America. The Women's Centenary Aid Association succeeded in its purpose and met in 1871 to disband. The group decided that it wanted to continue with its commitment of working together for the larger movement, and it voted to reorganize as an independent organization, dropping the word *aid*. It was chartered in 1873 with purposes that included: assisting weak parishes, building up Sunday Schools, educating ministerial students, relieving needy ministers and their families, distributing literature, and promoting missionary work. Its first president was the Rev. Caroline A. Soule. One of its first missionary efforts was with Scottish Universalists, who conferred ordination on Mrs. Soule, making her the first woman ordained in Europe.

By 1891 the association had raised $250,000, and distributed five million tracts. In that year the association was reorganized, and many state and local groups were formed. After the turn of the century, Japan became a major focus for the association, when it employed a missionary on its own payroll and then took charge of the Blackmer Home for Girls and two kindergartens. The association even added the word *Missionary* to its name. After 1913 their official publication was *The Bulletin*. The association became interested in camp activity, and junior groups were developed called Clara Barton Guilds. In 1911 the AUW assumed full responsibility for the superintendency of the North Carolina State Convention. This included assistance to small parishes, a Southern Building Fund, and a social service center,

Friendly House in Pigeon River Valley. One of the great success stories of the association began in 1920 with the purchase of the Clara Barton birthplace. The Universalist women wanted to create a shrine devoted to the great humanitarian and also carry on some kind of social service project. In 1932 an annual summer camp for girls with diabetes was begun, carrying on today as the Clara Barton Camp.

In 1939 the name of the organization was changed to the Association of Universalist Women, and new goals were launched as well. No longer satisfied to be only a missionary society, the association wanted a program to cover all the interests of Universalist women, including a program of personal spiritual growth. After the war, the Joslin Camp for diabetic boys was established to complement the girl's camp. After support for the North Carolina churches was given back to the convention, the association voted continuing support for the Jordan Neighborhood House, a nursery school, kindergarten, and social center for the black community in Suffolk, Virginia. The association increasingly tried to coordinate its departmental programs of service, education, and publications with those of the Universalist Church of America. In the early 1950s a committee of women began to meet with a like committee from the Alliance of Unitarian Women, and this resulted in closer cooperation and eventual merger in 1963. *See also* UNITARIAN UNIVERSALIST WOMEN'S FEDERATION.

ATHEISM. This implies the absolute position that there is no God. James Turner writes in *Without God, Without Creed*, that while the term was used in antiquity to describe those heretics who dissented from orthodox doctrines, genuine fear of disbelief did not surface until around 1600. Then it was almost another century before true atheists appeared. While there were some philosophers who questioned how knowledge of God was attained, and the materialist Thomas Hobbes became the most feared "atheist" of this time period; it was the break-up of medieval cosmology and the application of Newtonian science that resulted in further fears of the suspension of belief. Even though a denial of revelation and the birth of natural religion led the orthodox to see atheism everywhere, there were still only a handful of disbelievers in the world by 1750. Christian beliefs were diluted further by the application of reason to belief and the reduction of faith to morality.

Jonathan Mayhew, an important 18th-century liberal described Christianity as "principally an institution of life and manners, designed to teach us how to be good men, and to show us the necessity of becoming so." Liberals such as Mayhew encouraged their parishioners to believe in God only after impartially examining the questions. This rational and empirical path to God ultimately led most Unitarians to the position of Theodore Parker, the famed Transcendentalist, who said that the foundation of religion is "laid in human nature." While Parker still affirmed that the Divine could be experienced inwardly, God's role in the observable world became less tenable. Universalist minister **Abner Kneeland** was accused of atheism in the 1830s and holds the distinction of being the last person in the United States to be convicted and imprisoned for blasphemy. While trying to assert his belief in pantheism, his words were misconstrued when he wrote: "Universalists believe in a god which I do not; but believe that their god, with all his moral attributes (aside from nature itself) is nothing more than a chimera of their own imagination." By the end of the 19th century the idea of believing in God became more a matter of individual choice.

In 1867 Unitarian Charles Eliot Norton declared that religion had become "the most private and personal part of the life of every man." He felt the "decay of belief in creeds" was due to the "progress of science." Christian beliefs that were tested by the empiricism of science were found wanting. This is precisely why atheism became a common theological position among Unitarian Universalists. In *The Faith of a Religious Atheist*, a denominational pamphlet, W. Bradford Greeley writes, "For many of us who accept the description atheist, the growing understanding of life and living provided by the sciences leads to the final dissatisfaction with traditional theologies. We believe the evolution of knowledge and reason has moved us beyond the necessity of such belief." In the report *The Quality of Religious Life in Unitarian Universalist Congregations* (1989) 18 percent of Unitarian Universalists said that God is an irrelevant concept and the central focus of religion should be on human knowledge and values. Another 2 percent said God is a concept that is harmful to a worthwhile religion. This represented a decrease in percentage from the 1967 *Report of the Committee on Goals*, where 28 percent said God is an irrelevant concept and 1.8 percent said God is a harmful concept. These percentages led *Newsweek* to report on April 17, 1967: "To many mainstream Christians, Unitarians are largely atheistic intellectuals who can't kick the habit of going to church." While the idea of denying God has existed since ancient times (Psalm 14:1—The fool says in his heart, "There is no God.") it has only become possible in the last two centuries. In the attempts to make God more and more like a human being—intellectually, emotionally, and morally—the shapers of religion made it feasible to abandon God and believe simply in humanity. *See also* DEISM.

ATONEMENT. Atonement generally refers to the reconciliation between God and humankind, usually accomplished in Christian theology through the sacrifice of Jesus Christ. It became an important concept to Universalists through the seminal work of **Hosea Ballou**, ***A Treatise on Atonement*** (1805). Traditionally Christ had to atone for the sins of humanity by pacifying the Father with his sacrifice. In Ballou's view, Christ's role is to reconcile humanity to God and not the reverse. God is not a vengeful being seeking infinite satisfaction for the sins of humanity but rather a benevolent Father who sends Christ to show His infinite love. Ballou wrote: "To say that God loved man any less after transgression than before, denies his unchangeability; but to say that man was wanting in love to God, places him in his real character. As God was not the unreconciled party, no atonement was necessary for his reconciliation . . . but if man were the unreconciled, the atonement was necessary to renew his love to his Creator" (Ballou, *Treatise*, 99–100).

ATWOOD, ISAAC MORGAN (1838–1917). Coming from a poverty stricken, self-educated background, Atwood became one of the foremost leaders of the Universalist church in the late 19th century. Atwood went to work when he was 11 and experienced farming, stable cleaning, and mule driving on the Erie Canal. He managed to educate himself, convert from the Baptist faith to Universalism, and begin a life devoted to the church and its ministry starting at the age of 23 when he was ordained in September 1861 at Clifton Springs, New York. That same year he married Almira Church; they had five children. He served a succession of churches in New York, Maine, and Massachusetts. He was also editor of the *Universalist* (later merged with the *Christian Leader*) from 1867 to 1872. He was minister of the Third Universalist Church in Cambridge, Massachusetts, in 1879 when he was chosen the second president of Canton Theological School at **St. Lawrence University**. Not known as an educator, Atwood had to be convinced to take the position. That same year he received an honorary D.D. from Tufts. He was a decisive leader for the school, but he was handicapped by a lack of funds, especially in his role of fund-raiser for the College of Letters, which he helped save in 1886 by working to raise $52,000. During his early years there, the theological school built and moved into its own building, Fisher Hall.

In 1898 the **Universalist General Convention**, under intense pressure from a group of ministers who wished to promote denominational unity through "a spirit of loyalty and subordination," created the position of **general superintendent** of the Universalist church. Atwood was the first person to assume this position, and he tried ably to unite the denomination—not an easy task with some Universalists fearing that the denomination would become an episcopacy and Atwood a bishop. Atwood traveled widely in his new role (32,000 miles in the first year alone), visiting churches and state conventions and encouraging missions in the South, the West, and in Japan. He tried to increase fund-raising by establishing a "Twentieth Century Fund," but it fell short of its goal. Atwood did succeed in giving the far-flung and often rural Universalists a sense of common purpose and goals and a more centralized organizational basis. After his first year he wrote, "I believe more than ever in the Universalist Church—in its ideas, in its usefulness, in its ministry, in its membership, in its mission. I feel that our call has been renewed, and it is, as it was, the call of God." **Robert Cummins** writes that Atwood was an "eloquent and able preacher and an inspiring teacher," but was somewhat less skilled in administration. Over the years he published many books and articles. He retired from his leadership position in 1907 and returned to St. Lawrence University (New York), where he taught philosophy and theology for the last five years of his life and also ministered to the Universalist church in Canton. He died on October 26, 1917.

ATWOOD, JOHN MURRAY (1869–1951). The longtime dean of the Theological School at St. Lawrence, Atwood had deep roots in both

Universalism and upstate New York. His father, **Isaac Morgan Atwood**, was president of the Canton Theological School for 20 years and the first general superintendent of the Universalist church. John was born in Brockton (then Bridgewater), Massachusetts, on September 25, 1869, when his father was minister there, but they moved to Canton, New York, the site of **St. Lawrence**, when the boy was 10. He attended Canton Academy and then St. Lawrence, where he graduated Phi Betta Kappa in 1889. John was a reporter in Denver for a year, but then enrolled in the seminary. After graduation in 1893 he was called to the Universalist church in Clifton Springs, New York. He soon married Addie Ford and they had three children. Within a short time Atwood moved to Minneapolis where he served the Third Universalist Church. After completing a master's degree back in Canton, he moved on to serve a congregation in Portland, Maine. In 1905 he was invited back to serve on the faculty of St. Lawrence, and he taught sociology and ethics in the Theological School and Greek at the University. Atwood is remembered as a marvelous teacher—"the great object of education is to assist the individual to be what it is in him to be."

In 1914 he became dean of the Theological School, and subsequently academic standards were raised. Atwood was active with his local church and also with the New York State Convention. In 1923 he was elected president of the Universalist General Convention, where he spearheaded the "Five Year Program of Advance" and helped raise funds for the Universalist National Memorial Church in Washington. As the leader of the Theological School, Atwood used meager resources to keep the seminary on a steady course, and by 1947 a $100,000 endowment had been raised. Theologically, Atwood helped bring Universalism into the modern age of rational religion, as supernaturalism was left behind. A lover of baseball and a friend to all students, Atwood was associated with St. Lawrence for 47 years as teacher and dean. He died on November 4, 1951.

AUSTRALIA AND NEW ZEALAND. The origins of liberal religion in Australia began in the 1850s when Unitarians who emigrated from Great Britain founded congregations in Adelaide, Melbourne, and Sydney. The first meeting of Unitarians in South Australia occurred on July 11, 1854, when 12 people came in response to a public notice in Adelaide. In October 1855 the first service was held with the Rev. John Crawford Woods, who was sent by the British and Foreign Unitarian Association. Membership peaked at nearly 750 in 1881 and has fluctuated greatly, with about 100 at present. Woods had a long and successful ministry in Adelaide from 1855–1889. Catherine Helen Spence (1825–1910) was a significant member of this congregation. As a lay leader she helped increase public awareness of the need for greater opportunities for women in education, employment, and political participation. She played a major role in helping women gain the right to vote in 1894. This amazing woman became South Australia's first female preacher in 1878, helped establish the first government secondary school, and also became an important novelist. Spence now appears on the Australian $5 bill.

The Unitarians erected their first church building in 1856, and the congregation held services there until 1971. At that time the land on Wakefield Street was sold and a new church was built in suburban Norwood. Another group in South Australia in the Adelaide Hills met at the Shady Grove Unitarian Church, a schoolhouse that had been built by John and Priscilla Monks in 1854 but was dedicated as a church in 1865. This property is now managed by the group in Norwood, the Unitarian Church of South Australia. The Melbourne congregation was served by a woman preacher, Martha Turner, during its early years. Later it became known as the Melbourne Unitarian Peace Memorial Church. Both Melbourne and the Sydney Unitarian Church or the Unitarian Church in the State of New South Wales have been plagued with political controversy, where radical ministers have brought in many disgruntled transient people. This has made Sydney and Melbourne less stable than Adelaide. An example of this in Sydney is found with the career of James Pillars. Pillars was a charismatic preacher who drew such large crowds, the congregation started to erect a new building, but it stood unfinished for years because they kept fighting with Pillars and calling for his resignation. Finally, he died in 1875 from injuries suffered in a fall from cliffs in Sydney Harbor.

Unitarianism has mostly declined in Australia since its peak in 1891, although there was a period in the mid-20th century when Melbourne grew under the ministry of William Bottomley. There are also a number of fellowship groups that have been established over the years in both Australia and New Zealand. The Australian Assembly of Unitarian and Liberal Christian Churches was expanded in 1974 to become the Australia and New Zealand Unitarian Association (ANZUA). Their publication is *The Unitarian Quest*.

The church in Auckland, New Zealand, was founded in 1898, but services were first held in 1863 when Franklin Bradley, who had trained for the Unitarian ministry in Ireland, conducted worship services for 18 months. Their first minister, William Jellie, arrived in 1900, and the main part of the current church building was constructed in 1901, at which time there were 468 members. The church declined after Jellie left around 1910, and like the Australian churches, membership has fluctuated greatly. All of these congregations belong to the British General Assembly of Unitarian and Free Christian Churches, and the Adelaide and Auckland groups are members of the **Unitarian Universalist Association (UUA)**. Among all these congregations there are more than 300 members and they belong to the **International Council of Unitarians and Universalists (ICUU).**

– B –

BALCH, EMILY GREENE (1867–1961). Born and raised in the Jamaica Plain section of Boston as one of six children, Emily Greene Balch found strength and determination through her Unitarian faith. As a child Emily was influenced by the ministry of Charles Fletcher Dole at the First Congregational Society (Unitarian) and pledged herself to "goodness" when she was 14. Dole was an opponent of immigration restrictions and believed that labor unions and socialism were humane responses to the harsh problems brought on by industrialization; lessons that Emily later taught and worked for. She attended the newly established Bryn Mawr and graduated with its first class in 1889. After studying abroad and a period of volunteer work, she helped to establish a settlement house. This gave her direct contact with many of Boston's reformers including Mary Kehew, director of the Women's Educational and Industrial Union and another Unitarian. Here she decided to combine a career of study and research with activity in the public sphere.

In 1896 Balch accepted a position as professor of economics at Wellesley College, where she remained until 1915. Balch was active in many reform movements helping to combat industrial accidents, childhood poverty, and overcrowded and dangerous housing conditions with various inspections and codes. She helped found the Boston Women's Trade Union League to help women establish trade unions. She declared herself a socialist in1906 and regularly taught a class on it at Wellesley. In his Province of Reason, Sam Bass Warner Jr. writes of Balch, "Beneath the respect for facts and the attention to the details of human experiences rested her deep commitment to the values of her Emersonian religion." Warner says her sense of wonder and fusion of heart and mind appear in her study of immigration, *Our Slavic Fellow Citizens*.

After 1914 Balch became increasingly interested in working for world peace. She used her previous knowledge and experience to foster effective political action, and her devotion centered on what was called the Wisconsin Plan—continuous negotiations among belligerents. In 1916 she worked for the International Committee on Mediation, gathering documents that eventually resulted in her work, *Approaches to the Great Settlement*. After the United States entered the war, she worked to defend pacifists. For a few years she had been taking unpaid leaves from Wellesley, and found, largely due to her political activities, that her contract was not renewed in 1918. For the next 20 years Balch served the Women's International League for Peace and Freedom, seeking to bring the forces of reason and good will to bear through open dialogue and respect for all sides.

Her struggles for peace and disarmament were seemingly lost with the rise of fascism, but she eventually supported American involvement in the war and worked to aid Jewish refugees and interred Japanese Americans. She applauded the launching of the United Nations, but said world government was meaningless unless it had a "moral quality." In 1946 Balch became the third American woman to win the Nobel Peace Prize, and she was given the Unitarian Distinguished Service Award in 1955. After a long life of service and activism, she died in 1961.

BALLOU, ADIN (1803–1890). Founder of the utopian community at **Hopedale** and a Universalist and Unitarian minister, Ballou was a major contributor to ideas of Christian nonresistance. He was born in Cumberland, Rhode Island, on April 23, 1803, into a large extended family of Ballous, many of whom became Universalists. His parents were Ariel and Edilda, farmers who also owned a sawmill and cidermill. Adin became a tall farm boy who attended school when he could, often only in the winter. He had to quit altogether when he was 16, and his father later discouraged him from going to college, despite a love for reading. In 1815 the entire family was swept up in a great revival and all became converted to the Christian Connection. Adin was baptized and his father became a deacon of a newly organized church. Adin remained active with the church and at 19 felt a call from God to preach when his deceased brother appeared to him in a dream.

After he became a Christian Connection minister he began to attack the heretic Universalists, especially his distant cousin **Hosea Ballou**. He decided that he needed to become more familiar with the scriptures and Universalist writings, but unexpectedly the study resulted in his conversion to Universalism. This also helped his love life, as he was able to marry his Universalist sweetheart, Abigail Sayles. After supplying Universalist pulpits, Adin was called to the First Universalist Society in Milford, Massachusetts, in 1824. He left to briefly serve in New York and then returned to Milford. Almost immediately, he became involved with the theological controversy that was embroiling the Universalists. He was a believer in **Restorationism**, that there would be a period of suffering for sin after death where the soul is purified and brought into harmony with God. He published a weekly paper, *The Independent Messenger*, which helped promote this belief. In 1831 the Restorationists withdrew from the denomination, and Ballou was dismissed by his congregation. Almost immediately the Congregational Church in Mendon, Massachusetts, invited him to be their pastor. He served there for 10 years promoting social justice causes especially temperance and abolition.

Becoming familiar with the ideas of William Lloyd Garrison, Ballou began to advocate nonresistance, and the first organization he participated in was the New England Non-Resistance Society. Ballou became especially committed to the idea of Christian Perfectionism and split from his fellow Restorationists in 1837. He developed a "Standard of Practical Christianity" and advocated nonresistance to human government before the Non-Resistance Convention in 1839. Ultimately this led to the principle of refusing to obey earthly governments, as the only law is the will of God. Many of his ideas were expressed in *The Practical Christian*, which he started in 1840. He conceived of living out his faith through an ideal community originally called Fraternal Community Number One. The principles of the new community included belief in the religion of Jesus, never to hate, no taking of oaths, and no participation in war.

In March 1842, 28 people committed themselves to forming a community where all property would be held in common and all work and profits would be shared. The community, now called Hopedale because they first occupied an overgrown farm that had no apparent promise, was a relative success. It survived for 14 years with 600 hundred acres added to the original farm. The venture collapsed when its two largest financiers withdrew their capital. This was a lasting disappointment to Ballou. His story of the experiment is recounted in *The History of the Hopedale Community* (1890). After its collapse, the community continued as a church with Ballou as its minister. It was organized as the Hopedale Liberal Christian Parish (1867) and joined the local Unitarian conference. Ballou was never able to find a community that could truly live out his principles of practical Christianity. For many years he corresponded with the Russian philosopher Leo Tolstoy, who greatly admired Ballou's thoughts and writings. He died on August 5, 1890.

BALLOU, HOSEA (1771–1852). The central figure in the Universalist movement in the 19th century. Ballou was born the 11th child of Maturin and Lydia Ballou on April 30, 1771. The family had moved to the backwoods of New Hampshire in the spring of 1768. His father was a Baptist preacher and farmer, and his mother died before he was two. Hosea had very limited schooling and learned the skills of farming in a difficult environment. After he joined his father's church, he began to have questions of faith. This was partly brought on by the preaching in nearby Warwick, Massachusetts, of the Universalist **Caleb Rich**. Hosea wanted to defend his faith, but found that his study of the Bible affirmed universalism. His father eventually accepted the new faith, but it took time. Once his father found him reading in the kitchen, and asked, "What is that book?" Hosea said it was a Universalist book. His father declared that he could not allow a Universalist book in his house. Hosea knew his father was watching as he hid the book in the woodpile. Later Maturin went to the woodpile and found that the dreaded book was the Bible.

Hosea was able to save some money, had one term of school at Chesterfield Academy, and showed such promise that he was given a teaching license. In 1791 Hosea and his brother David went to the Universalist convention in Oxford, Massachusetts. He listened to many sermons at the meeting and felt called to preach the Universalist gospel. Thereafter he started an itinerant ministry and taught school. This culminated in his being ordained at the convention in Oxford in 1794 by Elhanan Winchester. Ballou's first settled ministry was Dana, Massachusetts, which was the center for his circuit riding. Ballou became well known as he preached from Vermont to Rhode Island. He also filled **John Murray**'s pulpit in Boston for several Sundays.

Ballou's first published work was a correspondence with Joel Foster from New Salem, Massachusetts, where they discussed the issue of future punishment. Ballou also married Ruth Washburn from Williamsburg, Massachusetts, in 1796, and they eventually had eleven children, but two died in infancy. In 1803 the Ballous moved to Barnard, Vermont, where he again spent time on a circuit of congregations. Ballou's theology began to coalesce at this time. He encountered the deism of **Ethan Allen** and came to his Unitarian view of Jesus, which was published in his great work, *A Treatise on Atonement*. In this book, he affirmed the use of reason in interpreting scriptures, denied original sin and Christ's blood sacrifice, and said humans did not have the power to resist God's plan of salvation for all. Ballou also believed in immediate salvation for all upon death with no period of cleansing for the soul. This became known as Ultra or Death and Glory Universalism.

After his ministry in Vermont, Ballou moved on to Portsmouth, New Hampshire, in 1809 for six years, then two years in Salem, Massachusetts. In the meantime, some of the Universalists in Boston became dissatisfied with the Calvinistic version of Universalism that was preached at First Universalist. They formed the Second Universalist Society in 1817, two years after John Murray's death, and asked Ballou to come minister to them. He accepted a position that catapulted him into being the acknowledged leader of the movement. He remained in Boston for the rest of his career and helped give the denomination a solid foundation. Two years later he started and edited the ***Universalist Magazine***, which later evolved into the ***Christian Leader***, the prime denominational periodical.

In 1821 he helped publish a hymnal. A little more than 10 years later he found his views on immediate salvation coming under attack from those who insisted that there was a period of reprobation for sin. Ballou remained committed to the position that people suffer for their sins in earthly life. He rejected the idea of individual moral rewards for behavior and advocated a corporate view of salvation. The renegade Restorationists left the denomination in 1831 and remained out for 10 years. Universalism expanded rapidly in Ballou's later years, and he frequently went on preaching tours, including a visit to New York six months before his death. He died on June 7, 1852, the acknowledged leader and "Father Ballou" of the movement.

BALLOU, HOSEA II (1796–1861). An important educator and editor who became the first president of **Tufts College**. Ballou was born in Guilford, Vermont, on October 18, 1796. He attended local schools, and then became a teacher. In 1813 he began to work in a school in Portsmouth, New Hampshire, of which his great-uncle **Hosea Ballou** had oversight. "Father Ballou" encouraged him in the ministry, and while helping out in Portsmouth and doing itinerant preaching, he was a recognized minister within three years. Ballou's first regular parish work began in 1817 in Stafford, Connecticut, the only Universalist church in the state.

In 1820, he was married to Clarissa Hatch, his childhood sweetheart. He served the church in Roxbury, Massachusetts, from 1821–1838, and during 10 of those years operated a school with his brother Levi.

In the 1820s he was editor of the ***Universalist Magazine***. His major work as a scholar was written during this period, *Ancient History of Universalism* (1829), the first comprehensive work to study Universalist history using primary sources. It identified Universalist origins in the Christian church, especially in the thought of Origen. He also became the first president of the Universalist Historical Society when it was organized in 1834. Ballou became a mentor to many students, including **Thomas Starr King**. He was active in the Restorationist controversy, where he developed a reputation as a peacemaker. He played this same role at the New England Conventions, where he was clerk for many years. He was known as a scholar, writer, and thinker, but not for pulpit eloquence. He ended his ministerial career with a pastorate in Medford, Massachusetts, from 1838 to 1853. It was during this latter period that he became affiliated with the newly founded **Tufts College** and he became its first president. In 1847 an educational convention met in conjunction with the Universalist General Convention in New York. After the General Convention, where Ballou gave the principal sermon, he was earmarked to head up the new plans for a theological school. He took a seat on **Harvard**'s Board of Overseers when William Ellery Channing died in 1842, and he stayed until 1858. He held the first Doctor of Divinity degree ever given to a Universalist (1845). Ballou also drew up the rules for academic progress at Tufts and served on the State Board of Education. Ballou started his full duties at Tufts in 1854, where he taught courses, was school librarian, and conducted religious services, as well as carrying out his duties as president. Ballou died in office on May 27, 1861.

BAPTISM. This is one of two Christian sacraments (the other was the Lord's Supper) retained by most Protestants after the Reformation. Calvin defined baptism as "the sign of initiation by which [Christians] are received into the society of the church, in order that, engrafted in Christ, they may be reckoned among God's children." Baptism in the liberal tradition comes from Puritan ancestors who dissented from the Church of England in three ways: making the sign of the cross, for which they felt there was no biblical basis; the role of godparents, whom they believed were usurping the duty of parents to promise that children were brought up Christian; and private baptism, as it was a ceremony that should be celebrated publicly in church. Baptism became a major issue for the second generation of Puritans as piety declined, and few became converted saints of the church. After it was recommended by a synod in 1662 a devise called the "Half-Way Covenant" became popular throughout New England, especially in the churches of eastern Massachusetts that later opted for Unitarianism. Parents who were in sympathy with the church, but had not had a conversion experience, could be allowed to have their children baptized when they "owned the covenant."

After the Great Awakening, liberals began to baptize any infants whose parents made a request, and although most continued to use the word baptism well into the 20th century, they rejected the Puritan belief in the stain of original sin: "Don't you think that a child brings enough sin into the world to damn it forever?" Some Unitarians and Universalists rejected infant baptism because of its association with original sin, and others simply gave it other meanings, or devised their own ceremonies, especially so that the positive potential of each child was affirmed and the Trinitarian formula did not have to be invoked. *The Universalist Manual* (1839) declared that baptism was neither "necessary" nor "obligatory" and when baptism was used the following words were suggested: "I baptize thee in the name of the Lord Jesus, and into the faith and profession of his holy religion." This publication also provided for an alternative "dedication of children." Stating that there were many in the Universalist denomination who could find no scriptural basis for requiring baptism, they did not consider it a "duty incumbent on them, to offer up their children in the ordinance of water baptism, either by immersion or sprinkling." The public dedication of children had become a popular practice, as children were offered up to God's service. Leonard J. Livermore in his **American Unitarian Association (AUA)** tract, *Baptism*, declared that this rite was "only a symbol" of being born into the church of Christ and it "pledges the parent to fidelity in his efforts to make it a lasting and complete union by the Christian nurture and instruction of his offspring." Many churches made baptism a requirement for joining the congregation, but this mostly had fallen out of favor by 1900. Infant baptism began to be conducted less frequently and was less central to the worship experience. Some clergy used a variant of the Trinitarian formula when they conducted such services. In Winchendon, Massachusetts, Andrew Culp devised these words: "________, I baptize thee in the name of God the Father, whose child you are, in the name of Jesus Christ, who loved little children, and in the name of the Holy Spirit which is promised to you."

While some congregations still use the word "baptize," it was mostly replaced, even in Unitarian Universalist (UU) Christian congregations, by the word "christen" by 1950. Other UU congregations began to use the "naming ceremony" or, more frequently, "child dedication," especially after the Unitarian Universalist consolidation in 1961. Despite the differences in the use of terminology, most UU congregations practice some kind of ritual to welcome children into their faith community and the world. The ceremony may be public or private and its elements may include water and a traditional baptismal font or other symbolic representations of life such as a flower. Most clergy use whatever words or practices they are comfortable with ("I dedicate you to the love of God and the service of all," or some variation thereof). Despite the differences in theology, affirming the worth and potential of the child, the responsibilities of the parents, and the importance of a larger spiritual and ethical home are central to the dedication of a new life.

BARNUM, PHINEAS TAYLOR (1810–1891). The great circus master was also one of the most devoted Universalists in the 19th century. Barnum was born on July 5, 1810, in Bethel, Connecticut, into a family of entrepreneurs. His father was a tailor who also ran a tavern, a freight service, and a livery stable. He died when "Taylor" was only 15, leaving the family insolvent, although his childhood poverty was greatly exaggerated in the autobiography Barnum published in 1854–55 (*The Life of P. T. Barnum, Written by Himself*). Barnum was named for his maternal grandfather, a practical joker who also introduced the boy to Universalism. Brought up Congregationalist, Barnum became a Universalist about 1824 when neighboring Danbury called its first settled Universalist minister, and apparently Barnum was clerk of the society at one time. At the age of 16 he moved to New York and was a store clerk and purchasing agent. A little more than two years later, he was married to Charity Hallet on November 8, 1829. Upon his return to Bethel, he began to write editorial letters to the paper about the separation of church and state. When they would not publish his letters, Barnum started up a rival paper, *The Herald of Freedom*. The paper carried a series on the "Proofs of Universalism." During his editorship he was sued for libel and found that his own testimony was inadmissible because he was a Universalist and therefore not accountable to God. He was convicted and served two months in jail. He returned to New York and launched his career as a showman touring with jugglers, minstrels, and various oddities, including Joice Heth, reputed to be the 161-year-old nurse of George Washington.

The major turning point in his career occurred in 1841 when the American Museum went up for sale, and Barnum was able to purchase it. The museum was an ever-expanding five-story building of natural wonders and curiosities, which eventually included America's first public aquarium. He became an active participant in the Fourth Universalist Society in New York and was especially friendly with its minister **Edwin H. Chapin**. The two men were seen together so much that they were compared to the famous Chinese Siamese Twins, Chang and Eng, who were part of Barnum's exhibitions. After Chapin's death, Barnum began to attend Unitarian services given by **Robert Collyer**. Barnum was most committed to the First Universalist Society in Bridgeport, Connecticut. After 1848, he was the greatest financial contributor to that church by far, and also donated enormous sums for various building projects. He left the church a sum in his will that became known as the Barnum Fund. **Olympia Brown** was his minister from 1869 to 1875. He was very supportive of her work and, often, she said, complimented her preaching, but her women's rights advocacy led to a schism and her early dismissal. It was during this time that he emerged from a retirement brought on by fires at the American Museum.

Barnum's new career was the circus business. With his tremendous talents for promotion and publicity he greatly increased the size and variety of the circus and was the first to utilize railroads for travel, and advance agents. For 20 years he ran the "greatest show on earth." Another minister who became Barnum's friend was Elmer Capen, the third president of **Tufts College**. Barnum served on the Board of Trustees there from 1851 to 1857 and, with Capen's encouragement, endowed and built the Barnum Museum of Natural History, which opened in 1884. He often gave the museum mounted animal hides from deceased circus performers, including the elephant Jumbo, who became the Tufts mascot. Barnum also gave money to a number of other Universalist schools and groups around the country. Near the end of his life he published the best selling pamphlet *Why I Am a Universalist*. It had a wide readership, remained in print for many years, and so enthralled George Perin, missionary to Japan, that it became the first Universalist tract translated into Japanese. In it Barnum postulated that death does not end character development, but that the soul continues to develop in the world to come. By the time of his death 60,000 copies were in circulation. Barnum was a fascinating mix of the gospel of success and the "Prince of Humbug," with a free thinking faith that promised self-expression and salvation for all, and sometimes led to the circus master being called the "Reverend" P. T. Barnum. He died on April 7, 1891, and the funeral was conducted on the 10th by Collyer and his Universalist pastor from Bridgeport, Lewis B. Fisher.

BARR, A. MARGARET (1899–1973). She was a British Unitarian minister who was devoted to the Unitarian movement in the Khasi Hills in northeast India. Born into a Yorkshire Methodist family on March 19, 1899, she discovered Unitarianism while studying for her degree at Cambridge. Fitted to be a teacher, she then trained for the ministry at Manchester College, Oxford. Barr served as minister for six years at the Church of Our Father in Rotherham, in the industrial heartland of England. After hearing about the indigenous movement of Unitarians in India at a meeting of the British General Assembly, Barr became convinced that she must see the work of Gandhi and work in village life in India firsthand. She wrote: "Here I am: send me." Unfortunately, the General Assembly was reluctant to send a lone woman to India. Her heart's desire to work in India was realized in 1933 when she secured a position at a school in Calcutta that operated under the influence of the **Brahmo Samaj**. She spent two-and-half years there, producing a volume on how to teach interreligious understanding to children, *The Great Unity* (1937).

After receiving a one year exploratory commission in the Khasi Hills from the General Assembly, Barr set off for the remote region of Assam, where she would spend the rest of her active career. Here she helped establish a vibrant faith community with much social and educational outreach. Barr assisted the local congregations in opening schools and orphanages. For more than 10 years Shillong, the capital, was her base for assisting the Unitarian churches. By the late 1940s the two schools there were operating well and she began to search for a new field. Following Gandhi's lead of going to the villages, she settled in Kharang, where she established a Rural Centre with a residential school. She also became nurse, midwife, and counselor to many. There is a Memorial Hospital in Kharang named for Kong Barr (Big Sister). During this time she also remained the superintendent minister for the Unitarian Union of the Khasi and Jaintia Hills, a position she had held since 1936. She had charge of arranging services and training leaders. She disliked the idea that she might be considered a missionary. Rather she saw herself as a "Bridge-Builder" between cultures and religions who wanted to make Unitarian contribution to social progress. In 1963 she received the **Unitarian Universalist Association (UUA)** Award for Distinguished Service. She was also named a fellow of Manchester College, Oxford, the first woman to receive that honor (1971). At the end of her life she told her story in *A Dream Come True: The Story of Kharang* (1974). She died, on the job, in 1973.

BARTÓK, BÉLA (1881–1945). The great Hungarian composer was born on March 25, 1881, in what was then part of the Austro-Hungarian Empire, but is now Sinnicolau Mare, Romania. He received his first piano lessons from his mother and began composing at nine and playing in public when he was 11. His father was a school principal who died when Béla was only seven. The family moved around some after this. In 1899 Bartók entered the Royal Academy of Music in Budapest, where he graduated in 1903. He also began to seriously compose at this time, influenced by Liszt, Brahms, and Richard Strauss. His first major work was *Kossuth* (1903), named for the Hungarian rebel. Bartók became fascinated by the folk music of his native land after he heard some of it performed in the summer of 1904. One of the first people to propagate the use of popular Hungarian music was Samuel Brassai, a precursor to Bartók, who was also Unitarian. Bartók developed a friendship with Zoltan Kodaly and they collected folk music together.

In 1907 Bartók became a professor at the Royal Academy. He was an outstanding pianist whose concerts were usually limited to his own compositions. In the late 1920s he toured the United States and the Soviet Union, eventually playing in 22 countries in all. He resigned from the Academy in 1934, but continued his research on ethnic music as a member of the Hungarian Academy of Sciences. He became increasingly fascinated with the roots of meters, rhythms, and modalities of the spontaneous folk traditions of the entire region, including Romanians, Slovakians, Croatians, and others, as well as Hungarians. He was later criticized for including those areas that were no longer part of Hungary after World War I. Bartók also became interested in children's musical expressions. He once wrote, "I cannot conceive of music that expresses nothing." He left Hungary in 1940 to lecture in the United States and remained there during the war. He taught as a visiting associate in music at Columbia, from which he received an honorary doctorate.

Bartók's last completed score, the *Concerto for Orchestra*, became his most popular work. He was working on his third *Piano Concerto* at the time of his death, and it was completed by his student Tibor Serly. Bartók suffered some financial difficulties during his last years, and his recordings became much more popular after his death. He died on September 26, 1945, with a service held at All Souls Unitarian Church, New York. Bartók's remains were returned to Budapest for a state funeral in 1988. His son, Béla Jr., was the lay president of the Unitarian Church in Hungary at that time. The father had converted to Unitarianism in 1916 after visiting Transylvania. He joined the church in Budapest in 1917, attended there frequently, and for a time was involved with the music committee. Bartók once said he would cross himself before his version of the Trinity: "Nature, Art and Science." He was married twice and was the father of two boys, one from each marriage. Finding great inspiration in nature and his native heritage, Bartók advised others to drink only "from a clean spring."

BARTON, CLARISSA HARLOWE (1821–1912). The Civil War "Angel of the Battlefield" was also the founder of the American Red Cross. Clarissa Harlowe Barton was born on December 25, 1821, in North Oxford, Massachusetts, to an active Universalist family. The youngest of five children, Clara's father Stephen and her mother Sarah (Stone) both rejected their Baptist heritage. He was present at **Hosea Ballou**'s ordination, and later became an officer in the Universalist church in North Oxford. A shy child, Clara was a regular attendee at the Universalist church, but her memories were mostly of how cold it was in the wintertime. Although she did not join, Barton remained devoted to the institutional church and helped raise money for a new building in Oxford in 1844. Later in life she referred to herself as a "well-disposed pagan," but she also wrote that she considered herself a Universalist throughout her life and apparently joined the Universalist Church of our Father when she lived in Washington.

Encouraged to be a teacher, Clara began to teach in North Oxford when she was only 15, but left to enroll in the Clinton Liberal Institute in New York. After her graduation she moved to New Jersey, where some Universalist friends resided. Here she opened the first public school in Bordentown. The school was a great success and led to the establishment of a permanent public school there. When the job of principal that she wanted was offered to a man, Clara felt rebuffed and resigned. Feeling worn from her labors, Clara moved to Washington, D.C., and became a clerk in the U.S. Patent Office. When the Civil War broke out, Barton's compassion was activated by the sight of trains of wounded soldiers, specifically the Sixth Massachusetts Regiment. During the war years she organized field hospitals and tended to the sick, wounded, and dying, and her front line aid, especially at Antietam, earned her the Angel of the Battlefield nickname. After the war she traveled to Andersonville Prison in Georgia to help identify the dead. After a brief period on the lecture circuit, Barton went to Europe to try to recover her health. The Franco-Prussian War broke out, and Barton went to assist on more battlefields. Here she first saw the work of the Red Cross, and became determined to found an American branch. She worked hard to see it come to pass, and when Chester Arthur signed the Treaty of Geneva, Barton was appointed the first president of the Association of the American Red Cross. She remained in that position for 23 years, during which the Red Cross became directly involved in peacetime disaster relief, such as the Johnstown flood.

In 1900, she wrote to Vincent Tomlinson, the Universalist minister in Worcester, "Surely the love that surpasses fear should be the strongest stimulus to all good endeavor." This love made Barton a true international humanitarian who always defied the "tyranny of precedent" especially to relieve someone's suffering. She died in Glen Echo, Maryland, on April 12, 1912. In 1920 the Women's National Missionary Association began to discuss purchasing her birthplace as both a Universalist shrine and a service project for the Clara Barton Guilds, which had been established at many Universalist churches. The next year the property was purchased, eventually becoming the Clara Barton Camp for Diabetic Girls, the first such facility in the country.

BEACON PRESS. This is the denominational publishing house of the **Unitarian Universalist Association (UUA)**. Although one of the major enterprises of the **American Unitarian Association (AUA)** was the publishing of tracts after its founding in 1825, Beacon Press dates its beginning from 1854. On March 9 of that year AUA President Samuel Kirkland Lothrop addressed a small gathering at the opening of a new AUA headquarters on Bromfield Street in Boston and suggested that book publishing might be a major new undertaking of the denomination. He said, "We can send forth a thousand volumes, to be read by ten thousand persons for what it will cost to send one missionary to speak here and there to a few hundreds." Lothrop called for the establishment of a fund to be used to promote the publication, sales, and distribution of books. Over the next century the AUA published more than 500 titles. The Beacon imprint and colophon was first used in 1902 when Livingston Stebbins became publishing agent.

For most of its history Beacon Press has printed primarily denominational tracts. It began a modern thrust in religious education materials during the 1930s under the leadership of **Sophia Lyon Fahs**, when the first of the Beacon Curriculum was published. The press was substantially revisioned during the presidency of **Frederick May Eliot**, who appointed Melvin Arnold director of the division of publications in 1945. Under Arnold's leadership Beacon became a prominent voice for liberalism. Arnold tried to attract authors who would appeal to the general trade market, but he had little to work with for a backlist and had no funds. A major change occurred with the publication of Paul Blanshard's *American Freedom and Catholic Power*, one of the most controversial and successful books Beacon ever published. It detailed Catholic positions on many matters, including birth control and censorship, and showed its threat to democracy. The book's success made it possible for Beacon to expand its operation. In 1955 Beacon paperbacks were offered for the first time, published in full library size rather than the more common pocketbook editions. These "quality" paperbacks were an enormous success, so much so that when Arnold left in 1956, Beacon had a backlist of 321 titles, 302 more than when he had arrived.

Beacon Press found a secure place in the field with many of its scholarly titles, and it developed a strong reputation for courage and integrity. This was especially evident in 1971 when Beacon, under the leadership of Gobin Stair, and the UUA made a decision to publish the ***Pentagon Papers***. This 7,000-page collection of documents chronicled America's involvement in Vietnam. The Federal Bureau of Investigation (FBI) began to investigate the UUA, and a legal battle ensued. Gobin Stair wrote: "It was a watershed event in the denomination's history and a high point in Beacon's fulfilling its role as a public pulpit for proclaiming Unitarian Universalist principles." Over the years Beacon has continued to publish books that promote liberal values and has been especially strong in gay and lesbian and feminist studies. After 1990 best sellers by Marian Wright Edelman and Cornell West gave the press a more visible presence. Despite its relative independence from the UUA bureaucracy, every Beacon edition bears the notice "published under the auspices of the Unitarian Universalist Association." Since the mid-1970s many of the books that are more narrowly focused on Unitarian Universalism have been published by the UUA under an inhouse imprint, Skinner House Books. *See also PENTAGON PAPERS*.

BEACON STREET. Beacon Street and, especially 25 Beacon Street, is synonymous with Unitarian Universalist headquarters in Boston. Beacon Street was an undeveloped area during the early history of Boston. Once known as Poor House Lane because of a nearby almshouse, Beacon Street was laid out in 1708. The name came from the signal lantern on the summit of the hill. After the Massachusetts State House was built in 1795 by Unitarian architect **Charles Bulfinch**, stately row houses were built along Beacon Street. Just to the left of the State House is "25 Beacon." Only the first floor façade of the original house remains on the building constructed by the **American Unitarian Association (AUA)** from 1925 to 1927 for their new headquarters building. Prior to this the AUA occupied a building from 1886 to 1925 just to the right of the State House that had originally been assigned the number 25. Unitarian headquarters had been in Boston since its inception in 1825, but not on Beacon Street until 1886. Over the years the association has owned a number of office buildings on Beacon Hill, including a house at 16 Beacon Street that was once known as the Unitarian annex and was Universalist headquarters from 1933 until the merger in 1961. The Universalists always had trouble agreeing on a location for central offices and made Boston a temporary site in 1918. Other significant Unitarian Universalist buildings on Beacon Street include a former Unitarian Universalist Service Committee headquarters at #78, the **King's Chapel** Parish House at #63–64, and opposite the State House entrance on the border of Boston Common is the Robert Gould Shaw Memorial. Shaw, the commander of the famous 54th Massachusetts, a black regiment in the Civil War, came from a prominent Unitarian family.

BELLOWS, HENRY WHITNEY (1814–1882). The leading force in the organization of the Unitarians into an association of churches in the 19th century. Bellows was born a twin into a large family in Boston on June 11, 1814. His father was a successful businessman as president of a local bank and importer of dry goods. Bellow's mother, Betsy, died when he was less than two, and he and his brother were cared for by an aunt until John Bellows married again. Henry attended a boys' school in Jamaica Plain and later the Round Hill School in Northampton, Massachusetts. He was admitted to **Harvard College** at the age of 14, and graduated in 1832 with the intention of being a minister. He wanted to enter **Harvard Divinity School** that fall, but his father had met financial disaster, and Henry needed to develop some of his own resources. He taught in Cooperstown, New York, and then tutored on a plantation in Louisiana. He returned to school in 1834 and graduated in 1837. Bellows had a six-month trial ministry in the church in Mobile, Alabama, but the slavery issue was beginning to unsettle his conscience.

Bellows returned north and received a call to the First Congregational Church in New York City, now All Souls. He was ordained and installed there in January 1839, where he remained for 43 years. That summer he married Eliza Townsend, and together they had five children, three of whom died in infancy. Later he married Anna Peabody with whom he had three more children. Bellows's early years in the parish drew in many new people, a new building was completed in 1845, and the church was renamed the Church of the Divine Unity.

In 1846 he helped to start the *Christian Inquirer*, a weekly paper, which Bellows was editor of for 11 years. He also edited the *Christian Examiner* from 1865 to 1869. During the next several years Bellows cultivated his friendship with Peter Cooper, and together they raised funds for a variety of causes, including an endowment for Antioch College. Bellows worked with Cooper to establish the Cooper Union in 1859, a community center that provided classes for working people, and a forum, where President Abraham Lincoln later gave a famous address.

One of Bellows's great contributions came during the Civil War. After the war broke out, a group of women from Bellows's church organized an aid society to help the wounded and improve camp conditions. Bellows saw that this idea needed to be broadened so that there was a central agency for coordinating medical relief and other special services for soldiers. After a committee meeting in Washington, Bellows convinced President Lincoln of the need for such an organization, and the U.S. Sanitary Commission was organized in June 1861 and Bellows became its president. Under Bellows's direction, campsites were cleaned up and food, clothing, and medical supplies delivered while hospital conditions were improved. The government did not provide funding, so Bellows had to raise money and was especially aided in this effort by **Thomas Starr King**. After the war, the commission helped the soldiers adjust to civilian life through jobs, pensions, and medical care, and Bellows worked hard to see the United States ratify the Geneva Convention, but it did not occur until after his death when the American Red Cross was established.

Bellows's great denominational contribution was to affect the establishment of a national Unitarian organization for church membership. Prior to 1865 the **American Unitarian Association (AUA)** was an association of individuals who did little to organize and promote the extension of Unitarianism. Bellows had predicted a more active national mission for the church when he delivered *The Suspense of Faith* in 1859. He helped organize a meeting in New York for ministers and delegates from churches in April 1865. This was the first time that Unitarian churches had direct representation at an official gathering. Here the **National Conference of Unitarian Churches** was organized, giving churches an official voice within the denomination. Bellows was made president of this new organization, but perhaps a more worthy title was applied in a memorial address after Bellows's death when Frederic Henry Hedge referred to him as "our Bishop." Bellows was a particularly influential member of a group of Broad Church supporters who wished to welcome a variety of theological viewpoints under the banner of Unitarianism. Bellows died on January 30, 1882, and was buried in Walpole, New Hampshire, near the family ancestral home he had purchased in 1854.

BELSHAM, THOMAS (1750–1829). The able leader of British Unitarianism who stabilized the foundations established by **Theophilus Lindsey** and **Joseph Priestley**. Belsham was born at Bedford in 1750. His father was a dissenting minister and Thomas was educated at the dissenting academy at Daventry to be an Independent (Congregational) minister. He tutored at the school for seven years following graduation and then, after a brief ministry, he returned to Daventry to be principal. As the instructor in divinity he began to question his own teachings and finally had to resign his post in 1789, when he became Socinian. Lindsey, Priestley, and Richard Price urged Belsham to accept the position of tutor at the New College at Hackney, where he taught until 1794. Then he was called to serve the Gravel Pit Church in Hackney, which Priestley was leaving to move to America. In his farewell, Priestley charged Belsham with carrying on the work of championing the Unitarian faith in Britain. He had already begun to do this. During his tutorship he had proposed the formation of the Unitarian Society for Promoting Christian Knowledge and the Practice of Virtue by the Distribution of Books (1791). This organization succeeded in unifying the Unitarians by giving them a common purpose and name, although all Arians, as worshipers of Christ, were excluded.

In 1805 Belsham was called to serve Lindsey's old pulpit at Essex Street, London. He now became the chief public defender of Unitarian views. One of his major projects was the editorship of *The New Testament* in an improved version (1808) by the Unitarian Book Society. In the meantime, a monthly magazine had been established by Belsham's successor at Hackney, Robert Aspland, and a Unitarian Fund for mission work was started. Shortly thereafter, Belsham published what he considered his most significant work, *Memoirs of Theophilus Lindsey* (1812). A chapter of this work on American Unitarianism was later reprinted by Jedediah Morse in America to show that American and British views on Jesus were identical. In fact most of the Americans were Arian, while the British were Socinian. Of greatest importance at this time was the passage of the Trinity Bill (1813), which finally made Unitarianism legal. Several Anglican clergy attacked the Unitarians and said the old laws denying civil rights to deniers of the Trinity should be restored. Belsham courageously defended the Unitarian faith in print and from pulpit against all challenges. An assistant came to join Belsham in 1825. By this date there were over 200 Unitarian churches in England, whereas when he became Unitarian in 1789 there were only two. Belsham had always had weight problems, and this became even more problematic as he aged. He finally had to use crutches constantly in order to get around. Being obese contributed to failing health, and he died in 1829.

BENEVOLENT FRATERNITY OF CHRISTIAN CHURCHES (BFCC). Starting out as a mission effort to the poor, the Benevolent Fraternity has evolved into the Unitarian Universalist Urban Ministry (UUUM). The organization had its origins on April 27, 1834, when nine Boston Unitarian churches united to form the Benevolent Fraternity of Christian (later, Unitarian) Churches (BFCC). The focus was to support **Joseph Tuckerman**'s Ministry at Large, which was inaugurated in 1826 to work with the poor in Boston. Within four years the BFCC had built two chapels, employed four ministers for outreach, and had 100 volunteers to help instruct children and adults in such skills as reading and sewing. The first chapel, Friend Street Chapel, was constructed in 1827. Friend Street closed in 1836 when the larger Pitts Street Chapel opened. Two of the early ministers in the ministry-at-large as it evolved into the BFCC were Charles Francis Barnard and Frederick T. Gray. Barnard later left the BFCC and ministered to the independent Warren Street Chapel for 32 years. Warren Street Chapel closed in 1925, but it lives on as the Barnard Memorial Fund, administered by the UUUM. John Turner Sargent served the Northampton Street Chapel (1837–1839) and then its successor, the Suffolk Street Chapel, which became the largest chapel under the auspices of the BFCC.

A significant event in BFCC history occurred in 1844 when Sargent exchanged with **Theodore Parker**. The Executive Committee of the BFCC declared that none of its ministers should exchange pulpits with the heretical Parker again. To defend the principle of the free pulpit, Sargent resigned his position. One of the longer term BFCC ministries was that of Andrew Bigelow who came to be minister-at-large in 1845 and stayed until 1877, first at Pitts Street Chapel, and later as visitor and spiritual advisor. The Hanover Street Chapel was founded in 1853 and it later evolved into the North End Union, a social work agency. In 1869 the Pitts Street Chapel was succeeded by the Bulfich Place Chapel. It was served for 33 years (1894–1927) by Christopher Rhodes Eliot, the brother of the famous poet T. S. Eliot. It finally closed in 1962 after many years as an effective social work center.

When the BFCC was organized in 1834, Joseph Tuckerman also formed the Association of Delegates from the Benevolent Societies in 1834 to help coordinate the relief work of 21 Boston agencies or charities. All of the congregations in Boston organized their own BFCC auxiliaries that raised funds and recruited volunteers. The programs of services and Sunday School at the chapels, and teaching of practical skills and visitation were primarily to produce a moral and economic improvement in the working class population. Historically the task of the BFCC was to aid individuals directly by providing a religious presence and social services. During the 1860s as immigrant populations increased, a ministry to Italians, Spaniards, and Greeks was formed. The **American Unitarian Association (AUA)** also helped support the establishment of the ministry-at-large in other cities, including New York. Fifty-seven Unitarian Universalist congregations in greater Boston are members of what is now the Urban Ministry. Programs today include Renewal House, a shelter for battered women and their children, which opened in 1980; a variety of Youth Programs for both teens and younger children that grew out of the presence of the First Church in Roxbury, which merged into the Benevolent Fraternity in 1976; social action ministries, which include advocacy in a number of areas; and an Asian Food Pantry. Throughout its history from BFCC to UU Urban Ministry this organization has advocated for the economic and educational reform of society through active social ministry.

BERRY STREET CONFERENCE. On May 30, 1820, **William Ellery Channing** invited those ministers who were identified as liberal Christians to meet at the Federal Street Church to organize some kind of group that would be mutually beneficial to all the clergy. The door leading to the Federal Street Church vestry was on Berry Street. In the address he gave at the formation of this organization, Channing said, "It was thought by some of us, that the ministers of this Commonwealth who are known to agree in what are called Liberal and catholic views of Christianity, needed a bond of union, a means of intercourse, and an opportunity of conference not as yet enjoyed" (Channing, *Life*, p. 218.). Channing proposed that the group meet annually especially to hear an address and also to spend time in prayer, hear reports on the churches, and to consider the best means for advancing religion. The Berry Street Conference is the oldest Unitarian organization still in existence today. An association of liberal congregations was first proposed at the conference's 1824 meeting, and the **American Unitarian Association (AUA)** was organized the following year. Octavius Brooks Frothingham reported that meetings of the conference were not advertised and attended almost exclusively by clergy. The normally placid setting occasionally provoked heated discussions such as when John Pierpont introduced the subject of slavery or Theodore Parker addressed rationalistic criticism. Today the essay is given in conjunction with the annual meeting of the Unitarian Universalist Minister's Association at the General Assembly. It is considered a high tribute to one's ministry to be chosen for the honor of giving the annual essay.

BIANDRATA, GIORGIO (1516–1588). A leading Unitarian voice in both Poland and Transylvania, his reputation suffered when he helped convict **Francis David** of heresy. He was born in 1516 at Saluzzo in Piedmont. He finished his degree at the University of Montpellier in 1533, where he became a physician, specializing in women's health. He wrote on women's health and attained a significant reputation in the field. Consequently he was employed as the court physician to Queen Bona of Poland and her daughter Isabella. He stayed there for 12 years, returning to Italy in 1553. Although Catholic, he began to study the reformers, and after he fell under suspicion, he fled to Geneva in 1556. He began to study the scriptures and questioned the deity of Christ more seriously. Coming under Calvin's suspicious eye, Biandrata eventually fled to Zurich and then on to Poland with Laelius Socinus.

In 1558 Calvin referred to Biandrata as a monster who could foster more monsters. He returned to Poland and settled in Pinczow, where he found anti-Trinitarian views being discussed, especially by Peter Gonesius. Biandrata became a significant leader of the movement and was chosen elder for the district of Krakow in 1560. Calvin warned the authorities of Biandrata's heresies, but the physician was able to convince them that he remained orthodox. In 1563 the young King John Sigismund of Transylvania became seriously ill. Biandrata, who had previously been the physician for John and his mother Isabella when Queen Bona sent him to Transylvania in 1554, was summoned to come to Transylvania again. As Calvin was pursuing Biandrata, this seemed like a fortuitous time for him to settle elsewhere. He accepted the position of court physician to the King of Transylvania. Biandrata became an important figure at court and a leading advisor to the king.

In 1564 **King John Sigismund** sent Biandrata to the Synod at Nagy Enyed, where the Calvinists were trying to achieve recognition. Here Biandrata encountered **Francis David** representing the Calvinists and was so impressed he used his influence with the king to have David appointed court preacher and bishop of the Reformed Church. Over the next several years there were many theological debates with David and Biandrata representing the Unitarian viewpoint. During this time, the king was converted to Unitarianism and the Edict of Toleration at Torda was approved in 1568. After King John's death, the fortunes of the Unitarians declined. Biandrata warned David about speaking out for innovations that became outlawed, but David refused to compromise his principles. Realizing that the Jesuits hoped to destroy the Unitarian movement, Biandrata summoned **Faustus Socinus** to convince David to moderate his positions especially on the worship of Christ. Biandrata decided he could no longer support David's radicalism. He turned against David and led the prosecution, which resulted in David's conviction and imprisonment at Deva. It is difficult to determine whether Biandrata was motivated by jealousy of David's leadership or feared that his radicalism would destroy the movement. After David died, Biandrata had a brief period of continuing influence in the church where he manipulated the clergy to adopt safe positions, including a confession of faith that accepted the adoration of Christ. Biandrata was also able to see that his candidate for bishop of the Unitarian church, Demetrius Hunyadi, was elected. He continued to retain his position as court physician, but increasingly disowned the Unitarians and gravitated toward the Jesuits. He died in 1588 in Gyulafehervar.

BIBLE. Even before the Protestant Reformation, scholars began to discover a biblical basis for Unitarian beliefs. During the early 16th century the great humanist Erasmus worked on a Latin translation of the New Testament. He discovered that the Trinitarian reference in I John 5:7 was a late textual addition and omitted it from his version. This use of reason in understanding scripture prefigured the liberal approach. Almost 300 years later **Joseph Priestley** based his religious beliefs on the scriptures as final authority, but he used critical freedom in rejecting sections regarded as additions to the original text. His friend **Thomas Jefferson** went even further when he produced the famous *Jefferson Bible*, which included a paste-up of Jesus' sayings and other passages Jefferson considered relevant but no miracle stories.

Liberals in New England at this time continued to hold to scriptures as the fundamental authority for believers. When **Henry Ware** was elected **Hollis Professor of Divinity** at Harvard in 1805, the only article of faith required was that "the Bible is the only and most perfect rule of faith and practice," and this was to be interpreted "according to the best light that God should give him." More than 15 years before this **James Freeman** had cited scriptural passages that led him to deny the Trinity, leading **King's Chapel** in Boston down the Unitarian path. Unitarianism was solely a biblical religion, but it was a biblical understanding by **Joseph Stevens Buckminster**. **William Ellery Channing**'s sermon "**Unitarian Christianity**" (1819) was a comprehensive exposition of a Unitarian approach to scripture. Channing viewed the scriptures as "the records of God's successive revelations to mankind, and particularly of the last and most perfect revelation of his will by Jesus Christ." While Channing affirmed the supernatural basis of the miracles, he also abandoned the theory of direct verbal revelation from God, and he held that certain parts of scripture were more important than others.

The **Transcendentalists** began a movement away from the belief in the Bible as the final arbiter of religious truth. **Theodore Parker** and others began to question the infallibility of the Bible and rejected the letter of the Bible in order to speak a more personal inner truth. He "would make it our servant, not our master." Controversy continued for many years for even as late as 1853, the **American Unitarian Association (AUA)** passed a resolution: "That the Divine authority of the Gospel as founded on a special and miraculous interposition of God for the redemption of mankind is the basis of the action of this Association." By the 1870s the Bible remained a rule of faith, but it had only a measure of divine authority, and **James Freeman Clarke** wrote that it is "not the only rule."

This was less true for Universalists who discovered their doctrine of salvation for all through studious readings of scripture. **Caleb Rich**, perhaps the first important native leader of the movement, had many charismatic experiences after intense Bible study. In his youth Rich's pupil **Hosea Ballou** read the Bible as the only book he knew. He used proof-texting to establish his Universalism; I Timothy 2:1, 6 clearly indicated that Christ gave himself as a ransom for all. In 1804 Ballou published *Notes on the Parables of the New Testament*. Universalists were not as quick as Unitarians to accept rationalism and biblical criticism. In 1850 most Universalists still believed in divinely inspired scriptures, and many of the clergy called themselves Bible Universalists, so there was no mistaking their loyalty.

Horace Greeley, the famed newspaper man and Christian Universalist wrote that those who rejected the authority of the Bible could not be part of the Universalist clan. This began to change toward the end of the 19th century. **Orello Cone**, a Universalist minister and world-renowned biblical scholar, brought an acceptance of higher criticism to Universalist circles. Cone taught that when reading the scriptures one must look for the spirit behind the letter of the texts for they should not be taken literally in many parts. He believed that science and religion could complement each other. Slowly the Universalists began to depart from the strict biblical foundations, but the Unitarians adopted a broader approach sooner. By the end of the 19th century, Unitarian **Jabez Sunderland** posited that there are two Bibles. One is an outgrown Bible of tradition and ignorance, and the other is the new Bible of inquiry and intelligence. From this time, the authority of the Bible began to wane considerably, so that its truth rested with the individual and not with the church or tradition. It was not until the mid-20th century that Universalist Brainard Gibbons called the Bible "a marvelous work of man, not the miraculous handiwork of God." This general superintendent of the Universalist Church of America (UCA) said "Universalists find God more fully and truly revealed in the universe and man than in the Bible. Brotherhood is more reliably demonstrated by biology than the Bible and is common to several world religions."

After 1920 a strong humanist influence was felt. Horace Westwood wrote: "Our doctrine of freedom recognizes the authority of neither church, Bible, sacred person, nor tradition save insofar as this authority confirms the verdict of one's own soul." Thus the Bible became a personal document. A modern view of the Bible was summed up by A. Powell Davies in a denominational pamphlet from the 1950s. He wrote that contemporary liberals view the Bible: "Not as a verbally inspired book but as a collection of many books of varying value, written over a long period of time. They do not think the Bible is a supernatural revelation, but they do find in it many insights and messages of enduring value." Most Unitarians hold that the scriptures of the great religions are of similar value, and that inspired words are still being written." So the Bible became one of many religious books that Unitarian Universalists draw inspiration from, picking and choosing those texts and stories that uncover universal truths. Unitarianism and Universalism began as protests about the interpretation of scripture. Early liberals sought a purer Christianity that went beneath the doctrines in the "religion about Jesus" to live the ethical truths found in the "religion of Jesus."

BIDDLE, JOHN (1616–1662). An English Puritan reformer who spent much of his life in prison for his heretical views. Biddle was born in 1615/16 at Wotton-under-Edge in Gloucestershire. The son of a woolen dealer, he attended Oxford. After graduation he attained a master's degree, became a teacher, and eventually the head of the Crypt School. Biddle began to study the Bible on his own and came to some startling conclusions. He circulated a paper denying the deity of the Holy Spirit, was called a heretic, and was jailed. For most of the final 17 years of his life he remained imprisoned. His paper, *XII Arguments Drawn out of the Scripture*, was published in 1647, and it helped keep him incarcerated. His second publication, *A Confession* *of Faith Touching the Holy Trinity, according to Scripture* (1648), questioned the doctrine of the Trinity as it had been corrupted by the Catholic church and also raised a furor. He was released on bail for a brief period, preached in Staffordshire, but then was returned to prison. He was finally released in 1652. He organized some private meetings for worship in London. At that same time a Latin edition of the *Racovian Catechism* was published in London, and an English one appeared in Amsterdam. The Parliament called it blasphemous, and declared that all copies should be burned. In the meantime Biddle was also busy reprinting his own works, a life of **Faustus Socinus** and two other Socinian tracts. Finally, he published *A Two-Fold Catechism*, drawn partly from the *Racovian Catechism*. This new Catechism resulted in attacks on Biddle in Holland where he was accused of Socinian Atheism, and in England, where he was brought before Parliament and charged with promulgating scandalous teaching. Even though he was released again, he soon engaged in a debate volunteering that Christ was not God. He was thrown back into prison again. In 1655 he was banished for life to the Scilly Islands. After two years he returned to London. In 1662 an Act of Uniformity was passed, and Biddle was again taken to prison after he was discovered holding private meetings for worship. This last imprisonment led to his becoming ill, and he died on September 22, 1662. Biddle believed that Christians are "obliged to be very Rational" in interpreting scripture, and this led to his denial of the godhead of Jesus Christ and the Holy Spirit. He believed that unreasonable doctrines must be rejected. For him the doctrine of the Trinity introduced three Gods and subverted the unity of God. Although he was not the founder of an organized Unitarian movement in England, John Biddle's Unitarian theological views, and the suffering he endured as a result of them, have led him to be called the father of English Unitarianism.

BLACK EMPOWERMENT CONTROVERSY. In the mid 1960s American society was torn by racial strife. Especially concerned by rioting in the cities and bearing the legacy of the civil rights battles in Selma, the **Unitarian Universalist Association**'s **(UUA)** Commission on Religion and Race and the UUA Department of Social Responsibility (with Department Director Homer Jack playing a significant role) organized "The Emergency Conference on the Black

Rebellion." The conference began on October 6, 1967, at the Biltmore Hotel in New York City. A movement supporting "black power" had developed at the Los Angeles church where Black Unitarian Universalists for Radical Reform (BURR) had formed. As people gathered for the conference, several black delegates were invited by BURR members to help form a black caucus. This black caucus formulated a plan to present to the conference. This included calling for greater black participation on UUA staff, board, and committees. The central request was for the creation of a new black controlled organization called the Black Affairs Council (BAC), which would be funded for $250,000 per year for four years with sole authority over its funds. While the conference voted to support this proposal, it had no binding authority with the UUA Board. The central issue was how much of an independent leadership role would be given to this group.

The UUA Board met in early November, voted down the new proposals in an emotionally charged session, and decided to reorganize the UU Commission on Religion and Race (created in 1963). The Commission helped subsidize a National Conference of the Black Unitarian Universalist Caucus (BUUC) in February 1968. This was attended by 207 black UUs and helped to solidify the impetus to create a new BAC to replace the old Commission. The conference recommended the creation of BAC with a quarter million dollar annual funding and also the creation of a permanent BUUC. A supportive white group also formed at this time, Supporters of Black Unitarian Universalists for Radical Reform (SOBURR) to organize nationwide white support. In March SOBURR wrote to all the ministers and board chairs in the UUA calling on them to recognize the validity of the Report of the National Advisory Commission on Civil Disorders, and support the creation of BAC. People sharing this perspective were asked to form a new group that would advocate at the next **General Assembly (GA)** in Cleveland for recognition of full funding for BAC. The new group was called FULLBAC.

In the meantime the UUA board had to address the issue of the creation of the National Black Caucus at the Conference in February. The board recognized the caucus and welcomed the application of BAC for affiliate status, but it also reorganized the Commission on Religion and Race and created a new group, a UU Commission for Action on Race, as well as a new Fund for Racial Justice. The association claimed that it could not forfeit its own responsibilities to have a programmatic response to racism, even though the BUUC had called for the dissolution of the commission. Members of BAC and BUUC were upset with the UUA Board for refusing to endorse groups with black leadership in confronting racism.

Prior to the GA, many UUs who opposed BAC and BUUC organized another group called BAWA (Unitarian Universalists for a Black and White Alternative). Led by Donald Harrington, minister of Community Church in New York, BAWA claimed that the Caucus was a segregated group and offered a more traditional integrated program that discounted racial differences. FULLBAC cochair David Parke responded that this approach perpetuated racism in middle-class rhetoric. The creation of BAWA did not address the issues of black leadership and power. At the General Assembly in Cleveland, the proposal for full funding BAC passed by a large majority. BAWA was denied funding. It briefly appeared that the denomination had decided to affirm black empowerment by these actions. However, in the wake of the GA, the board agonized over the issue of accepting an affiliate member group that segregated membership based on race (BAC had a majority of black board members, who were appointed by the all black caucus). Achieving affiliate status was not a problem for BAWA, which had now changed its name to Black and White Action. With no racial quotas stipulated, they received UUA recognition. During the year leading up to the next GA, financial concerns were raised. The board voted that the BAC funding would need to be reaffirmed each year. Matters worsened at the Assembly as the UUA Business Committee placed the new vote on whether to reaffirm BAC support several days into the agenda. **Jack Mendelsohn**, the minister of the Arlington Street Church called for a reordering of the agenda, but this failed to pass. With a sense of urgency BAC chairperson Hayward Henry declared that action on this issue was needed immediately. In a symbolic action black delegates stood by all the microphones on the floor of the assembly, with youth delegates next to them. Henry accused the UUA board of reneging on its commitment to fund BAC for four years that was made at the Cleveland GA. A motion to deal with the black agenda failed. Then the members of the BUUC walked out.

After the presidential candidates had spoken before the assembly to present their views for the upcoming election, the members of

FULLBAC returned to the platform led by Jack Mendelsohn. Mendelsohn said that the BUUC issues had not been addressed. Now he concluded he had to leave the Assembly, and he invited others to join him at the Arlington Street Church. More than 400 people filed in to the church. This group who made up "The Walkout" came to refer to themselves as "the Moral Caucus." President **Dana Greeley** convinced many of the members of the Moral Caucus to return the following day. Finally a vote was taken that BAC would be funded for another year and BAWA would not. Unfortunately the Board continued to struggle with whether they could afford to fund BAC. In January, 1970 the Board voted to cut the funding by $50,000. The leaders of BAC decided that they would not tolerate any more political wrangling with the UUA board over commitments they kept rescinding. As a funded affiliate they could not seek their own funding, and they decided to disaffiliate so that funding could go directly to BAC. This decision by BAC to leave the UUA umbrella effectively ended the UUA's commitment to racial justice for several years. It has been estimated that over 1,000 black UUs left the church over this controversy to affirm and fund black leadership within the UUA. BAC funded a number of programs between 1968 and 1973 with black self-determination central to its concerns, but a serious internal split eventually crippled its efforts. There was a contested annual meeting of the BUUC in 1973, and two BACs emerged and litigation followed. It was charged that a new group, the Black Humanist Fellowship, which was in favor of disaffiliating from UUA, was trying to usurp all the funds. Associate status for BAC in the UUA ended in 1979.

BLACKWELL, ANTOINETTE LOUISA BROWN (1825–1921). The first woman to be ordained by a congregation in America as a Congregationalist, Blackwell later fellowshipped with the Unitarians. She was born on May 20, 1825, to Joseph and Abby (Morse) Brown in Henrietta, New York, their fourth of seven children. As a girl she became a member of her parents' orthodox Congregational church, and later attended school at the Monroe County Academy. She became a teacher and soon saved sufficient funds to attend Oberlin College, from which she graduated in 1847. With some difficulty the school allowed her to take on a course of theological studies, but when she was finished they would not let her graduate or give her a preaching license. During her course of studies she preached as much as she could and taught at Rochester Academy in Michigan. After that she made a career out of lecturing on reform issues. She was a delegate to the first national Women's Rights Convention in 1850 in Worcester, Massachusetts.

Brown was called to the Congregational Church of South Butler, New York, and was ordained there on September 15, 1853. Unfortunately the Congregational General Conference protested the ordination, and **Olympia Brown**'s 1863 ordination is recognized as the first ordination of a woman with full ecclesiastical authority. She left that church within a year. By this time she was having doubts about Trinitarian Congregationalism. After she was married to Samuel Blackwell, she became a Unitarian. His brother was married to Lucy Stone, her friend from Oberlin and fellow worker for suffrage. Together the Blackwells had five children who survived infancy.

During the ensuing years, Blackwell continued to advocate for women to live lives with interests outside the home and to work part-time. She wrote eight books on a variety of subjects with special interest in science and nature. She was a well-known lecturer and frequently toured with **Susan B. Anthony** and **Julia Ward Howe**. She became one of the founders of All Souls Unitarian Church in Elizabeth, New Jersey, and later was named minister emeritus. Most of her married life was spent living in New Jersey, and she died in Elizabeth on November 5, 1821.

BOARD OF TRUSTEES. The **Unitarian Universalist Association (UUA)** is governed by a Board of Trustees consisting of district trustees selected by the various Districts (19 district trustees in 2003); and four trustees-at-large, who are elected by the **General Assembly (GA)**. The board meets four times per year; three times in Boston, and once at the General Assembly. The GA is the annual business meeting of the association. The UUA moderator, who is elected by the GA, presides at the GA meetings and the board meetings. In the original UUA bylaws of 1961 the board consisted of its officers (moderator, president, two vice presidents, secretary, and treasurer) and 20 trustees, who were elected directly by the GA. This changed in 1968 when the bylaws were altered so that the trustees were elected from the districts, allowing for more diversified representation. The organizing meeting of the UUA in 1961 considered a proposal for the board to select the president rather than the GA, but this was defeated. Prior to 1968 the board nominated the president, but this changed so that nomination was by petition thereafter.

BOSTON. Often called Unitarian Universalism's home city, it remains the site of the denominational headquarters, as it was for both denominations prior to consolidation in 1961. Boston is especially equated with the development of Unitarianism. Van Wyck Brooks wrote that Bostonians hardly knew that their old Puritanism had vanished and been replaced by a mild and tolerant faith "known far and wide as the 'Boston religion'" (Brooks, *Flowering*, p. 12). It was often said that the city was controlled by Unitarians in the period immediately after 1825. Henry Adams reflected upon this in a description of his childhood faith when he wrote: "Nothing quieted doubt so completely as the mental calm of the Unitarian clergy. In uniform excellence of life and character, moral and intellectual, the score of Unitarian clergymen about Boston, who controlled society and **Harvard College**, were never excelled. They proclaimed as their merit that they insisted on no doctrine, but taught, or tried to teach, the means of leading a virtuous, useful, unselfish life, which they held to be sufficient for salvation. For them difficulties might be ignored; doubts were waste of thought; nothing exacted solution. Boston had solved the universe; or had offered and realized the best solution yet tried. The problem was worked out" (Adams, *Education*, vol. 1, p. 35). Liberal religion began to dominate in Boston in the period after the **Great Awakening** leading up to the beginning of the Unitarian controversy in 1805. Liberal preachers were associated with Harvard College, with the majority being settled in parishes within the near environs of Boston and Cambridge. In the city itself the rational, entrepreneurial style of the faith proved effective when more than 70 Unitarian churches either evolved from the **Standing Order** of Congregational churches or were founded as separate institutions. In 1886 one of the denomination's leaders, **James Freeman Clarke**, offered a theology that offered five points of Unitarianism: "The Fatherhood of God, The Brotherhood of Man, The Leadership of Jesus, Salvation by Character, and the Progress of Mankind, Onward and

Upward Forever." The appearance that the origins and locus for the faith remained in the city were summarized in a shortened version of the five points: The Fatherhood of God, The Brotherhood of Man, and the Neighborhood of Boston. Henry Adams, who grew up on Beacon Hill, realized the social, cultural, religious, and political power that Unitarianism held in Boston from 1825 to 1865. First, the state church was disestablished in 1833, and after that demographics forever changed the character of the city as immigrant Catholics began to dominate.

BOSTON DECLARATION. This was a statement of faith passed by the Universalist General Convention in 1899 as an addition to the **Winchester Profession**. For some years prior to 1899 Universalists had been debating the "creed question." When the Universalists met in General Convention in Chicago in 1897, many groups feared that any changes in the Winchester Profession would result in disaster. Members of the Indiana Convention felt that a rewording of the creed would mean a "substantially new and different faith." While a revised profession had been defeated in 1895, this time a new "Boston Plan" was presented. The Boston area ministers recommended after surveying local congregations that the convention retain the Winchester Profession without amendment, but also adopt an alternate statement.

The new statement became known originally as the "Chicago Declaration" and it was proposed as article III in a new constitution. "The Five Principles" that were offered as an alternative were: The essential principles of the Universalist faith; "The Universal Fatherhood of God; the spiritual authority and leadership of His Son Jesus Christ; the trustworthiness of the Bible as containing a revelation from God; the certainty of just retribution for sin; the final harmony of all souls with God." Furthermore, the plan reintroduced the idea of a "liberty clause": "The Winchester Profession is commended as containing these principles, but neither this, nor any other precise form of words, is required as a condition of fellowship, provided always that the principles above stated be professed." There was none of the rancor of previous meetings at the 1899 sessions in Boston. Attendance exceeded even the centennial convention in Gloucester, Massachusetts. The new declaration was passed overwhelmingly, and without debate, becoming known thereafter as the Boston Declaration. Most

Universalists felt a new day had dawned in the history of the denomination. While acknowledging the important historic character of the old statement, a new profession was given equal status, and the freedom of choice was restored. the ***Christian Leader*** reported: "The Universalist Church has been reborn."

BRAHMO SAMAJ. A Hindu reform group that had important Unitarian ties in the 19th century. The Brahmo Samaj, or Society of God, was organized in 1828 by **Rammohun Roy**. Roy was a brilliant reformer who became a scholar of several traditions and was especially influenced by the New Testament and Jesus. With William Adam he helped found a Unitarian Committee in Calcutta. By 1828 Roy came to understand that he was not going to convert to Unitarian Christianity, and he decided to start a new group that would preserve many Hindu traditions. After Roy's death the next significant leader was Debendranath Tagore. In 1839 he started the Tattvabodhini Sabha to stem the tide of Christian conversions. He wanted to publish Hindu texts. In 1842 Tagore's organization merged with the Brahmo Samaj, and the following year it became a new sect of Hinduism. Unitarianism and the Brahmo Samaj intermingled again in the 1850s when the American Unitarian Charles Brooks arrived. Brooks had a short visit, but interest in India was rekindled so that an **American Unitarian Association (AUA)** missionary program was started with **Charles Dall**, who was sent to India to, among other things, investigate the Brahmo Samaj. In 1856 Dall met a young man named **Keshub Chunder Sen**, who became entranced with Unitarian writings and converted to the Brahmo Samaj in 1858. Initially Sen was interested in political reform especially in attacking the caste system and wanted to incorporate a spiritual Christ into the more Hindu oriented traditions. Tagore, who had been his mentor, resisted this, and a splinter group was formed in 1866 within the Adi Brahmo Samaj with the new group simply named Brahmo Samaj.

Sen's new movement was able to foment a Marriage Act, in which arranged child marriages were forbidden. Then great controversy developed in 1878 when Sen's own daughter was married in an arranged format at the age of 14. Moving away from a politically active faith, Sen emphasized a mystical approach now with a modified ascetic way of life. He said he had received a new revelation from

God and called his new group the Church of the New Dispensation (Navavidham). His former followers took on the name Sadharan Brahmo Samaj. Sen died suddenly, but a few years later there was an effort by the American **Jabez Sunderland** to unify the various factions. A joint Brahmo Samaj committee was created, and then the British and Foreign Unitarian Association voted in 1896 to support a variety of requests from Sunderland and Protap Mazumdar, who became the most important transitional leader. Mazumdar had written a book called *The Oriental Christ*, and had represented the Brahmos at the World Parliament of Religions in 1893. The British provided annual scholarships to Manchester College and support for joint educational efforts and a post office mission. The Brahmo Samaj became the first non-Western, non-Christian group to join what is now the International Association for Religious Freedom. The Sadharan Brahmo Samaj remains the central group today, but their class-bound Brahminism has given them minimal influence on cultural change. The Brahmo Samaj of today looks back to Rammohun Roy for inspiration. The New Dispensation has only a small following, and none are part of the Brahmo Samaj.

BROAD CHURCH MOVEMENT. In the late winter of 1865 **Henry Whitney Bellows** tried to devise a plan for unifying the theological factions within the Unitarian ranks. At a meeting in Boston on February 20, of 50 ministers, Bellows found that they could be divided into four groups. One faction he considered old-fashioned Unitarians who were interested in Brahmin self-culture and despised the Transcendentalists. A second group was the radicals who wanted to consider Christianity one of many great world religions. This group was especially suspicious of rallying around any standard of faith. A third smaller faction was made up of Evangelicals who believed in the miraculous nature of Jesus Christ. The fourth group, which included Bellows, **James Freeman Clarke**, **Frederic Henry Hedge**, and **Edward Everett Hale**, was considered the Broad Church movement. Their goal was to unite the factions because they saw elements of truth in all viewpoints.

Bellows wanted to develop a tangible platform for Unitarianism to stand on, but the radicals feared he was trying to impose a creed. Bellows insisted that the Unitarians use the Christian name, but he did not want to limit the growth of what the word meant. The name Broad Church came from a sermon by Frederic Henry Hedge. He argued that that there is no absolute religion for humanity, but only particular "given religions." Believing that religion is only expressed and communicated through the particulars, Hedge joined Bellows in the belief that the Broad Church had to remain Christian, but be defined as broadly as possible.

In April the organizing meeting for the National Conference of Unitarian Churches convened in New York. James Freeman Clarke gave the opening address calling for a new spirit of inclusiveness. The convention was able to unite upon the organizing principle of holding a common faith in Jesus Christ that was subject to the free interpretation of everyone. Bellows also wanted to adopt a broad Christian name for the group: the Liberal Christian Church of America. But this failed, not because of a rejection of the Christian name, but because of the loyalty to the Unitarian name. Although some of the radicals became involved in the **Free Religious Association** two years later, their influence at the convention was insignificant. The more conservative Christians failed at the convention to adopt a series of resolutions to give the convention a creedal basis, which probably would have split the group. By and large, the Broad Church group succeeded in finally giving the denomination a unified ecclesiastical body of churches when the **National Conference** was formed. Henceforth churches would always have delegate representation to a national (or continental) institution.

BROOK FARM (1841–1847). This was the most successful utopian community that grew out of the Transcendentalist movement. This cooperative venture was founded by Unitarian minister **George Ripley** and his wife, Sophia, in West Roxbury, Massachusetts, (now part of Boston) in 1841, after Ripley had resigned his pastorate at the Purchase Street Church in Boston the previous year and purchased the milk farm to try a social and economic experiment based on Transcendentalist principles. He wrote to **Ralph Waldo Emerson** that he wanted "to insure a more natural union between intellectual and manual labor . . . to prepare a society of liberal, intelligent, and cultivated persons whose relations with each other would permit a more simple and wholesome life" (Ripley as quoted in Hochfield, editor, *Selected*

Writings, p. 373). To accomplish this he proposed a communal venture on a small tract of land with a garden and farm associated with a school or college in which instruction was given from the simplest level to the higher moral philosophy.

Looking to ameliorate the materialistic conditions of society, Brook Farm attracted many of the great writers and reformers of the day, including Emerson, **Margaret Fuller**, and **Nathaniel Hawthorne**, who either visited or were residents for a time. Fuller visited so often, she had a cottage named after her, and Hawthorne, one of the original members, was inspired to write a novel based on his experience, *The Blithedale Romance*. There were 20 original members who took up residence with the Ripleys in the main farm house, which was renamed "the Hive." Stock could be purchased at $500 per share, and individuals received a fixed income regardless of the job they assumed at the farm. The community soon grew to 120 members. Especially successful was the Brook Farm School, which was housed in "the Nest." Highly regarded by local educators, the school provided the main means of income for the community. Numerous buildings were added between 1842 and 1844 including the Margaret Fuller Cottage, the Pilgrim House, a factory, a greenhouse, and the Eyrie, a residence for the Ripleys that allowed them to survey the entire complex of buildings. They hosted nightly gatherings at their home, which included chamber music, poetry readings, and parties. The Hive continued to be the principal dormitory, kitchen, and dining room.

The Brook Farm Institute for Agriculture and Education became the Brook Farm Phalanx in 1845 after reorganizing under the more structured principles of the French socialist Charles Fourier. The community also began publishing a journal, *The Harbinger*, in 1845. Unfortunately, a new central residential building for the community, The Phalanstery was consumed by fire in March 1846 while it was under construction. The building was uninsured; the already fragile financial condition became a complete bust and the experiment failed. In August 1847, only six years after its inception, the community disbanded. Later the site served as a Civil War training site and, eventually, a Lutheran orphanage.

BROWN, EGBERT ETHELRED (1875–1956). An early black Unitarian minister who struggled against the larger forces of denominational racism. Brown was born on July 11, 1875, in Falmouth, Jamaica, to James and Florence Brown. The oldest of five, Brown remembered that he liked to make speeches as a child. He entered the civil service after taking the exam in 1894. In 1899 he became first clerk of the treasury and he remained there until 1907 when he was dismissed possibly because of a question concerning missing funds. Brown decided to become a minister. Theologically he had many doubts and was attracted to Unitarianism by reading the literature, but he had no church. Ultimately, he decided he could not enter the African Methodist Episcopal Church where he had been active as member and organist. He felt he had to be honest about his faith. He wrote to Franklin Southworth of **Meadville Theological School**, who told Brown that white churches needed white ministers. Still Brown was accepted as a special two-year student at Meadville. **Louis Cornish** later wrote that he went to Meadville against all counsel. It was a great sacrifice for Brown. His wife, Ella, and their six children had to remain behind. Brown had immigration problems and was deported back to Jamaica. He formed, with some controversy, a Unitarian Lay Center in Montego Bay.

After another failed attempt, Brown made it to Meadville on his third try. He was the sixth black student to attend the school, but the first who was an avowed Unitarian. He enjoyed his years at Meadville and then was ordained at the school in June 1912 with the small group in Montego Bay acting by proxy. Brown returned to Montego Bay to be a Unitarian missionary supported financially by both the American and British Unitarian Associations. This three-year experiment ended when the two associations decided not to refund based partly on a report from Hilary Bygrave. In the middle of this effort, the **American Unitarian Association (AUA)** transferred Brown to Kingston to try the mission in a larger city, but this meant he had to start all over. Brown had a difficult time accepting the reality that AUA support of him was not wholehearted, and this began a long period of tension with the AUA. Brown pleaded his case for refunding before Samuel Eliot, the AUA president, whom Brown felt was condescending to black people believing they could never understand Unitarianism. Nevertheless, more funding was granted, but it was eventually withdrawn in 1917.

Brown remained in Jamaica until 1920, carrying on at the mission while holding another job for support. Then he came to America to try to fulfill a dream of building a Unitarian church in Harlem. After arrival he brought together a group of mostly Jamaicans to form the Harlem Community Church. Because of difficult relations with the AUA, Brown sought no financial support. He worked at a variety of jobs over the next 20 years. He had periods of employment as elevator operator and speaker for the Socialist Party, among others. His work in Harlem was hampered by AUA president Louis Cornish, who undermined his efforts by misrepresenting Brown to others. In the late 1920s the Fellowship Committee considered dropping Brown from the list of ministers for the second time and he was accused of begging the churches for donations for himself. His relationship with **John Haynes Holmes** prevented this from happening when Holmes intervened, but later he was dropped and he hired the American Civil Liberties Union (ACLU) to help him win back his status. Brown's family situation was also a source of great strain—his wife was mentally ill and a son committed suicide.

In 1937 **Charles Joy** visited the Harlem church and reported favorably. Support improved dramatically once **Frederick May Eliot** took the office of president of the AUA, as Brown received financial backing and pastoral support, and the now Harlem Unitarian Church became an official AUA congregation. Unfortunately, the advent of World War II hampered this effort. Brown kept his dream of building a strong black church in Harlem alive and it might have come to fruition if the denomination had supported him when he was younger. He remained at the church until his death on February 17, 1956.

BROWN, OLYMPIA (1835–1926). The first woman to be ordained with full ministerial standing recognized by a denomination, Brown was a pioneer preacher and women's rights advocate. She was born on January 5, 1835, in Prairie Ronde, Kalamazoo County, Michigan, to Asa and Lephia (Brown) Brown, the eldest of four. Her parents had moved to their log cabin home from Vermont. They had encouraged Olympia to be educated, and she attended an academy in Schoolcraft, Michigan. Then her parents sent her to Mt. Holyoke Female Seminary in 1854, but she found it too orthodox, having been brought up Universalist. Fortunately, she was able to transfer to Antioch College, the new liberal school in Yellow Springs, Ohio. The whole family eventually moved there, and Brown's siblings also attended Antioch.

Brown reported that the famed Unitarian educator **Horace Mann** was somewhat reticent about the prospects of women entering the professions. While she was at Antioch, Antoinette Brown Blackwell came to preach and this inspired Brown to pursue the ministry. She wrote to all the theological schools after graduation, but received little encouragement. After **Meadville** rejected her, Ebenezer Fisher, the president of Canton Theological School at **St. Lawrence University**, said that he would admit her, but he did not favor the idea of women preachers. Fisher was surprised when Brown entered the seminary, was able to do all the work, and, when she was done, applied for ordination. Again, his plan was to oppose the ordination. Yet the parish in Heuvelton wanted to call her to the ministry of their church and they also had a member on the ordaining council of the St. Lawrence Association. The association approved of Brown and she was ordained on June 25, 1863, with Dr. Fisher taking part in the historic ceremony.

Her political activity on behalf of women began during her years in Ohio when, in 1860–61, she circulated a petition seeking changes in the law for more rights for married women, which went before the Ohio legislature. After graduation Brown went to serve the church in Marshfield, Vermont, but she only stayed a few months before returning to Kalamazoo to care for her brother who was ill. In 1864 she was called to serve the church in Weymouth, Massachusetts. She took elocution lessons to improve her voice. She later remembered this pastorate, where she remained for six years, as her most enjoyable. During this time she took a four-month leave of absence to go on a tour of Kansas to advocate for a suffrage amendment to the state constitution. Although the amendment failed, Susan B. Anthony called it a victory in defeat.

In 1870 Brown was called to serve the Universalist church in Bridgeport, Connecticut. She later reported that she "preached better during my Bridgeport pastorate than at any other time of my life." Here her most famous parishioner and ardent church supporter was **P. T. Barnum** who she said "was very friendly to me and often made some complimentary remark" (Willis, ed., *Autobiography*, p. 40). Although the church improved its previously saddened state and broadened its vision, a small faction opposed Brown's ministry, including her advocacy of suffrage, and she was forced out. During her ministry in Bridgeport, she was married in 1873 to John Henry Willis, but kept her own name. The couple had met in Weymouth, where he was a member of her church board. They had two children Henry and Gwendolen, who edited her mother's autobiography.

After that Brown moved on to the Universalist Church of the Good Shepherd in Racine, Wisconsin, where she stayed for nine years. At that time she resigned to devote herself to suffrage work. She was president of the Wisconsin Woman Suffrage Association for more than 30 years. In 1893 Brown's husband died, and she managed his business, the Racine Times Publishing Company, until 1900 when it was sold. Brown was able to perform some part-time work in churches and did so in Columbus, Neenah, and Mukwonago, all in Wisconsin. Much effort went into the campaign for woman suffrage in Wisconsin, but the amendment to the state constitution failed to pass in 1912. After this the tide began to shift nationally and several states voted in suffrage, with the final national victory in 1920. At the age of 85, Brown cast her first ballot on November 2, 1920. She was one of the few long-term suffrage advocates to see the fruits of all her labors. After 1914 she began to spend winters with her daughter in Baltimore and died there on October 23, 1926, but was buried back in Racine. Throughout her life, Brown encouraged young women to enter the ministry, and many did, following Brown's example of devotion to liberal religion and advocacy of women's rights.

BROWNSON, ORESTES (1803–1876). A spiritual wanderer who left his Calvinist past to become a Universalist preacher, then a Unitarian minister with interests in class issues, and finally an ardent Catholic lay person and journalist. Born a twin in Stockbridge,Vermont, on September 16, 1803, to Sylvester and Rachel (Metcalf) Brownson, Orestes's father died shortly thereafter, and he and his twin sister were soon sent boarding with an older couple. Later in life Brownson remarked that he had no childhood. When he was 14, the family moved across the border into New York, and here he had his only formal schooling, a brief period in a nearby academy. Although he had an aunt who was a follower of **Elhanan Winchester**, Brownson joined the Presbyterian church. In his early twenties he became a teacher, first in New York state, and then in Detroit. During a long illness, Brownson rejected Calvinism and adopted Universalist views, and then applied to the **General Convention** for fellowship as a preacher. Back east he continued his studies and then was ordained in June 1826 in Jaffrey, New Hampshire. After that Brownson returned to New York, and preached regularly in three communities, including Auburn (1829), where he edited *The Gospel Advocate*. During this time he married Sally Healy.

Beginning to doubt Universalism, Brownson shifted his sense of sin from the souls of individuals to the social organization of society. This concern about social structure led him to the writings of Robert Owen. While he flirted with labor and politics, Brownson lost his faith in God. During his recovery, he read **William Ellery Channing**'s *Likeness to God* and was converted to Unitarianism. By 1831 he was declaring himself an independent preacher. The following year he was called to serve the Unitarian congregation in Walpole, New Hampshire, during which time he began to write for many of the Unitarian periodicals. Although Brownson called Channing his spiritual father and named one of his sons for him, the great Unitarian divine was cool toward Brownson because "he had not been brought up among us" (Schlesinger, *A Pilgrim's Progress*, p. 30).

In 1834 Brownson moved to Canton, Massachusetts, to serve the Unitarian church. **George Ripley**, with whom Brownson was developing a close friendship, preached the installation sermon. In 1836 Ripley and others began as the **Transcendental Club**, and although Brownson attended a couple of times, he was never a regular member. Brownson published his first book that year, *New Views of Christianity, Society and Church*. It provided the philosophical foundations for his new independent church, the Society for Christian Union and Progress, which was an attempt to bring liberal religion to the working class. He began to see more and more that religion had to address the needs of the poorest members of society. The injustices of capitalism became his prime focus, so that he became a forerunner of Karl Marx in the United States. During this time he began to publish the *Boston Quarterly Review*, which became a vehicle for Transcendental tracts. When the election of 1840 resulted in a Whig victory, Brownson decided that the Kingdom of God would not be coming to earth. He lost faith in humanity and turned back to God. Affirming the utopian community at **Brook Farm**, Brownson sent his son Orestes there, but this vision of the holy community did not keep the father's attention. Abandoning much of his radical social thought, he found solace in the Catholic church and converted in 1844. He continued to write and edit for many years thereafter, but his universal church of the future became the old universal church from the past. He died on April 17, 1876.

BUCHTEL COLLEGE. A Universalist school that was opened in 1872 and remained under denominational control until 1907. At the meeting of the Ohio Universalist Convention in 1867, the Committee on Education was asked to report on the possibility of opening a Universalist seminary. The idea was approved the following year, but then in 1869, the convention decided to support a college rather than an academy. In 1870 Akron was selected as the site, and by that date $62,000 was pledged to establish the school. The largest donor was John Buchtel, a Universalist first in Kent and later in Akron, where he was moderator for many years. The school took his name, and he became the first president. Buchtel opened for classes in 1872, and the first class graduated in 1873. It is now part of the state university system in Ohio, the University of Akron.

BUCKMINSTER, JOSEPH STEVENS (1784–1812). Destined to be the leader of the Unitarians, Buckminster's great potential was cut short by epilepsy when he died in 1812. He was born in Portsmouth, New Hampshire, on May 26, 1784. His father was a minister and his mother was the daughter of a minister. Buckminster was brilliant and this was evident from a young age—he began to study Latin when he was four. He went to local schools until he was 10, when he began attending Exeter Academy. By the age of 12 he was ready for college, but his father kept him at Exeter hoping he could arrange to send him to Yale, where he would find a more orthodox religious training. But Joseph chose **Harvard College** and began in the fall of 1797. His academic skills were evident throughout his career at school and he also had a speaking voice that was considered beautiful.

When he graduated from Harvard in 1800, he accepted an assistant teaching position at Exeter. During this time he began to consider the ministry, having just previously joined his father's church. In 1802 he had his first attack of epilepsy. The following year he had an opportunity to be a private tutor in Waltham, Massachusetts, and during this time he read widely and frequently met with **James Freeman** who was then minister at **King's Chapel**. His father said Freeman was responsible for making young Buckminster a Unitarian. His father tried to convince him to change professions. Buckminster was accepted by the Boston Association of Ministers and was invited to be an assistant at King's Chapel, but Boston's most prestigious congregation, the Brattle Street Church, began to court him. He was ordained and installed there on January 30, 1805, with his somewhat reluctant father preaching the sermon.

After an initial sickness, Buckminster took up his duties as pastor. He was active in the Anthology Club and published several articles in the *Monthly Anthology and Boston Review*. After a year of preaching and visiting, Buckminster was worn out, and his doctor recommended he go to Europe to recuperate. In 1806 he traveled there with Samuel C. Thacher and stayed nearly a year. He returned to his position where he was beloved, but it was clear that he was not well. In 1811 he was appointed Dexter Lecturer on Biblical Criticism at **Harvard Divinity School**, but he became fatally ill. He died on June 9, 1812. He had played an important role in bringing the German biblical criticism back from Europe. He began to explore theories about the inspiration and authority of the scriptures and was especially influenced by J. D. Michaelis's New Testament *Introduction* and Johann Jakob Griesbach's Greek New Testament, which he persuaded Harvard to publish. Buckminster said that not all scripture is equally authoritative and must be read in historical context. He believed that the Bible is not God's direct word, but the vehicle by which the word comes to us, and was not canonized because it was inspired, but because it was written by inspired men. He began preparing his class lectures for Harvard, but was never able to put his learning to use, except to influence his colleagues to use reason in interpreting scriptures and make this the bedrock of the Unitarian faith. It was said that in the pulpit Buckminster could hold his congregation in a trance. He gave the Phi Beta Kappa address at Harvard in 1809. Buckminster's death represented a great loss to the liberal Christians, and the mantle of leadership fell on **William Ellery Channing**.

BUEHRENS, JOHN A. (1947–). A recent president of the **Unitarian Universalist Association (UUA)**, he was born on June 21, 1947, in

Peekskill, New York. Raised mostly in the Midwest, Buehrens was a high school exchange student in Milan, Italy, and completed his schooling at a Jesuit *liceo classico*. He was admitted to Harvard University, where he studied the history and literature of the Renaissance and Reformation and earned his B.A. in 1968. He then went on to **Harvard Divinity School**, where, in addition to his academic work, he led youth groups, summer programs, and church schools in Lexington, Massachusetts, and Summit, New Jersey. He finished the seminary in 1973 with an M. Div. and was called to serve the Tennessee Valley Unitarian Universalist Church in Knoxville, Tennessee, where he remained until 1981. He was married to Gwen Langdoc, an Episcopal priest, in 1972, and they have two children. From 1981 to 1987, Buehrens served the First Unitarian Church in Dallas, Texas, and then the Unitarian Church of All Souls in New York City. His colleague at All Souls was **Forrester Church**, who coauthored *A Chosen Faith: An Introduction to Unitarian Universalism* with Buehrens in 1989. During his first 20 years in the parish, Buehrens advocated for civil liberties and interfaith cooperation for the homeless and the mentally ill. His organizational commitments included the National Parenting Association, the **International Association for Religious Freedom (IARF)**, and the Progressive Religious Partnership.

Buehrens left All Souls in 1993 when he was elected president of the UUA. He completed two full terms as denominational leader, finishing in June 2001. Important growth took place during his time in office, as he participated in 106 new building dedications. This growth was especially true in areas of youth (grew by five times) and young adult participation (six times as many college groups), and per capita financial giving by members, which doubled in constant dollars. Other emphases of Buehrens' term were affirming the denomination's commitment to antiracism work, decentralizing some of the UUA bureaucratic functions, forming a new president's council to advise the UUA administration, and renewed emphasis on global and interfaith activities. Whereas, his predecessor **William Schulz** advocated admitting international groups to UUA membership, Buehrens felt this was culturally insensitive and believed adequate services could not be given to congregations in Asia and Australia. He moved in the direction of supporting a new **International Council of Unitarian Universalists (ICUU)**, which was formed in 1995. This new group gave international groups the opportunity to come together and share resources and worship materials.

After his tenure as president, he served as a visiting professor at **Starr King School for the Ministry**, where he now serves on the Board of Trustees. He has also taught at Andover Newton Theological School and was a Merrill Fellow at Harvard. Once cited as "scholar, organizer, but above all, pastor," in the fall of 2002, Buehrens began a new parish ministry at the First Parish in Needham, Massachusetts. Believing that ministry is a matter of building trust, he wrote that he had longed to return to the close relationships he found in parish life after fulfilling many years as public spokesperson for the UUA. He also serves as special assistant to the Secretary General of the World Conference on Religion and Peace. Buehrens has recently completed a new book, *Understanding the Bible: An Introduction for Skeptics, Seekers, and Religious Liberals* (2003). He also wrote *The Uses of Memory* (1992). He has received honorary degrees from Starr King (1990) and **Meadville Lombard Theological School** (1995), as well as a degree from the federated theological school faculty at **Kolosvar**, Romania. Buehrens says Unitarian Universalism helps him proclaim: "Faith is not ultimately about believing some proposition in spite of the evidence, it is more like living with courage, gratitude, and integrity in spite of life's inevitable losses."

BULFINCH, CHARLES (1763–1844). The person who defined architecture in Boston with his design for many buildings, including the Massachusetts State House and five churches. Bulfinch was born on August 8, 1763, in Boston to Dr. Thomas Bulfinch, a physician, and Susan Apthorp, the daughter of one of the wealthiest Bostonians. Bulfinch, who grew to be a humble and retiring person, was educated at Boston Latin School. He developed an interest in architecture early in his life. His grandfather, Charles Apthorp, convinced his friend Peter Harrison to design the new King's Chapel, and then Apthorp gave most of the money to see that it was built. Apthorp also started an architectural library at the Bulfinch mansion that young Charles was able to use. Bulfinch attended **Harvard College** and graduated in 1778. His career there was marred by his being fined for a wild graduation celebration, but he went on to receive an M.A. in 1784.

Bulfinch became America's first professional architect as a result of following an aristocratic self-taught tradition. He went to Europe in 1785 and returned in 1787. It is often said that Bulfinch created Boston architecturally. He admired English Neoclassicists William Chambers and, most of all, Robert Adam. It has even been said that his style is American Adam, but most typically it is called Federal. Some of his early designs were the Massachusetts State House in 1795 and the first Harrison Gray Otis house in 1796. One great contribution of Bulfinch was his neoclassical town planning, as shown especially with the Tontine Crescent, a 500-foot sweep of 16 houses surrounding a tree-lined park. He also designed Boston's first theater in 1794, rebuilt and enlarged Faneuil Hall, and planned the Massachusetts General Hospital. In all he built five churches in Boston, including four for Unitarian congregations: Hollis Street (1787–88), New North (1802–04), Federal Street (1809), and New South (1814), the last being called his most beautiful. Of these only the New North survives today and is presently St. Stephen's Roman Catholic. In 1816 Bulfinch designed one of his great church buildings in Lancaster, Massachusetts, The Church of Christ, Unitarian.

Bulfinch also influenced many other young architects, including Asher Benjamin. Bulfinch's work was praised widely, but the architectural business was new, and he had a number of financial crises. This high born Bostonian was even imprisoned for debt at one point, after which architecture became more business and less pleasure for him. He was also active in the community, being chairman of the Board of Selectman and superintendent of police. In 1817 President James Monroe visited Boston and was pleased with the public buildings he saw. After Benjamin Latrobe resigned, Bulfinch was offered the position of Architect of the Capitol. The family moved to Washington, where Bulfinch finished the Capitol building and designed another Unitarian church. The society there was organized in the wake of William Ellery Channing's "Baltimore Sermon." Bulfinch was active in the congregation from the beginning and worshipped there while he lived in Washington. He designed their first building (1821–22 at the corner of 6th and D Streets, NE), and raised funds for its construction. Eventually his son Stephen served the church as minister. Bulfinch also returned in 1838 to supervise repairs to the building. The Bulfinches remained in Washington until 1830, after which Bulfinch retired to Boston. He died on April 15, 1844 with funeral services at King's Chapel two days later, where he was a lifelong member.

BURLEIGH, CELIA C. BURR (1826–1875). The first woman ordained to the Unitarian ministry. Little is known of Burleigh's background. She was born in Cazenovia, New York, on September 18, 1826. She had a long career teaching and writing and working for woman's suffrage. Her first marriage to Chauncy Burr ended in divorce. She lived in Syracuse for a time and taught there. She wrote articles for the ***Christian Register*** and lectured on temperance and suffrage. Later she moved to Troy, New York, and worked with Emma Willard, the educator. On September 7, 1865, she married William Henry Burleigh, a reformer and publisher who was working as harbor master for New York City at the time of the marriage. He was a native of Woodstock, Connecticut. Their marriage was later described by John White Chadwick as "co-equal of hearts and minds." They lived in Brooklyn, New York, where Celia continued her work in journalism. In 1868, her associate Jennie June Croly was excluded from a press club dinner. In response, 12 women, including Burleigh, formed Sorosis, an organization to promote deeper association between women writers and artists. Burleigh became a lecturer and fund-raiser for the group. The following year Burleigh helped organize a new organization, the Social Science Club, which was renamed the Brooklyn Woman's Club in January 1870, of which she was the first president. They also helped form the first woman's business union.

In May 1869 she was named a secretary to the Equal Rights Association. During these years she was a frequent attendee at woman suffrage conventions. She became an accomplished organizer and lecturer. In July 1871 she received an invitation from J. B. Whitcomb in Brooklyn, Connecticut, to be a summer minister for August. Although she had never preached, Burleigh was intrigued that the pulpit might be the place where she could give fullest expression to herself. During her time in New York, she had been a member of the Second Unitarian Society in Brooklyn where the minister, John White Chadwick, encouraged her. The summer in Connecticut was an unqualified success, and the society invited her to remain as their regular pastor. She agreed to do so as long as she did not have to subscribe to any creed or anything more binding than the highest truth that was revealed to her each day. Her husband, who had died in March, had encouraged her to be a minister.

At her ordination on October 5, 1871, **Julia Ward Howe** read a letter from Henry Ward Beecher, which read in part: "There are elements of the Gospel which a woman's nature ought to bring out far more successfully than a man can." She had a very active first two years, preaching and engaging in other activities such as woman suffrage work and participating in the ordination of the second woman to be ordained, Mary Hannah Graves. At Graves's ordination Burleigh said that both men and women were needed for the ministry, and that this was not new work for women. She was also the first woman to preach at a meeting of the Channing Conference. Then she became quite ill and tried to improve her condition with a water cure at a hospital in Danville, New York, where she remained for 18 months while serving the congregation in that town. Finally, she returned to Syracuse for a brief ministry, but became increasingly ill as a friend cared for her. She died there on July 25, 1875, and her body was returned to Brooklyn, Connecticut, for burial. Chadwick conducted a service at her old church, The First Ecclesiastical Society.

– C –

CALL, LON RAY (1894–1985). The founder of the **fellowship movement**, Call was one of the architects of 20th-century Unitarian extension. He was born in Advance, North Carolina, on October 6, 1894. From this rural setting, Call became a Southern Baptist preacher early in life. He attended Wake Forest College and received his B.A. in 1916. He became an ordained minister at the age of 21 and then went overseas to serve as a chaplain to the troops following World War I. Once he was back home, he decided to attend the University of Chicago Divinity School. While he was there he married Stevie Kennington. After graduation he was called to serve as an assistant minister at a Baptist church in St. Louis. At this time his studies of science began to conflict with traditional theology, and after falling under the influence of humanist **Curtis Reese**, he gave a sermon in 1923 called "Faith of a Modernist." It was his last in a Baptist church.

In September 1923 Call was invited to be minister at the First Unitarian Church of Louisville, Kentucky. In 1930 he went to the West Side Church in New York and the following year he became an assistant minister at Community Church in New York. Then his wife died of a heart attack. They had one child together, a daughter Marjorie. After briefly serving All Souls Church of Braintree, Massachusetts, Call was appointed secretary of the **Western Unitarian Conference (WUC)** and regional director for the Midwestern states in 1935. He became a specialist in revitalizing churches. He started new congregations in Ft. Wayne, Indiana, and Columbus, Ohio. In 1941 he became a minister-at-large for the **American Unitarian Association (AUA)** and went to Spokane, Washington, to revitalize that society. Here he was married to Lucy Powers. In 1946 he prepared a report on Unitarian extension. Call named 40 cities that might be good sites for new congregations, but he also proposed the establishment of small lay-led groups in towns that might not otherwise have ever been able to support a church. In Kentucky he had seen how small churches were able to keep going for years without having clergy. Soon thereafter a plan for creating fellowships was implemented by **Monroe Husbands**.

For the next five years, Call and his wife traveled extensively and started 13 new congregations from Washington to Tennessee. He remained minister-at-large until 1951 when he was called to the South Nassau Unitarian Church in Freeport, New York. He served there until 1960, when he was named minister emeritus. After that he retired and went on a long trip around the world. In retirement he became an interim minister and served four congregations. In 1967 Call received the Distinguished Service Award of the **Unitarian Universalist Association (UUA)** for his efforts in extending liberal religion. His later years were marked by ill health and he died after a long illness on October 7, 1985.

CALVINISM. Unitarianism slowly evolved within the Standing Order of Congregational Churches in Massachusetts. Theologically, Unitarian beliefs were a response to the tenets of Calvinism as followed and modified by the Puritans. John Calvin, who was born in 1509, believed in the complete sovereignty of God and tried to test his beliefs in Geneva, Switzerland, during his lifetime. His chief theological work was *The Institutes of the Christian Religion* (1536). After his death an important synod took place in Dort, the Netherlands, in 1618. This was held after a series of Arminian positions had been defended in the *Remonstrance*. In response to this Arminian Controversy a *Counter Remonstrance* was written, and then the five points of Calvinism were elucidated at Dort. These included: total depravity, unconditional election, limited atonement, irresistibility of grace, and perseverance of the saints. Total depravity signified a belief in the complete corrupt nature of humankind and an affirmation of the doctrine of original sin. Unconditional election meant that a person became saved not through his/her own merit, but that election was based solely on God's decree and not any human act or personal response to God's offer. Limited atonement meant that only some humans would be saved and most would be damned; therefore, Christ's saving act was only meant for some. The Arminians held that any person who accepts Christ will be saved, and that Christ died for all. This reduced the possibility of faith to a rational, human decision and refuted Calvin's idea of predestination that God has determined before the creation who will be saved and who will be damned.

This elevation of the meaningfulness of the human decision led to a decrease in the importance of the will of God. Irresistibility of grace underscored that God determines who will be saved, and that humans cannot refuse God's gift of grace if it is offered. Finally, the perseverance of the saints meant that once God filled a person with His grace, that person would always be a saint and could not backslide under any circumstance. Theologically, a fall from grace would mean that God could be defeated, and the Calvinists could not accept that. During the 17th and 18th centuries these beliefs began to be liberalized within the congregational churches so that the role individuals played in their own salvation became a primary one. Liberals began to deny original sin so that it became possible for human beings to choose the good and be saved based upon their own ethical choices. The Puritans emphasized a spiritual rebirth and a covenant theology that placed a prime emphasis on an agreement between God and humankind. In liberal thinking, the human role in this agreement grew greater and greater.

CAMBRIDGE PLATFORM. The definitive manual of Congregational organization, government, and ministry was published in 1648, two years after the General Court of Massachusetts had called for representatives from the independent Congregational churches throughout New England to meet to reestablish church discipline. Feeling that there were challenges to the "Congregational Way," this synod, which met in Cambridge, Massachusetts, produced a document that outlined some patterns of association that continue to the present day among Unitarian Universalist churches. These include the right of each parish to call its own minister, to control its own property and funds, and to determine criteria for church membership. These congregations were free to associate with one another without permission of any higher authority. Of the 65 extant congregations gathered in time to vote for the approval of the platform in 1648, 21 are members of the **Unitarian Universalist Association (UUA)** today.

Central to the Cambridge platform was the concept of the **covenant**. Today liberals often define covenant as the voluntary agreement among the people of a congregation to meet for public worship and mutual help and cooperation. The platform outlined four elements to a congregation's covenant: a voluntary agreement; a relationship with God; public worship; observance of the ordinances, which included the two traditional Protestant sacraments, baptism and communion (the Lord's Supper). The Puritans' understanding of covenant was that it was primarily with God, watchfulness over one another was a branch of the Lord's Covenant, and partaking of the ordinances enabled members to have fellowship with Christ. They found it difficult to maintain a church that consisted of only "visible saints" (those who experienced a conversion), and the number of people who could be welcome under the covenant was broadened after 1662, when the Half-Way Covenant was adopted. Under this system the children of those who were baptized, but unconverted, could henceforth bring their children to be baptized.

CAMPS AND CONFERENCES. Unitarians and Universalists have been attending summer conferences for spiritual renewal for over 100 years. The first Unitarian meeting on the Isles of Shoals was held July 11–18, 1897, after Mr. and Mrs. Thomas Elliott of Lowell, Massachusetts, had distributed a brochure to New England churches inviting them to gather 10 miles at sea for $10 a week. Prior to that, the

North Middlesex Unitarian Conference, of which Mr. Elliott was president, had summer conferences at the Weirs on Lake Winnipesaukee, New Hampshire. The Elliotts visited the Oceanic Hotel on Star Island in the summer of 1896 and that winter negotiated for a summer meeting creating a formal organization called the Isles of Shoals Summer Meetings Association. This first Unitarian conference held at the Oceanic was such a success that subsequent conferences were scheduled, including a Sunday School Institute. Despite a disastrous fire on Appledore Island, the meetings continued and the Star Island Corporation was formed in December 1915. The property was purchased by joint Unitarian and Congregational associations. Conferences are now held throughout the summer months.

Universalist summer meetings have an even longer history. As early as 1833 Universalists had erected a memorial to founder **John Murray** at a site that came to be known as Murray Grove in Lanoka Harbor, New Jersey. Murray was reputed to have preached his first sermon in America here in 1770. The Murray Grove Association was formed in 1887 after many years of fund-raising. The program facility was developed after that, but it never became the centerpiece of the denomination or the summer headquarters that it was intended to be. Beginning in 1882, Universalist missionary **Quillen Shinn** began holding summer conferences at the Weirs on Lake Winnipesaukee, New Hampshire. These continued until 1897. Wanting to have a setting that was exclusively Universalist, Shinn settled on an ocean site at Ferry Beach in Saco, Maine, where Universalists had held camp meetings as early as 1879. Since 1901 Ferry Beach has been the site of a full schedule of summer conferences.

In the 1920s Anita Trueman Pickett who had been a summer preacher in Rowe, Massachusetts, proposed that the church make its property available for broader uses. The following summer, 1924, the first Rowe Camp rally was held. What is presently the Rowe Camp and Conference Center was organized by Charles and Maude Wellman. By the late 20th century a wide variety of summer camps and conferences were held throughout the continent. These include: de Benneville Pines (California), Lake Geneva (Illinois), The Mountain (North Carolina), Southeast Summer Institute or SUUSI (Virginia), Unicamp (Ontario, Canada), Unirondack (New York), Unistar (Minnesota), and UU in the Pines (Florida). The Council of Unitarian

Universalist Camps and Conferences has 28 members in all. Of special note is the Clara Barton Camp for Girls with Diabetes. Started in 1921 by the Universalist National Missionary Association, this summer camp for girls who are insulin dependent is located on the birthplace site of the famed Universalist and founder of the American Red Cross, **Clara Barton**.

CANADA. It was difficult for Unitarianism and Universalism to establish a foothold and then flourish in what is known today as Canada. One of the significant issues was that the liberal faiths were not only seen as heresies, but their introduction was facilitated largely by immigrant Americans, and so they were generally characterized as foreign imports. This was the extreme opposite of Unitarian beginning in America, where many of the Unitarian congregations developed out of the oldest churches in the country. This has been a burden to the history of liberal religion in Canada ever since its beginnings. Unitarians in Canada have relied upon imported educational and polemical materials to extend their faith. About one-half of the ministers serving Canadian congregations between 1832 and 1982 have been Americans. Reliance upon American resources is illustrated even with John Cordner, the minister of the first Unitarian congregation in Canada in Montreal. Even though he was Irish, he was urged to look to the United States for support. Once he found it financially, the ties strengthened until Montreal played host to the Autumnal Convention of the **American Unitarian Association (AUA)** in 1854.

Several leading businessmen began having conversations about starting a Unitarian church in Montreal in the 1820s. Since it was British North America before it was Canada, it is not surprising that the first Unitarian service in Canada was conducted by a British minister, David Hughes, in Montreal on July 29, 1832. Hughes died shortly thereafter, but the pulpit continued to be supplied first by Joseph Angier, then Henry Giles, under whom the church was organized on June 6, 1842. Finally, William Lord came for a few months before **John Cordner** was discovered in Ireland. Cordner was called in the summer and preached his first sermon in Montreal on November 5, 1843. Their first building was dedicated in 1845, the same year as the first services in Toronto (July 6). The Toronto congregation was organized under the hand of Joseph Workman, the founder of psychiatry in Canada. Later, the first woman doctor in Canada, Emily Jennings Stowe, joined this congregation in 1879. Here she found support for her work for voting rights. Their first minister was William Adam, the Baptist minister who had been converted to Unitarianism in India by **Rammohun Roy** when they worked on a Bible translation together. Unitarians and Universalists were given legal rights to own property and conduct marriages in 1845. After Cordner left Montreal his congregation withdrew from official Unitarian affiliation in 1882 for a few years due to what was perceived as anti-Christian bias in the AUA.

The first Universalist preacher in Canada was Christopher Huntington, who was already 70 years of age when he moved to Compton in Lower Canada in 1804. The first Universalist congregation was organized in Stanstead, Quebec, in 1830. One of the most well-known preachers was David Leavitt, who preached all over Upper Canada after 1837. Leavitt was the first to push for organization; he helped gather a convention to form the Christian Universalist Association for Canada West and served as secretary for 30 years. The first woman preacher was Mary Ann Church, who built up a society around her in Merrickville. By the beginning of the 20th century the situation was generally not hopeful for expansion for either faith. The Universalists continued to have difficulties and, at the time of merger, only three Universalist congregations remained in all of Canada. Conversely, the Unitarians experienced a period of expansion. First, Toronto was revitalized under **Jabez Sunderland** and then expansion in the west took place. The first expansion was largely based in immigrations of Icelandic populations whose Unitarians members formed a Western Icelandic Unitarian Association in 1902.

In 1907 a new program jointly sponsored by the British and the Americans established a position of minister-at-large to western Canada with the responsibility of creating new congregations. Frank Wright Pratt, an American, served for six years and during that time congregations were founded in Winnipeg, Calgary, Edmonton, Vancouver, and Victoria. Horace Westwood, minister of the Winnipeg congregation became one of the most successful ministers in seeing this work implemented. He made the first efforts to form a Canadian Unitarian Association, but this never had substantial support, and no real national organization existed until the **Canadian Unitarian**

Council (CUC) was established in 1961. The association with the UUA after merger was often divisive. Canadians felt as though their national identity was slighted and they were treated like Americans. This had been true for a long time. Even though Montreal had participated in the formation of the National Conference in 1865, it was called National until 1911, when it was renamed General Conference. Budget cuts in 1969 led to threats of withdrawal from the UUA and, finally in 2001, a vote for a more separate existence with independent funding was achieved at the CUC annual meeting.

CANADIAN UNITARIAN COUNCIL (CUC). An organizing body for all religious liberals in Canada, the CUC began as a way for Canadian Unitarians to achieve an independent voice in the expression of liberal religious values. In 1911 the **National Conference of Unitarian Churches** (which included Canadians) changed its name at the urging of Canadian delegates to General Conference. With more congregations being organized in Canada, members of the Ottawa congregation began to feel that perhaps it was time for a national organization in Canada. In 1907 **Samuel Atkins Eliot** suggested the formation of a Unitarian Association in Canada funded with both United States and British support. This was delayed until 1913 when a church was dedicated in Winnipeg. At that time the Canadian Unitarian Association was formed to "diffuse the knowledge and promote the principles of Unitarian Christianity in the Dominion of Canada." Ultimately this organization failed after the **American Unitarian Association (AUA)** refused to support Horace Westwood's plan for a special commission to create a program of Canadian missions.

In 1909 Universalist minister Charles H. Pennoyer proposed a union of all religious liberals and organized the Canadian Conference of Universalists, Unitarians, and Kindred Religious Liberals. This group met periodically until 1945 but had limited Unitarian involvement. By this time the idea of a national Canadian organization was stimulating interest again. In 1955 the Vancouver congregation's board voted to address all Canadian congregations with a proposal for a new organization. A resolution was presented to the Western Canada Unitarian Association (WCUA) in June to form a council that would meet twice a year, publish a newsletter, arrange speaker tours, and be a public representative for all Canadians. By the following year a paper that had been published briefly in the 1940s, *Canadian Unitarian*, was revived. Then in June 1958 the WCUA voted to support the establishment of a Canadian Unitarian Council to further denominational activity in Canada. In the meantime Unitarians and Universalists in the United States were considering merger. In Canada the near total collapse of the Universalist movement meant that these considerations had less impact (this is also why the CUC does not contain the Universalist name). Most Canadian Unitarians favored the consolidation. After consolidation, Charles Eddis, a Canadian minister, became the chief spokesperson for a new Canadian organization. By March 1961 a draft constitution for a CUC was written. It was decided to vote on it at a meeting of the Meadville Unitarian Conference (the existing structure where eastern Canadian churches belonged) in April and then again at the first **Unitarian Universalist Association (UUA) General Assembly (GA)**. On May 14, 1961, the Canadian delegates from 11 congregations voted to bring the CUC into existence. Charles Eddis was elected the first chairman. The members now felt they could make plans to relate Unitarianism more effectively to their own country. At its first annual meeting the CUC adopted a bilingual name and by 1963 it had its own pamphlets. A major conflict erupted with the UUA in 1969 when funding, which was already low, was reduced. Canadians felt their concerns were given low priority in the UUA, but a separatist resolution was voted down at the annual meeting in 1969. In 1970 the UUA responded to these demands by agreeing to create a CUC office, expand publications, and give more service in the area of social responsibility. Further, the amount of money raised was evenly divided between the UUA and the CUC. The UUA also agreed to stop opposing independent membership for the CUC in the **International Association for Religious Freedom (IARF)**.

Tensions continued to exist between the UUA and the CUC over the years. The CUC tried to develop religious education materials and other publications and programs that were more responsive to specifically Canadian interests. In May 2001 the delegates to the CUC Annual Meeting voted to increase their autonomy as a religious organization. Many of the responsibilities for services and a portion of the UUA endowment were transferred to the CUC in July 2002. This came as a result of the more than 30-year conflict over dissatisfaction with the delivery of services to Canadians. More than 80 percent of the delegates at the annual meeting supported the change. At the time of the transfer of power there were 45 UU congregations in Canada representing 5,200 members. Organizing for liberal religious maintenance and growth in Canada has always been difficult. Limited resources and numbers of people coupled with great geographic distances, some degree of independence and apathy, and, finally, cultural insensitivity on the part of the United States have worked against the establishment of a strong Canadian organization.

CAPEK, NORBERT F. (1870–1942). Born the only son of a tailor in southern Bohemia, on June 3, 1870, Capek became the founder of the Unitarian movement in Bohemia (now Czech Republic). Although he was brought up Catholic, Capek discovered the Baptist church while living in Vienna with his uncle. The Baptists helped support his study of theology in Hamburg, and he became a Baptist minister at the age of 25. At first a Bible salesman and missionary preacher, he became a very successful evangelist in central Europe. Eventually he was head of all the Baptist churches in what came to be known as Czechoslovakia, but in his magazine articles his theology was becoming too liberal for his colleagues. He went into voluntary exile in the United States after writing some articles against the impending war, which angered authorities.

Capek was introduced to Unitarianism by the first president of the Czechoslovak Republic, Thomas Masaryk, and his wife, Charlotte, who was an American Unitarian from Brooklyn, New York. Through the influence of the Masaryks, Capek found and joined the Unitarian Church in Orange, New Jersey. He received some training and support from both American and British Unitarians and then returned to Prague in 1921. Announcing his new-found faith, Capek organized the Liberal Religious Fellowship, which grew into the largest Unitarian church in the world. His wife, Maja, and son, Eddie, were involved in this effort. The fellowship rented a concert hall initially, but soon purchased its own edifice, which was called Unitaria. Most of the members had strong reactions against their Catholic backgrounds and traditional rituals. Thus Capek led very simple services and introduced an alternative communion with flowers in 1923.

In 1934 Capek received a D.D. from the American **Meadville Theological School**. The Prague church and its outreach efforts were very successful until the invasion of the Nazis in 1938. Because of the monotheistic beliefs of the Unitarians many Jews were welcomed into membership who otherwise would have been rounded up by the Nazis. Soon many spies listened to Capek's preaching, and eventually he was arrested and all his writings were seized while he was charged with treason. Although he was initially released, the assassination of a local Nazi led to another arrest, with instruction papers for him to be sent to a concentration camp "return unwanted." It was judged that Capek's gospel of the inherent worth and dignity of every human person made him, as the Nazi court records revealed, "too dangerous to the Reich to be allowed to live." Eventually Capek was sent to Dachau where he was killed by lethal injection in a "medical experiment" on October 20, 1942, one year after his arrest. Before his death Capek was a source of inspiration to his fellow prisoners by the courage he displayed in the face of torture and starvation.

When news of his death reached America, **American Unitarian Association (AUA)** president Frederick May Eliot said: "Another name is added to the list of heroic Unitarian martyrs, by whose death our freedom has been bought. Ours is now the responsibility to see to it that we stand fast in the liberty so gloriously won." Capek is especially remembered today for his Flower Service, but he was also the author of some 90 hymns, and he was especially courageous in speaking out against the Nazis and covertly helping Jews escape their persecutors. Just before his death, Capek wrote a prayer that included these words: "It is worthwhile to live and fight courageously for sacred ideals."

CAPITAL PUNISHMENT. Beginning in the early 1800s a significant majority and eventually a near unanimous number of Unitarians and Universalists have been opposed to the death penalty. In 1835 the Universalists introduced a resolution at their General Convention, which stated that capital punishment is contrary to the spirit of the gospel. One of the most active proponents of abolishing the death penalty was Charles Spear, a Universalist minister who based his arguments on the sacredness of human life. Spear, who like many others was also active in the prison reform movement, wrote that capital punishment brutalizes both the criminal and the public at large. He called it a system of "retaliation" that is wholly subversive of any good. Universalist opponents claimed that criminals needed the fear of death in order to live upright lives—a similar argument to that used against Universalism itself, where orthodox preachers argued that the fear of hell must be used as a threat to coerce people into living moral lives. Early Universalists such as **Benjamin Rush** opposed the death penalty for any crime and called for converting the jails into houses of "repentance and reformation."

Because of founder **John Murray**'s experience in debtor's prison and a theology that taught that all people would be restored to happiness, more and more Universalists argued against the death penalty for some crimes and, eventually, for its complete abolition. Many considered it nothing more than legal murder. Spear was the leader of the movement for more than 30 years. The Massachusetts Society for the Abolition of Capital Punishment was organized at his house in 1845. John Pierpont, one of the leader Unitarians, was present at that meeting. Although Universalists had the largest number of reformers who advocated abolishing the death penalty, the Unitarians also contributed to the effort. Among those was **Thomas Wentworth Higginson**, who in 1849 tried to marshal support for an African American whom he felt was unfairly being used as an example, but he could not save him from execution. Abolitionist leader **Lydia Maria Child** advocated abolishing capital punishment in her *Letters from New York*.

Throughout the 19th century Universalists continued to voice their opposition to the death penalty with several resolutions at General Conventions, including one that was passed unanimously in 1882 in which capital punishment was called "barbarous, revolting and demoralizing, contrary to the spirit of the Christian Religion." This was introduced by George Washington Quimby, who led the successful campaign to abolish capital punishment in Maine in 1887. The Universalists also passed a resolution in 1927 just prior to the trial and execution of Sacco and Vanzetti. The following year Victor Friend, a Universalist trustee who became renowned for his Friend's Baked Beans, testified before the Massachusetts legislature to oppose capital punishment.

With merger in 1961 the Unitarian Universalists affirmed their long-standing commitment to the abolition of the death penalty with a **General Assembly (GA)** resolution. An additional resolution was passed in 1966 before the death penalty was outlawed by the Supreme Court in 1972. The reversal of this decision has led to renewed action on behalf of those who live on death row. The GA began to reaffirm its commitment to abolishing the death penalty in 1974 and 1979, as states began to enact new death penalty laws and executions started again. More recent actions include another GA resolution in 1989 and the establishment of a new grassroots organization, Unitarian Universalists Against the Death Penalty.

CHANNING, WILLIAM ELLERY (1780–1842). He was one of the most significant religious thinkers of the 19th century. His sermons from the pulpit of the Federal Street Church in Boston were a principal force behind the separation of Unitarianism from Calvinism. In these orations of "fervor, solemnity, and beauty," Channing gave voice to the supreme dignity of human nature, an unfailing advocacy of the free mind, and a mystical sense of imminent divinity. His influence in the fields of religion, literature, and social ethics extended far beyond sectarian boundaries and he developed a worldwide reputation. Channing was born on April 7, 1780, in Newport, Rhode Island, the fourth child of William Channing, a lawyer, and Lucy Ellery, the daughter of William Ellery, a signer of the Declaration of Independence. For a time during his youth he heard the preaching of the renowned Samuel Hopkins, whose threats of hell made Channing fear for his own soul and set him on the path to a more humanitarian faith, although he adopted some of Hopkins's thinking. At the age of 12 he was sent to live with his uncle Henry Channing in New London, Connecticut, to be tutored. After two years he was able to pass the entrance exams at Harvard College and started there at the age of 14. He graduated in 1798 and gave the closing oration for his class. An important learning experience followed when he went to live in Virginia to tutor the children of a United States marshal. He spent a year-and-a-half in the South, witnessing the slave culture and largely shunning social contacts. Sleeping on the floor, restricting his diet, and reading all day and night helped ruin his health; he was never very robust after that.

After returning to Harvard, as a proctor, Channing was able to undertake theological studies and then be accepted into fellowship by the Cambridge Association of ministers. His theology began to evolve from a moderate Calvinism and the more cruel deity of this system gave way after he read Francis Hutcheson, who helped Channing understand God as disinterested benevolence and the worth of human nature. In February 1803 he was called to the Federal Street Church in Boston, a charge only relinquished at his death in 1842. Due to his poor health he took a smaller, less prestigious church than he might otherwise have chosen, and he was ordained there on June 1, 1803. During the first few years of his ministry, Channing tried to avoid leadership roles during the emerging Unitarian controversy, but this became increasingly impossible after the death of **Joseph Buckminster** in 1812. Channing's reputation had begun to grow as a preacher, and a new building was constructed at Federal Street in 1809. On July 21, 1814, he married his childhood friend Ruth Gibbs and eventually they had four children, two of whom died in infancy. Soon after Jedediah Morse published a work depicting the liberal Christians as socinians. Channing responded by defending the liberals in *A Letter to the Rev. Samuel C. Thacher, on the Aspersions Contained in a Late Number of the Panopolist, on the Ministers of Boston and the Vicinity*. Channing's involvement prepared the way for his Baltimore Sermon, "**Unitarian Christianity**," a best-selling address that is often regarded as the first denominational manifesto providing a structured party platform for the liberal Christians. Prior to then, the liberals had been on the defensive, but this hour and a half address delivered in Baltimore, Maryland, at the ordination of Jared Sparks clearly presented Channing's position on the unity of God, the unity of Christ, and the use of reason in the interpretation of scriptures.

In 1820 Channing founded the **Berry Street Conference**, a minister's group that later helped provide the impetus for the founding of the **American Unitarian Association (AUA)** in 1825, but Channing, always one to shun sectarianism, refused to be the president of the new organization. He also received an honorary doctorate from Harvard in 1820. Channing's health continued to suffer and in 1822 he traveled to Europe in hopes of improvement. Back home, he was not much better, but the church provided him with a full-time assistant, **Ezra Stiles Gannett**, beginning in 1823. During the ensuing years Channing gave many of the addresses upon which his international reputation was built. This was especially true of *Remarks on National*

Literature, which helped formulate the idea of a true American literary tradition. In his 1828 sermon, "Likeness to God," in which he said "the divinity is growing within us," he helped pave the way for the Transcendentalists, who always acknowledged their debt to him.

Prior to 1830 Channing had not spoken out against slavery, but after a visit to the West Indies where he observed slavery under the British, he began to lift up his voice against its stain on the American character. In 1835 he published *Slavery* and increasingly wrote and acted for the abolitionist cause. In 1837 he wrote an open letter to Henry Clay against the annexation of Texas and he organized the protest meeting in Boston when Elijah Lovejoy, the abolitionist printer, was murdered in Alton, Illinois. Channing's views on slavery increasingly alienated his congregation and they especially hurt him when they refused to allow the use of the church for the memorial for Channing's friend **Charles Follen**. Slavery helped Channing to formulate his ideas on the moral nature of humankind. He said that every person has the right to exercise powers for the promotion of their own happiness and virtue and a slave's divine right to unfold his/her moral and intellectual nature was denied.

Channing's belief in freedom of expression led him to defend **Abner Kneeland**, the Universalist accused of blasphemy, and lead the petition drive to secure his release. Many people trace the beginning of the self-help movement in American culture to Channing's paean to an innate human ability to achieve moral improvement, *Self-Culture* (1838). He was also a longtime advocate for peace, and the Massachusetts Peace Society was founded at his instigation. In his last address, given in Lenox, Massachusetts, on the anniversary of West Indian emancipation, Channing invoked the moral force of human nature once again. Despite a small and frail physique, Channing had an uncommon spiritual magnetism, and his words wrought conversions to a revolutionary faith in human dignity and potential. He died on October 2, 1842, in Bennington, Vermont.

CHANNING, WILLIAM HENRY (1810–1884). A nephew of **William Ellery Channing**, he was a minor Transcendentalist who focused on social change and spent much of his life in England. Channing was born in Boston on May 25, 1810, the only son of Francis D. and Susan (Higginson) Channing. Channing's father, who was a lawyer, died before the boy was born, and his uncle became a surrogate father. He was educated at Lancaster (Massachusetts) Academy and the Boston Latin School. He went on to Harvard College and then the Divinity School there, where he finished in 1833. After graduation he preached around for a year and then traveled in Europe. He began his ministerial career as a minister-at-large in New York working with the poor and he also established a free chapel. He always had difficulty settling in one place. **Octavius Brooks Frothingham** said that he was outspoken and that settled ministry and its steady routine were boring to him. Frothingham called him "a prophet who went from place to place, with a message of joy and hope" (Frothingham, *Transcendentalism*, p. 336). After supplying pulpits for a time, Channing left New York to join a group of ministers who were headed west. He became minister in Cincinnati from 1839 to 1841. During this ministry he became coeditor of the *Western Messenger*, a Transcendentalist journal for the Midwest.

Channing became more focused on political reform and began to advocate for the organic unity of the church, partly because of his disdain for Unitarian individualism, a concern that nearly led him to convert to Catholicism after he completed the seminary. Finally, he returned to New York and was a minister for a couple of years to a newly formed independent church in Brooklyn (it later met in two other locations and was named Christian Union), where he showed his rejection of formalism by having the pulpit removed. The church was frequented by Horace Greeley and Henry James Sr. In 1843 Channing began to edit a social reform journal, the *Present*. He was also a contributor to the *Dial*. He became especially involved with the utopian community at Brook Farm and helped move that community in the direction of its eventual embrace of Fourierism.

In 1847 Channing became a founder of and minister to the Religious Union of Associationists in Boston, after having moved from New York in the fall of 1845 and preaching for a time in West Roxbury. This disparate Religious Union group expressed a common faith in "universal unity," but did not succeed. Channing preached more of the socialism of Charles Fourier to them. During his final year in Boston he edited the magazine *The Spirit of the Age*. He continued his advocacy for reforming society when he moved on to be minister in Rochester, New York, in 1850, where he also became active in abolitionism. His radicalism made it difficult to secure pulpits in America, and this helped influence his decision to go to England in 1854. For three years he served at the Renshaw Street Chapel in Liverpool and then assumed **James Martineau**'s old pulpit at Hope Street Chapel, also in Liverpool. Channing spent most of the remaining years of his life in England, which his wife and children enjoyed as their true home. He returned to America during the Civil War to serve as chaplain to the U.S. House of Representatives and also minister to the Unitarian society in Washington, D.C. He frequently helped with the war effort by visiting the battlefields and the hospitals. His literary output was primarily as a biographer. He published a three-volume *Memoir of William Ellery Channing* in 1848 and a biography of **Margaret Fuller Ossoli** (1852). He died in London on December 23, 1884.

CHAPIN, AUGUSTA JANE (1836–1905). The second woman to be ordained a Universalist minister, Chapin was also the first woman to receive an honorary D.D. She was born in Lakeville, New York, on July 16, 1836, to Almon and Jane (Pease) Chapin. The family moved to Michigan when she was six. She became a teacher when she was 14 and taught school in Lyons and Lansing, Michigan, but was unable to enroll at the University of Michigan for college, as it did not accept women. Eventually she went to Olivet College, where she converted to Universalism and decided to become a minister. She was an itinerant preacher in the Portland, Michigan, area for about four years. Chapin received a Universalist fellowship in May 1862 and was ordained in Lansing, Michigan, on December 3, 1863. She remained for another three years in Portland in a permanent settlement. After that she served many more congregations, a few of which were yoked parishes. The longer settlements included Iowa City, Iowa, 1870–1974; Oak Park, Illinois, 1886–1892; and Mt. Vernon, New York, 1897–1901. She was active in mission work for a number of years with short ministries in Omaha and San Francisco. She also helped organize the first Universalist State Convention in Oregon. When she was in Iowa City she was one of three delegates from her state to the Centennial celebration in Gloucester, Massachusetts. She addressed the Woman's Centenary Association and promised further assistance from the West.

Chapin became the first woman to serve on the council of the **General Convention** and she advocated that half of the trustees should be women. Prior to being called to a Hillside, Michigan, pastorate in 1884, she finished an M.A. at the University of Michigan, which had denied her acceptance years previously. In the period between her Oak Park and Mt. Vernon settlements, she taught at the University of Chicago as a lecturer on English literature. She was also active in national suffrage work and became one of the founders of the American Woman Suffrage Association. Chapin served on the organizing committee of the **World Parliament of Religions** in Chicago in 1893 and was chairwoman of the Women's General Committee. She gave comments at the opening and closing events of the World Parliament, read a paper **Antoinette Brown Blackwell** had prepared on women in ministry, and also moderated another session where two of the speakers were women. She was also on the committee to organize the Universalist congress there. At the World's Fair Chapin received her honorary D.D. from Lombard University. She had lectured there for some years in a nonresident capacity. In her later years she lead tours of Europe and was planning for one when she died of pneumonia in New York City on June 30, 1905.

CHAPIN, EDWIN HUBBELL (1814–1880). One of the leading Universalist ministers in the 19th century, Chapin made his name primarily as a marvelous orator who became a popular public speaker. He was born on December 29, 1814, in Union Village, New York. Rebelling from an orthodox background in the 1830s, Chapin was ordained in 1838. His first parish was in Richmond, Virginia, followed by service in Charlestown, Massachusetts, from 1841 to 1847. Early in his career he showed an interest in various reform movements and appeared at legislative hearings on the death penalty. In 1845 he helped edit, along with J. G. Adams, *Hymns for Christian Devotion; especially adapted to the Universalist Denomination*, which became the most widely used hymnal among Universalists. Chapin also published a popular "gift book" that year, *Hours of Communion*. He came as **Hosea Ballou**'s associate at the Second Universalist Society in Boston and was installed on January 28, 1846, but stayed only briefly. He encountered some problems with debt while he was in Boston. Eventually he came to differ from Ballou in his theological orientation. Chapin held Restorationist opinions so that he believed that there would be limited misery after death for those who sin, but eventual reconciliation with God for all. His preaching was less oriented toward theological subjects and more reform based.

In 1848 he was called to the Fourth Universalist Society (popularly known as the Church of the Divine Paternity after a new building was erected on Fifth Avenue in 1867) in New York, where he remained until his death in 1880. This growing parish bought the Church of the Divine Unity in 1852. While he was minister there he received the highest salary among Universalist clergy, $5,000 in 1855. In the 1850s he worked hard to relieve the debt of the Clinton Liberal Institute and even convinced Henry Ward Beecher to give a lecture to help out. Chapin was a strong supporter of denominational education efforts and spoke at the laying of the cornerstone for Canton Theological School. He was outspokenly antiwar and attended a World Peace Convention in Germany in 1850. He was also active in the temperance movement and gave an address at a Massachusetts convention in 1853. This reform spirit extended to women's rights, too. He called for legal equality with men and more educational opportunities. Many of his ideas for the social reform of society were summarized in *Humanity in the City*, (1854) where Chapin expressed his outrage at how poverty affected children and how Christianity must be put into practice to change society. The year before he had published a series of lectures, *Moral Aspects of City Life*, in which he called for the relief of poverty and the eradication of vice. In addition to food and shelter, he called for more employment opportunities for the poor.

During his active ministry in New York, he may have been the most well-known Universalist minister in America. He was especially friendly with **P. T. Barnum**, who was attracted to Chapin because he was a jokester and, like Barnum, loved puns. At one time the two friends were compared to Barnum's Siamese Twins, Chang and Eng. Beecher wrote that Chapin's speaking abilities could put a person in a trance. He died in New York on December 26, 1880, and the service commemorating him at the Church of the Divine Paternity was, according to **Henry Whitney Bellows**, more than three hours long. Reflecting on the class difference between them, Bellows referred to Chapin as "coarse," but also revered his unsectarian nature and "his kind, genial, hearty voice." Chapin's wife became active in helping to establish the Chapin Home for the Aged and Infirm in 1869, which became a fitting memorial to her famous husband.

CHAPLAIN. A layperson who has certain ministerial responsibilities, the position of chaplain was created in Canadian Unitarian Universalist congregations in 1970 after the **Canadian Unitarian Council (CUC)** took on the responsibility of registering ministers with the provincial authorities. A chaplain is appointed by his or her congregation and registered with the provincial government to perform rites of passage—weddings, memorial services, and child dedications. In congregations where there is no minister, the chaplain serves both the society and the local community, but in congregations with ministers, this unique form of lay ministry usually only conducts services for non-Unitarian Universalists. When the CUC voted to designate certain persons for this purpose, they named them chaplains to distinguish them from ministers and decided that they would perform no other ministerial functions. Shortly after the position was established, there were more chaplains than Unitarian Universalist ministers in Canada.

CHAUNCY, CHARLES (1705–1787). One of the leaders of the anti-revival movement during the Great Awakening, Chauncy helped precipitate the beginnings of Unitarianism in America. The oldest son of Charles and Sarah (Walley) Chauncy, he was the son of a merchant who died when Charles was only six. He went to Boston Latin School and entered **Harvard College** in 1717. He received his B. A. in 1721 and remained for another three years for his M.A. In 1724 he began candidating for pulpits, but his mediocre pulpit talents worked against him. In 1725 the assistant's position at Boston's First Church opened up and Chauncy was called there to begin in the fall of 1727. He stayed for 60 years. By 1731 the congregation had accepted the Half-Way Covenant to allow children's baptisms and by 1736 it was offering baptism to all adults. After 1731 a confession of faith was no longer required for membership. These changes indicate the general growing acceptance of rational choice in matters of faith.

Chauncy married Elizabeth Hirst in 1728, and they had three children. After her death, Chauncy married Elizabeth Townshend in 1739, and then Mary Stoddard in 1760. As a pastor at First Church, he became an automatic member of the Harvard Board of Overseers. In 1740 Samuel Osborn of Eastham was accused of Arminianism, and Chauncy went to serve on the council that decided his fate. Chauncy was among those who protested this action, but was especially concerned at the political implications of a dismissal. Challenges to traditional authority seemed to concern him more than theological hair-splitting. At this time Chauncy was plunged into the arguments that swirled around the **Great Awakening**, especially after George Whitfield appeared in Boston. It was matters of style and the political implications that continued to concern Chauncy. He was against the excessive emotionalism of the revival experience, and institutionally he worried about itinerants moving from town to town upsetting the established order of settled ministers. He came out against the revival in print and in the pulpit. He was soon drawn into battle with Jonathan Edwards and responded to Edwards's attacks with *Enthusiasm Described and Caution'd Against* (1742), where he traced the threat to the New England Way back to Anne Hutchinson. His most famous work against the revival was *Seasonable Thoughts on the State of Religion in New-England* (1743). For Chauncy, the individual gradually grew into a state of grace rather than experiencing an immediate, emotional conversion. The clergy who defended the structures and forms of order that had evolved since the Puritan foundations became known as "Old Lights," and Chauncy emerged as their main leader.

The effect of Chauncy's leadership against the revival was to irrevocably split the clergy of New England into "Old Lights" and "New Lights." The antirevivalists also increasingly developed a camp that could be discerned as liberal. Chauncy also took an interest in school affairs in the city. He tried to stay away from theological battles and did not return to theological writing until 1758 when he publicly rejected original sin. It was during this time that he began to formulate his ideas on universal salvation, but he only gave the manuscript to his friends. It was finally published anonymously in 1784, *The Mystery Hid from Ages and Generations*. Chauncy came somewhat late to supporting the American Revolution. By 1774 he felt the British government had lost its constitutional authority by destroying the colonies ordered way of life and he became an active supporter of Revolutionary causes.

CHILD, LYDIA MARIA FRANCIS (1802–1880). Known to most of America for her poem "The Boy's Thanksgiving Song," which begins, "Over the river and through the wood." Child was a prolific writer and reformer. Lydia Francis was born in Medford, Massachusetts, on February 2, 1802, the daughter of David Francis, a baker, and his wife, Susannah. The youngest of five children, whatever happy childhood memories she might have had were lost after her mother died when she was 12 and she was separated from her brother **Convers Francis** whom she adored. The young girl lived for a time in Norridgewock, Maine, with an older sister. She attended local schools and eventually became a teacher herself. When she was 20 she returned to Massachusetts to live with her brother, who was minister of the First Parish of Watertown, Massachusetts. She was baptized, joined the church, and subsequently gave herself the new name Maria. In 1824 she published her first novel, *Hobomok*, which depicts an independent white woman defying social conventions by marrying a Native American and having a child with him. Maria had also fallen in love with David Child, a law student who was ten years older than her. In 1826 she started a magazine for children, the *Juvenile Miscellany*, the first such publication in America. David and Maria were married in 1828, but their financial position as a couple was problematic. His law practice collapsed after he was jailed for libel and her work became their primary means of support, as it was throughout their lives. Their economical lifestyle was put to good use when Maria published *The Frugal Housewife*, which went through several editions and was followed by other advice books. She also became interested in women's history and produced a five-volume *Ladies Family Library*, which culminated in a history of women from all over the world. She and her husband became active supporters of the New England Anti-Slavery Society and in 1833 she published her most important work, *An Appeal in Favor of That Class of Americans Called Africans* in which she argued that personal freedom is the birthright of every human being. Child's book convinced Senator Charles Sumner that slavery must cease, but it alienated others. So many subscriptions to her children's magazine were canceled, she had to stop publication. She became quite active in the antislavery movement largely influenced by William Lloyd Garrison. Unfortunately she felt caught between factions in the movement, and after two years of editing the *National Anti-Slavery Standard* (1841–43) in New York she resigned.

During the next decade of her life she turned to further explorations in religion. She produced a three-volume work that took eight years to write, *The Progress of Religious Ideas through Successive Ages*. This work, which covers all the world religions and argues for the divine origin of each, was an attempt to foster understanding between the world's faiths. Child had been especially concerned that Christian descriptions of other religions usually concluded they were "childish fables" or "filthy superstitions." Many years later, Child complemented *Progress* when she published a work of worldwide quotations from religious thinkers (1878). Two years prior to that she had attended a meeting of the recently formed **Free Religious Association (FRA)**. She had been searching for a satisfactory religious home her entire adult life. When she was in her twenties her brother feared she would convert to Swedenborgianism, but she assured him that she was "more in danger of wrecking on the rocks of skepticism than of stranding on the shoals of fanaticism." She said, "I wish I could find some religion in which my heart and understanding could unite" (Child, *Selected Letters*, p. 2). She was especially disturbed when the Unitarians who spoke of the sacredness of freedom then went on to attack **Ralph Waldo Emerson** for his free expression of Transcendental ideas. She tried Unitarianism again in Northampton. She and David rented a pew at the church where there was considerable antislavery activity. They had gone there to start a beet sugar company in 1838, but it failed miserably. When she lived in New York she had been put off by the "cold intellectual respectability" of the Unitarian services. The FRA, founded mostly by radical Unitarians, was a group that hoped to bring together representatives of all faiths including non-Christians and agnostics. Child immediately joined the group as the living embodiment of the theme she explored in the book she had published 18 years earlier. Her view that religion was a universal instinct that knows no sectarian bounds had found an institutional home. She continued to attend their meetings and left the FRA some money in her will. Child was a socially progressive activist in the areas of racism and abolition, women's rights, and religious bigotry and she published works in every conceivable category of letters from domestic advice to history to fiction. She died at her home in Wayland, Massachusetts, on October 20, 1880. *See also* ABOLITION OF SLAVERY.

CHILDREN'S SUNDAY. This festival celebrating the importance of children in the life of the church was initiated by Charles H. Leonard at the Universalist church in Chelsea, Massachusetts, in 1856. The entire Universalist denomination adopted this special dedicatory day and scheduled the first one for the second Sunday in June 1868 so that flowers would be in full bloom. Special days for children were known by various names and the practice was soon a popular Sunday in other denominations as well. Many churches continue to celebrate some variant form of special recognition for children.

CHRISTIAN EXAMINER. An important 19th-century Unitarian periodical that began its life as the *Christian Disciple*. During the nearly 60 years of publication, the periodical was considered one of the most widely circulated and vital religious publications of its time. The *Examiner* had a wide diversity of writers and subjects, including such important luminaries as **William Ellery Channing**, **Ralph Waldo Emerson**, Francis Parkman Sr., and **Julia Ward Howe**. One of the central problems throughout its history was how to represent such theological diversity fairly. When Channing contacted Noah Worcester in 1813 he called for a new journal that would defend liberal Christianity from its enemies. The *Panopolist*, the chief orthodox publication, had been unmerciful in its attacks on the liberals. One liberal journal, the *Monthly Anthology*, had stopped publishing in 1811. Worcester agreed to edit the new periodical, and it started publication in May 1813. In its early years, Worcester, a pacifist, published many articles on war, and by 1819 he left under some pressure. Its critics felt it had strayed from its intended purposes that were practical piety, scriptural exegesis, and issues of congregational polity. **Henry Ware Jr.** became the second editor in 1819. Ware realized more the idea of promoting Unitarian views, and he made the magazine much more pastoral with its publication of prayers. Another editorial change took place in 1824 when John Gorham Palfrey started a brief term, during which the name was changed from *Christian Disciple* to *Christian Examiner*, with the idea being that it would examine the errors of orthodoxy more directly. After Palfrey left, there was controversy over the choice of a new editor, but its financial problems were also worsening, too. The editorship of Francis Jenks proved unpopular, and the Christian Examiner Society was reestablished to consider their future in 1829.

James Walker, with Francis W. P. Greenwood's help initially, gave the magazine a period of editorial stability in the 1830s. They opened up its pages to many of the younger Unitarians, but the emphasis on freedom of opinion would ultimately prove fatal to the magazine as the controversial views expressed in the *Examiner* led to denominational controversy. Later editors included **Frederic Henry Hedge** and **Edward Everett Hale**. The problems with finances and theological differences continued to plague the magazine until 1869, when editor **Henry Whitney Bellows** decided after four years of publishing in New York that the magazine should cease publication.

CHRISTIAN LEADER. There were countless Universalist journals published in the 19th century. The oldest publication was the ***Universalist Magazine***, which started in 1819 and became the *Trumpet*. It merged with the *Christian Freeman* in 1862 and together they became the *Universalist*. In 1875 a paper published in Utica, New York, called the *Christian Leader* was purchased and joined with the *Universalist*. The editor in Boston was George Emerson, who moved there from New York, where he was editing the old *Leader*. Slowly regional publications were being combined by the Universalist Publishing House, and by 1898, the *Leader* had a subtitle calling it "The National Universalist Paper" and it became the *Universalist Leader* at this time. This was also the year that Emerson died and was succeeded by Frederick Bisbee. During his editorship, the content of the *Leader* became less oriented toward religious articles and more toward organizational development and news. There was significant space given to mission work, including a column by **Quillen Shinn**.

The *Christian Leader* reached its literary peak in the 1920s when John van Schaick became the editor. Following a successful ministry in Washington, he had also been a frequent contributor of articles. He came first as acting editor in 1922 and then editor, a position he retained until 1945. Unlike his predecessor, he was a strong advocate of the Social Gospel, but his theology was quite conservative. In 1926 he had the name of the paper changed from *Universalist Leader* to *Christian Leader*. He made many contributions to religious journalism, including helping to start the Associated Church Press. The humanism of the Unitarian editor of the ***Christian Register***, Albert Dieffenbach contributed to feuding between the denominational papers. In 1929 van Schaick wrote "except for being mistaken most of the time . . . the *Christian Register* and its dynamic editor are perfect." The *Leader* was a weekly publication throughout most of its history, but low circulation and costs led to cutbacks, so that it was published twice a month beginning in 1941, and then monthly in 1948. When van Schaick stepped down in 1945, he was succeeded by Emerson Hugh Lalone, who had been the business manager of the Publishing House. Lalone's tenure brought another name change back to *Universalist Leader* in 1953, a move that some criticized because they felt it emphasized denominational awareness in a time when they were considering consolidation with the Unitarians. The paper became less known for its quality opinion articles and became a smaller, denominational newsheet. It was in a final transition period in 1960 when Lalone died, and Raymond Baughan filled most of that gap as editor.

The consolidation of the Unitarians and Universalists in 1961 brought some confusing name changes to the publication. At first it was published jointly with the *Unitarian Register* as the *Unitarian Register-Universalist Leader* in May 1961 with the Universalists covering only about one-quarter of the production costs. The next year it was the *Unitarian-Universalist Register-Leader*, which stuck until 1968, when the short term *UUA Now* appeared before it was finalized to ***Unitarian Universalist World***.

CHRISTIAN REGISTER. The major periodical of the Unitarians throughout their separate history, the *Christian* (later *Unitarian*) *Register*, was published in Boston from 1821 to 1961 when it was merged with the *Universalist Leader* to create the *Register-Leader*. The *Christian Register* first appeared on April 20, 1821, with David Reed acting as its editor. Reed wrote that the purpose of the paper was to "inculcate the principles of a rational faith, and to promote the practice of genuine piety" (Eliot, *Heralds*, p. 211). Reed, who was an ordained minister, remained the owner of the paper for more than 40 years and was its editor for many years, too. The paper was independent of the **American Unitarian Association (AUA)**, which was formed four years after the paper started publishing. It was a weekly paper that included not only liberal Christian views, but national and international political, social, and cultural news as well. At first, it carried little church news. Although the paper often advocated for various reforms, it was rarely controversial. The historian George W. Cooke referred to it as "mild and placid." The *Christian Register* also published a number of tracts, which were circulated by the Unitarian Book and Pamphlet Society.

One 19th century controversy occurred in 1872 when Thomas J. Mumford, the editor of the *Register*, wrote that the word "religious" did not belong in the name, **Free Religious Association (FRA)**. This helped precipitate the **Yearbook Controversy**. **William J. Potter**, the minister in New Bedford, Massachusetts, and the secretary of the FRA, later had his name removed from the list of Unitarian ministers because he refused to refer to himself as a Christian. The full correspondence between Potter and the association was published in the *Register*. The circulation of the *Register* had always been provided through subscriptions. Albert Dieffenbach, who was editor of the *Register* in the 1920s managed to increase circulation from 3,000 to 12,000 subscribers, but it became the subject of a Universalist joke when it was reported in the *Universalist Leader* that a friend of Dieffenbach's said, "When you took over the *Register* everybody respected it, but nobody read it. Now everybody reads it, but nobody respects it." There was a long, protracted debate with the Universalist editor John van Schaick over the issue of liberty, where Dieffenbach said there should be no limits to liberty when it comes to membership requirements in local societies. Circulation had declined to 3,300 and the paper was a monthly when **Stephen Fritchman** took over as editor in 1943. His tenure marked the greatest controversy in the history of the paper. Fritchman was named acting editor late in 1942 and then permanent editor early the next year. In the spring of 1941 the paper lost its editorial independence and was made responsible to an editorial board under the close scrutiny of President **Frederick May Eliot**. Editorial independence was only the beginning of his problems, as Fritchman initially revitalized the paper and increased circulation to 8,300 by 1947. A number of critics began to question his politics, including his editorials and prolabor activity. In

1946 a former AUA board member, Larry Davidow, wrote that Fritchman was carrying on a "deliberate campaign to use the *Christian Register* and other agencies as means of proselytizing the Communist Party cause" (Zwerling, *Rituals*, p. 29). Davidow became part of the Committee of Free Unitarians. Linscott Tyler, who also became a member of this group tried to smear **Charles Joy**, the head of the Unitarian Service Committee with accusations of communism as well. Then he turned on Fritchman. Both Tyler and Davidow tried to convince the AUA Executive Committee that Fritchman was a card carrying member of the Communist Party.

The controversy received national attention. Fritchman testified before the House Committee on Un-American Activities in Washington in October 1946. In 1947 Fritchman was told he must either cooperate with the editorial board or resign as editor. The Executive Committee suspended him as editor on May 9 and called a special meeting of the AUA board for May 20, 1947, days before the Annual Meeting of the Association. Fritchman was dismissed at this meeting for his failure to "cooperate" and his "insubordination." This was ratified by a voice vote at the AUA meeting days later, where A. Powell Davies had publicly criticized Fritchman's pro-Soviet editing. Fritchman had believed that his role was to advance "the struggle for human freedom." Such editorial independence was never regained. The name of the paper was changed to *Unitarian Register* at the annual meeting of the association in 1957.

CHRISTMAS. Coming out of a Puritan and Congregational tradition, early Unitarians rejected the celebration of Christmas until about 1830. This was not the case with the Universalists, who were perhaps influenced by **John Murray**'s Anglican and Methodist background. In 1810 William Bentley wrote in his diary that in Salem, Massachusetts: "Christmas has a public service in the morning for English Episcopalians and in the evening from the Universalists. Our Congregational churches stands fast as they were from the beginning." Unitarians began to feel the need to observe the holiday after **Charles Follen**, a German immigrant, introduced the Christmas tree to his congregation in Lexington, Massachusetts. After the custom spread throughout New England, Unitarians made many contributions to Christmas celebrations both in America and abroad. It has been claimed that Charles Dickens wrote *A Christmas Carol* after he heard a sermon by the Unitarian minister at the Little Portland Street Chapel in London. In 1849 W. P. Lunt, the Unitarian minister in Quincy, Massachusetts, asked his friend **Edmund Hamilton Sears**, the Unitarian cleric in Weston, to write a Christmas carol for the Quincy Sunday School Christmas celebration and the result was "It Came Upon the Midnight Clear," a classic carol that embodies the social message of "Peace on earth." The popular song, "Jingle Bells" was written in 1854 by James Pierpont of Medford, Massachusetts, the son of Unitarian minister John Pierpont, one of the founders of the **American Unitarian Association (AUA)**. **Henry Wadsworth Longfellow**, the famed poet and brother of a Unitarian minister, contributed "I Heard the Bells on Christmas Day."

The Christmas story has continued to inspire Unitarian Universalists over the last century and a half. While in some congregations the birth of the Christ child has become the universal symbol for the hope found in all births, and winter solstice celebrations (recalling the birthday of the sun, not the Son) have become common in many places, Christmas and its spirit of generosity make the holiday a popular Unitarian Universalist festival. Many Unitarian Universalist congregations light Advent candles, while others have incorporated celebrations of Hanukkah during the season. Whatever the emphasis in a particular congregation, Unitarian Universalists remember the words of **Francis Greenwood Peabody** from more than a century ago, "Let our ears hear the cry of the needy, and our hearts feel the love of the unlovely. . . . [L]et the gentler air of the Christmas Spirit touch our lives."

CHURCH, F. FORRESTER (1948–). The son of former U.S. Senator Frank Church and Bethine (Clark) Church, whose father was Governor Chase A. Clark of Idaho, Forrest Church was born on September 23, 1948, in Boise, Idaho. Raised a Presbyterian, Church began to drift away from formal Christianity, especially after his father presented him with *Thomas Jefferson's Bible* when he was 10. He was educated at Stanford University and then at **Harvard Divinity School** (M.Div., 1974). He was ordained in 1975 and served as the assistant minister at the First and Second Church of Boston from 1975 to 1978. Saying that he was "attracted by spiritual renegades,"

Church continued his studies in a doctoral program, completing his Ph.D. in early church history in 1978 with a dissertation on the Gospel of Thomas. As he was finishing his studies he was called as minister to the All Souls Church (Unitarian) in New York City in 1978 and has remained there ever since. Over the years Church has developed a reputation as the most visible proponent of a more evangelical Unitarian Universalist faith. His church has grown to have more than a 1,000 members and its social witness in New York has been important, too. In 1985 the church was responsible for placing 10,000 placards on city buses and subways with messages such as "AIDS is a human disease and deserves a human response." In 1991 All Souls received the Outstanding AIDS Ministry Award from the National AIDS Interfaith Network. In 1995 Church was appointed Chairman of the Council on the Environment in New York City. He helps direct many programs, including 32 green markets in the city. Under his leadership the church runs about 50 small community parks and oversees environmental and waste management programs. He has also served as a member of the Executive Committee of the Franklin and Eleanor Roosevelt Institute since 1998.

Church has become especially well known for his writing. He has written or edited 20 books. Early in his career these included: *Father and Son: A Personal Biography of Senator Frank Church of Idaho* (1985), *Our Chosen Faith: An Introduction to Unitarian Universalism* (1989, with **John Buehrens**), and *God and Other Famous Liberals* (1991). He also has written spiritual guidebooks for adults, *Life Lines* (1996) and *Lifecraft* (2000). Church has also published in the major areas of his scholarly background, including editing *The MacMillan Book of Earliest Christian Prayers* (1988). He has also brought out a new edition of the book that began his pathway to Unitarian Universalism, *The Jefferson Bible* (1989). Many of his addresses have been published in other volumes. His "Fear and Terror" was included in *Representative American Speeches 1937–1997* (1997). His voice has become an important one in the wake of the terrorist attacks on the World Trade Center in 2001. Soon after the attacks, Church edited *Restoring Faith: America's Religious Leaders Answer Terror with Hope* (2001). In 2002 two additional books were published. The first, *Bringing God Home: A Traveler's Guide*, a theological memoir, is Church's attempt to bring the message of a universal God to a wider audience and builds on his cathedral metaphor—one light, many windows. The other book, *The American Creed*, is what he calls a biography of the Declaration of Independence, or a way to understand America in spiritual terms. After its publication George McGovern said that Church "has become our preeminent preacher of faith and freedom." He calls for a patriotism that is respectful of international collaboration and understanding. Church has four children and is married to Carolyn Buck Luce. At other times in his career he has written newspaper columns for the *Chicago Tribune* and the *Sunday New York Post*. He has also served as a Montgomery Fellow and visiting professor at Dartmouth College. Church often uses this definition for what religion means: "Religion is our human response to the dual reality of being alive and having to die."

CHURCH OF THE LARGER FELLOWSHIP (CLF). The Church of the Larger Fellowship is known as the Unitarian Universalist "church-by-mail." In the late 19th century, there was considerable correspondence concerning doctrinal points, Sunday School helps, and where to find published materials in Unitarianism. In 1877 Charles Wendte founded a Missionary Society in Cincinnati with one of his church members, Sallie Ellis, serving as its treasurer. Ellis became the personification of what came to be known as the Post Office Mission. She helped spread the knowledge and influence of Unitarianism in the United States, but especially in the **Western Unitarian Conference (WUC)**, mailing thousands of tracts and letters to interested people. This outreach to isolated religious liberals by correspondence set the pattern for what later became the CLF. William Channing Brown revitalized the Post Office Mission in 1903 when he formed the Unitarian Church of All Souls. For more than 25 years he sent letters and sermons to people all over the country, but by 1943 his list was dwindling.

Under the leadership of **American Unitarian Association (AUA)** President **Frederick May Eliot**, CLF was formed in 1944 to serve and support these same isolated religious liberals through the mails. It was a reorganization of the Unitarian Church of All Souls, which represented only a handful of individuals who maintained their religious affiliation through correspondence. Some of them became charter members of CLF. It was intended that this organization be a church in the fullest sense with sermon publications, religious education materials, and personal contact with a minister. That first Acting Minister was Albert Dieffenbach. The Bond of Fellowship was: "Avowing as our sole bond of Fellowship our earnest desire to lead pure, reverent, and useful lives, to seek together the love which quickens fellowship, and the truth which makes us free" (Cavicchio, *CLF*, p. 23) Although initially part of the AUA's Extension Department, CLF became a separate organization with its own budget and board of directors in 1971 during the ministry of George Marshall, who served CLF for 25 years. During this period CLF grew to serve Unitarian Universalists who were isolated for geographic, medical, or emotional reasons. Today it has over 2,500 members throughout the world and remains the largest single Unitarian Universalist congregation. The Universalists organized their own CLF in 1947 to serve small churches and scattered members, and it grew to be especially meaningful for shut-ins. CLF has been an important source of growth for liberal religion, as over 400 congregations have been formed from a core of CLF members. This "church without walls" publishes a monthly newsletter, *Quest*. In 1961 the humanitarian Albert Schweitzer became an "honored member."

CLARKE, JAMES FREEMAN (1810–1888). One of the great Unitarian leaders of the 19th century. Clarke was born on April 4, 1810, in Hanover, New Hampshire, where his father was studying to be a doctor. He was the third child of Rebecca Hull and Samuel Clarke, whose stepfather was **James Freeman**, the minister of King's Chapel for whom the new baby was named. Clarke spent much of his time growing up on his grandparents' estate in Newton, Massachusetts. He did his college preparatory work at the Boston Latin School, which was located near a drug store his father owned. In 1825 he went to **Harvard College** at the age of 15. Clarke pleased his grandfather Freeman by choosing to enter the ministry after college and immediately going on to the **Harvard Divinity School** in 1829. During his training, he had to leave to help out his family when his brother Sam became ill. Clarke's friend **Margaret Fuller** helped him get a job teaching at the Cambridgeport Grammar School. He returned to school in 1831 and finished in 1833. That year James received an invitation to serve the church in Louisville, Kentucky, through John

Gorham Palfrey, the dean of the Divinity School, and he accepted. He was ordained on July 21, 1833, at Second Church, Boston. Those who were missionaries to what was considered western Unitarianism often felt cut off from Boston. This led Clarke to seek a special periodical for these sojourners. Together with Ephraim Peabody in Cincinnati, they drew up plans for the *Western Messenger* in 1835, and Clarke later became its editor (1836–39) after Peabody became ill. Clarke undertook a missionary venture to the deep South in December of that year. In Mobile he saw Anna Huidekoper, whom he had just met passing through Louisville on her way south for a winter vacation. She was the daughter of Harm Jan Huidekoper, who was an important figure in the extension of Unitarianism. He was a financial backer of the *Western Messenger* and he was the driving force behind the establishment of **Meadville Theological Seminary**. Clarke and Anna were married on August 15, 1839, in Meadville, Pennsylvania, and eventually had four children.

Theologically the *Messenger* often printed Transcendental works, and Clarke found little objectionable in **Ralph Waldo Emerson**'s controversial **Divinity School Address**, but he also published more traditional Christian-based Unitarian materials as well. Clarke's true radicalism was found in the way he advocated for a new kind of church organization. This bore fruit in 1841 when he returned to Boston to found the Church of the Disciples. It was based on three basic principles. The first of these was the social principle. The members, Clarke felt, needed to get to know one another through a wide variety of programs, including classes and discussion groups. The second principle was that all expenses were to be defrayed by voluntary subscriptions, and so pews were not to be rented or sold so that no social class seating distinctions were made. The third principle was congregational worship. Clarke hoped to involve the entire congregation in worship, including the option of lay sermons. He wanted to break down all social barriers within the church, and thus communion was completely open to everyone, too. Clarke helped inspire the congregation to be involved with reform work. He was a temperance advocate and a supporter of the Washingtonian movement, a precursor to Alcoholics Anonymous. He helped draw up a protest against slavery that was signed by 173 Unitarian ministers and he was named a member of the Boston Vigilance Committee to protest unlawful seizures of slaves.

In 1850 he became ill and was forced to take a sabbatical from his congregation. The family moved to Meadville, Pennsylvania, to live with Clarke's in-laws. Clarke was not completely idle during this time. He fended off invitations to serve other churches, worked with students, provided some pulpit supply, and wrote three books, a translation, and almost 50 magazine articles. He returned to reorganize the Church of the Disciples in January 1854. By the end of that year, plans were being completed for the congregation to merge with the Indiana Place Church and to occupy their building. In 1859 he was elected secretary of the **American Unitarian Association (AUA)**, a position that allowed him to keep his parish ministry, but also required much travel. He also became editor of the *Quarterly Journal* (became *Monthly Journal* in 1860), a position he retained after he stopped being AUA secretary after two years. Clarke also became involved in educational work. In 1863 he was appointed to the Harvard Board of Overseers, and Governor Andrew, who was a parishioner of Clarke's, named him to the State Board of Education. In 1865 he played a prominent role in the establishment of the **National Conference of Unitarian Churches**. He had always been a supporter of the institutional church being organized on a broad Christian basis. After 1866 he began to publish more. In 1872 the first volume of his most important work, *Ten Great Religions*, appeared. Clarke had been researching world religions for a quarter century, and this book was a major early contribution to the study of comparative religion.

In 1869 his congregation built a new building in Boston's South End on Warren Avenue, but many people found it ugly and gave it the nickname The Church of the Holy Gasometer. The church became reenergized after Clarke returned to it full time and annually gave thousands of dollars to charity. One of Clarke's great contributions later in his career came with the "Five Points of the New Theology," which were enunciated in a sermon in 1885. These five became a common Unitarian covenant of belief throughout the movement: The Fatherhood of God; The Brotherhood of Man; The Leadership of Jesus; Salvation by Character; and The Progress of Mankind, Onward and Upward Forever. Clarke remained minister of the church he called the home of his soul until his death on June 8, 1888.

COBB, SYLVANUS (1798–1866). The most important Universalist reformer before the Civil War. Cobb was born on July 17, 1798, in Norway, Maine, where Maine's first Universalist church was founded the following year. Cobb attended district schools and received some instruction at Paris Hill. He converted to Unversalism when he was 16 and at age 20 studied with Sebastian Streeter in Portsmouth, New Hampshire. He was an itinerant until July 1821 when he was called to serve societies in Waterville and Winthrop Maine, where he stayed for seven years. His ordination in Winthrop in 1821 marked the first Universalist ordination in the state. In 1828 he moved to Malden, Massachusetts, for a 10-year ministry.

In 1839 Cobb established the *Christian Freeman and Family Visiter [sic]*, which became the first Universalist paper to advocate for a number of social reforms, especially slavery. Cobb had briefly worked as an associate editor in Haverhill during his ministry in Malden, but knew little about managing a newspaper. He was roundly criticized for the primary political focus of his periodical, but he persevered. **Thomas Whittemore** had tried to avoid such controversial subjects in his *Trumpet*. Cobb began publishing while living in Waltham, Massachusetts, where he had been serving the Universalist church since 1838. He moved to East Boston in 1841 to serve a society that met in an old bath house. The church prospered, but Cobb resigned to devote more time to the paper. The church did not do well without him, and he returned, but then the owners moved the bath house and Cobb resigned.

In the meantime Cobb's paper was converting large numbers of clergy to various reform causes. By 1845 subscription had grown to 3,000 from an initial list of 300. Cobb was also having an effect on denominational actions against slavery. In 1840 he was one of the organizers of the Universalist Anti-Slavery Convention in Lynn, Massachusetts. In 1843 the **General Convention** met in Akron, Ohio, and passed a resolution condemning slavery. Cobb was part of a committee who worked on a petition, *Protest against American Slavery*, which was circulated among the clergy in 1846 protesting slavery. Eventually 313 Universalist ministers signed it. Cobb was also lecturing agent for the Middlesex County Temperance Society. His temperance views were tested during his East Boston ministry when the race track at Suffolk Downs was opened in 1842. He also actively spoke out against the death penalty. During these years Cobb acquired two struggling papers, *Gospel Messenger* and *Gospel Fountain*, and merged them with the *Freeman*. His paper also included denominational, theological, and secular news as well as the writing of abolitionists like Sarah Grimke and the proceedings of various meetings. In 1861 Cobb published a serial history of spiritualism. The *Freeman* lasted until 1862 when it was merged with the *Trumpet* after a complicated procedure. Cobb served briefly as senior editor until the paper was completely absorbed by the new New England **Universalist Publishing House**. He was theological editor for another two years until 1864, but he continued to write for other publications as well. He spent his last years finishing *New Testament with Notes* (1864). Earlier in his career he had supported a resolution before the Boston Association in 1847, calling for complete acceptance of the Biblical account of Christ's life, death, and resurrection. He died on October 31, 1866, in Boston.

COLLYER, ROBERT (1823–1912). He went from poverty to being one of the most famous preachers in America. Collyer was born on December 8, 1823, in Keighley, England, to Samuel and Harriet Collyer, who had both been orphans placed in a mill in Fewston, Yorkshire. Due to this inability to trace his family line, Collyer once said he had no family tree, "only this low bush." Collyer's father was a blacksmith. Young Robert had little formal education, but he learned to love books. He went to work in the mills at the age of eight and he continued as a child laborer until he was 14. After that he became an apprentice to a blacksmith, where he worked for 12 years. He made enough to get married and have a child, but he lost both his wife and the baby in childbirth. This tragedy turned him toward the church and he became a Methodist. His natural speaking abilities were discovered and he became a lay preacher. Collyer married again in 1850 and sailed for America. He found work as a blacksmith outside of Philadelphia. He continued to preach nearly every Sunday in nearby towns, but increasingly found he was unable to preach proper doctrine. He would later say that he never cared for dogma. After he heard Lucretia Mott speak, he became an abolitionist. This led him to be introduced to William H. Furness, the Unitarian minister in Philadelphia, and he eventually preached for Furness. This led to a trial before Methodist elders and Collyer's resignation. At the same time the Unitarians in Chicago wanted to start a mission to the poor, and Collyer was recommended by Furness in 1859.

Collyer's work as a minister-at-large proved successful and he was called to serve Unity Church, Chicago, that same year. He would remain with Unity Church for 20 years developing a nationwide reputation as the "blacksmith-preacher." During the Civil War he worked for the U.S. Sanitary Commission, first in Washington, D.C., and later at various battle fronts helping to care for prisoners. His first published work, *Nature and Life*, came out in 1867. In 1869 his congregation dedicated a new building, but when Chicago endured the great fire in 1871, the massive edifice burned down. By the end of 1873 a new church was dedicated. The next year, the Church of the Messiah in New York asked him to come as their minister. Collyer deflected their overtures for five years, but finally succumbed in 1879. He had another long, successful ministry that lasted until 1896 when **Minot Savage** came as his assistant. He came back to serve the church briefly after he had been made emeritus and, finally, John Haynes Holmes came in 1907. He died on November 30, 1912, in New York. A famed preacher and lecturer, Collyer's unique background of poverty and child labor coupled with a philosophy of seizing the power to save yourself and enjoying the simple things in life proved a winning oratorical formula that was put in print after Collyer's death in *Clear Grit*. He published a number of other works including the biography *Father Taylor* (1906) and an autobiography, *Some Memories* (1908).

COMMISSION ON APPRAISAL. This is a **Unitarian Universalist Association (UUA)** board-appointed group that consists of nine members who are elected by the **General Assembly (GA)**. Its role is to study and provide independent reviews of important denominational activities and report its conclusions to the GA. It is also required to report to the GA on the general program and accomplishments of the UUA. Over the years it has published printed reports on such issues as merger and racial conflicts. The two most recent studies are on congregational polity and membership. First established in 1934 by the Unitarians as the Commission of Appraisal, it provided an initial report in 1936, ***Unitarians Face a***

New Age, which proved essential in stimulating the 20th century rebirth of Unitarianism. In 1934 **James Luther Adams**, minister in Wellesley Hills, Massachusetts, and Kenneth McDougall, one of Adams's parishioners, led a group who advocated for an appraisal commission. At the 1934 May Meetings of the **American Unitarian Association (AUA)** a resolution was presented by Frank Holmes of the Committee on Resolutions from the Essex Unitarian Conference and the Ministerial Union urging a recovery program for the denomination and the establishment of a Commission of Appraisal. Holmes suggested that **Frederick May Eliot** be appointed chair of the commission. The commission consisted of eight members, but only one was from greater Boston and only two were ministers (Adams and Eliot). This was a clear signal of the desire for change. Other members included **Aurelia Henry Reinhardt**, the president of Mills College and the only woman on the COA, and Frederic G. Melcher, the editor of *Publisher's Weekly*, for whom the UUA's annual book award is now named. There were also two staff members.

The commission was formed because of the general perception that Unitarianism was not flourishing and growing. When the group issued its report it included structural recommendations such as the creation of a planning and review board and the new position of moderator. There was a larger sense of change that called for the entire denomination to be more organization conscious and less individualistic. When the report was published in 1936, it resulted in certain steps at the May Meetings that year to initiate bylaw changes that were voted in the following year. The general response to the changes was favorable, and the AUA embarked on a new era, sometimes called a Unitarian renaissance.

COMMITTEE ON GOALS. The **Unitarian Universalist Association (UUA)** Board of Trustees created a Committee on Goals in January 1965 with a charge of examining "the long range theological and sociological goals of the liberal religious movement." A questionnaire was developed, and after responses were received from more than 12,000 adult members, *The Report of the Committee on Goals* was issued (1967). The report suggested that a new religious liberalism was emerging based upon its radical pluralism and deliberate inclusiveness. Believing that liberal religion's growth potential lay with contemporary concerns rather than traditional formulations, the committee suggested building a common commitment to "the expansion of the quality of life." The report found that most Unitarian Universalist members "no longer regard their faith as distinctively Christian, and an overwhelming majority hope the denomination will move toward a universal or distinctively humanistic religion in contrast to liberal Protestantism or ecumenical Christianity." This seeming abandonment of Protestantism for a new universal fourth faith was disturbing to many of the denominations' Christians. The specific recommendations of the report were: the establishment of a Professional Graduate School for Liberal Religion; Metropolitan Centers offering programs for every aspect of church life; improvement in "communication." Few of these goals were ever met. The survey also provided information about the sociological makeup of the denomination. This showed that UUs were dominantly upper income levels, highly educated, professionally employed, and urban and suburban dwellers. The report also found that the typical UU "attends church primarily for intellectual stimulation, along with personal development and fellowship."

COMMUNION. This ancient Christian sacrament is still widely celebrated in Unitarian Universalist Christian congregations. It has also undergone many adaptations in forms and elements in other UU congregations. Puritans, like other Protestants, kept two sacraments, baptism and the Lord's Supper. While communion was reserved for church members (visible saints who were regenerate under the covenant of grace) in Congregational churches, this began to change with the Half-Way Covenant. Each church decided for itself whether people could became "half-way members" by professing their assent to the church covenant, so that their children could be baptized. These individuals were usually denied the Lord's Supper, but after 1660, many of the unregenerate were admitted to communion under a modification promulgated by Solomon Stoddard, whereby communion was used as a device to convert to full church membership. This device did not stop the decline of piety in New England, and communion was usually only partaken by a relatively few members of congregations.

Charles Chauncy, an early liberal, preached a series of sermons on communion in 1772, where he tried to convince his listeners not to fear participating in the Lord's Supper. "The bread and the wine are no otherwise holy, after their consecration, then as they are separated to an holy use, and in the use become capable of being improved to promote holiness in us." Early Universalists also practiced communion on a regular basis. In 1782 **Judith Sargent Murray** published a catechism where she explicated its meaning. She wrote: "The bread and the wine then is a standing memorial of the collection of the many individuals of Adam's race, in the person of Christ, and however we may become *ungratefully* forgetful of this all-comprehenisve figure, it will remain an emblem of grace, as long as time shall endure." Murray saw Jesus as symbolic of the oneness of the human race.

In 1790 Universalists recognized that there was a wide diversity of opinion on communion and stated in their platform of government that none of the ordinances, including communion, were obligatory for church members. This diversity was again acknowledged in *The Universalist Manual or Book of Prayers* (1839) by Menzies Rayner. Rayner wrote that some considered its observance binding upon Christians in all ages, while others felt its obligation was only temporary. He thought it *expedient* to continue this "symbolic and commemorative ordinance."

Communion was generally observed once a month and its form was that it be circulated by deacons among the communicants. Perhaps the most famous response to the obligation of conducting communion services in Unitarian history was given by **Ralph Waldo Emerson**. In September 1832 Emerson delivered a sermon arguing that there was no authority in the scriptures for the continued celebration of the Lord's Supper beyond Jesus' generation. Christ represented a living religion that replaced empty formalism; its observance, Emerson argued, will "produce confusion in our views of the relation of the soul to God. It is the old objection to the doctrine of the Trinity—that the true worship was transferred from God to Christ." Emerson did not mind that others observed the rite, but he did not have the heart to administer it. Unfortunately, because the Second Church of Boston considered it an "indispensable part" of his office, Emerson concluded he must resign from the ministry. Yet

Emerson represented a minority view, and communion was widely celebrated into the 20th century.

Orville Dewey (1794–1882), longtime minister of the Church of the Messiah in New York, was one of the great proponents of a widespread celebration of the sacrament. In his *On the Uses of the Communion* (1841), Dewey advocated for general participation in the rite, rather than keeping it confined to a small group of church members: "I would wish that every person who believes in Christianity, and seriously purposes to lead a life in accordance with it, would come and engage in the acts and offices and meditations of this holy season." Dewey also wanted to devote entire morning services to it, rather than simply making it a secondary event, such as at the close of a service. His interest in reforming communion and making it more central grew out of a childhood where he remembered viewing communion from the gallery "and pitying the persons engaged in it more than any people in the world—I thought they were so unhappy."

In 1914 biblical scholar Clayton Bowen gave the most extensive analysis of liberal views on communion. Bowen argued that the material and sacramental aspects should be eliminated, and "the memorial and fellowship aspects emphasized, rationally and devoutly received, it may still be an invaluable means of quickening the religious lives of the people in our churches." Although Vincent Silliman produced a communion liturgy in 1922, he realized that the celebration of communion was becoming unpopular. While a short and long form of communion were printed in *Hymns of the Spirit* (1937), a survey conducted by John W. Laws the following year found that only about half of the clergy said they celebrated communion. Those services in the hymnal were developed by Von Ogden Vogt, but many ministers designed their own celebrations. Laws argued that meaning could still be found in the rite. "It has a long historical tradition which makes that memorial [to Jesus] also an act of fellowship with the faithful of all ages." Despite his call that communion could help liberals dedicate themselves more fully to God, its meaning and usefulness in worship were lost on many.

Hymns for the Celebration of Life (1964) contained no communion services. There were those who continued to seek meaning in this ritual, including UU Christians, and two groups who sought liturgical renewal, first the **Humiliati** in the 1950s and Abraxas in the

1970s. Vern Barnet, who became active in Abraxas, wrote in *Unitarian Universalist Views of the Sacraments*, "The sacrament of communion has been corroded by beliefs. . . . For me, the Eucharist is experiencing what Christ experienced: the willingness to pay any price, even death, to maintain integrity, and to make the claim, I am God. With the wine I become both human and God. With the wafer, I share in the religious company of my friends and a history of great companions." While some liberals believe that communion is outmoded and artificial, others have found meaning in its celebration of our common origin and shared destiny as participants in a holy, living creation. Services may memorialize Jesus and/or other courageous religious people, and elements may included bread and wine, or other food or drink. Although the words and forms may vary greatly, many Unitarian Universalists still value the sacred significance of sharing a meal.

CONE, ORELLO (1835–1905). The most prominent Universalist biblical scholar. Cone was born on November 16, 1835, in Lincklaen, New York, and grew up on a farm. He was educated at the New Woodstock Academy and Cazenovia Seminary, and then taught school in Manlius, New York. After that he attended St. Paul's College in Palmyra, Missouri, where he became an instructor in Greek and Latin for a few years. Cone thought he would enter the Episcopal priesthood, but in the seminary found he could not hold such orthodox views. After he returned to New York for a period of private study, he was invited to preach Universalism, first in Cazenovia, and then on a local circuit. He became a Universalist minister and briefly served in Little Falls, New York. In 1865 he was appointed professor of biblical languages and literature at the Canton Theological School at **St. Lawrence University**. Here he began to make his name as a scholar, contributing many articles on biblical criticism to the *Universalist Quarterly*. He and Ebenezer Fisher were the only two members of the faculty. Cone became president of **Buchtel College** in 1880 and stayed until 1896. During this time he continued his biblical studies and published his most significant works: *Gospel Criticism and Historical Christianity* (1891) and *The Gospels and Its Earliest Interpretations* (1893). He also became coeditor of the *New World* in 1892. Buchtel had severe financial problems and a dearth of students when Cone assumed his new position. He tried to expand the student body to include many more non-Universalist students, so that by the end of his term they were no longer the majority. He also attempted to broaden the religious affiliations of the faculty. Unfortunately, he was not altogether successful. Cone came under great pressure from the Ohio State Convention to resign, as it was felt he emphasized scholarship too much with the result that his presidential duties such as fund-raising and community relations had suffered.

During the 1890s Cone was active in the American Congress of Liberal Religious Societies, an organization that helped broaden ties with other groups. After he resigned from Buchtel in 1896 he served a brief two-year ministry at a Unitarian church in Lawrence, Kansas, and then went back to St. Lawrence where he served as Richardson Professor of Biblical Theology until his death on June 23, 1905. Cone was the most effective of the Universalists in understanding science and religion as complementary in light of modern biblical criticism.

CONGREGATIONAL POLITY. The type of church government that has been historically associated with Unitarianism and Universalism and the consolidated denomination. Unitarians especially see the roots of their polity in the Puritan heritage. The basic governmental unit is the autonomous local congregation. Each congregation is a gathered community of believers who subscribe to a written covenant that outlines their relationship to one another and to God. The congregation possesses within itself the power to organize and administer its own life and does so through the establishment of bylaws, the election of officers, and the spending of its own funds. There is no limiting authority on the power of the local congregation either in representative synods or clerical or lay authorities. This does not mean that the congregation is an isolated entity. Beginning with the **Cambridge Platform** of 1648, there has always been an emphasis upon the larger wholeness of the church. In addition to the freedom of each congregation, there is a call to establish fellowship with others who have mutual concerns. Historically this larger fellowship developed into local associations, regional districts, and national or continental associations that are governed by elected delegates who are both lay and clerical. Under congregational polity, the ministerial leader has traditionally been seen as one who is called by God out of the midst of the people and is thus a member of the congregation, rather than a person set apart as a special class. Power and authority is derived from the relationship with the congregation who hold the power to ordain and thus to impart the clerical office.

Sacraments under congregational polity, as with all Protestantism, were limited to two: **Baptism** and the Lord's Supper, which Protestants saw as the two ordinances that Christ established in scripture. The Puritans believed that marriage was a civil compact between partners and not a sacrament. With no justification for ministerial celebration, no minister performed a wedding ceremony until 1685. After that they were usually conducted in the bride's home until Victorian times, so it was not a church celebration either. Today with both weddings and memorial services for the deceased, Unitarian Universalists are concerned with the needs of the couple and the family of the deceased. Thus both rites of passage are highly personal and reflect a noncreedal approach to faith.

COMMUNITY CHURCH MOVEMENT. The community church movement grew out of a conflict between **John Haynes Holmes** and the General Conference of Unitarians. A motion approving the conduct of World War I passed at the conference meeting in September 1917 after Holmes had given a speech calling for reconciliation. The following April the **American Unitarian Association (AUA)** Board voted that any congregation whose minister did not support the war effort would not be eligible for aid from the association (this was not reversed until 1936). Holmes was angered by the vote at the General Conference in Montreal and that December he presented five declarations to his congregation in New York. One of these was to make their institution "undenominational." The idea was that people would join not to profess their faith in Unitarianism, but because they were "lovers and servants of mankind." Holmes also asked them to change the church's name. Although the congregation agreed to change its name from the Church of the Messiah to Community Church in 1919, it never actually withdrew from the AUA to start a separate nondenominational movement. Nevertheless, Holmes saw the church as embodying his idea of community religion. For Holmes this meant an institution that dedicated itself first to the community and not any denomination. The church was to welcome all in a spirit of freedom and thus it was more humanistic than theistic. The idea of universal religion supplanted Christianity. Finally, the community church movement interpreted religion in terms of a social reconstruction of society so that it was more just and equal. Holmes's inspiration came from the Harvard philosopher, Josiah Royce.

After Community Church was transformed in 1919, the movement was expanded. In January 1920 Holmes spoke at a meeting in Boston. Working with the Universalist **Clarence Russell Skinner**, Holmes cofounded the Community Church of Boston. Some of the same spirit from the reorganization in New York inspired the first meeting in Boston. Many of the initial members were pacifists who opposed the war and wanted to unify all people in a church where there was no warring over sectarian or class divisions. Both Skinner and Holmes believed in forming a universal religion based on the unity of all people worldwide. In the Universalist denomination there had been some precedent for this. Otis Skinner tried to form a Universalist Free Church Association in the 1840s but it failed. The idea of free religion was institutionalized in the **Free Religious Association (FRA)** in 1867, and Holmes considered his Community Church a continuation of that organization. Both of these leaders remained with their congregations for many years, Skinner until 1936 and Holmes until 1949. Holmes's ideas on fashioning a wider nondenominational church movement were published in *New Churches for Old* (1922). The Boston congregation, especially, became known as a forum church for a wide ranging discussion of radical leftist social causes. Skinner was followed by Donald G. Lothrop, who served the church from 1936 to 1974. During his ministry, Community Church was called the greatest center of communist activity in the Boston area. The church typically attracted as many as 1,500 people to its services. It continues to support the fight for civil liberties and social justice.

COOK, MARIA (1779–1821). The first woman to preach in Universalist pulpits, Cook was a novelty and an inspiration to many in the early 19th century. Little is known of Cook's early life, but she apparently had a mother and siblings living around Geneva, New York, had income from what her deceased father left to her, and was single.

Nathaniel Stacy, the Universalist missionary, reported in his autobiography that she first appeared in Sheshequin, Pennsylvania, in 1810, where she held a number of religious gatherings. Then she asked to preach before the Western Association in Bainbridge, New York, in 1811. This caused a great controversy, but there was enough curiosity that she was finally allowed to address the meeting. Cook was given a letter of fellowship that allowed her to preach, but later she destroyed it, doubting its sincerity. Stacy said she exhibited sound faith, becoming zeal, was well educated, and had more than ordinary speaking talents. Cook received many invitations to preach in five different counties in New York over the course of the next year. She continued to preach until intolerance led to her being jailed in Cooperstown, New York, on a charge of vagrancy. She stayed in prison for a few weeks imparting her Universalist message to other prisoners, but retired from preaching after that. She experimented with the idea of starting a utopian community after she lived with the Shakers for a few months in 1811–12. Although she endured much harassment and abuse, Cook was courageous in her willingness to confront a prejudiced society. She died in Geneva, New York, on December 21, 1835.

CORDNER, JOHN (1816–1894). The first Unitarian minister in Canada. Cordner was born in Newry, Ireland, on July 3, 1816. Educated in Ireland, he trained for the ministry under Henry Montgomery in Belfast. At that time Montgomery had received a letter from Benjamin Workman in Montreal stating that the new Unitarian congregation was seeking a minister. On July 10, 1843, a call was extended to Cordner after a deadlock between supporters of him and William Lord, an American, was broken. The Remonstrant Synod of Ulster ordained Cordner on September 12, and he came to Montreal to preach his first sermon on November 5. The synod also made the congregation part of the Irish Synod as well. Cordner remained with the congregation for 35 years. Although there was significant opposition to Unitarianism within the city initially, Cordner persevered, and a new building was built and dedicated in May 1845. He received considerable financial support from the **American Unitarian Association (AUA)**, whereby contributions to the AUA were returned to Canada for extension work. He also tried to extend the Unitarian word by publishing the *Bible Christian*. He was interested in social reform and became active in public education causes and improving conditions for the insane.

Cordner was married in October 1852 to Caroline Parkman, the sister of historian Francis Parkman, and this helped cement his ties to Boston Unitarianism. The Autumnal Convention was held in Montreal in 1854 and Cordner gave one of the major papers. At that meeting the delegates acknowledged the role of the Underground Railroad for its work in Canada in helping slaves to escape. Within the congregation at this time there was some concern that they were drifting away from their Irish Presbyterian origins and becoming Americanized. In the midst of this conflict Cordner resigned, but a committee persuaded him to rescind it. Benjamin Workman was hoping to restore the Irish connection, but the church was identified now as part of the AUA. This association was also indicated by the invitation that came to Montreal to be part of the organizing meetings for the formation of the National Conference in 1865. Cordner's theology remained virtually unchanged throughout his ministry and was considered traditional liberal Christian. In 1858 a new building was erected on the original site. He received an honorary degree from McGill in 1870. When his health started to deteriorate, an assistant minister and then a colleague was appointed, but eventually Cordner had to resign. In 1878 he moved to Boston. He became involved on the building committee for the new structure that was planned for the AUA headquarters and was then erected in 1886 at 25 Beacon Street. He died in Boston on June 22, 1894.

CORNISH, LOUIS CRAIG (1870–1950). The president of the **American Unitarian Association (AUA)** during the depression, his reputation suffered partly due to the financial constraints of the times. Cornish was born on April 18, 1870, in New Bedford, Massachusetts, the son of a doctor. He attended Harvard College, but then finished his undergraduate degree at Stanford University in 1894. After graduation he was secretary to William Lawrence the Episcopal bishop of Massachusetts. He returned to Harvard for a master's degree and then became a minister. He had a highly successful ministry at the Old Ship Church in Hingham, Massachusetts, from 1900 to 1915. He also volunteered part time as the AUA's librarian. After that he entered the

AUA bureaucracy. Related by marriage to the Eliot family, he seemed well suited to be part of the inner circle of Unitarian leadership. He served for 10 years as an AUA secretary at large and then from 1925 to 1927 as an executive vice president of the AUA.

When **Samuel A. Eliot** resigned as president in 1927, Cornish seemed the logical choice to succeed him with his personal connections to all the sources of power. After his appointment by the AUA board, he had great predictions for growth, but everything turned sour after the Great Depression hit. AUA revenues declined greatly as personal incomes fell and gifts from the congregations completely dried up. Cornish found among his problems that salaries had to be slashed, the Pacific Unitarian School for the Ministry had to be bailed out from bankruptcy, and, finally, Lombard College collapsed after Cornish had tried to help arrange a joint Unitarian Universalist experiment to save it and its assets were given to the **Meadville Theological School**.

Cornish was also a cautious and inexperienced leader, and this indecision proved ineffective at a time of crisis. He came under criticism that the AUA was drifting. Kenneth MacDougall, a layperson from Wellesley, Massachusetts, wrote: "We content ourselves with exchanges of good will with a group of liberal Filipinos" (Murdock, *Institutional History*, p. 59). The failures of his administration to respond to the crisis led to the formation of the Commission of Appraisal, a new group formed to study the organization, administration, and leadership of the association. Its chair, **Frederick May Eliot**, called for a complete renewal of the denomination. The final report of the Commission, ***Unitarians Face a New Age***, helped sweep Eliot into office in the election of 1937. Cornish's administration had become, in Dave Parke's words, a "caretaker presidency." Yet there were positive accomplishments during Cornish's term. A hymnbook commission worked on updating the *Hymn and Tune Book* and in 1937 produced *Hymns of the Spirit*.

After 10 years as AUA president, Cornish turned to the work that was perhaps his greatest passion, the extension of Unitarianism around the world. From 1937 to 1946 he was president of the International Association for Liberal Christianity and Religious Freedom. He had previously investigated the persecution of religious groups in Transylvania, resulting in *The Religious Minorities of Transylvania* (1925). He had a special interest in the new Unitarian movement in

Czechoslovakia. Cornish traveled a great deal to help foster religious dialogue and understanding among nations. In *Unitarians Face a New Age*, Cornish wrote the chapter on international relations and was called, along with Charles Wendte, one of the two great international leaders in the denomination. Unfortunately, much of his work was blunted by the onset of World War II. He died on January 7, 1950, in Orlando, Florida.

COUNCIL OF LIBERAL CHURCHES (CLC). A joint meeting of Unitarians and Universalists was held in Andover, Massachusetts, in the summer of 1953, and the Council of Liberal Churches was established. This was the first important step in the final consolidation of the two denominations. The meeting also authorized the formation of a Joint Interim Commission, which would review the work of the CLC and make a report to the second biennial meeting in 1955. The CLC was incorporated that fall and a governing board was put into place. The hope was that the CLC would combine some administrative functions including religious education, public relations, and publications. There were practical problems in all of these areas, with the best success achieved in educational programming. Financing the organization was a serious problem. New Universalist **General Superintendent** Brainerd Gibbons reported at the **General Assembly (GA)** in 1955 that Universalists have never given enough authority to the headquarters nor supported it financially. Before the 1955 Biennial the Joint Interim Commission was able to meet two times. It finally recommended that a joint merger commission be established. The CLC presented the two denominations with the challenge of financing a third organization, whereas the best plan seemed to merge the two existing ones. While some wanted to give the CLC more time, a significant majority in both denominations favored establishing the merger commission, and it was so voted. The commission started meeting in 1956 with William Rice as chair. Two plans were formulated. One would result in a complete consolidation and the other an enlarged CLC. The CLC dissolved in 1959 when the denominations voted to proceed with complete consolidation.

COVENANT. Churches in the Puritan or congregational tradition were formed around a simple, written agreement called a covenant. The earliest covenants defined the relationship between the members of a single church. They were written and signed by all members of the newly gathered congregation and the words reflected their simple promises to one another and to God to worship God, forsake all evil, and give themselves to Lord Jesus, who was head of the church. Covenants were not statements of belief, but agreements that defined the nature of the church. The use of a covenant is expressly congregational in its usage. People become members of the community by agreeing to live with one another and look out for one another under the covenant. It derives from the covenant or federal theology of the Puritans, following the agreement first made in the Hebrew scriptures between God and His people. Covenant theology was especially developed in England by William Ames. Despite their common belief in predestination, Puritans differed on how much of the work of salvation was God's and how much was each individual preparing his/her heart to receive the covenant of grace.

In Puritan times, covenant was a well-used word. The covenant of grace usually referred to an experience of conversion. The Half-Way Covenant was a devise used after 1662 to enable unconverted members to baptize their children. They typically "owned the covenant" or agreed with the principles of the church covenant, and then their children could be baptized. Lines of membership were sometimes blurred under these guidelines. When the theology of the Puritans began to differ markedly within congregations, covenants were sometimes used by the orthodox as creedal tests. While liberals would never have interpreted covenant in this way, their belief in the increasing human role in salvation (Arminianism) made those who had experienced the covenant of grace feel as though this was an appropriate response. Some congregations still follow their covenant or some modern equivalent, as an agreement between members.

COVENANT FOR FREE WORSHIP. More commonly referred to as "Love is the Doctrine of this Church," a "Covenant for Free Worship" was written by the Universalist minister L. Griswold Williams (1893–1942) and included in his book *Antiphonal Readings for Free Worship* (1933). Williams served congregations in Reading, Pennsylvania; Barre, Vermont; and Floral Park, New York; and was a member of the hymnbook commission that produced *Hymns of the Spirit*.

(1937). Frequently used in worship, the original text reads: "Love is the Doctrine of this Church, The quest of truth is its Sacrament, And service is its Prayer. To dwell together in Peace, To seek knowledge in Freedom, to serve mankind in Fellowship, To the end that all souls shall grow into harmony with the Divine, Thus do we Covenant with each other and with God." Revised versions change mankind to humankind.

CRANCH, CHRISTOPHER PEARSE (1813–1892). A Transcendentalist poet and artist who has been characterized as a dilettante. Cranch was born on March 8, 1832, in Alexandria, Virginia. He attended Columbian College (now George Washington University) and **Harvard Divinity School**, where he graduated in 1835. After supplying pulpits around New England, he became associated with a number of Western radicals and worked with **James Freeman Clarke** on editing the *Western Messenger*, where he affirmed the religious nature of Transcendentalism as that "living and always new spirit of truth" (Cranch in Miller, *Transcendentalists*, p. 301). He preached in St. Louis and Cincinnati and finally returned east after five years. Perry Miller called Cranch one of the most delightful of the Transcendentalists, but also proved to be one of its most wasted talents. **Ralph Waldo Emerson** liked his poetry and encouraged him to publish in the *Dial*. He gave up preaching after 1841 and became a landscape artist in the tradition of the Hudson River School. He also published poems in the *Harbinger* and offered literary and musical criticism as well. Cranch traveled a great deal in the ensuing years, spending three years in Italy and 10 years in Paris. One of his most successful projects was a translation of *The Aeneid* (1872). He continued to publish poetry, including "The Bird and the Bell," with *Other Poems* (1875). He is best known for his caricatures based on passages from Emerson's writings, especially his depiction of Emerson's "transparent eyeball" from *Nature*. With his dabbling in painting, poetry, and music, Cranch is the best representative of the aesthetic sense in Transcendentalism. He died in Cambridge, Massachusetts, on January 20, 1892.

CUMMINS, ROBERT (1897–1982). Called "the modern architect of organized Universalism," Cummins was born in Sydney, Ohio. After graduation from college (Miami University–Ohio), he took charge of the Boon-It Institute in Bangkok, a Presbyterian mission. After only two years of teaching, Cummins helped engineer transferring responsibility for the school to local leadership. Upon returning to Ohio he became a Universalist because he said it was "big enough to allow me the freedom of conscience and intellect I seemed by nature to demand." He became the minister of three small congregations while also owning and operating his own insurance business. He soon accepted a call from the Universalist church in Cincinnati, where he served for six years while also earning an M.A. from the University of Cincinnati. In 1932 he became the minister of Throop Memorial Universalist Church in Pasadena, California. During this ministry he earned his M.Th. from the University of Southern California.

His successes in the parish led the Trustees of the Universalist **General Convention** to prevail upon him in 1938 to become the fifth **general superintendent** of what was called after 1942 the **Universalist Church of America**. Cummins was told "that we should try to check a decline which had been going on for fifty years." Cummins tried mightily to build Universalist confidence; he succeeded by introducing a departmental system and vastly increasing income and budget. But his 15 years of leadership could not restore Universalism to corporate health, even though he traveled all over the United States and Canada trying to bring regional groups into greater cooperation with a more centralized headquarters. Cummins also led the denomination's failed effort to join the **Federal Council of Churches**. The end of his tenure saw him supporting the establishment of the **Council of Liberal Churches**, which was the first step toward the final union of Unitarians and Universalists.

After his retirement Cummins served the Eisenhower administration by heading up the State Department's International Cooperation Administration. He was married to Alice Grimes, and they had three children, one of whom, John, became a Unitarian Universalist minister. In 1943 Cummins articulated the more inclusive basis of Universalist thinking when he addressed the **General Assembly (GA)** with these words:

> Universalism cannot be limited to Protestantism or to Christianity, not without denying its very name. Ours is a world fellowship, not just a Christian sect. For so long as Universalism is universalism and not par-

tialism, the fellowship bearing its name must succeed in making it unmistakably clear that all are welcome: theist and humanist, unitarian and Trinitarian, colored and color-less. A circumscribed Universalism is unthinkable.

CZECH REPUBLIC. After World War I many Czechs abandoned the Catholic church under the influence of the first Czech president, Thomas Masaryk. Although they had no heritage of religious freedom, the Czechoslovak National Church emerged as the major religious body of the nation. This church retained many of the Catholic forms and was somewhat broader in its message, but it still did not satisfy some. Norbert Capek, the founder of the Unitarian church, was brought up Catholic but discovered the Baptist church and trained for its ministry. Masaryk, who had married Charlotte Garrigue, an American Unitarian from Brooklyn, introduced Capek to Unitarianism. Capek went into voluntary exile in the United States and through the Masaryk's influence found and joined the Unitarian church in Orange, New Jersey. When Capek returned to Prague in 1921, he came as a missionary from the **American Unitarian Association** and the British General Assembly. After he announced his new faith publicly, he soon gathered those who wanted greater religious change into the Liberal Religious Fellowship. People came from many religious backgrounds and most did not want to be reminded of their former orthodox affiliations. They wanted no gown worn by the minister, no hymn singing, no ornate buildings, no formal or prescribed prayers, and refused to use the word church. The first services were starkly simple, but Capek slowly introduced hymns and in 1923 a new ritual, the **flower celebration**. The goal of the fellowship was to "provide spiritual and ethical education toward the establishment of a social order based on individual freedom and universal brotherhood." Capek's wife, Maja, organized a Women's Alliance and the fellowship became a center for cultural events, a book shop, a vegetarian restaurant, and a hostel, all located in an old palace in the center of Prague. This eventually grew into the Unitarian church with estimates of as many as 3,500 members (the largest Unitarian church in the world), with outreach congregations in eight other cities.

On June 30, 1930, the Unitarian movement was approved by the state as the Religious Society of Czechoslovakian Unitarians. Growth was hindered by the effects of the Great Depression, but Capek preached to large congregations until 1941 when, after speaking out against the injustices of the Nazi regime, he was arrested and eventually sent to Dachau concentration camp where he was killed. The Czech Unitarian movement was decimated during the Nazi occupation, but in the immediate postwar period Capek's son-in-law, Karel Haspl, assumed leadership of the church and membership was stabilized and much assistance was given to war orphans. Haspl underwent repeated interrogations at the hands of the communist regime, but the movement survived.

Sensing new possibilities for renewal after the revolution in 1989, the Czech Unitarian Association invited the Rev. Vladimir Strejcek, a Czech emigre to America, to return home and rebuild the church. Unfortunately, Strejcek transformed it from a democratic institution to an autocratic one with congregations answerable only to him. This resulted in a split in the Czech Unitarian movement. Strejcek and his followers took over the historic Unitarian church in Prague and all its funds, and the descendants of Capek and Karel Haspl, under the leadership of Haspl's daughter Livie Dvorakova-Hasplova and Eva Kocmanova (chairperson), met in a separate facility until June 2000. In May of that year the Czech courts ruled that the lockout by the dissidents under Strejcek was illegal, and Capek's descendants were able to regain control of their old building. Congregations in the United States maintain a partner church relationship with the three Czech congregations: Prague, Pilsen, and Brno.

– D –

DALL, CAROLINE WELLS HEALEY (1822–1912). Born the oldest child of a wealthy Boston merchant on June 22, 1822, Dall had full charge of a household that included a father, invalid mother, and seven siblings, when she was only 17. She was torn between her duties to family and an expanding religious consciousness. Writing Sunday School lessons and teaching at the West Church of Boston helped initiate her into a stimulating intellectual environment. Even as a young woman she realized that an independent woman would be scorned by society when she wrote in her diary in 1839, "how strange that when once a woman's earnest convictions are given to the world, the world seems to doubt her humanity." After marrying **Charles Dall** in 1844, she assisted him in his ministries and bore two children, but her marriage was not a happy one. When he left for a Unitarian mission in India in 1855, she remained behind and only saw him a few times during the next 30 years.

Caroline Dall was already a staunch women's rights activist. During the next few years she was coeditor of *The Una* and also published two collections of lectures she had given: *Woman's Right to Labor; or, Low Wages and Hard Work* and *Woman's Rights Under the Law*. Her most important work came out in 1867, *The College, the Market, and the Court; or, Woman's Relation to Education, Labor, and Law*. Dall argued that only work would give women the full human dignity they deserved. Going far beyond a plea for suffrage, she identified the cultural and legal barriers that confronted women everywhere. Especially interested in recovering historical examples, she published *Historical Pictures Retouched* to show the type of achievement women were capable of. Dall's fight for equal rights and opportunities for women continued thoughout her life. Later in life she published an account of **Margaret Fuller**'s conversations and a history of Transcendentalism. She died on December 17, 1912.

DALL, CHARLES HENRY APPLETON (1816–1886). Dall is chiefly remembered for his mission work in India. He was born in Baltimore, Maryland, on February 12, 1816, and graduated from **Harvard Divinity School** in 1840. Entering the ministry as a disciple of **Joseph Tuckerman**'s ministry to the poor, Dall worked in St. Louis, Missouri; Portsmouth, New Hampshire; and Baltimore, where he married Caroline Healey in 1844. He had brief pastorates in Needham, Massachusetts, and Toronto, Ontario, but poor health plagued him. In 1855, the **American Unitarian Association (AUA)**, following the urgings of Charles Brooks, established a mission at Calcutta, India. Dall volunteered for this duty and sailed in February of that year. His predilection for illness continued during his journey, and apparently upon arrival in India, he was carried unconscious from the boat. But there was never a word of illness again, and for the next 30 years, Dall carried out his duties faithful to the initial charge from the secretary of the AUA: "You go out as a Unitarian missionary, because we have reason to believe that many will receive the gospel as we hold it, who reject the errors which we believe others have added to the faith once delivered to the saints. But you are not expected to carry more doctrinal discussions and sectarian strife to those distant lands."

Dall was encouraged to establish friendly relations with all sects, and eventually the Unitarian schools gave very little overt religious instruction. Dall's work in the early years of the mission focused on establishing a strong church with preaching, baptizing, visiting, and publishing tracts. After 1860, the mission emphasis became education and the establishing of industrial schools. Especially successful was the School of Useful Arts. Dall had numerous conflicts with the European, English-speaking community, but made many enduring friendships with the Indian intelligentsia. The culmination of these relationships occurred in 1871 when Dall joined the **Brahmo Samaj** movement, partly owing to his friendship with **Keshab Chunder Sen**. In the later years of his mission, support for Dall, especially by the British Unitarians, began to wane. They preferred indigenous reformers. In a 25th anniversary report on his work, Dall emphasized the schools, his travels and speeches throughout India, and the publications. During this period, he only returned to America five times. In his final years support from the AUA was mostly silent, and Dall was worried that his work would collapse without his presence. Eschewing retirement, he died at Calcutta on July 18, 1886. *See also* DALL, CAROLINE WELLS HEALEY .

DAVID, FRANCIS (1510–1579). The founder of the Unitarian movement in Transylvania and the first Unitarian bishop. According to traditions, David was born in 1510, but it appears he was born closer to 1520 in **Kolosvar**, Transylvania. His father was Hertel David, a shoemaker of Saxon origin, and his mother was Hungarian. During his youth he went to school in his hometown and later at Gyulafehervar and Brasso. From 1546 to 1551 he studied abroad at German universities in Frankfurt and Wittenburg, where the spirit of the reformation began to capture his heart and mind. When he returned home, he became a teacher at Beszterce. The following year he became a minister in Petres, but he soon gave up the priesthood and became Lutheran. From 1552 to 1555 he was headmaster in Kolosvar, culminating with his election as chief minister. After 1555 Kolosvar became the center for religious reform, and David a key spokesperson for the reformation. His aim was to restore the Bible as the basis for gospel Christianity. From 1557 to 1559 he was the bishop of the Transylvanian Hungarian Lutherans, but he eventually resigned for doctrinal reasons. He began to believe that a more perfect reformation of Christianity could still occur beyond Lutheranism, and began to follow the Swiss reformers. David tried to reconcile the two factions but a Synod at Nagyenyed failed when they could not agree on communion. Then David was elected bishop of the Reformed group and also made the court preacher for **King John Sigismund**. This was only a brief stop for David, who began to question the dogmas of Calvinism.

David saw reformation as a continuous process, with its various stages helping to reach pure truth. In his biblical searching he rejected the doctrine of the Trinity as a human creation and began to preach the concept of one God, thus taking the reformation to Unitarianism. The first public Unitarian oration was in Kolosvar on January 20, 1566. After that he and Dr. **Giorgio Biandrata** provided leadership in the religious debates. David published four works in 1567 and several more the following year. One of the great events in Unitarian history took place in January 1568, at the Diet of Torda. Here David made a historic plea for religious toleration. The famous Edict of Toleration was passed whereby the king declared that all preachers should be allowed to preach according to their own understanding of the Gospel without having to suffer persecution. Only two months later, David was challenged to a debate with the Calvinist bishop Melius. Beginning on March 8 and lasting for 10 days, 11 debaters encountered one another. The debate at Gyulafehervar was considered an overwhelming Unitarian victory, and when David returned to Kolosvar, local tradition said that when the people asked him to speak to them, they were overcome by his eloquence and took him on their shoulders, resulting in the whole population converting to Unitarianism. That year David became a bishop for the third time, now for the Unitarians.

The Unitarians continued to plan a response and a new debate was called for in October 1569. David came to extol the virtues of religious liberty, but his opponents tried to condemn him. This debate at Nagyvarad sealed King John Sigismund's acceptance of Unitarianism. By 1571 David was concerned about the legal status of Unitarianism and convinced the king to increase to four the received religions of the kingdom: Catholic, Lutheran, Reformed, and Unitarian. This occurred at the Diet of Maros-Vasarhely in January. Unfortunately, the king died two months later on March 14. The new king, the Catholic Stephen Bathori, removed all Unitarians from positions of influence, including David as court preacher, which he had held since 1566.

In 1574 David's life came under the scrutiny of a synod after previous diets had decreed that any new innovations in religion were banned. David was made the lawful superintendent of the Unitarians in 1576. In 1578 **Faustus Socinus** was summoned from Switzerland in an attempt by Dr. Biandrata to have David curb his opinions, but this failed. In 1579, the year the Jesuits came to Transylvania, David was forced from his pastorate. Although he was sick and had to be carried into court, he was accused of preaching innovation for his teaching of "Non-adoramus," telling the Unitarians not to worship Jesus, but to follow him, and for "Semper Reformanda," the need for continuing reformation. He was eventually found guilty and imprisoned at the castle at Deva. The great Unitarian preacher did not survive long, dying on November 15, 1579. He became a great martyr to the Unitarian cause and a principal figure in the struggle for religious liberty.

DAVIDOFF, DENISE TAFT (1932–). A former **moderator** of the **Unitarian Universalist Association (UUA)**, she was born in New York City on March 11, 1932, to Allen and Bunnee (Zuckerman) Taft. After graduating from Vassar College in 1953, she worked on the Harriman for Governor campaign in New York. Then she went into promotional writing for *Time*, *Life,* and the *New Yorker* magazines. "Denny" was married to Jerry Davidoff in 1955, and they had two boys. After working for C. A. Smith & Company as an executive, she started her own public relations firm, Davidoff and Partners, in Norwalk, Connecticut. She was owner, chief executive, and president of this company until she sold it in 1991. Davidoff has been active in her local Unitarian Universalist congregation in Westport, Connecticut, since 1960 when she made the choice of moving beyond a Jewish heritage of emigrant ancestors from the Ukraine. In 1981 she was elected president of the **Unitarian Universalist**

Women's Federation (UUWF), after having been treasurer for four years. Here she played a key role in seeing that the **Principles and Purposes** debate did not become divisive and split the denomination. In 1981 several women's groups presented a nontheistic, degenderized version of the principles before the **General Assembly (GA)**. Davidoff decided that an immediate vote could cause a serious problem and instead supported the appointment of a committee to study the issue and report back a year later. Although this action divided many of the women delegates, it saved the denomination from a grave theological battle.

Davidoff was elected to the GA Planning Committee in 1985 and then became its chair from 1987 to1989. That was followed by her election to the position of UUA trustee-at-large. During this time she started a long-term period of service on the Committee on Committees, which fills many of the important volunteer roles in the UUA. She also served on the **Ministerial Fellowship Committee (MFC)**. In 1993 she was elected moderator of the UUA and then was reelected in 1997, serving two full terms until 2001 with President **John Buehrens**. She and Buehrens worked well together, and he credits Davidoff with helping the denomination move toward more interfaith efforts, especially because of her Jewish background. As moderator she served on the Executive Committee, Finance Committee, and was part of the Panel on Theological Education. During her time as moderator, the **Board of Trustees** embraced important antiracism initiatives. This commitment grew out of her former support for the black power group (FULL-BAC) during the **Black Empowerment Controversy** in the UUA. She traveled to many local congregations during her eight years in office, giving many people the opportunity to meet a denominational official. She came out of her experience with "a great sense of encouragement" about the future of Unitarian Universalism. Davidoff has also supported international outreach within the denomination and traveled to such places as the Khasi Hills in **India**. Her enthusiasm for UUA volunteer work did not wane after her term as moderator. She joined the board of the **Church of the Larger Fellowship** in 2001 (where she now serves on the Executive Committee) and then the board of the **Meadville Lombard Theological School** in 2002. Her international outreach efforts have also continued. She was a founding director of the Interfaith Alliance and is now president of the Interfaith Alliance Foundation in Washington, D.C. Davidoff is also a member of the Trustee Council of the World Conference on Religion and Peace. Professionally, she has worked as a consultant in recent years and she continues to reside in Norwalk, Connecticut.

DAVIES, A. (ARTHUR) POWELL (1902–1957). Perhaps the most important midcentury spokesperson for American Unitarianism, Davies was a foreigner who learned to love and understand the ethos of America more than most of its native born citizens. He was born on June 5, 1902, in Birkenhead, outside of Liverpool, England, of Welsh parentage. He had political interests from his youth and after graduating from secondary school, he worked as a secretary to a Labour Member of Parliament. In the period between the wars he became especially concerned about Great Britain's debt. Although George Bernard Shaw urged him to follow these political inclinations, Davies felt a call to the ministry. He entered Richmond Theological College (Methodist) at the University of London, where he received the highest theology prize. After graduating he served a church in Charing Cross for three years. Davies had long dreamed about sailing to the New World and left for America in 1928 with his wife of five months, Muriel Hannah.

Davies's first pastorates in America were to two small churches in rural Maine. After that he continued his Methodist ministry in Portland, but it was during this time that he developed a close friendship with Vincent Silliman, the Unitarian minister in Portland. A conversion to Unitarianism followed, and in 1933 Davies assumed his first Unitarian pastorate at the Community Church of Summit, New Jersey. He also became a U.S. citizen that same year. During this time, Davies campaigned for a limited type of world government, Federal Union, and was the first person to publicly endorse the principle. From 1933 onward he warned audiences about the looming threat of Nazism. While in summit, he published his first major book, *American Destiny* (1942), which called for America to assume leadership in the world. Davies belief in the freedom and equality of all led him to be an outspoken opponent of Nazism. After the war, a moderate stance toward communism turned to outspoken denunciation. He warned America that it must be prepared to oppose communism by introducing universal military training, continue American occupation of Europe, and also continue economic aid to war-torn areas. In some ways he helped the forces that shaped McCarthyism by his strident support for America. In 1953 he spoke at the Anniversary Service of the **American Unitarian Association**'s **(AUA)** May Meeting calling communism the ultimate evil.

In 1944 Davies was called to the ministry that brought him his enduring legacy, All Souls Church in Washington, D.C. Here he became a political force by urging his congregation, his city, and his nation to fight injustice everywhere. His major political achievements included a successful lobbying of Congress as chair of the Conference for the Civilian Control of Atomic Energy, so that nuclear power was placed under civilian jurisdiction rather than military. He also led a boycott of restaurants in Washington leading to their desegregation. Another project was a successful effort to establish an integrated Columbia Heights (Washington) Boys Club in cooperation with the Unitarian Service Committee. Davies was a founding member of Americans for Democratic Action, served on many organizational boards, and frequently testified before Congress. Immediately following the war he headed up efforts to feed starving people in Europe. He also defended a professor at George Washington University who was dismissed because he was an atheist. Davies went on to say that every campus should have at least one atheist on its faculty.

Davies had a tremendous faith in democracy. In 1949 he published *America's Real Religion* in which he said democracy has a religious base and we need to understand what it is spiritually. Davies wrote: "Democracy is the social and political expression of the religious principle that all men are brothers and mankind a family; *democracy is brotherhood: brotherhood unrestricted by nation, race or creed*." (Davies, *America's Real Religion*, p. 9) Davies believed this was the faith that could save the world.

Davies also believed in extending his Unitarian faith. In 1943 he became chair of the AUA's Program Committee, which was attempting to define "The Faith behind Freedom." He continued to give leadership to the program called Unitarian Advance in the 1940s, but found it difficult to deal with denominational bureaucracies and those unwilling to change. Davies believed that Unitarianism had to become a universal church and not just another Protestant denomination. He believed there could only be slight advance if they remained a liberal branch of Christianity. Much of his inspiration for church growth was evident in Washington from 1952 to 1957, where he helped create five satellite churches around the city, which in turn created three more congregations for a total of eight. Other metropolitan areas tried to emulate the growth in Washington. Davies had a heavy speaking schedule continuing his efforts for extension in the fall of 1957 when a recurring problem with phlebitis occurred, and he died on September 26, 1957. Davies declared in *The Faith of an Unrepentant Liberal* (1946) that Unitarianism was the greatest faith the world had known because it was liberal, universal, ethical, democratic and rational. He has been called one of the great ministers of the 20th century and he was certainly what *Time* magazine declared "a man who is heard." (Marshall, *Davies*, p. 4)

DEAN, PAUL (1783–1860). A leader in the Restorationist controversy in opposition to **Hosea Ballou**. Dean was born in 1783 in Barnard, New York. He became a talented itinerant preacher in central New York State around Utica from 1810 to 1813. In debates with orthodox opponents he agreed that there was a period of punishment after death, but that it would not be eternal. He showed at this stage of his career that he wanted to accommodate Universalism with the rest of Christianity rather than make attacks upon the orthodox. In 1813 he was called to serve as **John Murray**'s associate minister in Boston and was installed in August. Two years later, upon Murray's death, he became senior pastor at this very prominent pulpit. It was expected that Dean would become one of the major leaders of the denomination. He was given charge of denominational committees to found a seminary and write a church history.

In 1817 Hosea Ballou came to the Second Universalist Society in Boston and a major theological rift between Ballou and Dean began to divide Universalists. Ballou believed in immediate salvation upon death, and Dean represented a school of Universalists who advocated a period of reprobation before eventual salvation. This period of limited suffering after death became known as Restorationism. The small group of Restorationists published their views in the *Christian Repository* in 1822. A bitter war took place in the denomination's publications, and Dean and others were accused of jealously over

Ballou's dominant position as a denominational leader. Dean resigned from fellowship in the New England Convention, but was eventually restored in 1824 over the objections of **Thomas Whittemore**. The First Universalist Society formed an early Sunday School during his ministry. The congregation divided over the Restorationist issue in 1823 and some of them went with him to found the Bulfinch Street Church. In 1830 Dean went on an evangelical tour and preached the first Universalist sermons in Baltimore, Maryland, and Charleston, South Carolina, where societies were formed. In Charleston he was named "Bishop." The Restorationist controversy flared up again in 1831 when a group, including Dean, met in Mendon, Massachusetts, to form an organization for the defense of their beliefs. This new organization became known as the Massachusetts Association of Universal Restorationists. This group met annually for the ensuing 10 years, but interest waned and the organization finally disbanded, with those who favored social reform and utopianism following **Adin Ballou**.

This Universalist controversy was felt statewide when it came to deciding who would be the preacher of the annual Election Sermon. Dean was chosen for the 1831–32 session, but the ballot was nearly a stalemate with the other candidate being an Ultra Universalist, Linus Everett. During the 1830s Dean was editor of a Restorationist paper, the *Independent Messenger*, from 1835 to 1838, and then editor of the *Restorationist* for about two years. He had been drifting toward Unitarianism, as was true for many Restorationists. The Bulfinch Street Church became Unitarian in its affiliation as well. Feeling some pressure from his congregation, Dean retired from active ministry in 1840 feeling "broken" from all his hopes for his career gone awry. He later supplied the pulpit in Easton, Massachusetts. Like John Murray, Dean considered himself a Trinitarian, but the Holy Spirit had no real place in his beliefs. Some of his colleagues called him a Sabellian, a position where there are no eternal distinctions within the persons of the Godhead, but God is one being who operates in different modes. He believed in an "intermediate state" after death that was neither heaven nor hell. Here the sinners had an opportunity to hear the gospel and bring their souls into the right state to accept grace. He died in Framingham, Massachusetts, on October 10, 1860.

DEATH. Unitarian Universalist views of death and immortality have changed much over the centuries. From the late Middle Ages onward, Western thought increasingly focused on individual salvation. This culminated in the Romantic view of death in the 19th century when the beauty of death became a cultural obsession and cults of the dead, mourning pictures, and the rural cemetery movement began. Death became a peaceful deliverance from life with the assuredness of an eternal and heavenly reunion with loved ones instead of the ghastly vision of hell and damnation. Unitarians and Universalists were among those who banished the grim terror of death from their religious thought.

Beginning with Mt. Auburn Cemetery in Cambridge, Massachusetts, in 1831, the rural cemetery movement treated the dead differently by providing a beautiful garden home for the deceased so that the living could commune with them. Unitarians such as John Pierpont and Edward Everett were among the foremost leaders in this movement. Consolation literature from the 19th century became preoccupied with the nature of celestial destinations and activities. Hymns produced during this time highlighted the beauties of heaven while ignoring hell and its eternal flames. Unitarians such as **William Ellery Channing** and the Wares were among the greatest proponents of a domestic heaven. Here families could be restored and loved ones reunited. On Easter Sunday 1834 Channing said that Christ's resurrection confirmed the Christian doctrine of life after death. Channing held that heaven would be a place of continuing moral improvement. He said the work of education that begins here "goes on without end." The Transcendentalists did not hold such a literal view. In **Ralph Waldo Emerson**'s essay *Immortality* he speaks of the human soul sharing in a universal life, but it is not an everlasting personal consciousness.

Nothing could be more of a banishment of the negative overtones of death than the central belief of Universalism in salvation for all. For some Universalists their belief in the universal restoration of souls led them to a conviction that it was possible to communicate with the dead. **Adin Ballou** was among those who believed in spirit manifestations and he invited mediums to his Hopedale community. John Murray Spear was another well-known Universalist who advocated some form of spiritualism. Spear published accounts of his communications with the dead and even invented a table-top machine, The New Motive Power, that sat on a hill overlooking Lynn, Massachusetts. This occurred when an interest in mesmerism, phrenology, and spiritualism was sweeping the country, and some Universalists were attracted by the unusual mixture of science and mysticism. Even more divisive was the **Restorationist Controversy**. Some Universalists were disturbed by the belief in immediate salvation for all, "Death and Glory," and so promoted the belief in Restorationism, a 10,000-year period when the soul was washed clean, akin to the Catholic purgatory.

The assuredness of a domestic heaven began to vanish in the 20th century as a firm humanism and agnosticism took hold. Unitarians and Universalists refused to give comforting answers to the eternal question of life after death if they could not be sure of those answers. This rejection of a personal existence after death was reflected in the 1967 *Report of the Committee on Goals* (p. 26), which found that 89.5 percent of the respondents to the question of immortality said no. This question was broadened in the 1987 survey on *The Quality of Religious Life in Unitarian Universalist Congregations* (p. 36) to include a "not sure" response, as well as yes and no. While only 15 percent said yes in 1987, 38 percent said "not sure," and 46 percent said "no." Almost half of the respondents who called themselves Unitarian Universalist Christians did not answer yes to this question, so even those who adopt the traditional liberal Christian faith of the two denominations do not ascribe to the once popular belief in a personal afterlife. Many Unitarian Universalists attach the word immortality to the works of contributions that live on after a human life has ceased. Others associate immortality with the return of our bodies to the earth, where we merge with other atoms in the universe and assume immortality in a new form. Those who still affirm a personal existence after death often do so based on scientific evidence. They agree with fellow Unitarian, Oliver Wendell Holmes, who said we would enter ever more stately mansions in an after-life. We leave the shell of our bodies by "life's unresting sea." The variety of viewpoints underscores the Unitarian Universalist belief that everyone must answer for themselves.

DEATH WITH DIGNITY. Long believing that people should have the right to choose what is morally responsible, Unitarian Universalists support personal choice in relation to issues around death and dying. This means that Unitarians Universalists would support the decision by the individual or their proxy to withdraw artificial life supports, even if death results. In 1988 the **Unitarian Universalist Association (UUA)** became the first religious group to explicitly support the right to die with dignity. The **General Assembly (GA)** passed a resolution affirming that people have "the right to self-determination in dying and the release from civil or criminal penalties of those who, under proper safeguards, act to honor the right of terminally ill patients to select the time of their own deaths" (as quoted in Divine and Rosa, ed., *Resolutions and Resources Handbook*, p. 75). Although not all Unitarian Universalists would support assisted suicide where there are no medical options left, many do believe that in certain circumstances, it is the most humane choice for an individual who wishes to maintain some quality of life.

DE BENNEVILLE, GEORGE (1703–1793). An early preacher of Universalism, de Benneville represents a mystical, experiential type of the faith. He was born in London to French parents on July 26, 1703. His father, George Sr., was of noble birth, but he had been exiled from France due to Huguenot sympathies. George was the youngest of nine and his mother died in childbirth. The young boy received a noble upbringing when his Godmother Queen Anne brought him into the royal family. After a fine education, he tried a brief stint in the Royal Navy. After being influenced by Prince George's chaplain, de Benneville underwent a conversion that God's universal love and grace meant that all souls were to be restored. He then returned to France to preach and, although he was arrested and warned, he returned a second time to do more preaching. Arrested a second time, he was condemned to die. While his companion was executed de Benneville received a reprieve from Louis XV due to his noble background. He then went to Germany and Holland where he found many sympathetic listeners, among them a variety of pietists and mystics. Especially important were the Waldensians, who believed that Christ's sacrifice relieved all people of original sin. He also studied medicine and eventually was a practicing doctor for about 18 years.

Around 1740 de Benneville became very ill with what he called a "consumptive disorder." This led to a very high fever, which was so severe de Benneville had a vision that he had died and was drawn up into a cloud. He had two companions, one of whom told him that all creatures would be restored to happiness without exception. His extensive description of the experience was later published in *The Life and Trance of George de Benneville*. Finally, he was reunited with his body in a coffin, because his friends thought he was dead. They discovered that he was very much alive when he sat up to speak and the flabbergasted mourners helped him out of the coffin. This vision helped lead de Benneville to believe that he was called to preach in America and he went in 1741. He settled first in Germantown, where he assisted Christopher Sower, who was a Dunker and a Universalist, with printing. Eventually they produced a German edition Bible in 1743 and Paul Siegvolck's *The Everlasting Gospel* in 1753, which later proved instrumental in **Elhanan Winchester**'s conversion. Winchester helped make de Benneville better known by seeing that *Life and Trance* was published in 1800. In the meantime de Benneville continued to meet a variety of other religious groups. He was attracted to a group of followers of Casper Schwenkfelder and he also frequently visited the monastic community at Ephrata. He purchased some land in the country northwest of Philadelphia and went there with his new bride, Esther Bertolet, who emigrated from Germany. From here de Benneville frequently went on itinerant preaching tours, which took him as far afield as Virginia and Maryland. He also taught among the Native Americans. The couple moved back to Philadelphia in 1757 with their five children. Offering medical care to the wounded at the Battle of Germantown, de Benneville was able to take advantage of the intellectual life there and continued to work as a doctor. He died in March 1793. Though he was not a settled minister or the founder of churches, de Benneville is often called the first preacher of Universalism in America and was an important early influence in its development.

DEDHAM DECISION. The Dedham case, *Baker vs. Fales*, began in 1818 when a Trinitarian majority of church members (those who had made a confession of faith or assented to the church covenant) of the church in Dedham, Massachusetts, refused to agree with the parish's (all the voters of the town) choice of a liberal candidate, Alvin Lamson, for the ministry of the church. By custom the refusal of the "church" to concur with the parish's decision would have ended the young man's candidacy. The Dedham parish, however, assumed the legal right to contract Lamson, and they did so. This action was upheld by an ecclesiastical council dominated by Unitarians, and Lamson was ordained in October 1818. The church, although they only had a majority of two (17 to 15), refused to allow a liberal to become their minister and they withdrew from the parish taking the records, the communion service, trust deeds, and securities. Then the minority of church members promptly elected their own deacons and sued for the return of the property, which they said rightfully belonged to the parish. Baker and Fales were deacons who represented the Unitarian and Trinitarian factions respectively.

This case extended the controversial issues beyond theology (Unitarian vs. Trinitarian) to a political battle over the autonomy of the churches, the choice of ministers, and the control of property. Judge Isaac Parker presided over the jury trial beginning in February 1820. A decision was reached in October, but appeals held it up until April 1821. Parker affirmed that the portion of the church that remained with the parish, even if a minority, should have rights to the property since it was the parish that had created the church. After this ruling, the minority of church members in Dedham established a new congregation. The decision involved two fundamental questions: the choice of minister and the right to hold property. While the church had usually taken the initiative in choosing the minister, Article III of the Massachusetts Constitution said that the Parish had the legal right indicating "towns, parishes, and precincts," and not the old custom of church members. On the matter of property, the court decided that a Congregational church apart from the parish of which it was a part had no legal existence and could not hold property. While the deacons may have held property to be used by the church, the church could not "hold the same as a corporation, never having been incorporated as a body politic." The minority who seceded did so as individuals, and those who remained were the church of the parish. Thus the church had no power but that of divine worship and church order and discipline. Every Congregational church in Massachusetts was influenced by this decision.

The tenuous theological mix of Unitarians and Trinitarians within the churches was fully exposed, and quickly many towns witnessed the liberal and orthodox sides publicly declaring their differences, with minority groups withdrawing to form new societies. Within 20 years one-quarter of the Congregational churches in Massachusetts were Unitarian. *See also* STANDING ORDER.

DEISM. This theological perspective was not an organized religious movement in an institutional way, but it was profoundly influential, especially on the revolutionary leaders of America. Deists believed in God the creator who had set the universe in motion to function according to natural laws that human beings could readily perceive. God was symbolized by the "watch-maker" who set all the gears in motion but was not actively involved in anything that happened following the original creative event. Because God was not engaged with the world, Deists believed that God did not express approval or disapproval for the acts of humanity and thus did not reward or punish for the same. Deists tended to deny all Christian revelation. When **Thomas Jefferson** was preparing his own version of the Bible he employed a strict rational understanding of Scriptures and rejected all the miracle stories to affirm the purely human Jesus. The most important Deist work was **Thomas Paine**'s *The Age of Reason* (1794). He argued for a revolution in religion to accompany the political revolution. Like many other Deists, Paine was falsely accused of atheism, as Jefferson was during his presidential campaign.

THE DIAL. The periodical of the **Transcendentalists**, the *Dial* (after sundial) was published quarterly for four volumes, 1840–1844. In 1840 **Ralph Waldo Emerson**, **Margaret Fuller**, and **George Ripley** became the inspiration for starting this literary venture to record the thoughts of their group. Margaret Fuller served as its first editor and was succeeded after two years by Emerson, who was initially intended to share duties with her. Ripley served as business manager. The group hoped to pay Fuller $200 a year, but the magazine never made enough money to do so. Because they could not pay for articles, Fuller provided extra material of her own, including poems. She also managed to persuade most of the major Transcendentalists and others to contribute pieces, including **James Russell Lowell**. The banner for the periodical read: "The Dial: A Magazine for Literature, Philosophy, and Religion." The purpose was stated in the first issue July 1840. The Transcendentalists called for the "freest expression of thought" on the most important questions of the day. The *Dial* sought new contributions that expressed "the future," and not "the past," and "the living soul" and not the "dead letter."

Emerson took over as editor in July 1842 and held the position until April 1844, the date of the last issue. Unfortunately, the *Dial* was a commercial failure, as it never attracted enough sales to support itself. Efforts by Emerson to save it, including spending some of his own money, were not enough. The *Dial* was an important periodical despite its short life. It gave the Transcendentalists a forum for articulating and sharing their views and it gave many new and unknown writers an opportunity to publish.

DICKENS, CHARLES (1812–1870). The most popular novelist in the history of the printed word, Dickens became a convert to Unitarianism after he visited America in 1842. Born in Portsmouth on February 7, 1812, he was brought up in the Church of England, but apparently never subscribed to orthodox doctrines. One of eight children, during his childhood his father was imprisoned for debt and this left an indelible impression on the young boy. In 1836 he married Catherine Hogarth. An interest in Unitarianism was stimulated by the great liberal cleric **William Ellery Channing**. Dickens had an opportunity to meet many of the Unitarian elite, including **Henry Wadsworth** and **Samuel Longfellow**, **Andrews Norton**, and Washington Allston (Channing's brother-in-law). After his visit to America he attended worship services at the Essex Street Chapel, but settled on the Chapel in Little Portland Street in London's West End as his church of choice. He developed a friendship with the Rev. Edward Tagart. Dickens's antagonism to evangelical churches is evident in *The Pickwick Papers*. After Dickens's sixth child, Alfred, was christened, Robert Browning referred to him as an "enlightened Unitarian."

Dickens had a wide scope of interests and became especially concerned with the role of churches in society. He had little respect for the dogmatism of the Catholic church, and he considered it a tool of oppression, calling it "that curse upon the world." Dickens wanted to truly help victims of poverty and, coupling this with his virulent antidogmatism, he wrote: "Disgusted with our Established Church and its Puseyisms, and daily outrages on common sense and humanity, I have carried into effect an old idea of mine, and joined the Unitarians, who would do something for human improvement, if they could; and who practice Charity and Toleration." Dickens became a social crusader, and his hatred for all types of privilege is seen in many of his works, including *A Christmas Carol*, a story he poured himself into and over which he "wept and laughed, and wept again." Many of his novels were spiced with biblical phrases, and his disdain for self-righteous clergy, sectarianism, and irrational beliefs such as the virgin birth were touchstones for his liberal, benevolent faith. Dickens died on June 9, 1870.

DIETRICH, JOHN HASSLER (1878–1957). Called the Father of Religious Humanism, Dietrich was a key figure in the religious sea of change in Unitarianism in the 20th century. Dietrich was born on January 14, 1878, in Willow Hill, Pennsylvania, near Chambersburg. His father was a successful sharecropper, and the family religion was the Reformed Church. In 1893 the family moved to Marks, Pennsylvania, and John began attending Mercersburg Academy. After graduating in three years instead of the usual four, he went on to Franklin and Marshall College and became a teacher. Then he became a private secretary to Jonathan Thorne. Dietrich managed to save enough money to attend the seminary and he entered Eastern Theological Seminary in 1902. After graduation he became minister at St. Mark's Memorial Church in Pittsburgh. Although the church grew, some wealthy members objected to changes in the order of service and the use of a new hymnal and they withdrew. Eventually Dietrich resigned, but his problems with the Reformed Church had only begun. His unorthodox doctrines had come under the purview of the Allegheny Classis of the church.

Dietrich was eventually charged with heresy for denying the infallibility of the Bible and the deity of Christ. He was defrocked in 1911. Walter Mason, the Unitarian minister in Pittsburgh, was very supportive and recommended that Dietrich be given Unitarian fellowship, which he was, but he decided to decline Mason's invitation to become his assistant. That September Dietrich was called to the Unitarian Society in Spokane, Washington. It was here that he married his first wife, Louise Erb, with whom he had one child, but she died of cancer in 1931, and he remarried to Margaret Winston in 1933. The church grew from a congregation of about 60 to more than 1,500 by the time he left in 1916. Here Dietrich began to espouse humanism by 1915. He claimed that all traditional sources of religious authority were not valid, but that the only source of authority was the scientific method. When Dietrich affirmed this religion without God, he ruled out any kind of supernatural realm and said that the only reality is nature. While he was in Spokane he began to refer to prayer as aspiration, and his sermons became hour long lectures.

In November 1916 Dietrich became minister of the First Unitarian Society in Minneapolis, Minnesota. He met **Curtis Reese** at the **Western Unitarian Conference (WUC)** Annual Meeting in 1917 and found that they had both been preaching humanism. Dietrich had an article published in the ***Christian Register*** in 1919, which affirmed a religion that has faith in people and seeks no assistance or support from anything except human resources. This was the first sign of an impending storm that occurred after an address he delivered to the WUC in 1921, "The Outlook for Religion." This began the Humanist-Theist Controversy within the denomination's ranks.

That fall Dietrich addressed the **American Unitarian Association (AUA)** General Conference meeting and was verbally attacked by William Laurence Sullivan. Dietrich's congregation began to grow especially as he became involved in responding to the Scopes trial. In 1927 some of his sermons were published as *The Fathers of Evolution*. The burgeoning congregation moved to the Garrick Theater. Most of his published works were sermons found in the monthly *Humanist Pulpit Series*, which was published annually in book form. He also wrote two popular pamphlets for the denomination: *The Significance of the Unitarian Movement* and *Humanism*. Dietrich resigned from his pulpit when he was only 57, but he feared becoming ineffective and he wanted the church to remain vibrant. He was emeritus from 1938 to 1957. He moved to Berkeley, California, in 1941, where his theology continued to evolve. He became interested in the concept of God. His faith was never one that denied God, but he thought of himself as open-minded to the idea. He could never affirm theism, which for him meant a guiding intelligence working out some definite purpose. At the end of his life he tried to find a synthesis between humanism and theism. He may have seen this as a more mature humanism with a focus on the creative force or spiritual power that is the dynamic of the whole universe, but he always maintained that it was impossible to define God. He died on July 22, 1957.

DISTRICTS. When the **Unitarian Universalist Association (UUA)** was formed in 1961 the structure of intermediate organizations was not determined. At that time the Universalists had relied upon state conventions, which had a long history of failing to support a centralized ecclesiastical administration. The **American Unitarian Association (AUA)** had a number of small conference or council organizations in New England and larger conferences elsewhere. The new UUA bylaws called for the regional areas of responsibility to be known as "Regions." At the time of merger there were 18 Universalist state conventions, but some consolidations had already taken place. The powerful **Western Unitarian Conference (WUC)** merged with the Midwest Universalist Conference in 1961. Other merged groups included the Thomas Jefferson UU Council and the Pacific UU Council. Five other regional Unitarian councils or conferences still existed independently. The Unitarians had made some efforts to have regional professionals serving these local conferences, but this was never fully implemented.

The Interim Committee on regional organization recommended the establishment of 18 districts with suggested geographical boundaries. It was proposed that the districts be governed by a board elected by delegates from the member churches. The original plan was for each district to be staffed by an executive. The organization of the UUA into 22 regions known as districts was completed by 1964 (Michigan and Ohio Valley were combined, but later separated into independent districts, and now are merged as Heartland). In 1968 the **General Assembly (GA)** voted to have its board made up of district representatives, which helped give the regional interests a direct vote in UUA policies and it improved communication between the districts and the headquarters administration. Unfortunately, a UUA financial crisis in 1969 led to the establishment of an Interdistrict program, where the entire continent was divided into seven interdistrict area with professionals required to serve more than one district often covering huge geographical areas. The original plan to have each district served by a full time professional has been implemented in recent years, with many districts also employing a full time religious education professional as well. The UUA presently consists of 21 districts: Ballou Channing, Clara Barton, Central Midwest, Florida, Heartland, Joseph Priestley, Massachusetts Bay, Metropolitan New York, Mid-South, Mountain Desert, New Hampshire-Vermont, Northeast, Ohio Meadville, Pacific Central,

Pacific Northwest, Pacific Southwest, Prairie Star, Southwest, St. Lawrence, Thomas Jefferson, and Western Canada.

DIVINITY SCHOOL ADDRESS. When **Ralph Waldo Emerson** delivered the "Divinity School Address" in 1838 to the fledgling ministers at **Harvard Divinity School**, he had already left his own calling to the profession behind. Tired of what he saw as outmoded liturgical practices such as the celebration of the Lord's Supper and uncomfortable with the pastoral care of parishioners, Emerson had resigned his only parish at Second Church of Boston in 1832. Emerson was trying to carve a career out from lecturing, but he had been the regular supply preacher in East Lexington. In March 1838 Emerson was giving up this regular charge. On the 21st of that month he received a letter from the senior class at the Divinity School asking him to deliver an address before the graduates as they embarked on their careers. The address was scheduled for July 15 in the chapel at the Divinity School. There were probably fewer than 100 people present in the small space, including **Convers Francis**, **Theodore Parker**, and **Elizabeth Palmer Peabody**, who was reported to be "enraptured."

In the "refulgent summer" address that followed, Emerson outlined a much different philosophy than the one he learned when he was a student there. Rejecting much of what was considered inherited faith, Emerson spoke in favor of direct inspiration and creating faith anew. Three aspects of the address were critical. Haunted by his own misgivings about the profession, he had been listening to his own preacher in Concord, Massachusetts, Barzilai Frost with dire concerns. In a veiled reference to his preaching, Emerson writes that a worshiper is "defrauded" when the preacher is a "formalist." He said the secret of the profession was "to convert life into truth," and by implication, Frost had never learned this. Other parts of the address attacked the faith rather than the profession. Christian revelation was proven by the miracles of Christ, and Emerson said the word *miracle* as taught by the church was "monster." The other issue was a reference to the "soul knows no person." **Henry Ware Jr**. saw this as an attempt to reject the doctrine of God as person and preached "The Personality of the Deity," in response. These severe misgivings resulted in a controversy over "The Miracles." The following year at a meeting of the alumni of the School, **Andrews Norton** spoke on "The Latest Form of Infidelity" and equated Emerson's denial of the miracles with heresy. Emerson mostly remained aloof from the controversy and had others respond to the attacks. One of the great documents of Unitarian history, the "Divinity School Address" produced a firestorm of protest and radically challenged the Unitarian orthodoxy of the day with a fresh approach to discovering faith.

DIX, DOROTHEA LYNDE (1802–1887). Famed for her work with the mentally ill, Dix was one of the great social reformers of the 19th century. Born into a poor Methodist family on April 4, 1802, in Hampden, Maine, Dix once said that she never had a childhood. After early years of loneliness and abuse, she went at the age of 12 to live with her grandmother in Boston. Although she never adopted the society manners of her grandmother, Thea's quick mind made her a good student and eventually inspired her to become a teacher. She taught school for three years, with the exchanges between her and her pupils eventually evolving into a little book, *Conversations about Common Things*. (1824). In 1821 she opened her own "dame" school in Boston. Her Unitarian affiliations began in the early 1820s when she started to attend the First Parish of Dorchester, where her uncle, Thaddeus Mason Harris, was the minister. Eventually she affiliated with the Hollis Street Church, which was closer to home. She broadened her Unitarian church and social affiliations and attended as many sermons, lectures, and events as she could. Her new found religious interests resulted in another publication, *Hymns for Children* (1825), which made her believe she would become a writer. She produced three more religious works over the next few years, *Evening Hours* (1825), *Meditations for Private Hours* (1828), and *Selected Hymns for the Use of Children, Families, or Sunday Schools* (1833). It seemed that the rational Unitarian God was the perfect replacement for the more evangelical God of her childhood. She wrote:

> Awake, awake my mind!
> Thy reasoning powers bestow,
> With intellect refin'd
> The God who form'd thee, know.
> (as quoted in Gollaher, *Voice*, p. 51.)

Dix first heard **William Ellery Channing** preach in the fall of 1823, and began to attend the Federal Street Church and became friendly with him and his wife, Ruth. During these years Dix worked and studied beyond the physical capabilities of her body and became ill with tuberculosis. She became a private tutor to the Channing children and spent much time with the family. After her recovery she again ran a school for the next five years, but also fell ill again in 1836. During years of recovery and travel, Dix searched for a purpose in life. Channing especially inspired her to address the social problems of the day. Finally in 1841 she went to teach a class of convicts at the East Cambridge Jail (a place she visited many years before on a social outreach ministry with her uncle). Dix found that among those imprisoned were the mentally ill. The deplorable conditions and lack of aid made her vow that these people would be treated fairly. Her first small victory was a public exposé of the conditions at the jail and the subsequent installation of a stove. It was only the beginning. **Horace Mann** suggested that she inspect every jail in the commonwealth, and, eventually, she did.

With the help of **Samuel Gridley Howe**, Dix presented a petition to the legislature in 1843. A bill was passed to relieve the conditions and provide decent accommodations in Worcester. This strengthened Dix's resolve and she established a pattern of investigating conditions, publishing "Memorials," and then lobbying legislatures for new or improved insane asylums. In 1845 she published *Remarks on Prisons and Prison Discipline in the United States*. Her most effective work was in New Jersey, where she investigated 500 cases. Eventually the legislature passed a bill to build a model hospital for the mentally ill near Trenton, which was completed in 1848.

In subsequent years Dix traveled the breadth of the land from New Orleans to Nova Scotia. By the summer of 1848 she had covered 60,000 miles, documenting the sufferings of 10,000 people while soliciting aid for the insane in 30 states. In the 1850s she began to seek the support of the federal government in her work, but she ultimately failed when President Franklin Pierce vetoed a land bill for the establishment of hospitals. After her American experience, she spent years inspecting facilities in Europe. In 1861 President Abraham Lincoln appointed her superintendent of the United States Army Nurses. Under her supervision thousands of women were trained. After her dedication to the war effort was complete, Dix returned to her life's work, traveling from one hospital to another. The "Angel of Mercy" continued her furious working pace until she was 80 and then took a room at her "first child" (the state hospital in New Jersey) where she died on July 18, 1887.

– E –

EASTER. The Christian holy day that celebrates the resurrection of Jesus Christ from the dead, has often been reinterpreted by Unitarian Universalists to make it compatible to a liberal perspective. Puritan forebears rejected the observance of Easter, as they did Christmas and other religious holidays. By the early 19th century, Protestant congregations began to mark Easter with special services including appropriate sermons and, eventually, flower-laden sanctuaries. The theme of new life made it a popular time for baptism and eventually child dedication. While a literal resurrection from the dead has never been popular among liberals, they have found theological meaning through the hope of immortality and/or the victory of the spirit over apparent defeat. In 1834 **William Ellery Channing** confirmed this Easter emphasis when he said it was a time "to turn our thoughts, desires, hopes toward another world." While Channing accepted the resurrection of Jesus on scriptural grounds, this belief was undermined by the mid-19th century when **Transcendentalists** such as **Theodore Parker** downplayed the resurrection while regarding it as pure mythology. He wanted to emphasize Jesus' character more and said Easter should bring people to "a consciousness of that great soul." By the 1880s most liberals found scant reasons to affirm the resurrection. **William Furness** said that Christians accept resurrection upon trust, but that this faith is not a genuine conviction founded upon evidence. As the century turned, some liberals wanted to emphasize a universal belief that life was endless.

In the 20th century many liberals began to regard Easter as a time to celebrate the coming of spring. An article in the *Universalist Christian Leader* in 1933 stated that Jesus' life and message were being neglected in favor of celebrating a nature festival. By this date few Unitarians or Universalists found the concept of resurrection very inspirational. The traditional emphasis on immortality as an important religious value had also waned. Even those liberal Christians who affirmed the concept of resurrection, such as biblical scholar Clayton R. Bowen, viewed it in a nonmaterial fashion. The observance of Easter in congregations today often depends on its place in the theological spectrum. Some congregations blend many traditions, while others celebrate their roots with a Seder, rejoice in pagan rites of spring, or maintain a strong affinity for the Christian heritage with palms on Palm Sunday, Maundy Thursday communions where the deceased members of the congregation are commemorated, Good Friday tennebrae services, and finally glorious Easter celebrations. Despite the theological issues many liberals have with the traditional Easter message, a new life observance of some type continues to make it an important day in the cycle of the church year.

ELIOT, FREDERICK MAY (1889–1958). Born with a long Unitarian pedigree, Eliot spearheaded Unitarian revitalization in the mid-20th century. He was born in Dorchester, Massachusetts, on September 15, 1889, to Christopher Rhodes Eliot and Mary Jackson (May) Eliot. His father was minister of the First Parish of Dorchester, and there were Unitarian ministers on both sides of the family. His father spent a year in England when Frederick was four and, after their return, was minister of the Bulfinch Place Church in Boston. Frederick had two sisters and they all attended a local grammar school. After that Frederick went to Boston Latin, where he graduated in 1907, and then on to Harvard College. Eliot was especially interested in political science. He did well at Harvard and after graduation in 1911 went to Europe on a fellowship to study city governments. He returned to Harvard to teach municipal government and subsequently received an M.A. In Cambridge, Eliot attended church at First Parish and fell under the influence of Samuel McChord Crothers. He went on to **Harvard Divinity School**, where he graduated in 1915, and then he immediately became an assistant to Crothers. That same year on June 25 he married Elizabeth Berkeley Lee and they had two children.

After only two years at Cambridge, Eliot received a call from Unity Church in St. Paul, Minnesota, in 1917. Not long after he started he became a chaplain overseas. He remained at Unity for 20 years and became especially involved in the life of the community. He became active in the development of a strong church school program, and eventually a new education building and a children's chapel were built. Eliot became a well-respected minister in the denomination and was a logical choice to head up the new **Commission on Appraisal** in 1934. Its purpose was to study the entire structure of the **American Unitarian Association (AUA)** to report on what the policies for the AUA should be and what changes in organizational structure might be implemented. The final report, published in 1936, was ***Unitarians Face a New Age***. The success of this project gave many fellow Unitarians the belief that this new leader of the plan for renewal should also be the one leading them into the future.

Eliot was elected president of the AUA in 1937 and then went on to be reelected five more times. He immediately transformed a weakened denomination into a strong one. Religious education continued to be a central focus for Eliot. **Ernest Kuebler**, who stayed on as director of the department, initiated a new curriculum planning with the addition of **Sophia Lyon Fahs** to the staff. The growth of the entire denomination was facilitated by the appointment of **Lon Ray Call** as minister-at-large in 1941. Eventually the AUA initiated the fellowship program under **Monroe Husbands**, resulting in the addition of hundreds of new congregations. The development of the **Church of the Larger Fellowship**, which was formed in 1944, helped to interest isolated liberals in joining a larger network.

Eliot also instituted a regular campaign for the solicitation of funds, the United Unitarian Appeal. Finally, the Unitarian Service Committee was formed two years after he took office. In 1947 he shared with the Universalists his dream of forming a greater liberal church that would include Unitarians, Universalists, and others. His support for this was reflected in his frequent joint meetings and declarations with Universalist leaders. As president, Eliot was very active on the local level, frequently making appearances and speaking at many events. He also played a direct role in many settlements of clergy in churches. His interest in the broader community that he exhibited in St. Paul was seen in many community roles. He was president of the Board of Trustees of Mount Holyoke College, a board he served on for 17 years. At one time he was a director of the American Civil Liberties Union (ACLU) and also served on the board of Procter Academy and the Hackley School. His interest in biblical scholarship resulted in service on the board of the Massachusetts Bible Society. His enthusiasm for action meant that he was likely to die while serving some larger cause and that was what happened when a heart attack struck while he was in New York for a meeting on February 17, 1958. Theologically, Eliot was a middle-of-the-road theist who was supportive of humanism but was not its advocate. He affirmed the liberal Christian center of Unitarianism, and its belief in

God: "When I use the word 'God,' I am using a symbol for the reality that I believe exists behind the deepest convictions of my own mind and heart" (from Stiernotte, ed., *Frederick May Eliot, An Anthology*, p. 262). Someone once said that Eliot gave Unitarianism a courageous heart to meet the challenges of the 20th century.

ELIOT, SAMUEL ATKINS (1862–1950). The architect of the transformation of the **American Unitarian Association (AUA)** into a strong institution, Eliot was president of the AUA from 1900 to 1927. Most of Eliot's ancestors were active Unitarians, including his namesake and paternal grandfather Samuel Atkins Eliot, who was one of the founders of the AUA. Sam was born on August 24, 1862, in Cambridge, Massachusetts, to Charles Eliot, a professor and later president of **Harvard College**, and Mary Lyman, who died when Sam was only six. At the age of 16 Eliot began to attend the William P. Hopkinson School in Boston, and his father soon remarried to Grace Hopkinson, the sister of William. Eliot always said his main education was outside the curriculum. He went on to Harvard College, where he graduated in 1884, and then spent time in Europe. He thought he would be a lawyer, but the idea did not last long. He became the Harvard president's secretary for one year. When he finally decided to enter the ministry, Eliot interpreted the call in his own way. "But what is the call of God? It isn't a sign you can see or a voice you can hear. I think it must be just the desire of a man to make the most of this narrow span of life and serve his fellow men in all the ways of honest thinking and helpful doing" (McGiffert, *Pilot*, p. 17). He entered **Harvard Divinity School** and graduated with an M.A. in 1889. Prior to his graduation, Eliot wanted to prove his mettle as a preacher and went on a missionary journey to the Pacific Northwest in 1887–88. He also became engaged to Frances Hopkinson at this time, the niece of his stepmother, and they were married in October 1889. Eventually they had seven children.

In the fall of 1889 Eliot filled the pulpit in Denver, Colorado, on a trial basis and then received a unanimous call there to Unity Church. He was ordained in November 1889, saying at that time that the minister's "only authority is the reasonableness of his arguments, the strength of his convictions, and whatever truth it may be given him to utter" (McGiffert, *Pilot*, p. 38). Eliot became active in the community, including the Indian Rights Association. When he went to Denver he was the only Unitarian minister between Kansas and California, and this spurred on his missionary zeal. He left Denver in 1893 to serve at the Church of the Saviour in Brooklyn, New York. Here he began to focus on involvement in denominational affairs. He became a member of the AUA Board of Directors in 1894. He began to make innovative proposals, including a new budget plan so that the AUA would stop spending down the endowment. In 1897 he was made secretary of the AUA and had to resign from Brooklyn. Some board members, such as William Wallace Fenn, opposed Eliot because they feared he would centralize all power in the AUA.

In 1900 the board agreed to reorganize the administration so that the president of the board (not the secretary) would become the chief executive of the association. From the beginning of his term as the first salaried AUA president, Eliot fought for a more militant church. He said he would be a "missionary executive" who would stop subsidizing dying churches and expand the vision of the denomination. Eliot favored a number of new initiatives, including a Foreign Missions at Home program, which offered outreach to Icelanders, Finns, Swedes, Norwegians, and Italians. Eliot also favored the establishment of Unitarian secondary schools. He was involved with the Hackley School (New York) from the time of its founding and served as its board president from 1909 to 1929. He also became a member of the board of Procter Academy (New Hampshire). In 1909 he was appointed to the United States Board of Indian Commissioners. In 1914 the denomination produced a new hymnbook, *Hymn and Tune Book*, of which Eliot chose most of the hymns and was senior editor.

Eliot's greatest contribution was to revise the way the AUA was structured so that it could conduct its business more efficiently and effectively. This use of his personal authority to wield power subjected him to the accusation of running a "personal Episcopalianism." The budget grew significantly financed by successful giving campaigns. During his long tenure in office Eliot was challenged only once for the presidency. **John Haynes Holmes** and others opposed the new business management techniques of administering the AUA and protested that the religious nature of the organization had been lost, but in the final vote in 1912 Eliot won an overwhelming majority. In 1907 Eliot proposed the forming of a **Unitarian Laymen's League** and helped found it two years later. It was revitalized after the war. Eliot urged the organization and development of Sunday Schools and he brought together the Sunday School Association and the Department of Education. They published complete graded lessons and included nonbiblical materials. One of the final accomplishments of his presidency was the construction of a new headquarters office building at 25 **Beacon Street** in Boston.

After he left the presidency, Eliot was called to be minister at the Arlington Street Church in Boston. Here he was able to accomplish on a small scale what he had been able to do at AUA headquarters. A budget system was established and the endowment began to grow once again. He remained at the church until 1935, but when he turned 70, he began to agitate to be replaced by a younger person. During his long career Eliot distinguished himself as a historian. He was the editor of the four volume, *Heralds of a Liberal Faith* (1909–1910). In 1950 he received the AUA's Distinguished Service Award. That fall on October 19, he died in his 89th year.

ELIOT, THOMAS LAMB (1841–1936). A Unitarian apostle to the Pacific Northwest, and the founder of Reed College. He was born on October 13, 1841, in St. Louis, Missouri, where his father, **William Greenleaf Eliot**, was a minister. His education was local, concluding with an 1862 B.A. in the first class to graduate from the school his father founded, Washington University. His studies were interrupted for a time when he went to the West Coast to try to nurse his eyes back to health after an injury. While he was there he met **Thomas Starr King** who urged him to come back and spread the faith. Back in St. Louis he began to prepare himself for the ministry by working as a minister-at-large at a Mission House under his father's direction. Then he went to **Harvard Divinity School**, where he graduated in 1865. After that he served briefly as an associate in St. Louis. On November 28, 1865, he married Henrietta Mack, embarking on a 67-year marriage.

Then in 1867 Eliot was offered the choice of three pulpits and made the startling choice of picking Portland, Oregon, where a church was only beginning to form. King had preached the first Unitarian sermon there in 1862, and a Ladies Sewing Society had been formed. A church was gathered and the following year a chapel built in the summer of 1867. Only 26 at the time, Eliot defied the convention of settling in more established locations and took the risk of something new and exciting. He built a strong church through active parish calling. He was especially sensitive to human isolation and he countered the idea that humans must stand alone with a vision of a church that emphasized human sympathy and understanding. He saw the church as a "fellowship of striving souls." Theologically, Eliot tended toward the more conservative Christian side, but he avoided controversy and positions that would draw him into denominational battles. During the early years of his ministry, Eliot was often the sole Unitarian minister in the Northwest. A new church building was dedicated in 1879. He built an incredible record of community service. His greatest contributions were in the field of education. He became superintendent of schools in Multnomah County in 1872. Like the personal visits he had used to build up his parish, Eliot implemented a system of visitation for the schools, including 241 visits in one school year. Eliot had a child-oriented philosophy of education, which continued to be reemphasized as a goal of self-direction for each student.

Eliot retired from parish work in 1893, although his son-in-law **Earle Morse Wilbur** had arrived as an associate three years earlier. Eliot now turned toward a greater emphasis on community building. He helped form the Portland Art Museum and the Portland Library Association. He was also president of the Oregon Humane Society, helping to set up orphanages. He was active in a number of reform movements including prison reform, ballot reform, and woman suffrage. In 1908 he became a founder of Reed College, named for Oregon pioneers Simeon and Amanda Reed, who had set up a fund to make plans to start an educational institution. Reed was not a denominational school, but its vision was an expression of Eliot's self-directed Unitarian philosophy. The Reeds had been parishioners of Eliot's, and were, like him, determined that this would be an institution centered on equality and secularism. Classes were first held in 1911, and Eliot was president of the board. He and his wife had eight children, of whom there was William G. Eliot Jr., who succeeded to the Portland pulpit in 1906. His father died on April 26, 1936, after two years when both father and son were simultaneously ministers emeriti. Thomas Lamb Eliot, who followed his own father by becoming a missionary to a western outpost, made Portland the center of Unitarianism in the Northwest.

ELIOT, WILLIAM GREENLEAF JR. (1811–1887). One of the most important exponents of Unitarianism in the Midwest, Eliot also was an accomplished educator. He was born on August 5, 1811, in New Bedford, Massachusetts. His father suffered some financial reverses during the War of 1812, and the family ended up in Washington, D.C. The boy returned to New Bedford to attend the Friends Academy and then went on to Columbian College (now George Washington University), where he graduated in 1830. He worked for a year in the United States Postal Department with his father, and then entered **Harvard Divinity School** in 1831. Before he graduated Eliot had determined that he would pursue a ministry in the west. He was ordained at the Federal Street Church in Boston in August 1834. He received a call in 1834 to a new society forming in St. Louis, Missouri.

In 1835 the First Congregational Society of St. Louis came into being and Eliot remained as its minister until 1873. In 1837 he was married to Abby Cranch. Eliot became a civic-minded minister from the beginning. The church had a ministry-at-large to the poor, and when famed author **Charles Dickens** visited he commented, "The Unitarian Church is represented in this remote place, as in most other parts of America, by a gentleman of great worth and excellence. The poor have good reason to remember and bless it; for it befriends them, and aids the cause of rational education" (Holt, *William Greenleaf Eliot*, p. 33). Eliot became involved in many educational efforts and eventually served as president of the school board in St. Louis. His most significant contribution occurred when his friend Wayman Crow fulfilled a vision of Eliot's when he received a charter for a new college he named the Eliot Seminary. Eliot requested that the name be changed and Washington Institute (later University) of St. Louis came into being, with Eliot named the first president of the board in 1854, a position he retained until his death.

Eliot was involved in the extension of Unitarianism in various places and was even referred to as the "Unitarian bishop" or "apostle" of a wider region, as he traveled as far south as New Orleans and as far north as Milwaukee. He was elected secretary of the American Unitarian Association (AUA) in 1847, but declined the position after he returned from a trip to Europe, where he had gone to recover his health. Despite his widespread evangelism, Eliot's theology was increasingly in conflict with many of the members of the new **Western**

Unitarian Conference (WUC). His Christology was conservative by Unitarian standards, and in a proposed preamble to the WUC constitution that drew upon Eliot's *Unitarian Views*, the conservatives referred to Jesus as the Son of God and Redeemer of the World and not a "mere inspired man." Then in Alton, Illinois, in 1857, Eliot and the members of his congregation (now called The Church of the Messiah) withdrew from a meeting of the WUC in the wake of a discussion on slavery and an attempt to pass a binding resolution on the delegates. Yet Eliot became a key figure in keeping the state of Missouri in the Union prior to the Civil War. Once the war commenced, Eliot collaborated with James Yeatman to create the Western Sanitary Commission. Like its national model, the United States Sanitary Commission, this regional version provided hospitals, rest homes, and a camp for freedmen, plus clothing, comfort, food, and reading materials to thousands of soldiers.

After the war Eliot found that he could not physically complete the tasks of a parish minister and decided to devote his life to education full time. In 1870 he became the interim chancellor of Washington University and then was installed two years later as the permanent holder of the position. After that he resigned from his pastorate and was able to serve nearly 15 more years as chancellor before he died. In 1870 he had published a "Confession of Unitarian Christian Faith," a statement that showed he was giving more authority and honor to Jesus Christ as the denomination generally drifted away from its Christian foundations. One of Eliot's sons was Henry Ware Eliot, who was the father of famed poet, T. S. Eliot, and another was **Thomas Lamb Eliot**, who spread Unitarianism to the Pacific Northwest. William Greenleaf Eliot died in Pass Christian, Mississippi, on January 23, 1887.

EMERSON, RALPH WALDO (1803–1882). Perhaps the most famous Unitarian, much has been written about his life and literary career, but the foundations of his fame flow from his religious background and his leadership of the **Transcendentalist** movement. David Robinson reminds us this progenitor of much of our American literary tradition spent the most important phase of his career devoting himself to "oratorical rather than literary endeavors." The roots of all his lectures and essays are in the sermon, where he first learned how to put words together and express himself. **Frederic Henry Hedge** said that Emerson was "always a preacher in the higher, universal sense" (Robinson, *Apostle*, pp. 1–2). Emerson was a native of Boston and a child of Unitarianism born on May 25, 1803. His father, William Emerson, was minister at the First Church of Boston, but he died when Waldo was almost eight. His mother, Ruth Haskins, was the daughter of a distiller. Emerson suffered from chronic illnesses as a young man, and the family had some difficult economic times. Nevertheless he attended Boston Latin School and then became the fifth generation of Emersons to go to **Harvard College**. After graduation he taught school for a time and then returned to **Harvard Divinity School** in 1825. Ready to enter a profession where he could test his public speaking skills, he was ordained at the Second Church of Boston on March 11, 1829. He a served as its minister for only three years before resigning from the ministry. Emerson had a difficult time reconciling the required pastoral duties of visiting the sick and observing the sacraments with the more creative aspects of writing and speaking. Rather than trying to change an institution, Emerson was more concerned with freeing himself from them. Throughout his life he developed a distaste for organizations and associations.

Emerson was married to Ellen Tucker in 1829, but she died two years later. In many ways Emerson followed **William Ellery Channing** in his devotion to self-culture, the evolution of the individual soul toward perfection. But from the beginning of his preaching career Emerson, unlike Channing, moved away from biblical revelation as a basis for his religious faith. By the time he left Second Church in the fall of 1832 he had completely rejected the miracles as proof of Jesus' authority. This also meant that the supernaturalism he learned in Divinity School had evolved into a confirmed naturalism. This was given full expression six years later when Emerson was asked to speak before the graduating class at the Divinity School and delivered the "Divinity School Address." Here he said: "the word Miracle, as pronounced by Christian churches, gives a false impression; it is Monster. It is not one with the blowing clover and the falling rain" (Wright, *Three Prophets*, p. 97). This address stirred a great deal of controversy among the Unitarians. James Freeman Clarke wrote: "Here comes Mr. Emerson, and utters some doctrines which sound strange. . . . Mr. Emerson they know and acknowledge to be a singularly pure-minded, devout and conscientious person. But what do some of them do? . . . They denounce him, and all who are suppose to think with him; and they get up a popular excitement, and a terror of dreadful heresies, and talk about 'the latest form of Infidelity'" (Miller, *Transcendentalists*, p. 247).

Emerson had already provided the first manifesto of the Transcendentalists in 1836 with the publication of *Nature*. Here he had written: "Why should not we also enjoy an original relation to the universe? Why should not we have a poetry of insight and not of tradition, and a religion by revelation to us, and not the history of theirs?" (Albanese, *Spirituality*, p. 46) That same year he was involved in the organization of the Transcendental Club. Emerson also remained an active preacher for many years as well, especially in East Lexington. In 1835 Emerson married Lydia Jackson, and together they had four children. The important essays "Self-Reliance" and the Over-Soul appeared in the first collection of essay in 1841. Emerson took over the editorship of the ***Dial*** from **Margaret Fuller** in 1842, but the famed journal did not last long. By this time Emerson had settled into life in Concord, Massachusetts. His home became a gathering place for friends, writers and reformers, including Fuller and **Henry David Thoreau**. At first Emerson's new career of writing and lecturing kept him in New England, but eventually he traveled as far as San Francisco, gaining great fame as he went. He also made several trips to Europe. He continued to publish throughout his life, especially his poetry in his later years. He died in Concord on April 27, 1882.

EMLYN, THOMAS (1663–1741). An important precursor to the Unitarian movement, Thomas Emlyn made his contributions in Ireland rather than in the centers of Arian and Socinian thought in England. Born in 1663, he was educated in Dissenting Academies even though his parents were Anglicans. He trained to be a Presbyterian minister and he began his career as a private chaplain in Northern Ireland. While he was serving a congregation at Lowestoft in Suffolk, he met William Manning in 1689 (1630–1711), and they both read and discussed William Sherlock's *Vindication of the Trinity*. The result was that Emlyn became an Arian, and Manning a Socinian. Manning was one of the 2,000 ejected clergy from the Church of England in 1662.

He lived in rural Peasenhall and eventually gathered what has sometimes been considered the earliest Unitarian congregation in England. In 1691 Emlyn became an associate minister at a Presbyterian church in Dublin. He had an extremely successful ministry preaching on practical subjects, but after 11 years a parishioner noted that he never mentioned the Trinity. He took a leave of absence and then returned only to be arrested for blasphemy. To defend himself he had published just prior to his arrest *An Humble Inquiry into the Scripture Account of Jesus Christ* (1702). Following a very prejudicial trial, he went to prison for more than two years, the last dissenter to be imprisoned for denying the Trinity.

Prevented from preaching in Ireland, Emlyn went to London where he preached for a time to a small congregation. His writings became extremely influential. His *Humble Inquiry* was still controversial in London, and it became the only English Unitarian book printed in America prior to 1805. He was the first minister willing to take the Unitarian name. Emlyn was offered a pulpit in Exeter in 1726, but he decided he was too old. He believed in worshiping Christ, and accepted a divinity in him that was inferior to the Father, so he should be considered an Arian. His writings helped lead the more radical dissenters toward an avowed Unitarian position. He died in 1743.

ENGEL, JOHN RONALD (1936–). A denominational leader in the area of environmental ethics, Ron Engel has spent most of his career teaching at **Meadville Lombard Theological School**. He was born in Baltimore, Maryland, on March 17, 1936. As a youngster he became an active hiker, birder, and canoe enthusiast. Later he studied piano and theory of composition at the Peabody Conservatory of Music from 1954 to 1958. Engel majored in biological sciences at Johns Hopkins University and received an A.B. in 1958. The year before he graduated he was married to Joan Gibb, and they have two children. After graduation, he received his teaching certification for Maryland secondary schools, but he taught only briefly. He especially cultivated his interest in the environment when he served as a seasonal ranger at the Isle Royale National Park in Michigan. Deciding on the ministry as his chosen calling, Engel went to Meadville Lombard Theological School and received a B.D. in 1964. During his seminary training he was student minister at All Souls Church in Washington, D.C. He organized a University Neighborhoods Council during that time. From 1963 to 1965 he served as minister of the Unitarian Universalist Fellowship of Berrien County, Michigan. From 1965 to 1970 he was the minister of the Second Unitarian Church in Chicago and he began to teach as an instructor at Meadville Lombard during this same period. He demonstrated his commitment to social justice when he cofounded the Neighborhood Commons, a cooperative housing project for low income persons. Engel received his final fellowship as a Unitarian Universalist minister in 1967. He combined his interest in the environment with social justice when he pursued the Ph.D. degree in the field of Ethics and Society at the Divinity School of the University of Chicago, and he finished in 1977 (M.A. in 1971).

Engel has served Meadville Lombard and the Divinity School of the University of Chicago in a variety of capacities. From 1983 to 1999 he was Meadville's professor of social ethics and has recently been named research professor of environment and social ethics. He was a lecturer in ethics and society for the Divinity School from 1977 to 2000 and presently serves as part of the Environmental Studies Faculty, The College, University of Chicago. Engel has been active with a number of professional groups. Most recently he has been codirector of the Chicago Program on Ecology, Justice and Faith, Association of Chicago Theological Schools (1998–2001); executive committee member, International Development Ethics Association, 1992–2002; and codirector, Nature, Polis, and Ethics: Chicago Regional Planning (1995–). Within the interfaith religious community he has played a key role in the emergence of the movement for ecojustice. In the Unitarian Universalist denomination he was a codirector of the Unitarian Universalist Center for Urban Ministry in Chicago from 1964 to 1970, has been active in Collegium: Association of Liberal Religious Scholars, and is presently a member of the Third Unitarian Church in Chicago.

His most important publication has been *Sacred Sands: The Struggle for Community in the Indiana Dunes* (1983). In this book Engel combined his concern for environmental science with democratic political reform and religious myths to make an important contribution to the field of environmental ethics. He and his wife moved to the

Dunes in 1970. Here in the birthplace of "ecology," Engel became involved in the 80-year struggle to save the Dunes and he became convinced of the need to develop an "ethic that links the imperative of social justice with the imperative of environmental preservation." The book received the **Unitarian Universalist Association**'s (UUA) Melcher Book Award for making the greatest published contribution to Unitarian Universalism in a given year (1984). Engel has also had a hand in numerous other books and many articles. He has edited **James Luther Adams**'s *Voluntary Associations: Socio-cultural Analyses and Theological Interpretation* (1986) and also written *James Luther Adams: Religious and Political Liberalism* (1996). He has coedited two volumes, one with his wife Joan, *The Ethics of Environment and Development: Global Challenge, International Response* (1990), and with Julie Denny-Hughes, *Advancing Ethics for Living Sustainably* (1993). Finally, he has written *Ecology, Justice and Christian Faith: A Critical Guide to the Literature* (1996) with Peter Bakken and Joan Gibb Engel. He also served on the international drafting committee for the *Earth Charter*.

ENLIGHTENMENT. The most important intellectual movement influencing the development of liberal religion, the Enlightenment firmly established the idea that the universe could be understood rationally, and new scientific methods could be attached to every aspect of life. Those who were influenced by Enlightenment thought began to believe that traditional institutions and attitudes had prevented them from discovering the natural order. They spoke of the laws of nature and nature's God as a way of showing that they could discover the divine and learn how to live by their understanding of the world. Generally speaking, those who were influenced by the Enlightenment came to say that religious beliefs should be rooted in reason rather than based on faith. More emphasis was placed on human potential and the focus of religion was on moral behavior rather than theology or ritual. Both Unitarianism and Universalism grew from this liberalizing trend in thought.

ESSEX HALL. The location of Unitarian headquarters in the United Kingdom also marks the site of the first Unitarian church. On April 17, 1774, 200 people gathered to hear the Rev. **Theophilus Lindsey**

conduct the first avowedly Unitarian service. Among those attending were Benjamin Franklin and **Joseph Priestley**. Six months earlier Lindsey had resigned from the Anglican priesthood, moved to London, and decided that the time had come for Unitarians to publicly proclaim their then illegal faith. During the winter of 1773–74 he and his friends searched for a suitable chapel in which to hold services. They found a building on Essex Street, just off the Strand. Called Essex House and used as an auction room, the building stood on the site of the residence of the Earl of Essex. The congregation constructed a chapel at this site with box pews in 1778 and it became known as the Essex Church. They remained at this site until 1887, when they moved to a new location at Palace Gardens Terrace, Kensington, following a decision of the British and Foreign Unitarian Association to form a Free Christian Church in the West End of London. They erected their present building in 1977. While architect T. C. Chatfield-Clarke was building the new Kensington church in 1887, he also redesigned and expanded the old Essex Church into what became known as Essex Hall; the headquarters building for British Unitarianism. Essex Hall was destroyed by bombs in 1940, but a modern headquarters building at 1–6 Essex Street, Strand, was constructed in 1959. The staff at the headquarters under the leadership of the general secretary provide advice and assistance to the member congregations of the General Assembly of Unitarian and Free Christian Churches.

EUROPEAN UNITARIAN UNIVERSALISTS (EUU). This organization is the European Conference of the Unitarian Universalist Association. EUU was organized in 1981 to provide mutual support and programs for English-speaking Unitarian Universalist fellowships and individuals living in Europe. An earlier network of fledging groups organized in the 1960s and 1970s could not maintain continuity of programming, and six out of seven congregations disbanded (Wiesbaden, Germany, founded in 1964, remains active). With limited numbers and resources, keeping a Unitarian Universalist presence active in Europe has been difficult.

EVANGELICAL UNITARIANS. In 1855 Frederic Dan Huntington of the South Congregational Church of Boston declared that a group of Unitarians believed in a "special, supernatural redemption from sin, in Christ Jesus" the "eternally begotten Son of God." This lofty view of Christ characterized a group of Unitarian evangelicals who were often uncertain as to whether they belonged in the denomination or not. Some, like Huntington, went beyond Unitarianism in their Christology, and others, including Huntington again, decided they could not stay within the Unitarian fold. At first he hoped the more evangelical Unitarians would exhibit a catholic spirit that would "take the place of all sectarian strifes." But Huntington felt an increasing conflict between his old ties and a growing evangelical faith. In 1859 "the light entered his soul" and he preached a sermon in December on "Life, Salvation and Comfort for Man in the Divine Trinity." He subsequently resigned a teaching position at **Harvard College** and was admitted to the Order of Deacons in the Episcopal church in September 1860. Of those who remained Unitarian, Rufus Ellis of the First church of Boston and **Edmund Hamilton Sears** of Weston, Massachusetts, were the most prominent.

The evangelicals were characterized by a desire for a more personal relationship with Jesus Christ and worship services that were more highly liturgical. Jesus was the central figure of their more emotional religious expressions, and they generally feared that Unitarianism was losing him as its central focus. Ellis refused to attend the 1865 National Conference in New York because he did not want to underscore Unitarian differences with mainstream Christianity. George E. Ellis was another "right wing" Unitarian who published a series of articles in the *Christian Examiner* on why the Unitarians might become reconciled with the Congregationalists. When he was made a professor of systematic theology at **Harvard Divinity School**, he said the "old orthodoxy" had returned and that Unitarian preaching was moving away from the excesses of rationalism to a "more fervent and heart-satisfying Christology." Many of the Unitarians felt the pull of a more compassionate orthodox God, as Arminian doctrines liberated human will in both liberal and evangelical camps, plus the radicalism of Theodore Parker's Transcendentalism made them leery of an advancing humanism, but the principles of evangelical Unitarianism were never widely accepted.

EVERETT, EDWARD (1794–1865). The great 19th-century orator, politician, and president of Harvard. Everett was born on April 11, 1794, in Boston. His father was a liberal Christian minister at the New South Church, Boston. After he died, Mrs. Everett brought her boys to the Brattle Street Church where Everett was influenced by **Joseph Buckminster** to pursue the ministry. He graduated with highest honors from Harvard in 1811 and tutored in Latin for a time. There was great sorrow at the Brattle Street Church after Buckminster died in 1812 and the congregation approached Everett about succeeding his friend and mentor. He preached during the summer of 1814 and then was called to the pastorate in November and ordained on February 9, 1815. Everett was under 20 years old, but his incredible preaching skills made him widely accepted. **Ralph Waldo Emerson** used to sneak over from his father's church just to hear him. Everett and other colleagues were transforming the sermon into a very personal tool of moral reflection for their parishioners. The largest parish in Boston was a demanding post for a 19-year old, and he only remained thirteen months.

Everett accepted an appointment to teach in a new endowed chair of Greek literature at Harvard College. Before he took the position, he traveled in Europe for further study and became the first American to receive a doctorate from Gottingen University in Germany in 1817. Everett would sometimes preach after this and was always admired for his literary knowledge and speaking eloquence. He put this to good use in his professional career, as he became the second most sought after orator in America to Daniel Webster. He launched his public speaking renown with the Phi Beta Kappa address at Harvard in 1824. He remained Eliot Professor until 1826, when he began a career of public service. A congressman for 10 years and then governor of Massachusetts, Everett helped set up the state board of education and the normal school system. After that he was minister to Great Britain, 1841–45. In 1846 he was named president of Harvard, but he found it difficult to implement the program he wanted to and subsequently resigned. Later he was U.S. Secretary of State and a U.S. Senator. He spent his final years working for the Union cause. Everett was the prime speaker on the program on the day in November 1863 when Lincoln gave the more famous and shorter address at Gettysburg. He died in Boston on January 15, 1865.

EVERY DAY CHURCH. This was the name given to the Shawmut Avenue Universalist Church in Boston after it began to offer a number of social services to its immediate neighborhood operating seven days a week. In 1837 Otis Skinner opened the first Every Day Church in Boston to assist homeless people, which lasted until the late 1850s. The term was later applied to the Shawmut Avenue Society under the leadership of George Perin and his associate, Florence Kollock Crooker. After 1894 Perin helped the church acquire a vacant house which became headquarters for day and evening classes in skilled areas such as dressmaking and cooking. A day nursery for working mothers was established and free legal services were provided. Universalists operated many community centers such as this throughout the country during this period. When the Shawmut Avenue church merged with another congregation 10 years later, its activities were greatly reduced, but two enduring legacies continue today.

In 1889 John D. W. Joy, a member of the church, conceived of the idea of a home for "respectable, indigent young women, who from general debility, or inability to work, are unable to support themselves." The effects of urbanization and industrialization led to numbers of poor and/or sick young women in the city without homes or medical care. The result of Joy's vision was the Bethany Home (now Union) for Young Women, whose doors opened in 1890. Today residents come from all over the world to three connected buildings on Newbury Street, and they are selected on the basis of financial need. The other program was a large housing facility for young working women or students. In 1901 the Franklin Square House was established in Boston's South End with a homelike atmosphere and services for its residents. Russell Miller calls it "an enduring monument to Perin and Universalist philanthropy." Later the building became housing for the elderly.

EXTENSION. There has often been an antipathy to proselytizing among Unitarian Universalists. When the **American Unitarian Association (AUA)** was established in 1825, its primary purpose was to publish tracts, and this became the central means of extending the faith. This was not always successful, especially in the rural areas, where ministers such as Alpheus Harding in New Salem, Massachusetts, noted that his members were "not a reading people." The use of tracts was also a prominent feature of the Post Office Mission, formed in 1881. The written word was an important means of extension for Universalists in the 19th century as well. This was especially true of Universalist newspapers, of which there were about 180 published in different times and places.

The Universalists were especially noted for spreading the word of universal salvation by means of circuit riding preachers who would travel from town to town and preach anywhere they could. Often involved in vicious debates, the Universalists became frequent victims of attacks from other denominations. Erasmus Manford, who preached for "25 years in the West," heard that Universalism "is a loathsome spawn from Hell, the meanest of all the devil's work." Nevertheless, these circuit riders enabled Universalism to experience tremendous growth resulting in estimated numbers in the mid-19th century of 800,000 members. Among those who helped spread the word in New York, Pennsylvania, and westward were **Nathaniel Stacy** and Stephen Smith. Less willing to proselytize, the Unitarians have always been disturbed by the methods of evangelists and missionaries. This began with the Great Awakening when the liberals opposed the disruption of the **Standing Order** and the passionate methods employed to convert members. Unitarians have also respected the rational individual choices of people, and have refused to preach one revealed truth, even though they have wanted to share their religion with others. Despite having more evangelical origins than the Unitarians, many Universalists were also repelled by the techniques of evangelists, feeling that much of their work was for their own self-aggrandizement. Westward expansion for Unitarians often occurred when a Unitarian from the east moved west and wanted to replicate what he/she had already experienced. There were Unitarians who wanted to spread the word in a more missionary style. In the late 19th century these included **Jenkin Lloyd Jones**, the secretary of the **Western Unitarian Conference (WUC)**, and the group of women preachers known as the **Iowa Sisterhood**.

From the beginning Unitarians used the technique of having a well-established minister make preaching visits to other cities. **William Ellery Channing**'s famous Baltimore Sermon was given to mark the formation of the Unitarian church in that city, and in California, later in the century, **Thomas Starr King** went on preaching tours. The most well-known Universalist missionary in the United States in the late 19th century was **Quillen Shinn**, who spent many years preaching in the South.

When **Lon Ray Call** made a report on church extension in 1946 he said that "no well-founded policy of church extension is apparent since 1900." Two years later he said that there were no active Unitarians in 11 states: Alabama, Idaho, Montana, North Dakota, South Dakota, West Virginia, Arkansas, Mississippi, Nevada, New Mexico, and Wyoming, with no Unitarian sermon having ever been preached in the last five. His groundwork helped lead to the formation of the fellowship movement, the development of lay centers. This effort, which was carried out under the direction of **Monroe Husbands**, found tremendous support in an advertising campaign sponsored by the **Unitarian Layman's League**. In 1944 the **Church of the Larger Fellowship (CLF)** was organized. This home church for isolated liberals became the spawning ground for countless local Unitarian Universalist (UU) societies, where none previously existed. In 1975, 1,007 UU congregations were listed in the Unitarian Universalist Association (UUA) Directory, of which 346 had been formed from a group of CLF members. At that time much of the work of extension was carried out by interdistrict representatives, field staff of the **Unitarian Universalist Association (UUA)** who helped provide local congregations with services, develop strong district organizations, and extend the faith by starting new congregations with the assistance of a UUA Extension Department at the headquarters. Since then more resources have been used to employ a greater number of field staff. Growing new congregations and finding ways to expand its mission have been central emphases of the UUA in recent years. Extension ministries in targeted geographical areas where growth was demographically favorable and intentional start-up churches have been part of a larger plan were implemented in the last 25 years by a UUA staff much more oriented to expanding membership.

– F –

FAHS, SOPHIA LYON (1876–1978). The greatest Unitarian religious educator of the 20th century, Fahs lived a long and productive life.

She was born on August 2, 1876, in Hangchow, China, the daughter of Presbyterian missionaries. The large family left China when Sophia was three, and she grew up in Wisconsin and Ohio, where she attended public schools. It was her intention to follow the careers of her parents, but this began to change in college. She attended the Presbyterian University of Wooster (now the College of Wooster) in Ohio. Here she began to have questions about the divinity of Jesus, and this concern continued at the University of Chicago Divinity School, where she learned about biblical criticism. On June 14, 1902, she married Charles Harvey Fahs, and they subsequently moved to New York. She then attended Teachers College, Columbia University for an M.A. where she studied under Frank McMurry, a follower of John Dewey. Fahs worked at an experimental Sunday School at Teachers College that McMurry had founded.

During the next 20 years she primarily devoted herself to motherhood, eventually having five children, learning much about the needs of children. In 1918 she became the director of the Sunday School at the Manhattan Congregational Church in New York. She returned to school at Union Theological Seminary and graduated with a B.D. in 1926. Taking a position on the faculty of Union that year, she remained a lecturer in religious education for many years. Fahs also served as the director of the Sunday School at Riverside Church, which developed a reputation for experimental classrooms. During her work at Union she discovered the Beacon Course in Religious Education and learned about Unitarianism. In 1930 she taught at a Star Island summer institute on religious education. In 1937 when she was 60, she was invited to serve as editor of children's educational materials for the **American Unitarian Association (AUA)**. At this time she was not even a member of a Unitarian church, but that changed when she joined Community Church of New York in 1945.

Frederick May Eliot, AUA president, had given the education department a directive to produce new materials after the **Commission on Appraisal** report in 1936, which said that Unitarians did not take seriously the religious education of their children. Fahs tried to produce a curriculum that had a broad base to it that would appeal to more than Unitarians. Over the next few years, the New Beacon Series came to include more than 30 books of classroom materials and teachers' guides. Fahs wrote much of the material herself. She felt strongly that religion and science must be integrated, wanting to make religion as relevant as possible in the modern world. Under her direction the Bible was no longer the center of the curriculum but only one source book. She wanted children to experience the mystery of life and understand the universality of religious experiences.

Fahs's philosophy of religious education is summed up in *Today's Children and Yesterday's Heritage*. (1952) "We need to learn how to help children to think about ordinary things until insights and feelings are found which have a religious quality." Not long after she assumed the position of editor, she wrote *Consider the Children; How They Grow* (1940). She continued as editor until 1951 and even remained a member of the Curriculum Committee until 1964. The year she left as editor she received the AUA's Award for Meritorious Service. In 1959 Fahs was ordained to the ministry in Bethesda, Maryland. She continued to write about religious education until 1971. Her works became the central expression of Unitarian Universalist religious education for more than 30 years, and many of her books are still used today. She had a special interest in story telling, and this is reflected in all her books from creations myths (*Beginnings* series, 1937–38) to retelling biblical tales (*Jesus the Carpenter's Son*, 1945). She was held in esteem in many ways, including receiving numerous honorary degrees. Fahs also had a great interest in children's worship and wrote extensively on it, reflecting a deep spirituality, including *Worshiping Together with Questioning Minds* (1965). Fahs died on April 17, 1978, in Hamilton, Ohio, after a long life in which she enriched the religious lives of countless children, youth, and adults.

FEDERAL COUNCIL OF CHURCHES (FCC). The Federal Council of Churches was formed in 1924 as a means for Protestant denominations to work together in common voice and action. Beginning in 1939 Universalist leaders were encouraged to apply for membership by council members. **Robert Cummins**, the **general superintendent**, made this recommendation to a **General Assembly (GA)** meeting in 1941, believing that cooperative efforts were especially needed with the world at war. The GA authorized the **Board of Trustees** to make application. At a meeting of the Council in May 1942, the Universalists were informed of the necessity of belief in "Jesus Christ as . . . divine Lord and Savior." The Universalists felt as though differences of interpretation of this phrasing should not separate the churches in their common faith and experiences. There had also been many years of cooperation at the state and local level. At a council meeting in December1942 the application was never brought up, as the Advisory Committee recommended more conferences with the Universalists. The trustees reaffirmed their desire to apply for membership in 1944, but the Universalists were refused membership at the council's meeting in November. Cummins responded by saying, "that which happened in Pittsburgh was the imposition of a creedal definition of Christianity; and it is against such definition that Universalists protest. We cannot imagine Jesus of Nazareth barring the door to any church which accepts his name and leadership." Harry Emerson Fosdick wrote, "My blood boils at this nonsensical obscurantism." In 1946, the Universalist GA voted to reapply for membership. In October the Council asked the Universalists to redefine their official Universalist doctrinal position from the evangelical point of view and to omit references to their Bond of Fellowship, which was interpreted by most of the members as being Unitarian in its doctrinal impact. The Universalists refused to dilute their position to pacify the opposition. Once again, their application was rejected at the council meeting in December 1946. At the Universalist GA in 1947, the GA voted to support the program of the council "in such matters as are compatible with the liberal tradition and outlook of the Universalist Church." The Universalists were never able to convince the council to move from their position of doctrinal purity to a more inclusive understanding of the oneness of the churches working in "the spirit of fellowship, service and cooperation." Currently, the council is known as the National Council of Churches (NCC), and the **Unitarian Universalist Association (UUA)** has official observer status but not membership. The Unitarians never applied for membership.

FEDERAL STREET CHURCH. The former building in Boston where the **American Unitarian Association (AUA)** was organized, the church was the site of many historic events. Land at the corner of Long Lane and Burry Streets was purchased in 1729, and a barn on the site was converted for use by a congregation of Scottish Calvinist immigrants who used a presbyterian form of church government.

A second meetinghouse was built in 1744. The congregation adopted congregational government in 1786 and called a liberal minister, Jeremy Belknap. The Massachusetts State Convention ratified the United States Constitution in 1788 in this building, and thereafter Long Lane became known as Federal Street. The congregation was served by the spiritual leader of American Unitarianism, **William Ellery Channing**, from 1803 to 1842. During his ministry a third meetinghouse was built in 1809 designed by **Charles Bulfinch**.

In 1803 Burry Street was changed to Berry Street. A group of clergy who entered by the side door of the church became the **Berry Street Conference** in 1820; now the oldest organization for liberal ministers. It was this group who entertained a proposal to organize a Unitarian Association on May 25, 1825. That afternoon a second meeting was held in the vestry of the church and the AUA was voted into being. The **Benevolent Fraternity of Christian Churches (BFCC)** (now the Unitarian Universalist Urban Ministry) was also organized in this building in 1834, as was the Peace Society of Massachusetts on December 28, 1815, the first of its kind in the country. In 1858 land in Boston's Back Bay was purchased, and the Federal Street Church congregation moved to Arlington Street in 1861 when a new building designed by Arthur Gilman was completed. The Second Society of Universalists, once served by **Hosea Ballou**, and the Church of the Disciples, founded by **James Freeman Clarke**, both merged with the Arlington Street Church in 1935 and 1941, respectively. Annual meetings of the AUA took place in the spring in Boston every year until merger in 1961. The Anniversary Service for these "May Meetings" was held at the Arlington Street Church. The church has also maintained a distinguished history of social activism. In the 1960s it gained fame as the sight of numerous draft card burnings in protest of the Vietnam War. Especially because it houses the congregation once served by Channing, the Arlington Street Church continues to be a symbolic "Mother Church" for Unitarian Universalists.

FELLOWSHIP MOVEMENT. An important Unitarian program for extension launched in the period after World War II, it resulted in the creation of hundreds of new congregations. As early as 1895 **Jabez Sunderland** had encouraged the formation of a movement to found "parlor churches." In 1907 the **American Unitarian Association (AUA)** issued a handbook and voted funds toward a plan for the organization of "Lay Centers." Little came out of these earlier efforts, but the idea surfaced again in 1945. AUA president **Frederick May Eliot** was reminded of the old program that floundered and he took the matter up with the AUA Board, which created a study committee. The committee included Albert Dieffenbach, the **Church of the Larger Fellowship (CLF)** minister, George Davis, the AUA extension director, and Roland Burbank of the New Hampshire Unitarian Association. One other person who played a significant role was **Lon Ray Call**, the AUA minister-at-large.

In 1946 Call issued "A Research on Church Extension and Maintenance Since 1900: A Progress Report." Despite finding many previous failures, Call said that the best solution to extension of the faith would be the creation of "Lay Groups." With this recommendation the study committee was able to formulate a plan for the creation of such groups in communities where it was felt a church could not succeed. The resulting recommendation was that the new groups be allowed as much independence as possible in creating a mission, methods, and content for their local group. In October 1947 the AUA Board granted a request for funds for a Fellowship Office and a full-time director, and soon thereafter **Monroe Husbands** was named to fill the position. The plan became reality in 1948 when the Unitarian Fellowship of Boulder, Colorado, organized in June and was voted into membership on July 28, 1948.

The most difficult part of the process of creating new fellowships was to define what a fellowship was. The *Unitarian Fellowship Manual* said a fellowship was a group of 10 or more religious liberals who expressed their approval of the purpose of the AUA, had bylaws, and continued to make financial contributions to the AUA. In practice a fellowship was not intended to be a church in the making, but rather a lay-led group who would develop spiritually satisfying programs. It was difficult to maintain the distinction between church and fellowship, as many of the fellowships grew larger and eventually wished to achieve church status. While the fellowships were formed to encourage the development of lay leaders, many of them became anticlerical. Others remained small insular groups that floundered when the organizers died or moved. While most of the initial groups had no buildings or ministers, these criteria changed as societies grew and expanded their programming.

Fellowships were often characterized as casual, informal, highly personal, and democratic. Sometimes highly individual needs conflicted with organizational development, but groups were encouraged to develop their own style. After 10 years Laile Bartlett concluded in the book *Bright Galaxy* that the fellowship movement was a success in providing opportunities to give group liberal religious experiences to those who were scattered and isolated. Much credit for contact information must go to the CLF and the Unitarian Layman's League for its advertising campaign. Within the first 10-year span of time, 249 still active fellowships had been organized in all areas of the United States (315 were organized in all, of which 40 died but 11 were later reorganized, and one merged; 26 became churches). In 1967 Lon Ray Call noted that 80 fellowships had become churches. The movement was also successful in having a larger influence on the denomination in terms of developing lay leadership and making worship and organizational styles more informal.

FELLOWSHIP OF RELIGIOUS HUMANISTS. A group that was formed after the American Humanist Association (AHA, established 1941) became increasingly secular in their concerns. Many of the clergy in the former American Unitarian Association were the nucleus of the "religious humanists" group. They started the Fellowship of Religious Humanists in 1963 with Lester Mondale as president. Their quarterly journal, *Religious Humanism*, had Edwin H. Wilson as its first editor. Many of the members were also drawn from the Ethical Cultural movement, which had long been associated with the Unitarians, and this gave them a common forum. Some clergy, such as Mondale, had served both Unitarian churches and Ethical Culture societies. These religious humanists also knew that they needed to develop methods to work with others, especially within the **Unitarian Universalist Association (UUA)**, which was more theologically diverse than the old secular humanists that made up a wing of the AHA, many of whom were decidedly against the institutional church and Christianity. The fellowship maintains a noncreedal approach in its philosophy and gives religious humanists a common voice within the UUA

FENN, WILLIAM WALLACE (1862–1932). One of the leading theologians and professors among Unitarians in the 20th century. Fenn was born in Boston on February 12, 1862, to William and Hannah (Osgood) Fenn. His father died soon after he was born, and his mother made a life for herself and her son by running a boarding house. After attending the Boston Latin School, he entered **Harvard College** in the class of 1884. He was especially interested in languages and majored in Greek and Latin. After that he immediately went on to **Harvard Divinity School**, where he specialized in biblical studies, helping one professor assemble a Greek New Testament Lexicon. Although he had been brought up in more orthodox faiths, Fenn converted to Unitarianism in the seminary. In 1887 he was ordained and installed at Unity church in Pittsfield, Massachusetts, and after three years was called to another pastorate at First Unitarian in Chicago. In 1890 he married Faith Fisher, and they had five children, including Dan Huntington Fenn, who became a Unitarian minister.

Fenn made a name for himself in Chicago, first by being a key player in helping the **Western Unitarian Conference (WUC)** and the **American Unitarian Association (AUA)** reconcile on the theological and extension issues that were dividing them and were resolved with the Saratoga Conference. Then he played an important role in beginning the process that resulted in the **Meadville Theological School** moving to Chicago. Fenn helped oversee the erection of Hull Chapel near the University of Chicago, which later became Meadville's chapel. For a time he served on the WUC and AUA Boards, while also working at his own church and the chapel. He also served as a lecturer for Meadville in biblical literature. After 11 years he was hired to the position he would hold for the rest of his life: Bussey Professor of Theology at Harvard Divinity School. He was also dean at Harvard from 1906 to 1922. Concerned about the overly optimistic nature of liberalism, Fenn published an important essay, "Modern Liberalism" in 1913. He asked liberals to consider whether their faith could bear up in response to human tragedy and evil. There was also some question for Fenn whether liberals could still call themselves Christian "in any proper sense." In "Thought of God" Fenn showed that he believed that the key attribute of humankind was not sinfulness but freedom. He emphasized human responsibility so that people became coworkers with God in an unfinished evolutionary process, and thus God was less of a static being and more of an unfolding becoming.

During his years at Harvard, Fenn influenced countless students. In one story a student told Fenn how hard it was to write sermons. Fenn replied, “Into every sermon a certain amount of pain must always go; it is your choice whether it will be yours or your congregation’s” (as quoted in Wintersteen, *Christology*, p. 108.). Fenn also made important contributions to a Unitarian understanding of Jesus, expressed most succinctly in a series of summer school lectures at Harvard in 1905, “The Theological Method of Jesus.” Fenn’s main idea was that Jesus’ authority was derived from personal experience and not from tradition. Jesus responded to nature and found God in the common life around him. Fenn said we should look to Jesus’ inner life for inspiration and not external events. The idea of the Kingdom of God was that there was a time coming when we would all live together as one human family. Fenn died on March 6, 1932, and is buried in a family plot in Weston, Vermont, where he had always spent his summers. **Charles Edwards Park** said that he combined a forceful personality and a great mind.

FILLMORE, MILLARD (1800–1874). The 13th President of the United States is usually remembered for his undistinguished record as Chief Executive. Fillmore was born on January 7, 1800, in central New York State; his family having migrated from Vermont only the year before. Fillmore apprenticed to a Quaker lawyer, and was admitted to the bar in Buffalo. He married Abigail Powers when he was 25. Fillmore entered politics when he was elected a representative to the New York State Legislature. His legislative efforts included bills prohibiting use of state funds for sectarian religious schools and ending religious tests for witness testifying in court. In 1831 the Fillmores became founding members of the Buffalo Unitarian Church. Robert J. Rayback reports that Fillmore, having no childhood affiliation, may have been attracted by the church’s rejection of all dogma that offended reason. He and his wife remained lifelong supporters of the church. Fillmore continued to seek political office, serving for a time in the U.S. House of Representatives, and finally was rewarded in 1848 with the Whig Party’s nomination for vice president of the

United States. After the Taylor-Fillmore ticket won the election, Fillmore soon saw himself vaulted to power when Zachary Taylor died in July 1850. Fillmore's term was marked by the passage of the Compromise of 1850, which included the Fugitive Slave Act. His fellow religionist **Theodore Parker** wrote to the president saying that he was harboring fugitive slaves, and challenged Fillmore to arrest him. Fillmore quietly filed the letter. Back in Buffalo, Fillmore's minister, George Washington Hosmer, denounced the president for his support of the law, but Fillmore continued to believe that the compromise was the only way to preserve the Union. Fillmore failed to win renomination in 1852. He retired to Buffalo in 1856 after making a futile run for the presidency. He became active in local civic groups and even entertained President-Elect Lincoln in 1860, taking him to a Sunday service at the Unitarian church. Fillmore died on March 8, 1874.

FLAMING CHALICE. The Flaming Chalice is widely recognized as the symbol of Unitarian Universalism. Its formal association with the movement dates to World War II when it was adopted as an emblem for the newly organized Unitarian Service Committee (USC). The USC was founded in 1939 to assist refugees from Eastern Europe who needed to escape Nazi persecution. Han Deutsch, an Austrian who had escaped from the Nazis in Paris, met Charles Joy, the executive director of the USC, in 1940. While Deutsch was serving as an assistant to Joy, he was asked to create a symbol for the relatively unknown USC so that they would be recognized, look official, and also incarnate the spirit of their work. Deutsch devised a chalice with a flame making use of familiar elements but open to the interpretation of people with different religious or cultural backgrounds. The chalice was a sacred symbol to many faiths representing a common drinking vessel that is shared among many. The flame may represent the triumph of truth over fear and superstition. For some the flame hovering over the chalice represents the cross of Christianity. The USC adopted it for a seal for papers, an emblem on vehicles, and a badge for agents moving refugees to freedom. It embodied the shared meaning that was the work of the USC—service to others.

The Flaming Chalice remains the symbol of the **Unitarian Universalist Service Committee (UUSC)** today, but its use has spread widely. In the last 25 years, the **Unitarian Universalist Association**

(UUA) has used a variety of design variations, but most written materials carry the chalice logo. What is perhaps most significant is its use by a majority of its congregations as a focal point for worship when it is lighted at the beginning of a service. Prior to its adoption other symbols had appeared periodically. Many Universalist churches used a circle containing an off-center cross, developed by the Humiliati and created to represent the faith's Christian origins having grown to include a wider circle of the universal spirit. Immediately after the consolidation of the two denominations, two intertwined circles were used to represent the joining of Unitarianism and Universalism.

The Flaming Chalice is also shrouded in indirect historic origins. Jan Hus was a Czech priest and forerunner of the Reformation who was burned at the stake in 1415 for heresies that included the sharing of the communion chalice with the laity. Before this, only the priests shared the cup, but Hus intended the communion to indicate that all people are equal. Tradition tells that when he was being burned, Hus shouted out: "Today you are cooking a skinny goose, but from these ashes a swan will arise which you will not be able to burn." So the flame of prophecy and sacrifice was joined to the chalice, which is for all the people. In Bohemia and Eastern Europe, a great movement began, using the flaming chalice as a symbol. In 1433 the Hussites forced the church to accept the giving of the communion chalice to all the people. In the 16th century the Czech brethren used the chalice as a symbol of the egalitarian equality of the laity and the clergy. These Czechs were a strong influence on the Polish brethren, who also used the chalice as a symbol for equality and peace. Some of the modern Unitarian roots in Europe are traced through this Polish group. Etched on the Jan Hus memorial in Prague are these words: "Love one another. Always tell the truth." With both ancient and modern roots, the flaming chalice continues to grow in meaning.

FLOWER CELEBRATION. Widely known as the Flower Communion, it is a ritual that is celebrated in Unitarian Universalist churches all over the world, frequently at the last service in the spring before the summer break. The celebration was initiated by the Rev. **Norbert Capek** in the Unitarian Church in Prague on June 4, 1923. Realizing the importance of symbolic rituals, but eschewing the inherent theological difficulties the people had with Christian communion, Capek turned to the natural beauty of the countryside for the elements of a new ritual. He invited members to bring one flower representing their individual uniqueness and beauty to a service.

For the ritual the flowers were collected into a common bouquet representing the church body, and each person added their own contribution showing that it was of his/her own free will that he/she joined with others. Then at the end of the service each person took a different flower than the one he/she brought, representing his/her acceptance of one another and how much each person received from the community. Because Capek was later martyred by the Nazis, today the ritual also commemorates his life and the fight against tyranny. Capek never used the word "communion" since this ritual was developed to supersede traditional Christian rituals. In the prayer at the first flower celebration, Capek said: "In this holy resolution may we be strengthened knowing that we are God's family; that one spirit, the spirit of love unites us; and endeavor for a more perfect and more joyful life leads us on."

FOLLEN, CHARLES THEODORE CHRISTIAN (1796–1840). The man who introduced the Christmas tree to America was also a courageous advocate for freedom. Follen was born on September 4, 1796, in Romrod, Germany, the son of a judge. His mother died when he was only three, but he remained with his father, who remarried when the boy was seven. Follen excelled in ancient and modern languages at the gymnasium. Here he also became interested in radical politics and had a profound religious experience. In 1813 he entered the University of Giessen to study law. His studies were interrupted when he joined a group of student rifle volunteers who were organizing to oppose French domination. He finished his studies in 1818 receiving a degree in civil and canon law. After that he taught and then was employed defending villages against unfair taxations. Follen began to lose jobs over his radical political views, a problem that would plague him throughout his life. He eventually fled to Paris and taught at the Cantonal School of the Grisons in Chur, and then in Basel where he lectured at the university, but each time he was forced to move on until, finally, the Prussian government demanded his arrest in 1824.

This forced Follen to flee to America, where, thanks to General

Marquis de Lafayette, he lived in Philadelphia for a year learning the language and culture. In 1825 he received an appointment at Harvard College teaching German. Just prior to this he had visited New York, to meet Catherine Sedgwick, whose novel, *Redwood*, he admired. Sedgwick and her brother sent Follen to Boston with letters of introduction, including one to Eliza Lee Cabot, Catherine's friend. Eliza and Charles developed a friendship that blossomed into marriage on September 15, 1828. Eliza was a teacher in the Sunday School at the **Federal Street Church**, and Follen attended one meeting of teachers where **William Ellery Channing** was discussing the significance of the death of Jesus. Channing was impressed with Follen's thoughts and encouraged him to enter the ministry.

During the next five years Follen filled a number of pulpits, but remained unordained. In the fall of 1828 he was appointed an instructor in ecclesiastical history and ethics at Harvard Divinity School and he continued to teach German as well. In 1830 he became an American citizen and was offered a permanent ministry in Newburyport, Massachusetts, but when Harvard offered a full professorship in Germanic literature, he accepted that. It was during this time that Follen introduced the German tradition of the Christmas tree to the special delight of his young son, Charley, as it was reported by the British writer Harriet Martineau in 1838. Follen also began to agitate against slavery at this time, although he was warned not to by some of the more conservative elements in Boston society. He joined the New England Anti-Slavery Society in 1834 and testified before the Massachusetts legislature. He discovered at this time that his Harvard position would not become a permanent post.

There was a group of people in East Lexington, Massachusetts, who were trying to form a Unitarian church, and Follen began to work with them. In 1836 he traveled west and was invited to be minister in Chicago, but he declined. Another opportunity opened up in New York City, where William Ware had left the First Congregational Church (Unitarian). Follen received a temporary appointment, hoping it would become permanent. He was finally ordained on October 30, 1836, at the Federal Street Church in Boston. Despite a positive start, he alienated many of his parishioners with a Thanksgiving sermon that mentioned slavery. Follen returned for a second year still hoping to receive the permanent position, but his name was associated with a protest of Elijah Lovejoy's murder. Finally, the church told him he could stay another year, but they would be looking over other candidates. Follen resigned and returned to Boston in the spring of 1838. As he was preparing a trip to Europe he was invited to return to East Lexington to the society he had helped organize in 1835. Follen designed a building for the new church and helped them construct it. Before the building was dedicated, he was invited to New York to lecture. When he was returning for that building dedication, the steamship *Lexington* that he was traveling on sank on January 13, 1840, and Follen was lost at sea. He was survived by his wife and son, who were not on the trip. Eliza won fame in her own right as the author of the classic children's story, "Three Little Kittens." When the Federal Street Church refused to allow Channing the use of the sanctuary for Follen's memorial service, a despondent Channing said he had "poured out his soul in vain."

FRANCIS, CONVERS (1795–1863). He was a moderate Unitarian who tried to peacefully maintain the institutional church while being open to the radical thought of the Transcendentalists. Francis was born in West Cambridge, Massachusetts, on November 9, 1795, the fifth child of Convers and Susannah (Rand) Francis. His father gained a reputation as a successful baker in Medford, Massachusetts, and young Convers spent many boyhood hours wiping the excess flour from barrels of crackers. From an early age he had a passion for reading and was especially successful in "whatever required memory." He entered Harvard College, where he graduated in 1815, and then commenced training for the ministry. He was called to the church in Watertown, Massachusetts, in the spring of 1819 and ordained there on June 23, 1819. Francis remained with the Watertown church for 23 years. During the early years of his ministry he lived with his sister **Lydia Maria (Francis) Child**, who adopted the name Maria after being baptized in Watertown in 1821. Her older brother became her intellectual mentor, and she wrote her first novel Hobomok, while still living in the parsonage.

In May 1822 Francis married Abby Bradford Allyn, the daughter of the minister in Duxbury, Massachusetts. Together they had four children, but only the two youngest, George and Abby, survived infancy. Francis was also the mentor of **Theodore Parker**, who came to Watertown to start a school in 1832. Intellectually, Francis had few equals. He was a historian who wrote the history of Watertown and a biography of John Eliot. He was an early scholar of the German language. He was a charter member of the **Transcendental Club** and was chosen moderator, perhaps owing to his being the eldest and also skilled in diplomacy. He was a longtime admirer of **Ralph Waldo Emerson**, of whom he said: "Was ever a mind cast in a finer mold than Emerson's? He seems to have already anticipated the purity of the spiritual state." In 1836 Francis published a tract, *Christianity as a Purely Internal Principle*, which argued that the religion of Christ is purely internal. In his *Natural Theology*, he embraced the idea that the principles of thought and moral feeling come directly from the "fountain itself of heavenly light."

Despite his adoption of the radical new theological ideas, his peaceable ways enabled the parish in Watertown to bypass the Unitarian and Trinitarian battles altogether, and the church became Unitarian with little cost in personal pain. The life of the church was always more important to him than the promulgation of particular notions of truth. Wishing to avoid a catastrophic division within the ranks, Francis refused to exchange pulpits with his friend Theodore Parker in the wake of Parker's infamous "Transient and Permanent" sermon in 1841. Francis was accused of conformity and desertion when he announced this action, but he wanted to show tolerance for everyone in this divisive battle. In 1842 Francis was invited to help prepare students for the ministry at Harvard and became the Parkman Professor of Pulpit Eloquence. It was his view that the students should be allowed to pursue any line of questioning, so long as it was undertaken in a "proper pious spirit." For the next 20 years he encouraged his students to decide all kinds of religious and social questions for themselves. Eventually he was reconciled with Parker. In 1845 he was one of 20 clergy who called for a meeting to register the first denomination-wide opposition to slavery. In his career Francis showed great leadership by respecting both the history and traditions of the church and embracing the new currents of thought. Harvard College needed the kind of openness and tolerance he brought to the institution. He died on April 7, 1863.

FREE CHURCH FELLOWSHIP. An attempt by liberals to facilitate cooperation between faiths, it never became popular, but it was an important first step in the final process of consolidation between Unitarians and Universalists. Conceived by **American Unitarian Association (AUA)** president **Louis Cornish** as a federation of all liberal Protestants, it was an organization intended to affect the final union of all liberal religions. In 1931 the Annual Meeting of the AUA passed a resolution calling for a joint commission with the Universalists to look into uniting the two communions. Victor Friend, of Baked Bean fame, chaired the commission, which first met in December 1931. Rather than endorsing merger, the commission voted to form a new ecumenical group, which would be a wider fellowship than Unitarian and Universalist. It also called for more joint cooperation. A year later the final proposal was ready for the Unitarian May meetings and the fall Universalist convention in 1933. It received a much more enthusiastic response from Unitarians, as many Universalists were concerned that the organization had no mention of Christianity in its statement of purpose.

Originally called the Free Church of America, it was established in 1933 after the Universalists agreed to join. In 1934, the name "Fellowship" was added, and Jesus and God went into the Preamble. Although it began with high hopes, less than a year after its start, leaders such as **John Haynes Holmes** were wondering what happened to it. For one thing, it developed little support outside Unitarian and Universalist circles, as most other denominations showed little interest. Within Unitarianism especially there was concern that merger had been tabled so quickly. The fellowship also had bad luck when its first annual meeting was held during a horrendous snow storm. One problem was that so few churches joined, only 81 by early 1935. While some leaders pushed for its development, there was very little grassroots support. The fellowship accomplished very little and after three years there was little reason to continue operating. An appeal to the churches for funds resulted in one response. Without funds or purpose the fellowship came to an end in 1937, but, at the least, it helped continue the discussion of wider cooperation between Unitarians and Universalists.

FREE CHURCH IN A CHANGING WORLD. An important self-assessment of the denomination that was undertaken prior to consolidation in 1959 and published in 1963 as *The Free Church in a*

Changing World. The study was started with the hope that it would help provide a vision for the future of the denomination. Six commissions were established under a coordinating council with **Dana Greeley**, the **Unitarian Universalist Association (UUA)** president as chairman. The first commission was called "The Church and Its Leadership" and was chaired by Duncan Howlett. This commission included ministry in its discussions and called for a greater recognition of nonparochial (community) ministers, upholding the integrity of the profession, contracting for sabbaticals, and also for the greater recruitment of Negroes and women. The second commission was on "Theology and the Frontiers of Learning," chaired by Robert Tapp. This commission discovered significant theological diversity in the UUA and outlined six theological positions taken by individual UUs: Christian Liberalism, Deism, Mystical Religion, Religious Humanism, Naturalistic Theism, and Existentialism. This commission struggled with the continuing theological problem of finding religious consensus in a movement that emphasizes freedom of belief. The third commission was on "Education and Liberal Religion" and was chaired by Irving Murray. This commission recommended that our children need to be able to declare their faith by the time they emerge from our education classes, that they must be educated in a spiral curriculum rather than a linear one, that there be more parent and adult education, and that the UUA must make a greater financial commitment to education. The fourth commission on "Religion and the Arts," chaired by John Hayward, called for greater variety and drama in worship services. The fifth commission on "Ethics and Social Action," chaired by Donald Harrington, recommended, among others things, the establishment of a UUA Department of Social Responsibility, which soon became a reality. The sixth and final commission, "World Religion and Outreach," chaired by Floyd Ross, called for more interfaith work on the local level and a greater understanding of non-Western religions, but the recommended Department of World Churches was never implemented. In his concluding remarks Paul Carnes said that the denomination must be more critical in its search for truth, and less whimsical in accepting a noncritical freedom as the foundation of sound conviction. Carnes said that sound religious convictions must be both reasoned and held in community and not casual, verbal opinions or feelings of the individual. The need to discriminate among many truths was an important challenge to UUs.

FREEDOM OF THE WILL. One of the key issues separating the liberal Arminians from the Calvinists. Liberals in the 18th century rejected the notion that human beings have an inherent corrupt nature known as original sin. A totally depraved creature in the Calvinist system is not free to choose between good and evil but is predetermined to walk in sin and is only saved from this state by a gift of grace from God. Early liberals believed that human nature was malleable and that human character was determined by the influences of the environment. Human beings were seen as free moral agents who could choose the good not based on any inherited characteristic, but solely as a result of training and experience. Liberals were particularly opposed to the idea that there was nothing they could do morally to change their situation, but were condemned to choose the sinful path. Liberals believed humans are free moral agents and have the ability to alter their character for the better by making good responsible choices.

After the Unitarian controversy, Unitarianism went beyond the view that humans were born morally neutral to say that people were actually born good while possessing the freedom to perfect their very nature. **William Ellery Channing** elucidated this in *Self-Culture*. He said that no bounds can be set to human growth. Self-culture was possible because we have an inherent power to act on, determine, and form ourselves. The denial of original sin and the free choices one makes to transform human character to produce a righteous person were crucial changes from a completely God-centered world inhabited by depraved creatures who had no free moral agency to a more human centered world inhabited by creatures who can exercise their freedom to perfect themselves.

FREEMAN, JAMES (1759–1835). The first avowedly Unitarian minister in America, Freeman was born in Charlestown, Massachusetts, on April 22, 1759. He attended Boston Latin School and then Harvard College, where he graduated in 1777. He trained troops on Cape Cod for a time and then sailed to Quebec in 1780, where he was detained after being captured by a privateer. When he returned to Boston in 1782, he preached in several places and was invited to be a reader at King's Chapel. Their rector, Henry Caner, had been a Tory who left the city, leaving the congregation with no minister. After Freeman was settled there, he asked if he could change the liturgy in the Book of Common Prayer. In a series of sermons he outlined his doctrinal problems with the Trinity and he amended the liturgy according to the forms of Samuel Clarke in England. The changes were approved in June 1785, and King's Chapel became the first declared Unitarian church in America. The church published the *Book of Common Prayer According to the Use of King's Chapel*.

Two years later Freeman was ordained by the church according to congregational polity, after he found that Episcopal ordination was not possible. In 1788 he married Martha Curtis Clarke. Francis William Pitt Greenwood was made Freeman's associate in 1824, and two years later Freeman's health had deteriorated so much, he gave up the ministry to Greenwood. He lived on a country estate outside Boston for another nine years and then died on November 14, 1835. Freeman was a member of the first elected Boston School Committee in 1792 and was a founder of the Massachusetts Historical Society.

FREE RELIGIOUS ASSOCIATION (FRA). This was founded in response to the 1866 meeting of the **National Conference of Unitarian Churches** in Syracuse, New York, where the congregations had declared their allegiance to Jesus Christ and the radicals had failed to convince the group to declare itself nonsectarian or organize to include independent congregations as well as Unitarian. On the trip back to New Bedford, Massachusetts, **William J. Potter** began to ruminate on the idea of creating a new organization that would promote complete spiritual freedom from irrational doctrines and traditional authorities. In October eight people met at the home of Cyrus Bartol, who was interested in revolting from the Unitarians and perhaps organizing a new denomination. Two additional meetings were held, and finally a group headed by Potter, Edward C. Towne, and **Francis Ellingwood Abbot** drafted a constitution for the new Free Religious Association. The majority of the 30 people present wanted to establish a new group, but they did not want to break with Unitarianism.

Finally, an organizational meeting was held in Boston on May 30, 1867. The gathering drew a large group to hear a number of speakers, including **Ralph Waldo Emerson**. Abbot said free religion was a transfer of loyalty from Christ to Christ's principles: truth, righteousness, and love. The new faith was meant to reconcile religion and science. The constitution was adopted calling for an association that would: "promote the interests of pure religion, to encourage the scientific study of theology, and to increase fellowship in the spirit."

Octavius Brooks Frothingham was the first president of the FRA, but Potter was the driving force behind the organization for many years. He conceived of the organization as a group that extended a welcome to all religions. In 1872 he helped add an amendment to the constitution that no form of theism was required for members. Historian Stow Persons said that the FRA became little more than a debating society as the group moved away from establishing a new religion to fit the needs of a rationalistic age and instead placed their emphasis on the universal, nonsectarian aspects of free religion. Unfortunately, the constitution did not allow the group to speak as a united front because members were only responsible for their own opinions and there were no restrictions upon their connection with other organizations. The executive committee agreed that using tracts and lectures were appropriate means for spreading the word that a universal religious feeling was shared in all religions, but when they tried to organize meetings to show that there was such a thing as absolute religion, they usually found religion expressed in contrary ways with sectarian opinions. The FRA sponsored regular lecture series that continued until 1878.

Secretary Potter corresponded with many other religious groups throughout the world, but again the promotion of complete freedom prevented the group from joining with others to promote pure religion. After 1880 the group tried to root out some of this individualism, but they did not succeed. Potter remained the most influential member until his death in 1894. The FRA's periodical was called the *Index*. It was established in 1870 with Abbot as its first editor, after he had gone to Toledo to serve the church there, which dropped its Unitarian connection and became an independent society. David Locke had offered to finance a weekly journal of free religion, and the *Index* was the result. The first few issues included Abbot's Fifty

Affirmations, which stated that free religion was the final form of religion. After 10 years Abbot gave the Index over to the FRA to publish, and Potter became one of its editors. The FRA also held annual conventions that included public meetings and lectures. After 1894 the group decided to have local chapters, but by then it was too late for organizational improvements, and the organization never numbered more than 500 members. Little organizational activity was ever carried out in a group that hallowed the individual beliefs of its members so much. The FRA lived on into the 20th century, but its effectiveness as an organization was largely restricted to the last two decades of the 19th century. In addition to its organizational problems around freedom, the group was sometimes identified as an anti-Christian cult. What may have been most telling though was its identification with immorality. Pornographers tried to use Abbot's Liberal League as a way to have the Comstock Laws repealed, and this prominent member of the FRA became associated with free love and infidelity. While never a success organizationally, the FRA had a profound influence upon transforming Unitarianism into a broader more universal and humanistic faith.

FRITCHMAN, STEPHEN HOLE (1902–1981). He was a Unitarian Universalist minister with a passion for social justice who developed a reputation for political radicalism. Fritchman was born on May 12, 1902, in Cleveland, Ohio. His background was in religious orthodoxy, as his parents read the Bible to him every morning before breakfast. After attending the Wharton School of Finance and Commerce at the University of Pennsylvania for a year, he transferred to Ohio Wesleyan University where he received his B.A. in 1924. Fritchman's interest in religion, politics, and the media became evident early in his career. For two years he was religious news editor for the *New York Herald Tribune* and then briefly associate editor of the *Methodist Church School Journal*. During this time he received his theological training. He was granted a B.D. from Union Theological School in 1927 and an M.A. from New York University in 1929. In the meantime he married Frances Palmer. Fritchman moved to Boston to teach in the School of Religious Education at Boston University. His affiliation with Methodism ended when he was ordained into the Unitarian ministry in 1930 after being called to the First Parish, Unitarian in Petersham, Massachusetts. After Petersham, Fritchman spent six years as minister at the Unitarian church in Bangor, Maine.

In 1938 he became youth director for the **American Unitarian Association (AUA)**, leaving parish ministry for administrative work. The most painful period of his career followed after he was named editor of the denomination's journal, the ***Christian Register*** in 1942. He continued in both the youth and publishing jobs until a controversy erupted over his editorial policies. In a time of great fear over communist expansion, Fritchman was accused of following a Communist Party line, while openly supporting Soviet policies in the periodical. His supporters, who argued that he had revitalized the publication, were not able to garner enough support for Fritchman to continue in his position, and he resigned after an 18 month battle in 1947.

When the so-called "Fritchman Crisis" passed, the Unitarian denomination had survived what has been called a bitter ecclesiastical fight over principles of freedom of the press. Fritchman moved on and accepted a call to become minister at the First Unitarian Church in Los Angeles, where he remained until his retirement in 1969. Here Fritchman found an accepting home for his espousal of radical issues. The church became a center for resistance to the Cold War. He continued to be active in many peace and civil liberties organizations throughout his life. He often appeared on the protest line either fighting against the bomb, advocating for striking workers, or supporting civil rights. During the 1950s Fritchman led a successful fight against the State of California, which was attempting to impose loyalty oaths upon all the churches in the state. After the **Unitarian Universalist Service Committee (UUSC)** named its annual award for him, Fritchman said, "If we truly believe that human beings are of supreme importance, we will *not* be neutral." Recognizing this free thinker who would not submit to any yoke, the Unitarian Universalist Association (UUA) honored him with its Annual Distinguished Service Award in 1976, Fritchman summed up his own response to his life when he called his autobiography *Heretic*. His other published works included *Men of Liberty*, *Unitarianism Today*, *Youth Work in the Liberal Church*, and a collection of sermons, *For the Sake of Clarity*. He received an honorary doctorate from the Starr King School in 1967. He continued to translate his beliefs in freedom and justice into action throughout his life. Stephen Fritchman died on May 31, 1981.

FROTHINGHAM, OCTAVIUS BROOKS (1822–1895). A religious radical and founder of the Free Religious Association, Frothingham was born in Boston on November 28, 1822, the second of five children of the minister of First Church, Nathaniel Langdon Frothingham, and his wife, Ann Brooks. Octavius attended Boston Latin School and then attended **Harvard College**, where he graduated in 1843. He had early intentions on a career in ministry and so he continued on at **Harvard Divinity School**, where he described life as being "half-monastic." After that he was called to the North Church in Salem, Massachusetts, where he was ordained on March 10, 1847. Soon thereafter, he was married to Caroline Curtis of Boston. Frothingham began his career as a theological conservative, but he was swept up by the influence of **Theodore Parker** and **Transcendentalism** and both his theology and politics were radicalized. He said, "Not only was religion brought face to face with ethics, but it was identified with ethics." His parishioners were disturbed by his new found faith, especially after he preached about their failures to aid the escaped slave Anthony Burns and he refused to serve communion. Frothingham found himself uncomfortable in Salem.

A search for a new congregation led Frothingham to a new society that was found in Jersey City, New Jersey. This group was highly motivated to consider social questions and gave Frothingham complete freedom of the pulpit and supported his disinterest in serving the Lord's Supper. He soon found Jersey City restricted his interest in developing his social conscience, and after five years, he moved on to minister to a new society, Third Unitarian, in New York City. Here he enjoyed a 20-year ministry of immense popularity from 1859 to 1879. At first **Henry Whitney Bellows** did not realize the degree of radicalism that had developed in Frothingham's thought and Bellows had supported the creation of this congregation especially for Frothingham. After it became the "church of the unchurched," espousing a vague non-Christian theism, Bellows had nothing to do with Frothingham. The congregation erected a building in 1863, but six years later it was sold. Frothingham convinced the church to assume independent status in the wake of the formation of Bellows's **National Conference of Unitarian Churches** in 1865. The Third Unitarian now became the Independent Liberal Church.

Recognizing his fame as a leading nonconformist and renowned preacher, Frothingham was courted by a group to help form the **Free Religious Association (FRA)** and was its first president from 1867 (when it was founded) to 1878. Like his mentor Parker, he led his own congregation to meet in large halls. First they met at Lyric Hall and then in 1875 they moved to the Masonic Hall, where Frothingham preached to 600 or more, the largest congregation in New York City. When he left the congregation in 1879 it disbanded shortly thereafter. His theology evolved from Transcendentalism to what he called Rationalism, a completely scientific view. He expressed his theology in *The Religion of Humanity* (1872). During his final years in New York he began working on historical subjects; he wrote a biography of Parker and wrote the only complete history of Transcendentalism by someone involved in the movement, *Transcendentalism in New England* (1876). After he retired form the active ministry, he tried to restore his health by taking a trip to Europe. When he returned, he lived in Boston and settled down to a period of writing and scholarly work. Frothingham contributed a number of historical works including biographies of **George Ripley** and **William Henry Channing** and *Boston Unitarianism*, which was partly biography of his father. He returned to the Unitarian fold in Boston, becoming an active member of his father's old church. He finished his own autobiography in 1891, four years before he died on November 27, 1895, in Boston.

FRUITLANDS. A short-lived utopian community in Harvard, Massachusetts, Fruitlands was the brain child of **Bronson Alcott** and Charles Lane, but it fell to bickering and economic failure. In an era of idealistic ferment, Fruitlands was one of a series of visionary communities in America where a more spiritual and ascetic way of life was intended to be cultivated. Beginning on June 1, 1843, Lane and Alcott started this high-minded outcropping of their shared Transcendental philosophy. Calling themselves the Consociate Family and their house Fruitlands, the group held that property should be liberated from human ownership, so Fruitlands was held by a trustee. The members were all vegetarians, since it was believed that animals should not be deprived of their freedom. Clothing consisted of tunics for the men and bloomers for the women—all made from linen, as sheep could not be shorn of their wool, nor cotton used as it was a product of slave labor.

In addition to the cofounders Fruitlands was populated by the rest of the Alcott family and a variety of notables. Isaac Hecker stopped here on his spiritual pilgrimage that eventually led him to Roman Catholicism and the founding of the Paulist Fathers. Other advocates of the simple life included Samuel Bower, who was an Adamite or nudist, and Samuel Larned, who lived for one year on crackers and then for a second year on apples. One member expressed his individuality by reversing his name from Abram Wood to Wood Abram. Other prominent visitors included a variety of Transcendental leaders, such as **Ralph Waldo Emerson** and **George Ripley**. The community started its life in high spirits, but one by one people began to leave for a variety of reasons. Both Alcott and Lane went off on proselytizing missions when they should have been gardening. But the most significant problems developed between the founders. Lane began to advocate celibacy and the dissolution of the family, while Alcott wavered briefly. Eventually, Lane joined the Shakers, and Alcott reunited his family in a nearby farmhouse. The leaders' ultimate faith in the fullest possible development of the individual was the dream of this venture in communal living, but unfortunately this noble vision had only the briefest of lives, disbanding in mid-January 1844.

FULGHUM, ROBERT (1937–). One of North America's most popular writers and philosophers in the 1990s. Robert Fulghum was born in Enid, Oklahoma, on June 4, 1937. Growing up in Waco, Texas, he remembers that his favorite part of childhood education was "show and tell" because it was education that came from life experience. Fulghum has had an extraordinarily diverse career. During his college years and beyond he worked as a singing cowboy and ranch hand in ranches from Texas to Montana. He also rode in many rodeos. He received a B.A. from Baylor University in 1958. Along the way to becoming a minister Fulghum also worked at a number of other jobs, including bartender, IBM sales, and folk music teacher. He received a B.D. from **Starr King School** in 1961, the year he was fellowshipped and ordained as a Unitarian Universalist minister. From 1964 to 1966, he was minister of the Unitarian Universalist congregation in Shoreline, Washington, and he also served the Unitarian Universalist congregation in Woodinville, Washington, from 1964 to 1968. From 1968 to 1985 Fulghum was minister in Edmonds, Washington, and was named emeritus minister at the end of his tenure. Fame followed his days in the active ministry. In 1998 his first book, *All I Really Need to Know I Learned in Kindergarten* was published and went to the top of the *New York Times* best-seller list and remained there for nearly two years. Subsequent books also became number one best-sellers, including *It Was on Fire When I Lay Down on It* (1989), and *Uh-Oh: Some Observations from Both Sides of the Refrigerator Door* (1991).

Fulghum built his writing reputation on short, uplifting, humorous essays. Many of them were originally written for church newsletters. Fulghum has lived on a houseboat in Seattle, with his wife who is a physician, for many years. He has four children. An accomplished sculptor and artist, he has taught drawing and painting in Seattle and has also had several exhibits of his work. He is also a musician who plays the guitar, bass, and mandocello and more recently has performed with other authors in a celebrity rock band, the Rock Bottom Remainders. His works have been adopted by PBS for two television productions, along with a stage adaptation as well.

Fulghum has continued to publish books in recent years, some of them compilations of readings and stories. These books have reflected a commitment to supporting charitable organizations. Proceeds have been donated to Habitat for Humanity and Human Rights Watch. In all, his books have sold more than 15 million copies in 93 countries and been translated into 27 languages. Fulghum always states that he never intended to be a famous writer, but that he had thoughts to share that people wanted to hear. He claims he will not win a Pulitzer for his writing talents, but that he has won the refrigerator door award. Fulghum also raises Bonsai trees and enjoys sailing. He has traveled a great deal. In 1974 he lived in a Zen monastery in Japan, and in more recent years he has lived in Thailand, Greece, and France. Fulghum once said that he did not believe there was any meaning in life, but that a person is "capable of making life meaningful." His most memorable work has been the *Kindergarten* essay, which first appeared in the *Kansas City Bugle*. The simple lessons from the sand box include: Share everything, play fair, put things back where you found them, and clean up your own mess, among others. His other works include *Maybe (Maybe Not)*, *From Beginning to End*, *True Love*, and *Words I Wish I Wrote*. He has also written unpublished works of fiction.

FULLER (OSSOLI), SARAH MARGARET (1810–1850). The most important feminist writer in the 19th century and a leading figure in the **Transcendentalist** movement. Fuller was born on May 23, 1810, in Cambridgeport, Massachusetts, to Timothy and Margaret Crane Fuller. Her lawyer father imposed an intellectual rigor upon her from an early age, so that she was reading by age four and translating Latin by age six. When he went to Washington to serve in Congress, she often wrote to him in Latin. The educational pressures from her father helped lead to a lifetime of migraine headaches. When she was 14 she was sent to Prescot's Young Ladies Seminary in Groton, Massachusetts, where she became quite attached to its principal, Susan Prescott. After that she continued her schooling back in Cambridge with George Perkins. Fuller dropped the Sarah from her name because she felt it made her sound like an old maid. In 1833 the Fuller family moved to a farm in Groton, where Margaret felt isolated from the intellectual stimulation of Cambridge. After her father died in 1835 Margaret took over responsibility for the family. By this time she had developed a reputation as a genius and brilliant conversationalist. **James Freeman Clarke**, a childhood friend, helped launch her publishing career when early essays and poems appeared in his *Western Messenger*.

After an extended visit with the Emerson family, Fuller was introduced to **Bronson Alcott**, who hired her to teach Latin and French at the Temple School. After that she was offered a teaching position at a new school, the Green Street Academy, in Providence, which was dedicated with an address by her friend **Ralph Waldo Emerson** in June 1837. She left after two very successful years. The entire Fuller family moved to Jamaica Plain, Massachusetts, in 1839. During these years Margaret continued a rigorous course of self-study, especially translating works about and by Goethe. Fuller had already been the first woman accepted into the **Transcendental Club**, but in November 1839 she began another group exclusively for women. She started her "Conversations" where 25 women would come together weekly (usually at **Elizabeth Palmer Peabody**'s bookstore) to discuss religious, political, and aesthetic aspects of life. Fuller facilitated these sessions with ideas of her own and they continued for five years.

In 1840 she and Emerson began to edit the Transcendentalist journal, The ***Dial***. Some of the most important writers of the day appeared in its pages. In 1843 Fuller provided an intellectual foundation to the feminist movement with her article, "The Great Lawsuit: Man vs. Men, Woman vs. Women." It was later expanded into the book *Woman in the Nineteenth Century*, the most important women's rights book of the day. In "The Great Lawsuit" she said, "What a woman needs is not as a woman to act or rule, but as a nature to grow, as an intellect to discern, as a soul to live freely, and unimpeded to unfold such powers as were given her when we left our common home" (Hochfield, *Transcendentalists*, p. 359). Fuller wrote that as men realize that some men have not had a fair chance, they will realize that no woman has had a fair chance. This article was a declaration of the importance of personal self-dependence and gender equality. After Brook Farm was formed, Fuller was a frequent visitor to the Fuller Cottage, but she never joined. Critics have often claimed that Hawthorne's character Zenobia in *The Blithedale Romance* was based on Fuller.

In 1843 Fuller took a trip west with James Freeman Clarke. Her daily diary of the trip evolved into *Summer on the Lakes*, a look at some of the recent settlers and how they had displaced the native tribes. One reader who admired its content and other works of hers was **Horace Greeley**. He also supported many of her feminist ideas and consequently invited her to become a reporter for his *Tribune*, for which she later contributed some important literary criticism. She was able to take a long delayed trip to Europe when she left to be a foreign correspondent. In London she met Thomas Carlyle, the writer, who called her "an exotic from New England." Once the confident Fuller told him, "I accept the universe," and he replied, "By gad, you'd better." She also met Giuseppe Mazzinni, an Italian patriot and exile. She became fascinated with his revolutionary tales. Once she was in Rome, she met and subsequently fell in love with the Marchese Giovanni Ossoli, a young nobleman who was supporting the revolutionary cause. Fuller became pregnant and their son, Angelo, was born on September 5, 1848, in Rieti, Italy, where Margaret had fled for safety. They were married in a private ceremony the following year. Ossoli became involved in some of the battles defending Rome, and Margaret directed nurses at a hospital. But Rome fell to counterrevolutionary forces, and they had to flee. The family struggled to survive in Florence, and Fuller was dropped as a correspondent for the *Tribune*. Finally, they decided to book passage to America. On the night before they were to arrive, a terrible storm threw the ship off course and it hit a sand bar off Fire Island, New York. The family all drowned on July 19, 1850.

FURNESS, WILLIAM HENRY (1802–1896). A minister who had a long and significant pastorate in Philadelphia and was also an important biblical critic. Furness was born in Boston on April 20, 1802. He attended Boston Latin School where he developed a lifelong friendship with **Ralph Waldo Emerson**. After that he attended **Harvard College** and then entered the **Harvard Divinity School** in 1820. He finished in 1823, preached his first sermon in Watertown, Massachusetts, and candidated at a number of places, but did not secure a position. The following May he went to Baltimore to serve in an assistant capacity for three months. While he was there he received an invitation to preach in Philadelphia one Sunday. The church there, which had been founded by Joseph Priestley, had been without a minister for 29 years but was still operating. They invited Furness to stay and be their permanent minister. He accepted and was installed on January 12, 1825, with his classmate **Ezra Stiles Gannett** participating in the service. This relationship with the Philadelphia congregation continued for 71 years—50 as pastor and the remaining time before his death as minister emeritus. In 1825 he married Annis P. Jenks, and they had four children, including the architect Frank Furness.

The tiny remnant of a congregation in Philadelphia grew rapidly and a new church was built within three years at the corner of Tenth and Locust, designed by William Strickland. Furness held some controversial opinions, but his accommodating manner kept him out of the limelight in the **Miracles Controversy**. He sent a copy of his *Remarks on the Four Gospels* to **Andrews Norton**, his old teacher. Although Norton disagreed with the ideas, the willingness to seek his opinion pacified much of the antagonism that was vented on others who held Transcendentalist views. Furness accepted that the miracles actually happened, but he interpreted them as purely natural events and said that faith did not require confirmation by the supernatural. Furness was especially interested in the historical Jesus. *Remarks* (1836) was followed by several other books, including *Jesus and His Biographers* (1838) and *A History of Jesus* (1850). Furness said that the divine truth in Jesus' life was expressed in nature. "Let it be that he taught nothing more than the religion of Nature, still by concentrating all its force and loveliness in his individual being, by incorporating it with his life, and so teaching it as it had never been taught by any other, he made natural religion, HIS religion, HIS truth" (Furness, Remarks in Miller, ed., *Transcendentalists*, pp. 125–126).

Furness was an active abolitionist who turned the cellar of his home into a station on the Underground Railroad, and he entertained William Lloyd Garrison and others. He wrote a number of hymn texts. **Frederic Henry Hedge** worked with Furness on translating works from the German. Furness took an active interest in his son's architectural profession. When the father gave the closing address to the fourth annual convention of the American Institute of Architects in 1870, he urged the organization to break out of established molds. He said they should create "new orders of architecture." He had some skill as a draftsman and may have influenced his youngest son in this way. Furness wrote to his friend Emerson in 1852 that "one has great satisfaction in living in one's children." After Furness's active ministry ended, his son Frank designed a new church building for The First Unitarian Church. Located at the corner of Chesnut and Van Pelt Streets, it was dedicated in 1886. William died on January 30, 1896, in Philadelphia. He was an important liberal presence outside of New England at a time when Unitarian churches were scattered and isolated.

– G –

GANNETT, EZRA STILES (1801–1871). An important early advocate of creating institutional Unitarianism. Gannett was born on May 4, 1801, in Cambridge, Massachusetts, and was named for his mother's father, who was president of Yale. His father, Caleb, was a minister who served as steward of **Harvard College**. His mother died when he was only seven. After attending local schools, Gannetts started at Harvard College when he was 15, graduated in 1820, and then went to the **Harvard Divinity School**. **William Ellery Channing** noticed him and invited him to come to the **Federal Street Church** in Boston for a trial to preach half the time. He was subsequently called as Channing's assistant in 1824 and they worked together for 18 years. Upon Channing's death he wrote: "After my connection with this society, he encouraged me in every plan I undertook, welcomed every sign of increasing sympathy and energy among us, and cheered me under every occasion of despondency" (Gannett, *Ezra Stiles Gannett*, p. 213).

Gannett took on many of the pastoral and administrative duties of running the church. His organizational skills were immediately put to use in his role with the fledgling **American Unitarian Association (AUA)**. While his senior colleague was reluctant to commit to a strong institutional presence for Unitarianism, Gannett became one of the AUA's guiding lights. In May 1825, he helped draft the constitution for the AUA and he was also chosen secretary, a position he held for six years. He performed much of the new organization's administrative work, including sending aid to churches and employing missionary preachers. He also became an advocate of Joseph Tuckerman's ministry-at-large, and when the **Benevolent Fraternity** was organized in 1834, he became the secretary of that group. Gannett's conservative support of institutions also made him tentative when it came to the subject of slavery. **Samuel A. Eliot** said Gannett was a lover of order and government, and thus he feared the threats to the Union made by abolitionists at first, but he slowly changed positions. Even though he was a member of the younger generation of Unitarian preachers, he did not support the Transcendental positions, but maintained a moderate Christian stance. He married Anna L. Tilden of Boston on October 6, 1835.

Gannett suffered from ill health for about two years and traveled in Europe with hopes of restoring himself. After he returned home, he suffered a stroke and was forced to use crutches for the rest of his life. His senior colleague died in 1842, and Gannett became senior minister, but Channing had not been active in his ministry for many years. The following year Gannett was Dudleian Lecturer at Harvard Divinity School, and he received a D.D. In 1844 he was asked to become AUA president and held that post for five years. His work in service to the denomination continued in 1847 when he was appointed editor of the *Christian Examiner*, a position he retained until 1851.The neighborhood around the Federal Street Church was changing by 1850 and at the end of the decade the construction of the Arlington Street Church began. It was dedicated in 1861. As he aged Gannett considered retiring, but he continued to fulfill his duties, until August 26, 1871, when he was struck and killed by a train near Boston.

GANNETT, WILLIAM CHANNING (1840–1923). A leader of the Western Unitarians who advocated a broad-based free faith, he was an important hymn writer as well. Gannett had a long Unitarian pedigree. His father was **Ezra Stiles Gannett**, who was **William Ellery Channing**'s associate and then successor at the **Federal Street Church** (later Arlington Street Church) in Boston. Gannett was named after and christened by Channing after he was born on March 13, 1840. His mother Anna Tilden died when he was only six. Despite this church heritage, Gannett was unsure what he wanted to do with his life. He graduated from **Harvard College** in 1860 and taught school in Newport, Rhode Island. He tried **Harvard Divinity School**, but then left to work in the Sea Islands off South Carolina. Here the New England Freedman's Society employed him for four years. The work was hard and he was frequently ill, but he made a lifelong commitment to freeing African Americans from oppression. Here he managed farms and organized a school.

After he went to Europe for a year with his father, he returned to Harvard Divinity School and graduated in 1868. He immediately went west and took the relatively new congregation in Milwaukee, Wisconsin. After his father became ill, he returned east and served the church in East Lexington, Massachusetts. His father died in 1871, and Gannett spent the next few years working on a biography, *Ezra Stiles Gannett: Unitarian Minister in Boston, 1824–71* (1875). By 1877 he was ready to return to the west and was called to Unity Church in St. Paul, Minnesota. He began to use his poetic skills more and more and in 1880 coedited *Unity Hymns and Chorals* (1880). He wrote several hymns that have remained popular in Unitarian Universalist congregations, including "The Morning Hangs a Signal."

In 1883 he became minister at large for the **Western Unitarian Conference (WUC)**. After this, his relationships with the Western radicals deepened, especially **Jenkin Lloyd Jones**. Gannett (with Jones) founded and edited the WUC's periodical *Unity* for a time and held the copyright. He also wrote many Sunday School lessons. At the meeting of the WUC in 1886, **Jabez Sunderland** and Gannett squared off with the delegates finally passing a resolution offered by Gannett that the WUC would follow no dogmatic tests as a condition for fellowship but would welcome all who want to establish "truth, righteousness and love in the world." Although Sunderland opposed creeds, the two could not find a compromise. Gannett was stuck on eliminating the use of the phrase "kingdom of God." At the 1887 meeting of the WUC Gannett presented his ***Things Most Commonly Believed Today among Us*** and the group approved it by a large majority, but Sunderland was not present.

Gannett's statement helped become the basis for reconciliation in 1894 at the National Conference meeting in Saratoga, New York, where the gathering agreed that there would be no authoritative tests and that the churches accepted the religion of Jesus summed up in a practical way as "love to God and love to man." In 1887 Gannett was married to Mary T. Lewis. He was settled in Quincy, Illinois, for two years and then moved on to Rochester, New York, for his final parish settlement. **Susan B. Anthony** was a member of his congregation in Rochester who helped influence him to work diligently on woman suffrage issues. Together they also worked to have women admitted to the University of Rochester. He retired in 1908 and was named emeritus at the church. He died in Rochester on December 23, 1923.

GAY, EBENEZER (1696–1787). A leading liberal minister in the 18th century who prepared the way for the development of Unitarianism in America. Gay was born in Dedham, Massachusetts, on August 15, 1696, the youngest of eight children born to Nathaniel and Lydia Gay. Ebenezer showed a natural inclination for scholarly achievement early in life, and his father decided to steer him toward the ministry. He went off to **Harvard College** in 1710 with a good training in the classics, and he developed a reputation as a scholar. After he graduated in 1714, he began to prepare for his second degree and worked as a teacher, first in Dedham, then in Hadley, and later in Ipswich, all in Massachusetts. When he finished the degree he was called to the parish church in Hingham, Massachusetts, in December 1717 with a unanimous vote from both church and parish. At the beginning of his ministry he introduced the Half-Way Covenant, a device whereby the children of church members could have their children baptized, but they did not have to be confessing members of the church. Two years after he settled in Hingham, Gay married Jerusha Bradford in November 1719.

Although Gay's theology was somewhat evangelical in the early years of his ministry, his scholarly reputation made aspiring clerics flock to him, and his significant contribution of training many future liberals began at this time. He began to seriously align himself with the liberals after he participated in an ecclesiastical council in Eastham, Massachusetts, concerning the dismissal of Samuel Osborn, a radical Arminian whom Gay wanted to see vindicated. His leadership of the liberal faction was confirmed by his response to the Great Awakening and its excesses. In an ordination sermon for his nephew Samuel, Gay stressed both the covenant of works and the covenant of grace. Revivalists had made Samuel's beginning in Suffield, Massachusetts, difficult, and their lack of training and threat to the order and unity of established churches drove Gay to condemn their behavior and tactics. Despite divisions in Hingham leading to new parishes in South Hingham and Cohasset, Gay maintained harmony within his own community. As the years went by he became the confessor for the entire community. In 1745 Gay was asked to deliver the Election Sermon, a sign of his leadership among the clergy. Then in 1746 he gave the annual Convention Sermon, and this proved to be an attack on the upheaval caused by the New Light preachers.

In 1747 he preached at the ordination of his most famous and controversial student, **Jonathan Mayhew**, in Boston. After this Gay worked on developing a powerful Hingham Association of clergy on the South Shore, most of whom were preaching an Arminian gospel. Members of this association, with Gay usually leading the way, participated in councils all over New England. The greatest of these battles was in Leominster, Massachusetts, where Gay, Mayhew, and **Charles Chauncy**, the three leading liberals, all went to defend John Rogers against accusations of doctrinal errors. Gay made his most significant published contribution to the development of liberalism with his 1759 Dudleian Lecture, *Natural Religion*. Here Gay counseled his listeners that God had made humans rational beings who can discern what is needed for salvation through their own natures and relations. With his long ministry of nearly 70 years in Hingham, Gay became a symbol for community solidarity. This peace was interrupted by the Revolution. Gay became more and more loyal to the social order as violence escalated in Massachusetts. After 1765 he became an acknowledged Tory, as he generally believed in passive obedience to authority. In 1776 his son Martin sailed with the British to Halifax where he was exiled for eight years. Even though there were many disaffected people within the parish, Gay eventually reconciled with his detractors. After the war, Gay received a D.D. from Harvard and was made a trustee of Derby Academy. Toward the end of his life, Gay became involved in anti-Trinitarianism. Although a believer in the Trinity early in his career, he came to have close associations with the Englishman William Hazlitt, who was a Socinian and a disciple of **Joseph Priestley**. Hazlitt was refused access to the Weymouth pulpit, but he apparently preached in Hingham more than 40 times. Gay became seriously ill in the fall of 1786 and died the following March 18. Although he shunned public controversy his belief in natural religion, a benevolent God, and an innate human capacity for goodness led Gay to be called the first Unitarian and "the father of American Unitarianism."

GAY AND LESBIAN. The **Unitarian Universalist Association (UUA)** took its first steps toward affirming gay, lesbian, and bisexual people in 1970 when the annual General Assembly passed a resolution that called for the "end to all discrimination" against people of minority sexual orientation and also urged congregations to incorporate programs that led to a "more open and healthy understanding of human sexuality." This action was followed by a resolution in 1973, calling upon the UUA to establish an Office on Gay Affairs (now called the Office of Bisexual, Gay, Lesbian, and Transgender Concerns) at the denomination's headquarters. In addition to affirming gay human rights, the UUA began to address specific congregational concerns. In 1980 the **General Assembly (GA)** called upon congregations to end discrimination in employment practices (reaffirmed in 1989 as "Equal Opportunity in Ministerial Settlement"). In 1984 the

GA voted to affirm ministers who performed gay or lesbian Services of Union and to encourage congregations to support these ministers. Other actions in the late 1980s included opposition to AIDS discrimination and support for legal equity for gays and lesbians. In 1987 a Common Vision Planning Committee found that many gay, lesbian, and bisexual persons felt unwelcome in UU congregations, and the committee initiated a program to make the congregations more affirming. The GA subsequently voted into being the Welcoming Congregation Program in 1989, which in the past 10 years has proved enormously successful in breaking down barriers of homophobia. The most recent resolution by the GA was "Support for the Right to Marry for Same-Sex Couples" in 1996. Over the last 30 years Unitarian Universalist have been consistent advocates of affirming the human worth and dignity and legal rights of every gay, lesbian, bisexual, and transgendered person.

GENERAL ASSEMBLY (GA). The annual meeting of the **Unitarian Universalist Association (UUA)**. Every year since the consolidation of the **American Unitarian Association (AUA)** and the **Universalist Church of America (UCA)** in 1961, lay members and clergy have met to conduct the official business of the association. The schedule includes a wide assortment of program events, including speakers, worship services, and meetings of various affiliate organizations. Professional days are held prior to every GA. Each UUA congregation, depending upon their membership size, is entitled to send delegates. The meetings are held every June in the United States, except every 10th year when the GA must be held in Canada. General and Business Resolutions and Resolutions of Immediate Witness become the focus for the denomination. A General Resolution deals with issues of public policy with recommendations for action by groups not directly controlled by the UUA. These resolutions have represented a wide variety of peacemaking and social justice issues. Some of these have included: arms control, penal reform, gay and lesbian rights, opposition to capital punishment, and pro-choice on abortion. These resolutions are now called Study/Action Issues for Social Justice. A Business Resolution directly involves the administration and structure of the UUA. The business meetings may also include the amendment of bylaws and rules. Elections of UUA officers and trustees and members of UUA standing committees may also take place. The first General Assembly, which was the organizing meeting for the UUA, was held in Boston on May 11–15, 1961. The **Universalist Church of America (UCA)** also used the term General Assembly to denote their biennial business meetings from 1942 to 1960.

GENERAL CONVENTION. The Universalists first met in "General Convention" in 1793 in Oxford, Massachusetts. This group encompassed New England and New York, but it soon superseded the Philadelphia Convention (1790), and evolved into the Universalist General Convention. In 1803 the convention adopted its famous **Winchester Profession of Faith** and established a Plan of General Association with guidelines for meetings, rules for delegate status, and the professional standing of ministers. Churches were represented by both ministers and laity from the beginning. The Universalist organizational plan included church delegate representation, a statement of belief, and clerical guidelines, but they were slow to implement bureaucratic institutions to oversee publications or extension. These aspects of church life tended to be individualistic (certain ministers decided to publish periodicals) and haphazard (circuit riding house ministries).

At first the New England Convention was one of many regional groups, but it became the General Convention of Universalists in the United States in 1833. It was designated as a representative group of clergy and laity chosen by state conventions, which were first organized in 1825. The state conventions were made up of local associations formed by neighboring churches. The General Convention only had the power to act in an advisory capacity, with actual power residing within the state conventions, which usually had the authority to ordain ministers. Polity was Congregational at the local level, but more Presbyterial at the regional level.

Attendance at the General Convention was often poor, and there were many proposals to give it more power and central authority, all of which came to naught in the 19th century. After 1858 the convention established some committees on organization, but these groups could not administer programs efficiently. The convention incorporated in 1865, the year it adopted a new constitution. This document allowed for a permanent secretary—the first full-time salaried employee—and a treasurer. In 1870 the convention celebrated the centennial in Gloucester with the adoption of a new set of "Laws, Rules, Constitutions, and By-Laws." These new rules tried to give more authority to the convention. Local parishes were given recommended bylaws to follow, and state conventions were given authority over the parishes. The convention was given the authority to mediate disputes and raise funds. It was governed by a Board of Trustees and its delegates were representatives from the state conventions. Although it could recommend policies with its structure of appointed committees and not professional bureaucrats, it lacked the machinery to carry out effective policy management.

Many of the more effective programs were carried out by independent organizations. The Women's Centenary Association was responsible for much of the mission work, and the independent **Universalist Publishing House** became the denominational locus of print materials to spread the faith. The office of general secretary had been intended to give the convention a full-time executive when it was established in 1867, but this type of position did not work out until 30 years later when the office of general superintendent was created. After the 1889 meeting in Lynn, Massachusetts, the convention met on a biennial basis until 1960, which was a special and final session held in Boston. Early conventions were literally festivals of preaching, and although this tradition of hearing numerous sermons, including the important Occasional Sermon, continued into the 20th century, more time was given to business and plenary sessions to adopt resolutions, especially those with a social concern. For example, in 1925 the convention voted to allow members to be conscientious objectors. In 1942 the convention, which had been a forum for opinion and a source of funds, but never a central authority, became the **Universalist Church of America (UCA)**.

GENERAL SUPERINTENDENT. The office of general superintendent of the Universalist church was formed in 1898. Its creation was largely motivated by a speech given by Willard C. Selleck on "The Organized Church" at the New England Conference in Portland, Maine, on October 21, 1896. Selleck argued that the churches needed more central oversight, especially the large number of small congregations.

The position was conceived as a spiritual leader who would be a representative of the whole church. In October 1897 the General Convention meeting in Chicago passed a resolution calling for greater unity and continuity in the work of the parishes. The ministers, who were meeting in the Western Universalist Ministers Institute, had forwarded a memorial to the Convention affirming such action. Out of this came the "Chicago Covenant" calling for greater loyalty and subordination in the practical administration of the church. Other voices also began to support the idea of an executive position. The Vermont-Quebec convention called for a superior officer who would be called the "Bishopric of the Universalist Church." Action was already being taken by the trustees.

In January 1898, a field secretary plan was discussed, and a committee to consider the proposal was appointed in May. Finally in October, the committee recommended the appointment of a field secretary called the general superintendent. They chose Dr. **Isaac Atwood** of St. Lawrence for the position. A year later there was a proposal put before the General Convention by the New Jersey Universalists to change the title to the more dignified name of bishop, but this failed. Soon thereafter a system of state and regional superintendents was established.

Many Universalists were unsupportive and continued to be opposed to the position. They argued that under Congregational polity each congregation and ministers had a large degree of independence and freedom. Therefore, no authority would ever bevested in such a position. During his first year Atwood traveled and spoke a great deal. After Atwood retired in 1906 William H. McGlauflin was appointed to the post. He tried to reinvigorate the low morale in the denomination and also advocated for more social service work. The general superintendent had no direct responsibility to the General Convention, but the powers of the position were enlarged in 1917 when the general superintendent was given membership on the Board of Trustees. McGlauflin was followed by John Smith Lowe, who tried to emphasize world service. Next came Roger Etz, who wanted to make local churches more vital, but the depression era made for limited resources and energy and many of Etz's proposals were not implemented. Various suggestions were made in the 1930s to centralize leadership, even proposing that the general superintendent mediate congregational disputes and have the authority to remove ministers.

Robert Cummins, who held the position from 1938 to 1953, did much to effectively organize the denomination and move it beyond its narrow limitations as a Christian sect. Cummins was succeeded by Brainerd Gibbons, who, like Cummins, wanted to see Universalism moved beyond its narrow Christian orientation. He resigned in 1956 frustrated that the position made him "neither a minister or a businessman." The general superintendent job was abolished in 1961 when the two denominations consolidated, although the issue of whether the executive of the denomination is a spiritual or administrative leader has never been resolved. The last person to hold the office was **Philip Giles** (1957–61). He implemented a goal-setting plan called Operation Bootstrap. During his tenure a development program was started and the publishing house revitalized. Over the years the Universalists always struggled with issues of giving the position some authority and providing a sound financial base for its operation.

GILES, PHILIP RANDALL (1917–). The last **general superintendent** of the **Universalist Church in America (UCA)**, Giles steered the Universalists into the final stage of merger with the Unitarians. He was born in Haverhill, Massachusetts, on January 23, 1917. Giles received his degrees from **Tufts College** and began a long and varied career in the ministry with pastorates in Southbridge, Massachusetts, and Concord, New Hampshire. This was interspersed with stints of military service as an air force chaplain. He joined the Universalist headquarters staff in 1949 and served in the capacity of director of fund-raising (Unified Appeal), assistant to the general superintendent, and finally director of Ministry and Church Extension. He was named general superintendent on his 40th birthday.

Giles took charge of a disorganized and inefficient headquarters hampered by powerful independent state conventions. In response he proposed Operation Bootstrap, a four-year program to revitalize the faith. Although his plan was approved by the trustees, and a full-time extension director was appointed, and ministerial pensions increased, Giles found the Universalists were preoccupied with impending merger. After months of study of the information prepared by the Joint Merger Commission, Universalist congregations voted overwhelmingly to affirm the concept. After merger Giles's administrative skills were put to good use as a vice president for Field Services, a district executive, and later as head of development. Later in his career Giles served churches in Denver, Colorado, and Muncie, Indiana, and a number of interim positions. Giles recalled that merger "was a good idea and that it worked well," and that when he was appointed leader of the Universalists, they were "wary of power and institutions," and his goal was to strengthen the Universalist denomination "so it could carry more of its weight in the merger."

GLOUCESTER. The first Universalist church in America was organized in Gloucester, Massachusetts, in 1779, nearly five years after **John Murray** had first preached there in March 3, 1774. Under the leadership of Murray, the new sect attracted members from the First Parish in Gloucester. Although these dissenters had their membership suspended from the parish church in 1777 for attending Universalist worship services in members' homes, the tax assessors declined to consider them a legitimate religious sect. The group organized themselves into the Independent Church of Christ on January 1, 1779, with a covenant signed by 61 people, near equal numbers of men and women. A building was erected on the property of Winthrop Sargent and dedicated on December 25, 1780 (it was replaced by the present building in 1806). The Universalists were taxed and subject to property seizures until 1783, when some of the members convinced Murray to allow them to use his name in a suit against the First Parish. The case came to trial that year, but continued in litigation on appeal and review until June 1786 when the judges found that "teachers of any persuasion [are] entitled to the religious taxes of their adherents." As a result of this important test case, the Universalists moved to the forefront of the battle for the abolition of compulsory religious taxes in Massachusetts. In 1785, 85 members of the society signed a Charter of Compact. Among these people was Gloster Dalton, a freed slave. The town of Gloucester was a symbolic rallying place for Universalists and they held a huge centennial celebration there in 1870 to mark the anniversary of Murray's first sermon in America.

GOD. In response to their Calvinist faith, many liberals in the 18th century developed a fundamental belief that God was benevolent. This

God wanted His creatures to be happy and wanted them to develop their God-given capacities for the improvement of moral character to the fullest extent. This kindly God was made manifest in several doctrinal ways. The idea of a brutish God who would choose some people for salvation while condemning others to the fires of hell was rejected in favor of a God who gave all people a chance to embrace a universal offer of salvation. Because they believed that babies are born innocent, they rejected a God who would damn these infants to a life mired in sin. They also believed that human beings are free to respond to God's offer of salvation, and so they rejected the idea of a God who could create a creature who was not free to make the moral choices God required of them. In these ways the concept of God was reshaped in the development of Unitarian theology.

Universalists also affirmed a benevolent deity, but their emphasis initially was less on individual salvation and more on a God who promised salvation to everyone; thus the entire community was embraced by God's goodness. Both movements affirmed the unity of God, in which God is one and distinguished from the Son. This one God is chiefly understood by His moral character. This was also a break with Calvinism, especially for the Unitarians, who placed a greater emphasis on God's moral perfection rather than His power and majesty. God was viewed as a parent who educates, and thus the world was viewed as a place of education where humans pursue ever-growing virtue. Although **William Ellery Channing** and others expressed a belief in the miracles and Christian revelation, they also affirmed natural religion. The wonders of nature proved the existence of God. The concept of God evolved within the **Transcendentalist** movement from an external God to one that resides within everything, including each breast. Emerson believed that God is the moral law within us, and thus humans cannot only discern what is right and good, they can innately know what is right.

With the Transcendentalists, God began to lose its personality. When God the father became the Blessed Unity, then some liberals, such as **Henry Ware Jr.**, responded to this apparent blasphemy with diatribes on "The Personality of the Deity." **Octavius Brooks Frothingham** said that the idea of God as the father of humanity was nothing more than evidence of our intellectual limitation. He asked whether we could worship a force, a concept, or an abstraction. This became a special concern in the latter part of the 19th century when many liberals turned to a scientific naturalism as an outgrowth of the pantheism of Emerson, which saw the presence of God in every atom serving one universal end. While the 19th-century liberals stretched the concept of God, the early-20th-century liberals began to question whether God existed at all. Humanism as it first developed was defined as religion without God and affirmed that a worthwhile religion could be developed based wholly on human aspirations. When the **Humanist Manifesto** was published in 1933 it shook the **American Unitarian Association (AUA)**, but the Unitarians increasingly became defined more distinctly as a humanist movement. It became the dominant theological perspective in 1940s, 1950s, and 1960s. Universalists were slower to affirm the principles of humanism, with only one Universalist minister as a signer of the manifesto. The strong emphasis on humanism was evident in the **Unitarian Universalist Association**'s **(UUA)** "Committee on Goals" report in 1967. Here 28 percent of the respondents said that God was an irrelevant concept, while 44 percent affirmed that God could be equated with some natural process within the universe, such as love or creative evolution.

In the latter part of the 20th century, Unitarian Universalists began to embrace broader concepts of God beyond the anthropomorphic and patriarchal images of a father God in the sky who governed all affairs on earth. While there are still those in Unitarian Universalist congregations who do not find the concept of God useful, many new ideas about God have helped liberals embrace the idea of God more broadly. When the report on the "Quality of Religious Life in Unitarian Universalist Congregations" was published in 1987, the results were that 81 percent of Unitarian Universalists affirmed some concept of God, as compared to 70 percent in 1967. In 1987 only 18 percent found God an irrelevant concept (p. 34). This came only four years after a controversy over the development of new denominational principles and purposes, which were ultimately adopted in 1985. In 1983, *Time* magazine reported on "Deleted Deity: A Rather Radical Proposal" (p.62, June 27, 1983), a controversial UUA **General Assembly (GA)** in which the proposed principles did not mention God. This controversy was averted when the final version included a list of faith positions that were prominent within the pluralistic UUA fold, and this included "Jewish and Christian teachings which call us to respond to God's love." Some of the broader definitions of God have included feminist perspectives with emphasis on more inclusive language and images of the divine, liberation theology in which God is an advocate for the poor and oppressed and process theology in which two prominent Unitarian Universalist theologians have made important contributions. These are **Henry Nelson Wieman** who defined God as "creative interchange" whereby we listen and learn from one another and achieve greater spiritual understanding in these encounters and **Charles Hartshorne** who said that God draws human beings into becoming more loving and we in turn live our lives as the growing edge of an evolving God. Unitarian Universalists have long sought to speak of God in nonexclusive and nonsectarian ways, and this is reflected in the pluralism that characterizes liberal understandings of God.

GORDON, ELEANOR ELIZABETH (1852–1942). A member of the Iowa Sisterhood and important women's rights activist. Gordon was born on October 1, 1852, in Hamilton, Illinois, the oldest of six to Samuel and Parmelia (Alvord) Gordon. Born in a log cabin, she grew up on a large farm that was adjacent to where **Mary Safford** grew up. Sometime in the mid-1870s they pledged that they would work as a team for life. Gordon was an avid reader and, because of her mother's ill health, became the household manager. Gordon attended the University of Iowa in 1873–74, but her mother could not afford to pay for any more schooling. She became a teacher and assistant principal in Centerville and then a principal in Humboldt, where she was reunited with Mary Safford, who was serving the Unitarian church there. As a teacher she was accused of teaching "flagrant Unitarianism," as she encouraged the use of the scientific method. Gordon's religious background was a rich mixture, including an uncle and an aunt who were Unitarians. In 1885 Safford was called to the new Unitarian church in Sioux City and she convinced Gordon to go with her. For the next 20 years they would work together as a team extending the Unitarian faith and building churches. Under Safford's influence, Gordon decided to become a minister as well, and she was ordained in 1889 after she was able to go to Ithaca, New York, and study at Cornell for several months. She stayed in Sioux City for another seven years, but she primarily remained in Safford's shadow, who as the more charismatic figure often received more credit.

Gordon then struck out on her own as sole minister in Iowa City, Burlington, and then Fargo, North Dakota, and then back to an Iowa parish in Des Moines, where she relieved Safford who had become ill in 1904. In 1906 she combined ministry and social work with a stint at the Roadside Settlement House in Des Moines. She and Safford collaborated for many years on a Unitarian magazine, *Old and New*. She also served as field secretary for the Iowa Unitarian Conference until 1910. After that she left the Midwest and moved to Florida, where in 1910 she founded a church in Orlando with Safford. Many of her friends had moved to retire. She retired from active ministry in 1918. She later moved back to her old hometown of Hamilton, Illinois, where she died on January 6, 1942.

GREAT AWAKENING. The widespread growth of Arminianism was in many ways a response to the excesses of the great religious revivals of the 1740s. As the wave of evangelical pietism spread throughout New England, certain ministers spoke out against the unusual means. The revival created antagonisms among the clergy of the established Congregational churches. Many settled Congregational ministers felt itinerant preaching and its passionate style signaled a breakdown of the social and religious order. The schools of Old Light (antirevival) and New Light (prorevival) thought split the Congregational clergy into two parties. Then during the remaining years of the 18th century the two parties began to develop distinct and contradictory theological systems. A permanent bias against revivalism from some of the Old Light faction pushed some of them to an extreme wing of this group, and this became a catalyst for the future growth of the liberal or Arminian position.

While the New Light clergy were reviving and reemphasizing Calvinist doctrines, the Arminians concentrated on the natural reason of humanity and the benevolence of God. They increasingly began to believe that an individual's salvation was not solely dependent upon the grace of God, but while it was something that God offered, the person had to make the choice whether to act upon the offer. Salvation for them consisted of both faith and works. In the years following the American Revolution, the liberal position became better defined. Its greatest leaders in the 18th century were **Charles Chauncy**, **Ebenezer Gay**, and **Jonathan Mayhew**.

GREAT BRITAIN. Although there were several individuals, such as **John Biddle**, William Manning, and **Thomas Emlyn** (in Ireland), who held liberal religious beliefs, the beginning of liberal dissent in Great Britain is often dated to 1662, when 2,000 ministers left the Church of England because a new Prayer Book was published and an Act of Uniformity required all clergy to use that book. Those who were part of the Great Ejection were Puritans who included Independents and English Presbyterians and became known as nonconformists or dissenters. Most of the Presbyterians did not want to see doctrines used to test faith and were supporters of the Salters Hall petition movement, while the Independents were in favor of such tests. Much of the liberalizing of theology took place in Dissenting Academies, where more rational discourse and biblical criticism was allowed. The true organized beginnings of Unitarianism began with **Theophilus Lindsey**, an Anglican priest who discovered he no longer believed in the Trinity, resigned his pastorate, and moved to London. He turned an auction room on Essex Street into a chapel, and the first avowedly Unitarian service was held on April 17, 1774. Lindsey shared the early leadership with **Joseph Priestley**, who became famous for his scientific experiments, including the discovery of oxygen. The Presbyterians had mostly favored a more universal national church and feared being separated from other Christians, but Priestley wanted them to accept the anti-Trinitarian label. In addition to being against this sectarianism, many of the Presbyterians also disliked Priestley's radical political views, which eventually resulted in his emigration to America. Another dissenting group, the Baptists, joined with the fledgling Unitarian/Presbyterians and strengthened the movement. They offered a more evangelical style and became ardent supporters of the new Unitarian Fund for Promoting Unitarianism by Means of Popular Preaching set up in 1806 to promote the expansion of Unitarianism. The first missionary efforts were carried out by Richard Wright. He brought in a group of independent Methodist churches in Lancashire. Wright also evangelized in Wales and Scotland.

The leader of the liberal movement in South Wales was David Davis, who was minister at Llwynrhydowen from 1773 to 1827. Unitarian beliefs first developed in Wales much as they had in England within Presbyterian and Independent congregations that had formed in the 17th century, especially after 1662. This movement was particularly strong in rural communities in mid and south Wales where academies had been founded. The most important training center for Unitarian ministers developed at Carmarthen. One of the most influential early liberal tutors there was Thomas Perrot. Jenkin Jones, the great uncle of famed architect **Frank Lloyd Wright**, was a student of Perrot's. There are more than 35 congregations today in Wales, many of which are Welsh-speaking.

Back in England, **Thomas Belsham** began to establish his role as the leader of the Unitarians when he helped set up the Unitarian Society for the Promotion of Christian Knowledge and the Practice of Virtue by the Distribution of Books in 1791. This gave the Socinian dissenters an organized name and purpose, but any who worshipped Christ, including the Arians, were excluded. In 1813 the Trinity Act was passed, so that it was no longer a criminal offense to deny the Trinity. In order to defend their civil and property rights, the Unitarians established the Association for the Protection of the Civil Rights of Unitarians in 1819. All of the disparate groups for publishing, evangelism, and civil rights were united in 1825 in the British and Foreign Unitarian Association. By this date there were over 200 congregations in England.

As a direct result of the founding of the new Unitarian Association, a great mission effort was made in Scotland. George Harris drew large crowds and established 40 preaching stations there, but only the Aberdeen congregation remains today (four Scottish congregations in all). One strong influence on the Scottish movement was that a number of Universalist societies were formed there in the late 18th and early 19th centuries, including what is now St. Mark's Unitarian Church in Edinburgh. William Christie, a correspondent of Joseph Priestley, founded the first congregation in Scotland in 1781. Mission work also extended farther abroad. Contact was first made with Unitarians in Transylvania in 1822, and a missionary was sent to Madras, India, in 1831.

Liberal religion in Ireland began as a result of Presbyterians who refused to submit to confessions of faith. John Abernethy is considered the father of non-subscription in Ireland. He helped organize the Belfast Society for the discussion of theological problems, eventually resulting in the non-subscription controversy. In 1725 the Presbytery of Antrim, where Abernethy was settled, was excluded from the Synod of Ulster. One hundred years later another group, led by Henry Montgomery, was excluded from the General Synod. Three main groups of non-subscribers united in 1910 in The Non-Subscribing Presbyterian Church of Ireland. In their constitution, they affirmed the sacred right of private judgment and free inquiry in matters of religion. There are more than 30 congregations in Ireland. It is an affiliate member of the British General Assembly, but remains completely independent in its government.

In 1844 Parliament passed the Dissenters Chapel Bill, which protected the Unitarians and others from losing the chapels they had heretofore occupied. This grew out of the Lady Hewley case, where it was decided that trust funds could not go to groups who were illegal at the time that the trusts were established. With organizational beginnings and legal problems behind them, the Unitarians, under the leadership of **James Martineau**, began to search for a deeper spiritual life. He favored a more ecumenical organization that moved beyond mere sectarianism. He was rewarded in 1881 with the National Conference of Unitarian, Liberal Christian, Free Christian, Presbyterian, and other non-subscribing or Kindred Congregations. It was organized to bring together representatives from all the churches who affirmed a free search for truth. They began to meet on a triennial basis with the first gathering in Liverpool in 1882.

Unitarians were often active in social reform. An outstanding example is the work of Mary Carpenter, who founded the first girls' reformatory in Bristol in 1854, as well as a day school for poor children in 1846 and an industrial school for the homeless. John Pounds was a Unitarian shoemaker in Portsmouth, who though crippled by a fall into a dry dock started "ragged schools" (Carpenter preferred to call them free schools) where the poorest children learned to read and write. By the end of the late 19th century there were 360 Unitarian churches in the British Isles, but there was a problem with opposing factions. One group wanted the Unitarian name, and the other rejected the label in the name of freedom. By the early 20th century each side had its own college, newspaper, and hymnbook. This rift was finally healed in 1928 with the National Conference and the British and Foreign Unitarian Association merging into the General Assembly of Unitarian and Free Christian Churches. In the United Kingdom today there are more than 200 congregations concentrated primarily in Lancashire, the Midlands, and the London area. The General Assembly is headquartered in London, but the individual churches all have a congregational form of government. There are annual meetings of the General Assembly, held in April. Ministers are primarily trained at either the Unitarian College, Manchester, which was founded in 1854 by the Unitarian Home Missionary Board or at Manchester College, Oxford, which is a nondenominational school. The major publication is the *Inquirer*. There was very little growth in any churches, including Unitarian, in Great Britain in the wake of World War II

GREELEY, DANA MCLEAN (1908–1986). The last president of the **American Unitarian Association (AUA)** and the first president of the consolidated **Unitarian Universalist Association (UUA)**, Greeley was also a great advocate for many of the social issues of his day. He was born in Lexington, Massachusetts, on July 5, 1908. A fifth-generation Unitarian, Greeley's father recalled sitting behind **Henry Wadsworth Longfellow** in church in Portland, Maine. Seemingly destined for a role in denominational leadership, Greeley's path to ministry began when he was president of the youth group in his local First Parish in Lexington. He never looked back on his commitment to his faith. In college he served on the continental board of the **Young People's Religious Union** and eventually became its president. He also ran young people's conferences on Star Island, a denominational retreat that was always important to him. His undergraduate degree was from **Harvard College**, and then he went on to the **Harvard Divinity School** as well and received an S.T.B. in 1933. On December 27, 1931, he married Deborah Webster, who was literally the girl next door. Together they would have four children.

In 1932 he was called to the church in Lincoln, Massachusetts, and was ordained there on December 13, 1932. His ministry would only last two years there. He moved on to Concord, New Hampshire, for another short ministry before being called to one of three major milestone settlements in his life. This was a ministry at the Arlington

Street Church in Boston, where he was installed on November 4, 1935. Greeley was active in the community serving on the board of the Benevolent Fraternity throughout his entire ministry, with 10 years as president. He was also president of the North End Union, a settlement house that had once been a Unitarian mission church. He served on the AUA board for 12 years, and in 1945 he became its secretary. He left this position in 1953 to become president of the Unitarian Service Committee. He resigned from this post when he was running for the AUA presidency in 1958. During his time as president he helped bring stability to both **Beacon Press** and the Unitarian Service Committee. He was a complete advocate of merger with the Universalists, saying, "I believed in merger on the ground of our affinity with each other, and of our fidelity to the ideals of unity and brotherhood" (Greeley, 25 *Beacon Street*, p. 82).

Greeley's strong leadership abilities emerged after his election as president in 1961. This came at a crucial time, as his administration was beset with controversy over the issues of war and peace and race relations. As AUA secretary in the 1950s Greeley had been an outspoken advocate for human dignity in the midst of McCarthy era witch hunting, and this continued as president as he denounced the war in Vietnam, a conflict he had witnessed firsthand. Within the UUA and in society at large he wanted to see integration be successful, but he also understood the demands of the Unitarian Universalist Black Caucus. Most of all he wanted to save his beloved denomination from a split that would destroy it. The denomination survived, but many militant blacks left. In 1965 he led the UUA board to Selma, Alabama, to support Martin Luther King in his work for racial justice. At the end of his time as president, he taught briefly at the **Meadville Lombard Theological School**. Then he was called to be the minister at the First Parish in Concord, Massachusetts, in 1970, where he stayed for 16 years, retiring just prior to his death.

Before going there Greeley said, "My emphases in Concord will be both parochial and universal. I shall respect in one moment the integrity and self-sufficiency of the Concord parish yet in the next moment be eager for us to share with Copenhagen, Kolosvar, Capetown, Madras and Manila our devotion and our dollars" (Greeley, *25 Beacon Street*, p. 225). Greeley became devoted to internationalism. In 1986 he said that his most satisfying ministry had been the establishment of the World Conference on Religion and Peace. Starting in his own office in 1962 and making contacts all over the world, by 1969 he had built a world organization, partly forged through his friendship with Nikkyo Niwano, the founder of the liberal Buddhist group Rissho Kosei-kai in Japan. That same year he became president of the **International Association for Religious Freedom (IARF)**. Greeley was known for his great enthusiasm and tireless devotion to his faith. In 1969 he received the denomination's Distinguished Service Award. Before he died the Dana Greeley Foundation for Peace and Justice was established as a way to honor his vision that human conflict could meet with peaceful resolution. An athlete as a youth, Greeley was an energetic force and charismatic speaker. Historian David Parke called him "a field of force. He makes things happen." A powerful leader in turbulent times he had a 55-year ministry devoted to the dignity of the human person. Among Greeley's published works was the 1948 *A Message to Atheists*. His recollections of his presidency were published in 1971, *25 Beacon Street and Other Recollections*. He died on June 13, 1986.

GREELEY, HORACE (1811–1872). Known for telling people to "Go West!" and settle the land, Greeley was the founder of the *New York Tribune*. He was born on February 3, 1811, in Amherst, New Hampshire, to Zaccheus and Mary (Woodburn) Greeley. The family moved a great deal, as Greeley's father struggled to make a living. After residing for a time in Vermont, the family ended up in Erie County, Pennsylvania. Greeley's formal education ended when he was 14, but he was known as a champion speller as a child. In 1826 he became a printer's apprentice in East Poultney, Vermont. He later worked for the *Erie Gazette*, where he learned all the facets of journalism while still quite young. When he moved to New York City in 1831 he became a printer. He stayed in New York for the rest of his life. He married Mary "Molly" Cheney, a schoolteacher from Connecticut in 1836, and they had seven children together, but only two survived childhood, and their marriage was fraught with difficulty.

His first job as an editor came in 1834 with the *New Yorker*. Here he learned how to write editorials, but the publication collapsed after the economic panic of 1837. After that Greeley published two partisan political papers to support Whig candidates for office. The *Tri-*

bune first appeared on April 10, 1841, as a daily Whig "penny" paper. It soon won wide acclaim for its editorial quality, literary content and book reviews, and wide political and international coverage. Two important Transcendentalists served as literary critics. First **Margaret Fuller**, who wrote reviews of works by Edgar Allen Poe and others, and then the **Brook Farm** founder, **George Ripley**. He also employed Karl Marx as a European correspondent.

One of the central reasons for the paper's success was Greeley's ability to make it appeal to an international audience. By the Civil War, circulation for all *Tribune* editions was nearly 300,000. This included a weekly edition that was circulated throughout the country and gave Greeley a huge ability to influence public opinion. His editorials reflected support for a wide variety of social issues in 19th-century America. In commenting on one of the early women's rights conventions he said: "I recognize most thoroughly the right of woman to choose her own sphere of activity and usefulness." Despite this view, he was against woman suffrage. He also advocated for worker's rights including unionization and a belief in guaranteed employment, and also for temperance. For a time he was influenced by the socialist Charles Fourier, and he wanted to set up agricultural collectives. His invectives against the proslavery positions of U.S. House Speaker Albert Rust resulted in Rust using a cane on Greeley's skull inflicting a concussion when Greeley was reporting from the Capitol. His most famous editorial was issued in 1862, "Prayer of Twenty Millions," which implored Abraham Lincoln to declare immediate abolition.

Although Greeley was liberal on social issues, on financial issues he had a more probusiness approach to such issues as tariffs and the National Bank. In 1854 he helped form the Republican Party. During the Civil War his positions vacillated between pacifism and war drums, and he eventually wrote a history of the war in two volumes, *The American Conflict* (1864–66). Greeley was an active Universalist, especially after he moved to New York. He first encountered the faith in Vermont and decided he would choose this "kinder creed." In New York, Greeley joined **Thomas Jefferson Sawyer**'s church on Orchard Street, but after Sawyer left town in 1845, Greeley joined the Church of the Divine Paternity, where **P. T. Barnum** was a member. Greeley was familiar with its minister **Edwin Chapin**. He attended church frequently, arriving with the pockets of his long white coat filled with newspapers, and then would sleep before and sometimes during the service, opening his eyes only when Chapin was especially eloquent.

Greeley's Christology was Unitarian, but he also expressed a belief in Restorationism, a period of chastisement in the afterlife, but finally concluded that "all suffering is disciplinary and transitional, and shall ultimately result in universal holiness and consequent happiness." Greeley was a frequent delegate to Universalist **General Conventions** and was in Gloucester, Massachusetts, for the Centennial Celebration in 1870. Here he helped seat the Maryland delegation and read the report on "Diffusion of Universalism," which argued for the publication and distribution of more tracts. He called for the raising of an endowment fund for the establishment of a **Universalist Publishing House**, and this soon came to fruition. Years before he had given money toward the founding of the Canton Theological School at **St. Lawrence University**. In 1872 he was nominated for U.S. president by the Democratic Party and campaigned on a platform of returning control of the South to its "best men," but he lost to Ulysses S. Grant in a landslide. He died a month later on November 29, 1872, in a sanitarium, having been called insane. Dr. Chapin led the funeral for this pioneering journalist, who was one of the great public figures of the 19th century.

GULBRANDSEN, NATALIE WEBBER (1919–). A former **moderator** of the **Unitarian Universalist Association (UUA)**, Gulbrandsen was born on July 9, 1919, in Beverly, Massachusetts. The oldest of five children, her parents were Arthur and Kathryn (Doherty) Webber. Natalie grew up in the North Beverly Congregational Church and graduated from Beverly High School in 1937. She was active in girl scouting and led a troop while she was a student at Bates College in Lewiston, Maine, from which she graduated with a B.A. in 1942. During her college years she was also active in student government and was a dormitory proctor. She was hired after college to work with the Maine Child Welfare Department, but she was soon married to a dental student, Melvin H. Gulbrandsen. They moved to Boston, and Natalie became a Girl Scout executive for two years in Belmont, Massachusetts. In 1945 the Gulbrandsens had the first of five children and the next year moved to Wellesley, Massachusetts, where they joined the Unitarian Society of Wellesley Hills, and Natalie became active in the church. In 1958 she represented the Wellesley Women's Alliance at a meeting of the **International Association for Religious Freedom (IARF)** in Chicago.

By 1961, she was serving on the governing board of her local church, eventually served on most of its committees, and became president of the local branch of the **Unitarian Universalist Women's Federation (UUWF)**. She was also president of the local Girl Scouts council and with her husband, Mel, cochairs of Wellesley's METCO program, an education program where urban youth can attend school in the suburbs. She served for many years as a member of the Wellesley Town Meeting, was on the youth commission, and was president of the Wellesley Human Relations Service. In 1979 she and her husband received the Wellesley Community Center Service Award for devotion to volunteer work in their community. In 1971 Gulbrandsen joined the continental UUWF board, and eventually was its treasurer and then president from 1977 to 1981. During this time she began to serve on several UUA committees, including the Council on Ministerial Finances. She played a key role as UUWF president in surveying women leaders and helping to swing opinion to recognize the pervasive patterns of sexism in the UUA. In 1981 she was elected to the UUA Commission on Appraisal and IARF Council.

In 1985 Gulbrandsen was elected moderator of the UUA, the highest volunteer position in the association. She served two terms moderating **Board of Trustees** meetings and presiding over the **General Assembly**. She finished her eight years of working with President **William Schulz** in 1993. As moderator she was an active voice for establishing a partner church relationship with Unitarian congregations in Romania, and in 2002 she was honored by the Partner Church Council as being a founder of the program. During her term as moderator she joined the Coordinating Committee for a new interreligious peace action group, Choose Peace, in 1988. Gulbrandsen's interest in international liberal religion resulted in her being named IARF president from 1993 to 1996. Other denominational service included board chair of the **Church of the Larger Fellowship**, 1996–98, and chair of the Unitarian Universalist Women's Heritage Society, 2001–02. A humanist in her theological orientation, Gulbrandsen affirms liberal religion “because it gives me the freedom to pursue a lifelong search for truth.” Bates College honored her volunteerism with an honorary degree in 1996. She has also received the UUA’s Holmes-Weatherly Award for lifelong commitment to social justice and the UUA’s highest honor, the Distinguished Service Award, in 2001.

– H –

HALE, EDWARD EVERETT (1822–1909). Famed author and chaplain to the U.S. Senate. Hale was born in Boston on April 3, 1822. He was descended from the patriot Nathan Hale and his mother, Sarah, was the sister of Edward Everett, for whom he was named. He went to Boston Latin School when he was nine and the entered **Harvard College** when he was 13, the youngest member of the class of 1839. His father was a newspaperman and Hale learned much about writing and publishing as a boy. After college, he did not enter the Divinity School but prepared for the ministry under the tutelage of Samuel K. Lothrop, his minister at the Brattle Square Church, and John Gorham Palfrey. In 1846 he was called to the Church of the Unity in Worcester, Massachusetts, where he stayed for 10 years. In 1852 he married Emily Perkins, who was descended from Lyman Beecher.

In 1856 Hale went to South Congregational Church, Boston, where he had an active ministry until1899 and was then emeritus until his death. They erected a new building in 1861 on Union Park Street, which soon held one of the larger congregations in the city. Hale was a big man with a great deal of energy, always opening his doors to welcome visitors and always reaching out to those who needed assistance. During his career he was a prolific writer making frequent contributions to the *North American Review*, the *Atlantic Monthly*, and other publications. He was editor of the *Christian Examiner* for a time and also had editorial charge of his own magazine, *Old and New*. He was identified in the denomination with the **Broad Church Movement** and worked toward establishing the **National Conference**. During the Civil War he became known as a patriotic leader for the North and he also worked for the U.S. Sanitary Commission. This popular reputation was enhanced by the publication of his famous little book *The Man without a Country* (1863). He built on this fame with his story "Ten Times One Is Ten," which was first published in *Ten Times One Is Ten: The Possible Reformation* (1871). This led to the formation of Lend-a-Hand Clubs all over the country, eventually numbering 50,000 worldwide. These charity groups had the motto: "Look up and not down: Look out and not in; Look forward and not back: and Lend a Hand" (Eliot, ed. *Heralds*, vol. 4, p. 153).

Hale believed that ministers should be involved every day in reforming society. He was also a philanthropist, showing great generosity to many groups. Later in his career he became an advocate for an international confederacy, and a world court, showing he was far ahead of his time prophesying world government. In 1903 he was made chaplain of the U.S. Senate, a reward for his public gospel of patriotism and optimism. Here he was once asked, "Do you pray for the Senators, Dr. Hale?" and the chaplain responded, "No, I look at the Senators and pray for the country" (Brooks, *New England*, p. 418). Van Wyck Brooks called Hale the only rival of **Julia Ward Howe** for the title of national institution. Hale was an important public figure representing the best moral striving and social outreach of Unitarianism to the nation. He died at his home in Roxbury, Massachusetts, on June 10, 1909.

HANAFORD, PHEBE ANN COFFIN (1829–1921). The second woman ordained a minister in the Universalist church, Hanaford was born in Nantucket, Massachusetts, on May 29 (or May 6), 1829. Her mother died soon after her birth, and Phebe was the only child of this marriage. When her father remarried, he brought a son to the union, and together he and his new wife had seven more children. Phebe Coffin was a descendant of both the pilot of the *Mayflower* and the founder of the first settlement on Nantucket. She was brought up a Quaker. Trained as a teacher, she spent four years on the island practicing her profession before marrying Joseph Hanaford, a physician, in 1849. After her marriage she became a Baptist but was converted to Universalism following the deaths of two of her siblings. The Hanafords had two children, Howard and Florence. The couple separated in 1870. While raising her children Hanaford became a writer to help supplement the family income. She produced 14 books and also wrote poetry and prose for periodicals. After she became a Universalist, she edited the monthly magazine the *Ladies Repository* and a Sunday School paper, *Myrtle*.

Hanaford was encouraged to pursue the ministry by **Olympia Brown**, the first Universalist woman minister. Hanaford was ordained and installed at the First Universalist Church in Hingham, Massachusetts, in 1868, the first ordination of a woman in New England. **Julia Ward Howe** composed a hymn for the occasion. Hanaford was remembered for her "Floral Sunday" where the church was filled with flowers and canaries were suspended in cages. She was called to the Universalist Society of New Haven, Connecticut, in 1870. She brought with her the woman who became her life-long companion, Ellen Miles. While in Connecticut, Hanaford served as the first woman chaplain for the House and Senate. In 1874 she went to Jersey City, New Jersey, and she later served another congregation in New Haven and finally in Portsmouth, Rhode Island. She retired from active ministry in 1891. Always a strong advocate of social reform, Hanaford signed a pledge not to drink liquor at the age of eight. Throughout her career she was a strong supporter of women's rights and was involved in several organizations. She once wrote, "Man was not made subject to woman, nor should woman be subject to man. Neither men's rights nor women's rights should be considered, but human rights—the rights of each, the rights of all. Men and women rise or fall together." Hanaford was especially interested in the biographies of prominent women and published *Women of the Century* (later reissued as *Daughters of America*) in 1876. She lived for a time in New York City, continuing to be active in women's causes, including membership on the revising committee for *The Women's Bible*. Later she moved to Rochester, New York, and died there on June 2, 1921.

HARPER, FRANCES ELLEN WATKINS (1825–1911). An important writer and abolitionist, Harper was born in Baltimore, Maryland, on September 24, 1825. A free black, she was orphaned at an early age and raised by an aunt. She attended the William Watkins Academy for Negro Youth, which her uncle founded, and developed an interest in literature. Her first collection of poetry, *Forest Leaves*, was published when she was only 20. Moving to Columbus, Ohio, when she was 25, Harper taught domestic science at Union Seminary (now part of Wilberforce University), a school for free Africans founded by the African Methodist Episcopal Church. There she became committed to the abolitionist cause and, after moving to Philadelphia and giving up teaching, she became a prominent lecturer and activist, especially for the Pennsylvania Anti-Slavery Society. Apparently, she was such a powerful lecturer that some people refused to believe that a black woman was capable of this kind of effectiveness and accused her of being a man dressed as a woman or a white woman painted black. In 1860 she married Fenton Harper, and they had one child, Mary. But Harper was a widow in four years and returned to traveling and lecturing. She published several collections of poetry and her only novel in 1892, *Iola Leroy or Shadows of the Uplifted* (republished by Beacon Press in 1987). She lectured for the Women's Christian Temperance Union, especially fighting against the organization of segregated chapters.

Harper was one of the founders of the National Association of Colored Women. In 1894 she became the director of the American Association of Educators of Colored Youth. She also became active in the women's suffrage movement. Although she had a long association with the A.M.E. Church, she was a member of the First Unitarian Church in Philadelphia, where her funeral was held (she died February 20, 1911). In her essay, *Our Greatest Want*, she outlined her spiritual longings and her dreams of equality and justice. "We want more soul, a higher cultivation of our spiritual faculties. We need more unselfishness, earnestness and integrity. Our greatest need is not gold or silver, talent or genius, but true men and true women."

HARTSHORNE, CHARLES (1897–2000). One of the most important theologians of the 20th century, he developed the idea of "process" theology following the thought of Alfred North Whitehead. Hartshorne was born on June 5, 1897, in Kittanning, Pennsylvania. His parents were Marguerite Haughton and Francis C. Hartshorne, an Episcopal priest whom Hartshorne credited with gifts of compassion and thoughtfulness. His formal education began at Haverford College in 1915, but he left to serve in the army in World War I, where his experience as a stretcher bearer later influenced his theology. After the war he finished his college work at Harvard University, where he also completed a Ph.D. with a dissertation on "The Unity of All Things." For two years he studied in Europe. After his return to Harvard as a research fellow and instructor he helped edit the papers of Charles Sanders Peirce. It was during this time that he became an assistant to Whitehead.

In 1928 Hartshorne accepted a position in the Philosophy Department at the University of Chicago, where he remained until 1955. Shortly after moving to Chicago he married Dorothy Cooper, and they had one daughter, Emily. Somewhat isolated in the Philosophy Department, he received a joint appointment at the Divinity School. In the subsequent years, he developed his "process theology." His major works included: *Beyond Humanism: Essays in the New Philosophy of Nature* (1937), *Man's Vision of God and the Logic of Theism* (1941), *The Divine Relativity: A Social Conception of God* (1948), and *Reality as a Social Process: Studies in Metaphysics and Religion* (1953).

Difficulties in the philosophy department finally led Hartshorne to seek a position elsewhere and he moved on to Emory University until 1962 when he received an appointment at the University of Texas in Austin, which he retired from in 1976. Hartshorne viewed reality as dynamic and therefore had a worldview that stated that what is real is in process and everything that is static must be past or dead. This also applied to God, so that he believed God was in the flow of time and subject to change just like everything else. Hartshorne theorized that God has a dipolar nature, so that God exists no matter what else might be, but the character of God changes based on choices humans make. He created the term "panentheism," which means that everything in the world is experienced by God, but nothing in the world is God. Much of Hartshorne's thought focused upon God, but he did little to develop a broader Christian theology. He was a firm advocate of human freedom in a relational world and a believer that God is always with us responding and lovingly drawing us toward a greater fulfillment. While rejecting the traditional notion of God's omnipotence, Hartshorne said that God is the everlasting recipient and preserver of value and memory. He continued to publish in his later years, including *Omnipotence and Other Theological Mistakes* (1983). Hartshorne had a lifelong interest in birds and even theorized that birds sometimes sing for the pure pleasure of the song. He advanced this idea in *Born to Sing: An Interpretive and World Survey of Bird Song* (1973). He published an autobiography in 1990: *The Darkness and the Light: A Philosopher Reflects upon His Fortunate Career and Those Who Made It Possible.* He also enjoyed writing poetry. The man who said, "The reward for living is the living itself," died on October 9, 2000. His memorial service was held at the First Unitarian Universalist Church of Austin, Texas, where he was a longtime member.

HARVARD COLLEGE. From its beginnings Harvard College in Cambridge, Massachusetts, had a special relationship to the training of ministers and eventually the evolution of liberal religion. When the school was established in 1636 the vote of the General Court indicated a concern that the next generation of ministers be literate. Over the decades Harvard developed a reputation for being "free and catholic." By 1740 the influence of Harvard came to predominate in the pulpits of eastern Massachusetts and northeastern Connecticut. During the late 18th century, most of the pulpits in Connecticut and western Massachusetts began to turn over and be occupied by Yale graduates. Those who opposed the **Great Awakening** in Harvard territory tended to become Arminian or proto-Unitarians in their theology. Harvard also produced its share of moderate Calvinists as well as Arminians. Harvard gained the reputation of being "captured by the liberals" after **Henry Ware** Sr. was elected Hollis Professor of Divinity in 1805, and shortly thereafter a Unitarian, Samuel Webber, was elected president. The largest numbers of faculty members in the 1830s were avowed Unitarians and the Divinity School was formed in response to the orthodox center at Andover. Perhaps most significant of all is the fact that every president of Harvard in the 19th century was considered a Unitarian. Even the curriculum at Harvard centered on the Scottish Moral Philosophy that had direct associations with the Unitarians and their beliefs about religious morality that formed a part of human character and regulated all motives and actions. The character of Harvard began to change under President Charles William Eliot in the post-Civil War era. Harvard became a place for competing philosophies rather than a singular expression of Unitarian liberal arts.

HARVARD DIVINITY SCHOOL. The professional training school for clergy at Harvard University in Cambridge, Massachusetts, has had a long and significant relationship with Unitarianism. **Harvard College** was founded in 1636 to train ministers for service in a godly commonwealth. Increasingly during the 18th century, Harvard became the school that was identified with liberal factions within the Congregational church. These beginnings reflected a breakdown in the Standing Order of Congregational Churches in Massachusetts and the reality of greater religious diversity. Following the religious revivals known as the **Great Awakening**, Harvard and its students became identified with positions that were critical of the revival and affirming of plain, rational divinity. The tension between the factions within the Congregational church began to explode in 1805 with the election of **Henry Ware** Sr. to the position of Hollis Professor of Divinity. Once the college elected an acknowledged liberal, Samuel Webber, to the position of president the following year, the orthodox announced that Harvard had been "captured" by the Unitarians and further efforts to maintain a theological balance between unitarian and Trinitarian were fruitless. Feeling the need to train orthodox students in a setting that was more compatible to their theological orientation, Andover seminary was founded in 1807.

The Congregationalists established a pattern for all denominations, as numerous seminaries designed to perpetuate and spread the special teachings of their particular sect were established. In 1810 John T. Kirkland became Harvard's president. Although Harvard had been founded to train ministers, it concentrated its efforts on undergraduates and offered a liberal education rather than formal vocational training. Kirkland felt an urgent need to change this, especially after the founding of Andover challenged him to realize that vacant pulpits might be filled by Calvinists if they did not act. In 1811 a report on the "Theological Institution at Cambridge" was made and those who wished to become ministers were given more directed study. In 1815 Kirkland appealed for funds for divinity students culminating in the establishment of the Society for the Promotion of Theological Education in Harvard University in 1816. Although more resources and faculty were given over to the education of clergy, the seminary did not become a separate administrative part of the University until 1819. The school dedicated its first building, Divinity Hall, in 1826. Despite some organizational difficulties, the school made initial progress. The leading light until 1840 was Henry Ware Sr., who was seemingly always present at the school to offer stability and was the senior member of the faculty. The fields of study included: natural and revealed religion, Hebrew, biblical criticism, ecclesiastical history, and pastoral theology. Henry Ware Jr. was commonly thought to be the ideal parish minister, and through his classes in pastoral care he became a spiritual guide and friend to most of the students. Life at the school was relatively stable into the 1830s, but this was disrupted by the great controversy surrounding **Ralph Waldo Emerson**'s address to the graduating class in 1838. The ***Divinity School Address*** brought forth all the wrath of leading Unitarian theologian **Andrews Norton**, who responded with *A Discourse on the Latest Form of Infidelity*.

After this period one controversy after another followed around such issues as **Transcendentalism**, evolution, and slavery. The Divinity School remained small throughout the 19th century. There were less than 25 students enrolled and the faculty was small. Finally, the controversies coupled with legal hassles led to a complete decline of morale in the Reconstruction period. **Francis Greenwood Peabody**, who graduated in 1872, said his education was "a disheartening experience of uninspiring study and retarded thought" (as quoted in Sidney E. Ahlstrom, "The Middle Period [1840–1880]" in Williams, ed., *The Harvard Divinity School*, p. 91). Peabody was an important figure in the revitalization of the school. He became Plummer Professor of Christian Morals in 1886 and eventually became dean. Hoping to implement an approach following a German model of theological education, the school came to be described by three frequently used adjectives: "unsectarian, scientific, and broad." Harvard became the first collegiate institution to adopt voluntary religious exercises rather than compulsory chapel.

By 1900 Harvard was on its way to being the nondenominational seminary it is today thanks largely to the efforts of Charles C. Everett, who was dean at the Divinity School from 1878 to 1900. Everett was especially responsible for introducing non-Christian religions, and so by the late 19th century the demands of comparative religion made it impossible for the divinity school to be called a Unitarian institution any longer. Harvard President Charles W. Eliot maintained two Unitarian professors on the faculty, but this was done primarily to recognize the support the school received from a group of churches. The efforts to broaden its approach seem to have proven successful. By 1927 there were 18 faculty members and 104 students. Through the early decades of the 20th century registration soared, and the faculty included such luminaries as Albert Darby Nock, **William Wallace Fenn**, and Dean Willard Sperry. By the 1950s the school was suffering from low morale, much as it had in the post–Civil War period. Fortunately, the president of the University, Nathan M. Pusey, carried out his intentions to revitalize the school and helped fulfill a pledge to make it the finest theological school in the country. In recent years, this nondenominational school has seen an increasing number of Unitarian Universalist students enrolled. It remains the central East Coast seminary for the training of Unitarian Universalist ministers.

HAWTHORNE, NATHANIEL (1804–1864). The first great American novelist was one of the original subscribers to the utopian community at **Brook Farm**, but his thought had a deeper sense of sin and evil than most of his Transcendental friends. Hawthorne's ancestors came to America in 1630. Judge John Hathorne served as a magistrate in Salem during the witch trials. Because of this, Hawthorne always remembered the evil that good men and women can commit. Born in Salem, Massachusetts, on July 4, 1804, his early years were difficult. His father, a ship's captain, was lost at sea when Nathaniel was four, and the family was plunged into relative poverty. At a young age Nathaniel began to make up stories where the main character ended up at the seashore declaring that he would never come home again. Hawthorne's mother was reclusive—a trait that also describes the son, whom **Herman Melville** referred to as "the shyest grape." After his graduation from Bowdoin College, there was a period of about 12 years when Hawthorne lived in Salem at what he referred to as "castle dismal." Even though there was a family pew at the First Church of Salem, Hawthorne was a nominal parishioner. Religiously, Hawthorne wanted his readers to understand on a profound level that each and every person is capable of committing great evil. He was critical of those who were convinced of their own virtue, especially the upper classes. This is depicted in the *The House of the Seven Gables*, in which the failed artist Clifford is wrongly imprisoned by Judge Pynchon.

Hawthorne had a strong understanding of history and believed that the past haunts each person until we find a way to creatively reconcile ourselves to it. Hester Pryne in Hawthorne's *The Scarlet Letter* was based on Anne Hutchinson, the brave woman who spoke up for religious freedom but was scorned for her willingness to break with the conventions of society. His first novel, which depicted life at Bowdoin, was published in 1828. During these years he traveled and hiked all over New England and began writing and publishing stories, some of which were collected in *Twice-Told Tales* (1837). He became engaged in 1838 to one of the famous Peabody sisters, Sophia. Prior to their marriage in 1842, Hawthorne worked at the Boston Custom House and was a resident of Brook Farm, the socialist cooperative that was started by the Unitarian minister **George Ripley**. He invested the large sum of $1,500 in this experiment, which he undertook to observe communal life, but it also helped him postpone his marriage date. His experience there was later captured in the novel *The Blithedale Romance* (1852), in which the character based on **Margaret Fuller** is compared unfavorably with her Transcendental heifer. After their wedding Nathaniel and Sophia moved to Concord, where they lived in **Ralph Waldo Emerson**'s ancestral home, The Old Manse. Eventually they had three children: Una, Julian, and Rose.

Only a few years later, the family returned to Salem, where Hawthorne was employed at the Custom House. His fortunes changed with the publication of *The Scarlet Letter* in 1850. After a brief period in the Berkshires where Herman Melville wanted to pursue a deeper friendship than Hawthorne was willing to commit to, the Hawthornes moved back to Concord. Some of his greatest literary output occurred in the next few years, including *The House of the Seven Gables* in 1851. After his Bowdoin friend Franklin Pierce became president, Hawthorne was rewarded with a position at the U.S. Consul in Liverpool, England, where he rented a pew in Renshaw Street Chapel (Unitarian). His last novel came about as a result of this appointment. His family had a long holiday on the continent, and the resulting *The Marble Faun* (1860) had an Italian setting. Hawthorne brought his family back to Concord in 1860, and he died there four years later on May 19. The service was conducted at the Unitarian Church by **James Freeman Clarke**, the same minister who had united Nathaniel and Sophia in what became a "holy and equal marriage" years before.

HEDGE, FREDERIC HENRY (1805–1890). A brilliant and far-sighted minister who reconciled his Transcendental thought with a firm belief in upholding the institutional church. Hedge was born on December 12, 1805, in Cambridge, Massachusetts. His father, Levi, was a professor at **Harvard College** of logic and philosophy. When he was only 13 Frederic sailed for Europe with his tutor George Bancroft, the future historian. Hedge attended a private school while his mentor went to the university and, as a result, acquired a good working knowledge of the language and the literature. In 1823 he came back to begin his education at Harvard with advanced standing. Within two years he was finished, and although he had hoped to be a poet at one time, he entered Harvard Divinity School, following his father's wishes. He started a lifelong friendship with **Ralph Waldo Emerson** who was also there. After graduation in 1828 he was settled in West Cambridge (now Arlington), Massachusetts, the following year. In 1830 he married Lucy Pierce, the daughter of the minister in Brookline, Massachusetts.

Hedge wrote a number of articles for the *Christian Examiner*, in which he introduced some of the German Idealism and the thought of Immanuel Kant to America. Because of this, he is often acknowledged as one of the early Transcendental voices with the publication of an article on Samuel Taylor Coleridge in 1833. During this time he proposed that the young group of friends that was interested in the new philosophy ought to get together to discuss their ideas. The idea was adopted but Hedge was called to the ministry of the Unitarian Society in Bangor, Maine, in 1835, after some conflict at West Cambridge. He then tried to remain active in the **Transcendental Club**, which met when he returned to Boston for visits and became known as Hedge's Club. Hedge was "exiled" to Bangor for 15 years. Yet the distance between him and the controversies in Boston may have helped him develop a greater insight into the positive aspects of the institutional church than many of his radical friends who saw it as outmoded. Near the end of this pastorate he became president of the **American Unitarian Association (AUA)**, a largely honorary title at that time. In 1853 he produced two liturgical works with Frederic

Dan Huntington. One of these, *Hymns for the Church of Christ*, marks the first appearance of Hedge's translation of Martin Luther's famous "A Mighty Fortress Is Our God." Unlike many of the other Transcendentalists, Hedge had a great respect for tradition and historical authority. In 1846 he wrote that a true church must combine "the spiritual rights of the individual with the spiritual interests of society." He is identified with **Henry Whitney Bellows** and **James Freeman Clarke** in the "Broad Church" group that wanted to strengthen the institutional church and he gave an important sermon with that name before the AUA in 1860. Hedge believed that the divine purpose is carried out through the church, and that that church must one day put aside all of its division into sects and denominations and see its essential unity. He is often credited with being the first person to use the term *ecumenical*.

After Bangor, Hedge was called to the Westminster Congregational Church in Providence, Rhode Island (1850–56), and then finally the First Parish in Brookline, the longest settlement of his career of 16 years. The ministry in Brookline allowed him the opportunity to take on two other roles. From 1856 to 1878 he taught ecclesiastical history at Harvard Divinity School and also served as editor of the *Christian Examiner* from 1857 to 1861. When he retired from active ministry in 1872 he moved to Cambridge to become a professor of German language and literature at Harvard College. Theologically Hedge embraced Darwinism, saying that God and history were both evolving into higher and higher forms. Hedge once characterized his views as "enlightened conservatism." Many of his views were summarized in *Reason in Religion* (1856), where again he parts with the Transcendentalists who are those who "disparage what is outward in religion." Hedge says, "Those churches are the strongest that have most of it; strongest not only in the way of efficient action and ecclesiastical power, but strongest in spiritual vitality" (Hedge, *Reason in Religion*, p. 306). Hedge plays a particularly crucial role in blending radical religious intuition with a vision of a strong church based on ecclesiastical traditions and history. He died on August 21, 1890, in Cambridge.

HIGGINSON, THOMAS WENTWORTH (1823–1911). Called a man whose whole life was a "sermon on freedom," Higginson had a fascinating career as minister, editor, writer, and abolitionist. He was born on December 23, 1823, in Cambridge, Massachusetts. His father died when he was 11. The youngest in his class, Higginson matriculated at **Harvard College** when he was 14 and graduated in 1841. He was already writing poetry and had four poems published in 1843. He entered **Harvard Divinity School** in 1844 and although he dropped out for a time, he graduated in 1847. His Visitation Day student sermon was on the clergy and reform. That same year he was called to serve the First Religious Society, Unitarian, in Newburyport, Massachusetts. He also was married to Mary Channing at this time. His radical social views quickly led to his dismissal from the pastorate in Newburyport, but he remained in the area to begin a lecturing career. He became an ardent abolitionist and helped form the Boston Vigilance Committee to resist the Fugitive Slave Law. He also helped convene the Worcester Woman's Rights Convention in 1850, and ran for Congress on the Free Soil ticket but lost.

In 1852 Higginson was called to serve Worcester's Free Church. He was twice involved in cases involving runaway or former slaves, Thomas Sims in 1851 and Anthony Burns in 1854. He was indicted in the Burns case but never prosecuted. His sermon "Massachusetts in Mourning" was about the response to the Fugitive Slave Law. Later in the decade he recruited and armed settlers in Kansas to keep it from becoming a slave state. He met with John Brown in 1858 and agreed to support him financially. After Brown was captured, he made a plan to rescue him. After this he wrote about many slave revolt leaders. Although he is frequently remembered as an activist, Higginson's chief reputation was as a writer, and he became a regular contributor to the *Atlantic Monthly*, especially nature essays.

After the Civil War began, Higginson showed interest in forming a regiment. Eventually he became a colonel of the first regiment of freed slaves and, after the training period, went into battle with them. He received a medical discharge after he was wounded. Articles began to appear on this experience, which later evolved into the book that became a classic in American history, *Army Life in a Black Regiment* (1870). Higginson continued his other literary interests as well. In 1862 he began a correspondence with the reclusive poet Emily Dickinson and later edited her poems. His first book, *Outdoor Papers*, essays on nature, was published in 1863. He moved to Newport,

Rhode Island, where as a member of the local school board he worked on integrating the schools.

Higginson became one of the founders of the **Free Religious Association (FRA)**. One lecture for them, which was later republished for the World Parliament of Religions, was called "The Sympathy of Religions." First written in 1855, he wrote, "The human soul, like any other noble vessel, was not built to be anchored, but to sail. . . . Every year brings new knowledge of the religions of the world, and every step in knowledge brings out sympathy between them" (Howard, N. Meyer, editor, *The Magnificent Activist*, pp. 354–355). He continued to write and publish essays, but achieved his greatest popularity with a best-seller, *Young Folks' History of the United States*. In 1877 his wife Mary died after a long illness. That same year he began two long standing associations. First, he signed on as a contributing editor of the *Woman's Journal*, which was the principal publication of the American Woman Suffrage Association. He also began a stint as poetry editor of the *Nation*, a position he held for 26 years. He was remarried within two years to Mary Thacher, and they moved back to Cambridge. In 1881 a daughter Margaret was born.

In 1884 Higginson published a biography of **Margaret Fuller** Ossoli. He also began to write a regular column for *Harper's Bazaar*, "Women and Men," in which he continued a lifelong fight to end the stereotyping of women. Higginson was one of the first people to show the connection between smoking, addiction, and cancer. In 1888 he ran for Congress, but lost. Even though Emily Dickinson had died four years previous, Higginson found a publisher and coedited her first volume of poems. Another volume soon followed, as he continued to write and publish essays at a prodigious pace. In 1895–96 Higginson published a two-volume edition, *Massachusetts in the Army and Navy during the Civil War*. Seven volumes of his collected works were published in 1900. Into the new century he continued to write, especially biography including one on his father, Stephen Higginson. More essays followed, including the beginnings of a series on beliefs about immortality, but its completion never occurred. Thomas Wentworth Higginson died on May 9, 1911, at the age of 87.

HOLLIS PROFESSOR OF DIVINITY. The election of Henry Ware as Hollis Professor of Divinity at Harvard in 1805 is considered the precipitating event in the Unitarian controversy, the splitting of the **Standing Order** of Congregational Churches in Massachusetts along Trinitarian and Unitarian lines. In August 1803 David Tappan, who had been Hollis Professor since 1792, died. Tappan was considered a moderate Calvinist, a theological centrist who was acceptable to the liberal Arminians. The president of the school, Joseph Willard, hoped to arrange for another moderate to be elected. He knew that Henry Ware, the revered minister from Hingham, was the most likely candidate, but he was an acknowledged Arminian. For more than a year Willard avoided the issue and no discussion took place. Then in September 1804, Willard died. Professor Eliphalet Pearson, who hoped to gain the presidency for himself, was the interim president due to his position as senior faculty member. The members of the Corporation met in December after there had been criticisms in the press over the delays in filling the professorship. The Corporation split over two candidates—Ware and Jesse Appleton. Judge Oliver Wendell Holmes proposed a compromise that Ware be elected president and Appleton professor, but this failed and Ware finally received a majority of votes—four to three on February 1, 1805.

Pearson believed that theology was the most significant factor in the election, but other problems, including his own ambitions, prevented the compromise from working. After this, Ware's name had to be approved by the Board of Overseers, which met on February 14. At that meeting, representatives of the orthodox party inquired about the terms of Thomas Hollis's grant. They believed that London merchant Thomas Hollis, who created the first endowed chair in America in 1721, was not an Arminian and he would not have wanted someone of unsound doctrine holding the position. Their arguments failed and the election of Ware was confirmed and he accepted. Jedediah Morse of Charlestown, the leader of the orthodox party, believed that this election meant the loss of Harvard to the liberals, which signaled the beginning of a revolution in the Congregational church. Shortly after the election, Morse published *The True Reasons on Which the Election of a Hollis Professor of Divinity in Harvard College Was Opposed at the Board of Overseers*. Ware's election in 1805 was followed by the election of another liberal, Samuel Willard, to the presidency in 1806, thus confirming Morse's fears that the liberals had captured Harvard.

HOLMES, JOHN HAYNES (1879–1964). One of the greatest social activists in Unitarian history, Holmes was born in Philadelphia on November 29, 1879. He returned to his Boston roots soon thereafter. He attended public schools in Malden, Massachusetts, and then entered **Harvard College** in 1898. He graduated in 1902, although his work was finished in three years. Holmes knew early in his college career that he wanted to enter the ministry. He began at **Harvard Divinity School** in 1902 and finished in 1904, serving as student minister in Danvers. Holmes married Madeleine Baker on June 27, 1904, and they had two children.

He served the Third Religious Society in Dorchester, Massachusetts, for a little more than two years. Then following the retirement of **Minot Savage**, Holmes saw an opportunity to serve what he considered one of the "Cathedral churches" of Unitarianism. He began a long ministry at the Church of the Messiah in New York. Heavily influenced by the social gospel message of his day that he learned at Harvard under the influence of **Francis Greenwood Peabody**, Holmes began a social action ministry, which had an unprecedented record of involvement in countless issues. In 1908 he joined with others to found the Unitarians for Social Justice. This was followed in 1909 by a joint effort with Oswald G. Villard to start the National Association for the Advancement of Colored People (NAACP).

Holmes also had a close working relationship with Margaret Sanger. He became an advocate of voluntary parenthood and with the help of two of her associates founded a parish based Marriage Consultation Service, which was especially concerned with birth control and sexual issues in marriage. He began a long friendship with Rabbi Stephen Wise; together they worked protesting industrial abuses and later collaborated to start the Civic Affairs Committee to uncover corruption. Another organization grew out of his concern for civil liberties. During World War I he founded the American Union against Militarism. Later this became the American Civil Liberties Union (ACLU) under the influence of Roger Baldwin, Holmes's parishioner. Holmes became its chairman in 1940. His opposition to the war and his overall pacifism made him the target of attacks.

Holmes especially came to loggerheads with leaders of his own denomination, including former President **William Howard Taft**. In 1917 Holmes delivered a major speech before the General Conference. He outlined four positions Unitarians had taken in response to the war. Holmes classified himself with the nonresisters who see all war as one of the "supreme abominations of history." Holmes wanted to lead the churches in preventing war and especially to see the spirit of nationalism fade away. In response Taft offered a resolution supporting the war effort. It was passed and then was followed in April 1918 with a vote of the **American Unitarian Association (AUA)** Board to make any congregation that employs an antiwar minister ineligible for aid. Holmes then tried to lead his congregation out of the AUA into a new church movement. Although his congregation pledged their allegiance to the concept of a larger community ministry that went beyond sectarian boundaries, they refused to withdraw from the AUA, but in 1919 they took on the name Community Church. Holmes decided to resign from the General Conference and from his life membership in the AUA.

After the war Holmes continued his peace work. In the 1920s he became a disciple of Gandhi, whom he considered the greatest living person. He admired his nonviolent resistance to war and other evils. He met Gandhi in 1931 and later published *My Gandhi*. His **community church movement** was dedicated to adopting a wider religious identity and the social reconstruction of society. He worked with **Clarence Russell Skinner** in founding a Community Church in Boston in 1920. Back in New York, Holmes built an institution that reflected his vision for ministry. During the early years of his ministry, his preaching on socialism caused some consternation and he became friends with Eugene Debs and Norman Thomas. He became concerned that the congregation not split over his pacifist stand during both World Wars, and each time he offered his resignation. Both times he was turned down. The church itself reflected a broad-based program. In worship it honored all religious traditions. In social justice it expanded its mission to include a mental health clinic and a clinic to provide health care to the poor. Holmes edited the periodical *Unity* for many years. He retired from active ministry in 1949. In 1951 the Unitarian Fellowship for Social Justice initiated an award honoring the names of its two founders, Holmes and Arthur Weatherly. Despite the fact that Holmes separated himself from the AUA, he received the denominational Distinguished Service Award in 1954. He also resumed his membership in the Unitarian Ministerial Association, from which he had withdrawn. His autobiography, *I*

Speak for Myself, was published in 1958. In his later years Holmes suffered form Parkinson's disease and died in New York on April 3, 1964.

HOLMES, OLIVER WENDELL JR. (1841–1935). The famed Supreme Court justice was also one of the formulators of pragmatism. Holmes was born on March 8, 1841, in Boston to Oliver Wendell Holmes Sr., the renowned writer and doctor, and Amelia Lee Jackson, whose father was a judge. The elder Holmes had rejected his father's Calvinism and joined King's Chapel. Later he championed liberal religion in his columns in the *Atlantic Monthly*. Despite his liberal faith, Holmes did not subscribe to a liberal social vision, but like many of the Harvard Unitarians supported the status quo, the upholding of private property, and law and order. Holmes feared the disruption of government by the abolitionists who would "inflame the evil passions." The younger Holmes, who was the oldest child, attended Harvard College like his father. While he was there he became a member of the Christian Union, a liberal group that advocated for broad interpretations of faith as opposed to the more narrowly defined Christian Brethren. Later in life, Holmes could be characterized as a skeptic or an agnostic who refused to believe in any absolutes. His wife, Fanny, once informed her husband's secretary that "in Boston one has to be something, and Unitarian is the least you can be." He defined his faith as "bettabilitarianism." Since we could not *know* eternal truths, we could bet on the behavior of the universe in its contract with us. In fact, the Pragmatism that he helped develop in the discussions of the Metaphysical Club with William James and Charles Sanders Peirce was a philosophy that all believing is betting, as there is no certainty.

He enlisted in the army at the outbreak of the Civil War, but he was not called up before his graduation in 1861. After that he entered military service as a first lieutenant in the 20th Massachusetts Regiment. The war was a searing experience for Holmes. He was wounded three times, but, moreover, its destructiveness destroyed his idealistic Brahmin youth. All the learning and self-culture of Boston could not prevent such horror and later he said that after the war "the world never seemed quite right." In 1864 he entered Harvard Law School, finishing in 1866. He traveled for a year and returned to pass the bar.

He practiced law with a number of firms for 15 years. From 1870 to 1873 he was editor of the *American Law Review*. During this time he married his longtime love, Fanny Bowditch Dixwell, on June 17, 1872. In 1881 Holmes published *The Common Law*, which developed out of a series of lectures he gave for the Lowell Institute. In 1882 he was made the Weld Professor of Law at Harvard and that same year was appointed to the state Supreme Court in Massachusetts. He remained there for 20 years, eventually becoming chief justice. Finally in 1902 Holmes was appointed an associate justice with the United States Supreme Court. He remained on the bench for 30 years, retiring when he was 91.

During those years Holmes developed a remarkable reputation as the "Great Dissenter." Often thought of as a cynic and an enemy of social reform, Holmes was an incredibly gifted scholar who in his constitutional opinions refused to violate the will of the people through their elected representatives in the legislature, even when he thought them wrong. Not a democrat, he believed that reason would prevail in a free exchange of ideas. He was also a protector of free speech and won fame for articulating the idea that the only time free speech could be curtailed was when there was a "clear and present danger." However, as a judge his views were based on what he perceived as best for the society as whole rather than on individual freedoms. When Fanny died on April 30, 1929, Holmes's fellow Unitarian and Supreme Court justice **William Howard Taft** made the arrangements, as it was said, he "knew how to run a Unitarian funeral." Holmes died nearly six years later on March 6, 1935, and his funeral was conducted at All Souls Unitarian Church in Washington, D.C.

HOPEDALE. An intentional utopian community formed under the leadership of **Adin Ballou**. The Hopedale Community grew from a group of radical Universalist ministers that had formed a splinter Restorationist Association from their denomination, rallying around the belief in a period of purification following death rather than immediate salvation. During the winter and spring of 1839, Ballou and his colleagues developed the "Standard of Practical Christianity." Its publication caused a split in the Restorationist Association, which was dissolved after the radicals left to form Hopedale. In September Ballou addressed the New England Non-Resistance Society and gave the basic premises for forming Hopedale in that speech. Ballou later said that upon their Practical Christian platform they had to try to "build a new civilization." Initially, Ballou and **George Ripley**, who founded Brook Farm, discussed possible cooperation, but they split over Ballou's insistence that the "Standard" had to be used as a test of membership. Ballou's intention was that Hopedale would be a "living example of moral reform—a city set on a hill." They decided to buy a farm to pursue their plan to live a life of greater purity. In 1840 Ballou worked on a constitution that was adopted by his Restorationist friends in January 1841. Article one set out that this Fraternal Community would be the first of many more. Article 2 listed the standards to join the community. Other articles included the economic basis for the community, including all housing being owned in common.

The community vision was a series of small communities economically based in agriculture. Ballou contracted to purchase a farm in August 1841 and people began to move in during the spring of 1842, the Ballou family on April 16. Ballou stated at that time that he and his fellow communitarians had separated themselves from the world in order to reform the world. From the beginning the community was short of funds, and a controversy developed over whether they would continue their common-stock system in which the largest initial investors received the most shares. The communists, led by fellow minister David Lamson, argued for a joint-stock system, but Ballou, who had sunk all his money into Hopedale, feared that all the wealth would go to the poorer members. Lamson left by the end of the year. Certain constitutional amendments furthered the ability of capitalistic gain on the part of some members, but new amendments in 1844 put the industries under greater control. At the end of 1845, one of the founders, George Stacey, withdrew because he felt his personal liberties were being infringed upon. The community was reorganized in 1847. Ballou's daughter Abbie started a public school. There was continued fighting over business arrangements, as they became more consolidated and outside labor was hired. Progress was indicated by the purchase of more land and the establishment of a post office and bank. By the end of the first decade the community owned 500 acres and had built 30 new buildings, including three mechanic shops, a chapel, and several barns. There were 36 families in all with a total population of almost 200. By 1851 Ballou was able to resign as president and he was succeeded by Ebenezer Draper. Ballou wanted to develop more communities and establish an education institution, but his son Adin died, and the community showed an operating loss within a year. Ballou made plans to expand west and started to write his perfectionist vision. Unfortunately, Draper and his brother, who together owned most of the stock, decided in 1856 that the debt was too great. The community had to sign over most of its property to them and Hopedale had to close. Despite its sad end, which left Ballou embittered, Hopedale had a reasonable record of success as his reform impulse had created for a time a "miniature Christian republic."

HOSMER, FREDERICK LUCIAN (1840–1929). One of the premier Unitarian hymn writers. Hosmer was born in Framingham, Massachusetts, on October 16, 1840, the son of Charles and Susan Hosmer. He graduated from **Harvard College** in 1862 and then went on to **Harvard Divinity School**. Here he became friends with **William Channing Gannett**, with whom he would later collaborate to produce hymnals. When he finished Divinity School in 1869, he was ordained in the fall at the church in Northborough, Massachusetts, where he remained as pastor for three years. This was followed by a ministry in Quincy, Illinois. He then went on to a very successful ministry at the First Unitarian Church of Cleveland, Ohio, from 1878 to 1892. It was during this time that he began to work on hymns in earnest.

In 1880 Hosmer collaborated with Gannett and James Vila Blake to produce *Unity Hymns and Chorals*. Then in 1886 he and Gannett produced *The Thought of God in Hymns and Poems*. His hymns began to find their way into other hymnals, especially after 1900. Thirty-five of his hymns appear in *Hymns of the Spirit* (1937). From 1894 to 1899 Hosmer served the Church of the Unity in St. Louis, Missouri. His final ministry was at the First Unitarian Church of Berkeley, California, from 1900 to 1915. While he was minister in Berkeley, he wrote the popular "Forward through the Ages" (set to the tune "St. Gertrude") for the dedication of the Oakland church. He also delivered a series of lectures at Harvard Divinity School on hymnody. In Berkeley he was made emeritus and remained there until his death on June 7, 1929. The author of eight hymns in the current **Unitarian Universalist Association (UUA)** hymnal *Singing the Living Tradition*, his reputation as a hymn writer rivals that of **Samuel Longfellow** in Unitarian history.

HOWE, JULIA WARD (1819–1910). The author of the "Battle Hymn of the Republic," Howe was an important writer, reformer, and peace advocate who was also an active Unitarian. Born in New York City on May 27, 1819, her mother died in childbirth, leaving six young children. Julia was the third oldest and thought of her childhood as "more in shadow than in light." Her formal education ended when she was 16. Her family connections gave her access to a wealthy, privileged circle. **Henry Wadsworth Longfellow** and Charles Sumner brought her to Boston when she was 21 to tour the Perkins Institute and see the famous Laura Bridgman, the first deaf and blind person to use language. There Julia Ward met, fell in love with, and then married in1843 the Perkins director, **Samuel Gridley Howe**, the radical abolitionist who was 18 years her senior. Over the years she felt stifled by Howe, who preferred that his wife not take an activist role in the world. She lived for many years on the campus of Perkins, but this small house was a sharp contrast to the wealth and privilege she enjoyed in New York. In Boston she had six children born between 1844 and 1859, four of whom survived until adulthood. The youngest, Samuel Jr., died in 1863, and this was a special agony to the couple. Despite Samuel's attempts to control her and his frequent absences, Julia stayed in the marriage. She devoted time to her own education and that of her children. Before the Civil War she supported Samuel's causes and also worked for a time on an abolitionist newspaper, the *Commonwealth*, with him.

Howe began to find much solace in her religious affiliation, which was in sharp contrast to her strict Calvinist upbringing. At first she was a regular attendee of **Theodore Parker**'s 28th Congregational Society, which met in the old Melodeon. She was impressed with Parker's preaching and once wrote that she would rather hear him than go to the theater. Unfortunately, Parker's church was very informal and unsuitable for children to receive a religious education. Therefore, Howe began to take her children to **James Freeman Clarke**'s Church of the Disciples and eventually developed a deep friendship with Clarke, even though she preferred Parker's preaching and his personal responses to her poetry. After Sammy's death, she was even more devoted to Unitarianism. She became an official member of the church and published a paper in the *Christian Examiner* on "The Ideal Church." She decided she wanted to spread the word about this liberal faith of hers and, under the encouragement of Clarke, she began to lecture and preach. Over the next few years she struggled with her husband over this new career as a lecturer. In 1861 she was visiting military camps near Washington and was dismayed by the obscene words she heard sung to the tune of the popular "John Brown's Body." She decided to write new words, which were published in the *Atlantic Monthly* within two months and soon became a rallying cry for Union soldiers.

Howe became more independent as she aged, and, despite her husband's objections, she increased her outside interests and even became active in women's suffrage. She was the first president of the New England Woman Suffrage Association. In 1868 she helped organize the New England Woman's Club. She was also beginning to publish more at this time, including a third book of poems in 1865. Some of her publications included: *A Trip to Cuba* (1860), *Sex and Education* (1874), *Modern Society* (1881), *Margaret Fuller* (1883), and *Reminiscences* (1899). After the war, Howe became especially concerned with two causes: the ministry of women and world peace. Howe delivered her first sermon in Harrisburg, Pennsylvania, in 1870 and gave the charge to the congregation at the ordination of the first Unitarian woman minister, Celia Burleigh. In 1873 she organized a women's preaching convention in Boston and then in 1875 she organized the Women's Ministerial Conference, which helped lead a group of women to form the **Iowa Sisterhood**.

In the 1870s Howe began to crusade for peace. She formulated a plan for gathering women together for world peace congresses. The first one in New York in 1870 included an address by the Unitarian **Octavius Brooks Frothingham** and the Universalist **Phebe Hanaford**, who was a vice president. After a convention in Boston the next year, Julia helped organize an American branch of the Women's International Peace Association. When she returned from England in 1872 she developed a plan for Mother's Peace Day festivals, a predecessor of our modern Mother's Day. Her proclamation for Mother's Day included a cry from the devastated earth, "Disarm! Disarm!" After her husband's death in 1876, Julia traveled in Europe and then lectured on these travels. She continued to work for women's suffrage, including its defense before the Massachusetts legislature. In the mid-1890s she worked for the defense of Armenians, who were being persecuted by the Turks. In her final years, she was truly a national institution, received a series of honorary degrees, and in 1908 became the first woman elected to the American Academy of Arts and Letters. She died on October 17, 1910, and a service was held at the Church of the Disciples on October 19.

HOWE, SAMUEL GRIDLEY (1801–1876). He was an embodiment of the great reform spirit of the 19th century, which he expressed through abolitionist fervor and institutional reform for a variety of neglected and mistreated people. Howe was born the second son of Joseph and Patty (Gridley) Howe on November 10, 1801, in Boston. Like his friend **Horace Mann**, he attended Brown and graduated in 1821. He was known for his mischief making in college when he put hot ashes in a tutor's bed and when he led the president's horse to the top floor of University Hall. After college he earned an M.D. from Harvard and immediately implemented his skills on the battlefield when he became inspired by the Greek revolution. After serving for a time as a soldier and surgeon in the war, he was appointed chief surgeon to the navy. When he returned to Boston his career direction became unfocused. One day while visiting a college friend in 1829 he learned about the New England Asylum for the Blind, which was seeking a director. A passion for righting wrongs in the world that had been ignited in Greece was now galvanized into pioneering work in the education of the blind. Under Howe, what came to be known as the Perkins Institution and Massachusetts School for the Blind (now in Watertown, Massachusetts) developed into the most outstanding educational agency of its type in the world and Howe the foremost educator of the blind.

By 1843 the school was world famous. Laura Bridgman, the first deaf and blind person to learn language, helped this occur when she came to live in residence six years previously. Believing that all people deserve the right to be educated to reach their full potential, Howe achieved amazing results with Laura, and she became an international celebrity and a source of revenue for the school. Howe hoped to prove the Unitarian belief in the innate moral goodness of the soul by portraying Laura as a person who was untainted by the world. Howe had to defend his use of Laura as a refutation of Calvinism. Writers for the *Christian Observatory* attacked his "Fifteenth Annual Report" as director of Perkins and accused him of propagating Pelagianism—the view that human beings are naturally holy. His opponents said he was trying to make converts to Unitarianism. Although his religious theory did not prove entirely successful with Laura, his successful educational methods established him as one of the great humanitarian reformers of his day. Rejecting the Calvinist view of the inevitability of sin, Howe taught that everyone has distinctive talents and needs that merit individual attention. Laura Bridgman's fame led to a visit by a young society woman from New York, Julia Ward, in 1841. Howe fell in love at the age of 40 with a woman 18 years his junior and they were married in 1843. Together they had six children, the first born in Rome the following year and christened there by Theodore Parker. Howe was able to travel to Greece again, but was unhappy with the changes in the country he had grown to love. All during this trip, Howe stopped everywhere he could to inspect schools. The education of those who were mentally handicapped became his new passion. Howe issued a report to the Massachusetts Senate in 1848 on "Idiocy," in which he proved that the "feeble minded" could benefit from education. That same year the first publicly supported school for the instruction of idiotic and feeble-minded youth in the United States was established in South Boston. It later became the Walter E. Fernald School (now in Waltham, Massachusetts).

Howe's humanitarianism led him into the increasingly active abolition movement. In 1851 he took on the editorship of the *Commonwealth*, a new paper established to promulgate Free-Soil views. Later he became active with the Vigilance Committee and then with those who raised money to aid the crisis in Kansas, where he traveled in 1856. Howe became one of the "Secret Six" supporters of John Brown, along with the Unitarian ministers **Theodore Parker** and **Thomas Wentworth Higginson**. After Brown was executed and his friends, Mann and Parker, both died, Howe began to feel the effects of physical and mental strain. During the war, Howe was reinvigorated by government service and after the war continued his education and charity work. His voice was heard in the establishment of a new school for the education of the deaf in 1867. On January 9, 1876, Laura Bridgman came to bid him farewell as he lay on his death bed. The Rev. **James Freeman Clarke** was called, and Howe died shortly after noon. Despite some difficulties in their marriage at times, Julia wrote shortly after his death that nearly every class of unfortunates had been blessed by her husband's benevolence.

HUMANISM. Humanism became an important religious expression within Unitarianism in the early 20th century. Humanists said that God was not necessary to a worthwhile modern religion. Early humanists sought religious expressions of ethical values and common human aspirations. **John Hassler Dietrich**, who became minister in Minneapolis in 1916, first used the term *humanism* to explain the message he started preaching in 1913 in Spokane, Washington. He and **Curtis Reese** discovered they were promulgating a similar message, although Reese called his faith a "religion of Democracy." Both agreed that people were the rulers of their own affairs and there is no supernatural authority whose approval they had to gain. In "The Content of Present-Day Religious Liberalism" summer school lectures at Harvard University in 1920, Reese declared, "If liberalism can be reduced to a single statement, I think this is it: Conscious commitment and loyalty to worthwhile causes and goals in order that free and positive personality may be developed, intelligently associated and cosmically related" (as quoted in Parke, *Epic*, p. 134). Reese went on to say that liberalism was building a religion that could stand "even if the thought of God were out-grown." His book *Humanism* was published in 1926. Bringing his ideas to the East Coast produced a firestorm of controversy. In 1921 Dietrich gave an address before the annual meeting of the **Western Unitarian Conference (WUC)**, in which he said religion had no future unless it became humanistic. George Dodson, a professor from Washington University, responded by writing an article for the ***Christian Register***, "Clear Thinking or Death." This started a humanist/theist controversy within the denominational ranks that sometimes surfaced over the next 30 years. Initially, much of it was played out at the General Conference meeting in Detroit in October 1921. William Laurence Sullivan became the outspoken defender of theism. In a speech he attacked Dietrich and lost much of the support he might have had for a planned resolution calling for a crudely worded statement that Unitarians must affirm the existence of God.

Humanism did not begin with a 20th-century rejection of God. Drawing on Greek roots, it first developed in the Renaissance in Italy in the 14th century with a strong emphasis on classical learning. Within Christianity, humanism downplayed the importance of doctrine, advocated using reason in scriptural interpretation, and emphasized the ethical leadership of Jesus. These humanists began to focus less on the rewards of an afterlife and more on making the best of this life. Religious humanism, as it developed in the 20th century among several prominent Unitarians and others, recognized the value of the scientific method and insights. Religious humanism claimed that orthodox religious belief and practice must be reformed in light of modern knowledge. These religious humanists were all part of a larger group that can be called naturalistic humanists, or humanists who say that nature is the sum total of reality. Here there is no supernatural, nor can there be a belief in a transcendent God or personal survival after death. The humanist/theist controversy came up again in 1928 when Marion F. Ham from Reading, Massachusetts, said humanism as a religion without God is a religion without meaning or power. Ham became involved in a printed exchange with Dietrich. The controversy surfaced yet again when 13 Unitarian ministers signed *The Humanist Manifesto*, which was issued in 1933. The 1930s turned out to be a period of reconciliation for the humanists and theists. Humanists felt as though new **American Unitarian Association (AUA)** President **Frederick May Eliot** respected their positions, and both sides worked together on the new hymnal *Hymns of the Spirit*. Religious humanism became dominant among Unitarians in the 1940s, 1950s, and 1960s (less so among the Universalists), and according to polls, it remains the theology held by the largest number of UUs. During its heyday it developed a kind of orthodoxy in certain liberal circles, so that the discussion of topics such as God or the afterlife was not tolerated. The denomination worked actively to avoid this. In 1954 the AUA published a pamphlet by Charles E. Park called "Why the Humanism-Theism Controversy Is out of Date." Park said that both sides say they cannot know if God exists, but they have different conclusions. Because of scant resources, Park argued that the two sides needed to be friends.

Religious humanism is sometimes confused with secular humanism, which addresses many of the same themes and concerns as religious humanism (issues of ethics and morality) but finds no need for religion. In the 1960s some humanists began to see a need to develop an organization that could work more directly with other theological groups within Unitarian Universalism such as the UU Christians, and the **Fellowship of Religious Humanists** was organized. With today's renewed interest in spirituality, with postmodern distrust of science and technology, and new definitions of God, religious humanism has sometimes been looked upon as an outmoded belief in scientific progress that has lost its relevance, but much of religious humanism welcomes fresh approaches to spiritual experiences and it should remain a strong component of UU religious thinking.

HUMANIST MANIFESTO. A succinct statement of the philosophy of humanism that was published in 1933. By 1930 humanist ideas had spread, particularly among the Unitarians. Raymond Bragg, the associate editor of the *New Humanist* magazine, initiated the project. Bragg was also the secretary of the **Western Unitarian Conference (WUC)** who found in his denominational travels that many people urged him to publish a definitive statement about humanism. After giving a talk at the University of Chicago, Roy Wood Sellars, professor of philosophy at the University of Michigan, agreed to formulate a first draft. An editorial committee worked on revisions and then a confidential draft was sent out to about 20 readers. While some of this group signed on, others refused to sign. Some Unitarians felt it smacked too much of creedalism, and others, such as **John Haynes Holmes**, felt great respect for theism and thought he would be misunderstood if he signed. After the editorial process was complete, 65 persons were asked to sign, and 34 (half were Unitarians, of which 13 were ministers) did so in time for publication. The *Humanist Manifesto* appeared in the May/June issue of the *New Humanist*. It began: "The time has come for widespread recognition of the radical changes in religious beliefs throughout the world." Following the introduction the editors listed 15 affirmations. Among the more significant were: "First: Religious humanists regard the universe as self-existing and not created. . . . Fifth: Humanism asserts that the nature of the universe depicted by modern science makes unacceptable any supernatural or cosmic guarantees of human values. . . . Seventh: Religion consists of those actions, purposes, and experiences which are humanly significant. . . . Eighth: Religious humanism considers the complete realization of human personality to be the end of man's life." Signers included important humanist leaders **John H. Dietrich**, **Charles Francis Potter**, and **Curtis Reese**, and other clergy, academics, the famed educator John Dewey, and one Universalist, **Clinton Lee Scott**. A disclaimer at the end attempted to disavow the view that this was a creed. The response to this statement that traditional views of religion were no longer relevant was often negative. The *Chicago Tribune* published "Liberals See New Religion without God," and called the statement a "new creed: Religion must formulate its hopes and plans in the light of the scientific spirit and method." The Universalist publication, the ***Christian Leader***, shot back its response: "These humanists do not want God and they will not have God. . . .Well, we are just as strong in our view. When we say God we mean God. . . ." Finally, the *Christian Century* was especially critical, saying: "The manifesto is an astonishing exhibition of irrelevant and immature statements touching philosophical subjects."

Although the *Humanist Manifesto* became the most famous statement on humanism, it was largely ignored outside philosophical and Unitarian circles. Forty years after its publication, the manifesto was followed by *Humanist Manifesto II* in 1973. The second manifesto acknowledged some of the flaws of the first, such as: "Events since then make that earlier statement seem far too optimistic." It also said: "Science has sometimes brought evil as well as good." But the new publication still set out to provide "an affirmative and hopeful vision" and based that partly on a rejection of traditional theism, which is called an "unproved and outmoded faith." While continuing to affirm the scientific method, the second manifesto called for the affirmation of individual dignity, democratic rights, and a vision of world community. Both manifestos document the development of religious and philosophical humanism throughout the 20th century.

HUMILIATI. A group of young Universalist ministers who joined together in 1945 for both personal religious experience and denominational renewal. Concerned over a declining and lethargic denomination, the Humiliati wanted to promote a new Universalism that was more universal in its theological approach and tied less to the Protestant Christian mainstream. They termed their ideas "emergent Universalism" and published "Theologically Speaking." Despite their rejection of an exclusive Christian theology, the group emphasized a much more elaborate liturgy, vestments, and other visual symbols of religion than was usual for Universalists. Many were involved in the design of the circle with the off-center cross, a new symbol for Universalism that recognized Christian origins but intended to signify that Universalism had grown beyond its beginnings. The name Humiliati derives from a 12th-century Italian lay order. Seeking deeper emotional experience and a faith liberated from "dead dogma," the Humiliati were often seen as an "insurrectionary group." The eclectic Universalism they preached began to be the dominant denominational voice, and even though the group only lasted for 10 years, its influence was felt for decades, with most of its members becoming significant leaders of the consolidated **Unitarian Universalist Association (UUA)**. These included Raymond Hopkins, the first executive vice president of the UUA, and **Gordon McKeeman**, a candidate for president in 1977.

HUNGARY. Although Unitarianism's long history in Europe is associated with the Hungarian-speaking people of Transylvania, its history in what is now the nation of Hungary is not as extensive. When Unitarianism spread in Transylvania in the 16th century, there was some activity in Hungary. Stephen Balasz was a key figure in this mission work, which established key centers in Temesvar and Pecs. The Turks proved much more tolerant than the Catholics. In 1687 the Turks were forced out and the Unitarians were banished from Pecs. By 1710 all the Unitarian churches were outlawed. There were no Unitarians in this region until the latter portion of the 19th century when Transylvania was reunited with Hungary and some of the Unitarians (who spoke Hungarian) migrated to other portions of the Austro-Hungarian Empire and organized congregations there. This was a result of the Compromise of 1867 in which more home rule was returned to portions of the empire. Jozsef Ferencz, then a minister and professor in Kolosvar, but later bishop, delivered the first public Unitarian sermon in Budapest on June 13, 1869. The

Unitarian congregation in Budapest was organized in 1873 with its first minister appointed in 1881 and a building was erected in 1890. Several other churches were established in Hungary and a second one at Budapest in 1923. In 1902 these congregations were made an independent church district. After Transylvania was ceded to Romania as a result of the Treaty of Trianon in 1920, a boundary was created between the newer congregations in Hungary and the older ones in Transylvania. This forced the Unitarians in Hungary to establish a more formal bureaucracy separate from that of the Unitarian church in Romania. They were led by a deputy-bishop who was responsible to the Transylvanian bishop. During World War II, Alexander Szent-Ivanyi, a former minister in Kolosvar, worked to bring relief to refugees and prisoners in Budapest. In 1945 he became deputy-bishop, but he left soon thereafter. Today this church is much smaller that that of Romania—2,000 members as compared to as many as 80,000—and they have 10 congregations and some scattered fellowships. During the communist ascendancy, the repression in Romania was much greater, since the Unitarians were part of the Hungarian minority and Nicolae Ceausescu's totalitarian regime forced many intellectuals to undergo "conceptual trials." A total ecclesiastical separation from Romania was achieved in 1971 when Jozcef Ferencz, the grandson of the great Transylvanian bishop, became the first bishop of Hungary.

HUSBANDS, MONROE (1909–1984). As implementer of the **fellowship movement** in the **American Unitarian Association (AUA)**, he oversaw the greatest extension effort in the 20th century. Husbands was born on September 11, 1909, in Spokane, Washington. He graduated from the University of Utah in 1931 and then attended the Leland Powers School of Radio and Theatre. He then joined the speech department at the McCune School of Music and Art. He stayed there until he joined the service during World War II. After the war he went into public relations work for Blue Cross of Massachusetts, but his opportunity to make a name in Unitarian Universalist history came a year after he started. The AUA Board had approved a new program for extension named the Fellowship Plan, in which small lay-led groups would be formed in places that did not have a Unitarian church. The director of extension, George Davis, found his ideal candidate for the director of fellowships and associate director of extension, in his home church of Needham, Massachusetts, where Husbands was an active lay member. Husbands took on the job with great enthusiasm, saying, "The project can be the most successful thing the Unitarian association has ever undertaken."

The first meeting of the Fellowship Plan working committee was held in May 1948. Over the next 20 years, Husbands traveled to every corner of the country and beyond to meet with interested groups and address them with the question: "Who Are These Unitarians?" Then he guided the fledgling groups into formulating their plan for organization. It was important that Husbands brought the talents of a lay leader to his position, as he immediately won the respect of other lay people who would develop leadership roles and prove their organizational abilities in the new groups. He strongly believed that fellowships were not to be established as potential churches but special institutions unto themselves. The largest number of fellowships organized during the period of Husbands's leadership was the result of his own field trips. He also served as clerk for the **Church of the Larger Fellowship (CLF)** and could easily familiarize himself with all known liberals in an area targeted for a new group. He was thus able to personally guide many of these societies responding to their individual needs. The program proved an important tool for nurturing spiritual development and lay leadership training, and Husbands, drawing upon his PR background, produced outstanding organizational materials for everything from managing finances, to editing a newsletter, and starting a church school. Most of all Husbands loved his job: "Never in my life have I had a job that I enjoyed so much." He retired from the UUA in 1967 and then received the **Unitarian Universalist Association**'s **(UUA)** Distinguished Service Award in 1974, by which time more than one-third of the UUA's approximate 1,000 active congregations had their origins as fellowships. Husbands died in Needham, Massachusetts, on January 4, 1984.

HYMNODY. In early America, congregational singing was confined to Psalm singing. Psalms were thought of as the proper way to praise God. There were no instruments to accompany the people and the congregations usually only knew a few tunes. A method called lining-out was used to teach new tunes. The tune "Old Hundredth" is an example of this tradition where the words of Psalm 100 were set to music in the Genevan Psalter of 1551. In the early 1700s Psalm singing gradually declined, and the first musical instruction books were written. The use of biblical texts other than Psalms became known as hymnody. With the use of hymns in church, congregations of different theological persuasions began to come forward desirous of singing their own gospel. The English Universalist James Relly and his brother John used common hymn tunes of the day and wrote texts of the proper meter that reflected their belief in universal salvation. This was the pattern that repeated itself again and again in Unitarian and Universalist traditions. Throughout our history, common hymn tunes have been chosen for congregational singing, but new words have been written for those tunes. The first collection of hymns that could be called Unitarian was collected by the Rev. **James Freeman** and Joseph May of King's Chapel, *A Collection of Psalms and Hymns for Public Worship* (1799). In 1807 **Abner Kneeland** was appointed clerk of the Universalist General Convention and was asked, along with **Hosea Ballou** and others, to produce a hymnal. His own hymn text, "A View of Christendom," proved controversial. Kneeland said that the modern Christian world is "in superstitious error hurl'd," and then that Christians "have tortured, persecuted, slain, those who could not agree with them?" Kneeland and the committee eventually published *Hymns, Composed by Different Authors* (1808), including 138 hymns by Kneeland.

The Unitarians tried to omit those hymns that emphasized the Trinity or the sinfulness of humankind. The most popular collection, one that even received **Ralph Waldo Emerson**'s seal of approval in 1831, was edited by Francis W. P. Greenwood, *A Collection of Psalms and Hymns for Sacred Worship* (1830). Hymns began to be written for every special occasion, including ordinations and national holidays. After the advent of Sunday Schools, hymns for children began to be written. Eliza Cabot Follen published *Hymns for Children* in 1825. Hymn writing was not only about finding texts to suit theological needs. Many hymns became popular in other Protestant traditions. This was especially true of **Frederic Henry Hedge**'s translation of Martin Luther's "A Mighty Fortress," the English Unitarian Sarah Flower Adams' "Nearer, My God, to Thee," and **Edmund**

Hamilton Sears' Christmas carol "It Came Upon the Midnight Clear." The most important Universalist collection from the 19th century was edited by John Greenleaf Adams and the famed New York preacher Edwin Hubbell Chapin. Called *Hymns for Christian Devotion* (1845), it contained 1,008 hymns and included many social reform themes. Many of the New England poets had their writing set to music, including **James Russell Lowell**.

The most important hymn writers that emerged from the Transcendental flowering of writers included **Samuel Longfellow**, who wrote some 50 hymns and edited *A Book of Hymns for Public and Private Devotion*, which went through 12 editions. Much of his work was done in collaboration with Samuel Johnson. They later edited *Hymns of the Spirit*, a title reused in 1937. In 1867 the **American Unitarian Association (AUA)** published its first denominational hymnbook, *Hymn and Tune Book*. It was the first Unitarian hymnal to include tunes on the same page as the text. Prior to this time hymn books included only the words, and the church musicians chose the tunes. Two more Unitarian hymn writers made major contributions in the latter part of the 19th century: **William Channing Gannett** and **Frederick Lucian Hosmer**. They collaborated with James Villa Blake to produce *Unity Hymns and Chorals* (1880). After this period the two denominations increasingly made hymnal publications the responsibility of central offices and not private churches or individuals. The **Universalist Publishing House** produced a hymnal in 1907, and the Unitarians issued *The New Hymn and Tune Book* in 1914. Unitarians and Universalist began to work together in the period between the World Wars. In 1935 a joint committee published a hymnal for children called *The Beacon Song and Service Book* (1935). This was followed by *Hymns of the Spirit* (1937), a hymnal compiled by the Unitarian and Universalist Commissions on Hymns and Services. These two commissions were chaired by Henry Wilder Foote and L. Griswold Williams. Von Ogden Vogt played a significant role in compiling the services that were included. Many of the resources were nonscriptural and included material for humanists. This trend toward humanism continued.

In the 1950s **Beacon Press** published the hymnal *We Sing of Life* (1955), which was intended to reflect religious development as it was embodied in the AUA's church school curriculum. It was produced in collaboration with the American Ethical Union and included a readings book called *We Speak of Life*. Shortly after the consolidation of the Unitarians and Universalists, a new hymnal, *Hymns for the Celebration of Life* (1964), was assembled by the Unitarian Universalist Hymnbook Commission chaired by Arthur Foote II. Using Von Ogden Vogt's definition of worship as its title, the new book included many humanist readings, especially highlighting the work of Kenneth Patton, and also folk tunes and material from non-Christian religions. Growing out of the theological need to move beyond patriarchal language in worship, the Commission on Common Worship produced two paperback hymnals (*Hymns in New Form for Common Worship*, 1988) that revised the words of more than 50 hymns so that references to God or people were not cast in only masculine forms. This trend continued in the most recent Unitarian Universalist Association (UUA) hymnal, assembled by the Hymnbook Resources Commission chaired by Mark Belletini. Called *Singing the Living Tradition* (1993), it followed the UUA's Principles and Purposes, using them as "touchstones of our decision to proclaim our diversity." Its musical choices are quite eclectic and include many more folk tunes and jazz. Authors and texts represent many more worldwide cultures and living people than any previous hymnal collection, and the language employed is inclusive of both men and women. Throughout liberal religious history hymn texts have been written, rewritten, and adapted to fit the changing theological needs of the times. Hymns have given Unitarian Universalists a way to sing texts that echo their common beliefs: faith in human potential, the wonders of nature as revelation of the divine, and the struggle for justice and peace.

– I –

ICELANDIC UNITARIANISM. Liberal religion in Iceland was largely confined to a presence within the state church, but many Icelandic immigrants to various parts of North America established a unique and enduring legacy of Icelandic Unitarianism. In the early 19th century, the Church of Iceland hymnbook (Lutheran) was radically altered when Chief Justice Magnus Stephensen removed all references to the devil and eternal punishment. This hymnbook was later used by the Icelandic Unitarians in North America. Magnus Erikkson, an Icelandic theologian in Denmark, was expelled from the Lutheran church for supporting dissenters and profoundly influencing a young Lutheran minister, Matthias Jochumsson, who later became the author of the Icelandic national anthem and a missionary for the British Unitarians in Iceland. In the late 19th century a large number of people migrated from Iceland to Manitoba and Saskatchewan in Canada and North Dakota, Minnesota, and the Pacific Coast. A group of liberals met in North Dakota in 1888 and formed the Icelandic Cultural Society, which helped organize liberal viewpoints but not congregations. One of its members, Bjorn Petursson had previously begun to call himself a Unitarian after speaking with Kristofer Janson, a Norwegian minister in Minneapolis. He had secured some aid from the **American Unitarian Association (AUA)** in 1887 to publish pamphlets in Icelandic. With this support he moved from North Dakota to Winnipeg and founded the First Icelandic Unitarian Society in 1890. Petursson was attacked by the Lutherans as "the paid tool of American infidelity, labouring zealously toward the goal of unchristianizing the nation."

The spread of Unitarianism owes much to Magnus Skaptason, a Lutheran minister who rejected divine revelation and convinced five congregations to follow him out of the Lutheran Synod. They formed the Icelandic Free Church in America, which immediately asked for affiliation with the AUA (Skaptason later served the Winnipeg church). After the turn of the century the AUA started an Icelandic Mission, as orthodox leaders were trying to stamp out the liberal heresies. After conferences in 1900 and 1902, the Western Icelandic Unitarian Association was formed "to promote freedom in matters of religion and to awaken and uphold in the hearts of men rational living and inspirational ideals, in love to God and service to man." In 1905 the denomination established an Icelandic Week to raise funds to benefit "fellow-citizens of Icelandic birth," and this continued at least until 1923. By 1911 the AUA had a Department of New Americans that employed eight: two among Swedes, one each among Norwegians, Finns, and Italians, and three among the Icelanders. At this date Manitoba had the most Unitarians of any province in Canada—1,541. Several young Icelanders also began to study for the ministry, including Rognvaldur Petursson, who served the Winnipeg congregation and became the AUA field secretary for the Icelandic Churches (there were 11 Icelandic ministers who served Canadian congregations).

In 1923 several New Theology Congregations (a group who separated from the Lutherans in 1909) joined with the Icelandic Unitarians to form the United Conference of Icelandic Churches. By 1930 approximately 30 societies had been organized within this conference. But decline came swiftly when AUA money dried up, ministers returned to Iceland to serve parishes in the state church, then Petursson died in 1940. After the war, Petursson's nephew, Philip Petursson, became the new leader of the Icelandic Unitarians with a goal of establishing ethnically diverse congregations, and in 1952 the Icelandic conference became the Western Canada Unitarian Conference. By 1990 only two congregations that were primarily Icelandic remained: Arborg, Manitoba, and Blaine, Washington.

INDIA. More than 200 years ago a Hindu named Thirvengatam traveled to London while in the service of the East India Company. Having been orphaned and then enslaved in Madras, Thirvengatam was baptized William Roberts. Taking advantage of his newly won freedom, he fell under the influence of the writings of **Joseph Priestley** and **Theophilus Lindsey**. When he returned to India he founded the Madras Unitarian Christian Church in 1795. Roberts regularly reported back to England and began a correspondence with William Adam in the 1820s after Adam arrived in Calcutta. This Madras congregation has retained many of its traditions over the years, including the use of a revised Book of Common Prayer. Its present meeting house was erected in 1813, while many of the original families remain part of the congregation. The church has 120 members and sponsors a night school for underprivileged students.

In the early years of the 19th century, **Ramohun Roy**, a Brahmin from the province of Bengal began to agitate for a new reformed faith. Roy rejected Hindu mythology, but was also dissatisfied with the Christian doctrine of the Trinity. He decided that Unitarianism came closest to genuine Christianity. In 1833 he traveled to England to visit Lant Carpenter in Bristol, but he fell ill and died. His influence lived on in the religious reform movement, the **Brahmo Samaj**, which he had founded in 1828. Close ties continued between the English and the Brahmo Samaj. Mary Carpenter visited India three times in the 1860s and 1870s. A religious community was organized by Debendranath Tagore, the father of Rabindranath Tagore, poet and Nobel laureate. A new leader arose in the 1860s, Keshub Chunder Sen. Keshub's orientation differed from that of the elder Tagore who did not want to expand the influence of the Brahmo Samaj in non-Bengali areas. Keshub also wanted more emphasis on Jesus in the movement. In 1878 a crisis over an arranged marriage resulted in the founding of a splinter group, Sadharan Brahmo Samaj. They are the Brahmo group that continues to the present day.

The largest branch of liberal religion in India appeared in North East India when Hajom Kissor Singh objected to the mass conversions of his tribal kin to Christianity. In 1887 Singh formed his own church, which included the teachings of Jesus, Buddha, Sikh prophets, and also Hindu and Islamic scriptures, as well as a tribal faith, Seng Khasi. A Khasi Brahmo gave Singh some literature from **Charles Dall**, a Unitarian missionary to India who was living in Calcutta. After Singh read the works of **William Ellery Channing**, he decided to call his new church The Unitarian Church of North East India. He spread the faith throughout the region and by the time of his death in 1923 there were 10 groups with a total membership of 500. Singh also wrote many of the hymns that the Khasis still sing today. The Khasi Unitarians have consistently enjoyed financial support from the West. In the 1930s the British General Assembly sent **Margaret Barr** as church representative. Barr, who had studied with Gandhi, opened schools in Shillong and Jowai. Eventually Barr moved to the remote village of Kharang where she started a school and opened her doors to orphans. She became known as Kong Barr (Big Sister), continuing her work until her death in 1973. Since then the culture has been subjected to more Western influences and the land has suffered widespread deforestation, but this fiercely theistic Unitarian faith flourishes in many villages where there are now 35 congregations and approximately 9,000 members in the Khasi and Jaintia Hills. Most of the churches also operate schools. The Union is also affiliated with a Unitarian Christian Fellowship in Hyerabad.

Both American and British Unitarians have labored in India over the years. These efforts started with William Adam (1796–1881), who was born in Scotland, worked in India 1821–1829, and later became active in the antislavery movement. In the 1850s the American Charles Dall began a 31-year missionary effort. This more traditional effort to convert Indians to a liberal form of Christianity failed to succeed except in the area of education. The British sent the American **Jabez Sunderland** in 1896 and 1913. His arrival signaled a change in approach to mission work. Rather than an emphasis on conversion, Sunderland hoped to work with the Brahmo groups and make them an effective liberal religious voice among Hindus. Sunderland also helped the Unitarians in the Khasi Hills print their hymnbooks and write their first constitution. In 1987 a council of all the Unitarian groups in India was organized.

INTERNATIONAL ASSOCIATION FOR RELIGIOUS FREEDOM (IARF). The oldest continuing interfaith organization was started in 1900 at a meeting organized by the Unitarian minister Charles Wendte. The impetus came from the World Parliament of Religions held in Chicago in 1893, which was a ground breaking event celebrating understanding and respect among people of different religious traditions. The IARF's original name was the International Council of Unitarian and other Liberal Religious Thinkers, but this changed again in 1930 while meeting in the Netherlands to International Association for Liberal Christianity and Religious Freedom. The current name was adopted in 1969 after a Congress in Boston when a liberal Buddhist group, Rissho Kosei-kai, joined. Rissho Kosei-kai with its six million members has become an institutional force in the IARF. They had been encouraged to join by the Japanese Unitarian minister Dr. Shinichiro Imaoka.

After its founding in 1900, the IARF held frequent Congresses, and these triennial events continue to be its major program. By 1910 there were nearly 2,000 delegates who came to Berlin to hear such luminaries as Adolph von Harnack, Walter Rauschenbusch, and Ernst Troeltsch. Today the IARF has more than 56 member groups in 25 countries. The IARF supports interfaith coalitions for social service, justice, and world peace. It has a Social Service Network that sponsors community development programs in several countries. The IARF has also tried to develop materials and train people to provide leadership in interfaith work to promote religious freedom and prevent religious conflict.

The headquarters, The Secretariat, is in Oxford, England. An executive position was created during a reorganization instigated by **Unitarian Universalist Association** (UUA) president **Robert West**. This new full-time professional, Diether Gehrmann, a minister who was born in Germany but was trained in the United States, replaced a volunteer arrangement in 1972 in Frankfurt, Germany. The IARF sponsors regional meetings and conferences and has local affiliates, including a U.S. Chapter. Conferences frequently bring together leaders from different faiths to promote dialogue and understanding and sponsor several young adult programs in different parts of the globe. There is a women's organization, the International Association of Liberal Religious Women (IALRW), which holds a triennial conference before the IARF Congress. This group first met in Berlin in 1910 and then was formally organized three years later in Paris as International Union of Liberal Christian Women. The name was changed to IALRW in 1975.

Strong North American links with the IARF were reinforced during the presidency of **Eugene Pickett**, who became the IARF leader after he left the presidency of the UUA in 1985. Former UUA **moderator Natalie Gulbrandsen** also became an IARF president. In 1999 the 30th IARF Congress held that year in Vancouver, British Columbia, drew 650 delegates and observers from around the world. The IARF is recognized as a nongovernmental organization (NGO) by the United Nations and works with other NGOs and UN officials in New York.

INTERNATIONAL COUNCIL OF UNITARIANS AND UNIVERSALISTS (ICUU). The **International Association for Religious Freedom (IARF)** had been the traditional international gathering for Unitarians and Universalists since the group's founding in 1900. By the late 1980s the IARF had broadened its focus so much that Unitarian Universalists were no longer the majority of members. Responding to this need for a more narrowly defined Unitarian Universalist group, David Usher, an Australian who had been a minister in both the United States and Great Britain, proposed the formation of an international Unitarian Universalist organization to the British General Assembly in 1987, and the idea was endorsed. In 1992, **Unitarian Universalist Association (UUA)** president **William Schulz** invited Unitarian Universalist leaders from around the world to a meeting in Budapest, but no formal plans for a new organization were made. Because some UUA Board members were becoming uneasy with international groups joining the North American UUA, a proposal was made to the UUA Board by Polly and Ted Guild, the UUA's International Program Coordinators, to create an international council of Unitarians and Universalists and some funds were appropriated. A founding conference was held in March 1995 in Essex, Massachusetts, with 14 countries represented.

The International Council of Unitarians and Universalists (ICUU) was officially created with a constitution that was ratified by 18 initial members (now 20). (*See* appendix). The ICUU has council meetings that are held every two years. The mission of the group is to provide a worldwide communications network, to support new congregations, and to foster the growth of the faith. The group has members in traditional strongholds of Unitarianism such as **Australia and New Zealand**, **Canada**, **Czech Republic**, **Great Britain**, **Hungary**, **India**, **Nigeria**, **Philippines**, **Poland**, Romania, **South Africa**, and the United States, but other small or burgeoning groups are also involved including **European Unitarian Universalists (EUU)**, Denmark, Finland, Germany, Russia, Spain, Sri Lanka, and Pakistan, and there are some additional emerging groups as well in places such as Argentina and Latvia. At the ICUU Council Meeting in May 2001 in Montreal membership policies were established. The council publishes a newsletter, *The Global Chalice*, and has also published worship materials.

IOWA SISTERHOOD. The group of 21 Unitarian women ministers who served churches in Iowa and elsewhere, who brought a revolutionary style to the ministerial profession. Between 1870 and 1890 about 70 women were ordained to the Unitarian or Universalist ministry. Few of them had a chance to practice their profession in full-time positions. Women were often settled in the least viable pulpits that men would not take or were relegated to second class positions by denominational leaders or clergy spouses. Their struggle for recognition and the opportunity to make important contributions came on the Great Plains, and especially in Iowa, far from the neighborhood of Boston, where new opportunities were possible and new rules could be applied.

The shortage of men who were willing to help start liberal religious congregations in this region led to the formation of the Iowa Sisterhood. The idea for a sisterhood rose out of the Women's Ministerial Conference, organized by **Julia Ward Howe** in 1875. One of the primary leaders of this group was **Mary Safford**, a farmer's daughter from Quincy, Illinois. Between 1880 and 1910, she founded or organized seven churches, six of them in Iowa, and also served as the secretary of the Iowa Unitarian Association whose primary purpose she saw as mission work. In addition to Safford's seven congregations, she influenced other members of the sisterhood to start nine more congregations. Its members included Florence Buck, Caroline Bartlett Crane, **Eleanor Gordon**, Marion Murdoch, and Eliza Tupper Wilkes. While Wilkes founded only one of the Iowa churches, she started seven others elsewhere, including Sioux Falls, South Dakota, where Crane was the first permanent minister. Safford had charge of the Sioux City church for 14 years, where she was assisted for a time by her childhood friend Eleanor Gordon. Together they edited a missionary magazine, *Old and New*.

The sisterhood's style of ministry brought many program opportunities to these congregations, so that the church became a true home for families. In addition to many classes and social events, the churches addressed the practical needs of home and family. Their church spaces often reflected domestic uses as well. They encouraged that the church be used on a daily basis for many kinds of activities. Many of the women were also involved in civic affairs. While she was serving in Kalamazoo, Michigan, Caroline Bartlett Crane started the first daily public kindergarten. The sisterhood's success was a difficult pill for many of the East Coast bureaucrats to swallow and little was done to support their efforts. Nevertheless, the Iowa Sisterhood built a tremendous record of achievement blending traditional ministerial skills like preaching with sound business skills and especially maternal care taking to nourish these rural outposts of liberal religious life.

IRELAND. *See* GREAT BRITAIN.

ISSUE IN THE WEST. The *Issue in the West* was the title of a pamphlet written by **Jabez Sunderland** that attacked leaders of the Western Unitarian Conference who Sunderland believed were trying to remove Unitarianism from its historic Christian basis to a "Free or

Ethical Religion." In 1886 the conference was scheduled to meet in Cincinnati, but about a week before it commenced the pamphlet was mailed to ministers and key church leaders, and then distributed when delegates arrived at the meeting. Sunderland wrote that he could not remain silent on the issue of whether a Unitarian church would be reduced to stand for nothing more than free religion. He also opened the question of whether ministers who were known disbelievers in Christian Theism could be called to Unitarian pulpits. Sunderland said Unitarianism would be destroyed by removing the theistic and Christian flags and replacing them with an ethical one. He called for a conference that was broadly Christian.

The immediate result of the controversy was the establishment of a new alternative group called the Western Unitarian Association, which organized offering more support for the **American Unitarian Association (AUA)** coupled with work to diffuse the "interests of pure Christianity." Recognition of the maverick group was not forthcoming. The AUA did not renew Sunderland's contract as Western Agent, and he returned to his pastoral duties in Ann Arbor. When the conference met in 1887 in Chicago, **William Channing Gannett** introduced his important statement, "**Things Most Commonly Believed among Us**," which was later adopted on the understanding that it did not bind members to a single declaration of faith. Unfortunately, the theological rift was not healed until 1894.

– J –

JAPAN. A country where both Unitarian and Universalist missionaries tried to extend the faith. **The American Unitarian Association (AUA)** sent Arthur May Knapp there on a mission in 1888 to inquire into the progress of liberal thought in Japan and provide the intelligentsia with a liberal faith that corresponded with their values. Within two years a building had been purchased in Tokyo and many tracts had been published. The Japanese Unitarian Association was founded in 1890. By the following year, Clay MacCauley had succeeded Knapp, and there was one organized church and three other meetings. There were also four other outposts in different parts of the country. A school for training ministers, the School of Liberal Theology, was also founded. In 1894 Unity Hall, the headquarters for the mission and the school was dedicated. The church had between 150 and 200 members at this time. Although MacCauley stayed in Japan until 1900 and returned from 1909 to 1920, the mission suffered from financial cutbacks, and was effectively ended after he left. Shinichiro Imaoka, a native trained minister, worked to reestablish a Unitarian presence after the war and succeeded in 1948 when the Tokyo Unitarian Church was established. He also helped start the Japan Free Religious Association and actively promoted membership in the International Association for Religious Freedom by other Japanese groups. He died in 1988 at the age of 106 always maintaining a vision of Jiyu Shukyo, a universal religion beyond all particular religions.

The Universalists started a mission fund for Japan in 1886, and by 1889, they had raised sufficient funds. George Perin was selected to lead this missionary effort. Arriving in July 1890, he dedicated the first Universalist church by the end of December. Their program was to provide religious services, teach English, and give lectures. In less than three years they had started a training school for ministers and had 10 students enrolled. They were also able to establish mission outposts in five places other than Tokyo, and a girls' school was established in Shizuoaka. They also published a monthly magazine and other religious tracts.

The Universalist mission was augmented by the efforts of the Women's National Missionary Association (established as the Women's Centenary Association in 1869 and renamed in 1905). In 1894 Catherine Osborn went to Japan to replace the first teacher, Margaret Schouler. Two years later Osborn established a girls' boarding school in Tokyo called the Blackmer House, where orphans and the poor could be trained in English, homemaking, and kindergarten teaching skills. Within a few years a second worker was appointed to assist Osborn, a kindergarten was established, and an endowment raised for Blackmer House. By 1910 the Universalists had 13 missionaries, and although they were more comfortable with the idea of mission than their Unitarian counterparts, they still preferred to think of their efforts as friendship and service rather than religious conversion. The social service aspect of the program was funded and administered by the women's association, but they also became involved in the church work. In 1918 Hazel Kirk was appointed director of the Blackmer House, but two years after that she was sent to the Shizuoaka Church as minister.

The peak years in Japan occurred just prior to World War II when the Universalists had five churches in Japan and one in Korea and several secular buildings, including two kindergartens. The leader of the mission during this time was Henry M. Cary, who arrived in 1924. He successfully rebuilt the mission after a devastating earthquake, and a few years later a Japanese Universalist Convention was established. Universalist funding continued until the outbreak of war in 1941, when the American missionaries had to leave. The native Japanese missionary, John Shidara, continued to work throughout the war years. After the Tokyo mission was destroyed, he and his wife, Tsune, relocated to the rural Nagano area where they founded the still extant Komagame Universalist Church. When the Japanese mission was surveyed after the war, only one kindergarten, Ohayo Kindergarten, remained. Once again the **Association of Universalist Women** and the **Universalist Church of America** worked together to stimulate activity. The Koishikawa Universalist Center was built in Tokyo on the site of the Blackmer House. The Ohayo Kindergarten operation was merged under the name of the Dojin House (translated as All People or Universalist), which had been established in 1924. Today the Dojin Church has a large modern building and an American-trained minister, Rev. Chiyozaki. Their kindergartens and social work programs remain active elements of the movement. Other liberals in Japan are involved in the Japanese Free Religious Association and Rissho Kosei-kai, a large liberal Buddhist group.

JEFFERSON, THOMAS (1743–1826). The third president of the United States has long been claimed by the Unitarians even though he never joined a liberal church. Raised an Anglican, Jefferson came to embrace the deism that was common to many of the founders of America. Much of what he learned of Unitarianism came through his friend **Joseph Priestley**, whose writings convinced Jefferson to reject the miracles, the atonement, original sin, and Jesus' divinity. While Jefferson maintained his childhood church affiliation he also attended Unitarian and Universalist church services in Philadelphia. When he ran for president he was accused of being a "howling atheist" and it was said that his election would be a "rebellion against God." On December 8, 1822, he wrote to James Smith, thanking him for the pamphlets on Unitarianism. In that letter he declared, "No historical fact is better established, than that the doctrine of one God, pure and uncompounded, was that of the early ages of Christianity." He went on to say that the doctrine of the Trinity was "the hocus-pocus phantasm of a God like another Cerberus, with one body and three heads, had its birth and growth in the blood of thousands and thousands of martyrs." Jefferson thought that the belief in the unity of the Creator would spread throughout the country, and wrote, "I confidently expect that the present generation will see Unitarianism become the general religion of the United States" (Jefferson to Smith, *Selected Writings*, pp. 703–704.) But Jefferson never even found a Unitarian community to be part of for himself and wrote to Benjamin Waterhouse on January 8, 1825, that his neighborhood was "too much divided into other sects to maintain any one Preacher well. I must therefore be contented to be an Unitarian by myself, although I know there are many around me who would become so if once they could hear the question fairly stated."

Jefferson was especially proud of his advocacy of religious freedom and is frequently quoted today for his famous letter to the Danbury, Connecticut, Baptists in which he declared a "wall of separation" between church and state. He worked mightily to see his home state disestablished and to keep the University at Charlottesville free of sectarian influences, but he was accused of creating an "alliance between the civil authority and infidelity" and teaching the youth of the country "a refined and civilized heathenism." Jefferson's most famous exposition of his liberal faith occurred with the publication of *The Life and Morals of Jesus of Nazareth*. In 1800 Jefferson wrote to his friend Dr. **Benjamin Rush** that he was carrying out a promise he had made to Rush to write down his view of the Christian religion, saying, "To the corruptions of Christianity. I am indeed opposed; but not to the genuine precepts of Jesus himself." What became more commonly known as *The Jefferson Bible* was a massive redaction of the four Gospels, so that the revelation and miracles were removed. Jefferson simply cut out and pasted together those passages that made sense to him. He told Rush how attached he was to Jesus' teachings, "ascribing to himself every human excellence; and believing he never claimed any other." Religion for Jefferson was an intensely personal matter, and the true test of religion was moral conduct not dogma: "It is in our lives, and not our words, that our religion must be read."

While religion was always a central concern for Jefferson, his beliefs would have been considered too radical for most of the Unitarians of his day. His correspondence with **John Adams** in their later years of life is well known, and their thoughts frequently turned to religion. In April 1823 he told Adams, "It would be more pardonable to believe in no God at all, then to blaspheme Him by the atrocious attributes of Calvin" (Jefferson to Adams, *Selected Writings*, p. 706). Born on April 13, 1743, Jefferson died on the same day as Adams, July 4, 1826, the 50th anniversary of the Declaration of Independence. After his death and, especially, in the 20th century Jefferson became one of the saints of the church he never officially joined. Because of his faith in freedom of mind and spirit, tolerance of religious difference, and trust in reason and science, Jefferson was embraced as a prophet of modern liberalism.

JENKINS, LYDIA ANN MOULTON (1824/25–1874). An early advocate for women's rights, Jenkins is now considered the first woman to be ordained by a denomination in the United States. Born in Auburn, New York, Lydia Ann Moulton embraced Universalism as a young woman and sometime after 1846 married Edmund S. Jenkins, a Universalist minister. They began a team ministry in the late 1850s. Research by Charles Semowich has shown that she was ordained by the Ontario Association of Universalists in Geneva, New York, in 1860. Three years before that **Thomas Whittemore** wrote in the *Trumpet and Universalist Magazine* that she "has commenced preaching to good acceptance." **Horace Greeley** heard her in New York City and responded favorably as well. When she was given a license to preach, the *Christian Freeman* reported, "This is the first instance in our denomination, and we think in the world, where a woman has received a formal license of Letter of Fellowship as a minister of Christ."

In 1858 the Universalist General Convention was presented with a resolution supporting the fellowshipping of women as preachers, but it was tabled and postponed. There was still strong resistance to the idea, even though in Jenkins's case it was reported that "there was great beauty in the lady's style." In May 1860 she and her husband became coministers in Clinton, New York, and they were ordained on June 23. They also worked with students at the Clinton Liberal Institute, a Universalist secondary school founded in 1831. After leaving

Clinton in 1862, she continued to be an itinerant preacher until 1866. After that time she became a physician in Binghamton, New York, where she remained until her death on May 7, 1874. Throughout her adult life she was a speaker for women's rights, and her effectiveness as a preacher convinced many, including Universalist leaders like Whittemore, that women belonged in the pulpit and in other fields of labor on equal terms with men.

JESUS. Jesus has always been a central figure in Unitarianism and Universalism, but mostly as an ethical leader or teacher and not the Christ of salvation. For centuries liberals have always emphasized the more human Jesus, and thus even the Arian and Socinian views of Jesus have affirmed that he is less than God, even when it is said that he is the Son of God or called by God for a special divine mission. **Charles Dickens** believed that allegiance to the spirit of Jesus is "sustained by the best in humanity ever since his day." Dickens became Unitarian not because he rejected Jesus, but because he loved him so much. Unitarians have generally followed what **Ralph Waldo Emerson** said of Jesus in the Divinity School Address: "Alone in all history, he estimated the greatness of man. One man was true to what is in you and me. He saw that God incarnates himself in man" (Wright, *Three Prophets*, pp. 96–97). This ethical view of Jesus dates to the time of Francis David in Transylvania who said that Jesus should be followed and not worshipped. In Unitarianism there was a constant striving for self-improvement and Jesus was the model to follow. *See also* ARIAN, ANTI-TRINITARIAN, LIBERAL CHRISTIAN, SOCINIAN.

JOHN SIGISMUND, KING OF TRANSYLVANIA (1540–1571). The only Unitarian king in history released the first religious Edict of Toleration in Europe. John, son of Queen Isabella of Transylvania and King John Zapolya, was born on July 7, 1540. Isabella was the daughter of Queen Bona, the second wife of King Sigismund of Poland. She had a brief marriage to Zapolya, who died two weeks after John was born. Isabella was left with an infant son and the Transylvanian crown, which Zapolya had won with the help of the Turkish sultan Sulayman I. In 1543 Transylvania was declared independent with John Sigismund named king. This arrangement did not last though—in 1551, the parliament, under the influence of Bishop George Martinuzzi, seized the crown for Ferdinand. Isabella and young John had to flee to her brother's court in Poland. John was 11 years of age at the time of the exile, which lasted for five years.

During the time in Poland Isabella became increasingly influenced by her mother's doctor, **Giorgio Biandrata**, an anti-Trinitarian. Sulayman once again came to Isabella's aid when King John and Isabella were restored to the throne as part of a peace treaty in 1555. The Reformation had spread quickly in Transylvania and was completed when Isabella returned the following year to a triumphant welcome in Kolosvar. She issued a decree in June 1557 that everyone could worship according to their own faith. She died in 1559, but her son continued to reassert the freedom of conscience she had helped inculcate. He came of age in 1561 and continued to struggle with Ferdinand and the Hapsburgs. John had an intense interest in religious questions and also wanted to promote peace among the warring religious factions. A Diet at Torda in 1563 renewed and confirmed his mother's decree from 1557. In 1564 his childhood physician, Giorgio Biandrata, arrived to attend to an illness. Biandrata immediately became the king's personal representative in the battle to restore peace to the religious community. During the next few years King John participated in some of the many debates that took place at synods or diets. **Francis David** became his court preacher in 1564, and the Trinity was first debated in 1566. The king was committed to the belief that debate could restore harmony to the religious community. His most important act as king was issuing the Edict of Toleration as a result of the Diet at Torda in January 1568. This debate lasted for 10 days, after which the King adjourned it and issued a decree that reaffirmed four recognized faiths in Transylvania: Catholic, Lutheran, Reformed, and Unitarian. They were not allowed to abuse or punish one another because their teachings varied, summed up as "Faith is the gift of God."

Two months after Torda, Francis David won a great debate on the doctrine of the Trinity at Gyulafehervar. The debates over the doctrine of the Trinity came to a close after John called for a debate at Nagyvarad in 1569, which was held under his supervision. After this he ordered that the Unitarians not be interfered with and his entire court seems to have been won over to the new faith. King John's health had always been frail, including chronic intestinal problems and epilepsy. During his life he often tested his body with active sports involvement. He was also a promoter of schools and a patron of music and the arts. His last crucial act as monarch occurred shortly before he died. Despite the Edict of Torda, the Unitarian churches did not enjoy full legal recognition. This was granted at the Diet of Maros-Vasarhely on January 6–14, 1571. He was severely injured in a hunt on the day after the diet concluded. He died on March 14, 1571, at the age of 30. King John lived a brief life that was mostly spent in fighting for the right to assume and keep his throne. In a time of religious intolerance and bigotry when any contrary opinion from the ruling majority usually meant persecution, he fought for religious liberty. His was a remarkable voice for tolerance in an era of coercion.

JOHNSON, SAMUEL (1822–1882). An important hymn writer and Transcendentalist, who made significant scholarly contributions to the study of comparative religion with his books on religion in Asia. Johnson was born on October 10, 1822, in Salem, Massachusetts, where he continued to live throughout his active life. As a boy he was interested in academic pursuits and went to **Harvard College** at age 16, graduating in 1842. One of his classmates was **Samuel Longfellow**, with whom he began a long collaboration as hymn writers. They traveled together in Europe and also worked on a hymnbook, *Book of Hymns*. First published in 1846, it was later enlarged and revised as *Hymns of the Spirit* (1864). After he decided to enter the ministry, Johnson went to **Harvard Divinity School**, where **Octavius Brooks Frothingham** called him the "ardent disciple of the intuitionist philosophy," finishing in 1846. He tried out for a ministry in Dorchester, Massachusetts, and then he preached in a number of pulpits in greater Boston, but none worked out, largely due to his radical political ideas. After that he found a responsive group of listeners in Lynn, Massachusetts, at the Central Unitarian Society. Because of his nonsectarian, individualistic beliefs, he convinced the church to disaffiliate from the **American Unitarian Association (AUA)** and they formed the Independent Church of Lynn. He served them from 1853 to 1870. He so distrusted institutions that he would not even join the radical **Free Religious Association (FRA)** after it formed.

Johnson was a minor Transcendentalist whose faith was centered in naturalism, and he rejected much of Christian tradition as revelatory and held little faith in established institutions always refusing to join any organized groups. His later years were devoted to study and writing. He often looked outside of Christianity for his inspiration. In his hymn "Life of Ages" he writes, "Never was to chosen race that unstinted tide confined." His work on eastern religions was especially important. He published three volumes of his *Oriental Religions*. These were *India* (1872), *China* (1877), and *Persia* (1885). Johnson believed in many of the reform movements of his time, including abolitionism. He contributed to the *Liberator* and the *Anti-Slavery Standard*, among other periodicals. He was frequently asked to speak on reform subjects. He moved to a family home in North Andover, Massachusetts, after the conclusion of his ministry in Lynn, and he died there on February 19, 1882.

JONES, JENKIN LLOYD (1843–1918). One of the prime leaders of the Unitarians in the 19th century, he came from a long tradition of Welsh Unitarians. Jones was the youngest of six children born to Richard Lloyd and Mary Jones on November 15, 1843, near Llandyssul, in Cardiganshire, Wales. His farmer parents were lifelong Unitarians, and Jenkin grew up in the Unitarian congregation in Pantydefaid. The family came to North America when Jenkin was only one, living first in Canada but then settling near Spring Green, Wisconsin, where Jenkin spent the winters in school and worked all summer farming with his father. In the summer of 1862, when he was 19, Jones joined the Union army, and was sent to northern Mississippi. He survived the war and the 11 battles he fought in with a foot injury that caused a limp for the rest of his life, but he came home with money in his pocket and an urge to get a college education. He had been corresponding with the **Meadville Theological School** in Pennsylvania and soon decided he would go there. He worked his way through the seminary, holding every conceivable job from janitor to wood splitter, and graduated in 1870. While he was there he fell in love with one of the secretaries, Susan Baker, and they were married the day after graduation. They spent their honeymoon at the annual meetings of the **Western Unitarian Conference (WUC)** in Cleveland. Right away Jones realized the deep split within Unitarian ranks. One group in Cleveland wanted to impose creedal tests on the clergy, and the other group, which Jones joined, argued for freedom of belief.

Jones's first settlement was at the Liberal Christian Church in Winnetka, Illinois, but he moved on a year later to Janesville, Wisconsin, to serve the First Independent Society for nine years. He broadened the programs the church offered, including all sorts of classes. He also began to develop his own Sunday School materials and started a periodical, the *Sunday School*, based on "Love, Service and Devotion." Jones also became the missionary secretary of the WUC in 1875, a position that frequently required exhausting responsibilities. One year in the 11 years he held the position included traveling 14,676 miles, preaching or lecturing 78 times, and visiting 41 places. Finally, in 1879 he became editor of the WUC publication, ***Unity***, of which he had charge for 40 years. The theological division in the Midwest continued until 1886 when the conference revised its constitution to say no creedal tests were necessary for fellowship in the conference. In response the Western Unitarian Association was created as a splinter group from the WUC.

In 1882 Jones decided to live out a lifelong dream of serving a church in Chicago. He arranged this by starting his own congregation, the Church of All Souls. Jones attracted people from all kinds of backgrounds; they soon outgrew their space and in 1887 moved to a new building. Designed by Jones it had a first floor meeting room and offices and a second floor apartment. Eventually this space had to be redesigned to allow for more needs. Under Jones's direction the church also acquired property that was used for summer retreats. All Souls became a school for a wide variety of educational opportunities and its outreach included a Thanksgiving dinner for the homeless. Jones was also active in the community lending his support to several civic groups and teaching literature at the University of Chicago. He was the executive secretary for the committee arranging for the World Parliament of Religions, held in Chicago in 1893, making the arrangements for bringing in speakers from all the world's religions. His next major project was the establishment of the Abraham Lincoln Centre in Chicago. The center became an interfaith institution for educating and improving the whole person. It included concerts, classes, gym workouts, and an art gallery among its multifold offerings. During his later years, Jones was frequently employed as a lecturer. Politically, he became very active in antiwar movements and for a time his publication, *Unity*, was denied use of the U.S. mails. His death came at the time the ban was lifted, so that after he finished reading the issue, a final sleep came over him on September 12, 1918. Jones was the great leader of the Western conference during a critical time in its history. He helped expand the faith with his mission work, but moreover, his guidance as secretary of the conference for 11 years assured its bedrock position of freedom for all followers.

JORDAN, JOSEPH H. (1842–1901). The first black Universalist minister was from Norfolk, Virginia, where he returned to begin a Universalist mission effort. Jordan was born in West Norfolk, Virginia, in 1842 and was converted to Universalism mostly through the writings of important leaders such as **Thomas Whittemore**. He visited Philadelphia in the late 1880s and attended the Church of the Messiah, where he was eventually received into fellowship. Edwin S. Sweetser, the minister there, presided over Jordan's ordination in 1889. Jordan wanted to start a Universalist church in his hometown of West Norfolk. The congregation, which had begun to gather in 1887, was accepted into fellowship by the General Convention at the same time as Jordan. Within two years he had organized a day school and a Sunday School. In 1893 he made an address before the Universalist General Convention, at which he asked for support for the mission. The support was voted and a building was erected in Norfolk in 1894, which served as church and school. It was dedicated in November 1894 as the First Universalist Church of Norfolk with Edwin Sweetser preaching on the occasion. **Quillen Shinn**, who was a missionary in the South, organized a youth group and preached there in September. A second mission was established in Suffolk by Jordan's assistant, Thomas Wise. He had preached and taught school there previously. After raising some funds, a building was erected in Suffolk in 1898. Jordan died on June 3, 1901, in Huntersville, Virginia, but the work was carried on initially by Wise, who was placed in charge of both missions. Unfortunately he soon became a Methodist, and the Norfolk mission collapsed. The Suffolk mission was carried on by **Joseph F. Jordan** (no relation).

JORDAN NEIGHBORHOOD HOUSE. In 1898 the Universalists founded what later became known as the Jordan Neighborhood House. This mission and educational center in Suffolk, Virginia, was started by Thomas Wise and flourished under the direction of one of the early black Universalist ministers, **Joseph F. Jordan**. When his daughter, Annie Willis, succeeded him, the services included a prenatal and well-baby clinic, as well as the school, which had offered educational opportunities to thousands of black children during its first years of operation.

Known as the Suffolk Normal Training School when Jordan was its principal, its identity as a school changed when opportunities for blacks in the public schools opened up. In 1939 and 1940 the eight grades for school classroom work were discontinued. The name changed to the Jordan Neighborhood House in 1939, as it was becoming more of a social service center. Eventually the Universalists set up a day care center and a nursery school for working mothers. After a negative conditions report in the 1950s the **Universalist Church of America (UCA)** Board of Trustees voted to renovate the building and offer financial support. Many other denominational groups pitched in, too. Work camps were often held in the summertime. An early Head Start program was operated in the 1960s. General oversight of the programs was provided by the Universalist **General Convention**. These programs continued under Unitarian Universalist auspices until 1969 when the merged **Unitarian Universalist Service Committee (UUSC)** decided to discontinue funding. The name was changed again to the Jordan Community Center and many of the programs were assumed by other agencies.

JORDAN, JOSEPH F. (1863–1929). Known for his work at the Suffolk Normal Training School, Jordan was one of the earliest black Universalist ministers. Born on June 6, 1863, in Gates County, North Carolina, of slave parents, William and Anne, Jordan became an apprentice bricklayer and plasterer. His attendance at a Methodist church led to an early career of preaching and an appointment as a presiding elder in the Methodist church. He graduated from the State Normal School for Negroes at Plymouth, North Carolina. He was married and widowed twice. His concerns about endless punishment were alleviated by his conversion to Universalism by hearing the preaching of **Quillen Shinn**. Jordan spent a year studying at St. Lawrence as a special student, received a preaching license in 1903, and then went to work with Thomas Wise in Suffolk, Virginia, who was continuing the work started by **Joseph H. Jordan** (no relation), the first black Universalist minister.

Joseph F. Jordan received Universalist fellowship when he became principal of the Suffolk Normal Training School in 1904. He also served a congregation that had 50 families and a church school of 44. In 1909 the school had 129 students. Both school and church were remarkable reversals from near defunct organizations in 1904. Jordan also published what was intended to be a monthly paper, the *Colored Universalist*. He was active in the temperance movement as well. At first Jordan called his school the St. Paul Mission School, and he hoped to make it into an industrial college. By 1915 the students were divided in half, attending on alternate days. Jordan also served as a probation officer for about 700 black youths in Suffolk. He maintained cordial relationships between blacks and whites. Despite some prejudice toward his Universalist faith and prevailing racism, Jordan's work seems to have been respected. He remained there as the principal of the school at Suffolk until his death on May 1, 1929, after which the church dissolved, but the school continued under his daughter, **Annie Willis**.

JOY, CHARLES RHIND (1885–1978). Primarily remembered for his outstanding work with the Unitarian Service Committee (USC), he was sometimes misunderstood for his efforts. He was born in Boston on December 5, 1885, to Robert and Arabella (Parke) Joy. He attended Boston public schools, including Roxbury High School, and then went on to Harvard University and the **Harvard Divinity School**, but received his S.T.B. from Andover Theological Seminary in 1911. He married Lucy A. Wanzer, and they had four children. His interest in overseas work started when the Young Men's Christian Association (YMCA) put him in charge of their operations in Northern France and western Belgium during World War I. He served Unitarian churches in Portland, Maine, and in Pittsfield, Dedham, and Lowell, Massachusetts. Joy had some political difficulties in Portland. In 1915 he delivered an Elks Flag Day speech in which he condemned the war in Europe. A pacifist, he was forced from his pulpit in 1917 when he called World War I “an unrighteous war.” Joy said his prayers went out to both Germans and Americans, and the next day he was burned in effigy outside the church. He worked for a time at the headquarters of the **American Unitarian Association (AUA)**, where he was administrative vice president to Louis Cornish during his presidency, 1927–37. He was also the adult advisor to the continental board of the **Young Peoples Religious Union (YPRU)**, the continental youth organization. For a time in 1937 he was a candidate for the presidency of the AUA, but he withdrew during a bitter contest when **Frederick May Eliot** was accused of being a humanist.

Following up on an effort to aid Unitarians in Czechoslovakia, the Unitarian Service Committee (USC) was formed in 1940. Joy was sent to work with Waitstill and Martha Sharp in September and by the end of the year he had replaced them in the Lisbon office. He continued there working with Robert and Elisabeth Dexter. During his years with USC Joy became embroiled in a number of controversies, but he worked and traveled tirelessly for its promotion and extension. It was during his time in Lisbon that the USC adopted the **Flaming Chalice** as its official symbol. Joy had commissioned Hans Deutsch, a refugee from Paris, to create the artwork for the design. After the USC was organized in 1940, Joy described its immediate work as “Rescue.” His chapter in the book *Together We Advance* (1946) was called “Lives Were Saved.” Countless lives were guided to freedom from Nazi occupied areas. In late 1944 the Dexters accused Joy of incompetence and dishonesty. The USC Board decided the charges were baseless. The Dexters soon resigned, and Joy was appointed executive director in the Boston office.

After the war, Joy characterized the work of the USC as “Restoration.” In addition to providing the basic needs of food and clothing, the USC opened medical teaching missions and children’s homes as some of their many projects to restore war-torn Europe. In June 1946 the USC staff was accused of being dominated by communists, including Jo Tempi and Charles Joy. These two were also charged with sexual improprieties. Although he always denied these charges, the political and sexual accusations led to Joy being fired as executive director in August 1946. President Eliot continued to support him and later appointed Joy to the AUA’s Editorial Board. Raymond Bragg replaced

Joy as AUA vice president in charge of the USC (still the official designation for the USC executive director). When he left the USC, Joy went on to work for the Save the Children Federation and later a Korean Relief Program for CARE. In 1945, while still with the USC, Joy had authorized the sending of a grant to Albert Schweitzer's Hospital in Lambarene, Africa. On the verge of financial collapse, the grant saved the hospital. Joy was instrumental in helping to introduce Schweitzer to the world. Later Schweitzer joined the Unitarian Church of the Larger Fellowship; Joy visited Schweitzer and wrote several books about him. Joy also wrote a textbook on Africa and a popular Bible concordance, *Harper's Topical Concordance*. During his lifetime, Joy became devoted to Star Island, the Unitarian conference center.

JUDD, SYLVESTER (1813–1853). A Unitarian minister and pacifist, he made his name primarily as the author of the novel *Margaret*. Judd was born in Westhampton, Massachusetts, on July 23, 1813, the son of the editor of the *Hampshire Gazette*. The family moved to nearby Northampton when Sylvester was nine. Judd hoped to prepare for college, but had to work for a few years at a number of odd jobs, including clerking in a store, but was finally able to return to school, and did so in 1831 at Hopkins Academy in Hadley, Massachusetts. He took part in a revival during this time and joined the First Congregational Church in Northampton. After a year he entered Yale College hoping to become a minister, but his faith underwent a liberal transformation and he decided that the conversion experience was an unnecessary part of faith. In 1836 he took a job teaching in Templeton, Massachusetts, to pay off his debts. The following year he went on to **Harvard Divinity School** and became friends with Jones Very, the Transcendentalist poet. He heard **Ralph Waldo Emerson** deliver "The American Scholar," but, even though nature became a vital part of his faith, Judd was not a Transcendentalist, as he also affirmed the centrality of Jesus Christ. He also believed that Unitarians needed to be more evangelical in spreading the word of their faith.

In 1840 Judd was called to serve the East Parish in Augusta, Maine, and he was ordained there on October 1. On August 31, 1841, Judd married Jane E. Williams the daughter of Reuel Williams, a U.S. Senator, and they would eventually have three children. As soon as he began to preach on some of the reform issues of the day, he began to alienate some of his parishioners and others. He became an outspoken pacifist and even condemned the American Revolution as a moral evil. This resulted in his being dismissed as chaplain to the state legislature. In 1843 Judd began to write his best work, *Margaret*. It was followed in 1850 with two other publications: *Philo: An Evangeliad*, a long dramatic poem, and *Richard Edney*, another novel. *Margaret* received critical praise. **Margaret Fuller** called it a "work of great power and richness," and **James Russell Lowell** said *Margaret* was "the first Yankee book, with the *soul* of Down East." It is perhaps the only Transcendental novel with **Octavius Brooks Frothingham** describing it as setting "forth the whole gospel of Transcendentalism in religion, politics, reform, social ethics, personal character, professional and private life" (Frothingham, *Transcendentalism*, pp. 382–383). Judd's career was cut short when he died at the age of 39 on January 26, 1853. One of his goals in the Augusta church had been to open communion and church membership to all, including birthright membership for children, an issue he also brought before the Unitarian Autumnal Convention in Baltimore in 1852.

– K –

KING'S CHAPEL. Often called the first Unitarian church in America, but its historical development as a liberal congregation is an anomaly in Puritan and Congregational New England. In June 1686 the first Anglican service was held in Boston. The following Easter the first royal governor of New England, Edmund Andros, seized the keys of South Meetinghouse and forced the Puritans to share their house of worship with the Anglicans for two years. The first King's Chapel, a small wooden structure was dedicated in June 1689. The present church, a stone building, was completed in 1754. The coming of the American Revolution brought great divisions within the congregation. By 1776 nearly one-half of the pew holders, as well as English soldiers and officers who helped fill the pews, had left. When it came time to reorganize in 1782 the leadership of the church chose **James Freeman**, a Congregationalist, as their "reader" candidate for the ministry. Freeman embraced the Anglican liturgy, but he expressed doubts about the theology, especially the doctrine of the Trinity. When the congregation asked him to set forth his own interpretation, he did so with misgivings about how it would be received. When support for him continued, he also began to revise the prayer book based on one revised by the Englishman Samuel Clarke through the teachings of the Polish Socinians. In 1785 explicit Trinitarian passages were dropped and a unique Unitarian version of the *Book of Common Prayer* was adopted by vote of the congregation (the Apostles Creed was deleted in a second revision in 1811). While Freeman still considered the church Episcopalian, he found the first American bishop, Samuel Seabury, opposed his liberal views. Finally, on November 18, 1787, Freeman was ordained entirely by lay members of the church in an unprecedented ceremony. A group of Episcopal clergy denounced it as invalid and Freeman was effectively excommunicated. Thus King's Chapel lost its link to its founders and assumed its present unusual character: Unitarian in theology, Anglican in liturgy, and Congregational in church government. Despite its position of not being part of the Standing Order of Congregational Churches where the Unitarian controversy was eventually centered, King's Chapel became the first church in America to avow itself Unitarian. With more than 200 years of congregational life since and a recent revision of the prayer book, King's Chapel maintains its position as the most prominent exponent of Unitarian Universalist Christianity.

KING, THOMAS STARR (1824–1864). Known as "the preacher who saved California's soul," Thomas Starr King was born to the Rev. Thomas Farrington King and Susan Starr King on December 17, 1824. At the time, his father, a Universalist minister, was serving a church in New York City. Known by his mother's maiden name, Starr, the boy showed scholarly aptitude at a young age. In 1835 the family moved to Charlestown, Massachusetts, when the Universalist church called King's father to be the minister. Starr's hope for a college education was derailed when his father died four years later. He was called upon to support his family, as the eldest of six children. He took on a variety of jobs, but found the most satisfaction as a bookkeeper at the navy yard, and later in life he referred to himself as a "graduate of the Charlestown Navy Yard." King was determined to enter the ministry, and was encouraged by **Theodore Parker**, who said, "He has the grace of God in his heart and the gift of tongues."

After some supply preaching in Boston, King was called to the Charlestown church his father had served and was ordained there on August 2, 1846. Less than two years later the Hollis Street (Unitarian) Church invited him to revitalize their divided congregation, but King declined in order to cruise to the Azores to restore his already fragile health. When he returned, the congregation again asked him to come, and in early December 1848 he was installed. A few days later he married Julia Wiggin. King served Hollis Street for 11 years, during which time the congregation increased in size fivefold.

King was forced to take on a dual career in order to support his family. He won fame as a lecturer, but this took its toll on his body. He tried to renew himself by vacationing in the White Mountains of New Hampshire. He wrote letters to a Boston newspaper, recounting the legends and beauty of the mountains, and eventually these were published as his only book, *The White Hills*. In 1860 an opportunity arose for King to leave the "cozy stove of civilization" in Boston, and he accepted a call from the First Unitarian Society of San Francisco. His ministry there began on April 29. The forthcoming presidential election soon occupied his attention. He became the spiritual leader of the Republicans who supported Abraham Lincoln's candidacy and spoke whenever he could on themes of national unity. Through countless cities and mining towns King carried his patriotic messages that California not secede from the union. He also campaigned for Leland Stanford, a parishioner of King's, who won the governorship in 1860.

Once Republican control of California was secure, King turned to fund-raising for the U.S. Sanitary Commission, helping this precursor to the Red Cross raise about $1.2 million in contributions in California, one-quarter of the entire national total. Despite his political activities King did not ignore the growth of his congregation, where overflowing Sunday attendance and financial health resulted in the construction of a new church building during 1863. It was dedicated on January 10, 1864. A little more than a month later, King was ill with diphtheria. This turned desperate when pneumonia set in, and King died on March 4, 1864, at the tender age of 39. A great but fragile hero who worked himself to death, a statue honoring his life in Golden Gate Park, San Francisco, says: "In him eloquence, strength and virtue were devoted with fearless courage to truth, country and his fellowmen." As a result of his Civil War era leadership, California has honored him as one of two representatives in the Statuary Hall of the United States Capitol.

KNEELAND, ABNER (1774–1844). Known primarily as the last person to be jailed for blasphemy in America, Kneeland was a consistent and outspoken advocate for free speech. Kneeland was born on April 7, 1774, to Timothy and Marie (Stone) Kneeland in Gardner, Massachusetts. He received little formal education, but learned Latin, Greek, and Hebrew. He became a school teacher and moved to Dummerston, Vermont, to head a school. He married Waitstell Ormsbee in 1797. His ministerial career began when a nearby Baptist society in Putney, Vermont, invited him to be their regular preacher. Sometime after starting this ministry, Kneeland had read a book by the Universalist **Elhanan Winchester** and was converted to Universalism. He received a Universalist license to preach and was ordained in Langdon, New Hampshire, in 1805. He served there for six years, and became well known through the circulation of pamphlets. He also served in the New Hampshire legislature for two years. But these years were also marked by sadness, as his wife and a child died.

At the meeting of the Universalist General Convention in Newtown, Connecticut, in 1807, Kneeland was made clerk. He also became part of a hymnbook committee with **Hosea Ballou**. Kneeland was next called to serve in Charlestown, Massachusetts, and he was installed there in 1811. The society had considerable problems with debt and had trouble paying Kneeland's salary. To supplement his income he joined with his new wife in running a store in Salem, Massachusetts, and decided in 1814 that he could not devote enough time to parish work. Kneeland was beginning to have some theological doubts. He carried on a correspondence with Hosea Ballou in which Kneeland revealed his belief that the scriptures came out of human experience rather than divine revelation, which was published in 1816. He was soon back in the pulpit though and took a parish in Whitestown, New York, in 1817. This was followed after a year by a ministry at the Lombard Street Universalist Church in Philadelphia.

This was his most successful pastorate, although some members left after he declared his belief in no period of punishment after death. The growth of Lombard Street allowed another church to be organized in 1820 (Second Universalist) and Kneeland served both with the help of an associate. He left after seven years to serve the Prince Street Universalist Church in New York City. This congregation followed the more conservative theology of **John Murray** and found Kneeland's radical thoughts too disarming. He soon resigned.

He stayed in New York to edit a new paper, the *Olive Branch*, which was produced by the New York Universalist Book Society. Kneeland used the paper to criticize the churches, but he had enough supporters to back him in a new ministry at the newly formed Second Universalist Society. Unfortunately, Kneeland had Frances Wright, an advocate of communitarian experiments, speak in his pulpit. The congregation resented her presence and Kneeland's advocacy of a radical economic restructuring of society, and they dismissed him. The next year, Kneeland attended a meeting of Universalists in Hartford, and presented his theological views. He asked that his Universalist fellowship be continued, but this was refused and he was withdrawn from the list of acceptable ministers. For a time he lectured before a group called the Moral Philanthropists. In 1831 he moved to Boston to edit a new paper, the *Boston Investigator*. He also became the leader of the First Society of Free Inquirers.

Kneeland became a popular lecturer and traveled back to Philadelphia and New York. His editorship of the paper became especially controversial. He supported a large number of radical causes. He spoke in favor of labor reform, including a 10-hour work day. He spoke for women's rights, too, advocating the practice of birth control. He was the publisher for the first published advice on birth control in America. This was Charles Knowlton's pamphlet, *The Fruits of Philosophy: The Private Companion of Young Married People* (1832), a controversial work that landed Knowlton in jail. What especially caused controversy was Kneeland's insistence on free thought and the right of conscience. His attacks on Christian doctrine were handed over to the Grand Jury and he was indicted for blasphemy. In his paper he wrote that he thought that people's concept of God was a figment of their imagination, that the story of Jesus was a fable, that miracles did not happen, and that there is no eternal life.

After many delays and several years of new trials, Kneeland was finally convicted and sent to jail for 60 days. A petition campaign spearheaded by **William Ellery Channing** to secure his release was refused. From his prison cell, Kneeland continued to call for liberty. Once he was released, he decided to go west. He settled in a new community he called Salubria where neighbors were gathered together united in respect for freedom of opinion. He died on September 25, 1844.

KOLOSVAR (Cluj in Romanian). The center of Unitarianism in Transylvania, Kolosvar was the hometown of **Francis David**, the great prophet and martyr of the Unitarian faith. According to legend, David returned to Kolosvar after the great debate at Gyulafehervar in March 1568 and met a large crowd who had heard of his victory defending the truth that "God is One." He climbed on a large rock to tell them that because of the debate they would not be persecuted for whatever doctrinal views they held. Then the crowd mounted him on their shoulders and carried him to the church in the square where he could be heard better. The entire city was said to have been converted to Unitarianism that day. Soon after David declared his anti-Trinitarianism, a Unitarian college was established in Kolosvar in a former Franciscan cloister. The Unitarian Theological School of Kolosvar developed from these beginnings and remained unified with the college until 1914, when it was decided to administer the theological school separately. Over the centuries, life has often been difficult for the Unitarians in Kolosvar. This is exemplified by government seizures in 1716 when the main Unitarian church was seized, along with other Unitarian churches, as was their printing press, and government troops destroyed and pillaged the homes of leading Unitarians. Shortly thereafter the church was given to the Catholics and renamed St. Michael's Cathedral. Two years later the Unitarian college was taken.

In more tolerant times a new Unitarian church was completed in 1796 and then a few years later the "Old College" was built and operated there for 100 years. The old church was never returned. After World War I, when Kolosvar and the rest of Transylvania became part of Romania, Americans and British became concerned about their sister churches and sent investigative teams. As part of the relief effort in 1921, King's Chapel in Boston chose the church in Kolosvar as a sister congregation. More than $5,000 was sent. In 1949 the various Protestant schools were unified into a Protestant Theological Institute with university rank in Kolosvar, with shared faculty. One of the Unitarian professors, Lajos Kovacs, later became Bishop. Repression became even worse during the communist rule when there was a plan to raze villages and an attempt in Kolosvar to destroy all vestiges of Hungarian culture and language. Despite centuries of turmoil, the city of Kolosvar remains the center of the Unitarian faith, where its headquarters is located and its theological students train for the ministry.

KUEBLER, ERNEST WILLIAM (1903–1992). An important leader in Unitarian religious education in the 20th century. He was born in Kansas City, Missouri, on October 29, 1903, grew up there, and attended Kansas City Junior College. He briefly attended Northwestern University and then moved east to go to Boston University, where he received a B.R.E. from the School of Religious Education and Social Work and an M.A. in psychology. In the late 1920s he was involved with Sunday School administration in Dauphin County and then Harrisburg, Pennsylvania. After that he studied at Yale Divinity School, where he tried to work out his dynamic theories about education with theological doubts. His dean, Luther Weigle, told Kuebler that he had become a Unitarian. During this time he worked in religious education in Bridgeport, Connecticut. He had to leave when the depression wiped out his scholarship. Then in 1932 he became Director of Religious Education at the Central Congregational Church in Newtonville, Massachusetts, as a Unitarian. His innovative work there brought him to the attention of the Boston Curriculum Committee.

In 1935 Kuebler was appointed secretary of the Department of Religious Education at the **American Unitarian Association (AUA)** and then three years later he was named director. Working with a supportive AUA president in **Frederick May Eliot** and a creative curriculum developer in **Sophia Fahs**, Kuebler implemented a progressive philosophy of religious education, which he termed a "Revolt in Education." In this essay he said that religion for liberals is "everything that contributes to the growth and enrichment of personality through the complete participation in living." He saw education as an entire process of growing or becoming a person (Kuebler in *Together We Advance*, p. 159). In 1935 he appointed a Curriculum Study Committee who brought new education objectives before the AUA May Meetings in 1936. The committee emphasized a child-centered approach to education with trained teachers, teacher manuals, and, especially, new curriculum. Then the **Commission on Appraisal**'s report ***Unitarians Face a New Age*** recommended that the whole church program be "redefined in terms of education."

Sophia Fahs came to work with Kuebler as an editor in 1937. In 1938 Kuebler was ordained to a special educational ministry at King's Chapel. In 1939 Kuebler and Fahs wrote an open letter to all the ministers and education workers in the AUA describing the new plan for curriculum. After much hard work, especially with the Curriculum Committee, this dream became the New Beacon Series in Religious Education. Kuebler became an executive vice president of the AUA in 1949, and then as merger approached he was appointed to the position of administrative director of the Division of Education of the Council of Liberal Churches. He became concerned that seminaries offered little training in religious education. He wanted to establish a research center and a laboratory Sunday School at one of the seminaries, but it never materialized. In 1958 Frederick May Eliot died, and Kuebler ran for the presidency against Dana Greeley, but was defeated in a close election. He remained with the Council of Liberal Churches until 1961 when he briefly became a director of the education department at the **Unitarian Universalist Association (UUA)**, but then he resigned with 27 years of service to his credit. After that he was project director for the Hugh Moore Fund for two years and then ended his active career with district work. First, he was executive director for the new St. Lawrence District in upstate New York and then was a minister-at-large for the New York State Convention of Universalists from 1969 to 1976, which continued to have a programmatic function but was no longer a political division for the newly formed UUA. In 1980 he was given the UUA's Distinguished Service Award. He died at age 88 on January 2, 1992, in Syracuse, New York. His voice in promoting religious education helped the denomination reverse its decline in the 1930s and become a growing religious movement.

– L –

LATIMER, LEWIS HOWARD (1848–1928). An outstanding inventor and engineer who was also talented artistically and was a founder of the Flushing, New York, church. He was born in Chelsea, Massachusetts, on September 4, 1848, only six years after his parents, George and Rebecca, had escaped from slavery in Virginia. Shortly after arriving in Boston, George was recognized as an escaped slave. After the courts determined that he still belonged to his owner, abolitionists helped purchase his freedom. Lewis was the youngest of four children. He enlisted in the navy when he was 16. After the Civil War ended he returned to Boston and took an office job in a patent law firm. Latimer had always loved to draw and taught himself mechanical drawing. He was soon promoted to the much higher-paying job of draftsmen. Latimer met Alexander Graham Bell, who asked him to draws plans for the telephone, and he eventually provided Bell with blueprints and filed the papers so that he had the first telephone patent on file. In 1880 Latimer began working as a draftsman and assistant manager for Hiram Maxim, who was a founder of the U.S. Electric Light Company in Brooklyn, New York. This helped him to understand light bulbs and lamps, and he soon developed a reputation for making improvements in electric lighting. One problem with Thomas Edison's light bulbs was that they only lasted a few days. Latimer was able to design a new bulb that encased the carbon filament in an envelope so that the bulbs lasted longer and became cheaper to produce. He helped to install electric plants for Philadelphia, New York, and Montreal.

Thomas Edison became aware of Latimer's amazing skills, and hired him in 1884. His knowledge of electric lighting and patents proved invaluable. Edison made him a draftsman and engineer at first and later his chief draftsman and patent expert who investigated those who used Edison's inventions without permission. In 1890 Latimer wrote *Incandescent Electric Lighting: A Practical Description of the Edison System*, which explained how the lamps worked. Latimer was married to Mary Wilson in 1873, and they had two children. He was also a brilliant poet and playwright who also painted and played the flute. His poems were published as *Poems of Love and Life*. Latimer was one of the founding members of the First Unitarian Church of

Flushing, New York. The church began to have informal meetings in 1905 and incorporated in 1908 with Latimer being a charter member. The church started a building fund in 1914 and began to erect their building in 1916, with Latimer involved in some ways. He also served as a church auditor. His wife and family members also helped provide music for the society and led them in singing. He also used his skills to help immigrants by teaching drawing and English at the Henry Street Settlement House. He was involved in patriotic activities with the Grand Army of the Republic (GAR) and was also active in civil rights work. He closed out his work life by working for a patent consulting business. Latimer died on December 11, 1928. His granddaughter Winifred Norman served on the Board of the **Unitarian Universalist Association (UUA)**. His remarkable legacy of inventions meant that his name appeared on seven patents issued by the U.S. government. These included not only the more famous lamp fixtures, but also toilets for railway cars, a cooling and disinfecting system, and a locking rack for hats, coats, and umbrellas. He was named an Edison Pioneer as a founder of the electrical industry—the only African American to be so honored. Latimer can be credited with making it possible for society to have widespread use of the electric light.

LEND-A-HAND CLUBS. Edward Everett Hale, Unitarian minister of the South Congregational Society in Boston, inspired the organizing of over 50,000 Lend-A-Hand Clubs throughout the world. The guiding philosophy came from his story *Ten Times One Is Ten*, published in 1870. The hero of the story was Henry Wadsworth, whose friends gathered at his funeral and began to recount stories about how he had done something for each one of them that had awakened respect, gratitude, admiration, and love. Hale first voiced the motto for these groups at his Lowell Institute lectures on "The Divine Order of Human Life" in 1869: "Look up and not down; look forward and not back; look out and not in; and lend a hand." They were also known as Harry Wadsworth Clubs and Look-Up Legions, among other names. The first Lend-A-Hand Club was organized in New York among street boys. The mission of these clubs was summarized in Hale's verse, "How all shall lend a hand . . . to help the faint and weary." The clubs were formed primarily among young people for moral and social improvement always with a plan to lend a hand to help other people. Many of these clubs were informally organized, but the movement to invigorate communities with a greater public spirit and lives of service to others was a resounding success. One successful exponent of the Lend-A-Hand Clubs were the Look-Up Legions that were organized in more than 500 Methodist Sunday Schools. Although the organizational influence is virtually gone, the words "lend a hand" are used throughout the world, and the specific charitable activities, as started by Hale, are still carried on in an existing Lend-A-Hand Society in Boston, which was organized in 1886 and incorporated in 1891. Hale was its president until his death in 1909.

LIBERAL CHRISTIAN. The name preferred by those rational Christians in the **Standing Order** of Massachusetts who shunned the sectarian Unitarian label until it was forced upon them. They rejected the name at the beginning of the theological controversy in 1805 for fear of being thought of as exclusive or intolerant. Following the latest trends in biblical criticism, the liberal Christians were a group that wished to remain within the Congregational fold even as their orthodox opponents, led by Jedediah Morse, tried to disassociate themselves.

The liberals followed certain major points of faith. They believed in the unity or oneness of God, who is distinguished from the Son, who received his power from God but does not identify himself with God. This one God is chiefly understood through His moral character and not His sovereignty. There is a benevolent nature to this parental God who desires the happiness of His creatures. The world is a place for human education resulting in ever-growing virtue. Humans can achieve the ultimate goal of virtue because they have the free ability to respond to their moral duties and are not handicapped by predestination or original sin. The mission of Christ is for the moral and spiritual deliverance of humankind, but there is no sense of atonement. Jesus' mission is not to change God's mind, but to change human minds. It became Morse's goal to separate the two factions of Unitarian and Trinitarian Congregationalists, and he was largely able to fix the Unitarian name after 1815 when he published the pamphlet *American Unitarianism*, which actually described the more radical version of Unitarianism (complete human view of Jesus) that was prevalent in Great Britain. When Morse published a review of *American Unitarianism* in the orthodox journal *The Panoplist*, he called for the expulsion of the Unitarians, whom he said were heretics that were trying to overthrow the true faith. Although they wanted a purer understanding of Christianity within the established ecclesiastical structures at first, the liberals finally submitted to the pressure and named their new association Unitarian in 1825.

LIBERAL RELIGIOUS EDUCATION DIRECTORS ASSOCIATION (LREDA). The professional and support organization for Unitarian Universalist religious educators. In 1949 **Sophia Lyon Fahs** organized a week-long workshop on religious education at the Meadville Institute, which was a summer conference held in Lake Chautauqua, New York. This attracted thirty people who were mostly religious educators. At the workshop a laboratory school was set up from the children of families attending the conference. One important outgrowth of this workshop was that those religious education directors who were present organized themselves into an association. In 1954 this association became LREDA. This group began to develop standards for the profession. They have worked closely over the years with the **Unitarian Universalist Association**'s **(UUA)** education departments in an advisory capacity to assist with the development of programs and resources, as well as with professional recognition and leadership development. With the advent of the UUA bylaw change in 1979 allowing for the fellowshipping of the Ministry of Religious Education, the name of this organization was changed to Liberal Religious Educators' Association. Its membership includes ordained ministers who specialize in religious education and lay religious educators, many of whom are part-time professionals.

LIBERAL RELIGIOUS YOUTH (LRY). The youth organization created in 1953 by the consolidation of the American Unitarian Youth and the Universalist Youth Fellowship. It was the first joint group to be created from the separate denominations on the path to merger. Over the years the LRY developed a reputation for independence and rebelliousness, and leaders frequently saw themselves as catalysts for change. After merger in 1961 the LRY executive director became a staff member in the Department of Education. The director of the youth office at that time was C. Leon Hopper Jr. The college age portion of youth programs was called the Channing Murray Foundation, later renamed Student Religious Liberals (SRL). The LRY delegates to the General Assembly in 1969 played an important supportive role of protest with the Black Affairs Council. Unfortunately, reports of youth conferences became legendary during this volatile time period with respect to drug use and sexual activity. The LRY's reputation threatened its very survival as some congregations refused to affiliate.

Declines in interest and affiliation led the **Unitarian Universalist Association (UUA)** to establish a committee to study the LRY in 1976. They reported that youth programming "was inadequate and a disservice to youth," with adults completely abrogating their role. In 1979 a new youth office was formed with Wayne Arnason as its first full-time director in 10 years. The publication of the youth office was *People Soup*. A complete overhaul of youth programming was achieved after a continental youth conference in 1981, Common Ground. After that the LRY board voted to dissolve and support the new UU youth organization, **Young Religious Unitarian Universalists (YRUU)**, on January 1, 1983.

LIBERTY CLAUSE. Appended to the **Winchester Profession** of 1803, the liberty clause was an important Universalist statement affirming the rights of individuals not to be bound creedally to any professions of faith. It stated: "Yet while we adopt a general profession of belief . . . we leave it to the several churches and societies or to smaller associations of churches, if such should be formed, within the limits of our General Association, to continue or adopt within themselves, such more articles of faith . . . as may appear to them best under their particular circumstances, provided they do not disagree with our general profession or plan." The liberty clause remained part of the profession until 1870, when the denomination adopted a revised constitution. In an effort to achieve denominational unity and organizational efficiency, the Winchester Profession was made part of the document but for the first time a required "expressed assent" to its wording became a necessary condition for fellowship. Many Universalists argued that this gave them more doctrinal authority and a firmer legal status.

This new quest for doctrinal unity was put to the test in 1872 with the Bisbee Heresy Trial. Herman Bisbee was pastor at St. Anthony Universalist Church in Minnesota. He had fallen under the influence of the **Free Religious Association (FRA)** and came under attack for a series of lectures he gave on natural religion. Bisbee denied the miracles and said the infallibility of the Bible was an unsupportable myth. He said that natural religion was "the effort man makes to perfect himself, not the effort that God makes to perfect him." The denominational press editorialized that Bisbee was unworthy of fellowship and that his teachings were subversive. While Bisbee admitted that he wanted to counter the conservative tendencies of Universalism, he believed that the liberty clause allowed him liberty of interpretation and that it was a freedom that Universalists had always held to. The Committee on Fellowship and Discipline of the Minnesota Convention met in June 1872 and heard the report charging Bisbee with "unministerial conduct." The issue was that Bisbee was teaching doctrines that the committee felt were not in keeping with those held and taught by the Universalist denomination, and they voted to withdraw his fellowship. A Board of Appeal upheld this ruling, and it later came out that the board was convinced that Bisbee was being antagonistic to organized Universalism. Although his church voted that he could remain as minister, Bisbee resigned and never served a Universalist church again. He died in 1879. The deletion of the liberty clause and the Bisbee trial began a period of nearly 30 years of denominational wrangling over whether the principles of Universalism could be codified in a fixed creedal statement. The issue was resolved with the adoption of a new liberty clause in Article III of the constitution ("neither this, nor any other precise form of words, is required as a condition of fellowship, provided always that the principles above stated be professed") in the Boston Declaration of 1899.

LINDSEY, THEOPHILUS (1723–1808). The founder of the first Unitarian church in England was a courageous early leader for the movement. He was born on June 20, 1723, at Middlewich, Cheshire. A good student, he entered St. John's College, Cambridge, finished his degrees, and became a fellow in 1747. After a brief pastorate, he became chaplain to the Duke of Somerset and traveled in Europe for two years. After that he became rector at a parish in Kirkby Wiske in

Hosea Ballou. *Courtesy of Unitarian Universalist Association*

Nathaniel Stacy. *Courtesy of the author*

William Ellery Channing. *Courtesy of Unitarian Universalist Association*

Theodore Parker. *Courtesy of The First Parish of Watertown, Massachusetts*

Thomas Starr King. *Courtesy of Unitarian Universalist Association*

Dorothea Dix. *Courtesy of The Schlesinger Library, Radcliffe Institute, Harvard University*

Lydia Maria Child. *Courtesy of The Schlesinger Library, Radcliffe Institute, Harvard University*

Olympia Brown. *Courtesy of Unitarian Universalist Association*

Mary Livermore. *Courtesy of the author*

Clarence Russell Skinner. *Courtesy of Unitarian Universalist Association*

Aurelia Henry Reinhardt. *Courtesy of Mills College Art Museum*

William Sinkford. *Courtesy of Unitarian Universalist Association*

Yorkshire. Here he became friendly with Archdeacon Blackburne and eventually married Blackburne's stepdaughter, who was a firm supporter of Lindsey when all others deserted him. After three years he moved on to a parish in Dorset at Piddletown. He remained there for seven years and had a promising ministry, but he began to have questions about the Trinity. Becoming a serious student of the Bible, he finally concluded that Christ was a mere human being. In 1763 he moved back to the north of England to serve at Catterick, near Richmond. Here he set up Bible classes for village children and schools for the poor, but his parish successes were outweighed by the loss of integrity he felt about his beliefs. In 1769 he met **Joseph Priestley**, who would become his friend. At the time Lindsey was being advised by others to revise the liturgy in order to accommodate his beliefs but not resign from the church. For a time he became involved in a movement for clergy who opposed subscribing to doctrinal formulas, the Feathers Tavern Petition, but it was defeated, and Lindsey became more insistent that he would resign. After he did so, many of his friends refused to speak to him. Lindsey was not deterred and settled on a plan to organize a purely Unitarian congregation in London. Nearly destitute, the family sold most of its belongings, including the furniture and Lindsey's library. During the journey to London, Lindsey saw Samuel Clarke's revised *Book of Common Prayer* for the first time. He also wrote an account of the errors of Christendom and the development of Unitarian thought, which was later published as *The Apology of Theophilus Lindsey*.

After settling in London, Lindsey found a site for a chapel in a room on Essex Street that was used for book auctions and set up a liturgy based on an adapted version of Clarke's revisions. On April 17, 1774, Lindsey conducted the first avowedly Unitarian service in England without wearing the usual white surplice. There were about 200 people there, including Benjamin Franklin, who continued to attend while he was in England. The congregation grew, and a little less than four years later a newly renovated Essex Street chapel, which they now owned, was opened with a large chapel on one floor and minister's residence on another. Not long after this, Lindsey became ill and the congregation started to search for an assistant. John Disney was called to that position in 1783. After this Lindsey was able to spend more time writing. In 1783 he produced the first attempt to link all the Unitarian movements in one history, *An Historical View . . . of the Unitarian Doctrine and Worship from the Reformation to Our Own Times*. A few years after that Lindsey publicly defended his friend Priestley when the president of Magdalen College, Oxford, attacked him and pronounced him unfit to write. In 1788 he published *Vindiciae Priestleianae: An Address to the Students of Oxford and Cambridge*, and then followed that two years later with a work that more directly addressed the question of Christ's nature: *A Second Address, . . .* etc. Here Lindsey questioned the historical validity of the Gospel stories and the miracles and said that the human Jesus was subject to the same frailties and errors as everyone else. He also omitted the Apostles' Creed from the final version of the liturgy he produced. Lindsey resigned from his pastorate when he reached the age of 70 and enjoyed a relatively peaceful retirement. He was active with a new publishing organization, the Unitarian Society for Promoting Christian Knowledge. When John Disney resigned from Essex Street, Lindsey hoped his successor would be from among the ranks of dissatisfied Anglican clergy, but a Dissenter, Thomas Belsham, was settled. Much to his dismay, Lindsey's hope for a mass exodus from the ranks of Anglican clergy never materialized. Early in 1808 he became quite ill and died that year on November 3. Although he was not an original thinker, Lindsey was a courageous and determined leader for the early Unitarian movement in England. By 1810 there were 20 Unitarian congregations in England, and Lindsey had laid the groundwork for the future expansion of the faith.

LIVERMORE, MARY ASHTON RICE (1820–1905). Lived a long, productive life advocating for reform and women's rights. She was born in Boston on December 19, 1820, into a faithful Calvinist Baptist family. The fourth of six children born to Timothy and Zebiah (Ashton), Rice was an active, athletic girl, who loved learning. At about the time that she finished attending the Hancock School, her sister Rachel died, and Mary was tormented with the question of salvation. She was sent to the Charlestown Female Academy and graduated when she was 16. After a year of teaching, she defied her parents by accepting a position as a governess with a family in Virginia. For three years she experienced slavery firsthand and became a committed abolitionist. During this sojourn she found books by Deists

Ethan Allen and **Thomas Paine** in her employer's library and acquainted herself with these radical views, which she could not reconcile with her childhood orthodoxy. When she returned home, she moved to Duxbury in 1842 to run a school. On Christmas Eve she went out walking and heard a Christmas hymn coming from the Universalist church. Although her childhood church had never celebrated Christmas, and she had heard that Universalists were disreputable, she went in and sat in the back pew. The minister Daniel Livermore preached that God brings everyone safely home, no matter how lost they might feel. After the service Mary met Livermore and asked for a copy of the sermon. This began a relationship that progressed to marriage in 1845.

During the next few years the Livermores moved frequently. Daniel served several churches including Fall River and Weymouth, Massachusetts, and Stafford, Connecticut. Both the Livermores found their views on social issues to be controversial wherever they went. They were advocates for temperance, women's suffrage, and abolition. Because of the difficulties they encountered in parish settings, they developed a new vocation. In 1858 the family, now with three children, moved to Chicago so that Daniel could become owner and editor of a Universalist paper, the *New Covenant*. Mary wrote for her husband's paper and for other publications as well. She was active in the Universalist Church of the Redeemer and served on the Board of the Northwest Conference of Universalists as well. She once said, "This faith in Universalism, during the years that I have believed it, has grown upon me, until it is the central thing in me. I do not engage in anything that is not, as I see it, the outcome of this faith. My later comprehension has given me a noble and abiding faith in human destiny" (as quoted in Scott, *These Live Tomorrow*, p. 145).

In the city she helped found the Chicago Home for Aged Women and the Hospital for Women and Children. When the Civil War started, **Henry Whitney Bellows** chose Mary and another Universalist, Jane Hoge, to be associates of his in the U.S. Sanitary Commission. Livermore visited battlefields, did organizational and administrative work, public speaking, and fund-raising for the organization. She helped arrange two gigantic fairs that raised thousands of dollars. After the war, she devoted much of her time to women's suffrage. She started and edited a paper, the *Agitator*, which later merged with a Boston paper, *Woman's Journal*, of which she became editor. The Livermores moved to Melrose, Massachusetts, where they lived for the rest of their lives. After two years of editorial work, Mary switched to the lecture circuit for her prime means of employment. Frequently touching on controversial topics, despite the warning of her agents, she became a popular speaker on topics such as "What Shall We Do with Our Daughters?" and "Concerning Husbands." From 1875 to 1878 she was president of the American Woman Suffrage Association. In 1878 the Livermores went to Paris to attend the International Women's Rights Congress. Mary lectured all over Europe, and in England was dubbed the "Queen of the Platform." Back home she continued to advocate for women's suffrage and equal rights. She received an L.L.D. from Tufts University in 1896, the first honorary degree they conferred to a woman. She recounted her war experience in *My Story of the War* and her entire autobiography in *The Story of My Life* (1899). She died on May 23, 1905.

LOCKE, JOHN (1632–1704). Perhaps the most significant figure in the development of Enlightenment thought, Locke influenced political developments with his *Two Treatises of Government* (1690) and religious thought with his *Essay Concerning Human Understanding* (1690). Locke became an advocate of toleration for all beliefs unless they were a threat to peace and he voiced this in *A Letter Concerning Toleration*. His "sensationalist" philosophy was grounded in empiricism, which many of the American Unitarians modified into common sense realism. They argued that God had implanted common sense in the mind so that human beings can trust their senses and come to know God through natural signs.

LONGFELLOW, HENRY WADSWORTH (1807–1882). The best-known poet in mid-19th-century America, his brother **Samuel Longfellow** became a Unitarian minister, and Henry played an active part in all the liberal circles of his day. Henry was born February 27, 1807, in Portland, Maine, to Stephen Longfellow and Zilpah Wadsworth Longfellow. Sent to school at the age of three, he was drawn to writing and words at a young age. Although his father wanted him to become a lawyer, Henry was asked to teach in a new department of modern languages at Bowdoin College during his senior year there. Traveling to Europe before taking up the new position, he went from country to country for three years, preparing his own English-language texts of European literature. After teaching at Bowdoin for two years, he married schoolmate Mary Storer Potter in 1831, after he saw her at the First Parish Church in Portland where Longfellow's mother had long been active and his father became increasingly so due to a friendship with **William Ellery Channing**, who had been his classmate. Stephen Longfellow became one of the first vice presidents of the **American Unitarian Association (AUA)** after it was organized in 1825. Samuel Longfellow said, "It was in the doctrine and the spirit of early Unitarianism that Henry Longfellow was nurtured at church and at home. And there is no reason to suppose that he ever found these insufficient, or that he ever essentially departed from them. Of his genuine religious feeling his writings give ample testimony. . . . He did not care to talk much on theological points; but he believed in the supremacy of good in the world and in the universe" (as quoted in Cooke, *Unitarianism in America*, p. 432). His lifelong Unitarian revulsion toward obscuring the teachings of Jesus with theological creeds and blind faith is reflected in the relatively unknown *Divine Tragedy* (1871).

During Longfellow's tenure at Bowdoin he became a founding member of the Unitarian church in Brunswick, Maine, in 1830. He became a professor at **Harvard College** in 1834 and set off for Europe again to prepare himself. His wife died in Rotterdam after suffering a miscarriage. Seven years later he married Frances Appleton with the service being conducted by **Ezra Stiles Gannett** of Boston's **Federal Street Church**. He and his wife had six children. During this time he established himself at Harvard, published his first book of poetry, and sided with the abolitionists as shown in *Poems on Slavery* (1842). Longfellow was among the first writers to develop American themes in his writing giving a powerful mythology to the country in such figures as Paul Revere and the village blacksmith. His Bowdoin classmate **Nathaniel Hawthorne** provided him with the story for *Evangeline* (1847) in the forest primeval, which proved quite successful.

Deciding that teaching was a hindrance to his writing, Longfellow resigned from Harvard in 1854. That year he began *The Song of Hiawatha*. He joined with others to found the *Atlantic Monthly* in 1857.

The Courtship of Miles Standish was published in 1858. In 1861 his wife died from burns she received in a house fire. Thereafter, Longfellow threw himself into his work of translating Dante. During his later life, his fame spread and he received numerous honors throughout Europe, including a bust at Westminster Abbey. Longfellow was widely read the world over and everyone from poet to monarch who came to America wanted to visit the most famous writer in the world, including **Charles Dickens** who once shared breakfast with Longfellow and the "Unitarian pope," **Andrews Norton**. Longfellow died on March 24, 1882, and was buried in Mt. Auburn Cemetery, Cambridge.

LONGFELLOW, SAMUEL (1819–1892). The youngest brother of **Henry Wadsworth Longfellow**, Samuel made his reputation primarily as a hymn writer. He was born on June 18, 1819, in Portland, Maine, and brought up in that city's First Parish. Henry was already teaching at Harvard College when Samuel matriculated there in 1835. Graduating in 1839, he taught for a number of years and then entered the **Harvard Divinity School** in 1842. He developed an enduring friendship with Samuel Johnson, and together they collaborated on writing and assembling hymns. This resulted in the joint publication *A Book of Hymns for Public and Private Devotion*, which went through 12 editions. After it was adopted by his congregation, **Theodore Parker** apparently referred to the hymnal as the "Book of Sams."

When Longfellow graduated he was called to Fall River, Massachusetts, where he was ordained and installed in February 1848. After a three-year ministry, which included some wrangling over the slavery question, Longfellow traveled to Europe. Upon his return he became minister at the Second Unitarian Church in Brooklyn, New York, where he remained until 1860. Here he wrote the first Unitarian vesper service, including the hymn "Now on Land and Sea Descending." Again Samuel went traveling to Europe, where, for a time, he collaborated with Johnson again to produce *Hymns of the Spirit* (1864), a title that was reused in the 20th century for the first joint hymnal of the Unitarian and Universalist denominations.

Longfellow did not assume another pulpit until 1878 when he began his final ministry at Germantown, Pennsylvania, where he remained for five years. He spent the last years of his life in Cambridge, where he compiled biographies of his brother Henry (1886) and Samuel Johnson (1883). Longfellow sensed the divine as made manifest in all aspects of nature and throughout the world's religions, and this is reflected in some of his more popular hymns, "God of the Earth, the Sky, the Sea" and "Light of Ages and of Nations." In all, he wrote some 50 hymns. **Octavius Brooks Frothingham** considered him a mystical Transcendentalist who had a reflective and meditative personality. Samuel Longfellow died on October 3, 1892.

LOVE IS THE SPIRIT OF THIS CHURCH. A popular covenant in Unitarian Universalists congregations written by James Vila Blake (1842–1925) and adopted by the Church of All Souls, Evanston, Illinois, on April 29, 1894. Blake also served congregations in Quincy and Chicago, Illinois. He was a hymn writer as well and was the coeditor of *Unity Hymns and Chorals* (1892). The text is: "Love is the spirit of this church, and service its law. This is our great covenant: To dwell together in peace, To seek the truth in love, And to help one another."

LOWELL, JAMES RUSSELL (1819–1891). A poet of great renown in the 19th century, Lowell was one of six children born to Harriet B. Spencer and Charles Lowell, the Unitarian minister who served the West Church of Boston for many years. The elder Lowell was theologically Unitarian, but he refused to attach himself to any definitive denominational label other than Christian. "Jemmie" was born on February 22, 1819, in Cambridge, Massachusetts, at what became the family estate, "Elmwood." After attending a number of local schools he enrolled at **Harvard College** at the age of 15. Lowell was attracted to the power of words at an early age and especially enjoyed his class in rhetoric taught by **William Ellery Channing**'s brother, Edward. He proved a lackluster student though and was suspended in his senior year for neglecting his work. He was tutored by Barzillai Frost, the pastor of the parish church in Concord, Massachusetts, and there had the opportunity to meet **Ralph Waldo Emerson**. He liked Emerson personally, but seemed to find his doctrines too ethereal.

Lowell was elected class poet, a label that worried his father, who wondered if he would ever amount to anything. After his graduation from Harvard in 1838, Lowell considered being a preacher like his father but decided to take a law degree instead. The year of his graduation he said, "I am an infidel to the Christianity of today." Later in a letter to **Henry Wadsworth Longfellow** he wrote that the church must be reformed "from foundation to weathercock" (as quoted in Cooke, *Unitarianism in America*, 434). Like Emerson he drew much of his inspiration from nature and considered himself an intuitionalist. At times in his later life he showed some interest in more traditional faiths, but ultimately he rejected the idea of creeds and founded his church in "universal Love."

In 1840 Lowell married Maria White of Watertown, Massachusetts, who was an accomplished poet in her own right. She became part of one of **Margaret Fuller**'s Conversations groups. Maria and her brother William, who had been Lowell's classmate at Harvard helped stimulate his interest in the social problems of the day. By 1842 he became convinced that he would never succeed as a lawyer; he turned his attention full-time to writing and published his first book of poems. His interest in reform grew after he moved to Philadelphia to edit an antislavery periodical. In the late 1840s the *Biglow Papers* began to appear. These were political satires meant to express opposition to the Mexican War, which Lowell depicted as an effort to extend slavery. Before 1850 he published three other significant works. First, there was his contribution to the Arthurian legend, in which Lowell democratized the search for the Holy Grail in *The Vision of Sir Launfal*. The other publications that helped secure his fame as a major figure in American literature were *Poems: Second Series* and the witty, biting evaluation of contemporary American authors, *A Fable for Critics*. Here he confronted the Unitarians when he asked if they formed a religious union based on total dissent, how they could label **Theodore Parker** a heretic? During these early years of publishing success, Lowell began to suffer a series of devastating personal losses. By 1852 three of his four children had died, and Maria, his wife, died the following year. In 1855 a series of lectures on English poets led to his appointment to a professorship at Harvard. He married Frances Dunlap, the nanny for his remaining child, Mabel, in 1857.

He published a second series of *Biglow Papers* on the subject of the Union cause. He also served as the first editor of the *Atlantic*

Monthly and later with Charles Eliot Norton of the *North American Review*. Lowell became one of the founders of the Saturday Club, a monthly gathering of local writers for dinner and conversation. As he grew older the reform impulse of his youth faded as he embraced his aristocratic heritage. Much of his later writing consisted of critical essays on important literary figures. He won political appointments from 1877 to 1885, first as U.S. Ambassador to Spain and later to England. Lowell died on August 19, 1891.

– M –

MACLEAN, ANGUS HECTOR (1892–1969). A principal Universalist educator in the 20th century. MacLean was born on Cape Breton Island, Nova Scotia, to Neil and Peggy (MacRae) MacLean in 1892. Described later as a big rugged man with a Scottish accent, he had a Presbyterian background and left high school before he graduated to go on a recruiting mission with the Presbyterian Missionary Society. He enrolled at Westminster Hall Seminary in Vancouver, British Columbia. For a time, he was a horseback riding lay preacher and recounted this experience in *The Galloping Gospel* (1966). After that he went to McGill University. Before he could finish he entered military service in the medical corps for fours years during World War I. He attended the University of Edinburgh for one term and then returned to McGill and finished his B.A. Then he attended the Theological College at McGill, where he was first exposed to modern biblical criticism. He had difficulty getting licensed as a Presbyterian preacher because of his liberal views. He married Ruth Rogers in the spring of 1922, and they had two children. The Teachers College at Columbia University in New York granted him a fellowship and awarded him a Ph.D. in 1930. Before he graduated he had been working as an instructor and then the Canton Theological School of **St. Lawrence University** hired him in 1928. Eventually, he became the Richardson Professor of Religious Education and Psychology. During his training he had become concerned about how the idea of God was taught to children because assumptions were made about what God looked like and whether or not God existed in the first place. After he went to St. Lawrence, he published *The New Era in Religious Education* (1934).

MacLean remained an uncommitted liberal Christian until the 1940s when he embraced Universalism. Then he was ordained in 1945 at the Church of the Divine Paternity in New York. In 1946 he was named chairman of the first Department of Education in the **Universalist Church of America (UCA)**. He was appointed dean of the Theological School in 1951 to succeed **John Murray Atwood**. As dean he saw the immediate need to bolster the financial base and a Development Office was established in 1957. He placed a strong emphasis on pastoral duties in preparing students for the ministry. MacLean retired from his position in 1960, as the two denominations were preparing to consolidate. As dean he also carried a heavy teaching load as well. Despite his best efforts, the school's enrollment had not increased and financial problems still beset it. As a religious educator, MacLean placed prime value on the family as the base for religious growth. He spoke of modeling religious ideals by the whole community, so that in his educational model, "The Method is the Message" (UUA Pamphlet, 1962), he said that education must be relevant to the child, the church, and the problems of the world. He did much to revolutionize religious education while he was at St. Lawrence, including adding courses in philosophy, psychology, and youth work, as well as incorporating arts and crafts as a regular part of religious education curriculum. MacLean addressed many important religious questions in his *The Wind in Both Ears* (1965). After he left St. Lawrence, he served in retirement as minister of education at the First Unitarian Universalist Church in Cleveland. His ability to develop an educational structure that nurtures both children and adults was recognized in 1971 when the St. Lawrence Alumni Association established the Angus MacLean award for excellence in the field of religious education.

MCGEE, LEWIS A. (1893–1979). Called a black pioneer in a white denomination, McGee was the first minister of an experimental interracial congregation in Chicago. He was born on November 11, 1893, in Scranton, Pennsylvania. Ministry was in his blood, as his father, an emancipated slave, was an African Methodist Episcopal (AME) minister. The family moved frequently as his father changed positions. McGee graduated from high school in 1912 and then attended the University of Pittsburgh for a year before going to Payne

Theological School at Wilberforce University, where he received a B.D. in 1916. The following year he was ordained an elder in the AME church.

In 1918 McGee joined the army as a chaplain and later was minister of a number of AME churches in Ohio and West Virginia. In 1927 he moved to Chicago and became a social worker with Illinois Children's and Home Aid Society. While he was there he took college courses and subsequently received a B.A. from Carthage College. He returned briefly to the ministry, leaving a church in Gary, Indiana, when he joined the army again as a chaplain in 1943. He remained until after the war was over and was discharged as a captain. That fall McGee married Marcella. In the spring of 1946 he enrolled at **Meadville Lombard Theological School**, where he studied for a year, after which he received Unitarian fellowship. He had encountered Unitarianism many years previously when he came across a copy of the ***Christian Register*** while delivering mail. He visited a church then and decided that he was one of those people who were a Unitarian without knowing it.

In 1928 McGee met Unitarian minister **Curtis Reese** and read his book of humanist sermons. Reese told him then that the Unitarian church offered no opportunities for blacks. After the war, McGee felt like the time for integration had arrived, and he decided he wanted to be part of an interracial church. Wallace Robbins tried to help him find a position, but a new opportunity opened up in Chicago. The **American Unitarian Association (AUA)** approved the idea for a project that had been suggested by McGee to Randall Hilton, the secretary of the **Western Unitarian Conference (WUC)**. This was to be a survey of black Chicagoans on the South Side. The AUA was looking for a way to address the black community, and they hired McGee to see if this survey would show they had the potential for a Unitarian church. Harry Jones, following a discussion at the Ethical Society, had helped organize a few meetings in June 1947 to explore founding a Unitarian fellowship. The first regular service of the Free Religious Fellowship was held on October 5, 1947, with Kenneth Patton preaching.

McGee's final report to the AUA confirmed that there was room in Chicago for an interracial church. On April 25, 1948, the fellowship was organized. McGee was installed as minister in June. During its early years the fellowship grew to have 98 members and offered a variety of other programs. Membership fell after they moved to the **Abraham Lincoln Centre** for services, but McGee worked hard to build the congregation back up. Not a charismatic preacher, McGee offered humanist sermons in highly reasoned fashion. Although he had a strong social conscience, he was never divisive. In June 1953 he left the Fellowship, and worked for a time at the **American Humanist Association (AHA)**. In 1958 he returned to the parish as associate minister in Los Angeles and then served as the first minister of the congregation in Chico, California. This was the first time that a black man had served as senior minister of a white church. He ended his career with three short ministries, first as interim in Anaheim, followed by Throop Memorial in Pasadena and finally, Bayside, California, where he was named emeritus in 1966. He died on October 10, 1979 in Pullman, Washington, leaving his wife and two children, Ruth Harris and Charles McGee. McGee made a significant and successful effort to bring the liberal religious message to the black community.

MCKEEMAN, GORDON B. (1920–). A former president of the **Starr King School**, McKeeman also ran for the presidency of the **Unitarian Universalist Association (UUA)**. Known variously as "Bucky" and "Mac" he was born in Lynn, Massachusetts, on September 12, 1920, the oldest child of William and Lena (Goodridge) McKeeman. His father was a letter carrier, and the family lived on the upper floor of a triple decker. McKeeman went to a Congregational church as a child, but his father was interested in spiritualism and referred to himself as a "Home Baptist." As a child, young Gordon went to local public schools and graduated from Lynn English High School. In junior high school, McKeeman began to attend the First Universalist Church in Lynn, where all his friends were going, and he fell under the influence of Alice Harrison, the director of religious education.

McKeeman became the first person in his family to attend college and finished under some financial duress with a B.S. in education from Salem State Teachers College (Massachusetts) in 1942. During his college years, McKeeman began to date Phyllis Bradstreet. They were engaged in 1940 and married in 1944. Throughout his career,

Phyllis played a prominent role in most every endeavor—when the UUA awarded its Distinguished Service Award in 1993, the McKeemans were corecipients. Together they had three boys. During the war, he received a student deferment so that he might attend the **Tufts College** School of Religion. He graduated with a S.T.M. in 1945 after having served as a student minister in South Action, Massachusetts. In 1944, he received a full call to the All Souls Universalist Church in Worcester, Massachusetts, where he remained until 1950. During his Worcester ministry, a group of young Tufts graduates formed an organization in his living room called the **Humiliati**. This group tried to revitalize Universalism with a liturgical vitality, including the symbolism of an off-centered cross reflecting that Universalism was "more than Christianity with a difference." After that McKeeman moved on first to Stoughton (1950–55) and then to Palmer (1955–61), Massachusetts. Phyllis became especially active with the Girl Scouts in Stoughton, and Gordon became a community leader in Palmer, where the church constructed a new fellowship hall during his ministry. In Palmer he served on the hospital board, and was president of the local Rotary club.

In 1961 McKeeman was called to a large, dynamic congregation in Akron, Ohio, where he remained until 1983. During this time he began to be more active in the denomination. He began two terms on the UUA **Board of Trustees** in 1969 and was its vice moderator from 1975 to 1977. He also began a 10-year period of service on the board of the **Unitarian Universalist Service Committee (UUSC)** in 1969, including being its president from 1973 to 1977. In 1976 McKeeman decided to run for the presidency of the UUA and became part of the "**Jack (Mendelsohn)**, Paul (Carnes), and Bucky Show" all over the continent, with Carnes winning in a close election. After Carnes died in office, the UUA Board had to pick a successor until the next election. McKeeman lost in a close election to **Eugene Pickett**. McKeeman also served as a ministerial settlement representative in the Ohio Meadville District of the UUA from 1970 to 1983. During a preaching engagement on the West Coast, several people approached McKeeman about serving as president of the **Starr King School** after he had agreed to serve on a presidential advisory group the previous year. Eventually the search committee chose McKeeman, and he spent five years (1983–88) as the president, helping to put the school on a sounder financial base. After that he retired, and he presently resides in Charlottesville, Virginia.

In his religious odyssey, McKeeman wrote, "I believe in institutions. I even believe in the conservative mission of institutions. I believe institutions, if they are to fulfill their purpose, must be conservative. But to be viably conservative, they have to change." McKeeman said that he always hoped some other job than minister might leap off the want ad pages in the Sunday newspaper, but he never found anything else he was qualified for. He edited several volumes of devotional materials including a UUA meditation manual of Universalist materials, *To Meet the Asking Years* (1984). He received the UUA's religious education **Angus H. MacLean** award, and he was the **Berry Street Conerence** essayist in 1993. He and Phyllis were honorary cochairs of the celebration of the 200th anniversary of Universalism. He received an honorary D.D. from **Meadville Lombard Theological School** in 1969.

MANN, HORACE (1796–1859). The most powerful influence on the development of public schools in Massachusetts during the 19th century, Mann's liberal views of human nature and perfectibility profoundly influenced educational philosophy. Horace Mann was born in Franklin, Massachusetts, in relative poverty. The youngest of five, his father died when he was 13. The following year, 1810, his older brother Stephen drowned. Instead of going to church, Stephen had gone swimming. The minister at the funeral left no doubt as to his future state by describing the lake of fire and brimstone. Horace had long been troubled by bad dreams, and now following the death of his brother, he saw images of a God who enjoyed Stephen's torment. He decided that this unjust God was not for him and the road to Unitarianism lay open. Mann attended Brown College and graduated in the class of 1819. He attended the Litchfield (Connecticut) Law School, was admitted to the bar in 1823, and began practicing in Dedham, Massachusetts. In a few years he became a state representative and then a senator in the Massachusetts Legislature.

During these years he played a role in two cases that had a direct bearing upon religious issues. A bill before the house in 1828 would have allowed the First Church in Blandford to establish a fund for the support of a "Trinitarian" minister. Mann spoke out for religious freedom, stating that the populace needed to be left unshackled. The bill was deferred and eventually died. In Milton, Massachusetts, the members of the First Parish were involved in a suit with their minister, Samuel Gile, over property of the parishes that the minister had obtained title to. Mann successfully argued that Gile was living in violation of their agreement. His experience at the nearby First Parish in Dedham had shown that the parish had the legal authority to call the minister and hold the property. During Mann's service in the state legislature he helped to create the Massachusetts Board of Education, the first of its kind in the country. Then in 1837 he was appointed its secretary. He began to advocate for improving teacher pay and an improved system of teacher training. He learned something of educational philosophy in Europe when he visited there in 1843 to study conditions and learn methods. That same year he was married for the second time to Mary Peabody, one of the famous Peabody Sisters of Salem. Together they had three sons. His first wife, Charlotte Messer, had died in 1832 when she was only 23.

Mann began to alienate people when he returned from Europe and advocated the abolishment of corporal punishment. His Unitarian faith also led him to support nonsectarian education. Thus he incurred the wrath of church officials, who accused him of plotting to make all school children Unitarian. During the next 12 years, he transformed the state's system of normal schools, which were really charity schools for the poor, into the modern system of free public schools organized on principles that promoted the natural curiosity and goodness found in every child. This philosophy came directly from his religious faith. The school and the faith came together in Newton, Massachusetts, where the Mann's had moved in 1846. Horace helped found the church there that sits on the site of the Lexington Normal School, which Mann had moved there in 1844. (The church has a memorial to him.) He rejected that Calvinist God of his childhood which he believed was thwarting God's true plan by erroneously teaching that human nature is profoundly flawed and that any moral law within is scrambled by sin. Mann, and his friend **Samuel Gridley Howe**, believed that Boston society had created schools that expected and promoted the worst in human conduct because of their basic ideas about human nature and God.

A central theory for Mann was that acquirement of knowledge and pleasure should go hand in hand. He rejected external inducements like rewards and punishments because he said they destroyed the child's natural, God-given pleasure of learning itself. Mann once said that if we gave all the money we used for war to education, the millennium would surely come. He believed that public education adequately funded would bring peace and justice and humanitarianism to the world. Schools were the way that God had chosen for the reformation of the world. Education was the equalizer of social conditions. In 1848 he was elected to Congress, where he was an outspoken advocate of abolition. In 1854 he was appointed president of Antioch College. Eventually this nonsectarian school ran into financial difficulties and Mann was accused of trying to make it into an outpost of Unitarianism. He was aided in his fund-raising efforts by Unitarian ministers **Henry Whitney Bellows** and Rufus Stebbins, the first president of **Meadville** Seminary. Mann retained his position until his death on August 4, 1859. His statue flanks the entrance to the Massachusetts State House. His reformist spirit was captured in these famous words, "Be ashamed to die until you have won some victory for humanity."

MARTINEAU, JAMES (1805–1900). The most influential English Unitarian in the 19th century, born in Norwich on April 21, 1805. The son of a textile manufacturer, Martineau chose the ministry after becoming dissatisfied with his chosen career in engineering. His sister was the famous writer Harriet Martineau. Famous for her radical political views, her brother was much more reticent about expressing his more conservative political opinions. His ministerial education was at Manchester College, York, under the tutelage of Dr. Charles Wellbeloved. Ordained in 1828, his first pastorate was at a Unitarian church in Dublin, Ireland, where after four years he departed for the Paradise Street congregation in Liverpool. During this ministry he began to question the relationship between reason and scripture and published *The Rationale of Religious Inquiry or, the Question Stated of Reason, the Bible, and the Church* (1836). Here he rejected scripture as the final authority and stated that "reason is the ultimate appeal." This placed him with the liberal camp of Unitarians who defined Unitarianism more on inner conviction and less on external authorities. Martineau's sermons depended less and less on biblical thought. In 1840 he became professor of moral philosophy at Manchester New College, as well as continuing his pastoring. He continued to teach at the college for the remainder of his career. He published *Endeavors after the Christian Life* in 1843.

In 1845 Martineau became one of the editors of the Prospective Review. A year's study in Germany radicalized him even further. He abandoned the view that Jesus was a divinely appointed messiah and saw him as only a human being. In 1857 the principal of Manchester College resigned and this caused teaching positions to be reassigned. The board wanted to appoint Martineau to a chaired professorship. This resulted in a storm of protest, but the board gave him a vote of confidence and he assumed the position. He became principal in 1869 and then retired in 1885. In 1862 he published a handbook for congregational worship, *Common Prayer for Christian Worship*. He also edited and published important hymnbooks, including *Hymns for the Christian Church and Home* (1849).

Martineau convinced many of the British Unitarians to become less sectarian in their approach to matters of faith, but his attempts to organize them on a more inclusive basis regardless of doctrinal belief ultimately hurt the movement institutionally as he refused to support the creation of a strong national Unitarian organization. Toward the end of his career he published several works, including *The Seat of Authority in Religion* (1890). He achieved a great deal in helping British Unitarianism transition from traditional church and biblical authorities to a more mystical understanding of faith and a complete trust in human reason and conscience in religious matters.

MAY, SAMUEL JOSEPH (1797–1871). One of the most forthright advocates for abolitionism in the Unitarian movement. May was born on September 12, 1797, in Boston, the son of Colonel Joseph May, who was a warden at **King's Chapel**, and Dorothy Sewall, a descendant of the famous Sewall and Quincy families. Five of his 10 siblings did not survive childhood, and his sister Abigail was married to **Bronson Alcott**. May was sickly as a child, but completed his preparations for college and entered **Harvard College** in 1813. Although not an outstanding student, he decided to be a minister in his junior year being especially aware of the social impact of that position. He decided to go to the **Harvard Divinity School**, but he needed some preparatory work. Consequently, he studied with the Rev. Henry

Coleman in Hingham, Massachusetts. Once he was enrolled at the Divinity School, May became concerned with his increasing religious infidelity and wanted to quit the ministry, but **Henry Ware** Sr. assured him that doubt was part of the journey. He was helped further when he met Noah Worcester, the peace advocate. May began to see that his crisis could be resolved by putting his faith to work in transforming the world.

May heard of an opening in the church in Brooklyn, Connecticut. He also preached in New York, but William Ware, Henry's brother, received the call. May then turned back to Brooklyn and accepted their call on March 6, 1822. A little more than a week later he was ordained by the Boston Association as a missionary. After a year's trial he became the permanent minister in Brooklyn, but many of the members found his faith too liberal. He was married to Lucretia F. Coffin on June 1, 1825, at King's Chapel, and eventually they would have five children. His interest in the cause of peace continued and he helped organize the Windham County Peace Society in 1826. Temperance and education reform also occupied some attention. He hired Connecticut's first professional female teacher, organized the first national convention to reform common schools, and later established Syracuse, New York's, first desegregated and free public school.

In 1830 May heard William Lloyd Garrison speak and decided that he was a prophet who would shake the nation to its core. May became a convert to immediate abolitionism. May's role in the abolition movement became central after his involvement in the Crandall Case in Canterbury, Connecticut. Prudence Crandall was a teacher who decided to open a school for black girls. The Connecticut General Assembly then passed "Black Laws" to prevent the school from opening, and Crandall was arrested. The case convinced May to abandon colonization as a solution because he learned it was another manifestation of racism. May was an active participant in the founding of the American Anti-Slavery Society in 1833. He was asked to be its general agent, but he refused to leave his position in Brooklyn. May experienced many hostile crowds and much verbal abuse. As secretary of the Massachusetts Anti-Slavery Society (MASS) he issued a broadside defending their right to free speech. But in 1835 a riot took place at the church in Haverhill, where May was speaking. That same year he left his church to do antislavery work and then the following year he accepted a call to the church in South Scituate, Massachusetts. Here the famous Grimke sisters from South Carolina spoke from his pulpit in 1837. The experiences of many women in the abolition movement led them to use their skills in the new women's rights campaigns. May also played a key role in converting **William Ellery Channing** to be a supporter of the abolition movement.

During the next few years, May found that his sister Abba's family needed his help to pay off the mounting debts that her husband Bronson Alcott kept accumulating. By 1842 May had come into conflict with his congregation over segregated pews, and he resigned that year. He was hired to be president of the Lexington, Massachusetts, Normal School, and with **Horace Mann**, helped set up the normal school system in Massachusetts. In 1844 May was offered the pulpit of the church in Syracuse, New York, and by the following spring his family had arrived there. In the abolition campaign May became increasingly outspoken against the Founding Fathers, whom he said planted both freedom and slavery in the new nation. After 1842 he supported disunion. May also became involved in the women's rights movement. He was the first minister to publish a work advocating woman's suffrage. After the Fugitive Slave Law was enacted May became very vocal in his condemnation of it. At the denomination's annual meeting in 1850 he introduced a resolution condemning a group of Unitarians he believed had a hand in it: Daniel Webster, **Millard Fillmore**, **Edward Everett**, Samuel A. Eliot, Jared Sparks, Orville Dewey, and **Ezra Stiles Gannett**. It was defeated. May's involvement in the Jerry Rescue (of a fugitive slave) led him to be branded as one of the most dangerous men in New York State. After the Civil War, May continued to fight for black and female suffrage. Although he retired from the Syracuse pulpit in 1867, he preached until April 1868 when a replacement was found. He was hoping it might be his son Joseph, but some of the church members opposed this. He died on July 1, 1871.

MAYHEW, JONATHAN (1720–1766). One of the three great leaders of an emerging liberal thought in 18th-century America, Mayhew was an ardent political revolutionary as well. He was born on the island of Martha's Vineyard, Massachusetts, where his father, Experience

Mayhew, had carried on a family tradition of missionizing the Native Americans. His mother, Remember Bourne, was Experience's second wife, with Jonathan being their fifth and last child to survive, as she died following childbirth with the sixth child, when Jonathan was two. Jonathan had little formal schooling but probably gained much from his father and his father's library. He entered **Harvard College** when he was 19, considerably older than most of his classmates. During his time at Harvard he was fined a number of times for misconduct. The Great Awakening may have played some role in Jonathan's decision to enter the ministry. His theology was in flux at this time, but as he read of the excesses of emotional response, he began to distrust such revival techniques. After he finished at Harvard in 1744, he received grants to continue his studies. During this time he seems to have fallen under the liberal influence of **Ebenezer Gay** in Hingham, Massachusetts, who would later preach his ordination sermon.

In 1747 Mayhew was called to be minister at the West Church in Boston. His ordination had to be postponed after the Boston churches boycotted the council meeting fearing that the new minister would destroy their fragile ecclesiastical peace. This also meant that once he was eventually settled in his parish, Mayhew's colleagues would not exchange pulpits with him, nor would he be a member of the Boston Association. Mayhew, along with Gay and **Charles Chauncy**, became the leaders of the Arminian faction in Puritan Massachusetts, but Mayhew developed the most outspoken style of all. Four Boston newspapers helped flame the controversy over doctrinal differences. Mayhew argued that all people can use reason to discern religious truth. In his collection, *Seven Sermons* (1749), Mayhew said creeds are "imperious and tyrannical: and contrary to the spirit and doctrines of the gospel. They are an infringement upon those rights of conscience, which ought to be sacred" (Mayhew as quoted in Akers, *Called Unto Liberty*, p. 69). Mayhew refused to submit to any yoke of bondage and urged people to exercise private judgment in religion. He said original sin was not agreeable to truth, reason, or scripture.

The central emphasis in Mayhew's preaching was on morality. He was later accused of pure natural morality as the basis for his faith when he refused to draw a line between the work of God in conversion and the works of human beings. His book *Seven Sermons* won him a major reputation in Europe. In 1750 he preached his most famous sermon, "A Discourse Concerning Unlimited Submission and Non-Resistance to the Higher Powers." Here Mayhew argued that it is not Christian duty to always submit to rulers but only to obey good rulers, and that it is our duty to rebel against tyrants and oppressors. Rebellion was the right thing to do when a monarch exercised arbitrary power. Years later **John Adams** referred to this sermon as indicative of those principles and feelings that produced the Revolution. In 1752 Mayhew was afflicted with small-pox, but he survived. In 1756 he married Elizabeth Clarke, and they had three children, two of whom died in infancy. During the last 10 years of his life, Mayhew continued to be swept up in controversies. He became part of the opposition to the governor of Massachusetts when it was feared he would assert his right to issue charters. Mayhew frequently wrote against the Church of England, especially concerned that bishops would increase in numbers and power. His political controversies finally reached a climax in the Stamp Act Crisis. Opposition to the British government was expressed by Mayhew in the context of a state of slavery, in which the "slaves labor for the pleasure and profit of others." He preached "The Snare Broken," the most widely circulated sermon on the repeal of the Stamp Act. It also proved to be his last published sermon. After returning from a church council meeting in Rutland (now Barre), Massachusetts, Mayhew was subject to severe headaches, and then either had a stroke or cerebral hemorrhage, and died on July 9, 1766. Mayhew did not live to see the American Revolution or the birth of Unitarianism, but he laid much of the groundwork for both these revolutions in religious and political freedom.

MAY MEETINGS. The American Unitarian Association (AUA) was organized in 1825 and thereafter met on an annual basis to hear reports and elect officers. This also became a time when related organizations met as well. The annual meeting of the AUA was always held in Boston in May, and these became known as the May Meetings. During part of the 19th century, there were two annual gatherings. The other, known as the Autumnal Convention, was always held in different locations, including Montreal in 1854. The fall meetings were started in Worcester, Massachusetts, in 1842 and held for more than 20 years, the last in Springfield, Massachusetts, in 1863. Some of the discussions at these meetings centered on the need to organize more as an ecclesiastical body. The **National Conference** was established in 1865, only two years after the Autumnal Convention stopped meeting. It continued to meet separately from the AUA. While the AUA met in May for its annual meeting, the National Conference (later the General Conference) met in alternate years outside of Boston until 1925, when the General Conference and the AUA merged. The General Conference met for the last time in Cleveland in 1925. When the **Unitarian Universalist Association (UUA)** was established the bylaws called for an annual meeting in April or May.

MEADVILLE LOMBARD THEOLOGICAL SCHOOL. One of two Unitarian Universalist theological schools in the United States, it came about from the merger of Meadville Theological School and Lombard College. The first meeting of Meadville Theological School was held on October 1, 1844, in Meadville, Pennsylvania, in the home of Alfred Huidekoper. The opening of the school was the result of years of planning to further the cause of Unitarianism in the west. Harm Jan Huidekoper, a wealthy landowner who had helped establish the Unitarian church in Meadville in the 1820s, developed a plan for a joint undertaking for theological education between Unitarians and Christians. As a vice president of the **American Unitarian Association (AUA)**, he took this idea to Boston and won the approval of denominational officials. His younger son, Frederic, a student at **Harvard Divinity School** at the time, became one of the first faculty members. The elder Huidekoper also purchased a building for the fledging school, a former Presbyterian church. The school's first building, Divinity Hall, was bought at auction for $400, but was then renovated to accommodate the nine students who came that first year from three denominations. At the building's dedication the new president, Rufus Stebbins, spoke for more than two hours saying that the school would encourage freedom of thought and opinion. In the ensuing years more than 30 students registered each year. It was expected that they would complete their course of study in three years with the third year devoted to "constant preaching."

Meadville received its charter in 1847, which stated that no doctrinal requirements would ever be imposed on those who studied at the school, except a belief in the divine origin of Christianity. This was put to the test during the school's early history when the biblical criticism of Huidekoper was questioned by some of the faculty, including Stebbins. They voted in 1854 to exclude anyone who doubted the biblical miracles, and Huidekoper immediately resigned, feeling that this would force him to compromise his teaching. With waning support, Stebbins resigned in 1856. He was succeeded by Oliver Stearns, a Harvard graduate who immediately rescinded the exclusion rule. Huidekoper was invited back to teach church history.

Stearns was followed in 1863 by A. A. Livermore, who guided the school until 1890. In the first few years of his presidency all the members of the Christian denomination resigned from the faculty, but the early alliance had been important to enable the school to succeed. Under Livermore's leadership the curriculum was broadened to include course work in non-Christian religions and the impact of Darwinism. Meadville voted to admit women for the first time in 1868, and thereafter it assumed an important role in educating and recruiting women to the ministry. In 1870, the **Western Unitarian Conference (WUC)** president Artemus Carter declared that the ministerial schools were doing an inadequate job of supplying preachers in the West. Carter urged the Conference to accept a $50,000 offer from a group of Chicago laypeople to move Meadville to that urban setting. This bold plan came to fruition under the direction of **William Wallace Fenn**, the minister of First Church, Chicago, and Daniel L. Shorey, who was on the board of both the church and the University of Chicago.

In 1902 Shorey's Harvard classmate, Franklin Southworth, who was head of the WUC, became president of Meadville. A revolution was wrought during Southworth's 27-year presidency. Meadville started a Chicago semester that resulted in the purchase of a building there in 1921. Among Southworth's appointments during this time was Anna Garlin Spencer, who was a social ethicist of national renown. Great efforts were made to recruit new students. Another important faculty appointment was Clayton Bowen, a biblical scholar. Based on the feeling that an urban setting offered many more opportunities for the enrichment of students, and the success of the short term in Chicago, the board decided to move to Chicago in 1926 and establish an affiliation with the University of Chicago. After a successful capital campaign under the direction of the new president,

Sydney Snow, the school dedicated a new academic building in 1932. Snow, who was described by the ***Christian Register*** as "buoyant, inspiring, lovable," remained at the school until 1944.

In 1933 the trustees of Lombard College, finding their school in financial upheaval, voted to transfer its academic program to the Meadville School in Chicago, while sharing faculty but keeping the charters and endowed funds separate. Lombard College was founded as the Illinois Liberal Institute in Galesburg, Illinois, by the Universalists in 1851. Its **Ryder Divinity School** had been established in Chicago in 1881. It united with Meadville in 1928, and then two years later Lombard closed down and its charter was conferred on Meadville. After World War II, Meadville/Lombard became increasingly involved in the pluralistic mix of theological schools in Chicago. This evolved from the Federated Theological School faculty within the university to the Chicago Cluster of Theological Schools, which had been created in October 1843, to the current Association of Chicago Theological Schools (ACTS). Meadville/Lombard has developed a library of outstanding resources in the study of liberal religion. The Center for the Advanced Study of Religion and Science was established at the school by Professor Ralph Burhoe, who later received the Templeton Prize for his efforts. The school was a pioneer in using Clinical Pastoral Education as part of training during the tenure of faculty member Carl Wennerstrom. Important 20th century theologian **James Luther Adams** was a faculty member for a number of years. The school numbers among its graduates many recent leaders of the denomination, including Presidents **O. Eugene Pickett** (1979–85) and **William F. Schulz** (1985–93).

MELVILLE, HERMAN (1819–1891). The great novelist and author of *Moby Dick* grappled with religious issues throughout his life. Melville was born on August 1, 1819, in New York City. His father was a struggling merchant and a Unitarian by background. His eventual bankruptcy and early death plunged the family into oceans of debt. Melville went to sea at the age of 20, a tale he retells in the novel *Redburn*. After that he had some exciting South Sea island experiences that he recounted in *Typee*, a novel that **Margaret Fuller** called "entertaining and pleasing." In 1847 Melville married Elizabeth Shaw, the daughter of the chief justice of the Massachusetts

Supreme Court. A number of important events occurred in his life in 1849. These included the birth of his son Malcolm, the publication of *Mardi* and *Redburn*, and a trip to London to arrange publication of *White-Jacket* (1850), a book that recalled Melville's time in the U.S. Navy. After *White-Jacket* came out, young Malcolm was baptized by the Unitarian minister **Henry Whitney Bellows** of the Church of the Divine Unity (later All Souls), where Elizabeth had recently become a pew-renter. That fall the family left New York and Melville bought a farm, Arrowhead, near Pittsfield, Massachusetts. After this Melville met **Nathaniel Hawthorne**, who became his close friend. He stayed in the Berkshires in order to draw inspiration from his new friend and then dedicated *Moby Dick* to him. The following year *Moby Dick* was published, but it was a commercial disaster.

Within a few years Melville decided he would need to find a new way to support his family. Eventually he secured a position at the U.S. Customs House in New York, where the family had moved back to in 1863. These were difficult years for them. There was a plot involving the minister Mr. Bellows at one point to feign the kidnapping of Elizabeth Melville to get her away from Herman. It is sometimes said that she was not supportive of his writing and/or that he abused her. Mrs. Melville later thanked Bellows for all his help with her problems. In 1867 their son Malcolm committed suicide. The Melville family had rented a pew at the Unitarian church at various times since 1850, and finally Melville went to the minister Theodore Chickering Williams between 1883 and 1885 and asked if he could be listed as an official member of the church. Their old church now had a new building that was within walking distance of their house. It was now called All Souls, and its new building with alternated stripes of yellow stone and red brick was sometimes called the "Beefsteak Church" or the "Church of the Holy Zebra." Melville's thought was not a very stereotypical Unitarianism. *Moby Dick* depicts a radical conflict between good and evil. In his later years Melville may have come to some religious reconciliation when he officially adopted the religion of his father and his wife. His final character *Billy Budd, Sailor*, published after his death, exemplifies that goodness and beauty are possible even in a world where tragedy is commonplace. Melville died on September 28, 1891.

MENDELSOHN, JACK (1918–). One of the leading political activists in the denomination, Mendelsohn was born on July 22, 1918, in Cambridge, Massachusetts, to Anna M. Torrey and Jack Mendelsohn Sr. His father was a nonpracticing Jew who published music and met his future wife in her capacity as a professional pianist. The family broke up when Jack's beloved mother died of peritonitis when he was eight. Jack went to live with his Torrey grandparents in Cambridge, and his father moved to New York City. Jack was primarily interested in books and athletics. He received an A.B. from Boston University in 1939, and after studying at **Meadville Lombard Theological School**, he finished his ministerial training at **Harvard Divinity School**, where he received an S.T.B. in 1945. Ordained in 1945, his first parish calling was at Chicago's Beverly Unitarian Church. Mendelsohn spent much of his ministerial career serving urban churches. He was settled in Indianapolis, Indiana, from 1954 to 1959 and then was called to Boston's historic Arlington Street Church in 1959 and remained there for 10 years. He received an honorary D.D. from Meadville Lombard in 1962.

The reputation of Arlington Street Church as a hotbed of political activism was lived out during that time. Mendelsohn became involved in the Civil Rights Movement and black empowerment. He was president of the Boston Urban League and later CEO of the Civil Rights Projects, Inc. He also played a key role in the Unitarian Universalist **Black Empowerment Controversy**. At the **General Assembly** in 1969, a large contingent of black delegates walked out in protest. Mendelsohn, who was vice chair of the Black Affairs Council (BAC), spoke before the assembly of his anguish that black people were being returned to the "back of the bus." This fomented a walkout of the Assembly, and 400 people regathered at the Arlington Street Church. The show of solidarity with the black delegates mobilized by Mendelsohn eventually resulted in a vote for full funding for BAC for another year, but this was later rescinded by the **Unitarian Universalist Association (UUA)** Board.

The 1960s also marked a time of active antiwar protests and the Arlington Street congregation was infiltrated by informants from the Defense and Justice Departments and the FBI as a result of these activities. Perhaps the most famous event occurred in October 1967 when thousands gathered on Boston Common to protest the Vietnam

War and then regathered in the Arlington Street Church so that 67 men could burn their draft cards and another 214 turn them over to various clergy, including William Sloane Coffin, to forward the cards to the Justice Department later that week. Arlington Street Church members were also leaders of the movement that offered sanctuary to draft resisters.

In 1969 Mendelsohn was called to the First Unitarian Church in Chicago, and his last settlement was at the First Parish in Bedford, Massachusetts, from 1979 to 1988, when he retired and was named minister emeritus. He also served a brief interim ministry in Santa Barbara, California, in 1991–92. In Chicago he continued to work against racism, becoming the chair of the Alliance to End Repression in Chicago. He always tried to support new programs to involve marginalized groups in the life of the church and the city. During his Chicago ministry he was also a candidate for the presidency of the Unitarian Universalist Association in 1977 but lost in a three-way election to Paul Carnes. In Bedford he tried to encourage stronger connections between the suburbs and the city. He also continued a long personal history of being a friend and advisor to public figures, including Adlai Stevenson, Robert Kennedy, and Jesse Jackson. In 1983, Jackson asked Mendelsohn to accompany him to Syria to negotiate for the return of Lieutenant Robert Goodman, and the trip proved successful.

Some of Mendelsohn's renown within the denomination has come as a result of his writings. He was first asked to write an introductory pamphlet on Unitarianism in the 1950s. "Meet the Unitarians" was first published in 1957 and has remained in print ever since with Mendelsohn offering frequent updates (now "Meet the Unitarian Universalists"). This ability to introduce people to and help them understand liberal religion was also developed in a full length book. First published as *Why I Am a Unitarian* (1960) and revised with Universalist added to the title in 1963, the book was completely updated in a new edition in 1985, *Being Liberal in an Illiberal Age*. Here Mendelsohn recounts his lifelong struggle to free the human spirit from "the failings, the shortcomings, the repressions, the egocentricities, the hypocrisies" that are ever present in the human condition. His ability to write historical works exemplifying scholarly abilities is found in his biography of William Ellery Channing: *Channing, the*

Reluctant Radical (1971). He also published several other books, including *God, Allah and Ju Ju*; *The Forest Calls Back* (Dr. Binder in Peru); and *The Martyrs* (sixteen who gave their lives for racial justice).

Within the denomination Mendelsohn has served as president of the **Unitarian Universalist Minister's Association (UUMA)** and the **Unitarian Universalist Service Committee (UUSC)**. He was honored in 1997 with the UUA's Distinguished Service Award for his courage and conviction to live a "prophetic presence" among his fellow liberals. In 1975 Mendelsohn delivered a paper at a UUMA Convocation saying that there was one thing ministers could not do, "They cannot leave things as they are." Mendelsohn has fathered three children, is presently married to Judith A. Frediani, and resides in Maynard, Massachusetts.

MERGER COMMISSIONS. Both Unitarians and Universalists had seriously considered merger of their respective denominations in the 19th century. When the **National Conference of Unitarian Churches** was established in 1865, the convention passed a resolution "looking to union with the Universalist body." In the 1890s the Universalist **General Convention** meetings twice tabled motions calling for greater Unitarian and Universalist cooperation. In 1931 a Joint Commission was created to consider methods of union. One result of this was the creation of what became the **Free Church Fellowship (FCF)**, a generally ineffective joint venture. In 1947 another Joint Commission was organized. By 1953 the two denominations had established the **Council of Liberal Churches (CLC)** to work together on education and publications. Finally, a Joint Interim Committee recommended in 1955 that the two religious movements determine a step by step process for union. In 1956 the Joint Merger Commission was appointed with **William B. Rice** as its chairman. It became a facilitator of dialogue within the two groups and its work led directly to merger.

The commission hired professional consultants who produced a number of documents. These included a complete report on the state of the Universalist Church of America (UCA) and the American Unitarian Association (AUA), a proposed plan for merger, and other papers that summarized advantages, disadvantages, and opposition. A final document outlined a complete plan for how the consolidation would be accomplished. All the congregations were involved in the discussion process and were regularly supplied with reports. The final report of the commission was presented to a joint meeting of the UCA and the AUA in Syracuse, New York, in October 1959. This meeting approved the name **Unitarian Universalist Association (UUA)**. The greatest discussion centered around whether the purposes of the UUA would refer to the Judeo-Christian Tradition or to "truths taught by Jesus," and after both were removed at one point, the Judeo-Christian Tradition was eventually restored. An enabling resolution was passed subject to a final plebiscite in the churches. When this was conducted it showed that 88 percent of those Unitarian congregations and 79 percent of those Universalist congregations who participated approved of merger (after 1958 the word consolidation was generally substituted for merger). Nearly 95 percent of all congregations participated in the process. After that the plan had to be approved by the separate denominations at their respective meetings in 1960, as the plebiscite had no legal standing. This was held in adjoining rooms in John Hancock Hall in Boston on May 23, 1960. The vote was followed by a special service in Symphony Hall, where the pulpits of **William Ellery Channing** and **Hosea Ballou** were used. The last act of the creation of the new UUA was the approval of the constitution and bylaws when the first General Assembly was convened on May 12, 1961. Both groups had long histories of congregational autonomy and noncreedal faiths that were incorporated in the new consolidated body.

MINISTERIAL FELLOWSHIP COMMITTEE. The policies for determining how to grant professional credentials to their ministers have changed throughout Unitarian and Universalist history. Although the **American Unitarian Association (AUA)** did not assume ecclesiastical authority for credentialing ministers when it was established in 1825, the Unitarian/Congregational tradition of a Standing Order of churches usually followed the practice of having newly settled ministers appear before the local clergy association to determine if they had fit qualifications to hold the office of minister. The question of who would determine whether a candidate was fit to be a minister came up after the **National Conference** was organized in 1865.

In 1870 the conference voted to ask each local conference to create a Committee on Fellowship. This agitation for change continued until 1878 when the National Conference established a central Committee on Fellowship. This committee was then able to admit ministers to fellowship, but it had no means of removing ministers until a new set of rules was adopted in 1899. This committee became centralized as part of the AUA in 1924 just a year before the General Conference was merged with the AUA in 1925.

Dan Fenn wrote an important paper on fellowshipping for the report ***Unitarians Face a New Age***. (1936). He was especially concerned that there was no control over the quality of who was fit for the ministry. Fenn was dismayed that a certificate of fellowship would be granted to any minister serving a Unitarian church based only on the holding of that position and not on an examination of his/her qualifications for ministry.

Universalists were always less formal about granting credentials to their clergy. They had a tradition of welcoming new clergy by conversion, and at first, there was an antipathy toward an educated clergy. When the New England Convention adopted a Plan of General Association in 1803, it provided that the convention could examine the qualifications of candidates. After that the convention meetings examined candidates, but local associations often did so, too. When the U.S. **General Convention** was organized in 1833 the Universalists planned to have this national ecclesiastical organization be responsible for credentialing. In practice the State Conventions usually held this power to ordain and to examine the candidates after they began to be organized in the 1820s, and therefore a minister or someone who wished to be licensed as a lay preacher would appear before a committee of the convention that would examine him as to his fitness for ministry. Prior to consolidation, the credentialing process was far more centralized for the Unitarians who had one continental committee, while the Universalists had individual state committees, which were creatures of the state conventions, which were also the bodies with the ordaining power. In the Unitarian tradition the individual churches retained the ordaining power. At the time of consolidation a **Unitarian Universalist Association** Ministerial Fellowship Committee was created following the Unitarian pattern. This committee alone had the right to grant (and remove) fellowship within the association, but the power to ordain was retained by the individual churches. Since 1961 more rigorous standards for granting credentials have been adopted. Over the years the committee has granted fellowship for ministries other than the parish. Recently there have been three different tracks of ministry: parish, religious education, and community.

MIRACLES CONTROVERSY. The central battle between the traditional Unitarians and the Transcendentalists began in November 1836. That fall **George Ripley** and **William Furness** published materials that publicly showed that they advocated biblical interpretation that stated the miracles of Jesus were not performed to validate his teachings. **Andrews Norton**, the former Dexter Professor of Sacred Literature at **Harvard Divinity School**, concerned that this might destroy the reputation of the Unitarians, wrote a letter to the *Boston Daily Advertiser* on November 5 attacking Ripley's views, after the ***Christian Register*** had refused to publish it. Furness's book *Four Gospels* escaped Norton's public concern because Furness had previously asked Norton to read the manuscript, which Norton refused to do because he did not want to render a stamp of approval. Ripley's ideas were expressed in a review of a book by the English Unitarian **James Martineau** in the *Christian Examiner*. Ripley said that acceptance of miracles was not necessary in order to call oneself Christian. In his letter, Norton said that the miracles were the only evidence Christianity stood upon to make it a true revelation. A few days later Ripley responded by saying that this kind of mud slinging makes all Unitarians look bad and he was offended at being called a heretic. Now the *Christian Register*, at Ripley's request, agreed to publish the exchange. Then in December an anonymous letter, possibly by **Ezra Stiles Gannett**, appeared in the *Register*. While this writer expressed appreciation for the spiritual emphasis the Transcendentalists brought to the faith, he went on to say that Christianity had to be more than a mere set of ethical principles. He said that God's sending of his son was a supernatural event and could only be confirmed by supernatural events like miracles.

By the middle of 1837 the first stage of the controversy was over, but it resurfaced the following year in the wake of **Ralph Waldo Emerson**'s "Divinity School Address." In that famous oration Emerson called for a return to direct inspiration, saying that when Christ spoke of miracles, he meant all of life is a miracle. After he was finished, the seniors at the Divinity School expressed their gratitude for his speech and said that some of them disagreed with his viewpoints. The dean of the school, John Gorham Palfrey, was later reputed to have said that the address was part folly and part atheism. Two days after its publication, Norton responded again in the *Boston Daily Advertiser*. He attacked the entire Transcendental school and feared that the latest address would destroy principles that were basic to the continuation of the good society. He also wondered how Emerson could have been allowed to speak on such an important occasion. "It will be sufficient to state generally, that the author professes to reject all belief in Christianity as a revelation, that he makes a general attack upon the Clergy" (Norton as quoted in Miller, *Transcendentalists*, p. 195). While some of the Unitarians agreed that the address was dangerous and they wondered if Emerson should be considered a Christian, others felt that Norton's response was intolerant and destroyed the spirit of free inquiry. The *Christian Register* tried to steer a middle ground with its editor Chandler Robbins, who was a friend of Emerson's but disagreed with his ideas, yet still considered him a Christian. This angered Norton, who thought this atheist and infidel did not deserve to be called Christian.

Another important player in the controversy was **Henry Ware Jr.**, who had been Emerson's colleague at the Second Church of Boston. Ware's concerns were voiced in the sermon "The Personality of the Deity" in September 1838. Although he did not name Emerson in this address, he criticized the attempt to reduce God to an abstract idea ("There is a personal God, or there is none."). Previously he had stated that acceptance of these ideas would overthrow the authority of Christianity. Ware's colleagues brought these ideas into the public arena, and Ware expressed his unhappiness that he was drawn into opposition with his friend. The *Christian Examiner* reviewed Emerson's address and Ware's sermon together, giving the impression that Ware was a leader of the opposition. The *Western Messenger*, a monthly magazine published in Cincinnati, came to Emerson's defense and wondered about the spirit of free inquiry. **Orestes Brownson** also contributed a response that extolled the expression of the free spirit. He had another chance to enter the fray in January 1839 after Norton's masterpiece *The Evidence of the Genuineness of the*

Four Gospels was published in late 1838. Emerson played virtually no role in the fight over his address. Oliver Wendell Holmes compared him to Patroclus when the Greeks and Trojans were fighting over his body. The leading voice in the Transcendental counterattack was again that of George Ripley. In July 1839 Norton had delivered "Discourse on the Latest Form of Infidelity" before an alumni association at **Harvard Divinity School**. Here Norton said that miracles authenticated Christianity. Ripley responded with "The Latest Form of Infidelity Examined." Ripley said that Norton's belief that miracles were the only possible way to prove the truth of Christianity was just personal dogma. Then Norton fired back in "Remarks on . . . 'The Latest Form of Infidelity Examined,'" that miracles show that these truths come from God. The two adversaries found some measure of accommodation, as Norton admitted that truth can be discovered by other means than through the empirical. At this point **Theodore Parker** entered the debate under the pseudonym of Levi Blodgett. Parker said that faith in Christ cannot depend upon faith in miracles, but that faith must come by intuition. In his final salvo, Norton published *Two Articles from the Princeton Review,* which called the German philosophy "hideous and godless."

After 1840 Norton withdrew from the debate, as most other Unitarians refused to support his policy of exclusion. Ripley, too, dropped from the action shortly thereafter when he resigned from the Purchase Street Church in Boston in 1841 and found his energies absorbed in **Brook Farm**. After 1840 both the *Christian Register* and the *Examiner* were arguing for a neutral position suggesting greater attempts to understand the foreign philosophies without hysterical reactions against them. The miracles question would surface again. Most of the mainstream Unitarian ministers defended the belief in miracles and the supernatural underpinning of Christianity, and yet few refused to follow Norton in his desire to withdraw the name Christian from the Transcendentalists. One other result of the controversy was that after 1838 the Harvard Divinity School faculty reserved the right to approve graduation speakers.

MITCHELL, MARIA (1818–1889). The astronomer who discovered a comet, born on August 1, 1818, on the island of Nantucket, Massachusetts. Raised a Quaker, Mitchell never officially joined any church but regularly attended the Second Congregational Meetinghouse Society (Unitarian) on Nantucket. Once when confronted by a woman who feared her daughter was not Christian, Mitchell wrote that she was strongly tempted to avow her Unitarianism. Largely self-educated in the sciences, she was elected to the American Academy of Arts and Sciences in 1848. This was a year after she had discovered the comet that now bears her name, "Mitchell's Comet." She worked for 19 years for the *American Nautical Almanac* computing tables for the planet Venus. The U.S. Coastal Survey employed her in an astronomical party at Mt. Independence, Maine. For many years she was chairperson of the American Association for the Advancement of Science. In 1865 Vassar College appointed her as director of their observatory and professor of astronomy. Mitchell became a well-respected teacher who was devoted to helping her students develop their own abilities. Perhaps remembering her own lack of a college degree, she became especially interested in the higher education of women and was so devoted to this that she sacrificed her own scientific work. She died on June 28, 1889.

MODERATOR. The position of **Unitarian Universalist Association (UUA)** moderator was created in response to a recommendation of the Commission of Appraisal in its 1936 report, ***Unitarians Face a New Age***. The proposal was made "to give a titular head apart from the administrative work." The commission recommended that the moderator be an official representative of the denomination to exalt "the function of spiritual leadership." This was an unsalaried position for a two-year term with the initial intention that the person not be reelected. An important part of the job description was the role of presiding at all meetings of the association. The first moderator was Sanford Bates, followed by **Aurelia Henry Reinhardt**, the first woman, in 1940. Under the new bylaws created for the UUA in 1961 the moderator, who was now the chairperson of the board of trustees (the president had served in this capacity before), was elected to serve a four-year term with a possibility of being reelected. The first UUA moderator, Marshall Dimock, resigned before the end of his first term. He had hoped to have a greater role in the administrative workings of the UUA, but this was not realized under the strong presidency of **Dana Greeley**.

MONTANA INDUSTRIAL SCHOOL. After 1871 several religious denominations became involved in the education of Native Americans. The most significant Unitarian effort was the Montana Industrial School, opened in 1886 just south of Custer Station, Montana, under the direction of the Rev. Henry F. Bond. The purpose was to provide children with a practical education, and several buildings and shops were erected. Despite some early success and the financial support of Mary Hemenway, this **American Unitarian Association (AUA)** effort began to flounder after Bond retired in 1891, and the school was turned over to the federal government in 1895.

MONTREAL. This city was the site of the first Unitarian church in Canada. Unitarians, including the brewery owner John Molson, began to gather in the 1820s to begin considering the formation of a congregation. Literature from Boston was distributed on a regular basis, and finally, David Hughes, a Unitarian minister, arrived from England in 1832. The first Unitarian service in Canada was held on July 29, 1832 (the service was held in the Union Schoolroom), during the height of a cholera epidemic, and the new minister soon fell victim to the disease. The fledgling congregation was unhappy with a second British minister who arrived and requested that an American minister be sent. The **American Unitarian Association (AUA)** responded by sending a recent Harvard graduate Joseph Angier, who stayed for 18 months, established a Sunday School, and defended the Unitarians from attacks in the local press, but he was never formally settled. After a number of false starts the church began to coalesce during the brief ministry of an ex-Catholic Irishman, Henry Giles. The church formally organized on June 20, 1842, when 24 men signed the constitution of the Christian Unitarian Society of Montreal. The following year Benjamin Workman wrote to Henry Montgomery in Belfast asking for assistance in settling a new minister. Montgomery's suggestion was John Cordner, a young man who had recently finished his education and was willing to go to Canada. The call was extended, and by September 1843, the congregation knew that a new future lay before them.

William Hedge, whose wife, Elizabeth, was the sister of **Frederic Henry Hedge**, wrote to the AUA for help with a new building fund, for the congregation now occupied a converted house owned by the

Hedges. He also asked for "more zeal for the defense and spread of the great truths of Unitarianism." The Unitarians of Ireland (organized as the Non-Subscribing Presbyterian Church) gathered to ordain Cordner in September, and he arrived in Montreal in early November. Montreal's first choice for a settled minister was a completely dedicated servant of the church who soon established a monthly publication. After 10 years their numbers had tripled—not an easy task in a city where the liberals were constantly under attack. In 1854 the Autumnal Unitarian Convention came to Montreal, giving the Canadians true recognition that they were on an equal footing with their U.S. counterparts. By the late 1850s the congregation had grown in size and affluence and they decided to build a new church even though they had dedicated a structure in 1845. This successor building was dedicated in September 1858 and given the name the Church of the Messiah to show that Unitarianism was not as radical as some suggested it was. Cordner's ministry extended for a total of 35 years, leaving a remarkable legacy for the congregation, the city, and the country.

MORRISON-REED, MARK D. (1949–). A minister who has played a key role in helping the denomination confront issues of racism. Mark Reed was born on June 16, 1949, in Chicago, Illinois. Raised in Chicago, he is a lifelong Unitarian Universalist. His parents were among a tiny group of African Americans who attended the First Unitarian Church of Chicago, and he and his siblings were the first black children ever dedicated there. He sang in the famous Chicago Children's Choir. After, what he describes as a circuitous journey through several colleges, Reed worked as a Vista volunteer and then taught in Europe before finally deciding upon a career in ministry. He trained for the ministry at **Meadville Lombard Theological School**. He first received an M.A. from the University of Chicago in 1977 and then a D.Min. from Meadville Lombard in 1979. His thesis there was developed into an important book examining the roots of racism in Unitarian Universalism, *Black Pioneers in a White Denomination* (1980). The book examines the story of two black ministers, **Ethelred Brown** and **Lewis McGee**, and their efforts to bring the Unitarian message to black communities despite blatant denominational racism. On the day after he and his fianceé received their M.A. degrees in 1977, Reed was married to Donna Morrison, a native of Canada and a ministerial colleague with whom he took a joint name. They have two children and they have shared in cominisry throughout their careers with both being fellowshipped and ordained in 1979. Their first settlement was at the First Universalist Church of Rochester, New York, from 1979 to 1988, and now they serve the First Unitarian Congregation of Toronto, Ontario, where they were called in 1989.

Morrison-Reed's book *Black Pioneers* eventually evolved into an adult religious education curriculum, *How Open the Door? (Afro-Americans' Experience in Unitarian Universalism)* (1989). At that time he served on the denominational Curriculum Team, which developed ways to strengthen Unitarian Universalist identity. When he was minister in Rochester, Morrison-Reed wrote, "One of my visions has been for that church to become fully integrated." Remembering the rare UU congregation he grew up in and a few others that were thoroughly integrated in every aspect of their programs, he said, "I have always hoped that more of our churches could be like them, including my own." Morrison-Reed went on to say that diversity can come in many forms. In 1991, Morrison-Reed coedited a meditation manual, *Been in the Storm so Long*, with Jacqui James. In a selection called "Let Me Die Laughing," he writes, "Let me die laughing, savoring one of life's crazy moments. Let me die holding the hand of one I love, and recalling that I tried to love and was loved in return. Let me die remembering that life has been good." Morrison-Reed has also published "A Fear of Mass Appeal: Religious Liberals in Retreat" in *Unitarian Universalism* (1984) in which he calls for the Unitarian Universalist church to have a vision with a broader more universal appeal. He has served on several **Unitarian Universalist Association (UUA)** committees, including the **Ministerial Fellowship Committee (MFC)** and the **Commission on Appraisal**. He was a founding member of the African American Unitarian Universalist Ministries. He has also been president of the **Canadian Unitarian Council (CUC)** and has been active for many years as a volunteer with the Family Service Association. As a minister Morrison-Reed has tried to build communities where people are accepted as they are and that the church "assures us that we are not struggling for justice on our own, but as members of a larger community."

MURRAY, JOHN (1741–1815). One of the founders of Universalism in America. John Murray was born on December 10, 1741, in Alton, England, southwest of London. The oldest of nine children, John and his family moved to Ireland when he was 10 to live in a village near Cork. The family was converted from a strict Anglicanism to Methodism, and John became the leader of a boys group that met to pray and sing. After Murray's father died, John went to live with a couple named Little whose large library led to new educational opportunities. Shortly thereafter, John returned to London and took on a job in a cloth mill. Here he met Eliza Neale, whose grandfather despised Methodists. Despite his opposition, Eliza left his house and married Murray. John's leadership in the Methodist church was tested when he was asked to visit a woman from his church who had been converted to the Universalism taught by a preacher named James Relly. Murray became disturbed by this visit and decided to read Relly's pamphlet, ***Union***, and go hear him preach. He tried to divide his time between the two congregations, but the Methodists finally questioned him and found he had been converted to Universalism. Unfortunately, Murray's new faith was tested almost immediately. He and Eliza had a baby who died at the age of one, and then Eliza died soon thereafter. Finally, he went to prison because he could not pay his debts. Relly urged him to preach after he was released from prison, but he found he had too much heartbreak and resolved to discover a new life in America.

In July 1770 he sailed for the New World, landing at Philadelphia, but then headed to New York. Before they arrived the ship became stuck on a sandbar on the southern New Jersey coast, near Cranberry Inlet in a place later called Good Luck Point. Going ashore, Murray met a man named Thomas Potter. Potter explained that he had built his own meetinghouse because he expected that a preacher would come who would declare that all people were meant to be saved. When Murray admitted to Potter that he had preached, Potter tried to convince him that he was the man God sent to fill the pulpit. Murray said he vowed never to preach again. Finally, Potter struck an agreement with him. If the winds did not change and the ship remained stuck on the sandbar, then it would be a sign from God that Murray was meant to preach there. If the winds changed then Murray could proceed on his journey. It had been two days, but by Sunday morning the winds had not changed, and Murray, keeping the agreement believing it was a sign from God, preached the first Universalist sermon in America on September 30, 1770. For the next few years, Murray became an itinerant preacher of universal salvation. By 1772 he had reached southern New England, and finally Boston in 1773. When he returned to Boston in 1774 a stone was hurled through the window where he was preaching. Murray picked it up and remarked, "This argument is solid and weighty, but it is neither reasonable or convincing." He was attacked with stones again in Gloucester, where a small group led by Winthrop Sargent had invited him to preach. They had already been converted by reading a copy of Relly's *Union*. In 1775, Murray left Gloucester for nearly a year to serve as chaplain to a Rhode Island regiment in the war. After his return he continued to preach.

On January 1, 1779, a group of 61 people formed the Independent Christian Church in Gloucester. In less than two years a meetinghouse had been built. Soon thereafter the church was embroiled in litigation surrounding its legitimacy. Murray's named appeared on the suit against the Parish Church in Gloucester, which was attempting to tax the Universalists. This suit was finally settled in 1786 when the Universalists won the right to have their taxes support the church of their choice. Murray had to continue to battle state authorities over his ability to legally perform weddings, and this was resolved the following year when his legitimacy and ordination (which occurred at the December 25, 1780, church building dedication) were confirmed by state legislature. In October 1788, Murray married Judith Sargent Stevens, a widow and the daughter of Winthrop Sargent. During the next few years Murray took a leading role in attempting to organize and unite Universalist churches—first at the convention in Oxford in 1785 and later in Philadelphia. Murray finally left Gloucester in 1793 to settle with the First Universalist Church in Boston, where he remained until his death on September 3, 1815. Theologically Murray completely rejected transubstantiation and celebrated communion as a memorial service only. He also could find no scriptural basis for baptism with water, and so he initiated a long-held Universalist practice of child dedication. His views on Jesus and salvation were being challenged by the end of his ministry. Murray never deviated much from the theology he learned through Relly. He was a Trinitarian and remained clear about the divinity of Christ. In terms of the doctrine of election, he universalized Calvin's idea of the elect so that all people will eventually be saved due to a mysterious union between Christ and humankind that took place before the fall. All who believe in Christ on earth would be saved upon death. Others would go through a period of suffering, but all would be reconciled with God in the Final Judgment. Murray was not an original thinker, but his message of universal salvation for all brought a new optimism to America echoed in his words to give the people "not hell, but hope and courage."

MURRAY, JUDITH SARGENT (1751–1820). An important writer and early advocate for equal rights for women, Murray also made many contributions to the development of Universalism. Judith Sargent was born May 1, 1751, the daughter of Winthrop Sargent, a wealthy sea merchant and intellectual, and Judith Saunders Sargent. Her father had been rethinking his faith when he invited **John Murray** to preach in Gloucester, Massachusetts, in 1774. Judith was the oldest of eight children, and under the tutelage of her father received a fine education. The family had a large library, and Judith practiced writing constantly, mostly poems. In 1769 Judith married John Stevens, a sea captain. They had no children of their own, but Judith cared for her husband's orphaned nieces and also took on boarders. She became an advocate for equal education for boys and girls, and in 1782 she wrote a *Catechism*, which was her first publication and one of the earliest Universalist writings.

After the Revolutionary War, her husband fell into debt and left for the West Indies to escape debtor's prison, and he died there. Widowed and poor, Judith took up writing in earnest. Ever since her father had brought John Murray to Gloucester, Judith had corresponded with him, and in 1788, they were married. Judith had two children, the first was stillborn, but the second, Julia Maria, survived, even though she was a sickly child. Judith's writing bore fruit with poetry at first, but later she turned to essays. Her most famous essay, "On the Equality of the Sexes," perhaps the first published argument in America for women's equality, appeared in 1790. Here she wrote "our souls are by nature equal to yours; the same breath of God animates, enlivens and invigorates us." Murray said that women were equal in mental powers of reason, memory, judgment, and imagination. Because they did not have a positive sense of themselves, she said women were unable to resist the marriage market. Her poems appeared in *Massachusetts Magazine* and she also wrote an anonymous column called "The Gleaner" under the pseudonym Constantia. Here she argued for many political issues including equal education for women and the raising of children. She said that women should be accustomed to habits of industry and order and that "independence should be placed within their grasp." She even argued at one point that if women were made physically weaker, then they must have been given greater intellectual gifts.

In 1791 the Murrays moved to Boston. She was writing poetry at this time and it proved more popular than her essays, but she often had no forum after 1796 when the *Massachusetts Magazine* stopped publishing. Murray's skills as a writer were multifaceted. She also wrote plays, the first of which, *The Medium or Happy Tea Party*, was performed in Boston in 1795. Here the main character is suspected of wanting to marry for money, but she proves her worth by refusing to marry unless the man she loves does so on equal terms. In 1798 she published three volumes of "The Gleaner" columns. In 1802 she assisted two other women with the formation of the Ladies' Academy in Dorchester, Massachusetts. After her husband's death in 1815, she helped finish his biography, *Records of the Life of the Rev. John Murray, Written by Himself, with a Continuation by Mrs. Judith Sargent Murray*. With some trepidation she left Boston in 1818 to live with her daughter and son-in-law in Natchez, Mississippi, where she died on July 6, 1820. During her life she wrote more than 2,000 letters beginning at age 14, which serve as an important record of her life and times, including meeting President and Mrs. Washington, and exploring such issues as education reform and the independence of women. Murray was an important figure in setting a precedent for 19th-century feminists to become outspoken advocates of equality.

– N –

NATIONAL CONFERENCE OF UNITARIAN CHURCHES. The first national Unitarian organization in which churches were given delegate status was formed in 1865. Prior to the establishment of the National Conference, the Unitarians had two means of association. The **American Unitarian Association (AUA)** was an association of individuals, not congregations, but it was the only true national instrument of influence and organization. Second, from 1842 to 1863, the Unitarians had also met in Autumnal Conventions, but these were more informal meetings rather than a truly representational or authoritative assembly in the structure of the church. **Henry Whitney Bellows**, the minister of what is now All Souls Church in New York, wanted to rejuvenate and organize the Unitarian denomination and create a sense of corporate identity with a truly national church. He wanted to create a separate organization for churches rather than trying to reform the AUA from within. Bellows also wanted to help the church find and elucidate a creed, as he felt the Unitarians and other liberal groups were not a church but a protest and that they had a "petty piddling operation" beside the popular church. He was present at a special meeting of the AUA held in Boston on December 6–7, 1864, and asked for the development of a more effective denominational organization. After a discussion of raising more funds for the AUA, Bellows proposed the appointment of a committee of 10 to plan a convention.

On February 1, 1865, a notice was sent to all Unitarian churches that they could send a minister and two delegates to meet in New York to affect "a more thorough organization of the Liberal Church of America." After speaking in Boston on February 20, there was fear among some that Bellows intended to impose a creed. By mid-March responses from churches made it clear that the churches would be well represented. The planners, the so-called Broad Church men, decided to open the convention on April 4 with a conciliatory speech given by **James Freeman Clarke**. They adopted a resolution for funding denominational expansion and the establishment of a paper, *The Liberal Christian*. A resolution that anticipated merger with the Universalists was presented. The plan for organization allowed for a Christian basis for its platform, but this was subject to free interpretation. Efforts to adopt a creedal basis for the convention were defeated. Trying to establish a broad Christian basis for the denomination, Bellows proposed they be called the Liberal Christian Church of America, but loyalty to the Unitarian resulted in the name the National Conference of Unitarian Churches. With 202 churches represented, the denomination now had a national, representative, ecclesiastical organization to shape a common purpose, while the AUA could carry on its administrative and publishing work.

At the first National Conference meeting in Syracuse in 1866 Bellows proposed that a more effective means of local organization needed to be undertaken. This resulted in the creation of local conferences and by the time the conference met again in 1868, there were 14 such structures. Mostly these organizations served as a means of fellowship between the churches rather than effective bureaucratic or missionary entities. The meeting in Syracuse also marked an attempt by the radicals to revise the constitution so that all sectarian differences would be disregarded, but this failed. The disgruntled radicals founded the **Free Religious Association** the following year. Women were not permitted as delegates until 1868, when there were 37 women delegates, including **Julia Ward Howe**.

One result of the organization of the National Conference was the expression of the belief that the AUA should also have a formal relationship with the churches as well. Rather than consolidating, the AUA voted in 1884 to admit voting members from the churches, but they also continued to have their old system of individual life members of the AUA, so there were two categories of membership. Determining membership characteristics of Unitarian Churches was also a controversial subject. A Commission on Membership suggested that the National Conference should have this theological authority, but it never assumed it. In 1887 the editor of the ***Christian Register*** declared that no ecclesiastical body had the authority to decide what constitutes a Unitarian church. The National Conference was renamed the General Conference in 1911 and saw much of its work absorbed by the AUA after **Samuel Atkins Eliot** became president. In 1921 a Commission on Polity was appointed. This commission recommended to the General Conference in September 1923 that it be merged into the AUA, and after this was voted, the General Conference met for the lasttime in 1925. By this merger, the AUA decided to phase out lifetime members, so it would eventually be a delegate body only. They also decided to proportion delegates based on the size of churches, rather than the equal representation that had prevailed in the National Conference. Finally, they agreed to hold a more informal fall meeting away from Boston to correspond with the old biennial structure of meetings that the National Conference had. The creation of the National Conference had given the denomination its first truly national organization of churches and an effective means for developing a unified church. *See also* MAY MEETINGS.

NATURAL RELIGION. During the Middle Ages, nature and revelation were distinguished as the two sources of human knowledge. Revealed religion comes from those sources of knowledge that represent the word of God, which is found in the revelation in scriptures and is dependent upon the recorded experiences of others. Natural religion is based on those truths that are apprehended through human reason and is purely empirical evidence. The 18th- and early-19th-century liberals kept the wedding between faith and reason as the building blocks of religious truth, but the truth of revelation increasingly depended upon reason and what was perceived through the senses. Edward Holyoke's 1755 Dudleian Lecture defined Natural Religion as "that regard to a Divine Being or God which Men arrive at, by mere Principles of natural Reason, as it is improvable, by tho't, consideration, and Experience, without the help of Revelation" (Wright, *Beginnings*, p. 140).

NEW BEACON SERIES. The new curriculum developed by the **American Unitarian Association (AUA)** under the direction of **Sophia Fahs** and **Ernest Kuebler** during the 1930s, 1940s, and 1950s. After Fahs was appointed curriculum editor in 1937, it was thought that the old Beacon Course books would be revised, but this plan soon changed under Fahs's inspiration. At first the new books were referred to as the Beacon Books in Religious Education, but it soon became the New Beacon Series. The first books, a *Beginnings* series of creation stories and modern scientific explanations, appeared with the assumption that the same great life questions were asked by human beings throughout the ages. With a philosophy consistent with the work of John Dewey, the New Beacon Series focused on the child with the only aim being continuous growth. In 1939 Fahs and Kuebler wrote a letter to all ministers and church school workers outlining their new plans. They said the new books would be ones the children could read rather than textbooks. The new curriculum was used to emphasize a broad appreciation for religion and also help the children directly relate their own experiences. There were to be stories at every age level stressing religious values in the family and community. Out of this preparation came the *Martin and Judy* stories, with the first series appearing in 1939.

The New Beacon Series also had a number of biblically based biographies, including Fahs's own *Jesus the Carpenter's Son* (1945) and others on Abraham, Moses, and Joseph. Thanks to the cooperation of Riverside Church in New York where Fahs had previously worked, many of these curricula were field tested extensively, including the *Martin and Judy* series. This also reflected that many of the curricula were appropriate for churches other than Unitarian. Parent and teachers' guides were available as well. A Curriculum Committee also helped Fahs formulate and refine her ideas and plans. The New Beacon Series marked a crucial turning point for Unitarian Sunday Schools. The dynamic new curriculum helped revitalize the entire denomination under the inspirational leadership of Sophia Lyon Fahs.

NEW ZEALAND. *See* AUSTRALIA AND NEW ZEALAND.

NIGERIA. The Unitarian Brotherhood Church was organized in Lagos in 1919 by a group of liberals who were come-outers from other denominations. The chief leader was Dr. Adeniran Adedeji Ishola, who found the word Unitarian in a dictionary. He had been a member of an Anglican church and was married to the priest's daughter. He began to question the Trinity and then in 1918 formed an indigenous group called "1st Free Thinkers." He also wrote hymns in the native Yoruba language. Many of those are still used today along with other translated hymn texts. Their first place of worship was in the Lagos Public Hall, where they held two Sunday services. In 1919 they became the United African Church and then changed the name to Unitarian Brotherhood Church in 1921, after they made the dictionary discovery of the word that summed up their beliefs. The church suffered some persecution when new members began leaving established Christian churches to join the Brotherhood Church. Some members lost jobs, were denied education, or became subject to abusive language. Dr. Ishola was called a devil, charged with disturbing the peace in the Assize Court, and eventually was forced from his job with the civil service. He even survived an assassination attempt.

The church persevered and saved enough money to purchase an old Church of Zion building, where the Unitarians established their church and primary school in 1936–37. At this time the head of the church was Arinola Ibaru. Later the old corrugated metal building was torn down and a block building put up on the same site. Many of the services, which are given in Yoruba, are accompanied by drumming, making it one of the first churches to introduce African cultural elements into the liturgy. Children are baptized with names in their native Yoruba language. The membership is all drawn from the Yoruba, who are one of three principal ethnic groups in Nigeria, and it numbers about 200 adults and children. In 1966 the Rev. Opeolu Ademsu resigned his ministry after a major disagreement, but the Rev. A. Ajose Adeogun took over and began training new leaders. One of these people, A. A. Soyombo-Abowaba, is now the high bishop of the Brotherhood Church. Another person Adeogun mentored into a leadership position, Olatunji Matimoju, was head of the Egba diocese and then started a separate First Unitarian Church of Nigeria leaving the Brotherhood Church. The Unitarian Brotherhood Church is a member of the International Council of Unitarians and Universalists.

NORTON, ANDREWS (1786–1853). Known as the "Unitarian Pope," Norton was a scholar who helped establish the scriptural basis for not believing in the Trinity, but he became the defender of the first generation of Unitarians against the new school of thought represented by the Transcendentalists. He was born the youngest child of Samuel and Jane Norton in Hingham, Massachusetts, on December 31, 1786. A good student as a child, he prepared at Derby Academy and then under the tutelage of Abner Lincoln. He went on to **Harvard College** and graduated in 1804. He continued to study for another few years and then elected to be the supply preacher in Augusta, Maine, in 1809. He decided not to be parish minister, partly due to a weak voice, and went to be a tutor at Bowdoin College for a year. He returned to Harvard and held a number of positions. First he was a tutor in mathematics and then in 1812 he started a periodical, *General Repository and Review*, which lasted for two years. In 1813 he became the librarian for Harvard and stayed in that post for eight years. That same year he was also appointed a lecturer on biblical criticism. This evolved into the chaired position he was named to in 1819, the Dexter Professor of Sacred Literature in the **Harvard Divinity School**. At this time he began work on his most famous publication, *The Evidences of the Genuineness of the Gospels*, which was not published until 1837 (vol. 1). In 1821 Norton married Catherine Eliot, the daughter of Samuel Eliot, one of the founders of the **American Unitarian Association (AUA)**. In 1830 he resigned his professorship to work full time on finishing his masterpiece on the "evidences" of Christianity.

Norton is primarily remembered for his role in the **Miracles Controversy**. He began the controversy with a letter to the *Boston Daily Advertiser* in November 1836, but **Ralph Waldo Emerson**'s **"Divinity School Address"** ignited the conflagration. Norton responded in the newspaper saying "that the author professes to reject all belief in Christianity as a revelation, that he makes a general attack upon the Clergy" (Miller, *Transcendentalists*, p. 195). After that **Orestes Brownson** criticized the scholarship in Norton's *Evidences*. In response Norton gave an address before the alumni of the Divinity School called "A Discourse on the Latest Form of Infidelity" on July 19, 1839. Here Norton accused the Transcendentalists of rejecting all evidence that establishes the truths of Christianity. Norton went on to publish the second and third volumes of *Evidences* in 1844. Perhaps unfairly characterized as the villain of the Transcendentalist Controversy, Norton's academic leadership and defense of liberal Christianity were important in establishing the biblical basis for Unitarianism. One of his opponents, **George Ripley**, later remarked, "His thorough scholarship served to give form and substance to the literary enthusiasm which at that time prevailed in Cambridge" (Miller, *Transcendentalists*, p. 159). He died on September 18, 1853.

– O –

ORDINATION. The act that confers the title and authority of minister upon a person has in Unitarian tradition resided with individual congregations. This ceremonial act is expressive of Puritan and

Congregational tradition in which an independent and autonomous congregation elects a person by vote to serve as pastor and teacher for that group without any need for hierarchal sanction. Although election by a congregation was intended to be the most significant component of attaining ministerial status in Puritanism, by the early 1700s ordination took primacy over election. The act of ordination began to signify that a young man was being initiated into a clerical order, and the development of this pattern was preceded by a decreasing role for lay people in the services during the late 1600s. Approval of prospective candidates for ordination was usually provided by local councils composed of laity and ministers from neighboring congregations. Since the beginning of the period known as the Unitarian controversy (1805), ministerial candidates have presented themselves to one or more congregations and eventually been chosen by one and then elected to serve it. After some interval, ordination was conferred upon the candidate as the culmination of a relationship with a particular congregation.

Ordination in the Universalist tradition had always differed from the Unitarian pattern, as statewide fellowship committees sanctioned candidates and ordination was conferred by the denomination. By the early 20th century the approval of ministerial credentials in both denominations was formalized through state, regional, and continental committees. Since the Unitarian and Universalist merger in 1961 credentials for approved ministers have been granted by a continental Ministerial Fellowship Committee. While this has become the means whereby a minister achieves professional status, the importance of ordination as a distinct symbol of congregational polity and authority has been eroded. Ordinarily a minister is both fellowshipped and ordained when serving a local congregation, but the processes are completely independent of one another. Increasingly, ordination is conferred by a congregation that the candidate is not called to serve but rather one where he/she has either been an active member or served as its student minister. Thus ordination today usually precedes rather than follows the vote candidates receive when they are called to a congregation. While the **Unitarian Universalist Association (UUA)** affirms the right of congregations to call and ordain their ministers, ordination now symbolizes that an individual has completed his/her training and is credentialed by the denomination. Lost is the unique relationship a person has with one congregation that was the locus of authority in the Puritan—Congregational—Unitarian tradition, where one could not be an ordained minister apart from this specific relationship with one community. This raises questions as to the recognition and authority of all ministers, and especially community ministers, who have no special calling from a particular congregation, but are serving a broader constituency as teachers, counselors, and chaplains. Their relationships with individual congregations need to be nurtured and strengthened.

Historically, the Unitarian and Universalist denominations have set ground breaking precedents in broadening the pool of prospective people who could be ordained as full-fledged clergy. In 1863 **Olympia Brown** became the first woman to be ordained to the ministry with full denominational authority when the St. Lawrence (New York) Association (Universalist) affirmed her calling in June. Brown endured much prejudice and little support in her journey toward official sanction. The first Unitarian woman to be ordained was **Celia Burleigh** in 1871 in Brooklyn, Connecticut. A little more than a century later the UUA affirmed gay, lesbian, and bisexual ministers when the General Assembly of the UUA passed a resolution backing Ministerial Employment Opportunities (1980), which called upon the denomination to end job discrimination and lend full assistance in the settlement of openly gay, lesbian, and bisexual ministers.

ORIGINAL SIN. This was the first doctrine of Calvinism that came under attack during the **Great Awakening** by the **Arminians**. In response to the Calvinist belief that fallen human beings could do nothing to improve their moral condition, the early liberals began to argue that sin could be gradually overcome with the assistance of God and that sin was a personal matter that could be improved upon rather than a permanent condition of the entire human race. The Arminians did not deny that Adam had sinned or that people are sinners, but rejected the universal imputed guilt of Adam's sin on everyone and the total depravity that prevented people from acting on their own behalf to achieve salvation. The Arminians argued that Adam and his posterity are not one complex person, but that guilt is personal. In this context the Arminians emphasized humankind as individuals rather than as one race. The Arminians came to believe that human beings are a mixture of good and evil tendencies. Far from the later Unitarians who would emphasize the dignity of human nature, the Arminians believed that life was a process of trial and discipline and that overcoming sin was not easy, but that it could be done. After 1743 many communities experienced controversies around preachers who denied the doctrine of original sin. Arminians, such as **Jonathan Mayhew** (whose ordination in 1747 was controversial) and Lemuel Briant, were influenced by several dissenting clergy from England, including John Taylor. Within a decade they were asserting that people could strive for and achieve some measure of personal righteousness.

OWEN-TOWLE, CAROLYN SHEETS (1935–). She has been a pioneer in developing strong concepts of joint ministry with her husband Tom and was also a candidate for the **Unitarian Universalist Association (UUA)** presidency in 1993. Born in Upland, California, on July 27, 1935, her parents were Millard Owen Sheets and Mary Baskerville Sheets. Her father was an artist who has been called the "Father of Southern California Watercolor." She graduated from Scripps College in Claremont, California, in 1957 with a major in art and art history. She was married to Charles Chapman for 14 years and had three children. In 1973 she was remarried to Thomas Towle and took the name Carolyn Owen-Towle. Owen-Towle became a parish minister through the UUA's independent study program. This was undertaken at the Graduate School of Religion at the University of Iowa. She was fellowshipped into the ministry and ordained in 1978. Shortly thereafter, she was called with Tom, who was then serving in Davenport, Iowa, to serve the First Unitarian Universalist Church of San Diego, California. They served a 24-year ministry there as full-time senior parish ministers, retiring in June 2002. The church had 824 members with a church school of 318 at that time.

Owen-Towle was active in denominational groups from the beginning of her ministry. She served as president of the Ministerial Sisterhood, a prominent group of women ministers. For six years she was a board member of the **Unitarian Universalist Service Committee** (1980–86), finally becoming its president. From 1988 to 1889, she was president of the **Unitarian Universalist Ministers Association (UUMA)**. During this time she was also a board member of the **Meadville Lombard Theological School** (1998–92). A collection of her sermons, *Step off the Sidewalk*, was published in 1992. In 1993 she ran for the presidency of the UUA, but lost in a close election to **John Buehrens**. The next year she received an honorary D.D. from Meadville Lombard. When the Owen-Towles retired from the San Diego church they were both named minister emeriti and also had a garden dedicated to them and an endowment fund named in their honor. Retirement did not end her active role with the denomination, as she began serving a term on the UUA's Ministerial Fellowship Committee in 2002. She began her retirement by serving as a minister-in-residence at Meadville Lombard in the fall of 2002.

OXFORD CONVENTIONS. The Universalists began to organize themselves first with a regional meeting in Oxford, Massachusetts, in 1785, and then with a second meeting in Oxford in 1793, where the New England Convention was formally established. The first meeting in Oxford came about as a direct result of legal problems that **John Murray** and the Gloucester Universalists were experiencing. In Gloucester the First Parish Church had seized property for nonpayment of taxes, and Murray had countersued for the return of goods. Murray said that his opponents were trying to show that "God hates them, we hate them, and we hope that you will hate them." Adams Streeter proposed that the Universalists gather in association so that a unified and legal church body might be recognized on constitutional grounds. They met on September 14, 1785, and formed the Oxford Association, following the intended proposal that they be "cemented in one body" to assist one another. Delegates came from five churches under the leadership of **Caleb Rich** along with Rich, Murray, Streeter, and **Elhanan Winchester**. The group approved a "Charter of Compact" using language from the Massachusetts Constitution to prove their legitimacy. The problem in Gloucester passed when the case was settled in Murray's favor in 1786 and the association proved to be only a short-lived political alliance. The churches under Rich's influence never agreed to the charter, and the Universalists of New England did not develop any institutional stability until the next decade.

Trying to corral these independent New Englanders into a cohesive body bore some results in the 1790s. This first attempt at a national convention of Universalists was held in Philadelphia in 1790, but many New Englanders felt this was too much of a strain on resources to be represented there on a regular basis. In 1792 Universalists in Boston made a request to hold a New England convention. Although originally organized as an appendage of the Philadelphia group, the New England Convention gradually assumed more responsibilities. It met annually from 1793 until 1833 when it officially became the United States Convention. The invitation to the gathering in 1793 invited Universalists from 37 towns and by the following year, when they met in Oxford again, 71 towns were listed. Although the meeting in 1793 is considered the starting date for Universalist organization, little is known about the business transacted at that meeting. The convention in 1794 approved the Philadelphia Articles of Faith and Plan of Government, which provided for minimal order including congregational autonomy, validity of non-Universalist ordination and optional observance of sacraments, but assured Universalists of Gospel liberty in matters of faith. This convention also witnessed the spontaneous ordination of **Hosea Ballou** by Elhanan Winchester, although it appears that the convention did not assume this official power until 1800. This occurred in Orange, Massachusetts, where the delegates decided to do a better job of keeping records and making reports, work on settling disputes between clergy and churches, and for the first time, Walter Ferriss recommended they consider a profession of faith, which finally came at the 1803 convention in Winchester, New Hampshire. In subsequent years the convention named committees to take more responsibility for charity and mission work, publications, and oversight of ministers. The convention meetings included the approval of credentials, reports, and sermons, approving new societies, and granting licenses to preach and letters of fellowship to clergy. After 1805 the New England Convention came increasingly to be known as the "**General Convention**."

– P –

PACIFISM. *See* PEACE.

PAGANISM. This is a theological perspective that has become increasingly popular among Unitarian Universalists in recent years.

The word *pagan* derives from the Latin *paganus*, which means country dweller. Today pagan is identified with those who find their primary religious sustenance in an earth centered spirituality. Paganism is influenced by ancient practices when people were closer to the cycles of the seasons. Because it has roots in pre-Christian times, it has been unfairly characterized as false folk religion that was superseded by Christianity. Many of its practices were co-opted by Christians, especially in Easter and Christmas customs and rites. Paganism has largely enjoyed a revival due to the influence of the women's movement. An adult religious education curriculum, *Cakes for the Queen of Heaven*, inspired many Unitarian Universalists to find strength and hope in female images of God or Goddess. This has led to additional adult education curricula, worship services—especially for the solstices and equinoxes—and even the creation of entire congregations that centered their religious practices on paganism. Although Unitarian Universalism has a strong heritage of earth-centered practices, especially evident in the Transcendentalists who believed, like the pagans, in the direct experience of the divine through nature, the word pagan has only been commonly used in recent years.The importance of paganism in modern Unitarian Universalism was expressed in the 1995 bylaw change in the **Principles and Purposes** of the association, which added the following words as another expression of the sources of this liberal faith: "Spiritual teachings of Earth-centered traditions which celebrate the sacred circle of life and instruct us to live in harmony with the rhythms of nature."

PAINE, THOMAS (1737–1809). Known for his pamphlet *Common Sense*, a document that rallied the colonists to the cause of independence. His better known attack on the monarchy was also part of a larger belief in freedom, which was expressed religiously, too. Paine was born on January 29, 1737, in Thetford, England, northeast of London. By the time he was 37 he had run away from home, lost two wives, his house, and every job he had ever held. In 1774 he decided to remake himself in the New World and, with letters from Benjamin Franklin, embarked at the end of September. He became involved in publishing and his *Pennsylvania Magazine* eventually became a great success. *Common Sense*, a title suggested by **Benjamin Rush**, appeared in January 1776, and it proved dramatically prophetic in leading to the "free and independent states of America." In addition to the spark provided by *Common Sense*, Paine's letters on the American Crisis appeared in the press during a difficult time in the Revolution and helped the colonists believe in their cause and that in the end their triumph would be "glorious." Before Paine published *The Age of Reason: Being an Investigation of True and Fabulous Theology* (1794) in Paris, **deism** was largely confined to a more educated class. Paine endured some vehement criticism because it was felt he spread heresy to the common people with this publication. It was an attack on the authority of the Bible, but the arguments were made so that everyone could understand.

Paine had left America in 1787 to visit England, but he did not return until 1802. Some people were not happy to see him return. These included Benjamin Rush, who said, "His principles avowed in his *Age of Reason* were so offensive to me that I did not wish to renew my intercourse with him" (Koch, *Religion*, p. 135). The religious attacks were frequent in his later years, as his opponents often tried to associate republicanism with infidelity. In 1804 he wrote, "Deism is the only profession of religion that admits of worshiping and reverencing God in purity, and the only one on which the thoughtful mind can repose with undisturbed tranquility. God is almost forgotten in the Christian Religion" (Koch, *Religion*, p. 141). Paine died on June 8, 1809. The religious and political radical who also wrote *The Rights of Man* (1790), which led to his banishment from England, had a controversial life.

PANTHEISM. A theological position where God and nature are considered identical. Pantheism has traditionally been rejected by Christian theologians because it destroys the distinction between creator and creation. This is not to be confused with panentheism as it is understood in process theology. Panentheism posits that the world is part of God but does not exhaust the fullness of God. It is sometimes said that the **Transcendentalists** are pantheists with their emphasis upon the presence of the divine in nature. **Ralph Waldo Emerson** is usually most closely aligned with the pantheist perspective. In *The Over-Soul* he writes: "Let man then learn the revelation of all nature and all thought to his heart; this, namely; that the Highest dwells within him; that the sources of nature are in his own mind" (Albanese, *Spirituality of the American Transcendentalists*, p. 104).

PARK, CHARLES EDWARDS (1873–1962). An important preacher from the middle of the 20th century who is chiefly remembered for his long pastorate at the First Church of Boston. Park was born on March 14, 1873, in Mahabaleshwar, India. He was the son and grandson of congregational ministers who served as missionaries in India, his father completing his term there in 1881. Park went to Phillips Academy in Andover, Massachusetts, and then to Yale University, where he graduated in 1896. He trained for the ministry at the University of Chicago Divinity School, working with **William Wallace Fenn**, and graduated in 1899. He was ordained that year in Geneva, Illinois, and also met Mary E. Turner there. They were married on September 19, 1903, and had five children: Charles, Marian, Richard, David, and Edwards. From 1900 to 1906 he served as minister at the New North Church and the Second Church in Hingham, Massachusetts. Then in 1906 he was invited to be interim minister at the First Church of Boston but never left, becoming the permanent minister to the extent that he remained for 40 years, moving *Time* magazine to call him the "Grand Old Man of U.S. Liberal Pulpits" when he retired.

Park remained a Christian in a time of advancing humanism, as evidenced by his activity with a committee of 12 ministers that formed the Unitarian Christian Advance (now the Unitarian Universalist Christian Fellowship) in 1944, with the first meeting taking place at his church on December 12. He was editor of *The Unitarian Christian* from 1952 to 1958. During this time the periodical became more devotional and less argumentative about the religious direction of the denomination. Park was an important voice for compromise between the humanists and theists and was the author of an **American Unitarian Association (AUA)** pamphlet that attempted to reconcile the two camps. At one time he was referred to as "Mr. Unitarian." He did not believe that church was a place to tell people how to think about social issues. Hence, he placed a high value on the personal dimension of religion. He did the same with the life of Jesus, feeling that the person of Jesus was what animated Christianity. He said that God was incarnated in the creation and, especially, in humans. Our individuality is lived out through discovering God's expectations of us. This quiet, scholarly man preached a very human Jesus, who helps us find the way to God. He published *The Way of Jesus* (1956), and also was responsible for the Minns Lectures in 1947, *Christianity: How It Came to Us; What It Is; What It Might Be*. In 1945 Park delivered an address before the South Middlesex conference on "A Definition of Unitarianism" that was widely circulated by the AUA. Here he said that Unitarianism was not a body of beliefs but "a state of mind." He said the chief characteristic of Unitarianism was the open optimistic mind, which was ever ready to move on to better beliefs. He retired when he was 73 years old in 1946, and became minister emeritus until his death on September 23, 1962, in Boston.

PARKER, THEODORE (1810–1860). The great orator and important abolitionist, Parker is often credited with giving one of the three most influential sermons in Unitarian history, "The Transient and Permanent in Christianity." Parker grew up with the first stirrings of the American Revolution at his doorstep. His grandfather, Captain John Parker, uttered the famous words, "If they mean to have a war, let it begin here," on Lexington Green in Massachusetts. Parker was born there on August 24, 1810, the youngest of 11 children. He learned how to run his father's farm, and schooling often occurred only in wintertime. He had a brief term at the new academy when he was 16, but that marked the end of his formal schooling. Parker's mother, who died when he was 13, had encouraged him to go to **Harvard Divinity School**, but he could not afford it. Trying to save his money, he taught school in several locations. Finally, in the summer of 1830, he passed some exams at Harvard and enrolled as a nonresident student. After that he spent a year teaching in Boston and then moved to Watertown, Massachusetts, where he opened his own very successful school. Here he began to court Lydia Cabot of Newton, who taught in the Sunday School at the First Parish of Watertown. The minister of that church, **Convers Francis**, had a profound effect upon Parker. When Parker arrived in town, he told Francis, "I've come to learn," and his mentor then shared his large library and his knowledge of the new German criticism. After two years Francis helped introduce Parker to the faculty at Harvard Divinity School and he procured a scholarship for him to enter in the spring of 1834. He started as a junior and was able to finish in two years. During his training he tutored students in Hebrew, Greek, and German. Parker had a passion for languages and learned 10 or so more, while he was at the seminary.

After graduation Parker preached in several locations, including a summer on Cape Cod at Barnstable. Then in April 1837 he was called to the Spring Street Church in West Roxbury, Massachusetts, where he remained until 1846. He was married to Lydia the same month as his call and was ordained two months later. This small church afforded him the opportunity for further study. He was well liked by his congregation, but he stirred a hornet's nest of controversy after he had been there for four years, when he delivered the famous South Boston sermon "The Transient and Permanent in Christianity" at the ordination of Charles Shackford. When he further elucidated the ideas in "A Discourse of Matters Pertaining to Religion" (1842), he was all but ousted from the ministerial association in 1843 and virtually no one would exchange pulpits with him.

Parker scandalized the Unitarian establishment with his ideas that Christian doctrines and creeds were transient while the teachings of Jesus were permanent, but even his person was not necessary for their revelation. Parker said these great truths "spring up spontaneous in the holy heart." Parker began to attend meetings of the **Transcendental Club**, was a contributor to the ***Dial***, and a frequent visitor at **Brook Farm**. By the fall of 1843 he was exhausted after a long series of lectures and emotionally drained from his "heresy trial" before the Boston Association of Ministers, where he had refused to resign and left the meeting in tears. A trip to Europe was planned to restore his health. After that, he resigned from his beloved West Roxbury congregation in 1846 to serve the newly organized Twenty-Eighth Congregational Society in Boston. Here he began to exert an influence on all of American culture. He preached to a congregation of 3,000 first at the Melodeon and later at the Music Hall to accommodate the crowds. It was a congregation largely centered on Parker's powerful abilities as an orator and had little other organizational development. In 1847 the *Massachusetts Quarterly Review* was started with Parker serving as one of the editors until 1850. More than anything Parker was wedded to the reform movement. At his own installation service he had said that the "Christian Church should be the means of reforming the world."

While Parker addressed such questions as labor and prison reform, no problem was greater than slavery. For Parker freedom was an absolute good and slavery an absolute evil, and this evil must be assaulted with the most vehement force. He became an important figure in the abolitionist movement. He was central to the campaign to free the captured fugitive slave Anthony Burns and was arrested for the obstruction of the Fugitive Slave Law. He was one of the Secret Six who supported the violent rebellion fomented by John Brown, who had visited Parker in 1856. It is believed that President Abraham Lincoln borrowed Parker's phrase that government was "over all the people, by all the people, and for the sake of all," for the "Gettysburg Address." For all his political vigor, Parker's health deteriorated with the advance of tuberculosis, and he preached his last sermon in Boston January 1859. He traveled first to the West Indies and then on to Europe. During this time he wrote his *Experience as a Minister*. He died in Florence on May 10, 1860. His grave there is inscribed with the words "The Great American Preacher."

PARKMAN, FRANCIS (1823–1893). The great 19th-century historian who helped establish a tradition of literary historical writing. Parkman came from a Boston Brahmin background. His father, Francis Parkman Sr., was a Unitarian minister at the New North Church in Boston for many years. His father's father was a rich merchant and his mother, Caroline Hall Parkman, was a descendant of John Cotton and Cotton Mather. Francis or Frank was born on September 16, 1823, and grew up with four siblings in a mansion on Bowdoin Square. Not entirely healthy, Parkman spent some years on his grandparent's farm in Medford, where he began to develop his love for the wilderness. He attended Chauncy Hall School and entered **Harvard College** in 1840. Each summer he found an adventurous place to travel, and he published those accounts of his trips in the *Knickerbocker Magazine*. He was only an average student, but under Jared Sparks he developed a love for history. A year before graduation he had a physical and mental breakdown and traveled in Europe for seven months. He then went on to study law at Harvard and graduated in 1846. A recurring eye problem, which left him with vision too weak to use for research, led him to plan his great adventure on the Oregon Trail, which began in 1846. Parkman showed incredible powers of observation and reflection as he traveled from western Missouri to Oregon and lived for a time with the Sioux, but his perspective on Native American culture displayed a marked degree of privilege and prejudice. While he corrected many misconceptions of the west and wrote strikingly beautiful passages of observation, he also predicted the demise of native culture, which he found "savage," and was hard pressed to find much value in it. He once wrote, "He will not learn the arts of civilization, and he and his forest must perish together." Near the end of his journey he was near collapse, but he returned home to finish his narrative. *The Oregon Trail*, which had to be dictated to a cousin due to Parkman's poor eyesight, was published in 1849 (California was included in the original title). It has a unique place in Parkman's works because it represents a merging of history and autobiography written in a novelistic fashion. His work on *History of the Conspiracy of Pontiac* was published in 1851.

Parkman spent most of the next half-century working on his great seven volume work on France and England in North America. Among these books is *Montcalm and Wolfe*, known for its powerful portrayals of these two heroes. The works on the conquest of North America also reflect a deep seeded anti-Catholicism. Great sorrow and subsequent despair came to Parkman in the late 1850s. First a son died in 1857, and then his wife died the following year after the birth of a daughter. He gave up research for a period and became a horticulturist, even teaching briefly at Harvard. After the Civil War he lived the quiet life of a cultured literary historian who was looked after by his sister. Parkman enjoyed the company of his two daughters and also belonged to a number of clubs, including the **Saturday Club**. Despite ongoing struggles with health, he nearly lived to the age of 70, dying on November 8, 1893. Parkman's writing conveyed that the study of history should be part of American letters, and so he believed research and writing should create histories that are also good literature.

PATTON, KENNETH LEO (1911–1994). He was a Unitarian Universalist minister who achieved fame due to his liturgical contributions. Born in Three Oaks, Michigan, on August 25, 1911, Patton attended schools in the Chicago area. Always showing an aptitude for the arts he studied violin, sculpture, and painting. While he was a student at Eureka College, he worked as a commercial artist. Deciding to enter the ministry, he achieved a B.D. and an M.A. from the University of Chicago. At first a minister in the Disciples of Christ, he became minister of the Unitarian Church in Madison, Wisconsin, in 1942 where he gained prominence with a weekly radio program. He also actively engaged **Frank Lloyd Wright** to come design a new church building for the Madison congregation. In 1949 Patton was invited to be the minister of an experimental Universalist congregation gathered at the Charles Street Meetinghouse in Boston. The Massachusetts Universalist Convention wished to make this a center for the development of contemporary worship materials and services. Patton combined his artistic background and his belief in a universal religion that draws upon all the world's faiths to publish numerous volumes of liturgical materials on the newly established Meetinghouse Press.

In his *Religion for One World*, Patton wrote, "The liberal church should be a living prophecy of a new world to come. . . . It should be a community of universal peace and brotherhood, the beloved community, gathering the symbols, music, literature, idealism, and art of all times and places into one assembly and projection" (Patton, *Religion*, 226). Many of these readings and poems set to music were later printed in the **Unitarian Universalist Association (UUA)** hymnal, *Hymns for the Celebration of Life*, which was produced by a hymnbook commission of which Patton was a key member. He also actively collected songs and hymns. He remained in Boston for 15 years and then became minister of the Unitarian Society in Ridgewood, New Jersey, where he continued for another 22 years. Patton was also active in social causes, especially race relations and fair housing during his more than 50 years of ministry. He maintained an interest in writing poetry and in studying the arts of many worldwide cultures. In all Patton published seven books of prose, 14 books of poetry, and assorted pamphlets. In 1986 he received the distinguished service award of the UUA. Patton died on December 25, 1994, and was survived by seven children.

PEABODY, ELIZABETH PALMER (1804–1894). One of the famous Peabody sisters from Salem, Massachusetts; one sister, Mary, married **Horace Mann**, and another sister, Sophia, married **Nathaniel Hawthorne**. Elizabeth is often credited with being the founder of the kindergarten movement in America. She was born in Billerica, Massachusetts, on May 16, 1804, the eldest child of seven to Nathaniel and Eliza Peabody, who had been married in 1802. Both her parents worked at the Franklin Academy, but her mother soon opened a home school, which resulted in Elizabeth later commenting that she was "prenatally educated for the profession." The bookish girl opened her first school at her parent's house in Lancaster, Massachusetts, where they moved from Salem, when she was 16. She combined domestic activities with education and learned that educating a young mind required moral, physical, spiritual, and intellectual attainments. In 1822 she moved to Boston to teach school and help support her brothers in their educational plans. Over the years she maintained close family relationships with her parents and her siblings, especially Mary. Years prior to this the Palmer and Peabody families split over religious issues. Elizabeth first heard **William Ellery Channing** preach when she was a girl of eight or nine when he came to Salem.

Religious issues affected her during a stay in Hallowell, Maine, from 1823 to 1825. She was disturbed by a revival that took place and wrote a long letter to Channing about it. She also found that some of the Unitarians there found the faith was ill suited for the frontier because it "smelled too much of the lamp." After her return from Maine, Channing became her mentor and introduced her to his concept of self-culture. Peabody began to put her faith in the constant educational development of the self. She later wrote, "The final cause of human society is the unfolding of the individual man into every form of perfection, without let or hindrance, according to the inward nature of each. In strict correspondence to this, the ground idea of the little communities which are the embryo of the kingdom to come must be Education" ("Christ's Idea of Society" as quoted in Hochfield, *American Transcendentalists*, p. 337). She became a copiest of Channing's sermons and eventually transcribed about 50 of them.

In 1825 Elizabeth opened a school in Brookline with her sister Mary and in 1826 moved it to Boston. After the school closed in 1831, Elizabeth had the opportunity to reflect upon her educational philosophy. She worked on some historical study guides, but found by 1834 that she was desperate for some work for pay. This was solved when Bronson Alcott returned to Boston with a plan to open a school. She finally put her reform ideals into practice with Alcott at the **Temple School**. Elizabeth helped recruit 30 students for the school and eventually taught Latin, arithmetic, and geometry. She also kept a journal of the school, which was later published as *Record of a School* (1835). By 1836 she had become critical of some of Alcott's methods and was unhappy with her boarding situation with the Alcott family, too. She moved back to Salem with her family again, where she devoted much time to study and reflection. During the end of this period, she wrote a series of articles on the artistic work of Washington Allston, Channing's brother-in-law. In 1840 she opened the West Street Book Shop, which became a gathering place for her many friends in the larger Transcendental circle; she operated a lending library there as well. Here **Margaret Fuller**'s first "Conversations," which had a forerunner in Peabody's "conferences" for women, took place, and the Ripley's made their plans to start **Brook Farm**. Peabody contributed articles to the Transcendental journal the ***Dial*** and was its publisher from 1842 to 1843. She had already been a publisher for a couple of years, beginning with Hawthorne's children's books, *Grandfather's Chair* and *Famous Old People*. She also published the *Aesthetic Papers*, in which **Henry David Thoreau**'s "Civil Disobedience" first appeared. The 1850s brought considerable change to her life, including the deaths of her parents.

Peabody began to actively support public education through the use of Bem's charts for the classroom. She became an advocate of the kindergarten philosophy of Friedrich Froebel and then opened the first English-speaking kindergarten in the United States in 1860. With the kindergarten, **James Freeman Clarke** said she was "caught up with her mission." She taught Froebel's philosophy of kindergartens as art schools, where children blend free play with the discipline of nature. Her final years were devoted to the promotion of the kindergarten, a variety of reforms, and then in 1880 she published *Reminiscences of William Ellery Channing*. The mother of the kindergarten movement in America, Peabody did much to nurture the potential in all children and everyone else she encountered in her lifetime. She died on January 3, 1894, in Jamaica Plain, Massachusetts.

PEABODY, FRANCIS GREENWOOD (1847–1936). Dean of the **Harvard Divinity School**, Peabody is best known for bringing the social gospel to Unitarianism. He was born on December 4, 1847, in

Boston, the son of Ephraim and Mary Jane (Derby) Peabody, who had seven children, but only four survived childhood. His father was a Unitarian minister who served in Cincinnati and New Bedford, Massachusetts, and at King's Chapel, Boston, where he died in 1856. This made the subsequent years difficult, but the family found the means to educate Francis at **Harvard College** and then at the Harvard Divinity School. After graduation he had the opportunity to study in Germany under Friedrich Tholuck. He returned to teach briefly at Antioch College. Peabody became minister at the First Parish in Cambridge, Massachusetts, in 1874 and stayed until 1879, but his ill health made the duties of a parish ministry difficult for him to pursue. He began to lecture at Harvard Divinity School in ethics and homiletics and was soon appointed Parkman Professor of Theology, a position he kept for five years. In 1886 he became Plummer Professor of Christian Morals, where he remained until his retirement in 1913. He was dean from 1900 to 1907. Peabody was also the first chairman of the Board of Preachers at Harvard and oversaw a significant change in college worship from required attendance to the voluntary principle.

Peabody especially made a name for himself with the publication of *Jesus and the Social Question* (1900), which eventually saw five editions. He felt the message of Jesus affirms that the test of salvation is the individual's contribution to social service through saviors who have sanctified themselves for others' sake. The changing world economic situation demanded a response from the churches. Peabody felt that there was an opportunity for expansion of ministry and that social service work should be recognized as religious work. He spiritualized the social question. His ideas helped develop an entirely new field of religious study and he is often credited with being the first teacher in America to create a spot for Christian social ethics in a course of university study and theological education. He made this a crucial part of the education that prospective ministers received. His courses on ethics and social theory became known as "Peabo's drainage, drunkenness and divorce." He believed that modern economic conditions were changing the social order and political and economic problems must be considered ethical problems as well. Although he flirted with socialism, he never advocated a revolutionary change and, instead, tried to make the business community more virtuous. Seeing how widespread the problem was, Peabody advocated an ethic of justice and social democracy for all rather than the old fashioned charity for the poor. In 1909 he published *The Approach to the Social Question*, an interdisciplinary study. He died in Cambridge on December 28, 1936.

PEACE. Religious liberals have long been associated with many peace movements. Even before the development of formal organizations, Universalist **Benjamin Rush** advocated for a Peace Office in the federal government, after he noted that the Constitution called for a War Department, but no Peace Department. An active antiwar movement began with the War of 1812. In August of that year, Noah Worcester preached that the war was beginning without justification, and that all war is evil. In 1814 he published *A Solemn Review of the Custom of War*, and then the following year he was the leading light in the formation of the Massachusetts Peace Society in December. Others who were active included Francis Parkman Sr., **Henry Ware**, and **William Ellery Channing**. The society reached a peak of about 1,000 members, but then merged with the new American Peace Society in 1828. William Lloyd Garrison influenced a number of pacifists, but most Unitarian and Universalist clergy were not pacifists, including Channing. Channing wrote that war was a great evil, but there were some conditions under which it is justifiable. One pacifist was the Universalist **Adin Ballou**, who believed that true nonresistance was Christian nonresistance. The life and teachings of Christ was the primary impulse for the authority for pacifism. **Samuel J. May** was a Unitarian minister who struggled with the issues of pacifism and freedom, especially as he became more active in abolitionism. This was true for many of the peace advocates as the Civil War approached. **James Russell Lowell**, who had one of his characters in the *Biglow Papers* equate war with murder, was a pacifist who abandoned his views as his strong antislavery feelings made him a supporter of the Civil War. While there were not many resisters during the Civil War, many peace advocates had been active during the Mexican War. Thoreau refused to pay his poll tax to support the war, and spent a night in jail. Abiel A. Livermore of Keene, New Hampshire, wrote a book against the Mexican War and called for an international court to arbitrate these situations.

After the Civil War, **Julia Ward Howe** began a crusade for universal peace and especially advocated for a Mother's Peace Day. In her proclamation she wrote, "From the bosom of the devastated earth a voice goes up with our own, it says, "Disarm! Disarm!" Although the Spanish-American War was mostly a popular affair, Francis Ellen Watkins-Harper, an African American from Philadelphia, wrote a poem called "Do Not Cheer, Men are Dying." Resistance to war proved difficult in several instances in the 20th century. **John Haynes Holmes** was the most well-known pacifist. In 1915 he introduced a resolution at the **American Unitarian Association (AUA)** General Conference to keep America in "the way of peace." That same year he had declared from his pulpit: "The interests of human life are alone sovereign. War . . . is the enemy of life and all its interests. Therefore . . . I declare to you that war must be condemned universally and unconditionally" (as quoted in Voss, ed. *A Summons Unto Men*, p. 116). Holmes disagreed vigorously with former President **William Howard Taft**, who advocated a resolution in support of the war, which was passed in 1917. Later the AUA Board voted that any society that opposed prosecution of the war would lose its ability to receive aid from the AUA. This was finally repealed in 1936 at the request of Henry Pinkham of Newton, Massachusetts. Taft also made his influence felt in his home church in Cincinnati. Alson Robinson was dismissed by a congregational vote at the First Unitarian Church in 1918 after Taft helped convince fellow members that Robinson's pacifist sermons were unacceptable. In 1941 **Curtis Reese**, the managing editor of ***Unity***, was given equal editorial control with Holmes, when it was felt that a pacifist could not represent a sufficient response to fascism.

During World War I, three Universalist ministers declared themselves pacifists, including **Clarence Russell Skinner**, professor at Crane Theological School. He was attacked for his "un-American" views. Pacifist ministers received much more respect during World War II, thanks to **Frederick May Eliot**'s call for tolerance in 1942. Unitarian **Emily Greene Balch** won the Nobel Peace Prize for her work. The Vietnam War was an example of large majorities of Unitarian Universalists opposing a war. Members were active in the peace movement in many ways. The **Unitarian Universalist Association (UUA)** published the ***Pentagon Papers*** and supported conscientious objectors. On October 16, 1967, more than 5,000 people gathered on Boston Common to advocate for peace in Vietnam. Many burned their draft cards in front of the Arlington Street Church or handed them in to clergy. Within months many of these people were jailed. Many Unitarian Universalists in individual congregations left the church as a result of the conflicts over the war efforts. Involvement in antiwar movements during this time helped shift the majority of Unitarian Universalists in their political orientation to liberalism. Many church members became involved in disarmament movements and supported resolutions in their congregations designating them Nuclear Free Zones, following a **General Assembly (GA)** resolution in 1985. Between 1961 and 1985, thirty resolutions were passed by the GA seeking an end to the nuclear arms race. Unitarian Universalists have also voiced their opposition to other conflicts in the world in more recent times. In 1991 more than 400 Unitarian Universalist ministers signed a *New York Times* advertisement opposing the Persian Gulf War.

PELAGIANISM. Named for the British monk Pelagius (early 5th century), it is a theological position that argues that God would not command human beings to do what they are unable to do. Pelagius believed that freedom for the human race was not lost by Adam because of an individual act of disobedience and, therefore, he denied the doctrine of original sin. Taking a position for free will, Pelagius said that human beings are free to do good or evil. By this definition, sin is related to an individual's actions and not their innate condition. Augustine attacked Pelagius' position, stating that it meant that human beings could save themselves. Sometimes Pelagianism is attached to any position that advocates the freedom of the will. The denial of the imputed guilt of Adam's sin and the ability of human beings to exercise their free will to make good moral decisions were central beliefs for the liberals in the early development of **Arminianism** in America.

***PENTAGON PAPERS*.** The **Unitarian Universalist Association (UUA)** became involved in an important free press controversy when it published the *Pentagon Papers* in 1971. Mike Gravel, a senator from Alaska, who was also a Unitarian Universalist, was approached by Daniel Ellsberg, who was searching for a way to publish the entire 7,000-page report, which included classified material about the U.S. involvement in Vietnam. Gravel agreed to enter the papers into the *Congressional Record* and also asked Gobin Stair, the director of **Beacon Press**, if the UUA's own publishing house would be interested in making this remarkable document public. Several other publishers had already declined the opportunity for fear of government reprisals. When Stair put the question of publication before UUA President **Robert West**, the response was positive. In October 1971, *The Pentagon Papers: The Senator Gravel Edition* was published by Beacon Press with the help of a loan from the North Shore Unitarian Society in Plandome, New York. Within weeks, Federal Bureau of Investigation (FBI) agents arrived at UUA headquarters seeking the association's financial records and the names of those who supported the UUA. The UUA and Senator Gravel countered by suing the government. A Supreme Court decision in 1972 declared that Senator Gravel's immunity did not apply to Beacon Press. The case was never resolved though, as President Richard Nixon became deeply embroiled in the Watergate controversy, and eventually the Justice Department dropped it. The UUA performed a great service to the American public by exposing a deceptive government and upholding free speech.

PHILADELPHIA CONVENTION. The first attempt to organize Universalists into a national group occurred in Philadelphia in 1790. In September 1789 a group of Universalists from New Jersey and Philadelphia were discussing that no effort had ever been made to hold a common meeting. **Elhanan Winchester** bemoaned the fact that the Universalists were "without order, rule or system" and suggested a national convention. A committee was established to send out a letter to call for a gathering of all Universalists so that they might unite in a "General Church in bands of love and uniformity." Winchester wanted unity in matters of worship, ordination, and administering communion. Seventeen people came, including Winchester and **John Murray**. They met for two weeks beginning May 25, 1790. During this time they wrote a Rule of Faith and a Plan of Church Government, which were edited by **Benjamin Rush**. These articles affirmed the concept of self-government while each congregation was to be united by a covenant for electing officers, maintaining order, and conducting worship.

Great distance prevented the New England Universalists from ever becoming active, and their own convention was formed in 1793. A number of factors worked against the success of the Philadelphia group. The Universalists were a small sect in scattered locations with a shortage of clergy and few financial resources. There were also theological conflicts. Murray left the first meeting upset that the group promoted a Gospel liberty rather than affirming his Rellyian theology. They did not agree on a common form of worship or way of administering communion. They could not overcome their various problems and differences and, coupled with the rising ascendancy of the New England Convention, the Philadelphia Convention only continued to meet until 1809 when it dissolved.

PHILIPPINES. In 1951, the Rev. Toribio S. Quimada, an ordained minister of the Iglesia Universal de Kristo (Universal Church of Christ), was looking through an international church directory for an affiliate group and found the word *Universalist*. Curious about a possible connection Quimada wrote and eventually received a reply from the Universalist Service Committee. Materials about Universalism were sent and incorporated into the education program. This enraged the leaders of his church and Quimada was expelled from its ministry in 1954. Later that same year several members rallied around Quimada, and the Universalist Church of the Philippines was organized and affiliated with the **Universalist Church of America (UCA)** on December 29. After the merger of the Unitarians and the Universalists in America, contact was maintained, including a visit by the UUA president **Dana M. Greeley** in 1967.

In 1985 the church changed its name to the Unitarian Universalist Church of the Philippines (UUCP). Breaking with its tradition of not accepting international indigenous groups as members, the **Unitarian Universalist Association (UUA)** admitted the UUCP as a member congregation in 1988. Tragically, Quimada was murdered that same year and leadership of the church passed to his son-in-law. While this tradition continues to the present day, it was preceded by a Unitarian connection. A Philippine National Church was being organized about the time that Unitarian **William Howard Taft** was sent to the Philippines as governor. Taft became the vice president of the new church under the leadership of a former Catholic priest, Gregorio Aglipay. The services were much like the Catholic mass, and thousands converted to this Unitarian movement. Despite Unitarian interest in expanding there under **American Unitarian Association (AUA)** president and internationalist **Louis Cornish**, World War II intervened. After the war, the church was reconstituted as an Anglican communion. Those who did not follow were organized as the Independent Church of Filipino Christians with offices in Manila and are active members of the **International Association for Religious Freedom** (IARF).

PICKETT, (OLIVER) EUGENE (1925–). Helped redirect the **Unitarian Universalist Association (UUA)** toward stability and revitalization as its president from 1979 to 1985. Pickett was born the youngest of three boys on September 18, 1925, in Winfield, Maryland. He was an active Methodist growing up, and went to American University in Washington, D.C. Pickett had a difficult time at first due to inadequate background schooling but adjusted before enlisting in the U.S. Navy as World War II was going on. He began to be disillusioned with conventional religion and its entitlements when he attended a chapel service and found that the front rows were reserved only for officers. After the war, he finished his degree at American. Pickett visited All Souls Church in Washington, D.C., and liked the social conscience of **A. Powell Davies**, but Davies gave him little time—a behavior Pickett vowed never to replicate with others. He found Unitarianism open to new discoveries and would soon embrace its "holistic approach to life." He made a tentative decision to enter the ministry because he had a vague idea that he wanted to help people: "I simply wanted to do some good" (Owen-Towle, *Borne on a Wintry Wind*, p. 29). He enrolled at **Meadville Lombard Theological School** in Chicago. In 1951 Pickett met Helen Rice, who was a religious educator attending the Chicago Theological Seminary. They went from coleaders of a junior high youth group to being married on June 11, 1952, and eventually had three daughters. At the time Pickett was working as a student minister in Miami, Florida. He received his B.D. from Meadville in 1952.

During their time in Miami, Helen suffered a serious car accident, but recovered to appear at her husband's ordination on February 28, 1953. Pickett was in Miami for two years where Joe Barth was his primary mentor. Here he learned the importance of pastoral work, a human touch that he would put to good use throughout his ministry. When he was preaching at a summer institute, members from the Unitarian church in Richmond, Virginia, heard him and wanted him to become their minister. He stayed there for seven-and-half years. This was a positive experience where Pickett furthered his use of a collaborative style of ministry and worked on race relations in the community. After that Pickett moved on to Atlanta, Georgia. Here, in a 12-year ministry, Pickett took a 300-member church and helped it grow to 1,150 members with an attendance of about 850. His ministries were intensely personal so that he never took any time off and was available to everyone. This availability served him well in his years at the UUA headquarters. He left Atlanta in 1974 to work with theological students in the UUA's Ministry Department. He remained at headquarters after 1977 under new UUA president Paul Carnes, who died in office in 1979. By this time, he was director of the Department of Ministerial and Congregational Services. Many of the students who had worked with Pickett encouraged him to run for president. These included **William Schulz**, who would later succeed Pickett. When the final tally was made in a board election, Pickett defeated **Gordon McKeeman** by one vote.

During his years as president, Pickett had an open door to everyone and forged a good working relationship with the board. Pickett initiated a Friends of the UUA giving campaign and secured a $20 million endowment fund from the North Shore Unitarian Universalist Society in Plandome, New York. Giving to the UUA doubled during his administration. Membership declines were turned around, a new direction was formed for religious education, the UUA began to fully implement the **Women and Religion Resolution**, and the **Principles and Purposes** were approved during his term in office. Pickett will be remembered as an institutionalist. His theology is humanist with an acknowledgment that salvation only comes through pain and loneliness, "a small wave of light borne into my darkness on a wintry wind." After he left the presidency, Pickett ran the UUA's church-by-mail, the **Church of the Larger Fellowship**. In retirement he has stayed active in the UUA with membership on the **Ministerial Fellowship Committee**.

POLAND. Unitarian foundations in Poland began when Peter Gonesius stood before a Reformed Synod in 1556 and announced that the Trinity did not exist. Gonesius was initially a candidate for the priesthood, but he had converted to the Reformed church and had even encountered the works of Servetus in Switzerland. Although his views were eventually condemned, his influence soon helped propel the development of a Unitarian movement in a time of supportive nobles and tolerant monarchs. A key figure was Dr. **Giorgio Biandrata**, who had been in Poland previously as a court physician but returned in 1558 after being forced from Geneva, Switzerland.

The leader preacher of anti-Trinitarian viewpoints was Gregory Paulus from Krakow. Paulus, who had a more human view of Jesus than the prevailing **Arianism** and was a pacifist, became the new leader after Biandrata left for Transylvania in 1563 to become court physician to **John Sigismund**. After being shunned by the orthodox group within the Reformed Church, the anti-Trinitarians moved to form their own organization. In 1565 the Minor Reformed Church of Poland was formally constituted on June 10 (the group preferred to call themselves Christians, not **Socinians**, but they have most often been referred to as Polish Brethren). Forty-seven clergy attended the church's first synod in Wengrow that year. The synod decided to reject infant baptism and not worship the Holy Spirit as God. The church divided over beliefs about Christ. In 1574 a catechism was composed in Krakow, which was later revised in Rakow. This city had been founded in 1569 boasting freedom of religious worship. Gregory Paulus, who had fallen victim to persecution in Krakow, migrated to Rakow, which became the new center for the Unitarian faith.

The golden age of Unitarianism in Poland followed the arrival of **Faustus Socinus** in 1579. Rakow became the center for training ministers, and a press was established so that Socinian writings eventually were dispersed throughout Europe. Rakow was also the site of annual synods for the church. Earle Morse Wilbur estimated that there were as many as 300 congregations in present-day Poland, Lithuania, and Ukraine. Socinus died in 1604, but not before he had published many books and personally visited most of the congregations in Poland. He had also begun work on the catechism from 1574, which was finalized by others and published shortly after his death as the *Racovian Catechism* (1605). This document rejected original sin and predestination, and professed one sacrament, the Lord's Supper. Unfortunately, open attacks on the Socinians began during this period as persecution of all Protestants increased dramatically. The church at Krakow was destroyed in 1591, where three years later Socinus was attacked in the street and smeared with mud. The attacks became more frequent and vicious into the 17th century. In 1611 Iwan Tyszkiewicz was martyred for having blasphemed God and the Virgin Mary. A flourishing community in Lublin was attacked and anti-Trinitarianism banned in 1627; 11 years later Rakow itself was destroyed. Although the congregation met in a neighboring village for a number of years, eventually it became extinct. By the end of the century, what had been one of the most tolerant countries in Europe became one of the most repressive.

By 1660 all the surviving anti-Trinitarians were given the choice of either converting to Catholicism or leaving. Many of them took refuge in Holland. Ironically, as Poland became more repressive, the anti-Trinitarians became increasingly tolerant, especially under the influence of Simon Budny. The 1665 edition of the *Racovian Catechism*, which was published in Amsterdam, included in the preface: "While we compose a Catechism, we prescribe nothing to any man; while we express our own views, we oppress no one. Let each man be free to express his own mind in religion, provided we too be permitted to bring forward our own thoughts about religious matters, without wrongdoing or attacking anyone" (as quoted in Wilbur, vol. 1, *A History of Unitarianism*, p. 583). Polish Unitarians began to reappear after World War I and the Warsaw congregation was partnered with the U.S. congregation in Toledo, Ohio. But the Nazi invasion destroyed everything. The continuation of the Polish Brethren today is the Unitarian Church in Poland (Kosciol Unitarianski), which began to reorganize in the 1980s and achieved registered status in 1993. The Unitarian church is a member of the **International Council of Unitarians and Universalists (ICUU)** and **International Association for Religious Freedom (IARF)**. There are four congregations in Warsaw, Chorzow, Katowice, and one for at-large members.

POTTER, CHARLES FRANCIS (1885–1962). An important early humanist leader. Potter was born on October 28, 1885, in Marlboro,

Massachusetts, into a working-class family. Although he was a good student, he dropped out when he was 14 to work in the shoe factory where his father was employed. Determined to stay in school, he finally got a job working part time for the *Daily Enterprise* and returned to high school. His family had been active members of the Baptist church, and Potter obtained a preaching license. In 1903 he entered Bucknell University. He transferred to Brown University the following year, but it was too expensive and he returned to Bucknell. While he was at Brown, he fell under the influence of its president, William H. P. Faunce, who introduced Potter to the liberal German theologian Adolf von Harnack. Potter graduated from Bucknell in 1907 and then began seminary training at Newton Theological Institute in Massachusetts. After a year he became minister of a Baptist church in Dover, New Hampshire, and was ordained a Baptist minister. He also married Clara Cook at this time. After two years he moved to Mattappan Baptist Church, which was closer to the Newton seminary, where he received a B.D. in 1913.

Potter's theological training, especially the study of biblical criticism led him to question the tenets of his faith, and he became a Unitarian in 1914. His first assignment was in the remote field of Edmonton, Alberta, where the congregation grew and built its first church. Potter also became aware of **John Dietrich**, who was preaching humanism in Spokane, Washington. Potter had a parishioner in Edmonton who compared Potter's preaching on "personalism" to Dietrich's humanism that the parishioner heard when he was in Spokane on business. In 1916 Potter became minister of the Unitarian Church in his hometown of Marlboro, Massachusetts. He stayed for two years and then moved to Wellesley Hills, Massachusetts. After a year he moved to the West Side Church in New York City, where he remained for six years. Potter helped make this church a stronger institution and it moved to a new building. A highlight of his ministry was a series of debates with a fundamentalist Baptist, John Roach Straton, who was trying to win Potter back to the true faith. Called the Straton-Potter debates, they were held before huge crowds on subjects such as the infallibility of the Bible and the virgin birth of Jesus. Three of the four were held at Carnegie Hall.

Potter also attended the Scopes trial as a defense expert on the Bible. Just prior to the trial he resigned from West Side Church and worked briefly as a fund-raiser for Antioch College. He returned to the ministry to serve the Universalist Church of the Divine Paternity in New York, but his humanism was unacceptable to the congregation. After that he tried to organize the First Humanist Society of New York in September 1929. Prior to this he was struggling with his theology, and then in 1930 he published *Humanism: A New Religion*—one of a number of books he published in the 1930s. Potter continued to serve as a leader of the Humanist Society but also lectured and wrote extensively, especially for some popular periodicals such as *Reader's Digest* and the *Saturday Evening Post*. His leadership of the Humanist Society was reflective of his desire that humanists try to organize outside of Unitarian denominational structures, unlike Dietrich and **Curtis Reese**, who continued to serve Unitarian congregations. At the same time Potter was more interested in the Bible and Jesus than the other humanist leaders. In 1958 he published the popular *Lost Years of Jesus* and was interested in Dead Sea Scroll scholarship.

Potter believed in the authority of science and had a naturalistic view of the universe, but he was also curious about what lay beyond the senses. He dabbled in spiritualism and wanted to investigate more about extra sensory perception and physic phenomenon; the results of his work appeared in 1939 in *Beyond the Senses*. While Potter rejected traditional ideas of God and wrote that people must assume responsibility for their own destiny, he also believed that intuition was the highest form of knowledge and that there was a greater stage of human development called "cosmic consciousness." This was not God in a different guise though, as God played no part in his beliefs. Politically, Potter worked for a number of social causes and in 1938 he became a founder of the Euthanasia Society of America. He also advocated a collective social state with equal distribution of wealth. Potter developed cancer in his later years and died from the disease on October 4, 1962, in New York. Mason Olds, the author of *American Religious Humanism*, called Potter the "rebel" of religious humanism.

POTTER, WILLIAM JAMES (1829–1893). The driving force behind the formation of the **Free Religious Association (FRA)** in 1867, Potter was born in North Dartmouth, Massachusetts, on February 1, 1829, the youngest of nine children of a Quaker family. He attended a Friends School in Providence and then prepared to be a teacher at the Normal School in Bridgewater, Massachusetts. Forgoing teaching, he enrolled at Harvard College, where he graduated in 1854. He decided to study for the ministry and entered Harvard Divinity School in 1856 but then decided to further his studies in Europe after a year at Harvard. He studied theology at several German universities and returned home in 1858. He became a candidate for two churches and chose New Bedford, Massachusetts, which was close to home. His Quaker father had told him that if he was going to preach for money he should go where "thee will get the most." He was ordained on December 28, 1859. When the Civil War started he became a hospital inspector, and during a year's leave of absence from his ministry he married Elizabeth C. Babcock.

His interest in making Unitarianism more of a spiritual democracy came as a result of the **National Conference** meeting in Syracuse in 1866. Potter had begun to associate with a group of radicals that did not want to give Christianity any special rank within the denomination. When the radicals failed to amend the Preamble to the National Conference to affirm unlimited freedom rather than being disciples of Christ, Potter resolved on the train ride home to start a "spiritual anti-slavery society." In October 1866 a group met in Boston at the home of Cyrus Bartol. Potter was among those who wanted to organize outside of denominational boundaries. The group was organized on May 30, 1867, at another meeting in Boston. Potter helped draft the constitution for the group that advocated the interests of pure religion and the scientific study of theology. Potter was elected secretary of the Free Religious Association (FRA) and remained its guiding light for many years. He wanted the FRA to express a welcome to all religions, and in 1872 they voted that there would be "no test of speculative opinion or belief," so that even nontheists would be welcome. In 1882 Potter became president of the FRA. For six years he was the editor of the FRA's publication, *Index*. He contributed weekly editorials and often published his sermons from New Bedford. In 1873 he became embroiled in the Yearbook controversy after his friend Octavius Brooks Frothingham asked that his named be removed from the **American Unitarian Association (AUA)** Yearbook. When AUA Assistant Secretary George Fox wrote to Potter about this, Potter indicated that his name was listed with his consent. But after Fox told him he was relieved that Potter could still be listed as a Unitarian Christian, Potter said he was no longer a Unitarian Christian. Fox concluded his name should be dropped from the list after all. There was some controversy over this since Potter was a well-respected life member of the AUA and served a Unitarian church. There was also confusion over the criteria for being included and the definition of a Unitarian Christian. The decision was affirmed by the AUA, and Potter remained off the list of regular Unitarian ministers until 1883 when he appeared again on an "additional list" and then was returned to the regular list the following year.

Despite these problems, Potter had the tact to keep his congregation in New Bedford supportive of the theological changes he oversaw from more traditional Christianity, including communion to a radical, rational theism. Potter also preached on a variety of social causes, including support for educational programs for freed slaves. The church made regular donations to both the Hampton and Tuskegee Institutes. Potter also made frequent trips to the South to improve his health. In 1890 he helped organize the Bell Street Chapel in Providence, Rhode Island. He resigned his pastorate in New Bedford in December 1892, marking more than 33 years of service. The following year he preached across the continent, gave an address before the **World Parliament of Religions**, and then returned to preach and lecture some more in the east. Then on December 21, 1893, he had an apparent heart attack and died. He was an important influence on liberal religion by his advocacy of a faith that would not be confined to any specific tradition, but called instead for a broad, free approach that is open to the truths of science and other world religions in addition to Christianity.

PRESIDENT. The modern position of president in the **Unitarian Universalist Association (UUA)** bureaucracy was created after **Samuel Atkins Eliot** became secretary of the **American Unitarian Association (AUA)** in 1898. Eliot was elected to the board of the AUA in 1894. At that time there were only two paid staff members in Boston—secretary and assistant secretary. Feeling that the work of the association had outgrown its staff, Eliot advocated for greater authority for the secretary. He also felt that the position would have more executive authority if the title were changed to president. Many of his proposals for change to the structure of the bureaucracy were implemented despite the opposition of several board members, including William Wallace Fenn, who was concerned about increasing the power of the AUA administration at the expense of the churches. In November 1897 Eliot was elected to fill the vacancy in the position of secretary. In 1900 the bylaws were changed giving him the title of president.

As president, Eliot moderated the meetings of the AUA board and the association. Eliot remained in office until 1927 and created the first denominational bureaucracy. He was followed by **Louis Cornish**, who had the unenviable task of guiding the AUA through a difficult period, and his presidency is sometimes characterized as a failure. **Frederick May Eliot** succeeded to the position in 1937—the denomination was revitalized during his 20-year presidency. **Dana Greeley** was the last AUA president. When the UUA was created in 1961, the chief executive of the association continued to be the president, who was elected by the **General Assembly (GA)**. However, the president was an ex officio member of the board, without vote, and held the office at the direction of the board. Greeley became the first president of the consolidated UUA. After Greeley, there was a terrible financial crisis and some retrenchment, but the UUA was ably guided by **Robert West**. West was followed by Paul Carnes, who died in office after a brief presidency. Since that time, **Eugene Pickett**, **William Schulz**, **John Buehrens**, and **William Sinkford** have ably led the UUA to some modest growth and spiritual renewal. More recent attempts to change the structure of the presidency, especially after the UUA study by the Commission on Governance in 1993, have failed.

PRIESTLEY, JOSEPH (1733–1804). The famous scientist who discovered oxygen was also one of the most significant figures in the history of both British and American Unitarianism. Priestley was born on March 13, 1733, just outside of Leeds in the village of Fieldhead. He was the oldest child of a cloth maker and was orphaned at the age of six. Never healthy, he was brought up by an aunt who oversaw his studies. In addition to languages, he also became interested in science and was especially fascinated by spiders. At 18 he found he could not subscribe to Calvinist beliefs in his aunt's church, but he wanted to be a minister. With improved health, he entered the dissenting academy at Daventry, which encouraged free thought. He stayed there for four years and came out of school with Arian views of Jesus. He was settled in a Presbyterian church in Suffolk and took a teaching position, but together these two jobs barely paid him enough to survive. He immediately encountered difficulties with the congregation. In his preaching style he stammered, and his less-than-orthodox gospel offended some. He stayed for three years with a reduced salary, and then received a call to Nantwich. Here he secured a teaching job at Warrington Academy and was soon married as well. He then began a series of voluminous writings on theology, grammar, and science. After these contributions, Priestly received an honorary doctor of laws from the University of Edinburgh. In 1764 he met Benjamin Franklin, who was impressed with the young scholar.

Franklin told Priestley that he ought to write the history of electricity, and he did, *The History and Present State of Electricity* (1765). The book received wide acclaim and Priestley was elected to the Royal Society. In 1767 Priestley was called to the Mill Hill Chapel in Leeds. His continuing religious studies had led him beyond Arianism to the more accepted view of Unitarianism that Jesus was fully human and not to be worshipped. Yet he also believed in miracles and the Second Coming. In Leeds, the Priestleys lived next door to a brewery. The fumes helped stimulate Priestley to think about chemical reactions. The experiments that resulted made Priestley famous. He discovered the existence of oxygen in 1774 and later developed a process to produce carbonated water. He became a literary companion to Lord Sherburne and this enabled him to travel to the continent. When the American Revolution broke out, he sided with the colonists and his employer soon asked him to resign. Just prior to this, Priestley's friend **Theophilus Lindsey** had moved to London to start the first organized Unitarian congregation in England. Priestley was present at that first service. He was then called to serve at the dissenting church in Birmingham (New Meeting). Here Priestley spent Sunday preaching and teaching and was generally free during the week to pursue his literary and scientific studies. He became a member of the Lunar Society, a group of scholars who met near the time of the full moon so they could find their way home after dark. At this time Priestley produced his most significant theological works, but the result was increasing attacks by orthodox opponents. The most renowned was *History of the Corruptions of Christianity* (1782). These works tried to show that many views in the early church held that Jesus was not part of the Trinity and later theories had distorted Christianity.

Priestley also began to launch a campaign to win full legal rights for all dissenting religious groups. Many adversaries attacked him as being a subversive. On July 14, 1791, Priestley held a celebration in honor of the second anniversary of Bastille Day. Because of their support for the French Revolution, all the guests were accused in the days preceding the party of plotting treason. A mob gathered and attacked the house. Although all the family and guests escaped harm, Priestley's house and laboratory were destroyed. His books and papers were thrown into the street and burned. Further rioting took place in Birmingham, and the next night the Priestley family escaped. The family never returned to Birmingham, but settled outside of London where Priestley briefly preached and taught. His reputation for radicalism made it so no one wanted to associate with him. His sons were unable to find jobs and immigrated to America. The parents waited another three years and finally followed the children. Joseph Priestley had many friends in America who sympathized with his plight and offered support. In Philadelphia he became an active member of a circle of political and intellectual activists, including **Benjamin Rush** and **Thomas Jefferson**. In June 1794 Priestley became actively engaged in helping the Universalists raise money to complete their building. His sons had settled in Northumberland, Pennsylvania, and Priestley started a Unitarian church there in 1794. Then he helped start the First Unitarian Church in Philadelphia in 1796. Priestley died in 1804, leaving behind 25 volumes of religious and scientific writings and six books of chemical and electrical experiments. He recorded Benjamin Franklin's famous kite-flying episode. He believed in making the circle of liberty as wide as possible in both religion and politics. Jefferson once told him that his was "one of the few lives precious to mankind."

PRINCIPLES AND PURPOSES. Adopted by the **Unitarian Universalist Association (UUA) General Assembly (GA)** in 1985, the

Principles and Purposes is the major unifying religious statement of the denomination today. The current Principles and Purposes grew out of a similar theological affirmation, which was discussed during merger meetings in 1959 and 1960 and then voted as part of the UUA Bylaws in 1961. By the mid-1970s many people, especially women, had grown unhappy with the sexist language of the bylaws, which included references to "brotherhood" and the dignity of "man." Concerns were also raised over the importance given to the Judeo-Christian tradition at the expense of other world religions and the absence of any reference to the environment. After the passage of the Women in Religion resolution in 1977, members and groups began to ask whether the UUA principles affirmed women, and then in 1981 a nonsexist revision was presented to the General Assembly. This caused an uproar among Unitarian Universalist Christians because there was no reference to God. Seeing that a vote would be divisive, a confrontation was avoided and a motion was passed to study the issue. A special committee headed by Walter Royal Jones Jr., was set up and it began an extensive process of discussion and response with all the congregations. This included hearings at the General Assembly (the first report was presented in Brunswick, Maine, in 1982) and in districts, as well as extensive publications that fomented local discussion and feedback for the Principles and Purposes Committee. A draft proposal was sent to the congregations in September 1983 and a final draft was presented to the General Assembly in 1984, where it was first adopted. The second vote, required for bylaw changes, came in 1985. The final version included six principles and five historic sources for the living tradition. A sixth tradition, earth-centered religions, was added in 1995. The Principles and Purposes are:

We, the member congregations of the Unitarian Universalist Association, covenant to affirm and promote:

The inherent worth and dignity of every person
Justice, equity and compassion in human relations
Acceptance of one another and encouragement to spiritual growth in our congregations
A free and responsible search for truth and meaning
The right of conscience and the use of the democratic process within our congregations and in society at large

The goal of world community with peace, liberty, and justice for all

Respect for the interdependent web of all existence of which we are a part

The living tradition we share draws from many sources:

Direct experience of that transcending mystery and wonder, affirmed in all cultures, which moves us to a renewal of the spirit and an openness to the forces which create and uphold life.

Words and deeds of prophetic women and men which challenge us to confront powers and structures of evil with justice, compassion, and the transforming power of love.

Wisdom from the world's religions which inspire us in our ethical and spiritual life.

Jewish and Christian teachings which call us to respond to God's love by loving our neighbors as ourselves.

Humanist teachings which counsel us to heed the guidance of reason and the results of science, and warn us against idolatries of the mind and spirit.

Spiritual teachings of Earth-centered traditions which celebrate the sacred circle of life and instruct us to live in harmony with the rhythms of nature.

Grateful for the religious pluralism which enriches and ennobles our faith, we are inspired to deepen our understanding and expand our vision. As free congregations we enter into this covenant, promising to one another our mutual trust and support.

PURPOSES

The Unitarian Universalist Association shall devote its corporate powers for religious, educational and humanitarian purposes. The primary purpose of the Association is to serve the needs of its member congregations, organize new congregations, extend and strengthen Unitarian Universalist institutions, and implement its principles.

– R –

RACIAL JUSTICE. Following World War II, one of the great issues for all of American society was confronting racism. In 1963 **Unitarian Universalist Association (UUA)** president **Dana Greeley** led more than 1,500 UUs to the March on Washington. The UUA established a

Commission on Race and Religion at the **General Assembly (GA)** in June 1963. At that same GA the delegates had defeated a motion that would have required open membership without regard to race, nationality, etc., as a requirement for all societies applying to the UUA. This was defeated on the grounds of noninterference in congregational polity. Yet the delegates wanted to address the issue of segregation in some congregations directly and also begin to respond to civil rights issues with resources and programs. Walter Royal Jones was the chair of the new commission. The Task Force tried to address the issue of open membership.

A galvanizing event for all of America occurred in Selma, Alabama, in 1965. On March 8, Martin Luther King Jr. sent telegrams to many religious groups, including the UUA, calling upon them to come to Selma, where he was trying to stage a march, and join him in the struggle against racism and for the survival of democracy. Many UU clergy responded and marched with Dr. King the next day. The 2,000 marchers (including 50 UU ministers) were turned back by state troopers, and King decided to complete his fight in the courts. On the night of March 9, **James Reeb**, a UU minister, was clubbed by a group of white men and died two days later. The UUA Board had adjourned its meeting in Boston and voted to come to Selma to attend Reeb's memorial service. On March 17 the courts ordered that a march between Selma and Montgomery be permitted. The march began on March 25 with 300, but by the time the state capitol was reached, there were 40,000 marchers, including hundreds of UU ministers and laypeople. On the last day of the march, Viola Liuzzo, a UU from Detroit, Michigan, who had been chauffeuring civil rights workers back and forth between Selma and Montgomery, was shot as she drove along Highway 80 on her way to Montgomery to pick up marchers. Some people opined that the Voting Rights Act of 1965 was passed as a result of Liuzzo's and Reeb's martyrdom.

In response to urban rioting, the UUA called for an Emergency Conference in response to the Black Rebellion in 1967. Out of this conference, the UU Black Caucus was formed, which demanded the creation of a black-controlled Black Affairs Council (BAC). BAC leaders argued that black members needed to make their own leadership and financial decisions. An integrationist group, Black and White Action (BAWA), tried to develop its own programs, and received some UUA Board support. BAC sponsored many black controlled projects throughout the country, but eventually denominational funding was cut and there was a schism within BAC that undermined its effectiveness. After the painful debacles of the BAC/BAWA controversy, the UUA had no major initiatives on racial justice until 1980 when an institutional racism audit was undertaken. As a result of this completed audit report in 1981, an affirmative action plan was undertaken.

Within 10 years, the UUA reached the goal of 20 percent of the headquarters staff being people of color. In 2001, an African American, **William Sinkford**, was elected president of the UUA. In 1985 the UUA established the Black Concerns Working Group (BCWG) to help congregations battle racism. That same year, Yvonne Seon became the first African American woman to be fellowshipped as a UU minister. In 1984 the **Whitney Young Jr.** Urban Ministry Fund was started. The GA of 1992 adopted a long-range plan to become more racially and culturally diverse, and the UUA board appointed a Racial and Cultural Diversity Task Force. In January of that year the UUA Board had already affirmed the Ten Year Plan for Racial and Cultural Diversity. A new UUA Office for Racial and Cultural Diversity began to work with the task force and the BCWG to develop resources and programs. Most UUs in the 1950s and 1960s longed to bring justice to blacks in America and participated in a unified response in Selma, only to see it dissipated in battles over white middle class leadership and fears of black power in the late 1960s. Recent history has seen many efforts to heal the wounds of the **Black Empowerment Controversy**.

RACOVIAN CATHECISM. *See* POLAND; RAKOW.

RADICAL REFORMATION. The Protestant Reformation produced a left wing that has often been referred to as the Radical Reformation. In his book *The Radical Reformation*, historian George Williams distinguishes three types of religious radicals: Anabaptists, spiritualists, and evangelical rationalists. In addition to a large number of scattered Anabaptist sects and individual spiritualists, the humanists were mostly rational, Italian in origin, and often anti-Trinitarian. Sometimes it is difficult to distinguish between the three groups. One spiritualist, the German Caspar von Schwenkfeld (1489–1561), rejected a literal interpretation of scripture and argued that God speaks directly to each individual. The leading evangelical humanists who were emphasizing Christ's humanity included the Italian refugees Camillo Renato, whose followers spread his ideas to northern Europe; Celio Secundo Curione, a learned scholar and professor at Basel who opposed Servetus' execution; Matthias Gibaldo, who Calvin thought was the source of the heresies in the Italian church in Geneva; Valentino Gentile, who was accused of seven errors as to the Trinity and was beheaded at Bern; and **Giorgio Biandrata** and **Laelius Socinus**. The most famous and outspoken of all the anti-Trinitarians was the martyr **Michael Servetus**, who was burned by Calvin in 1553. Servetus was defended by a Frenchmen, Sebastian Castellio (1515–1563), who wrote an important book *On Heretics, Whether They Ought to Be Persecuted*. Castellio said truth had many aspects, and called for more love and understanding, saying that Christians did not deserve to retain the name if they did not show Christ's clemency and mercy. The radicals of the Reformation took Martin Luther's words to heart when, with increased literacy, they took their Bibles home and discovered truth for themselves. They broke ecclesiastical traditions by insisting that everyone has the right to feel the spirit speaking in his/her heart. Voices for freedom to speak the truth as each understood it, the use of reason in the interpretation of scriptures, and tolerance of others' views began to be heard in the evangelical humanist wing of the radical group; they found organized form in later years in Poland and Transylvania.

RAKOW. The 16th-century center of Polish Unitarianism grew from the joint efforts of a tolerant Polish noble, Jan Sienienski, and his theologically liberal Arian wife, Jadwiga Gnoinska. Taking its name from Jadwiga's family's coat-of-arms, the rak, or crayfish, and its philosophy from her influence, Rakow was established in south central Poland by a charter granted on March 27, 1567. A number of freedoms were accorded the citizens from the beginning, including complete freedom of belief. Freedom to choose a religion was possible on a few estates in Poland because the Lords of the Manors determined the policies. Members of the Minor Church were already beginning to feel persecuted by both Calvinists and Catholics, and a large migration of the Polish Brethren took place in 1569 where they became intent on creating a New Jerusalem living as the first Christians had lived. There was much controversy in the early years, especially when Gregory Paul tried to impose economic communism. The citizens differed on whether there should be an ordained clergy, and whether ritual should be abolished from church services. They agreed that baptism was necessary for admittance to the community. The effort at complete participatory democracy broke down, but fortunately Simon Ronemberg stepped in and reorganized the entire structure in 1572.

Rakow evolved from a closed utopian community to one that strived to reform the world in response to its religious ideals. For the next 60 years it was the capital of the Polish Brethren, especially after 1599 when Jacob Sienienski, the son of the founders, joined. It was the only town in the world where Unitarians made up a majority. The Brethren's press was moved there from Krakow, and more than 500 titles were published during the next 40 years, eventually being sent to Transylvania, Germany, and England. A school established by the church in 1602 soon attracted more than 1,000 students, including scholars from all over Europe. All of the church synods were held at Rakow. The entire community seriously attempted to follow the teachings of the Sermon on the Mount, including the advocacy of pacifism.

The great theological leader of the latter half of the 16th century was **Faustus Socinus**. He transformed the argumentative foundation that had been a perpetual synod into a united body of theological opinion capsulized in the Racovian Catechism, which was published the year following his death, 1605. The Catechism reflected a strong emphasis on following the ethical teachings of Jesus and the Ten Commandments and also commented extensively on social relations within the state. Rather than a teaching tool for children, it was a summary of church beliefs in question-and-answer format. With greater financial resources, the Brethren were able to publish more of Socinus's works after his death. This flourishing of Unitarian society and theology was destroyed almost overnight in 1638. Some students from the academy vandalized a crucifix erected by a Catholic landlord. The Bishop of Krakow used this incident as a pretext to incite public opinion, and he brought it before the Polish Senate. The decision was made to destroy the school and close down the Rakow press.

All "Arian" inhabitants were requested to leave town within four weeks. Within months, a cornerstone for a new Catholic church was laid where the Minor Church meetinghouse once stood. Although the movement struggled on for a few more years, it came to an abrupt end in its once great center in Rakow.

RANKIN, DAVID O. (1937–). One of the leading Unitarian Universalist preachers over the last quarter century. His parents, Oran and Reba (George) Rankin, came from McKeesport, Pennsylvania, where Oran spent his work life toiling in a steel mill. Beginning with U.S. Steel as a waterboy at the age of 16 to support his mother and sister, the elder Rankin remained there for 44 years. David, one of three sons, was born on June 10, 1937. Growing up, Rankin became an outstanding schoolboy basketball player and he worked four summers at the steel mill as a sweeper, laborer, and driller. His undergraduate work was completed at Westminster College with a B.A. in 1959. He received an M.A. from the University of Idaho in 1961. He became a political science instructor at Cornell College in Iowa, but was unhappy with academia. In reflecting on this time in his life, Rankin said he didn't want to be confined by one disciple, and wanted "more depth in teaching and in dealing with people of all ages." He also worked as an associate editor of the *North American Review*. He then enrolled at the **Tufts College** School of Religion and received a B.D. in 1965. Early in his career Rankin served two churches in Massachusetts; first in Watertown, 1966–69, and then New Bedford, 1969–73. In both these parishes, he demonstrated his concern for building a just world. He became active in draft counseling, drug rehabilitation, prison reform, and work with senior citizens. In 1968 Rankin met a young man who was AWOL from the army. Over the next few years he worked with more than 300 fugitives from the military in a modern Underground Railroad for war resisters. He also organized Parents Opposed to the War (POW). In 1971 he received the Clarence R. Skinner Award for the best Unitarian Universalist social action sermon, "The Salvation of New Bedford."

In 1973 Rankin was called to serve the First Unitarian Church in San Francisco, California, where he remained until 1979. During this time he published a sermon collection, *So Great a Cloud of Witnesses* (1978). He was also the author of the annual denominational meditational manual in 1978, *Portraits from the Cross*. In his first sermon in San Francisco, Rankin defined what the church is to him: "I have learned not to take my position too seriously. Or my image too seriously. Or myself too seriously. I have learned that the most important item in the religious community is the people of the religious community. And I have learned that the real church can be defined as our most intimate relationships:

How we smile and trust each other.
How we talk and touch each other.
How we share and protect each other.
How we welcome new friends and forgive old enemies.
How we love each other—in all the myriad ways that love can be expressed.
That is the church!

Following his ministry in San Francisco Rankin served what was then the largest Unitarian Universalist church—Atlanta, Georgia. He was named the **Berry Street** essayist in 1981. For the last 16 years of his active ministry, he served an independent liberal church, the Fountain Street Church, in Grand Rapids, Michigan. During his later years in the ministry he published *Theology through Humor, My Ending Is My Beginning* and, in 2001, another denominational meditation manual, *Dancing in the Empty Spaces*. Rankin has also served the denomination in a number of capacities. He has been a board member for the **Starr King School** (where he also taught homiletics) and served on the Unitarian Universalist Task Force on Urban Ministry. He has also maintained strong community involvement wherever he has ministered. He has served on the national board of Planned Parenthood and also been involved in fair housing, bail bond reform, prison chaplaincy, ERA Georgia, abortion rights, gay and lesbian rights, and suicide prevention. He is married to Virginia (Minor) Rankin, and they have three children and four grandchildren. In retirement, they live in Moscow, Idaho. In 1998–99, he briefly served the Unitarian church in Auckland, New Zealand. Rankin is also the author of a popular wallet card, "What Do UUs Believe."

REASON. This became an important concept for those who opposed the excesses of the Great Awakening and affirmed the moral discernment of religious understanding over the emotionally charged direct experience of divine revelation. Reason in religion became associated with a faculty that human beings were naturally endowed with, which they could use to discern God's goodness through the natural processes of uniformity and regularity that they could perceive in the universe. The faculty of reason made it possible for humans to organize and understand all the sense data of human experience. God had given people the ability to use reason to distinguish between right and wrong. Early Arminians stressed revelation and reason as equal approaches to truth. In "**Unitarian Christianity**," **William Ellery Channing** said that he "honored revelation too highly to make it an antagonist of reason." Channing, in that same address, argued for the use of reason in interpreting the scriptures. The historian Earle Morse Wilbur emphasizes reason when he suggests that there are three main principles in the liberal religious tradition: freedom, reason, and tolerance. Wilbur defines this as "the unrestricted use of reason in religion, rather than reliance upon external authority or past tradition" (Wilbur, *A History*, Vol. 1, p. 5).

REEB, JAMES (1927–1965). James Reeb was a Unitarian Universalist minister and civil rights activist, who became a martyr to the cause of equal rights. Reeb was born on January 1, 1927, in Wichita, Kansas, and grew up in Wyoming. He trained for the Presbyterian ministry at Princeton Theological Seminary. After making a transition to Unitarianism, he became assistant minister at All Souls Church in Washington, D.C., where he was popular and involved. Seeing the poverty that surrounded the church, Reeb decided to serve the poor directly in social service. He and his wife, Marie, moved to Boston, where he worked to help poor people receive better housing. In 1965 he responded to the call of Martin Luther King Jr. to go to Selma, Alabama, to participate in a civil rights march. While he was in Selma, he and two colleagues were attacked by four men who shouted at them, "Hey niggers, hey, you niggers." One of the men struck Reeb with a club, and he died within 48 hours. Many speeches and marches followed. President Lyndon Johnson appeared on television, and the 1965 Voting Rights Act was passed, when weeks before no one had given it much of a chance. Reeb's death made a significant difference in the battle for civil rights. In his final sermon at All Souls Church, Reeb said, "Let all who live in freedom, won by the sacrifice of others, be untiring in the task begun, till everyone on earth is free." James Reeb died on March 11, 1965.

REESE, CURTIS WILLIFORD (1887–1961). One of the outstanding humanist leaders in the Unitarian ranks. Reese was born on September 3, 1887, in Madison County, North Carolina. He came from a family of Baptist preachers and accepted Jesus as his savior when he was nine. He felt a call from God to the ministry and he attended a Baptist College at Mar's Hill, North Carolina, and was ordained to the ministry. He supplied a church in Alabama, where his brother was a preacher, and then he served two churches in Kentucky. At the church in Pleasant Home he met his future wife, Fay R. Walker, and they were married on February 7, 1913. Reese already had doubts about his faith as a result of encountering biblical criticism when he attended Baptist seminary in Louisville, Kentucky, where he graduated in 1910. He also became acquainted with Unitarianism in Louisville. After that he became a state missionary for the Illinois State Baptist Association. During this time he attended Ewing College and received a Ph.B. in 1911. Then he was called to serve the First Baptist Church in Tiffin, Ohio. Increasingly Reese was unable to accept his Baptist faith and after reading a book by the Unitarian **Francis Greenwood Peabody**, he went to see the Unitarian minister in Toledo. He made a profession of faith that included: "a Universal Father, God; a Universal Brotherhood, mankind; a Universal right, freedom; a Universal motive, love; and a Universal aim, progress." (Olds, *American Religious Humanism*, p. 101).

Reese entered the Unitarian fold and took a position at the church in Alton, Illinois, in 1913. Here he built a reputation as a community organizer against crime. He even managed to get himself shot at by underworld figures. He left Alton in 1915 to serve the Unitarian church in Des Moines, Iowa. Again he became active in the community and helped pass the Iowa Housing Bill; he was later appointed the first Housing Commissioner of the State of Iowa. In 1919 he accepted a position as secretary for the **Western Unitarian Conference (WUC)**. The famous humanist-theist controversy was ignited by an address Reese delivered at the Harvard Summer School in 1920. In the "Content of Present Day Religious Liberalism," Reese said: "Historically the basic content of religious liberalism is spiritual freedom. Out of this basic content has come the conviction of the supremacy of reason, of the primary worth of character, and of the immediate access of man to spiritual sources. Always religious liberalism has tended to replace alleged divine revelations and commands with human opinions and judgments" (Parke, ed. *Epic*, p. 133). Reese went on to say that personality had supreme worth. He also became active on the board of the **Meadville Theological School** and helped to arrange its move to Chicago, which the board approved in 1926. He also became president of Lombard College and worked toward preventing a financial collapse, but it was merged with Meadville in 1933.

For many years Reese was affiliated with the periodical ***Unity***, either as managing editor or editor. During World War II, Reese decided he could not support the pacifist positions of **John Haynes Holmes**, the editor, and took over the editorship. In 1930 Reese resigned as secretary of the WUC and became the dean at the Abraham Lincoln Centre. Here he was able to be engaged in community-based ministry again, as the center was an integrated community center that offered lectures, classes, forums, and social service programs. Just prior to this shift in his career he began to publish books on his evolving humanism. His first major effort was *Humanism* (1926), followed by *Humanist Religion* (1931), and *The Meaning of Humanism* (1945). Reese retired from the Abraham Lincoln Centre in 1957 following a heart attack, and he moved to Florida. He died on June 5, 1961, while attending a board meeting of the Meadville Lombard Theological School. Reese was one of the founders of the American Humanist Association and served as its president for 14 years. Reese appreciated his Baptist heritage of independence and the separation of church and state and, at first, referred to his humanism as "democratic" religion. As his religious thought evolved, the concept of God became irrelevant and he did not generally use the word, but it was harder for him to give it up than it was for **John H. Dietrich**, his fellow leader in the movement after 1917. Reese said he could place no reliance on either revelation or intuition and depended exclusively upon the "authority of evidence." He thought it was better to have a few beliefs rather than many that simply were not true. Reese believed that human nature was neither innately divine nor sinful, but rather it needed to be organized and directed toward worthy ends.

The more progress humankind attains, he said, the more the individual is valued. Reese played a major role in the development of the ***Humanist Manifesto***, in which "the complete realization of human personality" is seen as the religious goal.

REINHARDT, AURELIA ISABEL HENRY (1877–1948). Called by **American Unitarian Association (AUA)** president, **Frederick May Eliot**, "as distinguished a Unitarian as there is in the land," she was the first woman moderator of the AUA. Aurelia Henry was born on April 1, 1877, and grew up in San Francisco and Oakland, and attended the University of California at Berkeley with special interests in literature, music, and the classics. After briefly teaching at the University of Idaho, she began Ph.D. studies at Yale, receiving her degree in 1905. Her dissertation on Ben Jonson's *Epicoene or The Silent Woman* was published while she studied abroad. A teaching career was cut short when she went to care for her brother, Paul, who died in 1909. She fell in love with Paul's doctor, George Reinhardt, and they were married in December 1909. Mrs. Reinhardt was a busy faculty wife for less than five years, when she was tragically widowed at age 37. Before this she had given birth to two sons, George and Paul. She became a lecturer at the University in Berkeley, but her life course was determined when she was appointed president of Mills College in 1916. From then until the summer of 1943, Aurelia Henry Reinhardt transformed this small, local school into an institution of international repute. As Arnold Crompton has said, "She was Mills." In "The Aurelian Way," Evelyn Steel Little wrote of her, "You felt that she cared greatly about you as an individual. She believed in you and what you could become, and her faith in you, like her optimism, was contagious, giving you self-confidence and power so that you could not doubt yourself. She had a strange capacity for making you feel capable of anything."

Reinhardt became a speaker of national repute and this extended to many pulpits in Unitarian churches. She labored for the Pacific Coast Conference of the AUA and was briefly an interim minister in Oakland. At the May Meetings of 1932 she delivered the Ware lecture on "America and the Spiritual Frontier. This was a time when the Unitarian denomination was floundering, and the May Meetings in 1934 established a new Commission of Appraisal to study the church and find new directions for its reinvigoration. Reinhardt was the only woman and the only Westerner on this commission. She wrote the article on the place of worship in the liberal church. Feeling that some congregations had given minority views too much weight, she wrote, "There is visible proof that the liberal church cannot exist unless worship remains a distinctive and fundamental exercise of the congregation." In 1936 the commission's findings were published as ***Unitarians Face a New Age***. She also gave new direction to theological education by serving on the board of trustees, including the presidency, of the Pacific Unitarian School for the Ministry. In May 1945, she said: "We meet to plan for the future. Let us not forget that the future includes more women in the ministry than we have ever known before." She died on January 28, 1948.

RELIGIOUS EDUCATION. In 1912 a Department of Religious Education was established within the **American Unitarian Association (AUA)**. Prior to this, the Sunday School Society (SSS) had produced materials and offered direction for Unitarian Sunday Schools, but not under a single coherent plan. An attempt to combine the AUA efforts with those of the SSS had been rejected by the society in 1868. The president of the SSS became the secretary of the new department, and they jointly sponsored education programs until 1937 when they were completely merged. The new department developed a graded curriculum known as the *Beacon Course*, but financial difficulties in the 1930s limited what could be accomplished. In 1934 the *Beacon Hymnal* was produced for use in the church schools. When **Frederick May Eliot** took office as president in 1937 he built a strong education program. The head of the department, **Ernest Kuebler**, was retained. Working together with **Sophia Fahs** after 1937, they developed an outstanding program of curriculum materials, the *New Beacon Series*. The numbers of children enrolled in Unitarian church schools increased significantly after this. With Fahs the curriculum became child-centered, fulfilling **William Ellery Channing**'s vision of not stamping adult minds upon the young, but stirring up their own. Rather than biblically based and content-oriented, curriculum in the 1940s became experiential. This shifted again under the direction of Hugo Holleroth in the 1970s when large multimedia kits were developed. The emphasis of these was to show how human beings are meaning makers, and the intent was to develop tolerance and understanding for people all over the world. These kits were developed from a more secular viewpoint and included the controversial, but widely used, ***About Your Sexuality***. After the convening of the **Religious Education Futures Committee** and the publishing of their report in 1981, Religious Education took a turn toward developing a more religious orientation, especially emphasizing the need to nurture a stronger Unitarian Universalist identity. Religious Education became lifespan so that all ages would become involved in a church wide effort to nurture broader aspects of the spiritual dimensions of life.

Very little was done to promote Universalist Sunday School activities prior to the 20th century. The entire movement was local and neither organized nor coherent. The first Universalist Sunday School was established in Philadelphia in 1791. In 1840 the **General Convention** called for education for the young. State conventions were encouraged to form local associations. Both the Unitarians and Universalists used catechisms in the 19th century. The Universalist Publishing House printed *A Gospel Catechism for Sunday Schools* by A. St. John Chambre in 1869. A popular Sunday School paper was the *Myrtle*, which first appeared in 1851 and was continuously printed until 1924. The denomination did not create its own graded lessons until 1901, when the Murray Graded Lessons appeared under the editorship of John Coleman Adams, who also edited the *Helper* (began as the *Universalist Helper* in 1870), where uniform lessons were printed. Finally, after years of efforts to create a central organization, the General Convention established a Commission on Sunday Schools in 1899, but the commission did not flourish, and funding for a secretary was defeated in 1911. A General Sunday School Association of the Universalist Church (GSSA) was formed in 1913 after much debate and controversy. Some felt that Sunday School administration should be overseen by the State Conventions. Within fifteen years the GSSA had proven its effectiveness thanks to the efforts of George Huntley, who became its president and worked full time to assure its success. Huntley left **St. Lawrence** in 1917 to assume this new post with his salary subsidized by the General Convention. Its office was located in Boston, where the Universalists had finally established a national headquarters building in 1919. There was a dramatic reversal in Sunday School enrollments after this, even as adult membership declined. Religious Education also was emphasized more in seminary training. **Angus MacLean** became professor of education at the Canton School at St. Lawrence in 1928. It was not until 1948 that the GSSA was merged into a Department of Education as part of the UCA. Horton Colbert was the first Executive Director. During the 1930s representatives of the GSSA served on the curriculum committee of the Unitarian Department of Religious Education, and the two departments were then joined in 1954 under the Council of Liberal Churches. *See also* SUNDAY SCHOOL SOCIETY.

RELIGIOUS EDUCATION FUTURES COMMITTEE. A group that was formed in 1980 and planned the future of Unitarian Universalist religious education. In 1980 a special task force was created by **Unitarian Universalist Association (UUA)** president **Eugene Pickett** and the UUA Board called the Religious Education Futures Committee. They issued their report in October 1981, and it helped established a long-term plan for education in the denomination. When the group was formed in January 1980 with Christine Wetzel as the chair, their charge included assessing the needs of religious education, reviewing the present curriculum, and making recommendations for the future. Their final report was issued with the declaration that there must be a vision of religious education that saw the church as a worshiping and educating community for all ages. There was a special emphasis on developing Unitarian Universalist identity. The report also called for great preparation for ministers and religious educators.

Two major changes were already taking place in other related areas. A group called the Benson Commission had recommended the establishment of a Ministry of Religious Education, and a revolution was taking place in youth programming that would result in a Common Ground conference and the creation of a new continental youth organization. In their final report the Futures Committee made nine recommendations: 1. an advisory committee was to be set up to work with the UUA staff; 2. A new curriculum was called for that would be more explicitly religious, and also impart the Unitarians Universalist faith. They recommended that all curricula be based on certain principles, which were similar to what the UUA adopted as its new principles and purposes in 1985; 3. Better training for religious educators, which resulted in the UUA's Renaissance Training Modules; 4. A center for religious education created at **Meadville Lombard**; 5. A call for more satisfying worship for all ages; 6. Youth programs; 7. More UUA staff positions; 8. Retain many present programs; 9. Name change of the UUA department to emphasize religious education. The report and its recommendations resulted in a continent-wide shift of greater support for religious education programs, and after 1985 programs began to grow rapidly again after a period of stagnation and decline. There is an ongoing campaign to give greater respect to the position of religious educator and minister of religious education. The philosophical centerpiece to the Futures Report was the implementation of the philosophy that the entire church is an educating community. This report had important ramifications for a new vision for religious education.

RELLY, JAMES. *See* UNION.

RESTORATIONIST CONTROVERSY. An important confrontation within the Universalist ranks in the 1820s. During the early decades of the Universalist movement theological differences were largely ignored so that the movement could gain stability. Once it began to grow, these differences and other rivalries became more noticeable. Much of the wrangling centered around those who differed with Universalist leader **Hosea Ballou** over the doctrine of punishment after death. In the early stages of the controversy Ballou, who favored immediate salvation, was pitted against Edward Turner and **Paul Dean**, who favored a period of punishment before final happiness was granted. During 1817 Ballou and Turner, who were former friends, debated the matter in the *Gospel Visitant*. Party lines began to be drawn, especially after a hotheaded preacher named Jacob Wood tried to ignite controversy. Wood published a pamphlet and became convinced that a majority of the clergy favored Restorationism. It was probably about evenly divided, but Ballou maintained ecclesiastical control. Wood even suggested a Restorationist Association be formed. Ballou and his followers came to be disparagingly known as Leatherheads. The two sides began to exchange views in the *Universalist Magazine* in 1822. Restorationists participated in convention and association meetings less and less in the early 1820s. In 1822

Wood scheduled a counter convention at his house in Shirley, Massachusetts. Wood drafted a statement—the Appeal and Declaration—that was published in the *Christian Repository*. Eventually this led to the Restorationists having to sign retractions in order to not lose their fellowship in the denomination. After a relatively quiet period of a couple of years, there was a second phase of the controversy. David Pickering was transformed into a radical Restorationist during this phase. He was concerned by Abner Kneeland's theology, which had divided his church in New York. Kneeland, who was part of Ballou's Ultra Universalist Party, was doubting the authenticity of the scriptures, and this led the Restorationists to wonder if Ballou's theology ultimately led to infidelity.

A Universalist **General Convention** in Saratoga Springs, New York, in 1827 exposed some of the structural weaknesses of the denomination. Dean proposed a change that would transform the New England Convention into a national body. The new proposal suggested uniting into associations in convenient territories, but it was not to be officially considered for another year. The Restorationists responded precipitously by forming a new Providence Association in the fall of 1827. That summer Edward Turner decided he would leave the denomination, but asked Ballou for an apology before he did. Ballou refused, and Turner became a Unitarian. Feelings between the two camps were becoming more intense. In 1830 **Adin Ballou** preached an openly Restorationist sermon in Medway, Massachusetts. That spring the Southern Association (New England) met in Berlin, Connecticut. Two resolutions were passed to provoke the Providence Association. They intended to withhold recognition unless the Providence group accepted supervision, and they said the Providence group had to choose which association they belonged to. They either had to resign from the Providence Association or lose their fellowship. One immediate result was the dismissal of Adin Ballou from his parish, quickly followed by a call to the Unitarian church in Mendon, Massachusetts. In August 1831 the Restorationists met to form a new denomination, the Massachusetts Association of Universal Restorationists. The Restorationist group eventually filtered into Adin Ballou's community at **Hopedale**, but the split within Universalist ranks hastened the development of more stable state conventions and led the New England Convention to reconsider the development of a national convention.

RETIREMENT HOUSING. In the latter part of the 19th century, and continuing since, Universalists and Unitarians have founded retirement homes or living facilities to affirm the dignity of aging populations and to support their needs. The first such Universalist institution was the Chapin Home, named for the famed preacher Edwin Chapin and founded by his wife. It opened in 1869 as a nonsectarian home for both men and women. One of the more successful homes was the Messiah Home that was a Universalist home in Philadelphia that was started in 1900, with formal occupation beginning in 1902. It later merged with a Unitarian home, the **Joseph Priestley** House, to form the Unitarian Universalist House of the Joseph Priestley District in 1964. Messiah Home was a project of the Church of the Messiah, and one of the reasons for its founding was the fear that Universalists were being discriminated against for their unorthodox beliefs. A third Universalist retirement home, the Thompson Home, was founded in Waldron, Indiana, in 1913. A fourth such institution was the Doolittle Home in Foxboro, Massachusetts. It was founded in 1915 and was made possible by the gift of a 27-room house that belonged to Sarah Billings Doolittle. It became a popular institution and continues to operate, providing a homelike setting for its residents.

The tradition of organizing special housing facilities for elderly populations continued later in the 20th century. Congregations in Lexington, Kentucky, with Emerson Center and Manhasset, New York, with Hadley House have sponsored apartment living facilities. Other housing has included an older Unitarian-founded residence in Boston, the Frances Merry Barnard Home (1910), which merged with the **Edward Everett Hale** House (organized by the First and Second Church in 1965) in 1984. More recent developments have occurred in a variety of places including Sunset Hall in Los Angeles, which was built in 1965, and Culpepper Garden, in Arlington, Virginia, an existing high-rise facility, which opened an assisted living wing in 2000 for frail elders with low incomes. All of these facilities are meant to give their residences comfortable settings, while affirming their dignity and self-respect.

RICE, WILLIAM BROOKS (1905–1970). Remembered as the chairman of the Joint **Merger Commission** and the architect of consolidation of the Unitarian and Universalist denominations. Rice was born in Boston in 1905 and raised a Universalist. His father was an architect who had worked with the father of his future opponent for the Unitarian Universalist Association (UUA) presidency, **Dana Greeley**. Rice was active in youth work and was continental treasurer of the Young People's Religious Union (Unitarian). He was educated at **Tufts College** and then worked in the architectural profession for a few years. Then he returned to Tufts where he finally finished with an S.T.B. (1938). As a student he was director of education at the Church of the Disciples in Boston. He had a successful ministerial career first in Dover, Massachusetts (1934–45), and then in Wellesley Hills, Massachusetts, where he went in 1945 and died while still in service in 1970. Rice had been active denominationally before his appointment to the Merger Commission, having served on the **American Unitarian Association (AUA)** board and the **Ministerial Fellowship Committee (MFC)**.

While Rice was in Wellesley he help found the Wellesley Human Relations Service, a mental health organization. He was also Protestant chaplain at the Suffolk County Jail in Boston. His renown in the denomination was gained as the devoted leader of the plan to consolidate the American Unitarian Association and the **Universalist Church of America (UCA)**. Rice was named chair of the new commission in 1956. His greatest success as chair was not to be a proponent of consolidation, but to be a facilitator of a comprehensive discussion on the local level so that many viewpoints and opinions could be expressed. The commission, with the help of consultants, produced a remarkable number of documents and supporting materials to help the congregations make their decision. The thorough nature of the plan and the process made the decision possible, and much of the credit for guiding that process must go to Rice. After he had completed his mission, he became a candidate for the presidency of the newly formed UUA in 1961, as the candidate nominated by the UCA board. He ran on the platform of fiscal restraint and a weaker presidency than that envisioned by his opponent, Dana Greeley, but he lost a close election to Greeley by a vote of 1,135 to 980. At the **General Assembly (GA)** in 1963, Rice was active in helping to write the resolution that established a Commission on Religion and Race and he was later appointed to this commission. He received the **Unitarian Universalist Association**'s Distinguished Service Award in 1964. Rice died on February 22, 1970, in Peterboro, New Hampshire.

RICH, CALEB (1750–1821). One of the earliest preachers of universal salvation in America. Rich was born in Sutton, Massachusetts, on August 12, 1750, of Congregationalist parents, but his father became a Baptist in 1768 and this stimulated Caleb's religious interests. Rich came from a poor background and received virtually no formal education. He moved to the mostly forested town of Warwick, Massachusetts, with two of his brothers in 1771 to clear land for a farm and he became a member of the Baptist church there. Then he had two visions where a spirit guide came to him. In the second he visited Mount Zion, where he became convinced he was following an outpouring of God's spirit. He became a believer in universal salvation. When the Baptists heard about these ecstatic experiences, they called Rich a heretic and excluded him from their congregation. Losing members to Universalist conversions was a great threat to the Baptists. Samuel Bigelow of nearby New Salem said that universal salvation was "completely calculated to suit the carnal mind." Rich's exclusion led him to found his own "New Religious Society" in 1773 in Warwick. This was the first Universalist church organized in America, but it had no legal standing. So, **John Murray**'s church in Gloucester has usually been considered the first.

Rich's principal area of itinerant preaching and evangelism was in north central Massachusetts and southern New Hampshire but by 1776 he also had groups of Universalists in his home town of Sutton, Douglas, and in Oxford, Massachusetts, where the first Universalist convention was held in 1785. A "General Society" was formed in and around Richmond, New Hampshire, in 1777. Rich joined the Continental Army in 1778 and marched to Cambridge, but decided that he could not be a soldier. He found a substitute and returned to Warwick. He was also married that year after converting the entire family of his fianceé to Universalism. Rich also had more charismatic episodes in 1778. An angel came to visit and told him that all the children of Adam would pass from "death unto life." His ultra Universalism that all would be immediately saved upon death was adopted by his future disciple **Hosea Ballou**. Rich was ordained in 1781 to a regional ministry of three congregations in Warwick, Richmond, and Jaffrey, New Hampshire. The service was held in Richmond in a large townwide event with 300 people in attendance. He insisted that these congregations maintain separate organizations and they had complete liturgical freedom so that baptism and communion were not considered necessary for full membership. Rich succeeded in splitting the Baptist congregation in Richmond, converted several Ballou cousins and Hosea's brother David, and this may have played a significant role in Ballou's own conversion in 1790. He had a profound influence on Hosea's ideas and also introduced Ballou to his future wife, Ruth Washburn. Rich also converted Thomas Barnes, a future Universalist preacher, when Barnes became convinced that he could not set bounds to God's love. Rich's congregations sent delegates to the Universalist convention in Oxford in 1785. Rich also attended, but theological differences between Rich and **John Murray**, whom Rich once visited in Boston, prevented much progress in unifying the Universalists. The rural Universalists under Rich's leadership always refused to follow any plan of uniform church order, as they preferred to be ruled by "gospel liberty." Rich moved to New Haven, Vermont, in 1803 where he was reordained for legal reasons and continued to preach in a variety of places, including Shoreham, Vermont, and Hoosick, New York. He died in New Haven in October 1821, an itinerant preacher until the end. Stephen Marini has called Rich "the most important native New England Universalist leader."

RIPLEY, GEORGE (1802–1880). A brilliant scholar, he is best known as the Transcendentalist who founded the utopian community at **Brook Farm**. He was born in Greenfield, Massachusetts, on October 3, 1802. He was named for a brother who predeceased him. His parents, Jerome and Sarah, ran a tavern. **Ralph Waldo Emerson** was his cousin. Bookish from early in his life, and skilled at languages, Ripley went to **Harvard College** and graduated first in his class in 1823. He was still orthodox at this point and thought he might train at Andover, but he settled on **Harvard Divinity School** and began to abandon his Calvinist rearing. After graduation he was immediately called to the newly organized Purchase Street Church in Boston and ordained there on November 8, 1826. In 1825 he met Sophia Dana, and they were married on August 22, 1827. In 1832 he began to publish a series of essays in the *Christian Examiner*. Almost as soon as he had wholeheartedly embraced Unitarianism, he began to search among the European writers for a more pietistic strain of faith.

Ripley became one of the pioneers in introducing German idealism to America. He introduced the language and the literature of both French and German philosophy and was instrumental in creating American translations. In 1834 Ripley delivered an important sermon at the installation of **Orestes Brownson** in Canton, Massachusetts. In "Jesus Christ, the Same Yesterday, Today and Tomorrow," he said that the "Immutability of our Saviour consists in the Immutability of the religious truths which he taught . . . the great principles of religion to which Jesus Christ bore testimony are everlasting realities" (Miller, ed., *Transcendentalists*, pp. 285–286). Recognized as a founder of the Transcendental movement, he helped start the **Transcendental Club** and also worked on and contributed to the ***Dial***. He was a central figure in the **Miracles Controversy**, as the author of the review article on **James Martineau**'s publication, which outraged **Andrews Norton**. In replying to Norton in the *Boston Daily Advertiser* he defended the views that Norton called "injurious to the cause of religion." He called Norton to task with respect to his scholarship and defended the new philosophy.

In 1841 Ripley resigned from the parish where he was well loved to become cofounder with his wife, Sophia, of the utopian community at Brook Farm. This was a courageous act to give up his established career. He defined his faith in Transcendentalism in his farewell letter: "They maintain that the truth of religion does not depend upon tradition, nor historical facts, but has an unerring witness in the soul. . . . These views I have always adopted" (Miller, ed., *Transcendentalists*, p. 255). He put all of his financial resources into Brook Farm, and was left in complete despair when it failed in 1847. His mistake may have been trying to organize the community around Fourieristic principles. After the failure, he said it was like witnessing your own funeral. Ripley become a journalist in order to pay off his many debts from both Brook Farm and his journal, *The Harbinger*, which he tried to continue in New York. His wife was so forlorn over their failures, she converted to Roman Catholic, and then died in 1861. In his later years Ripley wrote some important literary criticism for the *New York Tribune*. He was remarried to a young German widow and was able to tour Europe. Most of his ties to his Unitarian and Transcendental past he let lapse. He died on July 4, 1880.

ROY, RAMMOHUN (1772–1833). The founder of the **Brahmo Samaj**, an important Hindu reform movement. Born a Brahmin in 1772, Roy became an important force behind social and religious reform. A number of influences combined to be a catalyst for his remarkable ability to bring together many different traditions. He was highly educated and fluent in several languages, including English. He prepared an English translation of the Upanishads and also prepared a translation of the New Testament into Bengali. His critical study of the scriptures enabled him to convert a Baptist missionary he was helping, William Adam, to a Unitarian viewpoint when he gave him proof that the Trinity could not be found in the scriptures.

Christian missionaries were able to teach and preach in Bengal after 1813 and this helped introduce reform ideas to Roy. He began to advocate in print for the rights of women, including the outlawing of *sati* (widow burning). Few of his works in Bengali, of which there were 32 published items, dealt with social questions. A greater number of reform ideas were reserved for his English publications, of which there were 40, and there he touched upon women's rights, freedom of the press, inheritance rights, and caste issues. Most of his publications in both languages were about religious subjects. Other missionaries were disturbed by his study of Christianity, especially, the Gospels. He wrote *The Precepts of Jesus*, which presented the Unitarian view that Jesus is the great teacher. Roy came to the attention of British and American Unitarians who found him "learned, eloquent, and opulent" and mistakenly assumed he was a liberal Christian. Englishman Thomas Belsham was excited that Roy was teaching the doctrine of the "divine Unity."

In September 1821 Roy and his convert William Adam and others founded the Calcutta Unitarian Committee whose purpose was educational and informational. A Calcutta Unitarian Society was also formed, but it closed after Adam left India in 1830. Back in the United States a number of articles were published about Roy, and also his views on Hinduism and Christianity. He struggled with Christian identity in the 1820s, but because of caste restrictions, he never intended to convert from his Brahmin caste Hinduism. In 1827 a new British Indian Unitarian Association was formed to reorganize the earlier Unitarian Committee. Adam and Roy had frequently been at odds over how Roy's Anglo-Hindu School would operate. Then during the early months of 1828 Roy decided on a new approach that would mean the organization of the Hindu Unitarians into a new group. The first service for the Brahmo Samaj, or Society of God, as a Hindu reform movement, was held on August 28, 1828. Roy decided to reject a specific Christian or Unitarian name for his new group, so that Hindu cultural, religious, and caste identity could be maintained. In 1830 he traveled to England, where he spent the last three years of his life, often in the company of British Unitarians. Moncure Daniel Conway, the American abolitionist, identified Roy's arrival as the "dawn of the new interest of cultured England in Hindu religion." Roy was met by all the leading Unitarians, including Harriet Martineau and Sarah Flower, the author of "Nearer My God to Thee." Roy is buried in the Unitarian churchyard in Bristol, where he had gone to visit the reformer Mary Carpenter, the daughter of the minister Lant Carpenter. When the American **Joseph Tuckerman** went to England, and visited Roy, he referred to him as "the most advanced Christian" he met there.

RUSH, BENJAMIN (1745–1813). The "Father of Psychiatry" and signer of the Declaration of Independence, was also an active social reformer and Universalist. Born on December 24, 1745, in Byberry, Pennsylvania, outside of Philadelphia, Rush was the fourth of seven children born to John and Suzanna Rush. His father, who was a farmer and maker of firearms, died when Benjamin was only five, and the family moved into the city where Suzanna set up a grocery and china shop. She spent some time educating her children, and then at age nine Benjamin went to the Academy in Nottingham, Maryland. He earned some college credit there, and then finished at the College of New Jersey (now Princeton). He received a B.A. in 1760 when he was 15 and decided to be a physician. He studied at the Pennsylvania Hospital (where he was later a staff member, 1783–1813) but then went abroad to finish his training. He studied at the University of Edinburgh in 1766 and two years later was granted a doctor's degree. When he returned home, he took a position at the College of Philadelphia as a chemistry professor. He later published the first textbook on chemistry written by an American, *Syllabus of a Course of Lectures on Chemistry*.

Rush was an active member of the Philosophical Society, and his impulse toward reform surfaced when he published a pamphlet against slavery and founded the Pennsylvania Society for Promoting the Abolition of Slavery. He had become a convert to republicanism in Edinburgh. He met **Thomas Paine** and worked with him on the drafts for *Common Sense*. He attended the Continental Congress, signed the Declaration, and later became a surgeon-general in the Continental Army. During his service Rush became concerned about conditions in the hospitals and wrote an influential but controversial report. He was eventually forced to resign. In 1775 he returned to visit his old school in New Jersey and met and fell in love with Julia Stockton. They were married a few months later, and eventually had 13 children, of whom nine survived infancy and childhood. After the war Rush began to argue for many types of reform. Essays, which were first published in the newspaper and later gathered in book form, advocated for penal reform, the abolition of capital punishment, and a new system of education. He set up the first free medical dispensary in the country. When the new federal constitution was being written Rush wrote a plan for a Department of Peace to complement the intended Department of War.

Many of his medical accomplishments occurred after Rush became the chaired professor of the theory and practice of medicine at the new University of Pennsylvania. After suggesting some curriculum changes there, he argued with the provost and then left to found a separate school, which is now Dickinson College. In 1793 he was criticized for suggesting that a yellow fever epidemic was caused by poor sanitation, and he also worked tirelessly for its victims. He had long advocated better treatment of the insane, and his book, *Medical Inquiries and Observations upon the Diseases of the Mind*, was a forerunner of the modern science of psychiatry. He made Philadelphia the center for medical education in the country. He was also a temperance advocate due to his medical concerns for how alcohol affects the body.

Religiously, Rush was active in a variety of churches, after being born a Quaker. In 1781 **Elhanan Winchester** became a universal Baptist and had to leave his pulpit to found a new Universalist congregation. They met at the University of Pennsylvania at first, Rush joined them, and wrote in 1787 that he had embraced Universalism. He saw a relationship between universal political and religious equality. Rush was active in the Philadelphia Convention in 1790, but his plan to invite all Christians to gather on a platform of reason and good works was rejected in favor of a more sectarian gathering of Universalists. A number of social reforms were voted for with Rush's support. His major contribution was to edit and arrange the Articles of Faith and Plan of Government, which became a basis for the **Winchester Profession**. It was at this time that he met **John Murray** and began a correspondence with him. After the convention Rush helped organize the first Sunday School Association in Philadelphia. He believed that the equality of the human race could be found in the creation accounts in the Old Testament. He said that conscience was planted in human beings to show our resemblance to God and humans have a moral faculty to discern good from evil. The great physician of his day, Rush has sometimes been criticized for his unrelenting support of bloodletting in medical cures, but his overall contributions in medicine, politics, and social concerns were monumental for his time. He died on April 19, 1813.

RYDER DIVINITY SCHOOL. This was one of three theological schools associated with the Universalists. Ryder had a crisis-ridden history before its final merger with the Meadville Theological School in 1964. It first opened its doors in 1881 at Lombard College in Galesburg, Illinois. The Ryder designation was given in 1890 in honor of its benefactor, William H. Ryder. The school moved to Chicago in 1912 in order to take advantage of the facilities at the University of Chicago, but much of the impetus came from a financial crisis at Lombard. Lewis B. Fisher, a former president of Lombard, became dean and served until 1923. The original plan was to build a Midwestern center for Universalism, but this never came to fruition. Fisher had a difficult time recruiting qualified students and complained to the **General Convention** in 1915 that Universalists had gone too long with low educational standards for their ministers. Ryder remained small, with 14 being the greatest number of students it ever had at one time, and the year after Fisher resigned there were only three.

In 1928, with Lombard College still suffering from financial problems, the trustees agreed to merge Ryder with the **Meadville Theological School** (Unitarian), which moved in 1926–27 from Pennsylvania to Chicago. The Ryder name was retained with an endowed chair, and their building was sold to the University in 1928. The Lombard campus closed in 1930, but a separate corporate identity was maintained until 1964 when the new name, Meadville Theological School of Lombard College was adopted. Even after merger with the Unitarians in 1928, the school failed to attract any substantial number of Universalist students, and it accomplished little in the way of improving standards or alleviating the shortage of Universalist clergy.

– S –

SAFFORD, MARY AUGUSTA (1851–1927). The leader of the **Iowa Sisterhood**. Safford was born on December 23, 1851, to Stephen and Louisa (Hunt) Safford on a farm in Quincy, Illinois. The family moved to Hamilton, where Mary attended public schools. Her father died when she was nine, but he had helped introduce her to Darwinism and radical religious thinking. After that she went to Iowa State University, but her own ill health and then the need to care for a sister who was sick prevented her from finishing. She became a teacher and taught in the Oakwood School for a few years. Before she became a minister she organized a church in her hometown of Hamilton, learning some of her skills through the Hawthorne Literary Society that she had started in 1871. Then she moved on to Humboldt, Iowa, where she was ordained in the Unity Church on June 29, 1880. She was at work at the same time organizing a church in Algona, Iowa. In 1885 she moved on to Sioux City, where she remained for 14 years. Here she teamed up with her childhood friend Eleanor Gordon, whom Safford convinced to enter the ministry. Safford organized many adult classes, clubs, and church gatherings and the church flourished. A new building was erected in 1889. Safford, who was a charismatic speaker, traveled and preached all over the state. After Gordon left, she was assisted by another member of the Sisterhood, Marie Jenney Howe.

Safford preached a humanist message, which was expressed institutionally when the congregation drew upon members' strengths with innovative lay-led services. From 1885 to 1910 she was especially active in the suffrage campaigns and was a frequent lecturer. She became president for a time of the Iowa Suffrage Association. In 1899 Safford moved on to Des Moines, where she remained until 1910. She helped that church get out of debt and then oversaw the erection of a new building in 1905.

Safford was active in a number of larger denominational groups in the region. She was Secretary of the Iowa Unitarian Association and coordinated the efforts of the members of the Iowa Sisterhood to extend and strengthen Unitarianism. In her role with the association, she published *Old and New*, an extension magazine. She served on the Western Fellowship Committee and was named a director of the **American Unitarian Association (AUA)** in 1898. At that time she was scheduled to be the next president of the **Western Unitarian Conference (WUC)**. Safford locked horns with AUA head **Samuel Atkins Eliot** who wanted to centralize AUA funding, while Safford wanted to keep it local. At one point she reminded him that the Iowa Association had raised more money and started more churches than any other conference. She was discouraged by Eliot's lack of support for women in the ministry, especially after the AUA began to advocate that women train to be parish assistants at places like the Tuckerman School rather than full-fledged ministers. Safford saw herself as a missionary for Unitarianism—she organized seven societies in all and helped members of the sisterhood start nine more. She retired from active ministry in 1910 and purchased a home in Orlando, Florida. Again she teamed with Eleanor Gordon, and they started a church there. She worked actively for suffrage in Florida and fully supported the war effort, helping lead the drive to sell Liberty Bonds. She died on October 25, 1927.

ST. LAWRENCE UNIVERSITY AND CANTON THEOLOGICAL SCHOOL. After **Tufts College** was opened in 1854, Universalists in upstate New York began to agitate to start a college connected to a theological school in their region. In 1855 the New York State Convention voted to establish the school at Canton and raised $50,000 to fund it. **Thomas Jefferson Sawyer** proved to be a prophet when he predicted the site was too isolated. He had gained some knowledge of the area when he ran the Clinton Liberal Institute and tried some ministerial training there before he left in 1852. Clinton later merged its resources with St. Lawrence when it closed in 1900. The St.

Lawrence University and Canton Theological School was organized in 1856 with an unsectarian college and a theological school intended for training and preparation for the Universalist ministry. Funds were separated, but the schools shared common trustees. The charter was amended in 1910 giving the theological school its own trustees appointed by the State Convention. Construction of Richardson Hall was begun in 1856. The first dean was Ebenezer Fisher. The school soon had nine students, and graduated five in 1861, the year **Olympia Brown**, the first woman to receive a divinity degree, arrived. During Fisher's tenure the school produced more clergy than it did graduates, as the denomination had lax standards for the completion of requirements. The school survived a financial crisis during the Civil War. Fisher was succeeded by **Isaac Morgan Atwood**. During his presidency, Fisher Hall was erected. It became the central building of the school until it burned in 1951. **John Murray Atwood** was the most significant figure in the school's 20th century developments. He came to the school in 1913, and stayed for 46 years, mostly as dean. After 1920 students of other religious persuasions than Universalist began to attend the school. Undergraduates in the university took all their religion courses at the theological school until 1955, when a Religion Department was established.

There was some emphasis in the approach of the school to attract students who would serve rural and smaller churches, where both Fisher and Atwood felt Universalism had its greatest strength. During World War II, a study committee decided the school needed to be larger, and by 1951 the school graduated its largest class (nine) since 1894. There was an effort after the war to increase the endowment. Two other significant events occurred in 1951. J. M. Atwood resigned as dean, and Fisher Hall burned down. A vote and fund drive to replace Fisher Hall was soon undertaken. In the 1950s the trustees voted to expand the faculty from four to six and make the seminary a graduate school only. During the deanship of **Angus MacLean**, the school developed a reputation for religious education work. MacLean also started the first development office. None of these actions prevented the decline of the school and Universalism. Enrollment had dropped to 14 students in 1960. The school suffered from faculty turnover and a lack of accreditation. The school also encountered a funding problem when the **Unitarian Universalist Association**

(UUA) created the Joint Fund for Theological Education. New York Universalists preferred to fund their own school and refused to send money to a general fund. The school was already suffering from a financial crisis when the Taylor Report was issued in 1962. This criticized the school for its outdated methods of teaching and recommended it set new standards. Despite protests, there were several proposals after this to merge the school with others. Finally, the **General Assembly (GA)** in 1964 voted that both Tufts and St. Lawrence should consider consolidation with some other institution. After consolidation discussions failed, the trustees voted in June 1964 to end classes after the completion of the academic year. In October the trustees voted to create the St. Lawrence Foundation for Theological Education, thus ensuring the school's name would live on in scholarship funding for theological education. This came as a result of a close vote, where the trustees nearly affirmed a consolidation with the Crane School at Tufts. There were five graduates in the last St. Lawrence class.

SATURDAY CLUB. A group of Boston's social and intellectual elite who met on a monthly basis mostly at the Parker House beginning in 1856. It is said that they met on the last Saturday of the month because this was the day **Ralph Waldo Emerson** made his regular visit to the Old Corner Bookstore. The group had an afternoon of conversation followed by dinner and the exchange of ideas. It mostly represented a society of friends who enjoyed being together. In all there were about 20 members, including **Henry Wadsworth Longfellow**, **James Russell Lowell**, **Nathaniel Hawthorne**, and, of course, Emerson.

SAVAGE, MINOT JUDSON (1841–1918). One of the great preachers and published voices of Unitarianism, Savage was born on June 10, 1841, in Norridgewok, Maine, the youngest of four children. His brother William H. was also a Unitarian minister. Due to ill health he never received much formal education, but he taught briefly after high school. Then he attended seminary in Bangor, having been brought up in a conservative Congregational church and experiencing a teenage conversion. He took time off one summer to be a chaplain in the army but returned to graduate in 1864. Savage married Ella

August Dodge, with whom he sailed for California. He served as a missionary in San Mateo and Grass Valley but returned east to help care for his parents. He settled in Framingham, Massachusetts, for two years, but then moved on to Hannibal, Missouri, where his brother William was already settled. Here he began to revolt against what he perceived as the cruelty of God and the infallibility of scriptures. Before he left Congregationalism, he converted to the science of Darwin. William, who later became a Unitarian minister, too, helped Minot in his search.

In 1873, Minot published *Christianity, the Science of Manhood*, and that was followed three years later with *The Religion of Evolution*. Later Savage would argue for belief in a "God who is in and through nature" and does not interfere with natural processes. By now he knew that Christianity was only one part of religious truth. No longer able to abide Congregationalism, he accepted a call to the Third Unitarian Church in Chicago, still unsure if he was a Unitarian or not. Here he came to know **Robert Collyer**, and his friendship with Lucretia Mott helped make him an abolitionist. Savage had stayed only briefly in Chicago when he received a call to Boston's Church of the Unity in 1874, where he remained for 22 years. He became known as a great preacher and lecturer, and volumes of his sermons were published. He would stand in front of the pulpit and speak without notes before throngs of a thousand and more. He died soon after he left the church.

By the 1890s many of his congregation were beginning to move to the suburbs, and he was looking to go elsewhere. In 1895 Robert Collyer was pleading with Savage to come to New York and be his assistant. Called the most "representative mouthpiece of Unitarianism," he decided a move to New York would be advantageous to his career. His fame grew even more, based primarily upon published sermons. As part of his definition of Unitarianism he said, "Character is no condition of salvation, it is salvation." In 1895 he was made chairman of the **National Conference** after he had helped revise the constitution. At the famous meeting in Saratoga in 1894, Savage was responsible for helping define the statement of purpose that remained in use until 1959: "These churches accept the religion of Jesus, holding, in accordance with his teaching, that practical religion is summed up in love to God and love to man." He had also been a board member of the **American Unitarian Association (AUA)**. He received a D.D. from Harvard University in 1896, the same year he settled in New York. Savage became deeply immersed in spiritualism later in life, especially after the death of his son Philip. In 1906 Savage's health worsened, and he resigned form the Church of the Messiah in New York. His son Maxwell became a minister as well. He came to Boston for the May Meetings in 1918 and died at the Parker House Hotel on May 22. One of the great preachers of the late 19th century, he was the first to attempt to reconcile evolution with religion.

SAWYER, THOMAS JEFFERSON (1804–1899). He was an important early educator in the Universalist movement. Sawyer was born on January 9, 1804, in Reading, Vermont. He received both a B.A. (1829) and an M.A. from Middlebury College (1833) after many years of financial hardship. In 1830 he was called to the Orchard Street Universalist Church in New York City, where he remained for 15 years. During this successful ministry he started the periodical the *Christian Messenger* and was its coeditor for a number of years. The society was able to purchase its leased building in 1834 and launched a Sunday School in 1835. As early as 1832 Sawyer became an advocate for a prescribed course of training for Universalist ministers. He was also a founder and prime mover of the Universalist Historical Society in 1834 and was its secretary and librarian for more than 50 years. In the 1840s he began to agitate more loudly for the establishment of a Universalist training school for ministers. He advocated combining many of the numerous Universalist periodicals to save money and eventually used these funds to start a theological school. When Sawyer was asked to develop a plan for the overall organization of the Universalist **General Convention**, he gave a final report in 1844 that was eventually enacted. In that report he called for a "more uniform and more wholesome Discipline" within the Universalist ranks.

Sawyer's direct involvement with education began in 1845 when he began to preside over the Clinton Liberal Institute (New York), a Universalist secondary school where he began some separate training for theological students. He remained there until 1852. In 1847 Sawyer issued a call for an education convention, and eventually

Tufts College grew from this meeting. At that time he returned to the Orchard Street Church for another nine years of ministry. He spent some of the 1860s in retirement, but took one hiatus to edit the *Christian Ambassador* for three years. He was then convinced to take a position as the first faculty member, a professor of theology, at the new divinity school at Tufts from 1869 until 1890 when poor eyesight forced his retirement. He died on July 24, 1899.

SCIENCE. One of the basic premises of Unitarian and Universalist beliefs is that faith is justified by the authority of human reason using observation and experience, more than by the authority of scripture. Observing and testing ideas with the mind became the scientific method for discovering truth. Early Unitarians believed that our senses were a reliable means for understanding the world but still relied upon the reasonableness of the scriptures and accepted them as religious truth, even if second hand. **William Ellery Channing** said, "The heavens, the earth, the plant, the human frame, now that they are explored by science, speak of God as they never did before. . . . Religion opens before the improved mind in new grandeur" ("Christian Worship" in *Channing's Works*, pp. 410–411). He believed that God and His plan for the world were observable through nature. Later the Transcendentalists said that the truth of God was directly knowable through nature, and as **Ralph Waldo Emerson** said in *Nature*, mind and matter are one continuous revelation. From their earliest days, the Universalists also tended to be a group that was open to both new ideas and the use of rationalism in their interpretation of scripture. Their openness was expressed by Elbridge Gerry Brooks when he wrote, "We should welcome discovery . . . and keep abreast of the most advanced knowledge." **Benjamin Rush** had been interested in the work of Larmarck, along with other members of a scientific circle that was brought together by **Thomas Jefferson**. This included the great chemist **Joseph Priestley**, who was also a Unitarian minister. Priestley thought of himself as an amateur scientist and professional theologian, but he discovered oxygen in 1774 and published a history of electricity.

Prior to 1850 some Universalists tried to harmonize the Mosaic account of creation with the geological record. They suggested the "days" in the biblical account actually refer to epoch or ages.

Thomas Starr King presented a pantheistic interpretation of the relation between science and religion in 1847. He said the tenets of the scriptures unfolded or were confirmed by the researches of science. The grandeur of the deity could be measured, he believed, by the delicate correspondence between beast and bird and flower and tree. If the Unitarians believed that God's unfolding purpose was understandable through our observation of nature, this remained possible even as Charles Darwin's evolutionary ideas became known in wider circles. Darwin's idea of a constantly evolving universe with a benevolent divine plan behind it confirmed what they had believed all along. Science gave a better understanding of the works of God. Their openness to science was tested by the period after the Civil War. Prior to that time God's loving care for His children was central to realizing God's presence in nature and in personal revelation. After the war scientific truth and advancing knowledge replaced God and became a greater hope for the advancement of humankind. Unitarians now saw that the world of science could open avenues for improving the world by making it more humane, whereas their old loving God had ordained a brutal conflict.

Universalists were not as quick to accept Darwin, and his theories of evolution presented serious challenges to Universalist beliefs. They were a biblically centered faith, who had not been threatened by the Transcendentalist controversy and, therefore, maintained the reliability of scriptures. The initial reactions to Darwin were hostile. They believed that human beings were the creation of a superhuman intelligent agency and that species were immutable. One of the Universalist leaders of this time, **Thomas Thayer**, felt that religion had nothing to fear from science, but also counseled caution. He did not want to hastily endorse every new theory, but be open to new truths as they unfold. He did not fear that Christianity would be outgrown. Evolution implied the working of intelligence just as much as any idea of creation, and evolution became the method by which God accomplished His will in the universe. **Orello Cone**'s texts on higher criticism endorsing the use of reason through the scientific study of scripture were influential among all Americans. Cone effectively reconciled science and religion with the support of biblical criticism. He wanted to apply the finding of many other areas of study to a comprehensive examination of the texts. He found no conflict between science and religion, saying one dealt with the facts and phenomena of the physical world and the other with the facts and relations of the spiritual world. The Unitarian astronomer **Maria Mitchell** also wanted to reconcile science and religion, believing that science needed imagination and beauty and poetry. She believed we could learn the certainty of spiritual truths through nature's laws. She wrote: "There will come with the greater love of science greater love to one another." The leaders of the **Free Religious Association (FRA)**, especially **Francis Ellingwood Abbot**, were among those who proposed a doctrine of Scientific Theism. This was a faith based on knowledge, and the prophet of the "known" God was science.

By the end of the 19th century most Unitarians believed in an evolutionary optimism. Humans began to think that they could become possessors of all knowledge and, in effect, solve all problems. After the turn of the century Marion Shutter became the great Universalist champion of evolution. He wrote in a series of popular lectures in Minneapolis that religion had gained much more from science than it lost. With science, validated truths replaced invented truths and evidence superseded dogma and superstition. Shutter defined God as eternal goodness and equated the deity with a real universe that is pervaded by unity and order, the universality of law, and the continuity of the processes of nature. His most famous work was *Applied Evolution*, in which he outlined what religion had gained from science. First, there was a quickened sense of truth; the right methods for discovery. Second, there was the value of evidence rather than unsubstantiated claims. Third, science taught religion about using methods of reasoning. Shutter concluded that society must abandon any conclusion that contradicts truth because truth is the safest thing. While debate on evolution raged among other denominations culminating in the Scopes trial in 1925, Universalists were mostly searching for ways to produce a partnership between science and religion. Universalists in the **General Convention** in 1923 concluded that the Bible "was to be interpreted as any other literature in light of experience and by human reason." Shutter said humans will discover a rational mind behind creation and nothing, not even God, was unknowable. The theologian Henry Nelson Wieman was an important voice in the 20th century for using the methods of science to build a strong faith. He wanted to see religion shape the scientific ethic, and be a method for discovering religious truth but not be the content of religion. Science was generally viewed as the savior of the world until the moral dilemmas of the 20th century began to multiply. Universalists along with Unitarians said religion must undertake the task of providing a conscience for science. **Clarence Russell Skinner** said, "Science says to religion: 'Your goodness is not wholly good if it is not true.' Will religion have the courage to say to science, 'Your truth is not wholly true if it be not good?'" This led Universalists to question their long held belief that scientific methods led to positive discoveries of truth, which always implied the betterment and advancement of humankind. The dropping of the atomic bomb in 1945 destroyed forever the optimistic outlook that science would allow the world to always unfold in new and greater ways.

After World War II Unitarians and Universalists played an important role in starting the Institute on Religion in an Age of Science in 1954. Ten years later the Center for Advanced Study in Science and Religion was established at **Meadville Lombard Theological School**. Two years after that the institute and the center began to publish *Zygon, Journal of Science and Religion*. Ralph Burhoe, who was professor of Religion and Science at Meadville, was the guiding spirit behind this wedding of science and religion. He said: "Many of us feel that our religious hopes and meanings as well as our moral convictions must be credible in light of the revelations of reality portrayed by the sciences." Burhoe believed in a science-based concept of transcendent purpose to which the immortal souls human beings are called to participate in. For many other Unitarian Universalists the general acceptance of knowledge from contemporary sciences made the belief that religion and science are not in conflict so obvious that there was a lack of interest in the sciences in the late 20th century. With the perception that science is too rational, these liberals may have sought more mystical experiences. Some liberals have tried to do this in the context of science, including the group Unitarian Universalist Psi Symposium. They are especially interested in metaphysics, holistic health, and healing and parapsychology.

The global ecological crisis has helped many Unitarian Universalists see the religious implications of the interconnectedness of creation and also the dangers in using scientific knowledge to attempt to remake nature. Some Unitarian Universalists are active in the environmental movement and are organizers of eco-justice projects. Liberals also realize that the desire to better humanity may produce catastrophic consequences, as we ponder a future of genetic engineering and cloning. At one time there were Unitarian Universalists, such as **Oliver Wendell Holmes**, who were part of the eugenics movement that favored attempts to control breeding for the betterment of the human race. What will society do to inhibit our technological choices when more options become available to engineer human improvements? There are also some liberals who have become interested in the new physics, including Unitarian Universalist minister Gary Kowalski, who in his book *Science and the Search for God* (2003) relates quarks and quantum theory to religious belief. From Priestley and Rush to Burhoe, Unitarians and Universalists have tried to find the truth using all the tools of thought and mind they have at their disposal so that humans might make choices that bring about a more just, humane, and peaceful world.

SCHULZ, WILLIAM F. (1949–). The Executive Director of Amnesty International USA and a former **Unitarian Universalist Association (UUA)** president, Bill Schulz, was born on November 14, 1949, to William F. and Jean Schulz in Pittsburgh, Pennsylvania. Schulz's father, whom Bill describes as someone who offered something "close to unconditional love," was a legal scholar and professor. Schulz developed a sense of the need for social change in the world from an early age. When his parents took him to visit the Custis-Lee house in Virginia, he recalls the "powerful sense of injustice" he felt from seeing the slave quarters. Schulz received his B.A. in sociology from Oberlin College in 1971. The year before graduation, he had a searing experience that sealed his commitment to ministry and social justice. He was serving as student minister in Kent, Ohio, at the time of the Kent State College shootings. Knowing that ministry would be his lifelong vocation, he immediately entered the seminary at **Meadville Lombard Theological School**, received an M.A. in 1973, and then a D.Min. in 1975. (Meadville Lombard also honored Schulz with a D.D. in 1987.) He also received an M.A. in philosophy from the University of Chicago (1974). While he was in the seminary he taught philosophy for two years at the Chicago "Y" Community College. In 1975 Schulz was called to serve the First Parish in Bedford,

Massachusetts, and he was ordained and installed there that fall. He says it was not the most distinguished of parish ministries, but this is primarily because of its brief duration. In early 1978 he was asked by UUA president Paul Carnes to be the head of a newly reformed Department of Social Responsibility at the UUA, and he accepted the post. He was active in many areas of social witness, but slowly began to offer more training opportunities for local leaders and started the *Ethics and Action* newsletter.

After **Eugene Pickett** was appointed UUA president in the wake of Carnes's death, Pickett placed Schulz's before the UUA Board as the candidate for executive vice president, and he was appointed. Only 29 years old Schulz became the administrative manager of the UUA. There were many important accomplishments during Pickett's six years in office, including the first successful capital campaign in the UUA's history. In 1985 Schulz ran for the presidency of the UUA and defeated Sandra Caron, who had been the UUA's **moderator**. He pledged to increase the public visibility of the UUA and to expand membership, not only in North America, but around the world. Many of Schulz's campaign promises were established as programs. Most visible of all was the transformation of the **Unitarian Universalist World** newspaper to a magazine format. Schulz also established a professorship in Unitarian Universalist studies at **Harvard Divinity School**, revived campus ministries and programs for young adults, and reaffirmed interfaith efforts by establishing observer status with the National Council of Churches. He also continued his long-term commitment to social justice issues, including his own arrest in 1987 at a nuclear test site. After two years in office, the UUA found itself in a financial crisis, which, with new management and budgeting procedures, was averted. Schulz was reelected to the presidency in 1989, but not without controversy. His dismissal of the African American director of the Social Justice Department resulted in charges of racism. The UUA at this time was changing its priorities to be less involved in social witness and more committed to local training, and despite Schulz's long-term commitment to racial and cultural diversity, he endured much personal criticism.

Schulz's second term as president included many new initiatives. There was continued growth in UUA membership throughout his years in office. There was also a renewed emphasis on "spirituality" in the local congregations. The UUA also developed the "Welcoming Congregation" program to welcome gay and lesbian members and also completed a new hymnal, *Singing the Living Tradition*. Schulz was especially interested in the international Unitarian Universalist witness. In 1990 he and moderator Natalie G. Kulbrandsen undertook a trip to Romania to visit the Unitarians in Transylvania. A partner church program with these ancient congregations was developed soon thereafter. In 1992 the first World Summit of Unitarian Leaders took place in Budapest. Schulz also hoped to extend UUA membership to international congregations and during his tenure the Unitarian Universalist Church of the Philippines was accepted as a member. He also gave his unflinching support for the **International Association for Religious Freedom (IARF)** and encouraged it to adopt advocacy programs for human rights throughout the world. From 1985 to 1993, he served on the Council of the IARF.

His passion for human rights helped Schulz transition easily into his next career, when he was named executive director of Amnesty International USA in March 1994. During his years with Amnesty, he has traveled broadly, including a mission to Liberia to investigate atrocities committed there. An outspoken advocate for many causes, in 2002, *The New York Review of Books* said "William Schulz . . . has done more than anyone in the American human rights movement to make human rights issues known in the United States." Schulz has served on many volunteer boards, including Planned Parenthood and People United for the American Way. In 2000 he was named "Humanist of the Year" by the **American Humanist Association (AHA)**. Schulz is married to Beth Graham, a fellow Unitarian Universalist minister, and he has two grown children from a previous marriage. He is the author of several books and articles. In 2001 he published *In Our Own Best Interests: How Defending Human Rights Benefits Us All* and then in 2002 a history of humanism, *Making the Manifesto: The Birth of Religious Humanism*. Prior to these books, he had edited a book on preaching, *Transforming Words: Six Essays on Preaching* (1984), and a selection of essays and reflections, *Finding Time and Other Delicacies* (1992). Raised in a Unitarian church, Schulz was dubbed "Bill the boy humanist" in theological school. This abiding religious humanism has been the basis of his faith, "How could we recognize ourselves without humanism's courageous faith that the future of the world is in our hands—not those of an angry God or inexorable fate? Humanism beckons us to believe that we can make a difference to history" (Schulz, *Finding Time*, p. 42).

SCOTT, CLINTON LEE (1887–1985). Called the "Revitalizer of Universalism," Clinton Lee Scott was born in Vermont in 1887. As a young man he worked as a granite and marble cutter. While employed as an organ pumper, Scott became inspired by the Universalist preaching he heard and subsequently entered **Tufts College**. He completed his undergraduate degree and then received the S.T.B. from the Crane Theological School at Tufts in 1915. He was ordained to the Universalist ministry in Northfield, Vermont, but after 1926 held fellowship in both Unitarian and Universalist denominations, as did his brother Harold. Scott's long career in the ministry was marked by liberal views in both politics and religion. From Northfield he went to Buffalo, New York, where he was attacked for his wartime pacifism, and then followed ministries in Atlanta, Philadelphia, and Los Angeles. During his pastorate in Peoria, Illinois (1930–40), he became the only Universalist minister to sign the ***Humanist Manifesto***. After a brief ministry in Dayton and El Dorado, Ohio, he was called in 1942 to serve the Gloucester, Massachusetts, church, where he composed many of the tales that were later published as *Parish Parables*.

After only four years in Gloucester, he was narrowly elected superintendent of the Massachusetts Universalist Convention. In a period of decline and malaise for the church, Scott managed to infuse the convention with new energy. In 1946 he initiated a series of radio broadcasts that he eventually delivered himself on a weekly basis. Many of these later reappeared in the book *Religion Can Make Sense*. The following year he organized a Larger Fellowship of Universalists that was based on the very successful Unitarian church by mail, **Church of the Larger Fellowship**. At the **General Assembly (GA)** that year, the Universalists from Massachusetts asserted their new found power when the assembly elected Scott's wife, Mary Slaughter Scott, to the **Universalist Church of America (UCA)** Board of Trustees. Scott was a widower with two daughters when he and Mary were married in 1930. They later had a son, Peter, who became a Unitarian Universalist minister.

One of the greatest difficulties for both Clint and Mary was the controversy surrounding the Charles Street Meetinghouse and its minister **Kenneth Patton**. Both of the Scotts had worked hard to establish a Universalist church in Boston. Patton gave the faith the kind of broad, innovative Universalism that the Scotts supported, as opposed to a traditional Christian emphasis. Unfortunately, Patton alienated many of the Christians with both his theology and his abrasive style. Despite efforts to cut off funds to the Meetinghouse, Scott continued to support Patton and the controversy finally subsided in the mid 1950s. In 1951 Scott took on the work of superintendency of the Connecticut state Convention, as well as Massachusetts. His tenure of both ended in 1956. During his service as superintendent, Scott brought a new found sense of confidence to the Universalist movement and actively supported merger with the Unitarians, especially as a member of the Committee on Consolidation. In 1957 Scott moved on to Tarpon Springs, Florida, for a 14-year ministry, not retiring from the active ministry until he was 84. He became the grand, old man of the Unitarian Universalist movement, being the oldest minister both in terms of age and years of service at the time of his death in 1985. Scott was also an important historian of the movement, publishing *The Universalist Church of America: A Short History* (1957) and *These Live Tomorrow: Twenty Unitarian Universalist Biographies* (1964). He also published an autobiography in 1976, *Some Things Remembered*.

SCOTTISH COMMON SENSE PHILOSOPHY. The philosophical foundation of Harvard Unitarianism was provided by the Scottish Common Sense Philosophers, primarily Thomas Reid and Dugald Stewart, who reinterpreted **John Locke** for an American audience. Daniel Walker Howe in his *The Unitarian Conscience* says there are three epistemological doctrines in Common Sense philosophy; observation is the basis of knowledge; consciousness is the medium of observation; and consciousness contains principles that are independent of experience and impose order on the data of experience (Howe, *Unitarian Conscience*, p. 30). The philosophers believed that God had implanted common sense in the mind so that we could come to know God through our perceptions. Locke's pure sensationalism made people distrust the truth of their knowledge, but the Common

Sense Philosophers allowed for an innate moral sense that could be trained to apprehend the truth in external objects. While humans are not born believing these truths, once they are revealed to us, they will seem self-evident. The most important American text elucidating Common Sense principles was written by Levi Hedge, Harvard professor and father of **Frederic Henry Hedge**. His *Elements of Logick* (1816) was reprinted several times.

SEARS, EDMUND HAMILTON (1810–1876). Known primarily for his authorship of the Christmas carol "It Came upon the Midnight Clear," Sears was also a pacifist and biblical critic. He was born in Grandisfield, Massachusetts, on April 6, 1810, into a farming family. As a boy he worked the farm and attended village schools and Westfield Academy. He graduated from Union College and then went on to Harvard Divinity School, where he finished in 1837. Briefly he preached in the west, but then was ordained and installed as minister in Wayland, Massachusetts, in 1839. He also married Ellen Bacon that same year. After a short ministry, he moved on to Lancaster, Massachusetts, in 1840, where he served for seven years. His work at this larger parish, which included the introduction of the first "church socials," exhausted him. Here he found his duties "extended and various." He returned to Wayland for recuperation following a nervous breakdown. It was during this period that he wrote "It Came upon the Midnight Clear." The power of his ministry was found in the poetic expressions of the spiritual life, so that his sermons were often compared to prayers. In all he wrote some 500 hymns, including another Christmas favorite "Calm on the List'ning Ear of Night." The more rural parish in Wayland proved to his liking, when he again began to serve the year following his return to town. He continued in this pastorate for 17 years. This contemplative and retiring soul who had difficulty speaking before crowds had facets to his personality beyond quiet meditation.

Sears's great carol, "It Came upon the Midnight Clear," may have been composed at a friend's request to be performed at a Sunday School in Quincy, Massachusetts. Also known as "The Angel's Song," it has a powerful antiwar message. Sears was a pacifist who felt great contempt for the Mexican War, and the call for peace underscores this carol. His social conscience led him to advocate abolitionism as well. From 1859 to 1871 Sears played an editorial role with Rufus Ellis in the *Monthly Religious Magazine*. In 1866 he was called to the parish in Weston, Massachusetts, where he served until his death on January 16, 1876. His religious orientation was more evangelical and mystical than most of his colleagues, as shown by his interest in the Gospel of John. Well versed in current biblical criticism, his more Christocentric approach is evident in the title of his most scholarly work, *The Fourth Gospel the Heart of Christ*.

SEN, KESHAB CHANDRA (1838–1884). One of the leaders of the **Brahmo Samaj** in India. Sen was born on November 19, 1838, in Calcutta, although his ancestors had come from a small village up the Hooghly River. When he was seven, he went to the Hindu College, where he showed a special interest in drama. He moved on to Metropolitan College, where a search for religious meaning led him to study under three missionaries, including **Charles Dall**, the Unitarian, whom Sen met when he was eighteen. Dall gave Sen numerous writings to absorb, including the works of **William Ellery Channing**, **Theodore Parker**, and **Frederic Henry Hedge**. Sen was married that same year, but the following year was ready to place marriage second to his religious devotions. Sen became one of the founders of the British India Society, a literary and scientific club. Once Sen converted to Brahmoism, he rose to a leadership role quickly. He believed that religion must also transform society, and so when the Goodwill Fraternity of Sangat Sabha was formed in 1861, it voted to end caste distinctions. Sen began to go on missionary tours in India, and he also published regularly in the Brahmo paper, the *Indian Mirror*, in which he called for educational reform and antipoverty programs.

Sen was involved in a number of debates and controversies with Christian missionaries. His basic faith was summed up in "Religion of Love," "Love God as thy Father and man as thy brother" (Sen as quoted in Lavan, *Unitarians*, p. 110). Sen earned some renown through a lecture he gave in 1866: "Jesus Christ: Europe and Asia." That same year he led a rebellion within the ranks of the Adi Brahmo Samaj, so that the more progressive elements split off from Debendranath Tagore's (father of the famous poet Rabindranath Tagore) conservative group and formed the Brahmo Samaj. Sen wanted to incorporate a universal Christ in the new Brahmo faith, but Tagore was more Hindu oriented. Sen wanted to inspire a young generation of Bengali youth to embrace the spiritual Christ, but he wanted a faith that did not embrace any narrowly defined theological traditions or social caste, whereas Tagore had built a Samaj that only accepted Brahmins as members. In 1870 Sen visited England and gave more than 50 lectures. He was extremely well received and was granted money by the British Unitarians, although Charles Dall was offended by all the attention Sen received and noted that he was not a Christian. Dall tried to remedy this by joining the Brahmo Samaj. Sen had encouraged the group toward a greater practice of Hindu devotionals, and it was increasingly ascetic in its approach to living.

By the late 1870s a new controversy tore the Brahmo Samaj apart. They had been successful in passing a Marriage Act, which reformed the practice of child marriage. To facilitate this, Sen had helped establish an Indian Reform Association and a Normal School for girls. Then in 1878 Sen announced an arranged marriage for his daughter, and he was sharply criticized because this violated the very Marriage Act they had worked for. Many of the members withdrew to join a new group, the Sadharn Brahmo Samaj, who are the active Samaj group today. The remaining members of Sen's group became known as the Church of the New Dispensation, with Sen claiming he had received a new revelation from God. Sen died suddenly in January 1884, and there was considerably less contact with American and British Unitarians in the next few years. **Jabez Sunderland** visited in the 1890s and tried with some success to unify the three factions of the Brahmo Samaj. Sen is primarily remembered today through his reading: "Unto the Church Universal," which was popularized at the Community Church of New York. "Unto the church universal, which is the depository of all ancient wisdom and the school of all modern thought; Which recognizes in all prophets a harmony, in all scriptures a unity, and through all dispensations a continuity. . . . We pledge the allegiance of our hands and hearts" (for complete text see #474 in *Singing the Living Tradition*).

SERVETUS, MICHAEL (1511–1553). An enemy of both the Catholic Church and John Calvin, Servetus became a martyr for his heretical anti-Trinitarian beliefs in 1553. He was born on January 12, 1511, in Villanueva in Aragon, Spain, the son of nobility and devout

Catholics. In his midteens, Servetus went to France to study law at the University of Toulouse. During this time he began to discover the Bible and soon concluded there was no central doctrine supporting a belief in the Trinity. His studies were interrupted when he was called into service to sail with Emperor Charles V to Italy for a coronation ceremony by the Pope. His disgust with the spectacle of this coronation led to his commitment to reform the church. After this Servetus went to Basel, Switzerland, where he began to write in 1530 and in the summer of 1531 he took his manuscript to Strassburg, Germany, where *On the Errors of the Trinity* was published when he was only 20 years old. For Servetus, the Logos, which became incarnate in Jesus, is eternal, but not the Son himself. Within a year, the book was resoundingly condemned. Thinking he could restate his position, Servetus published a second book, *Two Dialogues on the Trinity*. The Protestant reformers continued to condemn the views and the Catholic Inquisition decided it would try to lure Servetus back to Spain. His views led to 20 years of life in exile under the assumed name Michel de Villeneuve. Knowing that Lyons was safer than Paris, Servetus moved to the village of Vienne, France, where he first worked as an editor. But after a two-year hiatus in Paris, where he studied medicine, he returned to his village in 1538 to practice both professions. He even made an important discovery about the pulmonary circulation of blood. Unable to keep silent, Servetus published *The Restoration of Christianity* in 1552. In this work Servetus said that a person can only make the choice of emulating Christ as an adult, and that is when one should be baptized.

While the Catholic Inquisition hunted him for heresy, his outspoken views also enraged John Calvin. Apparently on his way to Naples, Servetus made the mistake of passing through Geneva. It is unknown whether he tried to bring martyrdom upon himself, had some apocalyptic vision, or made a poor choice of travel plans, but Calvin heard a report that he was spotted in church and had him arrested. He was imprisoned, brought to trial, and convicted of heresy, especially with regard to his anti-Trinitarianism, the eternal deity of Christ and infant baptism. During this period, Calvin interviewed Servetus and reported that he said those who "recognize God the Father, Son, and Holy Spirit, with a real distinction, created a three-headed hound of hell. I told him to beg the pardon of the Son of God, whom he had disfigured with his dreams, denying that he came in our flesh and was like us in his human nature, and so denying that he is a sole Redeemer. But when I saw that all this did no good I did not wish to be wiser than my master allows. So following the rule of St. Paul, I withdrew from the heretic who was self-condemned" (John Calvin, as quoted in *Hunted Heretic: The Life and Death of Michael Servetus*, 1511–1553 by Roland Bainton [Boston, 1953], p. 210). Servetus was burned at the stake in Geneva on October 27, 1553, with *The Restoration of Christianity* tied to his thigh. Both Catholics and Calvinists succeeded in burning nearly every copy of the book. Servetus's ideas lived on in renewed concerns for religious liberty and questions about the basic doctrines of Christianity. Servetus has a monument dedicated to him in Geneva directly behind the Hopital Cantonal.

SEWELL, MARILYN J. (1941–). A leader of a large church in Portland, Oregon, Sewell has achieved recognition for editing several significant works. She was born on July 9, 1941, in Washington, D.C., but grew up in Homer, Louisiana, with her father, an oil field worker, and her paternal grandparents. Her undergraduate training was at Louisiana Polytechnic Institute, where she graduated with an English Education major in 1962. Then she received an M.A. in English from the University of Arkansas in 1965. Sewell taught high school for several years and then was married to a doctor for six years. During this marriage she had two sons and lived for periods in Liverpool, England, and Lexington, Kentucky. She worked briefly in Lexington as a therapist and also broadcast a television advice show. She began to train for the ministry in 1983 at the **Starr King School for the Ministry** in Berkeley, California, and then, after receiving her M.Div. in 1987, she remained at the Graduate Theological Union in Berkeley to study for a Ph.D. in Theology and the Arts. After her ordination in 1987, she served as a consulting minister to the Unitarian Universalist Fellowship of Vallejo, California, and then was an interim minister at First Unitarian Church, Cincinnati, Ohio. Sewell was called to the First Unitarian Church in Portland, Oregon, in 1992, a congregation that has since grown to approximately 1,000 members and 500 children in the church school, and she has been an active force in the community. In June 2000 she was the preacher for the

Unitarian Universalist Association's **(UUA)** annual Service of the Living Tradition.

Sewell is perhaps best known for her published anthologies of women's writings. Foremost among these is the award-winning *Cries of the Spirit* (**Beacon Press**, 1991). In the introduction to this sourcebook, Sewell writes, "I hope that *Cries of the Spirit* will provide a source of nourishment, life-giving bread for a new day, to those women who are exploring their spirituality" (xvi). In 1996 she edited another sourcebook of women's poetry, *Claiming the Spirit Within*. In 2001, a collection of memoirs by people who had grown up Catholic was published, *Resurrecting Grace*. She has also published a collection of her sermons, *Wanting Wholeness, Being Broken*. Sewell notes that in seminary she was encouraged to "notice and mention." She writes, "Because I am serving a large, urban church, I notice. I notice the bedraggled strangers who camp out on the church steps, the confused and agitated who come in off the street, the lesbians and gay men who have been reviled and even physically attacked and who have sought a safe place of worship at our door, the runaway teenagers who hang out on our block, leaving used needles behind." Her attempts to encourage others to pay attention to the stranger affirm the power of relationships and the view that all life is sacred.

SEXUALITY, ABOUT YOUR. An innovative sex education curriculum that was both controversial and highly successful. In the 1960s **Unitarian Universalist Association (UUA)** education staff, under the direction of the Director of Curriculum Development Hugo Hollerorth, began to look to sex education materials for possible use in church schools. They decided to develop a new curriculum that would counter many of the moralistic and judgmental materials with a more positive understanding of sexual behavior. The perspective was to be that sex is a positive and enriching force in life, that some expression of it is normal at all ages, and that there is no one right norm. In the fall of 1968 a **Liberal Religious Education Directors Association (LREDA)** conference featured health education professor Deryck Calderwood. He led religious educators in a workshop about the questions junior-high-aged boys and girls ask about sexuality and strategies of helping them in dealing with these issues. As a result of this conference, a curriculum development team was created, including Calderwood. They met regularly for nearly two years and field tested materials in 25 congregations. The result was *About Your Sexuality* (first called *Human Sexuality*), published in 1971 (revised 1983). This new curriculum, written by Calderwood who was a UU, helped junior-high-aged youth to receive accurate information, build values, and learn some communication skills so that they could make responsible sexual decisions.

Prior to publication there were many concerns about the explicit nature of some of the materials. President Robert West of the UUA made the courageous decision not to be swayed by these views, but felt the importance of the material far outweighed the negative responses. The Brookfield, Wisconsin, church and the UUA received an injunction from the district attorney in Wisconsin for harassing the Brookfield church. This curriculum, despite its controversial beginnings was an important, ground breaking effort in sexuality education. It has recently been superseded by a new sexuality curriculum called *Our Whole Lives* (OWL).

SHINN, QUILLEN HAMILTON (1845–1907). The greatest Universalist domestic missionary in the post-Civil War period. Shinn was born on January 1, 1845, in Bingamon, Virginia (later West Virginia), to Elisha and Mary (LeFevre) Shinn. His father died when he was only two, but his mother remarried to a doctor. He had little formal education and at the age of 16 enlisted in the Union Army. He was taken prisoner once and then paroled and later saw action at Appomattox, where General Robert E. Lee surrendered. He attended an academy in Ohio and then taught school. Shinn's stepfather was a Universalist, and Shinn was converted after reading **Thomas Baldwin Thayer**'s *Theology of Universalism*. In 1867 he began attending Canton Theological School at **St. Lawrence**. On his way to school he stopped at the meeting of the Universalist **General Convention** in Baltimore. He listened to the debates and became disturbed by all the wrangling. Finally, he stood up and told the assembled delegates that he had been on his way to school to prepare himself for the ministry, but said he now felt like he would return home, "for evidently Universalist ministers could write better than they could talk." Harmony was apparently restored, and Shinn continued with his plans.

Shinn finished school in 1879 and was fellowshipped by the Vermont Convention and then ordained in Gaysville, his first church. He tried, without success, to start a church in Wheeling, West Virginia, and then he returned north to work for the **Universalist Publishing House**. In 1876 he married Maria Burnell, and they had three sons who lived to adulthood. During the early years of his ministry, Shinn served several brief pastorates, including congregations in Massachusetts, New Hampshire, Vermont, and Maine. He usually tried to establish preaching stations nearby as well. When he was in Plymouth, New Hampshire, in 1882 he set up 14 such stops on his circuit. It was during this time that he started summer gatherings that grew into National Summer Meetings, starting at the Weirs on Lake Winnipesaukee, New Hampshire. Others recognized that Shinn had a particular fitness for mission work. After a visit to Canada in 1883, he served in Omaha, Nebraska, where they built a church in less than two years. After 1891 even short pastorates would not suffice, as Shinn became an itinerant missionary moving from place to place. The "Grasshopper" eventually preached in every state in the union, as well as numerous locations in Canada. When he signed the Ferry Beach, Maine, summer register in 1904, he listed his home as "Everywhere."

Shinn formulated several plans as to how to missionize the country. In 1895 he was named "general missionary" by the General Convention. Even prior to then he had singled out the South as his field of special work, and then in 1900 the convention gave him the title of "southern missionary." Shinn was constantly traveling and preaching, covering as much as 700 miles per week, often by foot or horseback. He believed in having a new church construct a building as soon as possible after forming as a visible sign of their presence in the community. In Georgia six churches built buildings between 1896 and 1902. Russell Miller estimates that Shinn recruited hundreds of new members to Universalist churches and oversaw the erection of at least forty buildings. Despite his unflagging spirit for spreading the word, he was often criticized for preaching Universalism in rural places where it was not likely to grow and, especially, later in his career, he preached more in urban centers. There was also some conflict over authority after the Universalists established the office of general superintendent in 1898. In 1901 Shinn was placed under the general superintendent's authority. Shinn had a lifelong interest in temperance causes, frequently lectured on the topic, and was a member of the Prohibition Party and the Good Templars. Shinn's war record made him a popular speaker on patriotic themes. He continued to preach right up until the months before he died. In the summer of 1907 he visited four churches in South Carolina. By this time many of the southern states had district superintendents. He died on September 6, 1907, in Medford, Massachusetts, leaving a remarkable legacy of preaching Universalism in every nook and cranny of North America.

SINKFORD, WILLIAM G. (1946–). He was elected president of the **Unitarian Universalist Association (UUA)** in June 2001. Sinkford was born in San Francisco in 1946 and became an active Unitarian Universalist during his teenage years in Cincinnati, Ohio. After joining the First Unitarian Church in Cincinnati, he became increasingly active in youth programming, eventually serving as the president of the continental youth organization, **Liberal Religious Youth (LRY)** from 1965 to 1966. Sinkford found a spiritual home in local, district, and continental youth gatherings, which he describes as places of "inquiry and support, of celebration and commitment, of safety and challenge." After high school, when he was one of the first U.S. Presidential Scholars, he was admitted to **Harvard** University. He graduated in 1968. Some of Sinkford's activities during college included advising local youth groups in Boston and Lexington, Massachusetts, serving as Assistant Director of Rowe Camp, a Unitarian Universalist Camp in Rowe, Massachusetts, and directing a Harvard-Roxbury Summer Project. After that he spent a year in Greece as a Rockefeller Fellow. Sinkford worked in private business for many years. Mostly employed in the marketing field, he held management positions with Gillette, Avon, Johnson Products, and Revlon. During this time he received the Black Achievers in Industry Award from the Harlem YMCA. He also ran his own business, Sinkford Restorations, Inc.

After returning home to Cincinnati, Sinkford became active in his local church again and entered the **Starr King School for the Ministry**. During this time he served on the UU Urban Concerns and Ministry Program and also became active in African American Unitarian Universalist Ministry. As he neared the end of his seminary training he was hired to serve on the staff of the UUA. A close friend of president **John Buehrens**, in 1994 he became the director of the Congregational, District, and Extension Services departments, which oversee congregational health and growth. The following year he was fellowshipped as a community minister and ordained in his home church in Cincinnati. In 2001 he ran for president of the UUA against Diane Miller, the director of the UUA Department of Ministry. He won by a large majority, but soon after taking office, Sinkford found that as a religious leader, he had to respond to the terrorist attacks on New York. He believes that "the shared tragedy has heightened our appreciation of the importance of religious life and community." Sinkford, who lives in Newton, Massachusetts, has two children and is a member of the Unitarian Universalist Church in Marblehead, Massachusetts. The first African American to head the UUA, Sinkford says of his Unitarian Universalist faith, "We are committed to living as a religious community that honors and celebrates difference. We believe that our differences can be blessings, not curses."

SKINNER, CLARENCE RUSSELL (1881–1949). Skinner was the great Universalist social prophet of the 20th century. He was born in Brooklyn, New York, on March 23, 1881. He grew up in a family of actors and theater people. His father, who was a reporter, also wrote plays and was a drama critic. Young Clarence took part in plays at Erasmus Hall High School and also at **St. Lawrence University**, where he started in the fall of 1900. Skinner was also active in the Universalist church in Canton, New York, where his classmate Clara Ayres played the organ. After they graduated in 1904, Skinner was leaning toward the ministry as a career and went to work at the Universalist Church of the Divine Paternity in New York. He was in charge of the Sunday School and youth programs. He also attended programs at the University Settlement and eventually taught classes there in current events. Skinner was ordained in New York on April 8, 1906, and accepted a call that summer to the Universalist church in Mt. Vernon, New York. That fall he and Clara were married.

Skinner's ministry in Mt. Vernon was a success, as a building was erected and the church school prospered. He continued to be involved in the University Settlement and also finished his M.A. from St. Lawrence. Soon thereafter **John Haynes Holmes** was settled in New

York, and he and Skinner became friends. They agreed that the church must broaden its orientation toward reforming all of society. At this time congregations were taught about many of the social injustices of the day and public forums became popular. Christians across the country were applying Christ's teachings to the social problems of the day, calling it the Social Gospel. This reform impulse was spearheaded in the Universalist denomination by Skinner. In 1910 Skinner helped form the Universalist Social Service Commission and served as secretary for six years. The following year he left Mt. Vernon to accept a call to Grace Universalist Church in Lowell, Massachusetts. Here, in a community where the industrial revolution had started, Skinner had more firsthand experience in dealing with social problems. He tried to bring labor and management together for discussions and sponsored many forums. He was also named president of the Massachusetts Universalist Sunday School Association. Then in 1914 he was appointed to the new position of Professor of Applied Christianity at Crane Theological School at **Tufts**. This was the beginning of a long relationship with Tufts. Although some were concerned about Skinner's social radicalism, he was a popular teacher with the students. After he was there for only a year, his major work on *The Social Implications of Universalism* was published (1915). Here Skinner wrote, "The true social objective is the perfecting of human character by the progressive improvement of those conditions and environments which are within the social control" (Skinner, *Social Implications*, p. 33).

In 1917 the denomination approved a Declaration of Social Principles that Skinner had written. That year was a difficult one for Skinner, as his stand against World War I and his avowed pacifism was unpopular with much of the campus. After the war he once again joined forces with Holmes; together they formed a Community Church of Boston, similar to Holmes's venture in New York. Both believed that the church must move beyond sectarian boundaries and serve the broader community with a ministry that addresses social problems in the world. Organized in 1920, Skinner remained there for 17 years as leader. During the 1920s Skinner was especially active in the defense of Sacco and Vanzetti, whom he felt were unjustly convicted of murder based on their political radicalism. In 1929 Skinner was made vice dean of Crane, and then Dean Lee McColllester resigned three years later. There was some opposition to Skinner taking the position, but finally he received the appointment. He continued to teach during his term of 12 years as dean. The school also continued to grow and improve academically. After the stresses of World War II and ill health, Skinner decided to resign from his position. He died four years later on August 26, 1949. After his death many of his ideas on worship and spirituality were gathered from previously unpublished material in *Worship and the Well-Ordered Life* (1955). His teaching and writing, in addition to his concern for social justice, also contained a vision for a new Universalism as a religion of universals transcending all particulars, and some of this was articulated in *Religion for Greatness* (1945). Like his famed 19th-century predecessor Hosea Ballou, Skinner saw salvation as only possible when the entire world is saved, not just isolated individuals.

SLAVERY. *See* ABOLITION OF SLAVERY.

SMITH, GARY E. (1947–). The minister of the largest Unitarian Universalist church in New England. He was born in Waterville, Maine, on July 14, 1947, the youngest of three boys to Clarence and Anita Smith. He was educated in the local school system and then went on to the University of Maine, where he studied philosophy and graduated in 1969. Feeling called to the ministry at a young age, Smith went to the Divinity School of Vanderbilt University and graduated in 1972 with an M.Div. In the meantime he had married Elizabeth Masciadri in 1970, and they have two children. He was ordained into the United Church of Christ in 1972, and his first settlement was as an associate pastor at the First Church of Christ, Congregational, in Middletown, Connecticut, from 1972 to 1976. Smith returned home to Maine in 1976 to serve the First Universalist Church in Bangor, but he did not receive Unitarian Universalist ministerial fellowship until 1982 (with final fellowship confirmed in 1985). He left Bangor in 1985 to serve as a denominational official at **Unitarian Universalist Association (UUA)** headquarters. From 1985 to 1986 he was director of a new capital fund drive, Visions for Growth. Having developed a close relationship with UUA president **William Schulz**, Smith was named the UUA's director of public relations and special assistant to the president for public outreach.

Smith left the UUA in 1988 to become senior minister at the First Parish in Concord, Massachusetts, succeeding **Dana Greeley**. Under Smith's leadership the church has grown to more than 800 members with two Sunday services. He edited a book of readings on ministry, *Awakened from the Forest* (1995). Recognized by his colleagues for his leadership, he was president of the **Unitarian Universalist Ministers Association (UUMA)** from 1998 to 2001. Smith was also a participant in an important series of discussions that formulated a vision for the future of religious education in the UUA. Their findings were published as *Essex Conversations* (2001). More recently, he led 44 members of his congregation on a pilgrimage to Concord's partner church in the village of Szekeleykeresztur in the Transylvanian part of Romania. Smith has also been an active board member and workshop leader at the Wright Tavern Center for Spiritual Renewal in Concord since 1997. A proponent of the caring power of religious community, in a sermon in November 2002 Smith reminded his parishioners, "You do not have to go it alone. When you are awake in the dark of the night, there is someone else here who is also awake. We hold one another. We hold tight. What a blessing."

SOCINIANISM. A Reformation movement of the late 16th and early 17th centuries that flourished in Poland and was later exported to Holland and England. An early form of Unitarianism, it is often considered the more radical of the two main types of anti-Trinitarianism commonly distinguished: Arian and Socinian. The Socinian type draws its name from **Faustus Socinus** (partly through the influence of his uncle Laelius Socinus), the leader of the Polish Brethren in the late 16th century. Socinianism rejected certain orthodox doctrines and helped establish the freedom of the individual believer to interpret biblical texts for him/herself, always advocating the primacy of reason in this examination. Socinianism rejected the Doctrines of the Trinity, the Preexistence of Christ, Original Sin, and the Satisfaction Theory of the Atonement on the grounds that they were both irrational and unscriptural. Establishing a more ethical standard for Christianity, Socinianism proffers that if God forgives sin, then no satisfaction is necessary. Christ saves human beings not by dying for them, but by offering up an example to emulate. Perhaps the sharpest distinction between **Arianism** and Socinianism is that Socinianism denies any divine nature in Christ. He is wholly human, although he is considered the Son of God and the mediator between God and humans. In the Arian view, Christ is begotten and inferior to God, but he is regarded as a being that is neither fully human nor fully divine but rather an intermediate creature. This distinction became important in the development of American Unitarianism, when the Trinitarian Congregationalists tried to falsely portray the majority of American anti-Trinitarians as the more radical Socianism types rather than Arian types.

✓ **SOCINUS, FAUSTUS (1539–1604).** The leading voice in the development of anti-Trinitarianism in Poland, Socinus's name has become synonymous with a radical understanding of the nature of Christ as human. Socinus was born in Siena in 1539 into a well-established family of lawyers. Sadly, his father died when he was only two, and he received much of his education from family tutorials. Aware that his uncle Laelius had been harassed by members of the Inquisition, Faustus left Italy in 1561 and started a business in Geneva, Switzerland. After he inherited his uncle's library and papers, Faustus began to seriously study the Bible and came to the conclusion that Christ was divine only by office and not by nature. He returned to Italy and was a courtier in Florence, making the appearance that he was Catholic. During this time he published *On the Authority of Holy Scripture*. He remained until 1574, when he moved to Basel. Here he wrote *On Christ the Savior* (1578), which established his belief that Jesus was totally human, but that God shared his divine power with him, making him an adopted deity who could be worshipped and invoked in prayer. During this time he was called by **Giorgio Biandrata** to mediate a theological dispute in **Transylvania**. After several months there, he feared returning home, as he might be accused of heresy, and made the decision to settle in **Poland** at Krakow in 1579.

After this Socinus reached the zenith of his career by becoming the prime inspiration for the development of the Polish Brethren. What is unusual about his role is that he was rejected for membership and denied the Lord's Supper in the church after he appeared before a synod in Rakow in 1580. This was because he found no scriptural basis for considering baptism as prerequisite for church membership. He said it was only necessary for those who were born pagan and not required for born Christians. Socinus became a widely respected theologian and published many tracts defending the church against charges of heresy. He was also active in synod debates where the issues that divided the anti-Trintiarians were sometimes resolved. Many of his views were embodied in the *Racovian Catechism*, which was published shortly after his death. Several components of his faith stand out. Reason is the foremost authority in the interpretation of scripture. God's nature is one, not three. Original sin is denied in favor of free will. He claimed that the church must be pacifist. There was a strong ethical component of his faith, so justification by faith alone was insufficient. Socinus came under suspicion while he was living in Krakow and he moved to a noble's estate where he remained for four years until 1587. He married Elizabeth, his host's daughter, and they had a daughter together, but his wife died after they had moved back to Krakow.

The Catholic Church continued to regain power, and Socinus's person and ideas came to be increasingly under attack. He had to leave Krakow again and settled in a village less than 50 miles away. Here he remained for the final years of his life. His last published work was a critique of the Polish Calvinist Church. He spent these final years editing his earlier works and working on the catechism with his colleagues. He called together two meetings of clergy and lay leaders in **Rakow** in 1601 and 1602. These helped unify the church on doctrinal issues and established Socinus's legacy as the true leader of Polish Unitarianism who organized their disparate beliefs into a coherent system. Socinus died on March 3, 1604, in Laclawice. A monument was erected there in 1933 with money donated by American Unitarians.

SOCINUS, LAELIUS (1525–1562). The uncle of **Faustus Socinus**, he influenced many of the early anti-Trinitarians and rationalists. He was born at Siena on March 25, 1525, into a family of wealthy lawyers, including his father Mariano who taught jurisprudence. He also trained for the legal profession in Padua. His interest in humanism and rationalism led him to reject Roman Catholicism as a young man. He lived in Venice for a time and later at Chiavenna, where he was influenced by Camillo Renato, the leading Anabaptist in Italy. Laelius left Italy to explore the fruits of the Reformation in several countries. He visited many of the reformers in his travels, including John Calvin in Geneva, then on to Basel where he met Sebastian Castellio, and as far afield as England, where he met Bernardino Ochino. After further traveling, he settled in Zurich, Switzerland, in 1549. Socinus opposed the execution of Servetus, and it propelled him into further study of the Trinity. His theology fell under suspicion and he was questioned by his friend Bullinger, who accepted Socinus's vague response to charges of heresy. Thereafter Socinus became cautious about openly expressing his views. When his father died in 1556, the Inquisition seized the family estate and he never recovered it or his inheritance. Because of his caution, it is difficult to ascertain his beliefs. He died on May 14, 1562, in Zurich, donating his library and papers to his nephew Faustus, who used them to good benefit in developing his own anti-Trinitarian thought.

SOULE, CAROLINE AUGUSTA WHITE (1824–1903). Known as the first Universalist missionary, Caroline Augusta White was born in Albany, New York, on September 3, 1824. She was educated at the Albany Female Academy, and the year after graduation, she took charge of the women's department at the Universalist-founded Clinton Liberal Institute. Being only 17, many of her students asked her to "wear a cap" so that she would look "more matronly." At Clinton she met and later married the Rev. Henry B. Soule, who was head of the men's department at Clinton. In the next few years Henry had a succession of pastorates in New England and New York. He contracted small pox in 1852 and died, leaving Caroline a widow with five small children. She began to write in order to support herself, starting with a memoir of her husband. She published a number of stories in ladies' magazines, including the *Ladies Repository*. After moving to Iowa in 1853, she published three books, the last a temperance story, *Wine or Water* (1862). After moving to New York, she became the founder and editor of a Sunday School paper, the *Guiding Star*, and she edited the children's section of the ***Christian Leader***.

Raised a Universalist, Soule began to take a leadership role in the denomination. At the 1869 **General Convention**, she helped organize the Women's Centenary Aid Association, which began as a short-term organization meant to raise an endowment for the denomination (including funds for needy ministers and their families, of which Soule had personal experience). Soule was its first president and traveled extensively raising funds, lecturing, organizing, writing, and, most especially, mailing tracts all over the world to spread the Universalist message. Her efforts included the fund-raising for an endowed woman's professorship at Buchtel College. Two years later the group was reorganized as the Women's Centenary Association, the first national women's organization in the United States, and she remained president for eleven years. Always suffering from poor health, she traveled to England and Scotland in 1875 to try to recuperate. But Soule plunged into denominational work there as well and helped organize the Scottish Universalist Convention. By 1878 she became the first foreign missionary for the Universalists, being appointed by the Women's Centenary Association. She became minister of St. Paul's Universalist Church in Glasgow in 1879 and was ordained the following year. She remained there until her retirement in 1892. Soule continued to speak whenever she could, saying, "Fatigue in the cause of Universalism is infinitely better than inaction, apathy, indolence." She died on December 6, 1903. *See also* ASSOCIATION OF UNIVERSALIST WOMEN.

SOUTH AFRICA. The Unitarian Church in Cape Town was founded in 1861 by liberal Afrikaaners who became disaffected with the Dutch Reformed Church. Their leader was the Rev. Peter David Faure, who was educated for the ministry in the Netherlands, but found his liberal views were unacceptable once he returned to preach at home. He established the independent Free Protestant Church (later Unitarian), an outpost of liberalism in a country that has been historically unsympathetic to its aims. The church is the only mixed-race church indigenous to South Africa. It has maintained an affiliation with both the **Unitarian Universalist Association (UUA)** and the British General Assembly, with settled clergy from both groups. After 1948 when apartheid became the law of the land, the church struggled with racial restrictions. The church especially thrived under the leadership of Victor Carpenter in the 1960s, but he left in 1967 when it became apparent that his political activities might endanger the congregation and he was threatened with expulsion.

A decade later a native South African, Bob Steyn, was settled as minister. He served faithfully for 20 years, but died in 1997, leaving the congregation with an uncertain future. The church was served by visiting American ministers for a few years, until former Cape Town mayor, Gordon Oliver, was permanently appointed as minister in 2000 (initially as a minister-in-training). The church has supported interfaith dialogue, sponsored a social worker, and maintains an African Scholars Fund. More recently they have founded a sister congregation in a Cape Town suburb. Over the years there have been other small congregations in South Africa, including a fellowship in Johannesburg, founded in 1956, which was once affiliated with the UUA and is now served by a part-time minister. Another fellowship exists in Durban with part-time ministerial leadership. The Unitarian Church of South Africa is a member group in the **International Council of Unitarians and Universalists**.

SPEAR, CHARLES (1801–1863). An important Universalist leader in the movement to reform prisons. Spear was born in Boston and was dedicated in the Universalist church by John Murray, for whom his younger brother was named. Charles's career began as a printer, a skill he would put to good use as a reformer. He moved on to the Universalist ministry and was fellowshipped by the Northern Association in Vermont in 1827. Spear spent most of his career in prison reform after serving brief ministries on Cape Cod and in Boston. Influenced by the writings of **Benjamin Rush**, Spear became especially concerned about prison conditions, the reform of prisoners, and their lives after discharge. He taught Sunday School classes in both the state prison and the Charles Street Jail in Boston. His wife, Sarah, also became active in this work and traveled with him a great deal up and down the coast and as far inland as Michigan, speaking on the treatment of prisoners. In 1845 he began to edit a periodical called *Hangman*, which opposed capital punishment. He also joined forces with his brother for a time and edited *Voices from Prison: Being a Selection of Poetry from Various Prisoners, Written within the Cell* (1847). They founded the Prisoners' Friend Association in 1845, which published a journal, *The Prisoners' Friend*, which lasted in various forms until 1861. But John, who had an erratic career, drifted off to **spiritualism** after two years. This paper also introduced the first column devoted to the humane treatment of animals. Charles also spoke before numerous legislatures to implement penal reform. Spear became an outspoken advocate for the abolition of the death penalty after living in Connecticut in the early 1830s and later published *Essays on the Punishment of Death* (1844). In 1845 he was one of the organizers of the Massachusetts Society for the Abolition of Capital Punishment and became its first recording secretary and later its chief agent. In 1851 the governor of Massachusetts authorized Spear to go to England to speak on capital punishment.

Spear was devoted to a number of other reform issues. He was an outspoken advocate for peace and, with his wife, spoke out for the rights of women to hold property. He wrote on the economic exploitation of women. Like his brother, he was active in the abolition movement and offered a resolution against slavery that was passed by the Massachusetts State Convention of Universalists in 1843. He was also interested in the water cure (hydrotherapy) and phrenology. In prison, reform progress was slow and Spear received scant support from the denomination, although **P. T. Barnum** and his virtuoso singer Jenny Lind gave money. Spear made great progress in abolishing debt as a reason for being sent to prison. Penal reform continued to receive his devoted attention for his remaining years of life, as his goal was to apply "the spirit of charity to all outcasts." He died in 1863.

SPIRITUALISM. This religious movement developed a large following in the mid-19th century after two sisters who lived near Rochester, New York, Margaret and Kate Fox, heard what they believed were rappings of deceased people trying to communicate with them from beyond the grave. First promulgated by the Swedish mystic Emmanuel Swedenborg, spiritualism offered a spirit world beyond life in which humans could perfect themselves, and, under the proper environment, the living could communicate with those spirits. Communicating with the dead was especially powerful because it was an empirical method for assuring immortality and coincided with the growing belief in the power of science to uncover all truths. Because it sought broader ways to understand the natural laws of the universe, many Universalists became interested in the spiritualist movement. Two former Universalist clergy, William Fishbough and

Samuel B. Brittan, established the periodical *Univercoelum* in December 1847. Brittan went on to edit the most popular spiritualist paper of the 1850s, the *Spiritual Telegraph*. John Murray Spear, a radical reformer among Universalists, came to believe that he received direct communications from his namesake and the founder of Universalism, John Murray. Spear founded a utopian community, Harmonia, which drew its name from the Harmonial Philosophy of Andrew Jackson Davis, the "Poughkeepsie Seer," who believed in the wholeness of the universe and was one of the most well-known spiritualists.

Adin Ballou's **Hopedale** Community was also a center for spiritualist activity; Ballou also wrote a history of spiritualism. Many Universalists also opposed this wide assortment of seances, demonstrations of mesmerism (hypnotism), and other spirit manifestations. Charles Chauncey Burr, who had been minister of Universalist societies in Troy, New York, and Portland, Maine, gave a series of lectures on "electro-biology." For a time, Burr was a serious convert to spiritualism, but as he investigated it, he became convinced that it was a fraud. Thereafter, his demonstrations of mesmerism became a traveling exposé of its errors. He showed how the Fox sisters were able to crack their knuckles and toes to produce rapping sounds. One of them subsequently sued him for libel. **Thomas Whittemore**, the leading Universalist publisher, denied the credibility of spirit rappings and lamented how often Universalists became the receptacle for every strange thing under heaven.

STACY, NATHANIEL (1778–1868). The Universalist preacher who was called "the Ballou of New York and Pennsylvania," was born in New Salem, Massachusetts, on December 2, 1778, the son of Rufus and Anna (Day). At 14 he became an apprentice to a blacksmith, but after a long illness, he decided that he was not fit for a life of manual labor. In 1797 he entered New Salem Academy and he spent some time teaching before hiring on as a clerk in Dana, Massachusetts. Stacy's parents had been Universalists in Gloucester, but became "half-covenant" members in New Salem. As a child Stacy was not aware of their faith, but later "strange preachers of a strange doctrine" came to town and caused "considerable excitement, and called forth all the bitter censures, denunciations, and condemnations of the standing order." Stacy had embraced Universalism as a religion of "youthful vivacity" by the time he moved to Dana. There he fell under the influence of **Hosea Ballou**, who centered his circuit riding ministry in that town. Ballou became his mentor and encouraged Stacy to become a minister. One Sunday in October 1802, Ballou feigned a headache and told Stacy he must preach in his place: "You may say just what you please, and I'll get up and prove it all true, by Scripture." After Stacy conducted the service with "quaking knees and quavering voice," Ballou delivered a closing prayer and Stacy "heard no more of Mr. Ballou's headache" (Stacy, *Memoirs*, pp. 71–73). Stacy became an advocate of "God's Universal Grace" and promised "to defend the truth against the attacks of its enemies." He wrote that the first lesson he learned in this new school was that "the salvation of *all* was just as secure as the salvation of the Calvinistic elect." The belief that all would be saved "removed all slavish fear, and filled my soul with 'joy unspeakable'" (*Memoirs*, p. 466).

Soon thereafter, Stacy began itinerant preaching in Vermont. He was fellowshipped in September 1803 and ordained in Westmoreland, New Hampshire, in 1804. Stacy was a strong supporter of the **Winchester Profession**, feeling that a confession of faith helped to legitimize the legal status of Universalists and saying it "was absolutely necessary to save Universalists in New England, and particularly in New Hampshire, from Clerical oppression." He married Susan Clark of New Salem in 1806. They had eight children; three sons and five daughters. In 1805 Stacy began preaching in New York, with Brookfield as his headquarters. In April 1808 he accepted a call to the church in Hamilton, New York, where he remained for 22 years. He served briefly as a chaplain during the War of 1812.

A leader in organizing and spreading Universalism in New York, Stacy founded the Chenago and Black River Associations (1823), proposed the idea of starting a New York State Convention, and later took part in its creation in 1825. In his *Memoirs*, he wrote, "In the State of New York, I have witnessed its first breathings, its infantile struggles, its youthful fears and hopes, and ardent longings and anticipations, until it assumed a manly dignity" (*Memoirs*, p. 348). Stacy claimed that within less than 25 years the number of Universalist societies had grown from two to two hundred. The end of his tenure in Hamilton was unhappy, as an anti-Masonic group created some tensions within the congregation, and Stacy decided it would be better to move on. From 1830 to 1840 he traveled through Ohio, Michigan, and Pennsylvania, starting in Columbus, Pennsylvania, where he organized the church, and was its first minister. From 1835 to 1840, he was pastor in Ann Arbor, Michigan, the first settled Universalist in the state, but he felt constrained to leave there due to financial difficulties. After a return call to Columbus in 1841, he continued to further the cause of Universalism in western Pennsylvania. In 1859 the Universalist societies there were formed into the Stacy Association. This five-foot, 100-pound, diminutive, and modest man became a legend for his fortitude in organizing rural societies with constant itinerant preaching, traveling by day and preaching at night, spreading the gospel of Universalism. He wrote, "My travels, in all seasons, through all kinds of roads, amid all sorts of weather, and amidst almost all the variety of character that human nature is capable of sustaining, have been excessively fatiguing" (*Memoirs*, p. 349). Despite the strain, Stacy's health remained vigorous throughout a career that stretched from the Atlantic Ocean to the Great Lakes and back. He wrote that he was never "so happy as when proclaiming . . . and defending, with all the efforts of my feeble talents, the GREAT SALVATION" (*Memoirs*, pp. 17–18). He died on April 7, 1868, in Columbus.

STANDING ORDER. The term used to describe the church/state relationship in colonial New England. Towns and parishes were legally required to support public worship and generally did so through public taxation. In most New England towns all inhabitants were assessed a property tax that was used to build and maintain meetinghouses and pay the minister's salary. These arrangements were maintained until the early 19th century. Pressure from minority groups often led communities to allow voluntary support for some recognized religious groups. In those cases, town clerks issued exemption certificates to individuals who declared their affiliation with some group other than the established Congregationalists, such as Baptist, Universalist, or Church of England. In some instances these minority groups were harassed or arrested for trying to follow their own persuasion. For example, Isaac Backus reported that in New Salem, Massachusetts, a person named Goodale "looked every day to be caried [sic] to jail or have his goods taken by force for ministers rates." Universalists in Gloucester, Massachusetts, were excommunicated from the parish church and the tax assessors refused to consider them a legitimate sect. They were taxed and subject to property seizures until 1783, when some of the members convinced the Rev. **John Murray** to allow them to use his name in a suit against the First Parish. The case came to trial that year but continued in litigation on appeal and review until June 1786, when the judges found that "teachers of any persuasion [are] entitled to the religious taxes of their adherents." The battle to abolish compulsory religious taxes continued for many more years, with Massachusetts the last state to disestablish the Standing Order in 1833.

STARR KING SCHOOL FOR THE MINISTRY. The West Coast center for Unitarian Universalism was founded in 1904. At the sixth annual meeting of the Pacific Unitarian Conference held in Portland, Oregon, in September 1889, Charles Wendte, minister from Oakland, proposed the establishment of a West Coast training school for ministers. In his presentation he related the story of a minister who had been sent west, was settled in a church, and soon thereafter declared himself the reincarnated messiah, and when the congregation would not worship him, committed suicide. Wendte's told this dramatic story to illustrate how the West Coast congregations often received the ministers who were undesirable for one reason or another in the east. The conference responded favorably to Wendte's proposal that the school be started in Berkeley, where the state university system was centered. A committee was appointed, but Horatio Stebbins, the minister in San Francisco, later stepped down from the committee, fearing the **American Unitarian Association (AUA)** had prior commitments to **Meadville Theological School**. Wendte turned to Horace Davis, a Unitarian who was president of the University of California. Davis presented a proposal to the faculty and regents that the university invite all the theological schools to avail themselves of university resources. At the next meeting of the conference, Wendte said the supply of ministers was unsatisfactory, but, moreover, a school was needed to train clergy in the traditions and customs of the West, which were less abstract scholarship and more practical. The plan included drawing upon conference funds for one professor's salary and AUA mission money to establish a church in Berkeley, whose minister would teach at the seminary. The conference approved the plan, but the project was delayed mostly for financial reasons.

The plan for a school was revived again in 1900 when George Stone was appointed AUA Pacific Coast field secretary. On February 7, 1904, he presented the Oakland church with a proposal to use a few of their rooms for the Pacific Unitarian School for the Ministry. Horace Davis was still behind the planning, but this time he wanted to be sure that the school had a leader, money, a place to meet, and the association's backing. At the 1904 meeting of the conference, it was announced that enough money had been pledged and that **Earle Morse Wilbur** had agreed to be the first dean. After two years of meeting at the church, Francis Cutting bought the school a building in Berkeley. On March 2, 1906, AUA president **Samuel Atkins Eliot** came to the annual meeting of the Oakland church to ratify the Articles of Incorporation for the school. The school was chartered to "establish and maintain an institution for educating students for the Christian ministry, especially for Unitarian churches." Unfortunately, the San Francisco earthquake delayed progress, but the school remained open with 16 students continuing.

In 1921 a library building was given by the Unitarian Laymen's League. The depression era brought a period of financial crisis to the school. **Aurelia Henry Reinhardt** reported that its geographic separation and its financial problems had slowed its growth. In 1936 an AUA Advisory Committee recommended that the school remain open. After this it entered a new era of expansion when it moved to a new building in 1941 and renamed itself the Starr King School for the Ministry, after **Thomas Starr King**, the West Coast hero.

Although it continued to suffer severe financial problems and had a limited enrollment, the school somehow survived. Just after World War II, its president, Edward W. Ohrenstein, was part of a small group called the Committee of Free Unitarians. Concerned that the school was being taken over by a small group who wanted to turn Starr King into a "de-spiritualized pseudo-religious cult," Ohrenstein argued that Christianity must be at the center of Unitarianism. With few active alumni, and a skeptical headquarters staff, few people were left to support the school. Josiah Bartlett, its president during the 1950s and 1960s, said that the school had no curriculum and its eight students were all misfits and draft dodgers. Bartlett placed supervised field work in churches at the center of his curriculum and pioneered in individually tailored programs for students and clinical pastoral training. By the time Bartlett left in 1968 after 20 years of renewal, Starr King's academic standards had vastly improved, psychological tests were required of applicants, and students were given important roles in governing the school. During the 1970s, while Robert Kimball was president, there was a rapid expanse in the number of students, especially women. This led to a campaign to establish a chaired professorship for a full-time woman faculty member in the name of Aurelia Henry Reinhardt, who had served on the board from 1932 to 1947. The school was often criticized for its progressive and self-directed methods of education. It has also attempted to admit students of widely diverse backgrounds who could enrich the experience for all. In the 1990s much progress was made during the presidency of Rebecca Parker. The endowment was vastly increased, the building was renovated, and student enrollment increased from 50 to 70. By the end of the 20th century, Starr King was graduating the largest number of people entering the Unitarian Universalist ministry. Starr King has always encouraged nontraditional work beyond academic study, including experiences all over the world. The school has also benefited from membership in the Graduate Theological Union, a consortium of nine theological school and other related institutes.

STATE CONVENTIONS. During the 1820s the Universalists tried to organize a system of state conventions. Despite chronic fears of granting power to centralized authorities, the state conventions slowly came into being. This was especially true after the General Convention was organized in 1833, when a convention system was implemented in nearly every state. Several meetings in the 1820s tried to clarify the relationship between the New England Convention and the new state conventions. New York was the first state convention, organized in 1825, but the difficulties of implementing the new system are revealed there. Five local associations shared the authority of granting fellowship and ordaining the clergy and often refused to give up this local prerogative. Even after the Western Association took the lead in forming the Convention, the Genesee Association refused to join. Once the **General Convention** was organized, it had only advisory powers, and the state conventions could determine whether they wished to join or not. A uniform system of organization was not finalized until 1865, when the General Convention approved it.

The state convention in Massachusetts also grew out of the effort of the General Convention to organize a comprehensive state system. One local association, the Boston Association, provided the impetus, and it was organized in 1834 with all regular clergy and a delegate from each congregation as members. Delegates to the General Convention were appointed on the state level. Most of the state conventions were neither active nor powerful during the first 25 years of their history. This changed in Massachusetts after 1859 when the Massachusetts State Convention was incorporated and assumed control over ministerial fellowship, ordination, and discipline. Although there continued to be resistance to this state authority, the state conventions generally became the most effective ecclesiastical arm of the Universalist denomination. After 1900 many of the state conventions had state superintendents to act as executives for the organization. In many cases it was hoped that this person would act as the chief missionary for the Universalists in the state, but too many duties and lack of funds often prevented much development of this role. The New York State Convention first recommended a state superintendent in 1900 but did not fill the position until 1904. The state convention system began to be phased out after the **Joint Merger Commission** was formed in 1955. Ministerial fellowship was centralized and a regional arrangement of associations was recommended following the Unitarian system. Eventually the district became the regional/state unit of denominational organization. Several of the old Universalist state conventions, including the oldest in New York, continued to function after the consolidation of the Unitarians and Universalists. They continue to provide funding and programming in the local area.

STEBBINS, HORATIO (1821–1902). A principal West Coast leader of the Unitarians. Stebbins was born in South Wilbraham (now Hampden), Massachusetts, on August 8, 1821, the third son Calvin and

Amelia (Adams) Stebbins. His mother died when Horatio was young and he helped his father work a successful farm. He attended school during the winter months and later went to high school in Springfield. He hired out on a farm and also worked for his father. He was eventually licensed to teach and kept school for several years. Then he went to Phillips Exeter Academy in New Hampshire and then on to **Harvard College**, where he graduated in 1848. Stebbins had to earn his way through the early years of life—he once grew potatoes on a plot lent to him by a faculty member. As a result of his years of hard labor, he was more aged than all of his classmates by as many as 10 years. Three years later he graduated from **Harvard Divinity School**. He soon received a call from the Unitarian church in Fitchburg, Massachusetts, where he was ordained November 5, 1851. He also married Mary Ann Fisher at this time. In Fitchburg he was a colleague to Calvin Lincoln. After he was there for a year, he was invited to go to San Francisco, but declined so he could undergo more seasoning, not knowing the call would come again 12 years hence. In 1854 he was called to the First Parish in Portland, Maine, to be the associate for Ichabod Nichols and was installed the following January. Nichols died in 1859, and Stebbins succeeded to the senior position. His political sermons sometimes caused some consternation among the conservative congregation. On the Sunday following the fall of Fort Sumter, the pulpit was draped with an American flag, and some were concerned that the flag had nothing to do with religion, but Stebbins's loyalty to the Union was a major part of his faith.

In 1864 **Henry Whitney Bellows**, who had gone west to fill **Thomas Starr King**'s pulpit after his death, recommended Stebbins to the San Francisco congregation as the best person to follow the great Civil War orator, King. For a few months while Bellows preached in San Francisco, Stebbins filled the pulpit at All Souls, New York. In August 1864 Stebbins sailed for California with his wife and two children. Stebbins's personal life was plagued with sorrow in the years ahead, as his wife died, and then after her marriage, his daughter died as well. He drew close to his son Roderick, who later became a Unitarian minister as well. Later Stebbins was remarried to Lucy Ward, and they had two children.

Stebbins became a powerful figure in the development of Unitarianism on the West Coast. He was instrumental in the establishment of the church in Portland, Oregon, in 1866, and then the society in Santa Barbara, California, in 1877. He was active in starting the Pacific Coast Conference and the founding of the Unitarian Club of California; Stebbins made enormous contributions to educational institutions. The College of California graduated its first class in 1864. He was soon active as a member of the board of trustees and later president. This became the foundation for the University of California, which was eventually moved to Berkeley, and Stebbins became a regent for 26 consecutive years. He also became involved with Stanford University after its founding and served on its board of trustees. Stebbins was part of a committee to investigate the establishment of a training school for ministers in Berkeley, but he withdrew when he felt the **American Unitarian Association (AUA)** had to fulfill its commitment to help Meadville Theological School first, and that the Pacific Coast Conference was too small to take on such a large project. By the late 1890s his health became precarious. He finally resigned and was made minister emeritus in 1900, ending an active ministry of more than 35 years. He moved back to New England to be near his son Roderick, who was minister in Milton, Massachusetts, and his other children, Horatio and Lucy, who were studying in Massachusetts as students at Massachusetts Institute of Technology (MIT) and Radcliffe respectively. Stebbins set up home in Cambridge. Never the famed orator that Thomas Starr King was, Stebbins made his presence known by devotion to duty and hard work. The writer Samuel Clemens once said of him, "Stebbins is a regular brick." Stebbins once said of his life as a minister, "I would walk with anybody, and supplement my experience by his, and increase the breadth of my knowledge, and learn to know how little I know, yet standing firm as a rock in the eternal verities of moral and spiritual being" (as quoted in Crompton, *Unitarianism*, p. 161). He died on April 8, 1902, and was buried in Portland, Maine.

SULLIVAN, WILLIAM LAURENCE (1872–1935). The Roman Catholic priest who converted to Unitarianism and became a renowned preacher. Sullivan was born in East Braintree, Massachusetts, on November 15, 1872, the son of Patrick and Joanna Sullivan, who had come from Ireland the year before. Sullivan was a good student who loved books and sports. His father died when he was 14. He graduated from Quincy High School, went on to Boston College, and then to St. John's Seminary in Brighton, Massachusetts. Then he moved on to Catholic University of America, where he earned an S.T.B. and an S.T.L. Sullivan had longed to be a priest since childhood, and he was ordained a Paulist in 1899. He was an outstanding scholar who was steeped in the classics, and he became a professor at St. Thomas's College. During this time he became interested in Modernism. This was to prove his undoing as a Catholic, especially after Pope Pius X condemned Modernism in an encyclical in 1907. At this time Sullivan was a priest of a Paulist church in Austin, Texas. He was threatened with excommunication if he did not submit and ultimately decided he had to leave the church.

Sullivan lived in Kansas City for two years, wondering where his future lay. After he moved to Cleveland, he discovered the Unitarian church there and its pastor, Minot Simons. He went to New York and taught at an Ethical Culture school and then decided to become a Unitarian minister in 1912. Sullivan was called to the new Church of All Souls in Schenectady, New York, that year. Soon thereafter he published *Letters to His Holiness Pope Pius X*, in which he condemned the Vatican. He also began to build a reputation as a preacher and moved on to be associate minister at All Souls Church in New York City, traveling back and forth to continue ministering in Schenectady at first. In 1915 he became the senior minister at All Souls. He spent a period as a mission preacher for the **American Unitarian Association (AUA)** on the West Coast when he was at All Souls. This role as missionary preacher became his job in 1922 when he worked under the auspices of the **Unitarian Laymen's League**. From 1924 to 1928 he served the Church of the Messiah in St. Louis. Sullivan taught summer school at **Meadville Theological School** and also became a popular lecturer. Although he intended to write more, he finally took another parish, the Unitarian Society in Germantown, Pennsylvania, from 1929 to 1935, where he died while still active on October 5, 1935. His prime reputation was as a preacher, lecturer, and retreat leader both inside and outside Unitarian circles, but he still managed to publish some writings during his lifetime, especially ones in response to Catholicism. His most famous work was his autobiography, *Under Orders: The Autobiography of William Laurence Sullivan* (1944). He also reviewed books for the *New York Herald*

Tribune. Sullivan was known as an ardent theist and defender of Unitarian Christianity who felt that humanists were really atheists who were afraid to use the word.

SUNDAY SCHOOL SOCIETY. The Boston Sunday School Society was formed on April 18, 1827, with the Rev. Joseph Tuckerman as its first president. The earliest Unitarian Sunday School in Boston had been formed in 1822 at the West Church (the church in Beverly, Massachusetts, is considered the first Unitarian Sunday School, founded in 1810). By 1828 there were nine schools in the city and 30 more outside Boston with more than 3,700 students and 640 teachers. Initially an organization of teachers who wanted "to increase the number and usefulness of these nurseries of piety, the society met to consider the best ways to teach, to determine how to bring needy students into the schools, and to reprint and write materials for use in the schools. The educational philosophy of the Unitarians was profoundly influenced by an address given before the society in 1837 by **William Ellery Channing**. Still quoted today, Channing said, in part, "The great end in religious instruction, whether in the Sunday school or family, is, not to stamp our minds irresistibly on the young, but to stir up their own; not to make them see with our eyes, but to look inquiringly and steadily with their own." Channing wanted to awaken the moral conscience in each child rather than "impose religion upon them." He felt that the great danger was that the schools would fall into a course of mechanical teaching, imparting religion as a lifeless tradition. By 1850, 236 Sunday Schools belonged to the society. These schools became an important component in the extension of the liberal faith. In 1850 one church reported: "In the west, Sabbath schools are of peculiar value. For establishing of a religious society, one of the most efficient means, if not the most important move, would be to establish a Sunday School. People will pay for this who will pay for nothing else." Since 1827 several regional societies had been formed. To promote unified action by these local organizations, the society became a general denominational group in 1854. Many of these smaller groups published weekly or monthly magazines. The most successful of these was the *Sunday School Gazette*, which was first published by the Worcester Society. The society also published teacher's guides and held training institutes. Concerns for how best to develop a successful school centered on the recruitment of teachers, regular teachers meetings, parent interest, involvement of the minister, and a system of teaching Christian doctrines that was not overly mechanical.

In 1868 the society changed its name to the Unitarian Sunday School Society. It was about this time that graded lessons began to appear. In 1873 a Western Unitarian Sunday School Society was founded under the leadership of **Jenkin Lloyd Jones**. He was concerned about the character development of children, and he found the materials from Boston too formal and doctrinal. The year before he had started publishing a monthly lesson plan, *The Sunday School*. The general society passed a resolution in 1891 to the end that children may grow up to "become intelligent workers in our Unitarian churches." The year before, **Minot Savage**'s *Unitarian Catechism* was published. This has always been a debated issue in the liberal church, whether to indoctrinate our children to the faith. Channing had warned of binding children "by ineradicable prejudices to our particular sect." Sunday School walls at this time were frequently adorned with printed copies of **James Freeman Clarke**'s statement of "Our Faith": The Fatherhood of God, the Brotherhood of Man, the leadership of Jesus, salvation by character, the progress of mankind onward and upward forever.

By 1920 Sunday Schools had begun to use multimedia devices with the introduction of motion pictures. There was also an increased use of drama and music in the curricula. Choir festivals were held and in 1935 a hugely successful children's hymnal, *The Beacon Song and Service Book*, was published. In 1902 the society president Edward Horton wrote that the word Sunday School was becoming inadequate, and true to his prophecy, by 1925, "church school" began to come into vogue. The main speaker before the society in 1902 was **Julia Ward Howe**, whose subject was, "Problems to Be Considered in the Religious Education of the Young." Howe wrote that the great themes of faith, hope, and love could be presented now that they are "freed from the clouds which once obscured them." From its beginning in 1827 this independent society worked to advise and promote religious education among Unitarians, but its resources were limited. In 1912 the president William I. Lawrence was made secretary of a newly created Department of Religious Education of the **American**

Unitarian Association (AUA). After this the execution of the society's program was part of the AUA and they were completely merged by 1937. The society maintains a separate legal identity today and holds annual meetings with programs. Lawrence engineered this transition to one central education office between 1910 and 1925, always promoting his declaration that "the strength of any church is in the Sunday school." His work was complemented by that of Florence Buck, who edited a magazine, *The Beacon*, which was distributed after Sunday classes. She also edited a hymnal, wrote textbooks, and promoted the training of teachers. This society was responsible for the foundations of the liberal religious education program and with the aim of building good character in young people, created a denomination-wide network of materials and methods. *See also* RELIGIOUS EDUCATION.

SUNDERLAND, JABEZ THOMAS (1842–1936). A leader in the **Western Unitarian Conference (WUC)** who preferred to organize churches on the basis of Christian theism rather than a broader-based freedom, was also an important figure in promoting worldwide religious understanding. Sunderland was born in Yorkshire, England, on February 11, 1842. His family moved to the United States when he was a young child. He was educated at the University of Chicago, where he received a B.A. (1867) and an M.A. (1869). After that he received a B.D. from the Baptist Theological Union (Chicago) and briefly served two Baptist churches in Omaha, Nebraska, and Milwaukee, Wisconsin. He became a convert to Unitarianism at this point in his career, served a four-year ministry in Northfield, Massachusetts, and then served for two years at Fourth Unitarian Church in Chicago. At this point he became minister in Ann Arbor, Michigan, where he had a 20-year successful ministry (1878–1898). From the beginning in Ann Arbor, Sunderland was also the **American Unitarian Association (AUA)** state missionary for Michigan, and he helped found eight congregations there. His wife, Eliza, was also active in religious work. Sunderland was also an editorial contributor to ***Unity***, but came into conflict with **Jenkin Lloyd Jones**, the WUC secretary who wanted to incorporate the WUC in 1882 with objectives that sounded like the "freedom and fellowship" that were part of the motto of the radical Free Religious Association (FRA). Sunderland wanted to specify a connection to Christianity and began to work closely with Unitarian missionary Jasper L. Douthit, fearing that Jones and others were scheming to change the WUC to a branch of the FRA. Early in 1886, shortly after he had become secretary of the WUC, Sunderland's efforts to publish an alternative journal to *Unity* were rewarded with the publication of the *Unitarian*, of which he was coeditor. Later that year Sunderland published a controversial pamphlet, the ***Issue in the West***, which was mailed to all ministers and congregations and then distributed at the annual meeting of the WUC. Sunderland said this group of Unity men headed by Jones wanted to remove Unitarianism from its historic Christian and Theistic base to "Free or Ethical Religion."

In June Sunderland resigned from his post as secretary of the WUC and helped to form a rival conference, the Western Unitarian Association, which promised more cooperation with the AUA. The controversy raged during the following year when **William Channing Gannett**'s *Things Commonly Believed among Us* appeared. This finally helped bring reconciliation to the WUC in 1894 at a meeting in Saratoga, New York. In 1895 Sunderland resigned as editor of the *Unitarian* because he felt that the action at Saratoga had placed the denomination "unequivocally on the Christian basis." Shortly after this he took a leave of absence from his church in Ann Arbor. When he was in England, the British Unitarians asked Sunderland to spend a portion of his year off in India inspecting the conditions of the **Brahmo Samaj** movement. He had corresponded previously with Unitarians in the Khasi Hills and that fall he prepared for the trip. In addition to meeting with various groups and lecturing, Sunderland had the opportunity to attend meetings of the Indian National Congress at Poona. He was the first American to attend and speak at these sessions. The most satisfying of all was the trip to the Khasi Hills, where Sunderland is remembered to this day as a patron saint. He returned to England with proposals for a program that eventually helped revitalize the Brahmo Samaj movement. He had followed up the World Parliament of Religions in 1893 with an interchange that showed how worldwide religious cooperation could be achieved.

Sunderland continued to serve in the ministry, but India became his life's passion. He served briefly in Oakland, California, was in London for a year, and then was called to Toronto, Ontario, where he served for four years. After that he was in Hartford, Connecticut, and Ottawa, Ontario. All this time he lectured regularly on Indian religions and the Brahmo Samaj. In 1908 he published a significant article in the *Atlantic Monthly*, "The New Nationalist Movement in India." Sunderland's attack on British rule was the first indictment before a wide American audience. During the next 20 years, Sunderland found a new career as a spokesperson for Indian independence. He worked with nationalists in exile, published books, and supported freedom in any way he could. In 1913 he was appointed a Billings Lecturer for the AUA. Previous to this he had published an AUA pamphlet, "The World Mission of the Unitarian Faith," in which he said that the principles of Unitarianism were world principles and that it was a faith calculated for humanity as a whole. Sunderland was able to return to India on a tour that started in Japan. After he came back to America, Sunderland moved to New York City and commuted to a new church placement in Poughkeepsie, New York. He was there from 1914 to 1928, retiring when he was 86. He retired to Ann Arbor, where he died on August 13, 1936. One of the highlights of his later years was the publication of *India in Bondage* (1929), a book calling for India's right to freedom that was immediately suppressed in India. The book won Sunderland some degree of fame, including an article in *Time* magazine. Sunderland's efforts to support independence and freedom in India have continued to be an important component of relationships between American and Indians through the interchange between liberal religious movements and Unitarian Universalist funded programs that exist there to promote greater economic and social justice.

SUPERNATURAL RATIONALISM. A term applied to a certain group of theologians and ministers, including those who followed Arminian and later Unitarian tenets in the 18th and early 19th centuries. A supernatural rationalist affirmed both natural religion and revealed religion. Like the deists, they posited a God who created a uniform and orderly universe, and they accepted that revealed religions were based upon historical evidence and logical analysis. But they parted company with their rationalist compatriots on other issues. Accepting revealed religion, the supernatural rationalists said that doctrines could be above reason, but not contrary to it, and these doctrines included the miracles, for which they assumed historical evidence. Both supernatural rationalists and deists rejected claims of authority for Christianity based on religious experience, or tradition or the authority of the church. But the supernatural rationalists frequently found themselves making a rational defense of Christianity in opposition to the deists. In fact many Calvinists and Unitarians held supernatural rationalism in common as a basis for revelation but differed on the content of that revelation. In 1821 **William Ellery Channing** delivered "Evidences of Revealed Religion," stating, "To a man whose belief in God is strong and practical, a miracle will appear as possible as any other effect, as the most common event in life; and the argument against miracles, drawn from the uniformity of nature, will weigh with him only as far as this uniformity is a pledge and proof of the Creator's disposition to accomplish his purposes by a fixed order or mode of operation." For the supernatural rationalists, natural religion was not enough to discover the essential doctrines of religion but had to be supplemented by those doctrines that came through divine revelation.

SWEDEN. In the mid-19th century, Unitarianism was introduced by the author Viktor Rydberg, who was influenced by Theodore Parker. In 1929 the Unitarian organization Sveriges Religiosa Reformforbund was formed by Emanual Linderhold of Uppsala. In 1976 a fellowship was established in Malmo, Sweden, as an outpost to Det Fri Kirkesamfund in Denmark. The first Swedish Unitarian minister, Ragnar Emilsen, was ordained in 1987 at a service conducted by Bishop Lajos Kovacs of Romania. Thereafter the fellowship was declared independent of the Danish church and it took the name Fria Kyrkan i Sverige (The Free Church of Sweden). The fellowship has about 500 members. Emilsen also serves as bishop of the Free Church of Sweden and Norway.

– T –

TAFT, WILLIAM HOWARD (1857–1930). The 27th president of the United States, and the 10th chief justice of the Supreme Court, was also an active Unitarian lay person. Taft was born on September 15,

1857 in Cincinnati, Ohio. His family was affiliated with the First Unitarian Church in Cincinnati, founded in 1830, where there is a memorial to Taft. Taft's father Alphonso had rejected his Baptist faith to become Unitarian, and young Will attended Sunday School there. He was educated at Yale University (1878), and then returned home for the Cincinnati Law School. He also married a hometown girl in 1886, Helen W. Herron. After a brief legal career, he was appointed to the Ohio Superior Court in 1887. From 1892 to 1900 he served as a circuit judge of the Sixth Federal Circuit Court. In 1899 when it was thought he might be offered the position of president of Yale, Taft said that religion was one of the things which stood in his way. In a letter to his brother Henry he stated that he was a Unitarian, and although he believed in God, he did not believe in the divinity of Christ. He said that he thought religion had had an "elevating influence" in history.

In 1900 President William McKinley appointed Taft to head up a commission to end military rule in the Philippines. Soon thereafter he became governor general of the Philippines and proved an able administrator. During this time he was named honorary president of the Independent Church of the Philippines, which was formed from disaffected Catholics. His fine work in the Philippines brought him to the attention of President Theodore Roosevelt, who made him secretary of war in 1904. They became close friends, and by 1906 he was Roosevelt's hand-picked successor. Although he was reluctant Taft became the candidate and defeated William Jennings Bryan in 1908 saying he would continue all of Roosevelt's policies. During this campaign on the Republican ticket, his liberal faith surfaced after he received countless letters saying that a Unitarian atheist should not be allowed to occupy the White House. One paper accused him of looking upon the Savior as a "common bastard and low, cunning impostor."

Taft had a difficult term as president because he could not fulfill Roosevelt's dream of progressive reform. Some have said that Taft was ill suited for the hard work of the presidency. As a boy he had loved dancing, and this affable man was more inclined toward a life of fun and ease rather than intense labor and conflict. He loved to play golf and was most famous of all for his large size. Although many antitrust cases were settled during his presidency, and the income tax was established, Taft ran into conflict over several issues. Conservation issues became especially heated after Taft fired Gifford Pinchot, the symbol of Roosevelt's conservation policies. Taft was conservative by nature—ended up supporting capital over labor time and again and feared the progressives wanted to overturn the social order. Eventually, Roosevelt challenged Taft for the nomination of the Republican Party and ended up creating the Bull Moose Party. In the 1912 election Taft finished third. When he was president he appointed Unitarian President **Samuel Atkins Eliot** to the U.S. Board of Indian Commissioners.

After his term as U.S. president, Taft became president of the General Conference of Unitarian and other Christian Churches from 1915 to 1925, at which time the General Conference was absorbed by the **American Unitarian Association (AUA)**. In 1917 he was drawn into controversy over World War I. In his capacity as moderator of the proceedings, Taft gave an opening address. He called upon the conference to affirm President Woodrow Wilson's conduct of the war, only to be followed by **John Haynes Holmes**'s speech criticizing the war effort. In the fiery debate that followed, Taft called for and received a positive vote on a resolution to continue the campaigns and win the war. There was concern that some ministers were creating discord in their parishes; Taft affirmed this with his own role at his home church in helping to oust the pacifist minister. Taft was appointed chief justice in 1921 by President Warren G. Harding. When he became ill in 1930 he had to resign, and then died on March 8, 1930.

TEMPLE SCHOOL. With a long-term interest in educational reform and a commitment to opening experimental schools in his background, **Bronson Alcott**'s most famous school opened at the Masonic Hall in 1834 with 30 children enrolled. He had two prominent assistants: **Margaret Fuller**, who taught languages, and **Elizabeth Peabody**, who taught geography. Alcott had absorbed many of the techniques of the famous Swiss educator Henry Pestalozzi. These included encouraging his older students to keep a journal, in which they would write down their ideas each day. Alcott read stories and recited poems and then everyone would discuss them. He was also aware of children's physical needs to play and allowed for long exercise periods. The school had a "common conscience" so that punishments for bad behavior were determined by general consent. Alcott often conducted conversations using the Socratic Method to draw the children out. A series of conversations on the New Testament transcribed by Peabody was very controversial when it was published, *Record of Conversations on the Gospel* (1836–37, 2 volumes). There were a number of newspaper attacks on the book and its scandalous content. Enrollment soon declined as a result of the bad publicity. Alcott was forced to move the school first to the basement of the temple and then to his home in Boston. Things became worse when he allowed a black girl to enroll—all remaining students other than his daughters withdrew. The school was forced to close in 1838. Alcott's vision for transforming society through the classroom was transformed to a dream of a utopia society. After the school closed he traveled to England to visit the Alcott House, which was modeled on the Temple School. There he met Charles Lane and they soon began to formulate plans for the development of Alcott's next experiment, **Fruitlands**.

THAYER, THOMAS BALDWIN (1812–1886). The leading Universalist theologian in the late 19th century. Thayer was born in Boston on September 10, 1812. He had little formal education and began preaching Universalism in 1831. From 1833 to 1845 he was minister at the First Universalist Society in Lowell, Massachusetts. During this time he worked with Abel Thomas to establish Improvement Circles for girls who worked in the Lowell mills. When he was editor of the periodical *Star of Bethlehem* near the end of his ministry, he included some of their work in the publication. After Lowell he served as pastor at a Universalist church in Brooklyn, New York, and then returned to Lowell to again serve First Universalist from 1851 to 1859. Thayer moved on to the Shawmut Avenue Universalist Church in Boston and began editing the *Universalist Quarterly* while he was there. His great work was *The Theology of Universalism* (1862). It was widely read and relied primarily upon biblical foundations to support Universalist truths. It was described as "Being a Scriptural Exhibition of Its Doctrines and Teachings, in Their Logical Connections and Moral Relations." He said that evil is a school, and humans did not need to change their nature but the direction of their lives. Jesus was an example of the perfection that can be realized, and the example of Jesus can effect that change in humans.

Thayer edited the *Universalist Quarterly* for more than 20 years, (1864–86) and was a frequent contributor as well. Thayer believed the truths of science would not contradict the truths of the Bible, and so he was generally positive about the contributions science could make to religion. In 1881 in a review on missions he called into question why his own denomination had no presence in foreign countries. He pushed this issue for some time, and eventually the Japanese mission became a reality. Richard Eddy came as Thayer's assistant editor in 1885 and succeeded him the following year when Thayer died on February 12, 1886. Thayer was an important Universalist intellectual leader who tried to provide Universalism with a unified system of divinity.

THINGS MOST COMMONLY BELIEVED TODAY AMONG US. A statement of faith written by **William Channing Gannett** in response to a raging controversy over the theological basis for Unitarian churches. Gannett's proposal for doctrinal compromise came at the 1887 meeting of the **Western Unitarian Conference (WUC)** in Chicago, when his statement was adopted by a vote of 59 to 13. The controversy came to a head the previous year when **Jabez Sunderland** published the controversial pamphlet the ***Issue in the West***. The debate raged over the question of whether or not Western Unitarianism was to be grounded in Christian theism or a broader-based freedom advocated by **Jenkin Lloyd Jones** and Gannett. At the 1886 conference, Gannett introduced resolutions to appoint a committee to create a statement of "the things most commonly believed today among us." Although this was defeated, the conference passed a resolution stating that no dogmatic tests would be used as conditions of fellowship. These attempts at reconciliation did not prevent Sunderland from resigning his position as secretary and then help create a rival, the Western Unitarian Association, in June.

The **American Unitarian Association (AUA)** in Boston vowed it would not assist any group that did not rest on a Christian basis. Gannett wanted to respect the freedom of belief for both groups stating that the conference did not wish to bind anyone to declarations of faith. In its final form the statement *The Things Most Commonly Believed Today among Us* tried to articulate simple truths that a majority could agree upon. These included such ideas as "reason and conscience as the final authorities in matters of belief," the "nobility of Man," and an "unfolding, beneficent order to the universe" (Parke, ed. *Epic of Unitarianism*, pp. 130–131). Unfortunately, the passage of Gannett's statement did not heal the rift. This finally occurred in 1894 when its spirit of compromise provided the basis for unity. A new preamble stating the purposes of the **National Conference** was adopted unanimously at Saratoga, New York. After 50 years of division, unity was finally achieved

THOREAU, HENRY DAVID (1817–1862). The great Transcendentalist writer and naturalist born in Concord, Massachusetts, on July 12, 1817, the third child of four. Thoreau was a man of simple means and needs who lived the Transcendentalist vision of experiencing the immediacy of the world. He spent most of his life around Concord variously employed in surveying, lecturing, writing, and pencil making. Henry was a scholarship student at **Harvard College**, noticeably embarrassed in his green homemade suit, but he graduated with honors in 1837. He became a school teacher in Concord, but when he refused to flog the students, he decided to resign. After that he teamed up with his brother running a school. It was a progressive environment where students learned by doing and frequently went on field trips. Walking in the woods and picking the flowers prepared Thoreau for his complete embrace of Transcendentalism, as he found the great truths of the universe in nature. The school had to close after John became sick.

After 1837 Thoreau drew much inspiration and support from his friendship with **Ralph Waldo Emerson**. He tutored the Emerson children and was a handyman around the house. The attacks on Emerson after the "**Divinity School Address**" drew Henry closer to him, for Henry identified with being criticized by the Boston establishment. By 1840 Emerson wanted to see some of Thoreau's writing published in the ***Dial***. It was eventually, and Thoreau even edited the April 1843 issue. Emerson also invited Henry to a meeting of the **Transcendental Club** in 1840 for a session that was discussing the meaning of poetry. This was an important event in Henry's life because it affirmed him intellectually by making him part of this larger school of thought. Both Emerson and Thoreau read texts from world religions other than Christianity introducing them to America and starting a religious pluralism that would later be common in Unitarianism. Thoreau delved deeply into Hinduism and was familiar with the writings of **Rammohun Roy**. Thoreau may have experienced Transcendentalism more than any other member of the movement. He knew mystical experiences of sensing a oneness with nature that to Emerson were mere ideas or concepts. Thoreau twice lived at the Emerson home when they went abroad. His friend also acquired the land, where Thoreau built the cabin later immortalized in Walden (1854). Thoreau also went on frequent hiking and canoeing trips that were documented in *A Week on the Concord and Merrimack Rivers* (1849).

Although Thoreau's thought is often remembered in the context of the solitary man in nature, he also envisioned the creation of a just society. His nonviolent radicalism is seen in the night he spent in jail for refusal to pay his poll tax in protest of the Mexican War and in his great essays *Slavery in Massachusetts* (1854) and *Civil Disobedience* (1849), which later was an inspiration to both Tolstoy and Gandhi. Here he said: "Under a government which imprisons any unjustly, the true place for a just man is also prison" (Albanese, *Spirituality*, p. 284). These essays were followed by *A Plea for John Brown* (1859), whom Thoreau first met in 1857. Together the essays reveal Thoreau as the only Transcendentalist with a thorough antislavery program. He believed that government was subject to higher laws and when the government is an accomplice to slavery, then, morally, it must be resisted. For many years Henry was involved on and off in his father's pencil making business, which he took over after his father died. The graphite dust probably worsened his tendency toward tuberculosis, which claimed Henry's life on May 6, 1862. Thoreau's sister wondered if it was appropriate for Thoreau's funeral to be held in the church since Henry adamantly refused to join, but Emerson insisted. The families gathered on May 9 at the First Parish Church in Concord to hear Emerson eulogize his great friend. "The country knows not yet . . . how great a son it has lost. . . . [H]is soul was made for the noblest society, he had in a short life exhausted the capabilities of this world; wherever there is knowledge, wherever there is virtue, wherever there is beauty, he will find a home" (Smith, *My Friend*, p. 183).

THROOP UNIVERSITY. In 1861 the Universalist National Convention, acting on a recommendation from the California State Convention, reported favorably on the idea of establishing a combination college and theological school to serve Universalists on the West Coast. Although nothing happened at that time, part of the plan bore fruit when a wealthy Universalist businessman, Amos G. Throop, presented the idea of forming a school in the city of Pasadena. Throop had been a large donor to Universalist causes, including a professorship of theology at Lombard. Throop donated $200,000 and a site to start Throop University, and it opened in 1891. The school was a combination college and technical school. By 1892 there were 175 students at what was now called Throop Polytechnic Institute. Throop died in 1894, but the school continued to carry his name until 1920, when it adopted its current name, The California Institute of Technology. Although the original board was made up entirely of Universalists, the school never had much of a direct link to the denomination. Throop's hope for training ministerial students on the West Coast did not materialize in his lifetime, but the Pacific Unitarian School of the Ministry (later **Starr King School**) was established 10 years after his death.

TRANSCENDENTAL CLUB. A group of Transcendentalists who met for the first time at Willard's Hotel in Cambridge on the day before the publication of **Ralph Waldo Emerson**'s *Nature*, September 8, 1836. This first gathering brought together **Frederic Henry Hedge**, **George Putnam**, **George Ripley**, and Emerson as a way to protest the unsatisfactory state of American thought and letters. Purporting to represent "deeper and broader views," they were rebelling against what they perceived as the rigid conservatism of Harvard. After the first meeting, they never met in Cambridge again. After this initial meeting, the group met again 11 days later with a contingency of 10 and thereafter usually numbered this many, sometimes more. The group began to meet at a time when many of the members were first being published and the club became a forum for new ideas and open conversation.

The club was the brain child of Hedge. Because it often met when he could make the trip to Boston from Bangor, Maine, it was known as Hedge's Club. Emerson was the leading spirit, but the group also included **Orestes Brownson**, George Ripley, **Theodore Parker**, and its elder statesman, **Convers Francis**, who was chosen moderator, for his diplomatic skills. A year after its founding, Emerson induced the group to invite women to its meetings, with **Margaret Fuller**, Sarah Ripley, and Elizabeth Hoar the first to attend. The meetings usually focused on a single topic such as "Education of Humanity," "Pantheism," and "What is the essence of Religion as distinct from morality?" The group met five or six times a year over the succeeding four years for a total of about 30 meetings. Membership was open to any who wished to attend with more than 30 different men and women taking part, some, like **William Ellery Channing**, only once. The group consisted of the leading liberal intellectuals who generally held a common dissatisfaction with the religious thought of the times while affirming Kantian idealism and romanticism. The club and the magazine the *Dial* were the only two institutional expressions of Transcendentalism, which was not conducive to collective expression but taught that the religious spirit does not reside in eternal forms. Even the two entities could not exist simultaneously. The club stopped meeting in 1840, the year the *Dial* was founded.

TRANSCENDENTALISM. Transcendentalism was primarily a religious movement that developed as part of a rebellion against the liberal Christian Unitarians whose faith derived from rational biblical criticism and historical tradition. Transcendentalism was more a spiritual approach to life than a systematic philosophy. Its practitioners hungered for a religious intensity lacking in their experiences of a cold, formal Unitarianism. Transcendentalism was part of a larger Romantic movement that engulfed Europe and America in the late 18th century. Rejecting the dry rationalism of the Age of Reason, Transcendentalism evoked an immediate and emotional response to life. Its name derives from Immanuel Kant's *Critique of Practical Reason*, in which he calls all knowledge Transcendental. Echoing Kant's concern for how we come to know things, the Transcendentalists rejected John Locke's "sensationalism" and argued in favor of intuition and direct inspiration. The Transcendentalists believed that every person could experience the divine personally and immediately.

Transcendentalism had many sources. In 1837 **Ralph Waldo Emerson** said the differences between **William Ellery Channing** and the Transcendentalists required amputation, but Channing's emphasis upon the dignity of human nature and the indwelling God significantly influenced this second generation of Unitarians. They did not reject the religion but rebelled against some of its forms, thereby transforming the faith. In "Likeness to God" Channing had posited that the idea of God comes from our souls—a theory embraced by Transcendentalists. The Transcendentalists also borrowed the idea of self-culture, or the progressive quality of human nature, from their Unitarian progenitors. The rationalism of their Unitarian parents was the primary cause of their revolt, which was not against all tradition. In fact, the Transcendentalists found inspiration in earlier New England ancestors such as Jonathan Edwards and Puritan mystics who seemed to experience the divine more directly. The Puritans had also favored the Platonic system where an analogy was made between the material world and the spiritual realm. German philosophers, such as Johann Goethe and Frederic Schleiermacher, helped give Transcendentalism its mystical bent. The poetry and criticism of those English writers whom the Germans had a special influence upon included William Wordsworth, Samuel Taylor Coleridge, and Thomas Carlyle, whom Emerson met when touring Europe. The Transcendentalists were among the first to read scriptures from religions that were non-Christian and included the Bhagavadgita, the Upanishads, the Koran, certain Buddhist writings, and the teachings of Confucius, among their influences.

Despite its geographical confines to greater Boston and especially Concord, Massachusetts, and the Unitarian orientation of most of its adherents, Transcendentalism was not an organized party. Many Transcendentalists who were ministers continued to serve Unitarian congregations despite their radical religious leanings. The Transcendental Club, organized in 1836, provided a regular schedule of meetings for the group, and both their local publication, the ***Dial***, and its transplanted incarnation, the *Western Messenger*, gave a voice to their religious longings, but they were largely anti-institutional. **Margaret Fuller** also gathered people together for "Conversations." Rather than forming a new sect or organizing churches, the Transcendentalists wanted to experience truth directly and become students of God, especially through nature.

The beginnings of the Transcendentalist revolt are sometimes dated to 1832 when Emerson resigned his ministry at the Second Church of Boston ostensibly over the congregation's request that he continue to administer what he considered an outmoded meaningless ritual, the Lord's Supper. Emerson published the chief manifesto of the movement in 1836 with *Nature*, in which he wrote, "Why should we not also enjoy an original relation to the universe? Why should we not have a poetry and philosophy of insight and not tradition, and a religion by revelation to us, and not the history of theirs?" (R. W. Emerson, *Works*, I, p. 3). That same year **George Ripley** wrote an article in the *Christian Examiner* on the miracles of Christ. **Andrews Norton** countered with an essay in the *Boston Daily Advertiser*, and the **Miracles Controversy** ensued. In 1838 Emerson's "Divinity School Address" suggested that all of life is a miracle and that miracles as defined by the Christian church were "monster." Representing the traditional voice of Unitarianism, Norton responded to Emerson with his pamphlet *The Latest Form of Infidelity*. Ripley, who would resign his pastorate three years later to found the community at Brook Farm, defended the Transcendentalist view with *The Latest Form of Infidelity Examined*. During the 1840s **Henry David Thoreau** built his cabin at Walden and Margaret Fuller went to Rome and took part in a revolution. With Fuller's death in a shipwreck in 1850 and Thoreau's premature demise in 1862, the movement lost two of its greatest voices, but Emerson and others continued to write and publish for another 20 years thereafter.

Transcendentalism also had a strong social component. This was reflected in two famous utopian experiments at **Brook Farm** and **Fruitlands** and also in most of the important reform movements of the day. Transcendentalists like **Theodore Parker** and **Orestes Brownson** saw the main promise of Transcendentalism in social terms and wanted to remake the world itself rather than just their perception of it, as was true of some of the Transcendentalist poets. The particular reform movements that many of the Transcendentalists were active in included defenses of the working class by Brownson, the equality and rights of women by Fuller, the abolition of slavery by Parker, Thoreau's defense of civil disobedience, which later inspired Mohandas K. Gandhi and Martin Luther King Jr., and **Bronson Alcott**'s radical education reforms. The Transcendentalists made a strong demand for personal integrity and believed a social revolution could take place when every person makes his/her own life consistent with principle. The Transcendentalists believed in the redemptive power of humanity, and thus the ambiguity of human choices and politics was sometimes lost on them. Their vision of the world remained forever hopeful.

TRANSIENT AND PERMANENT IN CHRISTIANITY. Often considered one of the three great sermons in Unitarian history, "The Transient and Permanent in Christianity" was delivered by **Theodore Parker** at the ordination of Charles C. Shackford in the Hawes Place Church, South Boston, Massachusetts, on May 19, 1841. It is not clear why Parker was chosen to preach on this occasion. Shackford was not a close friend of Parker's, nor was the council prior to the ordination a Transcendentalist gathering. In fact, Shackford's training had chiefly come at Andover seminary and not the Harvard Divinity School. This meant there were non-Unitarians present. The content of the sermon produced a denominational firestorm, but this was not apparent at the end of the evening after Parker received the customary expressions of gratitude. The controversy was precipitated by the non-Unitarians who summarized the content of Parker's sermon as anti-Christian and submitted it to several orthodox papers. This was the perfect opportunity to discredit the Unitarians. Parker was a minister in good standing and generally well liked, but some of his colleagues found that preaching this kind of sermon for a ceremonial occasion was inappropriate.

The crux of the matter centered on his relationship with the Boston Association of Ministers. They asked to meet with Parker in January 1843. At this meeting Nathaniel Frothingham of the First Church of Boston stated that he did not want to have ministerial relationships with Parker because he denied the miracles. Chandler Robbins said Parker should withdraw from the association. Parker replied that the principle of free inquiry was at stake, and he would not resign. The colleagues were philosophically unable to apply a doctrinal test for membership because it would have violated their own principle of free inquiry. While many would have wished that Parker resign, they spoke instead of his integrity, and Parker left the room in tears. Although he would not technically resign, he was personally ostracized by most of his colleagues who continued to refuse to exchange pulpits with him.

The controversy made Parker famous. Soon he would move on from the small parish he served in Roxbury at the time of this sermon to preach before thousands in Boston. The sermon drew inspiration from German biblical critic David Strauss, who wrote an article in 1838 called "On Transiency and Permanency in Christianity." Parker's theology had evolved from where he once accepted the Christian miracles to the point where he questioned them all and even considered the resurrection a myth. In the sermon he makes the point that the doctrine and forms of the church are transient in nature. Among the transient doctrines that he felt had changed over time were the authority of the Bible and the personal authority of Jesus, but the words of Jesus were part of the permanent. He described the religion of Jesus as: "Absolute, pure morality; absolute, pure religion." Unlike the deists who mostly relied upon the natural religion embodied in **John Locke**'s sensationalist philosophy, Parker followed an intuitionalist philosophy where absolute religion such as love for God and humankind was perceived by instinct. In this address Parker affirmed the liberal principle that new truths can continually be revealed and challenged his colleagues to reaffirm their belief in the spirit of free inquiry.

TRANSYLVANIA. The first Unitarian sermon in Transylvania was given by **Francis David** in January 1566. He had been undergoing significant theological changes and had been observed by the court physician to Queen Isabella, **Giorgio Biandrata**, who brought anti-Trinitarian thinking from **Poland** in 1563. Religious debates on the Trinity were held at Gyulafehervar and Torda in 1566. Further debates occurred in 1568, culminating when David convinced the Diet at Torda in 1568 to accept full toleration for four churches, including Unitarian. David became bishop of the newly organized Unitarian church. After a debate at Nagyvarad, most of the royal court, including the king, had been won over to Unitarianism and then in 1571 Unitarianism won complete legal recognition as one of four received faiths, along with Catholicism, Reformed, and Lutheran. The timing was fortunate for the Unitarians, as King **John Sigismund**, the only Unitarian king in history, died soon thereafter. Although David had to step down as court preacher and no new innovations were allowed under King John's successors, the movement flourished for a few more years. Unfortunately, David and Biandrata began to disagree when David argued that since Christ was not God he should not be worshipped. Biandrata feared that David would be accused of innovation, and **Faustus Socinus** was brought in to mediate. The case was not resolved; Biandrata's fears proved true when David was arrested and Biandrata had to prosecute as counsel to the prince. David was found guilty and sentenced to life imprisonment at the castle at Deva. Already ill, he died soon thereafter.

At the time of David's death, there were nearly 500 Unitarian congregations in Transylvania, but preserving that heritage over the centuries has been difficult. At first there was resentment toward their fellow Unitarians who did not support David, especially Biandrata who some saw as a traitor. Initially the church survived under the conciliatory leadership of the new bishop, Demetrius Hunyadi, but things worsened soon after his death. Persecution under a Catholic regime began when Prince Sigismund arrested several Unitarians and beheaded them for conspiracy in 1594. A revolt took place in 1602 led by Mozes Szekely, but after some success, he was killed. After this the repressions were led by Calvinist princes. In 1638 the Accord of Dees mandated Unitarian beliefs under penalty of persecution. The Unitarians were compelled to worship Christ, baptize in the name of the Trinity, and submit all publications for approval. Most important, they could not introduce any innovations. This was the first time the word "Unitarian" was used as the recognized name for the anti-Trinitarians. By the early 18th century, when Transylvania was part of the Austro-Hungarian Empire, there had been a resurgence of Catholicism that took over many Unitarian properties, including the school and publishing house in Kolosvar. The main church building there has never been returned, and remains a Catholic cathedral. Unitarianism was primarily preserved in the country villages, while the urban remnants met in private houses in secrecy. By 1800 there were only 125 churches remaining, but the oppression had lessened. In 1781 a new edict of toleration from Emperor Joseph II allowed Unitarians and other Protestants to worship freely. Many of the churches, schools, and parsonages that had been previously seized were given back. Publishing was also allowed once again, including a major theological work by Bishop Michael Szent Abrahami, a great leader who is often credited with saving the movement.

The 19th century was less restrictive with Unitarianism becoming fully legal again in 1848, but this was postponed until 1867 when

Hungary was reunited with Transylvania. A second Unitarian college, in addition to the one at Kososvar, was established at Szekelykeresztur, along with a school at Torda and many other village schools. In 1861 the Unitarians met in synod to elect a new bishop, Janos Kriza. He tried to strengthen relationships with both the British and American Unitarians and precipitated a revival of Unitarianism. He had the works of William Ellery Channing translated into Hungarian and started a theological journal. By the time of World War I, there were 163 churches. During World War I, Hungary, which then included Transylvania, supported Germany, and Romania joined with the Allies. As a reward after the war, Romania received Transylvania. The ethnic Hungarians who made up the Unitarian population began to be persecuted almost immediately. The **American Unitarian Association (AUA)** sent a delegation to Romania in 1922 to inspect the churches to find the extent of the repression. Relief efforts were begun by the Americans, including the beginning of a sister church program. In the history of the late 19th and early 20th centuries, Bishop Jozsef Ferencz played a key role. He was elected bishop in 1876 when he was already senior minister in Kolosvar. He continued to teach at the Theological Academy for another 35 years. He had a strong literary output but most important of all was a Unitarian catechism, *Unitarius kate*. He died in 1928, after serving as bishop for 50 years. In the following years the Transylvanians were subject to the persecution of the Nazis and then the Romanians under communism, except for that small portion of the movement that exists independently in Hungary.

The life of Imre Gellerd illustrates the repression experienced by Unitarians in the 20th century. Gellerd was born in 1920, the year Transylvania was ceded to Romania. He was educated at the Unitarian seminary in Kolosvar. For decades he was the sole voice of Unitarian learning in Szekely-Keresztur, but after the advent of communism, he found it increasingly impossible to compromise his integrity, was eventually imprisoned, harassed by the secret police, and, finally, on his 60th birthday he committed suicide rather than face imprisonment again. After his death, his work *A Burning Kiss from God to Preach the Truth* was published. Overcoming this history of repression has been difficult. The Transylvanian movement has been strengthened since 1988 by increased ties to the **Unitarian**

Universalist Association (UUA) through the "Partner Church" program where congregations are linked financially, socially, and emotionally to one another. The Unitarians of Transylvania have endured centuries of oppression, but their strong faith endures.

A TREATISE ON ATONEMENT. The greatest work by Hosea Ballou and the most important theological book the Universalists produced in the 19th century. *A Treatise on Atonement* was written early in Ballou's career while he was circuit riding in Vermont. It was published in 1805 and reprinted many times thereafter. The *Treatise* represented Ballou's thought after he had an opportunity to become familiar with the deistical work of **Ethan Allen**, *Reason the Only Oracle of Man*. While he didn't accept all of Allen's ideas, Ballou was fully converted to the concept of using reason in the interpretation of scripture. With the thought that all truth could be made understandable, mystery was slowly being eroded from faith. Ballou began the book by arguing that he believed that sin was finite rather than infinite. He saw sin as limited to the human condition and, therefore, confined to this life. Consequently, Ballou's notion of God was a benevolent being who understood human frailty and loved his creatures and wanted to "happify" them.

The *Treatise* was the first book by an American to advocate an avowedly Unitarian position. Ballou said that Jesus Christ is a "created, dependent being." He often made his points in a humorous, homespun way. He wrote "that if Jesus is the Son of God, then he must be the Son of himself. . . . To say of two persons, exactly of the same age, that one of them is a real son of the other, is to confound good sense" (Ballou, *Treatise*, p. 91). Then he went on to say that if the Godhead is three persons who are infinite, then the whole Godhead is the "amazing sum of infinity multiplied by three." If sin was finite, Ballou said, then it could not have infinite consequences. So, he denied original sin as well as the concept that some had to pay eternal consequences for their sin. The *Atonement* was completely revised as well. Ballou said that Christ did not make a blood sacrifice to appease a wrathful God. Rather than believing that Jesus died to reconcile God to humanity, he thought that Jesus' role was to reconcile humanity to God. Christ lived to show human beings the nature of God and how they could live lives of love.

Despite the rejection of original sin, Ballou did not believe in free will. He said salvation means that God, not people, determines who is saved. Therefore, one's character makes no difference. We are all saved together as a community and not as individuals on our merit. Ballou offers that Universalism most honors the divine name by arguing that God would not create millions of rational creatures to hate him or live in endless rebellion against him, but rather would have creatures who would want to live in union and happiness with him. When first published, the *Treatise* represented an Arian view of Christ, but this changed in the ensuing years, and Ballou came to believe that Christ was purely human but on a divine mission. The second theological change for Ballou was his assuredness that there was no period of punishment following death. This viewpoint that salvation was immediate for all came under attack later, and a group of Restoratonists, believers in a period of reprobation, seceded from the denomination. The book proved popular among Universalists and established Ballou as a major leader of the denomination.

TRINITARIAN CONTROVERSY. After the death of **John Biddle**, Thomas Firman took on the mantle of Socinian leadership in England. Firman raised funds to help exiled Polish Socinians and became involved in other philanthropic activities. In 1687 he published *A Brief History of the Unitarians Called also Socinians* by Stephen Nye, the first of a number of Unitarian tracts. These publications started the Trinitarian Controversy within the Church of England. Firman wanted to broaden the theological understanding of Christ in the established church, and a massive pamphlet war ensued. In 1689 the king declared that dissenters could hold public worship by the Act of Toleration. Unfortunately, those who denied the Trinity were excluded from this act. In 1695 **John Locke** published *The Reasonableness of Christianity*, which called for more tolerance, but it resulted in Locke being called a Socinian. Two years later Thomas Aikenhead was executed for denying the Trinity, the last person to suffer such a fate. The Trinitarian controversy ended in 1697 by royal decree, and the following year anti-Trinitarians were barred from holding public office by the Blasphemy Act, which was upheld until 1813. Soon thereafter an Arian Controversy started, in which the person of Christ was questioned. William Whiston was forced from his position at Cambridge University for his Arian views. Samuel Clarke, an esteemed theologian, formulated an Arian "subscription," which allowed enough latitude of belief within the church that many Arians could hold their private beliefs without fear of persecution. In *The Scripture Doctrine of the Trinity* he said that Christ is subordinate to God and should only be worshipped as a mediator. Later Clarke made changes in the Book of Common Prayer, which were then followed by **Theophilus Lindsey**'s avowed Unitarian congregation in London and by **King's Chapel** in Boston.

TUCKERMAN, JOSEPH (1778–1840). Known for his ministry to the poor, Tuckerman is considered one of the founders of the social work profession in America. He was born in Boston on January 18, 1778, to Joseph and Elizabeth (Harris) Tuckerman. Tuckerman decided on the ministry early in life and prepared at Phillips Academy and then with the Rev. Thomas Thacher of Dedham, Massachusetts. He entered **Harvard College** and graduated in 1798 with **William Ellery Channing**. Licensed by the Boston Association Tuckerman was called to serve the church in Chelsea (now Revere), Massachusetts, where he was ordained on November 4, 1801. On July 5, 1803, he was married to Abigail Parkman, the sister of the Rev. Francis Parkman and aunt to the historian **Francis Parkman**. Tuckerman had a long ministry of 25 years in Chelsea. He later wrote that he gave "much time to pastoral intercourse, to communications with individual minds." He felt as though he was minister to the entire community and this was exemplified by his forming of the first religious mission to seamen in 1811–1812. As soon as he left this pastorate he took up a new kind of ministry-at-large, where he was employed by the **American Unitarian Association** to minister to the poor in Boston. As he had in Chelsea, he visited as many people as he could and eventually established free chapels for worship to serve the religious needs of the unchurched. He collected information about conditions that produced poverty; published reports; and worked with legislators to improve conditions, offer free public education, and enlarge charity programs. He met with Channing, who helped inspire this ministry, on a weekly basis.

In 1834 the churches of Boston organized the **Benevolent Fraternity** to support this work in the city (it continues today as the Unitarian Universalist Urban Ministry). Tuckerman became ill in 1833 and visited Europe to restore his health. He influenced the British Unitarians to establish "domestic missions" and he met **Rammohun Roy** from India. When Tuckerman returned to America he found he could no longer carry on this work due to his health. In 1835 he wrote that he had seven ministers-at-large employed, of whom four were Unitarians and the others were a Baptist, Congregationalist, and Episcopalian. Concerned about the gap between rich and poor and the moral implications, Tuckerman published *The Principles and Results of the Ministry at Large in Boston* (1838), in which he asked if God intended "that a few should enrich themselves by the toil of the many . . . while the many obtain . . . a bare subsistence" and are considered "below their employers in worth" (Rose, *Transcendentalism as a Social Movement*, p. 2). By that year the Benevolent Fraternity employed 100 volunteers to teach children and adults basic skills in reading and sewing. Tuckerman also helped form an association to coordinate the work of 21 different charities. Unfortunately, he had to continue to travel for health reasons and died in Havana, Cuba, on April 20, 1840. Tuckerman helped educate his colleagues to the causes of urban poverty and was a true pioneer in American social work.

TUFTS COLLEGE. Established as a "seat of learning in New England," Tufts was the first college opened under Universalist auspices and the fourth to be chartered in Massachusetts. In 1847 a group of Universalists who believed that the time had come to establish both a liberal arts college and a theological school gathered at the Orchard Street Church in New York for an "Education Convention." Among the leaders of the meeting were **Thomas J. Sawyer**, **Hosea Ballou II**, and **Thomas Whittemore**. The group voted to found a college if the sum of $100,000 could be raised. The **General Convention** heard a report from this meeting in September of that year when Ballou gave a sermon imploring members to support higher education. That week the Universalists voted to place Otis Skinner in charge of raising the funds for the school. By the spring of 1851 all the money had been subscribed. The committee considered two sites. One was a farm in Somerville, Massachusetts, owned by Charles Tufts and the other land owned by Harold Dean in Franklin, Massachusetts. The Tufts site was chosen, with the total amount of land at 100 acres, and the benefactor's name given to the new school. A story about the founding of the school states that Tufts was asked what he would do with his bleak Walnut Hill site and he replied, "I will set a light on it." The charter was issued on April 15, 1852, with the right to issue all degrees except M.D., which was added in 1867. Ballou was elected the first president and the first building also received his name. The college formally opened in 1855 with 30 students. Several buildings were erected during Ballou's presidency, which ended with his death in 1861. He was followed by Alonzo Ames Miner, who helped restore the financial stability of the college after some difficult times.

Sylvanus Packard, the largest original benefactor of the college, also left a bequest that stipulated that a professorship of Christian theology be maintained. This left the trustees with a dilemma because their original intention for the college was to maintain a nonsectarian character even though it was founded by Universalists. The original charter forbade a religious test of either faculty or students. This bequest evolved into the Tufts Divinity School, which was established in 1869 as a separate institution in connection with Tufts. Although he had declined an offer to be president of the college in 1852, Thomas J. Sawyer was appointed to the faculty of the Divinity School in 1869 and later served a 10-year term as dean. When he came to the school he brought the library of the Universalist Historical Society with him. Training for the ministry was a three-year course and resulted in the granting of the B.D. degree. A chapel was set up in West Hall in 1872. The school expanded to new buildings, including a dormitory.

The Tufts Divinity School became the Crane Theological School in 1906 as the result of a large gift from Albert Crane. This helped with one of its critical problems—lack of endowment. The school had also struggled with admission standards, academic performance, and the number of students enrolled. While the school maintained a separate organization from the college, it increasingly operated as a department of the college. It was possible to combine undergraduate training with the study for the ministry. The school also offered course work for Sunday School teachers and church management. There was serious wrangling over the future of the school at the time of the Unitarian Universalist merger. Despite a recommendation to close from **Unitarian Universalist Association (UUA)** committee reports, the trustees and the administration of Tufts tried to put the School of Religion on a secure footing. A combination of financial shortfalls, faculty resignations, and an uncertain denominational climate put the school's fate more in doubt. The theological school was dissolved in June 1968, with financial considerations listed as the major contributing factor.

Tufts College continued to expand during the presidency of one its own graduates, Elmer Hewitt Capen. In 1892 women were admitted to all departments on an equal footing with men. The great showman and Universalist **P. T. Barnum** was a benefactor of the college. In 1882 the Barnum Museum was begun. Barnum also gave a number of stuffed animals to the museum, which is how Jumbo the elephant began its reign as the popular symbol of Tufts. Eventually the college added both a dental and a medical school and evolved in the 20th century into a fine university, which it became by a charter change in 1955. The university was completely nonsectarian in its orientation during the late 20th century, although its chaplain throughout the 1980s and 1990s was a Unitarian Universalist minister, the Rev. William (Scotty) McLennan.

– U –

ULTRA UNIVERSALISM. This was a term coined by **Adin Ballou** to describe his opponents in the Restorationist controversy that rocked the Universalists in the 1820s and 1830s. Ultra Universalists were those who denied any punishment after death but instead believed in immediate salvation for all. In the early phases of the controversy, their opponents called them "Leatherheads." Another term applied to this belief was "Death and Glory" Universalists. Restorationists were those Universalists who believed in a period of reprobation following death. Although the controversy died out after 1841 when the Restorationist Association was disbanded, the majority of Universalists seem to have subscribed to the Restorationist view by 1870. Ultra Universalism was the belief of the great Universalist leader **Hosea Ballou**, who had died in 1852.

UNION. The major work by the English Universalist James Relly. Relly was a Welshman who became a preacher of Methodism after his conversion by George Whitefield in 1741. He moved to London in 1750 and broke with Whitehead, presumably over universal salvation. He preached to a congregation there until 1778, when he died. He was briefly followed by the American **Elhanan Winchester**, but the congregation eventually disbanded. Relly's ideas were published in *Union; or a Treatise of the Consanguinity and Affinity between Christ and His Church* (1759). This pamphlet was the chief means of the conversion of **John Murray** to Universalism while he was living in London. The pamphlet was first printed in America in 1779, but several people in Gloucester, Massachusetts, had seen it some years prior to this when a seafarer had brought back a copy from England. In the work, Relly argued that there had been a mysterious union between Christ and the entire human race assuring the salvation of everyone. A believer in original sin, Relly argued that this human stain was also Christ's sin and he was punished for human sin, but atoned for everyone as a result of his sacrifice. The elect became not the few who God predetermined, but everyone. Relly was also a Trinitarian, as was his disciple Murray, who followed most of the religious views presented in *Union*.

UNITARIAN. The beginnings of Unitarianism are often traced to a fourth-century belief promulgated by Arius, a priest from Alexandria. Arius taught that Christ was a created being who was less than God. He also maintained that Christ was created before the creation of the world and that his nature was somewhere between divine and human. The followers of Arius were outvoted at a church council meeting in Nicea in 325 when the view that Christ's nature was different from God was declared a heresy and the Nicean Creed was affirmed.

The organized beginnings of Unitarianism date from the stirrings of reform during the Renaissance to the establishment of congregations in the wake of the Reformation. During the Renaissance the humanist scholar Erasmus had shown that the doctrine of the trinity did not appear in the oldest New Testament manuscripts but was a later addition. Many of those who began to question the Trinity were Italian reformers who were forced to flee during the Inquisition. Although there was some organization of liberals in Switzerland, the primary places that it developed after the Reformation were in **Poland** and **Transylvania**. In Poland these anti-Trinitarians were mostly known as **Socinians**, after **Faustus Socinus**. Unlike the Arians, the Socinians primarily believed that Jesus should not be worshipped because he was human and not God. They also rejected the Arian view that Jesus was divine and preexistent. Jesus was a human being with a special mission. The word Unitarian was first used in Transylvania, but it did not become the commonly accepted term for the anti-Trinitarians there until 1638 when the Diet of Dees established a new creed, where the Unitarians were instructed to worship Christ but not as God. Many European writings were imported into England, especially via Holland after the Socinian movement was suppressed in Poland.

Scattered liberals in the British Isles preached and wrote in the years leading up to the establishment of the first official Unitarian congregation there in London in 1774 by **Theophilus Lindsey**, a disaffected Anglican. Most of the English Unitarians were Socinian, holding that Jesus was a human being with a divine mission but was not divine himself. Some Englishmen, such as **Joseph Priestley**, brought Socinian views to America, but most American Unitarians initially were Arian and preferred to be called "**liberal Christians**." In America mainstream Unitarianism developed out of the Congregational or Puritan church in Massachusetts, especially in response to Puritan doctrines concerning original sin and predestination. *See also* ARIANISM, SOCINIANISM.

UNITARIAN CONTROVERSY. The period between 1805 and 1835 when the "liberal Christians" in Massachusetts were identified as a distinct group within the **Standing Order** of Congregational Churches, culminating in organizational development following the formation of the **American Unitarian Association (AUA)** in 1825. It is generally considered that the controversy began in 1805 with the election of **Henry Ware** as the **Hollis Professor of Divinity** at **Harvard College**. This signaled to the orthodox that Harvard had been "captured" by the liberals, and they responded by founding Andover Seminary in 1807 as a training school for "orthodox" clergy. Historian **Conrad Wright** defined three distinct phases of the controversy. The first from 1805 to 1815 marked a time when battle lines of exclusion from established groups were drawn. This system of inclusion and exclusion often occurred on the local level and was played out in several ways. Some ministers, usually the orthodox, were unwilling to exchange pulpits with more liberal colleagues. Second, some ministers refused the hand of fellowship to others by failing to participate in the ordination services or ecclesiastical councils that were dominated by their opponents. These councils no longer provided any kind of mediating function with respect to church disputes, as theological divisions made unbiased opinions impossible to achieve. Finally, there were splits in many towns where parish and church members were typically alienated along theological lines with the more conservative church members supporting more orthodox ministers and the more diverse parish members supporting liberal preachers. Church members were those who had typically made a confession of faith and received communion. Parish members paid their religious poll taxes and lived within the geographical parish but were not as ideologically committed as the church members. This period of infighting ended with the publication of the pamphlet *American Unitarianism* by the liberal orthodox opponent Jedediah Morse, who tried to label the liberals as extreme radicals.

The next 10 years between 1815 and 1825 marked a period of theological debate, including **William Ellery Channing**'s landmark sermon "**Unitarian Christianity**" in 1819 and the famous "Woods 'n Ware" debate on human nature. Perhaps the most significant event during this period was the **Dedham Decision**, where the court decided that the majority of a parish has the right to choose the minister and retain the property. This led to a large number of splits within congregations in Massachusetts. Finally, the **American Unitarian Association (AUA)** was organized in 1825 marking the beginning of the final phase of the controversy. After this the Unitarians began to develop their own denominational consciousness, including the formation of several organizations. This period also marks the separation of church and state in Massachusetts in 1833, which forced certain parishes to identify their faith on an ideological basis rather than geographical area and Unitarians and Trinitarians could no longer be mixed in one large parish. Many of those church members who were in the theological minority withdrew from established societies during this period and organized separate churches. The Unitarians had little time to recover from controversy. Only a year later, in 1836, **Ralph Waldo Emerson**'s *Nature* was published and the controversy with the Transcendentalists began.

UNITARIAN FELLOWSHIP FOR SOCIAL JUSTICE. In the early 20th century Unitarians began to organize for social action. **American Unitarian Association (AUA)** president **Samuel Atkins Eliot** had urged the denomination to establish a Department of Social and Public Service, which was accomplished in 1907. Several younger ministers believed that the AUA was only interested in study and recommendations without action. Wanting to deal with practical matters of reform rather than philosophical ideals, this group, led by **John Haynes Holmes** and Arthur Weatherly, established the Unitarian Fellowship for Social Justice in 1908. They accused the AUA of "sculdugerous work" in keeping ministers with radical social ideals out of pulpits. When the United States entered World War I, the fellowship opposed the Conscription Act and universal military training. Eliot was opposed to the fellowship and rejected the suggestion that it become an officially recognized denominational agency. He called it "a safety-valve for explosive social reformers."

Despite Eliot's dismissal of the fellowship as a group filled with "hot air," the fellowship remained active for many years. It became a kind of social conscience for the movement and regularly passed resolutions at its annual meetings. Despite inadequate finances, the fellowship established a Washington, D.C., office and held an annual national workshop on public affairs. These programs are carried on today through the **Unitarian Universalist Association (UUA)**'s Washington office. Following the recommendations of the ***Free Church in a Changing World*** (1963), the work of the fellowship was absorbed by the UUA's Department of Social Responsibility. The spirit of the fellowship lives on in an annual Holmes-Weatherly Award given by the UUA to a person or group for outstanding work in the pursuit of social justice.

UNITARIAN LAYMEN'S LEAGUE. It was organized in 1907 with a plan to establish denominational lay centers where no Unitarian church existed. Although this plan did not succeed, the Laymen's

League was an important adjunct to the **American Unitarian Association (AUA)** and **Unitarian Universalist Association (UUA)**, especially in the area of public relations. The Universalists organized the National League of Universalist Laymen in 1907, but this group failed and was succeeded by the Order of Universalist Comrades in 1917. Both Unitarian and Universalist groups provided important social activities for men over the years, often coupled with community service or fund-raising efforts.

The Unitarian League was reorganized after World War I (1919), following a large laymen's conference in Springfield, Massachusetts, where former president and Unitarian layman **William Howard Taft** was a speaker. It immediately took on major responsibility for the Unitarian Mission, a two-year project in which 13 ministers visited 115 cities and towns and held rallies, public meetings, and interviews. Although only two congregations grew from this mission, many older societies were revitalized. By 1924 the league had 270 chapters and 12,000 members to help publicize the Unitarian faith. There were four cities with offices and agents, and in 1927 the Rev. Horace Westwood became staff mission preacher. There was also a fund-raising effort (the Unitarian Campaign) that between 1919 and 1934 raised over $1.6 million. The league also established the first Religious Education institutes held on the Isles of Shoals, New Hampshire. They campaigned to recruit new ministers and conducted a salary survey that led to substantial efforts to increase minister's compensation. They also worked to bring to fruition the first worldwide observance of United Nations Day. The league also established a Laymen's Sunday, an idea that many denominations adopted.

Perhaps the league's greatest success came through an advertising campaign. This was funded by a bequest from Henry D. Sharpe, one of the league's founders who died in 1953. A Public Relations Planning Committee placed advertisements in six different magazines. The campaign began in 1956 and ran until 1963 (Are You a Unitarian without Knowing It?). In all over 31,000 responses and inquiries were received and it was estimated that about 7,000 new members were added to Unitarian congregations across the country. In 1963 the Unitarian League merged with the less visible National Association of Universalist Men, and it continued operations for a number of years working closely with the UUA on developing new projects to further liberalize religion. Membership was open to women in 1966. Advertising remained its major contribution to extension efforts and it was among the first Unitarian Universalist groups to develop television programming.

UNITARIAN MISCELLANY. The first publication in America to carry the Unitarian name. The *Unitarian Miscellany and Christian Monitor* began publication in Baltimore in January 1821. Baltimore was the site of **William Ellery Channing**'s famous Baltimore Sermon in 1819, "**Unitarian Christianity**," and a society had been organized there two years prior to that. Jared Sparks, at whose ordination Channing spoke, was the first editor and remained so for three years. Its editorship was carried on for another three years by Francis W. P. Greenwood, but after he left Baltimore to go to **King's Chapel** in Boston, the paper ceased publication. What was important about this paper was that it was avowedly denominational four years prior to the actual formation of the **American Unitarian Association (AUA)**. In the first issue, the introductory observations made clear that the Unitarians did not want to be "condemned without a fair hearing." Thus, the paper was established to "assert and defend" Unitarian positions. It was published with the assistance of the Baltimore Unitarian Book Society, whose work was to publish books and tracts. This society, formed in 1820, was followed by many more such organization in other cities, all organized to promote the faith through publications.

UNITARIANS FACE A NEW AGE. The published report of the **American Unitarian Association**'s **(AUA)** Commission of Appraisal (COA) that proved pivotal in changing the direction of the denomination toward renewal in the 1930s. The COA, which came into being as a result of an AUA Annual Meeting resolution in 1934, issued two preliminary reports to the membership. One was given in May1935 at the AUA Annual Meeting and the other at the General Conference meeting in the fall of 1935 in Cincinnati. The COA held 11 regular meetings. *Unitarians Face a New Age* was a 342-page report, including appendixes. The report consisted of seven major areas of recommendations for the denomination. Under the "Larger Liberal Fellowship," there were hints of increased interest in merger when the report called for greater cooperation with other religious groups, including the **Free Church Fellowship**. The report also called for increased international contacts. There were broad changes called for under "Organization." In response to the prior presidential tendencies toward centralization, this report called for greater regional administrative roles. This section also recommended the creation of a Planning and Review Board and the new position of moderator who would provide a symbolic figurehead for the denomination. Overall, there was a recommendation for the AUA to assume the functions of the General Conference. Under "Leadership," the commission called for greater training of lay leaders, the formation of a Department of Ministry, and better practical training for ministers. Under a section on "Doctrine," the commission considered those religious values upon which Unitarians agreed, including the free search for truth, the importance of worship, and those areas of disagreement that included the question of whether the denomination was to maintain a definite Christian tradition. The commission suggested that there should be some attempt to formulate these theological views in written statements.

In the area of "Worship" there was a consistent call for new and creative work, including increased emphasis on symbols. The recommendations under "Education," which proved very far reaching, included the establishment of an AUA Department of Education with complete reorganization and extension of educational efforts. In the final section on "Social Relations," there was hesitancy to rest the need for action on the shoulders of an AUA department, but an affirmation of the centrality of the need on both the local and national level. The report showed the serious need for change in the denomination and its subsequent implementation under the leadership of its chair, **Frederick May Eliot**, who became president of the AUA in 1937, ushered in a new era of denominational growth.

UNITARIAN UNIVERSALIST ADVANCE. An organization for the promotion of scholarship and the discussion of ideas to help promote theological dialogue and religious renewal. UU Advance was founded in 1975, after a small group of ministers had solicited support from their colleagues. Thirty-five ministers and laypeople met in Minneapolis at the General Assembly to create the group. It has sponsored numerous conferences and published materials.

UNITARIAN UNIVERSALIST ASSOCIATION (UUA). A religious movement that was created by the consolidation of the **American Unitarian Association (AUA)** and the **Universalist Church of America (UCA)** in 1961. The UUA was legally constituted at an organizing meeting May 10–15, 1961, in Boston. The consolidation procedures were finalized with the adoption of a constitution and bylaws. Some Unitarians and Universalists had lobbied for closer cooperation for nearly a century. By the 1950s many local congregations had merged and several joint continental efforts had been undertaken. A Joint **Merger Commission** was formed in 1956. Congregational plebiscites and continental meetings in Syracuse (1959) and Boston (1960) finalized the consolidation. After the formal creation of the denomination, **Dana McLean Greeley**, who was the last president of the AUA, was elected the first UUA president. Greeley envisioned a strong executive position for himself, but he also had a grand vision for the association in terms of the expansion of programs and spending. He came to loggerheads with the UUA's first **moderator**, Marshall Dimock, who wanted equal power with Greeley and frequently interfered with UUA appointments. Dimock resigned after three years and was succeeded by a three-term member of the U.S. Congress, Joseph Fisher. Greeley dreamed of making the UUA an important international force and was especially interested in issues of war and peace. He took a leadership role in the civil rights movement, but the greatest struggle of his presidency was over the **Black Empowerment Controversy**.

Greeley was followed in the UUA presidency by **Robert Nelson West**. West inherited a financial crisis and has often been criticized for making vital decisions to save the UUA from bankruptcy. His presidency was also marked by the publication of the ***Pentagon Papers*** and the launching of the ***Unitarian Universalist World***, a tabloid paper that was sent free of charge to all Unitarian Universalists. The first Office of Gay Concerns was also opened during West's presidency. West was followed in the presidency by Paul Carnes, who was elected in 1977. Carnes died after only 18 months in office, but he was able to form a Commission on Worship, which eventually helped lead the way to the publication of a new hymnal.

The UUA began to turn around financially and demographically during the term of **Eugene Pickett** (1979–1985). He thought the greatest challenge of his presidency was to reverse the general malaise he found in the movement. Pickett launched a capital campaign in 1983, a trend that every succeeding president has followed. A new youth organization, Young Religious Unitarian Universalists (YRUU), was also created during his term. **William Schulz** was elected president in 1985 and came to the position with a number of ideas for growth, and the UUA's membership began to expand. His accomplishments included the transformation of the *UU World* to a slick magazine format, a great emphasis on international outreach, especially to Transylvania, and a renewed spiritual impulse among the membership. The UUA also received a substantial endowment gift from the North Shore Unitarian Universalist Society in Plandome, New York. **John Buehrens** came to the presidency in 1993. Continued growth occurred during Buehrens's eight years in office, including a substantial number of new building dedications for local congregations. What was especially encouraging was the revitalization of college-age programs. Buehrens's interest in international programs helped result in the establishment of the **International Council of Unitarians and Universalists (ICUU)**.

Finally in 2001, **William Sinkford** was elected president. Sinkford, the UUA's first African American president was expected to continue the UUA's renewed emphasis on spirituality and also help the denomination wrestle with its long standing concern for racism. Today the association is made up of about 1,050 congregations in the United States and Canada, with a few overseas congregations. The congregations are democratic in polity and govern themselves. The UUA headquarters in Boston exists to provide services to the congregations, with the Canadian congregations primarily served by the **Canadian Unitarian Council (CUC)**. Each congregation in the UUA is affiliated with a **district**, of which there are 23. Districts receive some funds from the UUA to help support the district executive program. The UUA receives some of its income from annual contributions from congregations in the Annual Program Fund (APF). The UUA has its own publishing house, Beacon Press, but it also publishes books of particular interest to Unitarian Universalists under another imprint, Skinner House Books. The UUA is governed by a **Board of Trustees** and an elected **president**, who is not only the spiritual leader of the denomination but also the administrative executive for the headquarters staff, which also includes all the field staff such as the district executives. *See also* VEATCH FUNDS.

UNITARIAN UNIVERSALIST HISTORICAL SOCIETY (UUHS). This organization is the result of a 1978 merger of the Unitarian Historical Society, which was founded in 1901 and incorporated in 1958, and the Universalist Historical Society, which was founded in 1834 and incorporated in 1877. Its purpose is to promote the study of the history of the denomination through scholarship, programs, and publications. Its major publication is: the *Journal of Unitarian Universalist History*, which succeeds the *Proceedings of the Unitarian Historical Society* and the *Annual Journal of the Universalist Historical Society*. A comprehensive collection of Universalist materials was for many years housed at **Tufts College**, but it was transferred to Harvard in 1975 and now forms part of the Unitarian Universalist collection at the Andover Harvard Library of Harvard Divinity School.

UNITARIAN UNIVERSALIST MINISTERS ASSOCIATION (UUMA). One of the first consolidated organizations of the **Unitarian Universalist Association (UUA)**, it was formed on May 10, 1961, bringing together once separate Unitarian and Universalist professional groups. Local associations of clergy were important organizations dating from the 18th century, but formal denomination-wide organizations came much later. The Universalist organization grew out of an increasing emphasis on professionalization. It was formed in 1929 as the Universalist Ministers Association for clergy to provide support and fellowship. The group also proposed a plan to establish a code of ethics, but this was not completed until 1951. It became a cosponsor with the Unitarian Ministers Association of the *Journal of Liberal Religion* in 1945. On the Unitarian side, clergy began to agitate for a professional organization after it was seen that no one had much control over who was admitted to professional status and what the rules of conduct should be. Local associations were mostly social and did not exist where pulpits were widely dispersed geographically. After the Autumnal Convention in 1863 a committee headed up by **Edward Everett Hale** set up an organizing meeting.

The Ministerial Union was formed in 1864 to help new ministers, offer support, and provide guidelines to maintain standards for membership. A Committee on Membership was given the power to determine who qualified for membership and who could be recommended for removal for moral infractions. Soon thereafter the Union had 200 members. Some of the issues that proved important in its early years were providing a means for relief for those who were sick, poor, or unemployed and providing pulpit supply. In 1922 the name was changed to Unitarian Ministerial Union (UMO) and then the Unitarian Ministers Association (UMA) in 1947. In 1933 the UMO called for a "recovery program" to raise salaries and revitalize the churches. Great improvements occurred after 1936 when the **American Unitarian Association (AUA)** established a Department of the Ministry and the UMA worked closely with them. The UUMA Guidelines is the current code of conduct. The UUMA began to publish an annual journal, *Unitarian Universalism: Selected Essays*, in 1985. In recent years there has been a greater emphasis on the UUMA as an organization that helps facilitate better ministerial skills through continuing education. Perhaps the greatest change in the ministry in the last quarter century has been the large influx of women. There are over 1,500 ministers in the UUA, and more than half of them are women. While the vast majority of ministers train for the parish ministry, the UUA also provides for fellowshipping in other tracks. These two additional paths are community ministry for those who work outside of the context of a parish in wider community settings, such as hospitals, campuses, and shelters, and the ministry of religious education for those who specialize in work with children, youth, and young adults. Interim ministers have also become a specialty for many clergy who wish to devote long periods in their careers to short-term affiliations with congregations.

UNITARIAN UNIVERSALIST SERVICE COMMITTEE (UUSC). The greatest chapter of organized service for Unitarians and Universalists began with the formation of the Unitarian Service Committee (USC) in response to fascism. In the wake of the Munich Treaty of 1938, many Unitarians leaders felt a personal involvement with the suffering of "our friends" in Czechoslovakia. In response, the **American Unitarian Association (AUA)** sent Martha and Waitstill Sharp on February 4, 1939, as representatives of the Commission for Service in Czechoslovakia. The Sharps primarily worked with refugees who needed to emigrate, but they were also involved in direct rescues. On March 23, Martha Sharp escorted 35 refugees to England. After more than a year of relief aid and refugee assistance, the Unitarian Service Committee was organized in May 1940 as a standing committee of the association "to investigate opportunities for humanitarian service both in America and abroad." (After 1948 it became independent of the AUA.)

Wartime activities for the USC included numerous medical, educational, and relief programs. The prime site in France was in Marseille, where the USC opened a medical clinic that continued to operate throughout the war, serving over 2,500 people during its busiest month in March 1942. The main office during and after the war was in Lisbon, where much of the case work for the refugees was done. There were other offices in Paris and Geneva offering medical care, refugee assistance, clothing, and additional services. A conflict within the organization arose in 1944, when the first executive director, Robert Dexter, and his wife, Elisabeth, accused **Charles Joy** of lying and incompetence. An investigation exonerated Joy, and the Dexters resigned, resulting in Joy, who had been in Lisbon, returning to Boston as the second executive director.

Postwar programs also concentrated on aiding the victims of Nazism. There was a great expansion of operations from 1944 to 1946. In addition to offices in Paris, Geneva, and Lisbon, and a center in Toulouse, the USC opened six additional offices in other European cities. There were also additional projects in Europe such as a dental clinic in Austria and a collection center in New York for food and clothes. These efforts were complemented by those of the Universalist Service Committee, which was organized in 1945. They helped take over a program for displaced children after the USC began to experience serious financial difficulties. The Universalist Service Committee under the direction of Dana Klotzle established a series of summer workcamp programs in psychiatric care beginning in 1949. Klotzle also promoted intercultural education. The expansive Unitarian Europe program shepherded by Noel Field soon fell apart due to internal divisions, which resulted in Joy's dismissal and continuing financial problems. In 1948 the large scope of 60 projects in

15 countries was cut back to 14 programs and 12 workcamps. The USC wanted to withdraw from the AUA, saying it could raise more money if it were independent. They finally seceded during the directorship of Raymond Bragg.

In the 1950s USC leaders realized the need to concentrate on serious problems at home. One project was the establishment of a community center in Gallup, New Mexico, for Native American populations, the brainchild of Tillie Moore. In this postwar period, the USC made a commitment to social work education under the direction of Helen Fogg, who began as director of the Child and Youth Projects Department. The organization began to move away from war reconstruction to medical and educational projects in collaboration with native peoples. In 1955 Helen Fogg helped start a teacher-training school in Cambodia. The Unitarian and Universalist Service Committees merged in 1963. For a few years they continued the long established work of the Jordan Neighborhood House in Suffolk, Virginia, the outgrowth of the work of the first black Universalist minister, **Joseph Jordan**.

International efforts reflected a growing interest in Third World development. Important advances in medicine were often a result of UUSC work. Internationally the traditional providing of services and relief was phased out with the empowerment of people to gain control over their political, economic, and social institutions. In 1972 Richard Scobie took over as permanent executive director after the unhappy departure of Harold Bejcek. Scobie's long term of office resulted in an expanded and stable service organization. A central philosophy of cultural respect, collaborative work, and combined educational, medical, and economic efforts proved successful. Over the years the UUSC had tremendous success in implementing medical programs. This proved especially true of a mothers' and children's health program in Haiti in the 1960s, under the direction of Dr. Ary Bordes. In Senegal the UUSC began to work with the Federation of Senegalese Women's Associations to help rural women who had migrated to the city. In 1984 a training center was set up, but the program eventually helped many of these women return home when a network of rural cooperatives to improve food production among farming families was established. In 1978 the UUSC began to sponsor fact-finding missions for congressional delegations. These missions provided information on political corruption and human rights violations in Central America. These were complemented by service projects such as a leadership training program in Guatemala.

Later in the century, domestic programs included a moratorium campaign on prison building, and then, starting in 1989, the UUSC sponsored a domestic program on children at risk, Promise the Children. Headquartered for many years in Boston on Beacon Street, the UUSC moved to a new site in Cambridge, Massachusetts, in 1990. More recently the UUSC has helped to train women to defend their human rights. Since 1992 a UUSC partner in the Congo, Promotion and Support for Women's Initiatives (PAIF), has sponsored such a women's group who are also an active force working for peace. The UUSC also continues a long tradition of offering humanitarian aid. Since the war in Afghanistan, assistance has been given to several organizations who especially offer programs for women and children. Over the years of its existence the UUSC has tried to help create a world where a much greater degree of equality of opportunity and justice marks the lives of those who society has disempowered, abused, or oppressed.

UNITARIAN UNIVERSALIST WOMEN'S FEDERATION (UUWF). The women's organization of the consolidated **Unitarian Universalist Association (UUA)** is an independent affiliate of the parent organization. Its mission "is to enable Unitarian Universalist women to join together for mutual support, personal growth and spiritual enrichment, and, through their combined strength and vision, to work toward a future where all women will be empowered to live their lives with a sense of wholeness and integrity in a world at peace that recognizes the worth and dignity of each individual." Its first executive director was Connie Burgess, who was also a member of President John F. Kennedy's Commission on Equal Rights for Women. Under her leadership the **Alliance of Unitarian Women (AUW)** merged with the **Association of Universalist Women** (AUW) in 1963, and she held the position of executive director for 10 years. Burgess received the UUA's Distinguished Service Award in 1972.

UUWF members played a key role in the passage of the **Women and Religion Resolution** in 1977. **Natalie Gulbrandsen**, who became UUWF president in 1978 and later UUA moderator, had worked on a survey of women in the ministry and in positions of power, and the results, which showed strong sexist assumptions and language, helped convince the **General Assembly (GA)** delegates to pass the resolution. This became a catalyst for the eventual revision of the UUA **Principles and Purposes**. The UUWF has a history of advocating for the Equal Rights Amendment, abortion rights, pay equity, children and family issues, and other social justice concerns. It has recognized leadership with its Ministry to Women Award and has developed programs, often in collaboration with other groups such as the Continental Women and Religion Committee and the Ministerial Sisterhood (MSUU). The UUWF published the curriculum *Rise Up and Call Her Name: A Woman Honoring-Journey into Global Earth-Based Spiritualities* (1994). The UUWF newsletter is the *Communicator*, a quarterly publication, which offers a diversity of opinions and news on local and district membership groups. The UUWF continued the legacy of Universalist women by operating the Clara Barton Homestead and Camp for Girls with Diabetes (and the Joslin Camp for boys) for many years. In December 2001 the UUWF sold the Camp real estate to the Barton Center, which is a separate corporation the UUWF established in 1985. The UUWF was one of the cofounders of the UU's Acting to Stop Violence against Women and also coconvened the UU Task Force on Sexual Abuse and Clergy Misconduct. Another recent program is the Margaret Fuller Award for work in feminist theology.

UNITARIAN UNIVERSALIST WORLD. The magazine of the **Unitarian Universalist Association (UUA)** started as a tabloid newspaper in March 1970 as a fulfillment of a campaign pledge by presidential candidate **Robert West** that every UU family would receive a free denominational paper by mail. The successor of the *Unitarian Register* and the *Universalist Leader*, which were for a time combined to be the *Register-Leader*, the *Unitarian Universalist World* was mailed to 100,000 UU homes to promote a sense of denominational unity and disseminate news in a timely fashion. Prior to this the magazine was available only through paid subscriptions. In 1985 the UUA Executive Staff followed President **William Schulz**'s suggestion and voted to have the newspaper become a magazine again with a slicker format. This publication premiered in January 1987 offering less denominational news and more articles of opinion and was renamed *The World* in the hope that it would appeal to a broader audience. It has now returned to the *UU World* name with more denominational news. The magazine publishes six issues per year, whereas there were usually 19 issues of the tabloid newspaper. Important readership surveys were conducted in 1978 and 1996. Both of these indicated that Unitarian Universalists had high levels of educational attainment and mean incomes with mostly professional or managerial jobs, and members largely described their ethnic backgrounds as white.

UNITY**.** The conference paper of the **Western Unitarian Conference (WUC)**, it was also an important mouthpiece for free religious thought. When **Jenkin Lloyd Jones** became secretary for the WUC in 1875, it had no periodical. In 1878 the conference launched the *Pamphlet Mission*, which evolved shortly thereafter into *Unity*, a semi-monthly journal of news and theological opinion. Its inclusiveness was embodied in the masthead of "Freedom, Fellowship and Character" and this caused dissent in the Unitarian ranks, especially at first with Jasper Douthit, who withdrew from the conference based on its non-Christian position. Working with **William Channing Gannett** as his coeditor, Jones welcomed contributions from such radicals as Robert Ingersoll and Felix Adler, of the Ethical Culture Society. The issue of whether the word Unitarian was broader than Christian became more heated, and, in 1886, **Jabez Sunderland** started a competitive monthly journal, the *Unitarian*, to represent a more Christian perspective. This came after he was asked to resign from the board of editorial contributors of *Unity*. The Western Unitarian Association was formed in June that same year. Those who advocated for open fellowship in the conference became known as Unity Men. There were also Unity Clubs, which were organized in Unitarian churches for educational programs.

In 1893 as a result of the **World Parliament of Religions**, a conference of Jews, Unitarians, and Universalists and ethical leaders met to consider forming a nonsectarian Church of Humanity. After this, *Unity* evolved into the *New Unity*, but this only lasted from 1895 to 1898. The periodical *Old and New* became the official organ of the Western Conference when *Unity* moved beyond its denominational foundations. After *Unity* returned, Jones remained editor until his death. He had a 40-year editorial record of social-justice publishing defending oppressed people and advocating a remarkable number of reforms, including defending birth control leader Margaret Sanger. The paper remained pacifist throughout Jones's editorship, and in 1918 during World War I, the U.S. Postal Service suspended mailing privileges briefly. Jones also used the paper to launch a successful public campaign to restore Abraham Lincoln's Birthplace. The paper remained pacifist during the editorship of **John Haynes Holmes**. Holmes's relationship with Gandhi resulted in *Unity* gaining exclusive rights to publish Gandhi's autobiography (1926–27). *Unity* continued to publish until 1965.

UNIVERSALISM. The belief that God's love will ultimately redeem all people from sin. Universalism as an organized movement was largely restricted to North America. One of its founders, **John Murray**, was an Englishman who immigrated to America and founded the first Universalist church in America in Gloucester, Massachusetts, in 1779. At approximately the same time other Universalists organized in the Philadelphia area, especially under the influence of **Elhanan Winchester**. Some earlier Universalist preaching had occurred near Philadelphia as early as 1741 when **George de Benneville** came to America. A third strand of Universalist beginnings occurred in the hill country of southern New Hampshire and north-central Massachusetts in Warwick, where **Caleb Rich** founded a church as early as 1773 (actually predating Murray, but not officially recognized). Early Christian Universalism was often Trinitarian and deterministic. This began to change with **Hosea Ballou**, the greatest Universalist leader of the 19th century and a disciple of Rich. Ballou was a Unitarian in his theology and also an advocate of ultra Universalism, which meant all people would immediately be saved upon death. The moral implications of this concerned some Universalists who turned to a view that some people would suffer for their sins in an intermediate period after death, where their souls would be cleansed for eventual salvation. This split in Universalist ranks was known as the **Restorationist Controversy**.

When Universalism celebrated its Centennial in Gloucester in 1870, Alonzo Ames Miner addressed the gathering with a reminder that Universalism as a belief had ancient Christian origins. Many

Universalists had been taught by the historians **Hosea Ballou II** and **Thomas Whittemore** that the Christians of the first centuries were Universalists. Many Universalists in the late 19th century named their churches after St. Paul, who declared a universal faith, to indicate this belief in the origins of Universalism. The theological connection was often made to church father Origen, whose works were condemned by an Ecumenical Council in 553. Concentrating on the perfection of God's love, Origen could not believe that wrath would be the final expression of that love. The Universalist expression of the salvation of all led many of its adherents to espouse reform causes in the 19th century, especially the liberation of women. Their notion of a spiritual democracy helped convince them to call for greater opportunities in the world. This also made them less God-centered, and, like the Unitarians, they began to concentrate more on human potential. Universalism, as an organized church in America, understood itself as a branch of the Christian church throughout most of its history, but this was interpreted in different ways. Once he developed his firm belief in ultra Universalism, Hosea Ballou began to see Universalism as being strikingly different from the rest of Christianity, but others wanted to affirm Universalism as the simplest or purest form of the Christian household of faith. Some saw it as the savior of the world whereby humanity would understand God's redeeming love for all and embrace their oneness.

After World War II a new emphasis on Universalism as a religion that went beyond Christianity began to be emphasized. **Kenneth Patton** and others began to support a universal religion that brought together symbols and beliefs from all the world's faiths in a new unified eclectic approach. This would restore all of humanity to a singular religious understanding and thus, in a new way, bring the Universalist message to all. Two Universalist general superintendents from the middle of the 20th century articulated some of this new message. Brainerd Gibbons rejected Universalism as a branch of Christianity, and **Robert Cummins** said that Universalism "cannot be limited to Protestantism or to Christianity, not without denying its very name. Ours is a world fellowship" (Cummins, as quoted in Cassara, *Universalism*, p. 269). Within a few years Universalism as a separate religious movement ceased to exist when it consolidated with the Unitarians in 1961.

UNIVERSALIST CHURCH OF AMERICA (UCA). The official name of the Universalist denomination after 1942 until the consolidation with the Unitarians in 1961. Steps toward greater organizational cohesiveness had begun to take place in the late 19th century, but the denomination was in a period of general malaise when **Robert Cummins** became general superintendent in 1938. The following year he made a presentation to the **General Convention** calling for wholesale church renewal. He wanted to consolidate programs under the General Convention so that it was not merely one of many auxiliary bodies representing one program function of Universalism, but was a strong, central church operated through a series of departments. To promote denominational unity, Cummins supported an idea that had been raised in 1937 that the corporate name of the church be changed to represent a unified church.

In 1942 the governor of New York, where the church charter was held, signed into law the name change from Universalist General Convention to Universalist Church of America. Previously the General Convention had been the delegated body of the denomination that met to transact business. After 1942 that body became known as the **General Assembly (GA)** and it met in biennial sessions. Cummins's dream of a series of centralized departments was authorized in 1949, but his reorganization plan was never completely fulfilled. Although some membership growth and financial stability was achieved, it only proved temporary, and the symbolic name change did not reverse the denomination's general decline.

UNIVERSALIST HERALD. The most important and longest lived Universalist publication in the South. In 1847 C. F. R. Shehane started a paper in Montgomery, Alabama. Within two years its named was the *Religious Investigator* and its place of publication was Notasulga. That same year, John C. Buruss purchased the paper and settled on the name *Universalist Herald* when he took over as owner and editor on January 1, 1850. Over the next few years a conflict developed with Shehane who was made an associate editor and for a time he ran a competitive newspaper. The *Universalist Herald* became the popular voice of Southern Universalism. After the Civil War the paper was revived in 1867 and Buruss continued to publish it until it was sold in 1896 to John Bowers, who published the *Geor-*

gia Universalist. Bowers decided to continue using *Universalist Herald* as the paper's name and it still continues publication in the new millennium. The *Herald* had a list of subscribers of more than 1,300 during the height of its popularity in the 19th century.

UNIVERSALIST MAGAZINE. The oldest continuously published denominational periodical, the *Universalist Magazine* began to be printed on July 3, 1819. Its direct successors included: the *Trumpet* and *Universalist Magazine* (1828–1861), the *Trumpet and Christian Freeman* (1862–1864), the *Universalist* (1864–1878), and the *Christian Leade*r (1879–1897). After that the *Leader*'s name changed a few times in the 20th century and was eventually consolidated with the *Unitarian Register*, finally producing today, the ***Unitarian Universalist World***. For its first two years, the *Universalist Magazine* was edited by **Hosea Ballou**. Then the publisher made an unfortunate choice of editor, Henry Bowen, who was removed within a year. After that the elder Ballou returned with his nephew **Hosea Ballou II** and **Thomas Whittemore**. In 1828 Whittemore and Russell Streeter decided to start a new paper, when the then editor of the *Universalist Magazine*, Eli Case, resigned, and they presumed the paper would fold. Whittemore and Streeter were able to purchase the subscription list for a new combined effort, the *Trumpet and Universalist Magazine*, which started on July 5, 1828.

After Streeter left, Whittemore began a long, successful period of editorship, which only ended with his death in 1861. Known for his forceful opinions, he was uncompromising in his views. Whittemore defended Universalism with an unswerving single-minded fervor. In 1831 it had the largest circulation of any Boston religious paper, 3,900, and this grew to more than 5,000. Several attempts were made to burn down the offices of the controversial paper and the building was lost to fire in 1839. The *Trumpet* absorbed several smaller newspapers during its lifetime. After 1838 it had direct competition from **Sylvanus Cobb**'s *Christian Freeman*, which was similar in content to Whittemore's effort, except that it included reporting of social reform activities. Other Universalist publishing ventures were nearby in the Cornhill section of Boston. Abel Tompkins produced a Sunday School paper and the well-known magazines *Ladies Repository* and *Rose of Sharon*. Cobb's and Whittemore's competing papers were combined after Whittemore's death. After 1865 a number of publishing ventures were consolidated under the **Universalist Publishing House**. Just prior to that George H. Emerson began a term as editor of the *Universalist*, the successor of the *Trumpet and Christian Freeman*. He later moved to New York to edit the *Christian Leader*, then he returned in 1872 to take over the *Universalist* again, and stayed until his death in 1898. Emerson was largely self-educated and an accomplished writer. He wrote biographies of two important Universalist educators, Ebenezer Fisher and Alonzo Miner. In 1879 the Publishing House acquired the *Christian Leader*, which, despite a few more name changes, remained the major denominational paper until consolidation with the Unitarians.

UNIVERSALIST NATIONAL MEMORIAL CHURCH. The idea of a national church was first discussed at a meeting of the General Convention in Baltimore in 1868. The thought resurfaced again in the wake of World War I at the General Convention in 1921. The plan then was to memorialize those who had served in the war overseas, and to build a strong local society in the nation's capital. A group of laymen, the Universalist Comrades, decided to raise funds and a plan for a building was made. There was some opposition to the plan, especially from the Midwest. Opponents said that the money could support a number of other projects, including small church maintenance or the Japan mission. Although it was difficult to raise money, plans for the National church moved forward and construction began in the fall of 1928. The cornerstone was laid on April 28, 1929, and a Peace Tower was dedicated in the name of Owen D. Young, a diplomat who had helped with a German reparation plan. The church, scaled back from the original design, was finally dedicated on April 27, 1930. There was a large cost overrun to the project, but a mortgage enabled the **Universalist Church of America (UCA)** Board of Trustees to finish the construction.

The project, despite its funding difficulties, made even worse by the Depression, was hailed as a wonderful realization of a great dream: "a national temple at the heart of the nation." It was one of the few successes of this period of Universalist history. Frederic Perkins, from Lynn, Massachusetts, had agreed to be the first minister of the new church, played a key role in construction, and enjoyed a successful ministry until he resigned in 1938. He was followed by Seth Brooks. The denomination had thousands of dollars tied up in the church, but this slowly changed until 1956, when the UCA Trustees voted to cut national funding, so that the church would become self-sufficient. The Universalist National Memorial became an important monument to the Universalist faith.

UNIVERSALIST PUBLISHING HOUSE. The publishing arm of the Universalists had a 100-year history of contributing important books and periodicals to the denomination. It was organized in 1862 as the New England Publishing House. Its purpose was to establish a paper for Universalists in Massachusetts and other states as interested. Prior to this there were many Universalist periodicals. The earliest with a continuing publishing history was the *Universalist* (1819). In 1828 it became the *Trumpet and Universalist Magazine*, which enjoyed the long editorship of **Thomas Whittemore**. It merged with another paper in 1862 to form the *Trumpet and Christian Freeman*. This paper was purchased by the Publishing House, which also began to produce a Sunday School paper, *Myrtle*. In 1873 another Sunday School paper was added, *Sunday School Helper*. In 1875 the publishing house purchased a paper from Utica, New York, the *Christian Leader*. This merged with what was now called the *Universalist*, the successor of the *Trumpet and Christian Freeman*. The combined effort was renamed again as the ***Christian Leader***. It became the major denominational paper until merger with the Unitarians in 1961.

The publishing house also published books, including a two-volume history of Universalism by Richard Eddy (1884–86). In 1871 the complete catalog of books, pamphlets, and tracts included 113 titles. Then in 1890 the publishing house produced what may have been its all-time best seller, *Why I Am a Universalist*, by **P. T. Barnum**. The publishing house purchased a building on Boylston Street in Boston in 1910, which became denominational headquarters. At this time the publishing house had net assets of $200,000 and published 150 volumes and five periodicals. Two other buildings in Boston were occupied prior to merger. The Publishing House operated independently of the **General Convention** until 1914. In the 20th century the publishing house continually had problems meeting its financial obligations. After World War II fewer books were produced, with a greater effort made to publish pamphlets. All operations were combined with **Beacon Press** in 1962.

– V –

VEATCH FOUNDATION. The financial savior of the **Unitarian Universalist Association (UUA)** in the second half of the 20th century. The Veatch Foundation began inauspiciously with the forming of the Port Washington, New York Sunday School Committee in 1941. By 1945 the founders decided to form a Unitarian congregation. Searching for community members who might make a one-time gift to the fledgling group, one of the members suggested a homebound widow, Caroline (Carrie) Veatch. Veatch was frequently visited by the congregation's minister, Gerald Weary. Her husband had been a stockholder in the North European Oil Corporation, and Carrie was in possession of some royalty rights. She and her sister began to make grants to the church, which moved to Plandome, New York. She left her royalty rights to the congregation when she died in 1953. A major boon occurred when natural gas was discovered in the German oilfields. In 1959 the Caroline Veatch Assistance and Extension Program was started.

The congregation voted to promote Unitarianism through loans and gifts to worthy programs. A tremendous variety of grants was made to the UUA, affiliated organizations, and individual congregations. The income from the royalties kept increasing until it reached a peak of $20 million. Worried that they might appear to be controlling UUA policies and programs, the Veatch Committee set up an endowment trust fund for the UUA, which transferred $20 million over in 1985 so that annual income would match the then current level of funding. Additional grants have also been made on an annual basis, including extension programs and religious education materials. The Unitarian Universalist Funding Program is now supported by Veatch funds and is given through three funds: for Unitarian Universalism, for social responsibility, and for a just society. The Board of Veatch also funds other affiliated UU organizations, such as the theological schools. These funds have provided a tremendous amount of support for new and creative programs to support and extend Unitarian Universalism.

– W –

WALKER, JAMES (1794–1874). A founder of the **American Unitarian Association (AUA)**, he was later a professor and then president of **Harvard College**. Walker was born in Woburn, Massachusetts, on August 16, 1794, the son of a major general in the army. After studying with Caleb Butler, the principal of Growton Academy, he went to Harvard College and graduated in 1814. He taught briefly at Phillips Exeter Academy and then went on to **Harvard Divinity School**, where he graduated in 1817 in the first class to complete its studies. After studying with **Henry Ware Jr.**, he was ordained on February 11, 1818, to the ministry of the Harvard Church on Main Street in Charlestown, Massachusetts, where he stayed for 22 years. He was appointed secretary of the group that met in January 1825 to consider the formation of what became the AUA in May of that year. He married Caroline Bartlett of Charlestown.

Walker was known as a minister who was active in his community. He was also a staunch defender of the **Standing Order**. He said that while the Puritans followed an outmoded Calvinism, they were "experienced and sober minded statesmen" who would not let vital religious institutions be "broken up and destroyed" (Howe, *Unitarian Conscience*, p. 214). Walker was very critical of revival techniques saying preachers such as Charles Grandison Finney and others were hypocrites who dispensed cheap, unearned grace. Although not a Transcendentalist, he was open to some radical views and related common sense to intuitionism. For Walker, the proof of the existence of a spiritual world rested upon "intuitive suggestion." In 1831 he became the editor of the ***Christian Examiner*** and his tolerance of divergent views allowed him to publish many of the Transcendentalists in its pages. In 1839 he resigned from his parish. He had been appointed a Fellow of Harvard, and then in 1839 he became the Alford Professor of Moral Philosophy. He was a follower of the Scottish moral philosophy and edited the works of Thomas Reid and Dugald Stewart. Finally in 1853 he was made president of Harvard, a position he retained for seven years before his retirement in 1860. His failing health prevented him from leading a very vigorous presidency, but he survived for another 14 years after retirement. He died on December 23, 1874, in Cambridge, Massachusetts.

WARE, HENRY (1764–1845). Ware's appointment as the **Hollis Professor of Divinity** at Harvard College in 1805 is often considered the principal precipitating cause of the Unitarian controversy. He was born in relative obscurity to a farming family in Sherborn, Massachusetts, on April 1, 1764. Ware's father, John, died when Henry was 15, but the rest of the family helped with financial support in his obvious aptitude for college. Before college he trained under the Rev. Elijah Brown. He graduated first in his class at Harvard College in 1785. He taught school in Cambridge for a year and was a student minister with the Rev. Timothy Hilliard. Ware was then called to serve the First Parish Church (Old Ship) in Hingham, Massachusetts, where Ebenezer Gay had recently died after a 70-year ministry. Ware was ordained on October 24, 1787. He had three wives: Mary, who was the mother of 10; another Mary, who died after eight days of marriage; and Elizabeth, who was the mother of nine. Ware outlived all his wives, and of his 19 children, six graduated from Harvard, including **Henry Ware Jr.**

While he was in Hingham, Ware tutored a number of students for college and, most important, came to the attention of some of the members of the Corporation at Harvard who were looking for a new professor. The controversy over the question of whether he was too liberal or not to be elected professor of divinity lasted two years. The historian **Conrad Wright** reports that Ware became the liberal candidate because he had obvious Arian tendencies as shown in the preparation of a catechism with the Rev. Daniel Shute. He also had a clean record of character and service and a gentle disposition. Ware accepted the controversial election after it was confirmed by the Harvard Board of Overseers. He was inducted into the office on May 14, 1805, and remained the Hollis Professor for the rest of his career, more or less retiring from active teaching in 1839 due to a cataract. The election elicited a response from the orthodox because it signaled that Harvard had been "captured" by the liberals. One of Ware's important contributions was the development of formal graduate education for the study of the ministry beginning in 1811 and leading to the formation of **Harvard Divinity School**. Following **William Ellery Channing**'s famous Baltimore Sermon in 1819, Ware carried on a scholarly battle about orthodoxy with Professor Leonard Woods of Andover Seminary (**Wood 'n Ware Debate**). Ware's writings are a witness to reason, conscience, and the value of human experience. He believed that humans have innate qualities for discerning right from wrong and these faculties are a human's rational "moral sense." Ware's lifetime of lectures, which influenced nearly 40 years of theological students, was collected in his two-volume *Inquiry into the Foundation, Evidence and Truths of Religion* and reflected his interest in nature and natural religion. He died on July 12, 1845. *See also* UNITARIAN CONTROVERSY.

WARE, HENRY JR. (1794–1843). The archetype of the pastoral minister, Ware gained his reputation as a professor at **Harvard Divinity School**. Ware was the oldest child born on April 21, 1794, to the Rev. Henry and Mary (Clark) Ware in Hingham, Massachusetts, where his father was minister at the First Parish Church. He was educated locally and with the Rev. Allyn of Duxbury, Massachusetts. He also studied with Ashur Ware, his cousin, and Samuel Merrill. In 1807 he attended Phillips Academy, Andover, Massachusetts, for a year and then went on to Harvard College. After he graduated in 1812, he became an assistant teacher at Phillips Academy in Exeter, New Hampshire, where he developed a close friendship with John Emery Abbott. Ware stayed for two years and preached at a new congregation in Exeter during his final months. He returned to Cambridge to study further for the ministry at Harvard Divinity School. He worked in the library for a time and received his license to preach in 1815. He preached at the Second Church of Boston in February 1816 and was invited to be their minister in November. He was ordained there on January 1, 1817. Just a few months later in October he was married to Elizabeth Watson, the daughter of the famed scientist Benjamin Waterhouse.

In March 1819 Ware became the editor of the *Christian Disciple*. He was instrumental in the formation of the first Unitarian congregation in New York and Ware's brother William became its first minister. By 1824 his youngest child and wife both had died, leaving him a single parent to two young children. He married again in 1827 to Mary Lovell, and they eventually had six children together. Ware was a supporter of the new **American Unitarian Association (AUA)** and served on its executive committee. By 1835 he saw the weakness of the AUA as an institution with little evangelistic inclination and little money. Wanting to root out apathy in the denomination he published *Sober Thoughts on the State of the Times* in 1835. Here he announced, "We are a community by ourselves." He suffered from chronic poor health, and in 1829 **Ralph Waldo Emerson** was called to help out and briefly served as his assistant and then his successor. Ware had won a reputation as an outstanding parish minister who exhibited both warmth in personal visits and in the pulpit with his extemporaneous preaching, which was available in *Hints on Extemporaneous Preaching*.

As a result of his renown, a position was created for him at Harvard Divinity School and he became the Professor of Pastoral Care and Pulpit Eloquence in 1830. He was unable to begin his duties right away. That same year he and Mary traveled to Europe for 17 months to try to restore his health. He visited several countries, including Hungary where he met with the Unitarians. In 1831 Ware produced his most important work, *On the Formation of the Christian Character*. This devotional manual was popular among Unitarians and proved that they were no strangers to the personal and emotional in religious fervor. This work came from the heart. Ware told his readers to "insure the predominance of a spiritual frame of mind, a perpetual, paramount interest in divine truth" (Ware, *Unitarian Universalist Christian*, p. 30). His students loved him and he became their counselor and friend. When he retired they said, "Your example, beloved Sir, even more than your instructions, has taught us the greatness and beauty of a Christian life" (Williams, ed. *Harvard Divinity School*, p. 57). He also became a defender of Unitarian orthodoxy against his old assistant Emerson whose teachings Ware thought made worship impossible. He felt the Divinity School Address ignored the concept of a personal God and wrote *The Personality of the Deity* (1838) in response. Ware said that God should not be confused with nature itself and to apply God's name to the universe was a disguise for atheism. Emerson did not respond, and Ware did not push the matter, as he and Emerson had been friends for many years. In the fall of 1841 Ware found that he was too ill to continue his services and although he tried a trip to New York and Washington, he was unable to complete his preaching duties. He died on September 22, 1843.

WASHBURN, ISRAEL JR. (1813–1883). Israel Washburn Jr. was one of seven brothers from Livermore, Maine, who forged distinguished careers, especially in public service. Israel Washburn, Sr. and Martha Benjamin Washburn had 11 children altogether, with three sisters and one brother who died in childhood, making up the remainder of the prolific clan. Israel Jr., who was born on June 6, 1813, and his siblings grew up in a rural village with a one-room schoolhouse nearby and a Universalist Church built half on Washburn property. When Israel was 67 years old he looked back on this era in his life and said, "There was a halo about these times." Yet life was not purely idyllic. Poverty threatened the family when Israel was only five, as his father went into bankruptcy. The family had a long history of political involvement dating back to the 1630s. Israel Sr. was a legislator and his wife predicted that their first born son would be governor of Maine, despite his diminutive stature. Israel more than fulfilled his mother's predictions for political fame. As an antislavery representative from Maine to the U.S. Congress, Israel was a leader in the battle to defeat the Kansas-Nebraska Act, which would extend slavery. Despite its passage, Israel remained undeterred in the wake of the vote, saying he was "alive, hearty, and indomitable."

Washburn was one of the founders of the Republican Party responsible for giving it its name. Then he was governor of Maine during the early years of the Civil War, 1861–62. Sounding like a true Republican, he warned against the "tendency of things in the direction of centralization." He later became identified as a Radical Republican. His brother Elihu was a close confidant of Abraham Lincoln. Recent research shows that Lincoln previewed the Emancipation Proclamation with Elihu, who also was responsible for promoting General Ulysses S. Grant. All of the brothers made a significant place in history. The fourth brother, Cadwallader, was the founder of Gold Medal Flour, which later became General Mills. The youngest brother, William, was called the father of Universalism in Minneapolis, Minnesota, and was once president of the National Universalist Convention.

Israel's career included other significant contributions as a railroad president, collector for the Port of Portland, Maine, and as a key lay leader in the Universalist church. Historian **George Willliams** has identified him as one of the pivotal figures in the Universalist church in the 1870s and 1880s. He served on national committees and was president of the board for Tufts College. He clearly identified the American Republic with Universalism, which was the most democratic faith in his view. His blending of Universalism and democracy foreshadowed our understanding of a "civil religion," which is expressed in the ideals of freedom and equality. This religious counterpart to democracy was seen as the future church of America. In an address he gave for the Universalist centennial celebration, he said the faith was "universal in its scope and ultimate membership—it will embrace the world." Israel's faith continued to be central in his later years. He was serving on a national committee which was considering revisions in the **Winchester Profession** when he died in 1883.

WASHINGTON DECLARATION. A Bond of Fellowship and Statements of Faith adopted by the Universalist church in 1935, it was the last formal statement of faith made by the Universalists prior to consolidation with the Unitarians. In 1923 the Universalists had reaffirmed the Boston Declaration of 1899 as "fundamental" to their faith. This avowal of faith had the Winchester Declaration (1803) and the Five Principles of 1899 appended to it. Many changes both within and without the denomination resulted in agitation for a new statement. **John Murray Atwood**, the outgoing president of the **General Convention**, stated in 1927 that a statement of faith should not be required for church membership. Some called for the deletion of Article II of their constitution: "provided that the faith thus indicated be professed." Other groups began to argue that the old statement was outdated in light of science and modern thinking. A commission to revise the old statement was appointed with Frederic Perkins as chair in 1931 to develop "a new statement of faith or covenant of fellowship more in harmony with the religious position of our church today, and with the principles of religious liberty which has been our guide in the past."

The new statement was brought to the floor of the General Convention in 1933. It had a strong emphasis on faith in God and the leadership of Jesus, but there was no mention of the Bible. It was meant as a statement of purposes rather than anything approaching a creed. The new Bond of Fellowship was defeated at first, but amendments with the two previous statements (1803 and 1899) were added and members were assured of historical continuity. The revised version passed unanimously and when it came to the floor again in 1935, it was also passed unanimously with no debate. A few Universalists felt the statement did not go far enough and would have preferred a nontheological statement without God, Jesus, or Christianity, but they were a small minority. Thus humanism did not gain a foothold in the formal statements of the Universalists. The text of the Bond of Fellowship was: "The bond of fellowship in the Universalist Church shall be a common purpose to do the will of God as Jesus revealed it, and to cooperate in establishing the Kingdom for which He lived and died. To that end, we avow our faith in God as Eternal and All-Conquering Love, in the spiritual leadership of Jesus, in the supreme worth of every human personality, in the authority of truth known or to be known, and in the power of men of good-will and sacrificial spirit to overcome all evil and progressively establish the Kingdom of God."

WAYSIDE COMMUNITY PULPIT. The famous "sermons in a sentence." The Wayside Pulpit began in 1919 when Henry H. Saunderson, minister of the First Parish, Unitarian in Brighton, Massachusetts, decided that church outdoor bulletin boards were completely ineffectual. Saunderson wanted to create "wayside sermons" where people would stop and read a message that would make them reflect on life's meaning. At first he posted quotations outside his church, and when people began to take notice, he thought it would have a wider usage. Soon Saunderson had one hundred ministers who were willing to subscribe to a series of messages that would fit on a 32" by 44" bulletin board and could be read from across the street. Saunderson was also secretary of the **American Unitarian Association**'s (AUA) publicity department. He composed the quotations initially, including one that was reputed to have saved the life of a person contemplating suicide: "When you come to the end of your rope—tie a knot in it and hang on." Eventually the AUA began to use worldwide literature sources.

By the mid-1920s there were hundreds of subscribers with 12 different denominations represented. The British Unitarians also had their own version of the Wayside Pulpit, started in 1920 in Manchester,

England, by H. Harrold Johnson. The Universalists in America also developed their own inspirational roadside service called the Universalist Community Pulpit. The two denominations agreed to merge efforts in 1932, and the now Wayside Community Pulpit appeared in 1933. After consolidation the messages continued to appear, but increasingly they became identified with a more liberal denominational focus, so that other denominations withdrew their subscriptions. By 1968 there were only 220 subscribers and manufacturing costs had risen markedly. The frequency of the service kept being reduced in the 1980s from 26 quotes per year, to the current printing of a set every other year.

WEISS, JOHN (1818–1879). Born in Boston on June 28, 1818, John Weiss attended the Chauncy Hill School and later the Framingham Academy. He graduated from Harvard College in 1837 and taught school for a few years in Jamaica Plain, Massachusetts, before attending **Harvard Divinity School**. Later on in his life he commented on the quality of learning he perceived that went on there, when he said, "Time was that when the brain was out a man would die, but now they make a Unitarian minister of him" (Eliot, ed., *Heralds*, III, p. 378). During his ministerial training he spent several months at Heidelberg University, which furthered his expertise in German philosophy. His sharp intellect was also nurtured by a Jewish background. He was ordained in Watertown, Massachusetts, on October 25, 1843, where he was settled twice, 1843–47 and then 1862–69. During his first ministry in Watertown he was an outspoken advocate of antislavery opinions and even resigned once from his pastorate over these views, only to be convinced to return by his parishioners. In 1847 he was called to the church in New Bedford, Massachusetts, where he served for 11 years. When he returned to Watertown, he was active on the school committee and was one of the founders of the public library, being the first chairman of its founding board of trustees.

Weiss was one of the first religious thinkers whose views were purely natural and scientific, but he had a difficult time making his views accessible to any but the most erudite and, thus, never achieved great success on the lecture circuit. He was one of a group of radical theists who rejected Christian traditions, calling himself a theistic naturalist. This led him to membership in a conversation group called The Radical Club and eventually to being one of the founders of the **Free Religious Association (FRA)** in 1867. Despite his unorthodox views, Weiss retained his Unitarian affiliation and served as a director for the **American Unitarian Association (AUA)** when others were calling for complete withdrawal from the movement. Despite his loyalty, Weiss felt there was a tendency in Unitarianism to be altogether too slow in adopting more liberal views. His biographer Minot Savage agreed with Weiss that the old radicals had been sacrificed so that their doctrines could be safely preached, "The process of killing them off had opened the eyes and broadened the minds of the community, and so I was enjoying a freedom which their martyrdom had purchased" (M. J. Savage in Eliot, *Heralds*, III, pp. 378–79). During his life he published many volumes of theology and history, including a biography of **Theodore Parker**. Remembered for his nervous energy and wit, his classmate **Octavius Brooks Frothingham** said of Weiss, "This man was a flame of fire. He was genius, unalloyed by terrestrial consideration; a spirit-lamp, always burning."

WENDTE, CHARLES WILLIAM (1844–1931). An important figure in the international organization of liberal religion. Wendte was born on June 11, 1844, in Boston, the son of German refugees. After his father died, when Charles was young, his mother supported the family by teaching German and running a boardinghouse. Theodore Parker was one of her students and became an important influence on Wendte. Unfortunately, Wendte developed tuberculosis and was advised to head west. When he was 14 he moved to California and worked in a store and a bank. He fell under the influence of **Thomas Starr King**, who became a minister in San Francisco in 1860. During the war he served as a drill sergeant, as his health became completely restored. In 1866 Wendte went back east and began to attend **Meadville Theological School** after discussions with **Henry Whitney Bellows** and **Edward Everett Hale**. His success at Meadville convinced officials at **Harvard Divinity School** to admit him even though he had no college education. He graduated in 1869. He was ordained that same year at Fourth Unitarian Society in Chicago, where the congregation grew and they built a new building.

In 1876 Wendte was invited to be minister at First Unitarian in Cincinnati. During his ministry there, one of his parishioners, Sallie Ellis, began the **American Unitarian Association (AUA)**'s Post Office Mission sending out AUA tracts to persons in the West. Although Wendte had a successful ministry, ill health forced him to take a less demanding position in Newport, Rhode Island, at Channing Church from 1882 to 1885. With his health restored Wendte was appointed secretary for the AUA on the Pacific Coast. He then embarked on a 12-year ministry of founding and organizing new congregations, including Salem, Oregon, and Spokane, Washington. He centered his labors in Oakland, California, where he was the founder and minister of the first church there. In 1886 he helped to reorganize the Pacific Coast Conference of Unitarian and Other Christian Churches. That same year he married Abbie Louise Grant.

The idea of establishing a training school for West Coast ministers surfaced at a Pacific Coast Conference meeting in 1889, and Wendte served on the committee to explore its formation, but nothing was organized until 1904. Wendte returned to his AUA job, from which he had resigned in 1889, in 1893 with a new title, superintendent of the AUA of the Pacific Coast, but then he resigned from the Oakland church in 1895. In 1898 he served as supply minister in Los Angeles. In 1900 the International Council of Unitarian and Other Liberal Religious Thinkers and Workers was organized in Boston at the time of the 75th anniversary of the AUA. Wendte was named executive secretary.

International work became the great mission of his life, but his dream of an international movement died with World War I. He traveled for part of every year, trying to extend the liberal message in Europe. He helped support himself by serving churches near or in Boston (Newton Centre, Parker Memorial in Boston, and Brighton) and by being secretary for foreign relations of the AUA. He helped organize biennial congresses of the International Council. He also became involved as executive secretary of another group, National Federation of Religious Liberals, which he helped organize. They promoted tolerance and freedom across denominational lines. Later it evolved into the Free Church Fellowship after Wendte had left its leadership. After World War I he turned his attention elsewhere. His main focus was the Pacific Unitarian School for the Ministry, which he had labored to found many years before. Wendte was a talented musician. He also wrote hymns and early in his career had edited a song book for Sunday Schools, *The Sunny Side*. He continued to publish widely including editing the papers of the International biennials, a hymnbook for children, *Jubilate Deo*, a biography of Thomas Starr King, and his own autobiography, *The Wider Fellowship*. He died on September 9, 1931.

WEST, ROBERT NELSON (1929–). The second president of the **Unitarian Universalist Association (UUA)** who is responsible for rescuing the UUA from a financial quagmire. Bob West was born on January 28, 1929, in Lynchburg, Virginia, to Samuel W. and Mary (Wells) West. After growing up in a Methodist household in Virginia, West joined the U.S. Navy for two years and was an aviation control tower operator. He completed his college requirements in 1950 earning a B.A. from Lynchburg College. Following graduation he went into the insurance business ultimately ending up as the manager of the firm. In the meantime he had married Nancy K. Smith in 1951, and eventually they had four children. Deciding upon a career in ministry, West entered the **Starr King School for the Ministry**, where he graduated with an M.Div. in 1957. That year he was called to serve the Tennessee Valley Unitarian Church in Knoxville. During the next five years he was active in sit-ins and other civil rights and desegregation efforts. In 1963 he moved to the First Unitarian Church in Rochester, New York. Here he became active in Vietnam War protests and continued his work on behalf of civil rights campaigns. His ministry in Rochester was enormously successful as the congregation quadrupled in membership. In the denomination West served on two **General Assembly** Planning Committees and also served on the UUA's Theological Education Commission and the Religious Education Advisory committee.

Although he was not yet 40 years old, West joined the campaign for the UUA presidency when his candidate, Harry Scholefield of San Francisco, dropped out. He took on the role of being a moderate candidate who would not take sides in the divisive fights over the **Black Empowerment Controversy** and the Vietnam War, and he won a majority of the votes even though there were seven candidates. When he took office, West inherited a critical financial situation. The

UUA had accumulated tremendous debts and was beginning to use unrestricted capital. In order to balance a budget that had a $650,000 deficit, West cut costs by 40 percent. He also eliminated about one-half of the 150 UUA staff positions and reduced 21 district services offices to 7 new interdistrict programs. West was criticized widely for his budget cuts, especially when he stretched out the payments to the Black Affairs Council (BAC), and BAC Chair Hayward Henry responded that this was "a shocking revelation of the institutional racism still rampant in the UUA." West was determined to bring institutional stability to the headquarters. He implemented professional management standards for staffing and budgeting and opened up UUA **Board of Trustee** meetings to observers.

As president, West also implemented a number of important, continuing programs. The denominational journals had only been sent to subscribers prior to 1970. President West believed that sending a newspaper to all members would keep them better informed, and so the tabloid *Unitarian Universalist World* was mailed to congregation membership lists beginning in March 1970. West also started the "Sharing in Growth" program to help congregations grow in size and religious depth. His years in the presidency also saw the publication of the ground-breaking sexuality curriculum ***About Your Sexuality***, the opening of the first Office for Gay and Lesbian Concerns, and the beginnings of a fruitful relationship with the **Veatch Foundation**. Another controversy that occurred during Bob West's years in office centered upon the ***Pentagon Papers***. In 1971, West gave Gobin Stair, the director of **Beacon Press**, permission to publish the complete documents that revealed the lies and cover-ups of the American government in the conduct of the Vietnam War. Subsequently, the denomination had to fight government harassment, especially by instituting a lawsuit against the FBI, Federal Grand Jury, and Department of Justice Internal Security Division. By the end of his eight years in office, West had renewed a sense of hope for the future. Despite the criticism he endured, especially for controversial financial decisions, he has often been given credit for saving the association from bankruptcy. During his presidency he received an honorary D.D. from **Meadville Lombard Theological School**. After leaving the presidency in 1977, West never returned to active ministerial work. He sent a sabbatical year in England, then from 1978 to 1981 was a senior consultant to the Arthur D. Little Corporation, and from 1981 to 1993 he was the executive director of two Boston law firms. He retired in 1993 and lives in Boston.

WESTERN UNITARIAN CONFERENCE (WUC). Isolated Unitarian churches in the Midwest began to organize after 1849 when a conference of ministers was held in Chicago in May. The organizers included Augustus Hammond Conant, an early Unitarian missionary in the area, William Adams, minister in Chicago, and Mordecai DeLange, minister in Quincy, Illinois. This group advocated for promoting Meadville seminary graduates to consider Western pulpits with special regard and passed a Christian profession of faith. Nothing happened for a couple of years, but plans were revived at the dedication of the Church of the Messiah in St. Louis. **William Greenleaf Eliot,** who had missed the meeting in 1849, was present to help the group formulate the founding of a formal Western association, and it was decided that all the churches and ministers should meet in May 1852 in Cincinnati to accomplish this dream. The purpose of the association was to unite in their work more closely and to "spread the truth." On May 7 representatives from 12 churches gathered and passed a resolution to form an Association Annual Conference of delegates from each of the Western churches who would meet once a year and advance the cause of "vital, rational, and practical Christianity." There was some discussion over whether they would call themselves Liberal Christian or Unitarian, but the latter prevailed. Eliot was chosen the first president.

There was tension within the conference from the beginning over theological issues. At the meeting in 1853 a delegate from Louisville offered a creed for the conference's approval, which included support for the New Testament miracles and a description of Jesus as the redeemer of the world. During the 1860s there was controversy over how independent the conference would be, as the **American Unitarian Association (AUA)** tried to centralize its efforts and funding for outreach. Many in the West felt they were motivated by a broader and more liberal spirit that looked to the future. This became especially true after 1875 when the conference withdrew from the AUA's outreach program and hired **Jenkin Lloyd Jones** to organize and lead them to embody "Freedom Fellowship and Character in Religion."

For a number of years they were divided by theological strife over whether they would consider themselves Christian and theistic or more broadly based in free religion. This became particularly divisive in 1886 when a rival association was founded, and **Jabez Sunderland** published the ***Issue in the West***.

Much of the conflict was finally resolved at the meeting of the **National Conference** in Saratoga in 1894 when the preamble to the constitution was revised giving some emphasis to the "religion of Jesus," while holding that nothing should be an "authoritative test." The WUC continued its somewhat independent methods of operation until the consolidation of the two denominations in 1961. At that time they had considerable funds, and they owned the Abraham Lincoln Centre. Despite pressure from denominational officials, they decided to support consolidation but not release their funds to the new **Unitarian Universalist Association (UUA)** and instead created the Midwest Unitarian Universalist Foundation.

WHITTEMORE, THOMAS (1800–1861). A man with a remarkably varied career as minister, publisher, musician, politician, and bank president. Whittemore was born the fourth of 10 children on January 1, 1800, in Boston. When he was five, the family moved to Charlestown. His father died when he was 14, and the boy was apprenticed to a leather maker. He tried a number of different trades, but none of them proved successful. In 1820 he was singing in a choir in a Baptist church in Boston, but was offered in May a position to play bass viol at the Second Universalist Society for $1 a service. **Hosea Ballou**'s preaching convinced him of the truth of Universalism and soon Ballou was encouraging him to train for the ministry. Whittemore undertook this study with Ballou and was called to serve the Universalist society in Milford, Massachusetts, where he remained for only a year. He was ordained on June 13, 1821, by the Southern Association of Universalists in Stoughton, Massachusetts. On September 17 in that same year he married Lovice Corbett of Milford, and eventually they had eight children. He moved on to serve Cambridgeport, Massachusetts, and was for a time also preaching in West Cambridge. Whittemore's writing career began almost immediately. In 1821 he prepared a catechism for children and then in 1823 he began a major project that culminated in the 1830 publication of *Modern History of Universalism*.

Beginning in 1822 Whittemore became one of three editors of the ***Universalist Magazine***. He thought for a time he would move the paper to Cincinnati, but then in 1828 he approached Russell Streeter about expanding the paper. Together they bought the *Universalist Magazine* and re-established it as the *Trumpet and Universalist Magazine*. After Streeter transferred his interest, Whittemore found that all of his time was swallowed up by engaging in the needed tasks of running the paper and found it necessary to resign his pastorate in Cambridgeport after nine years. He stayed on as editor of the paper for 33 years and was also its owner and chief clerk. The paper alone could not keep him occupied, so he made his debut in politics. He ran for the Massachusetts legislature in 1831 and served for five years as a representative from Cambridge. Here he worked hard for the separation of church and state, long a Universalist concern, and helped achieve disestablishment in 1833. He was a frequent speaker around the state, especially on the topic of temperance.

Whittemore's interest in music resulted in the production of five different collections by 1844. The first was *Songs of Zion* (1836), followed by *Gospel Harmonist* in 1841. He also published an instructional manual for the Sunday School choir and a popular guide to Universalism (1838). He was an advocate of denominational education efforts and was rewarded for his support when **Tufts College** granted him its first honorary degree (D.D.) in 1858. Whittemore was an outspoken advocate for Universalism and frequently found himself in newspaper battles over religious issues. Historian Russell Miller says that his writing was as blunt and direct as his personality. His bluntness showed up in a number of ways. He would name those writers who he felt were not brief enough, and he even published the list of subscribers who had not paid their bill. Subscribers seemed to like his controversial approach to religious issues, as he had 5,000 of them by 1836, and his paper was consistently the most important Universalist publication before the Civil War. Although he tried to avoid speaking out on reform issues, Whittemore became more forcefully antislavery by the end of the 1830s. As editor he feuded constantly with other religious groups. He was especially inclined to be critical of Unitarians, whose clergy he called clerical dandies, finally concluding that their theology had no grand design but left everything uncertain. He once referred to the Unitarians as those who "preach as near nothing as a man can who preaches at all." One ongoing debate in the Universalist denomination that surfaced on a regular basis was that over Restorationism. For years Whittemore fought with those who advocated some form of future punishment, especially **Adin Ballou**. Near the end of his life Whittemore admitted that he sometimes spoke out of turn and was not fair, but that he wanted to keep the denomination unified.

As he grew older Whittemore tried other sideline careers such as president of the Cambridge Bank, which was fortuitous when he was appointed president of the Vermont and Massachusetts Railroad in the 1840s and used his bank position to save the railroad from bankruptcy. He also served as a selectman in Cambridge and then was an alderman after it became a city. Whittemore followed his history of Universalism with a commitment to establishing the Universalist Historical Society in 1834 and became its first treasurer. He also wrote a four-volume biography of his mentor, *Life of Rev. Hosea Ballou* (1854–1855). He died on March 21, 1861, in Cambridge.

WIEMAN, HENRY NELSON (1884–1975). One of the great theologians of the 20th century was a Unitarian Universalist minister and teacher. Wieman was born on August 19, 1884, at Rich Hill, Missouri. He received his B.A. from Park College and a B.D. from San Francisco Seminary, after which he became a Presbyterian minister in 1912. He received a Ph.D. from Harvard in 1917. He also studied at Jena and Heidelberg, Germany. Wieman was influenced by Alfred N. Whitehead and John Dewey. His first teaching job was at Occidental College as professor of philosophy. Wieman became especially interested in relating contemporary scientific views to understanding religion. In 1926 he published *Religious Experience and Scientific Method*, in which he said that assertions about God or religion must be as objectively grounded as scientific assertions. For the rest of his life, Wieman considered what operates in human existence to sustain it and transform it toward the greatest good. He hoped science would help discover this creative power in human history that works through us with the "promise of growing good" and can be called God. He left Occidental in 1927 to teach philosophy and religion at the University of Chicago Divinity School, where he remained for another 20 years before he took his first retirement.

While teaching at the University of Oregon in 1949 he was asked why he was not a Unitarian by a Unitarian minister who had been a former student of his. Thereafter he joined the church in Eugene and became fellowshipped as a minister in 1950. He emerged from this retirement to become a professor of philosophy at the University of Southern Illinois from 1956 to 1966. He was active in the Unitarian Fellowship of Carbondale during this time. During the late 1960s he was a visiting professor at both **Meadville Lombard** and **Starr King** seminaries. He also helped develop *Zygon, Journal of Religion and Science*. The revival of interest in process theology also brought a revival of interest in Wieman's works. Among his best known books are *The Source of Human Good* (1946) and *Man's Ultimate Commitment* (1958). He died on June 18, 1975, still wrestling with critical questions in his 91st year up until two days before his death.

WILBUR, EARLE MORSE (1866–1956). The foremost historian of Unitarian development in Europe, Wilbur guided the Pacific Unitarian School (now **Starr King**) for many years as its president. Wilbur was born April 26, 1866, in Jericho, Vermont. He later described himself as a "country boy from northern Vermont, born in a family of churchgoing Congregationalists." After a local primary and secondary education, he attended the University of Vermont and graduated in 1886. He went to **Harvard Divinity School** and remained a Congregationalist, except when he went before the regional association he had some difficulty with the question about Christ's divinity, answering that while he did believe it was "not in the sense you probably had in mind." After this he was told not to come to Nebraska, where a position had been arranged for him. Fortunately, a friend told Wilbur that his father, Unitarian minister **Thomas Lamb Eliot**, needed an assistant in Portland, Oregon. Wilbur went and had his new faith confirmed by ordination into the Unitarian fold. He also became Eliot's son-in-law after he married Dorothea Eliot in 1898 and later gave him grandchildren.

When Eliot retired in Portland in 1893, Wilbur became senior pastor for five years until he returned east to serve the church in Meadville, Pennsylvania, from 1899 to 1904. Early in his career in Portland, he attended a Coastal Conference in Oakland, California, and returned a "full-fledged Rev." This would become the site of his grand remaking of a West Coast version of Harvard Divinity School. In 1904 he was asked to be dean of the new Pacific Unitarian School for the Ministry and the announcement was made at the Coast Conference in San Francisco in May 1904. He started immediately to organize the school and prepared a prospectus for "A New School of Liberal Theology." Wilbur worked hard to build up a library, which by 1923 consisted of 16,500 volumes and 13,000 unbound pamphlets from the liberal religious tradition, and then developed his own approach to curriculum. Rather than placing biblical studies at the pinnacle of the curriculum, he placed psychological or historical courses followed by biblical. He remained dean and professor until 1911 and then served as the school's president until 1931. Despite his loftier titles, he always listed himself as professor of homiletics. Looking to develop a series of lectures on the history of Unitarianism, Wilbur discovered there were no sources. He then began a lifelong interest in researching and writing about Unitarianism. The **American Unitarian Association (AUA)** Religious Education Department asked him to write a history of Unitarianism that would be suitable for teenagers. This became *Our Unitarian Heritage* (1925), a preliminary study of the much larger and more comprehensive work to follow, which he hoped to present "duly fortified with all the authorities that a history should give." Wilbur spent long periods studying in European archives, needing to use as many as eight languages to translate materials. He was first there in 1925–26 and then again between 1931 and 1934, partly on a Guggenheim Fellowship in Poland. During this second trip he was relieved of his duties as president of the Pacific Unitarian School and offered emeritus status in 1931. The school had suffered a severe financial reversal. This terrible setback was followed by the death of his only son, Thomas Lamb Eliot Wilbur, who was a student at Pomona College, in 1932.

Wilbur returned from Europe in 1934 and spent the remainder of his life researching and writing until his death in Berkeley, California, on January 8, 1956. The first volume of his magnificent *A History of Unitarianism: Socinianism and Its Antecedents* came out in 1945 and was followed by the second volume, *A History of Unitarianism: In Transylvania, England, and America* in 1952. Wilbur's study was groundbreaking in many ways. He came to believe that there were three principles of the liberal tradition that marked its continuing developments: freedom (freedom of thought rather than bondage to creeds or confessions), reason (use of reason in relation to revelation, external authorities, and tradition), and tolerance (understanding and acceptance of others rather than requiring uniformity). He first articulated these in a lecture in Copenhagen in 1934 that was later published by the Lindsey Press, *Freedom, Reason, Toleration: Our Distinctive Vocation*. Wilbur also saw the liberal religious tradition as one largely continuous stream of connected phases in Poland, Transylvania, England, and America, rather than as separate movements. Wilbur received the denomination's Distinguished Service Award in 1953.

WILLIAMS, GEORGE HUNSTON (1914–2000). Acknowledged as one of the great church historians of the 20th century, George Williams was once called "An Historian for All Seasons." He was born in 1914 in Huntsburg, Ohio, the son of David Rhys Williams, a minister to both Unitarian and Congregational churches. Educated at **St. Lawrence University** (A.B. 1936) and Meadville seminary (B.D., 1939), Williams also studied at the University of Munich and conducted special studies in Paris and Strasbourg. He was ordained in Rockford, Illinois, in 1940, marking the fourth generation of ministers in the family. He served that church as assistant minister from 1939 to 1941. After that he taught at the **Starr King School for the Ministry** and the Pacific School of Religion for a few years and then received his Th.D. from Union Theological Seminary in 1946. Thereafter his academic career belonged to **Harvard Divinity School**, where he began teaching church history as a lecturer in 1947. He retired in 1980 as **Hollis Professor of Divinity** Emeritus. Williams also served as acting dean of the Divinity School in 1953–1955. Williams was married to Marjorie Derr, and they had four children. Over the years the breadth and depth of his scholarship was enormous. He published some 15 books and nearly 200 articles. He was also active as an editor and translator. He served on several editorial boards of major journals and was fluent in all the major European languages and dialects, translating what seemed like the most obscure works. His breadth of knowledge was fostered by his teaching load from 1947 to 1954, when he taught the entire gamut of church history from ancient to modern. Early in his career, Williams adopted the perspective that church history would not be subsumed by secular history, as seemed to be the trend in his vocation. He wanted to study his discipline within the context of a historic community of faith. This meant that church history, in his view, should be understood as a theological discipline, giving a deeper vision to the human condition.

Williams's greatest work was *The Radical Reformation* (1962), a term first coined by Williams in his *Spiritual and Anabaptist Writers*. In *The Radical Reformation* he categorized the reformers into three distinct groups: Anabaptists, Spiritualists, and Evangelical Rationalists. Although he developed the standard study for this field, his diverse knowledge is exemplified by everything from *American Universalism: A Bicentennial Historical Essay* (1971) to chapters on the history of ministry in the early church in the anthology *The Ministry in Historical Perspective*. These particular examples show his lifetime role as a mentor to those who wished to follow him in the vocation of ministry, and particularly those who were preparing for the liberal ministry. Williams was never one to be confined by denominational affiliations though. As a historian he had a true ecumenical temperament, trying to tie Unitarian Universalist history to a broader context in Christian history. He was also a major player in Protestant-Catholic dialogue, including the authorship of a book on Pope John Paul II in 1981: *The Mind of John Paul II: Origins of His Thought and Action*. He later received the Order of St. Gregory the Great by the Vatican. Not confining himself to publishing and teaching, Williams was also an effective voice for social action. He had a lifelong interest in the natural world and especially encouraged the ecology movement in its infancy. He gave the sermon at the Arlington Street Church in Boston at the famous draft card burning service in 1968. The brilliance and variety of Williams's scholarship was especially noteworthy in the modern era of academic specialization. He was working on a history of Harvard Divinity School when he died on October 6, 2000.

WILLIS, ANNIE BIZZELL JORDAN (1893–1977). Born on May 30, 1893, Annie B. Willis devoted much of her life to the work of her father, **Joseph F. Jordan**, one of the first black Universalist ministers. Annie grew and learned under his tutelage at the Suffolk Normal Training School, a project funded by the Universalist General Convention and the most successful of three Negro missions. When her father died in 1929, Willis took on the role of superintendent at the age of 36. She had been teaching in the school prior to then and the family tradition continued with Willis's own daughter Dorothy, who also became a teacher there. Willis held the institution together through the depression. Instilling a sense of self-respect and pride in her students from an early age, Willis had as many as 210 students while the staff sometimes was reduced to three functioning in a dilapidated building with few books in an era of profound racism. The school became known as "Miss Annie's" and operated on a shoestring budget. In 1938 the Young People's Christian Union made the school one of their service projects and later the **Association of Universalist Women (AUW)** provided funds to give Willis a full-time assistant.

When public school opportunities became more prevalent for black children, the grades were phased out in 1939 and 1940 and the institution became known as the **Jordan Neighborhood House**, providing many social services. The kindergarten continued to operate and there were also programs for small children, which now included a day care and nursery school. A prenatal and well-baby clinic had been started in the 1920s. In the 1960s Willis helped oversee the first Head Start program for preschoolers. Universalist affiliation continued until 1969 with close supervision and support. Willis retired from the school in 1974, but remained closely affiliated until her death on February 1, 1977. She gave her last words of direction to her successor on the night before she died, "Watch out for my children."

WINCHESTER, ELHANAN (1751–1797). An early Universalist in Pennsylvania, Winchester was born in Brookline, Massachusetts, on September 30, 1751. His father was a farmer and shoemaker and a religious wanderer from New Light Congregationalist to residence at a Shaker village. Although he did not receive much formal education, Elhanan was largely self-educated and he became a master at languages. In 1769 he underwent a conversion and preached to "New Lights" at his father's house and elsewhere. But he left Congregationalism and affiliated with a group of Baptists who believed in an open communion. He married Alice Rogers of Rowley, Massachusetts, but she was only the first of four wives who suffered and died, along with seven out of eight children stillborn, leaving Winchester frequently grief stricken. In 1771 he was ordained during a revival in Rehobeth, Massachusetts, but he left when he became a convert to closed communion. This controversy continued, and eventually he left Rehobeth to live first in nearby Bellingham and then he preached in Grafton. In 1774 he was called to serve a Baptist church in Welch Neck, South Carolina. After his first wife died, he returned to Boston and married again, but she died soon thereafter. After a visit to Virginia, he married his third wife, but she died in 1779.

During this period of such sadness, Winchester read Paul Siegvolck's *The Everlasting Gospel*, a German book that apparently received wide circulation among the pietists who settled in the Mid-Atlantic States. For the first time he learned that all God's people would be redeemed by Jesus to a final state of bliss. He continued as a Baptist preacher, but his preaching was much more accepting of converts regardless of theological orientation. In addition, many slaves were welcomed into his congregation. While they were converted to Christianity, Winchester began to denounce slavery itself. In 1779, he left South Carolina for New England, intending to return. He continued to preach as his doubts about his faith increased and within the year he was convinced of the truth of Universalism. On his way back to South Carolina, Winchester happened to stop in Philadelphia. While he was there, he received an invitation to preach at a Baptist church with no minister. He won wide acclaim, but his parishioners began to notice that it appeared that in his preaching, salvation through Christ was available to all. His faith in Universalism was solidified when he read *Restitution of All Things* by Sir George Stonehouse. In January 1781 he was called before a group who asked him if he believed in Universal Restoration, and Winchester said he did. He agreed to leave that congregation, but many of his former parishioners ended up forming a Society of Universal Baptists, which was able to meet at the University of Pennsylvania for four years. He married for the fifth time in 1784. His congregation built their first meetinghouse on Lombard Street in Philadelphia.

Winchester also became a frequent visitor of Dr. **George de Benneville**, the Universalist preacher. In 1787 he traveled to England, where he did itinerant preaching in many locations and met **Joseph Priestley**, **Thomas Belsham**, and Richard Price. In 1788 he published *The Universal Restoration, Exhibited in Four Dialogues*. He returned after six years. In 1794 he preached all over New England and played a prominent role in the Universalist Convention in Oxford, Massachusetts, where he was moderator. In 1796 he returned to his old congregation in Philadelphia. He became ill during this time, but Dr. **Benjamin Rush**, his old parishioner, attended to him. That fall he went to Hartford. After a dramatic appearance at a funeral where he spontaneously preached on the resurrection, he received an invitation to speak, and he did so twice a week. He continued to preside over meetings there until his death on April 18, 1797.

WINCHESTER PROFESSION OF FAITH. The central Universalist statement of belief in the 19th century was adopted in 1803. A wide variety of Universalist beliefs were being preached in 1800. Concern about this diversity led to the formation of a committee after the New England Convention in 1802 to write a statement of faith to prevent misunderstandings and confusion. This statement was approved by the delegates to the convention in Winchester, New Hampshire, in 1803. Its three paragraphs became the basis for Universalist belief throughout the 19th century. Hosea Ballou believed that the profession was especially valuable because it affirmed the belief in universal salvation, but did not require a Universalist to profess whether he/she believed in future punishment or not. The committee drew upon the 1790 Rule of Faith adopted at the convention in Philadelphia. The complete Winchester Profession read:

> Article I. We believe that the Holy Scriptures of the Old and New Testament contain a revelation of the character of God, and of the duty, interest and final destination of mankind.
>
> Article II. We believe that there is one God, whose nature is Love, revealed in one Lord Jesus, by one Holy Spirit of Grace, who will finally restore the whole family of mankind to holiness and happiness.
>
> Article III. We believe that holiness and true happiness are inseparably connected, and that believers ought to be careful to maintain order and practice good works; for these things are good and profitable unto men.

A "Liberty Clause" was attached to the document so that individual societies or groups of societies could adopt articles of faith that fit their own circumstances. The driving influence behind the statement was Walter Ferriss of Charlotte, Vermont. He made the original motion in 1802 to formulate such a statement and wrote the final statement that was presented in September 1803 for the "Profession of Belief and Plan of General Association." Because of the Universalist belief in freedom, passing the profession was not easy. Some opposed adopting any common statement because they believed it violated the Universalist belief in private judgment. Those who favored the resolution said that it would help the Universalists be recognized as a legitimate Christian group prevailed. It was passed with a provision that it could not be altered in the future. The primary opponents of the Winchester Profession were Edward Turner and Noah Murray. Murray, a newcomer from Pennsylvania, said, "It is harmless now—it is a calf, and its horns have not yet made their appearance, but it will soon grow older—its horns will grow, and then it will begin to hook" (Stacy, *Memoirs*, pp. 95–96). Turner, who had been Hosea Ballou's friend, would eventually split with his old friend on the issue of Restorationism. The Winchester Profession remained the central Universalist statement of faith until 1899 when the Boston Declaration was adopted.

WOLLSTONECRAFT, MARY (1759–1797). The most important forerunner of the feminist movement who had a complicated and controversial life. She was born in London on April 27, 1759, the second-born of seven and the first daughter. Her father was always losing money and abusing his wife, and her mother doted on the oldest boy to the neglect of Mary and the others. Mary always felt that she was smarter and stronger than her spoiled brother Ned. In 1783 a younger married sister, Eliza, showing extreme stress in her relationship, fled the marriage with Mary's assistance. This was a key event in Mary's understanding of the need for female emancipation. With Eliza and another sister now dependent on Mary, the older sister started a school in Newington Green. Here she began a pattern of creating friendships with some of the great thinkers of her time.

The minister of the local group of dissenters was Richard Price, a correspondent of Benjamin Franklin, **Thomas Jefferson**, and **Joseph Priestley** and known political radical. Price was a world renowned philosopher, who was later especially admired at Harvard. **William Ellery Channing** once said that Price's intuitionist moral philosophy saved him from **John Locke**. Wollstonecraft began to attend the Newington Green chapel to hear Price's sermons. She gained much from the dissenters who helped give her a firm attachment to reason as the fountainhead for individual rights. Their views on human rights and equality taught her to think critically about society. Ultimately the school failed, but she wrote about her experiences in *Thoughts on the Education of Daughters* (1786). In need of money, she went to work as a governess but she resented the wealthy aristocrats and wrote about them in her first novel, *Mary* (1788). Wollstonecraft then went to live with her publisher Joseph Johnson. He was the distributor of all the Unitarian literature, so he was in touch with the dissenting academies and their rational and skeptical approaches to education. Mary also became friendly with Thomas Christie, who worked with Mary on a new magazine, *Analytical Review*. Christie was brought up in one of the earliest Unitarian churches in Scotland in Montrose, whose first minister Thomas Fysshe Palmer was convicted of sedition and sent to Australia for seven years.

These years of interchange with radical friends resulted in the publication in 1790 of *A Vindication of the Rights of Men*. Her main fame was founded on its sister publication, *A Vindication of the Rights of Women* (1792). Here Mary argued for the end of women's dependence on men. They should receive an equal education and the professions should be opened to them, she argued. She became infatuated with the painter Henry Fuseli, who, not wanting to risk his marriage, was not interested in a liaison. Disappointed, Mary then set up household in Paris. She was shocked by the failures of the French Revolution when she saw the Reign of Terror at firsthand. She became involved romantically with Gilbert Imlay and became pregnant by him but refused to get married. Although she loved her daughter, she became emotionally and financially dependent upon Imlay and her isolation led to two failed suicide attempts. In 1796 she started a relationship with the English novelist William Godwin. They married, but she died 10 days after childbirth. Her second child, another daughter, Mary, grew up to be Mary Bysshe Shelley, the author of *Frankenstein*. Wollstonecraft lived a remarkable life of independence and experimentation in an era when women were allowed little of either. She has been described as abrasive with no sense of self-restraint, but she had the most difficult task of creating how women could independently fashion who they would be in the world. Her book on women's rights is sometimes considered the founding document of the feminist movement

WOMEN AND RELIGION RESOLUTION. The **Unitarian Universalist Association (UUA)** officially called attention to the relationship between religion and sexism when the **General Assembly (GA)** unanimously adopted the Women and Religion Resolution in 1977. Proposed by the Joseph Priestley District and a group of women from the First Parish in Lexington, Massachusetts, who were **Unitarian Universalist Women's Federation** members, it called upon religious leaders to "put traditional assumptions and language in perspective and to avoid sexist assumptions and language in the future." This impetus for change grew out of the feminist movement of the 1970s and first surfaced in efforts to change the language in the original UUA bylaws, where all the officers were referred to as "he." The UUA published a meditation manual in 1974 that featured the work of women. One result of the resolution was a radical rethinking of the UUA **Principles and Purposes**. This proposal developed out of a Continental Conference on Women and Religion held in Loveland, Ohio, in 1979. Then UUA President Paul Carnes appointed a Women and Religion Committee.

By 1981 a draft set of principles was presented to the General Assembly with inclusive and nontheistic language. While a majority of Unitarian Universalists seemed to favor the changing of language from exclusive male terms such as mankind and Lord or Father to more inclusive words such as humankind to represent the whole human race and either gender neutral terms for God or equal affirmation of female attributes for God, many of the Unitarian Universalist Christians feared that the word God would be dropped from the Principles when they saw the draft. The final version proposed in 1984 represented the UUA's pluralism but also included God and was fully inclusive.

Two major changes occurred as result of the Women and Religion Resolution. First, most of the barriers to women's full participation in the power structures of the church were dismantled. Working with the Unitarian Universalist Women's Federation was an organization of women ministers called the Ministerial Sisterhood (MsUU). The number of women clergy increased dramatically, until by the turn of the century, women were the majority. All of the moderators of the UUA since 1985 have been women, and there have also been three women presidential candidates since 1985. Second, the UUA became committed to moving beyond gender in liturgies and celebrations of worship. The UUA established a goal of an inclusive, nonsexist language as an outgrowth of the Unitarian Universalist heritage of affirming the worth and equality of all. The 1980 General Assembly resolved to urge all congregations to provide opportunities to understand the sexist nature of our religious heritage and urged the UUA to develop materials to understand this heritage and change it to bring about full equality and participation. Religious education materials were developed including the popular "Cakes for the Queen of Heaven," which helped people examine biblical sexism. In 1981 the UUA published *Readings for Common Worship*, which eliminated sexist references in responsive readings. A UUA Commission on Common Worship developed changes in hymns as well and in 1982 published *Hymns in New Form for Common Worship*. This booklet was later enlarged to include 50 hymns. These language changes and the commitment to complete equality and the elimination of sexist language were continued with the preparation and the publication of the most recent hymnal *Singing the Living Tradition*. By the turn of the century feminism had affected the UUA in many ways. Ways of worship, usages of language, the ministry, and religious orientations were all transformed as a result of addressing the historic inequalities and discriminations in religious traditions.

WOMEN'S RIGHTS. Unitarians and Universalists were early leaders in the women's rights movement in the United States and elsewhere. Believing that women were created men's equals, women and men from the 18th century onward were active in reform efforts to change society and as authors of many kinds of literature. **Abigail Adams** was one of the first to make the connection between the freedom the revolutionaries were contending for and the freedom of women. She advised her husband to be more "generous to them than your ancestors." Adams and **Judith Sargent Murray** both pleaded for more educational opportunities for women. Perhaps the most important publication supporting the women's movement was written by **Margaret Fuller**. An article of hers was reprinted in 1845 as "Woman in the Nineteenth Century." This advocated the abolishment of the laws that gave men total rights over women and children and said that every occupation should become open to women. Fuller said women should be able to "unfold such powers as were given her." While Fuller provided the intellectual basis for a rising feminism, the reform movements of the 19th century provided much of training schools for political, economic, and social reform.

The antislavery movement especially gave women opportunities to speak and organize and publish that they might not otherwise have found available to them. The outstanding example from the Unitarian ranks was **Lydia Maria Child**. She made her initial contributions to society through her writings as a novelist and then as a domestic expert through the bestseller *The American Frugal Housewife*. Books for children and Sunday Schools, fashion magazines, and cook books opened up many publishing opportunities for women. Child then went on to publish one of the most important antislavery tracts, *An Appeal in Favor of That Class of Americans Called Africans* (1833), and edit an abolitionist paper. Her work was essential in converting **William Ellery Channing** to a more active position in the antislavery debates. While women continued to suffer discrimination and harassment in society, many men began to offer their support. **Horace Greeley**, the editor of the *New York Tribune*, was a supporter of women's rights and employed Fuller for a time as a correspondent. After 1850 women began to organize more vigorously to obtain the right to vote. Many times women were given more opportunities in the West. Prejudice within churches certainly made this true once women began to try to secure pulpits. The Universalists were the first to ordain a woman to the ministry with full denominational recognition. **Olympia Brown** achieved this position in 1863 after a difficult struggle to be accepted. Universalism had long been receptive to women taking important church roles as a reflection of a theology that promoted the spiritual equality of all. **Maria Cook** was an early preacher of universal salvation. By 1882 there were 30 women who were Universalist preachers, but they frequently encountered prejudice, as did Brown when she was forced out of her pulpit in Bridgeport, Connecticut. Brown became active in the fight for suffrage and was one of the few activists from the 19th century who lived to see the day when women could vote. The most important Universalist leader from this period was **Mary Livermore**. She participated in a great number of reform movements but was more of a gradualist in the campaign for women's rights. Nevertheless, she joined the increasingly powerful suffrage movement after the Civil War. She came to believe that the right to vote alone would make women the legal equal of men. She delivered her lecture "What Shall We Do with Our Daughters?" more than 800 times imploring her audience to support equal professional and moral educational opportunities for women. The Unitarians ordained their first woman minister, **Celia Burleigh**, in 1871. Many of these early ministers worked collaboratively in the **Iowa Sisterhood**, which was organized out of the Women's Ministerial Conference formed by Julia Ward Howe. Unitarians and Universalists alike played active roles in the great campaigns for equality. From Murray and Adams to **Susan B. Anthony** planning the Seneca Falls Women's Rights Convention in 1848 to the present, a strong feminist tradition has played an important part in the Unitarian Universalist faith. One fruit of the struggle for equality within the denomination is that in the new millennium there are more women ministers than men. Unitarians Universalists still struggle to make their institutions free of sexism so that full equality may be achieved. *See also* MARY WOLLSTONECRAFT; WOMAN AND RELIGION RESOLUTION.

WOOD 'N WARE DEBATE. An important pamphlet debate during the Unitarian controversy that pitted Harvard professor Henry Ware against Leonard Woods, the orthodox professor at Andover seminary. Largely centering on their conflicting views of human nature, the written debate eventually included more than 800 pages of opinion. Woods, who became Professor of Christian Theology at Andover in 1808, wrote for the *Panopolist* and was a founder of the American Tract Society. From 1820 to 1822 his published works in which he took on Ware included *Letters to Unitarians* (1820), *Reply to Ware* (1821), and *Remark's on Ware's Answer* (1822). For his part Ware published *Letters Addressed to Trinitarians and Calvinists* (1820) and *Answer to Dr. Woods' Reply* (1822). Ware, the Hollis Professor of Divinity, argued that the Calvinist doctrine of original sin would degrade people's sense of their own character and lead to despair. People would be repelled to believe that they had a moral tendency toward evil. Ware also warned that those who were likely to commit crimes because of circumstance would find the doctrine of depravity attractive since they could use it as an excuse to show they could not help themselves. In the long run the Unitarian moral argument forced the Calvinists to soften their positions.

WOOLLEY, CELIA PARKER (1848–1918). A leading citizen and reformer in Chicago, Woolley was born on June 14, 1848, in Toledo, Ohio, to active abolitionists, Marcellus Harris and Harriet M. Parker. She grew up in Coldwater, Michigan, and attended Coldwater Female Seminary. She married Dr. J. H. Woolley, a dentist, in 1868. After they moved to Chicago, Celia became very active in the social and cultural life of the city. She joined the Chicago Woman's Club, was its president for a time, and opened up its membership to blacks. She achieved this by working with her friend Fannie Barrier Williams, a black Unitarian lay woman. Woolley joined the editorial staff of the Unitarian publication ***Unity*** in 1884 and continued to help in some capacity until her death in 1918. She published articles in the ***Christian Register*** and several books, including *Love and Theology*. She became a director of the **Western Unitarian Conference (WUC)**, but she was alienated by the divisive politics involved. She was also in demand as a lecturer on such issues as woman suffrage.

In 1894 she was ordained to the Unitarian ministry and served for three years in Geneva, Illinois, and then for two more years in Chicago at the North Side Church, where she tried to evoke a social conscience in her parishioners. She was closely associated with **Jenkin Lloyd Jones**, who preached her ordination sermon, and she frequently supplied his pulpit at All Souls. Always concerned with issues of racism and human rights, Woolley and her husband moved to the black neighborhood on Chicago's South Side in 1904. Here she established the Frederick Douglas Center to provide programs and services that would open greater opportunities for blacks and foster greater cooperation between the races. She devoted many years to this community ministry, where she lived and worked. At first she hoped it would be a type of settlement house, but it evolved into a meeting place for middle-class blacks and whites to find common ground, and so concerts and teas, a poetry series, and lectures on topics such as vegetarianism became the more typical programs. Although she was criticized for not helping those with the greatest needs, Woolley did much for breaking down racial barriers. She died on March 9, 1918.

WORLD PARLIAMENT OF RELIGIONS. Held in conjunction with the World's Columbian Exposition in Chicago, the World Parliament was the first international gathering of representatives from faith groups all over the world. **Jenkin Lloyd Jones**, who gained the name "The World's Fair Unitarian," was a major catalyst in the planning for the Parliament. He saw the fair and the Parliament as expressions of the values of Unitarians. Jones was appointed as secretary of the General Committee on World Congresses. The committee hoped to organize 50 denominational and special interest congresses and the Parliament itself, which was to be convened on September 11–27, 1893. Responses to the World Parliament varied, but most liberals saw it as a victory for the forces of religious unity over those of Christian superiority. The opening celebration was spectacular with over 300 religious leaders from all over the world marching with their religious vestments and robes. Much of the plan for the coordination of events broke down, as there were many cancellations. Large crowds listened to a series of papers and presentations on the religious teachings of the world's faiths. Women were especially active in the planning and the presentations. **Augusta Jane Chapin**, a Universalist minister, was a member of the planning committee and she spoke at both the opening and closing events when she remarked that this event had seen the fulfillment of a dream witnessing the "solidarity of the human race." One outgrowth of the Parliament was that the large number of liberals present made plans for a Congress of Liberal Religions in 1894.

WORSHIP. Unitarian Universalist worship traditions are rooted in the Protestant, and more specifically, Puritan traditions. This means two significant things. First, the emphasis in worship has been on the preaching of the Word of God rather than on the sacraments. In Puritan meetinghouses this was symbolized by the architecture. The pulpit was placed in the center of the building where the word was spoken. In the Roman Catholic tradition, the altar, where the sacrifice of Christ takes place, is the center of the worship space. Second, the Unitarian Universalist worship tradition evolves out of a declaration of freedom from established forms and patterns of ritual and liturgy. Architecturally this was also symbolized by replacing stain glass windows with clear glass, the removal of all icons so that there were no visual representations of Jesus/God, and free forms of worship instead of a prayer book determining the elements of worship. The entire history of Unitarian Universalist worship can be described as freedom from "outgrown forms and obsolete phrases" that represented institutional authority to a more "spontaneous and flexible" worship service that reflects institutional freedom (**Aurelia Henry Reinhardt**).

The spoken word has dominated Unitarian Universalist worship throughout its history with little emphasis upon ritual. **Ralph Waldo Emerson** declared he was quitting the church over the outmoded ritual of communion. His "**Divinity School Address**" also advocated for preaching that converted "truth in to life" by emanating from life experiences rather than intellectual exercises. In recent years there has been greater emphasis in much of Unitarian Universalist worship upon ritual with the introduction of Candles of Joy and Sorrow, the involvement of lay people in the service as worship leaders, and greater symbology, especially with the widespread use of the **Flaming Chalice**. Nevertheless, the sermon continues to be the central act of the worship service, although its length has shortened considerably from Puritan days of two hours of biblical exposition to a current 15–20 minutes of reflection on any important topic of personal, theological, or social concern. The purpose of worship in the Unitarian Universalist tradition has also evolved from the worship of God in the divine/human encounter to a more inclusive celebration of life and community where we find spiritual meaning in the journey.

WRIGHT, (CHARLES) CONRAD (1917–). The outstanding scholar of American Unitarianism and Unitarian Universalism in the 20th century, Conrad Wright has made much more than intellectual contributions to liberal religion by asking UUs to reformulate many presumptions about their tradition and history. He was born on February 9, 1917, in Cambridge, Massachusetts, and never left the ivy-covered environment. Wright received all of his education at Harvard University, including the Ph.D. in 1947. After service in World War II, he became an instructor at the Massachusetts Institute of Technology (MIT) for a few years and then received his first appointment at **Harvard Divinity School** in 1954. He became a full professor of church history there in 1969 and is currently professor emeritus. Wright has also been an active lay member of his church and especially within the denomination with the Unitarian and later the **Unitarian Universalist Historical Society (UUHS)**. His writings, beginning with his major work *The Beginnings of Unitarianism in America* (Boston, 1955), have placed the American Unitarian heritage squarely within the Calvinist and Puritan traditions of New England. The father of three children, his son Conrad E. is also a scholar of the liberal traditions.

Wright has helped the denomination uphold the vision of the conservative Unitarians who supported institutional church life, while the more famous Transcendentalists were a detriment to organized Unitarianism. Wright also called into question some of the excesses of individualism and helped to provide a common sense of institutional unity with his "A Doctrine of the Church for Liberals" lecture (later published in *Walking Together*) in 1982. A teacher who has influenced countless numbers of students with his lectures and discussions, Wright was given the **Unitarian Universalist Association (UUA)**'s Distinguished Service award in 1988.

WRIGHT, FRANK LLOYD (1867–1959). The great architect was born in Richland Center, Wisconsin, on June 8, 1867, to William and Anna Lloyd (Jones) Wright. The oldest of three children, Frank and his family moved frequently. His father was a Baptist preacher who converted to Unitarianism when he was pastor in Weymouth, Massachusetts. Living back in Wisconsin, Wright began to spend summers on his uncle's farm. This was the area near Spring Green, Wisconsin, where his mother's large Welsh family had settled (where Rev. **Jenkin Lloyd Jones** was nurtured) and where Wright later built his home, Taliesin. The landscape had a profound effect on Wright, which would later surface in his designs. His parents divorced in 1885 and he never saw his father again. Wright worked in the Engineering Department at the University of Wisconsin and studied civil engineering there. He assisted the architect Joseph Silsbee on the Unity Chapel project, a Lloyd Jones family chapel. In 1887 Wright moved to Chicago, despite his mother's opposition, and worked for Silsbee as a blueprint tracer at first and then took a drafting job when he worked with the architect Louis Sullivan for six years. Here he absorbed Sullivan's style of using natural themes and a purely American approach to architecture. In 1893 Wright had to leave this job when Sullivan found him taking commissions for outside designs. In 1889 Wright married Catherine Tobin, and together they had six children. Wright designed a house for the family in Oak Park, Illinois.

The year he left Sullivan's employ, Wright declared he would be a revolutionary architect, started his own firm, and produced his first masterpiece, Winslow House. During this time Wright designed his "Prairie Houses," which were low, horizontal designs like the prairie. Wright's "Organic Architecture was intended to link nature with building, people, and the environment, using natural materials and simple design. The Robie House came out of this period. In 1909 he deserted his family and went to Europe with Mamah Borthwick Cheney. After his return he began work on Taliesin. In 1914 Wright was working on Midway Gardens in Chicago when a servant set fire to Taliesin and killed Cheney and two of her children plus four others. During the early 1920s he worked on Tokyo's earthquake-proof Imperial Hotel. He also married Miriam Noel, but they were later divorced. In 1925 Taliesin was destroyed a second time by fire. In 1928 he married Olga Lazovich. By the time of the depression era, Wright was receiving few commissions, but he published two important works: *An Autobiography* and *The Disappearing City*. In his life he would author 20 books. Wright also established the Taliesin Fellowship, an apprenticeship program for architects. Wright proved his critics wrong when he made a comeback from relative inactivity and advancing age. He designed a Johnson Wax administration building and a house on a waterfall, "Fallingwater," in Pennsylvania.

In 1937 Wright decided he wanted a permanent house in the West, and the Taliesin Fellowship began to construct Taliesin West near Scottsdale, Arizona. Here Wright tested many design ideas and developed his popular single-story, moderate-cost houses, "Usonian" homes. Wright's faith, like that of his ancestors, was Unitarian. He reflected this faith in two important church buildings he designed. One was the First Unitarian Society of Madison, Wisconsin, where he had attended the youth group's Contemporary Club and signed the membership book: "The Unitarianism of my forefathers found expression in a building by one of the offspring." The building was commissioned in 1946 and the first service there was held on February 4, 1951. His father had been secretary of this congregation when it was founded in 1879. During the summers he heard Jenkin Lloyd Jones preach at the family chapel. He absorbed Jones's nonsectarianism and once said, "I believe religious experience is outgrowing the church." His second important Unitarian Universalist building project was the Universalist, Unity Temple in Oak Park, Illinois (1908), the first important architectural work in poured concrete. Wright's views on Unitarianism were also published in a denominational pamphlet. In 1956 ground was broken for the Guggenheim Museum, which was finished after his death. Toward the end of his life, many of Wright's commissions were for public buildings. During his lifetime Wright designed more than 1,100 projects, of which one-third came during his last 10 years of life. Wright always strived to create a purely American architecture. Wright once said, "A building is not just a place to be. It is a way to be." Wright died on April 9, 1959 in Phoenix. Max Gaebler, the minister of the Madison, Wisconsin, society conducted his funeral service.

– Y –

YEARBOOK CONTROVERSY. This controversy occurred in 1873 when George W. Fox, the assistant secretary of the **American Unitarian Association (AUA)**, removed the name of **William J. Potter** from the list of ministers in the Unitarian Yearbook. The yearbook was an annual publication listing all the Unitarian churches and ministers, but the ministerial listings were not an official list of fellowshippped clergy, but only those who were generally acknowledged to be Unitarian. In 1873 **Octavius Brooks Frothingham** asked that his name be removed from the listings since he had declared for Free Religion and his church was now independent of the AUA. After this Fox wrote to several other clergy to see if they wished to continue being listed. These included Potter, who was the secretary of the **Free**

Religious Association (FRA), but the minister of a loyal Unitarian church in New Bedford, Massachusetts. Potter wrote back that his name was there with his consent, but since the list had been compiled by the AUA officers, they should decide. Fox wrote back saying he was glad that Potter could still be called a "Unitarian Christian," but Potter responded that he did not call himself a Christian. Fox then concluded that Potter's name should be dropped from the listings, and it was. Despite the fact that this was an unofficial list and that no one could possibly define Unitarian Christian, coupled with Potter being a life member of the AUA, the action was upheld by the Executive Committee of the AUA and at the annual meeting in May 1874.

This action resulted in protests from many Unitarian leaders, including **William Greenleaf Eliot** and **Henry Whitney Bellows** whose resolution welcoming Potter and his church delegates to the **National Conference** was tabled. In 1875 the **Western Unitarian Conference (WUC)** passed a resolution saying, "We deprecate and deplore the action of the AUA in its effort to limit the fellowship of the Unitarian body by defining the word 'Christian' so as to make it a dogmatic shibboleth instead of a symbol of righteousness." They went on to protest the removal of names and specifically Potter's as a "departure from Congregational and Unitarian principles which can only be rectified by its restoration." The resolution was approved unanimously. The WUC went on to say that it conditions its fellowship on "no dogmatic tests." But the AUA was unmoved by all the protests, and it asserted its ecclesiastical authority by ignoring the effort to return Potter to the list until 1883 when an "Additional List" of ministers, including Potter, appeared in the yearbook. After that the lists were consolidated and no more was said about this unfortunate incident.

YOUNG PEOPLE'S CHRISTIAN UNION (YPCU). The national youth organization of the Universalist church organized in Lynn, Massachusetts, in 1889. This organization recognized a growing youth movement in the denomination. Since 1881 more than a hundred local organizations of youth were formed, mostly either as Universalist Christian Endeavor Societies or Young People's Missionary Associations. One effort at organizing in 1884 had failed when many of the groups refused to give up their social orientation. Stephen

Roblin, a young minister from Bay City, Michigan, sent a letter to all denominational youth groups calling for the formation of a national youth organization. In 1889 the Universalist **General Convention** was scheduled to be held in Lynn. A Convention of Young People's Societies was held a day prior to and overlapping the convention. Fifty-six congregations were represented and the group adopted a constitution. It was generally known as the YPCU, but it was also called the National Union at times. Roblin and others had begun publishing a youth paper in 1883 and this became the official national youth paper *Universalist Union*, renamed in 1893 as *Onward*. Annual conventions were held in the fall in various cities, but this was later changed to July so as to not conflict with the National Convention.

The first YPCU convention was held in Rochester, New York, by which time there were 67 local groups with 3,200 members. The organization was involved in raising money to help churches and promote service projects, including the work at the **Clara Barton** birthplace. The YPCU raised so much money that it was able to help finance the building of five churches. The YPCU began to hold summer conferences within three years of its organization. These were held in four regions, including Ferry Beach in Maine and Murray Grove in New Jersey. Many congregations also supported the establishment of an annual Young People's Day in churches. The YPCU had official colors of white and blue (for purity and truth) and a national hymn, "Follow the Gleam." A membership peak was reached in 1895 with 436 local groups and 15,400 members. The YPCU was quite successful in fulfilling two of its initial goals: recruiting candidates for ministry and encouraging young people to join the church. In 1929, in responding to a general decline in membership, Dorothy Spoerl suggested that the YPCU had perhaps outlived its usefulness. Over the next 20 years Alice Harrison proved to be a key figure in national youth activities, as she became director of youth activities in the denominational Department of Education. In the 1930s Unitarian and Universalist youth groups began to cooperate when they created a Joint Commission for Social Responsibility, and they had their first joint convention in 1951. In 1953 the two youth organizations consolidated to form Liberal Religious Youth (LRY).

YOUNG PEOPLE'S RELIGIOUS UNION (YPRU). The Young People's Religious Union was organized on May 28, 1896, in Boston. It grew out of a prior movement to organize Unitarian youth for social activities and worship. Some impetus came from the National Bureau of Unity Clubs. Unity Clubs were first organized in the Midwest under the influence of **Jenkin Lloyd Jones** and had flourished as centers for educational and social activities. In 1889 a National Guild Alliance was formed and joined with the Bureau of Unity Clubs and the Temperance Society in 1890. The YPRU superseded this effort in an attempt to unite youth work and secure the interest of young people in the churches. The objects of the YPRU were: to foster the religious life; to bring the young into closer relations with one another; to spread rational views of religion, and to put into practice such principles of life and duty as tend to uplift mankind. Right from the beginning many joint union meetings and rallies between the Unitarian and Universalist youth movements were held. Several efforts were made to consider closer cooperation. In 1933 a Joint Commission on Social Responsibility was started growing out of a group that was created by the YPRU in 1930. The YPRU had a representative on the Unitarian Joint Student Committee after 1925. This was an effort by several Unitarian groups to coordinate work with students.

The Unitarians were the first to call for the merger of the Unitarian and Universalists youth movements in 1935, but the Universalists refused to act on the proposal. The YPRU was reorganized in 1941, when the word Unitarian was added giving it a denominational designation, American Unitarian Youth. It merged in 1953 with the Universalist group, the Universalist Youth Fellowship, which had also changed its named in 1941. The new youth organization **Liberal Religious Youth** was the first merged organization from the two separate denominations to be organized prior to the general Unitarian Universalist consolidation in 1961.

YOUNG RELIGIOUS UNITARIAN UNIVERSALISTS (YRUU). The **Unitarian Universalist Association (UUA)** Board voted to sponsor a continentwide youth conference in 1981. Two "Common Ground" conferences in the summers of 1981 and 1982 resulted in the creation of a new youth organization to replace **Liberal Religious Youth** (LRY). The LRY had suffered from poor relationships between youth and adults, and behavioral problems. As a result of these conferences the new organization, YRUU, was formed on January 1, 1983. YRUU was meant to have closer ties to the UUA and provide for greater participation by adults on all levels. The YRUU publication is called *Synapse*. Its bylaws stated that its purposes included: "fostering spiritual depth, creating a peaceful community on earth and peace within us, and clarifying both individual and universal religious values as part of our growth process." As a result of neglect of post-high school youth, the UUA supported the formation of a UU Young Adults conference in 1986, which was followed by the creation of a continental network (C*UUYAN). The UUA was especially successful in the 1990s creating college campus programs. By the end of the decade there were 125 such groups.

YOUNG, WHITNEY M. JR. (1921–1971). He was a prominent civil rights leader and executive director of the National Urban League. He was born in Lincoln Ridge, Kentucky, to Whitney M. and Laura (Ray) Young on July 31, 1921. His father was principal of Lincoln Institute, a private black high school modeled along the lines of Tuskegee. After attending Kentucky State College, he joined the army. He married Margaret Buckner in 1942. Later he received a master's degree in social work from the University of Minnesota. His first position with the Urban League was as executive secretary in Omaha, Nebraska. In the mid-1950s he became Dean of the Atlanta University School of Social Work and remained there until 1960 when he went north to New York to lead the Urban League. Originally a social service agency that tried to place blacks in middle class occupations, under Young's leadership the League made an important name for itself in the civil rights struggle.

Young has sometimes been criticized for accommodating rich and powerful white people while being out of touch with the grassroots black population. Although he originally condemned the "black power" movement, Young changed his views after 1968 when he started the Urban League's "New Thrust" program, which shifted its emphasis from social work to the political and economic empowerment of blacks. Young's moderation also reflected a long integrationist history that was supported by most African Americans and he played an important mediating role by advocating the civil rights agenda with political leaders and corporate heads. He became an advocate of a "domestic Marshall Plan," which would undo the network of racism and poverty among people of color. Young wrote, "Together, blacks and whites can move our country beyond racism and create for the benefit of all of us an open society, one that assures freedom, justice, and full equality for all" (Young, as quoted in *The Whitney M. Young Jr. Urban Ministry Fund*, UUA pamphlet). He was an active participant in the 1963 March on Washington. In 1968 **Starr King School for the Ministry** granted Young an honorary L.H.D. and the following year he was honored with the highest U.S. civilian order, the Medal of Freedom.

Young first attended a Unitarian church in St. Paul, Minnesota (Unity Church). This affiliation gave Whitney and Margaret Young greater interracial contacts beyond the separate black churches. This became a professional difficulty when the Youngs moved to Omaha. When they became active in the Unitarian church, Young found that it hurt his credibility with blacks and he was accused of abandoning the black church. His embrace of Unitarianism was seen as an act of racial disloyalty, and he returned to the African Methodist Episcopal congregation while his wife and daughter continued at the Unitarian church. Wherever he went Young was drawn back to Unitarianism. In Atlanta he became a board member of his local Unitarian Universalist church, gave Sunday sermons, and worked with the Thomas Jefferson Southern Regional Conference. Later he was drawn into continental Unitarian Universalist concerns and served on the board of the **Unitarian Universalist Service Committee (UUSC)**, the Commission on Religion and Race, and the Layman's League. He was an active member and frequent preacher at the White Plains Community Church when he lived in New York. He was the author of two books, *To Be Equal* and *Beyond Racism*. Young died in a drowning accident on March 11, 1971. In 1983 the Unitarian Universalist Association established a Whitney M. Young Jr. Urban Ministry Fund to "develop and strengthen the Unitarian Universalist presence in the city."

Appendix

SOME OTHER FAMOUS UNITARIAN UNIVERSALISTS WHO DO NOT RECEIVE FULL BIOGRAPHICAL TREATMENT IN THIS BOOK

Hannah Adams (1755–1831)—historian of religion, first woman to earn living as a writer
Washington Allston (1779–1843)—artist, brother-in-law of William Ellery Channing
George Bancroft (1800–1891)—historian
William Cullen Bryant (1794–1878)—poet
John C. Calhoun (1782–1850)—U.S. Senator from South Carolina
Fannie Merritt Farmer (1857–1915)—cooking teacher and publisher
Frank Furness (1839–1912)—architect
Elizabeth Gaskell (1810–1865)—British writer
Edvard Grieg (1843–1907)—Norwegian composer
Bret Harte (1839–1902)—poet
Oliver Wendell Holmes (1809–1894)—doctor, poet, and satirist
Frances Anne (Fanny) Kemble (1809–1893)—British actress and author
Arthur Lismer (1885–1969)—Canadian artist and teacher
Violet Liuzzo (1926–1965)—civil rights martyr
Harriet Martineau (1802–1876)—British abolitionist and author
John Molson (1763–1836)—founder of Montreal church, famous brewer
James Pierpont (1822–1893)—composer of "Jingle Bells"
Beatrix Potter (1866–1943)—British children's book illustrator and author
George Pullman (1831–1897)—railroad car manufacturer
Malvina Reynolds (1900–1978)—folk singer
May Sarton (1912–1995)—poet
Pete Seeger (1919–)—folk singer
Adlai Stevenson (1900–1965)—presidential candidate, U.N. Ambassador
Joseph Story—Supreme Court Justice
Lucy Stone (1818–1893)—abolitionist and suffragist

Emily Howard Jennings Stowe (1831–1903)—Canada's first woman doctor
Charles Sumner (1811–1874)—U.S. Senator, abolitionist
Jones Very (1813–1880)—Transcendental poet who was sent to McLean Asylum while a student at Harvard after he announced that the Holy Spirit was speaking through him.
Daniel Webster (1782–1852) U.S. Senator, orator
Josiah Wedgwood (1730–1795)—maker of fine china
Joseph Workman (1805–1894)—father of Canadian psychiatry
Newell Convers (N.C.) Wyeth (1882–1945)—illustrator and artist

General Superintendents—Universalist Church of America

Isaac Morgan Atwood, 1898–1907
William Henry McGlauflin, 1907–1916
John Smith Lowe, 1917–1928
Roger Frederick Etz, 1929–1938
Robert Cummins, 1938–1953
Brainerd Frederick Gibbons, 1953–1956
Philip Randall Giles, 1953–1961

Presidents—American Unitarian Association

Aaron Bancroft, 1825–1836
Ichabod Nichols, 1837–1844
Joseph Story, 1844–1845
Orville Dewey, 1845–1847
Ezra Stiles Gannett, 1847–1851
Samuel Kirkland Lothrop, 1851–1858
Edward Brooks Hall, 1858–1859
Frederic Henry Hedge, 1859–1862
Rufus Phineas Stebbins, 1862–1865
John Gorham Palfrey, 1865–1867
Thomas Dawes Eliot, 1867–1870
Henry Chapin, 1870–1872
John Wells, 1872–1876
Henry Purkitt Kidder, 1876–1886
George Dexter Robinson, 1886–1887

George Silsbee Hale, 1887–1895
John Davis Long, 1895–1897
Carroll Davidson Wright, 1897–1900
Samuel Atkins Eliot, 1900–1927
Louis Craig Cornish, 1927–1937
Frederick May Eliot, 1937–1958
Dana McLean Greeley, 1958–1961

Presidents and Moderators Unitarian Universalist Association

President

Dana McLean Greeley, 1961–1968
Robert N. West, 1969–1977
Paul N. Carnes, 1977–1979
O. Eugene Pickett, 1979–1985
William F. Schulz, 1985–1993
John A. Buehrens, 1993–2001
William G. Sinkford, 2001–

Moderator

Marshall E. Dimock, 1961–1964
Joseph L. Fisher, 1964–1977
Sandra M. Caron, 1977–1985
Natalie W. Gulbrandsen, 1985–1993
Denise Davidoff, 1993–2001
Diane Olson, 2001–

HISTORIC AFFIRMATIONS OF FAITH

Universalist—Articles of Faith, Adopted by the Philadelphia Convention, 1790

Section 1. Of the Holy Scriptures

We believe the scriptures of the old and new Testament to contain a revelation of the perfections and will of God, and the rule of faith and practice.

Section 2. Of the Supreme Being

We believe in one God, infinite in all his perfections, and that these perfections are all modifications of infinite, adorable, incomprehensible and unchangeable love.

Section 3. Of the Mediator

We believe that there is one Mediator between God and man, the man Christ Jesus, in whom dwelleth all the fullness of the Godhead bodily, who by giving himself a ransom for all, hath redeemed them to God by his blood; and, who, by the merit of his death and the efficacy of his spirit, will finally restore the whole human race to happiness.

Section 4. Of the Holy Ghost

We believe in the Holy Ghost, whose office it is to make known to sinners the truth of this salvation, through the medium of the holy scriptures, and to reconcile the hearts of the children of men to God, and thereby dispose them to genuine holiness.

Section 5. Of Good Works

We believe in the obligation of the moral law as to the rule of life; and we hold that the love of God manifested to man in a redeemer, is the best means of producing obedience to that law, and promoting a holy, active and useful life.

Universalist—Winchester Profession of Faith, Adopted Winchester, New Hampshire, 1803

Article I. We believe that the Holy Scriptures of the Old and New Testaments contain a revelation of the character of God, and of the duty, interest and final destination of mankind.

Article II. We believe that there is one God, whose nature is Love, revealed in one Lord Jesus Christ, by one Holy Spirit of Grace, who will finally restore the whole family of mankind to holiness and happiness.

Article III. We believe that holiness and true happiness are inseparably connected, and that believers ought to be careful to maintain order and practise good works, for these things are good and profitable unto men.

Unitarian—Article 2 of the Constitution of the American Unitarian Association, 1825

The objects of this Association shall be to diffuse the knowledge and promote the interests of pure Christianity throughout our country.

Unitarian—Preamble and Article I, National Conference of Unitarian Churches, 1865

Whereas, The great opportunities and demands for Christian labor and consecration at this time increase our sense of the obligations of all disciples of the Lord Jesus Christ to prove their faith by self-denial and by the devotion of their lives and possessions to the service of God and the building up of the Kingdom of his Son.

Therefore, the Christian churches of the Unitarian faith here assembled unite themselves in a common body, to be known as the National Conference of Unitarian Churches, to the end of reorganizing and stimulating the denomination with which they are connected to the largest exertions in the cause of Christian faith and work.

Unitarian—The Ames Covenant, 1880 (Written by Charles Gordon Ames for the Spring Garden Unitarian Society in Philadelphia, and Later Adopted by Many Unitarian Churches).

In the freedom of truth, and in the spirit of Jesus Christ, we unite for the worship of God and the service of man.

Unitarian—The Blake Covenant, 1894 (Written by James Vila Blake, and Adopted by the Church of All Souls, Evanston, Illinois, on April 29, 1894, and Later Adopted by Many Unitarian churches).

Love is the spirit of this church, and service its law. This is our great covenant: To dwell together in peace, To seek the truth in love, And to help one another.

Universalist—The Boston Declaration, 1899 (Five Principles Adopted by the Universalist General Convention in 1899 to Be Appended to the Winchester Profession).

The essential principles of the Universalist faith: The Universal Fatherhood of God; the spiritual authority and leadership of His Son Jesus Christ; the trustworthiness of the Bible as containing a revelation from God; the certainty of just retribution for sin; the final harmony of all souls with God.

Universalist—Covenant For Free Worship, 1933 (Written by L. Griswold Williams and Adopted for Worship in Many Universalist Congregations)

Love is the Doctrine of this Church, The quest of truth is its Sacrament, And service is its Prayer. To dwell together in Peace, To seek knowledge in Freedom, to serve mankind in Fellowship, To the end that all souls shall grow into harmony with the Divine, Thus do we Covenant with each other and with God." (Revised versions change mankind to humankind).

Universalist— The Bond of Fellowship, 1935, (Adopted in Washington, D.C.)

The Bond of Fellowship in the Universalist church shall be a common purpose to do the will of God as Jesus revealed it, and to cooperate in establishing the Kingdom for which He lived and died.

To that end, we avow our faith in God as Eternal and All-conquering love, in the spiritual leadership of Jesus, in the supreme worth of every human personality, in the authority of truth known or to be known, and in the power of men of good-will and sacrificial spirit to overcome all evil and progressively establish the Kingdom of God.

Unitarian Universalist—Article 2, Section 2, of the Constitution of the Unitarian Universalist Association, 1961

The members of the Unitarian Universalist Association, dedicated to the principles of a free faith, unite in seeking:

1. To strengthen one another in a free and disciplined search for truth as the foundation of our religious fellowship;
2. To cherish and spread the universal truths taught by the great prophets and teachers of humanity in every age and tradition, immemorially summarized in the Judeo-Christian heritage as love to God and love to man;
3. To affirm, defend, and promote the supreme worth of every human personality, the dignity of man, and the use of the democratic method in human relationships;
4. To implement our vision of one world by striving for a world community founded on ideals of brotherhood, justice and peace;
5. To serve the needs of member churches and fellowships, to organize new churches and fellowships, and to extend and strengthen liberal religion;
6. To encourage cooperation with men of good will of all faiths in every land.

Unitarian Universalist—Article II, Section C2.1 of the Bylaws of the Unitarian Universalist Association. Principles and Purposes Adopted at the General Assemblies, 1984, 1985

We, the member congregations of the Unitarian Universalist Association, covenant to affirm and promote:

The inherent worth and dignity of every person.

Justice, equity and compassion in human relations.

Acceptance of one another and encouragement to spiritual growth in our congregations.

A free and responsible search for truth and meaning.

The right of conscience and the use of the democratic process within our congregations and in society at large.

The goal of world community with peace, liberty, and justice for all.

Respect for the interdependent web of all existence of which we are a part.

The living tradition we share draws from many sources:

Direct experience of that transcending mystery and wonder, affirmed in all cultures, which moves us to a renewal of the spirit and an openness to the forces which create and uphold life.

Words and deeds of prophetic women and men which challenge us to confront powers and structures of evil with justice, compassion, and the transforming power of love.

Wisdom from the world's religions which inspire us in our ethical and spiritual life.

Jewish and Christian teachings which call us to respond to God's love by loving our neighbors as ourselves.

Humanist teachings which counsel us to heed the guidance of reason and the results of science, and warn us against idolatries of the mind and spirit.

Spiritual teachings of Earth-centered traditions which celebrate the sacred circle of life and instruct us to live in harmony with the rhythms of nature.

Grateful for the religious pluralism which enriches and ennobles our faith, we are inspired to deepen our understanding and expand our vision. As free congregations we enter into this covenant, promising to one another our mutual trust and support.

Purposes

The Unitarian Universalist Association shall devote its corporate powers for religious, educational and humanitarian purposes. The primary purpose of the Association is to serve the needs of its member congregations, organize new congregations, extend and strengthen Unitarian Universalist institutions, and implement its principles.

Preamble to the International Council of Unitarians and Universalists (ICUU) Constitution, Adopted March 23–26, 1995

We, the member groups of the International Council of Unitarians and Universalists, affirming our belief in religious community based on:

- liberty of conscience and individual thought in matters of faith,
- the inherent worth and dignity of every person,
- justice and compassion in human relations,
- responsible stewardship of the earth's living system,
- and our commitment to democratic principles,

declare our purposes to be:

- to serve the Infinite Spirit of Life and the human community by strengthening the worldwide Unitarian and Universalist faith,
- to affirm the variety and richness of our living traditions,
- to facilitate mutual support among member organizations,
- to promote our ideals and principles around the world,
- to provide models of liberal religious response to the human condition which uphold our common values.

Bibliography

There are rich resources for the study of Unitarian Universalist history. The European roots of Unitarianism were brilliantly scoured over many years by Earle More Wilbur, the former president of the Starr King School. Wilbur wrote the two-volume *A History of Unitarianism* (1945, 1952), which concentrated on Poland, Transylvania, and England with a brief section on America. This book has been the standard bearer for all European studies of the roots of rational religion. George H. Williams of Harvard Divinity School placed Unitarianism in the wider context of the Reformation in his monumental work *The Radical Reformation* (1962), a term he coined. Besides these standard works other books are listed in the Canadian, European, and Asian sections below. There is no good comprehensive history of Unitarianism in Great Britain, although the architectural history of Unitarian chapels, *The Unitarian Heritage* (1986), is especially helpful in understanding the geographical and architectural rise and decline of the movement. An insightful recent work is *Unitarian Perspectives on Contemporary Religious Thought* (1999), edited by George Chryssides. A number of works about Joseph Priestley, the great chemist and Unitarian minister, have been published, including a brilliant new volume by Jenny Uglow about the Lunar Society he belonged to. Called *The Lunar Men: Five Friends Whose Curiosity Changed the World* (2002), it also features material about Josiah Wedgwood, the famous Unitarian potter. The Center for Free Religion in Chico, California, has produced a number of books in recent years on Unitarianism in Transylvania. These publications have been coordinated by Judit Gellerd, the daughter of a Transylvanian Unitarian minister, and her husband, George M. Williams. The European background has been summarized in a brief history by Charles Howe, *For Faith and Freedom* (1997).

There have been a number of general histories of Universalism. The most comprehensive is the two-volume *The Larger Hope* (1979, 1985) by Russell Miller, which superseded an earlier study by Richard Eddy, *Universalism in America: A History* (1884–1886). Miller's work provides endless, encyclopedic detail about every aspect of Universalist development. This overall history has been adroitly condensed by Charles Howe, *The Larger Faith* (1993). Ernest Cassara has produced two important volumes. The best documentary history of Universalism is his *Universalism in America* (1971), and he also wrote the only modern biography of the great Universalist leader, *Hosea Ballou: The Challenge to Orthodoxy* (1961). Universalism has received much less scholarly attention than its Unitarian counterpart, but two studies from the last generation stand out. Stephen Marini in his *Radical Sects of Revolutionary New England* (1982) examined the evangelical roots of Universalism in the hill country of New England through the life of Caleb Rich and his followers. More recently Anne Lee Bressler has contributed *The Universalist Movement in America, 1770–1880* (2001), which explores the initial theological emphasis on the moral community of all people in the Godhead in contrast to a focus on individual salvation found with other early liberals. The book also shows how the theological implications of universal salvation led to a leadership role in the women's rights movement and how the desire to prove a scientific basis for life after death led to an embrace of spiritualism by a few Universalists. Peter Hughes has also written interesting essays on the history of the Restorationist Controversy for the *Journal of Unitarian Universalist History*. George H. Williams has contributed a brilliant essay, *American Universalism* (1971), which first appeared in the *Journal of the Universalist Historical Society* and was later published in book form. There are fewer biographies of Universalist leaders than there are for their Unitarian counterparts. One especially important work undertaken by the Unitarian Universalist Historical Society was Catherine Hitching's biographical dictionary of *Universalist and Unitarian Women Ministers* (1975). Many full-length biographies are listed in the bibliography below. In most cases only the most recent or most comprehensive biography is included.

While Earle Morse Wilbur advocated an international interpretation of the development of Unitarianism, scholars in the last half century have mostly emphasized the indigenous evolution of liberal religious thought from its Puritan roots. Much of this work was influenced by the great Unitarian scholar C. Conrad Wright of Harvard Divinity School.

His *The Beginnings of Unitarianism in America* (1955) firmly established Unitarian development in the context of emerging liberal doctrines within the old Puritan Standing Order of Congregational Churches. Wright was the editor of the only recent comprehensive history of Unitarianism, *A Stream of Light* (1975), which consists of brief sketches of chronological periods by several scholars. He has also published a number of other works, mostly collections of essays, such as *The Liberal Christians* (1970) and *The Unitarian Controversy* (1994). More recently he has written a history of *Congregational Polity: Unitarian Universalist Practices* (1997). Unfortunately, there have been few attempts at producing a comprehensive narrative history. The 20th-century standard was set by George W. Cooke's self-congratulatory *Unitarianism in America*, and more recently David Bumbaugh has attempted the first modern narrative outline of Unitarian Universalism (2000). A marvelous little book of primary documents, *The Epic of Unitarianism* (1957), was edited by David Parke. The breadth of Unitarian theological expression is found in a volume of primary materials edited by Sidney Ahlstrom and Jonathan Carey, *An American Reformation: A Documentary History of Unitarian Christianity* (1985). There are a number of important studies of the Unitarian controversy period. None is more helpful than Daniel Walker Howe's *The Unitarian Conscience: Harvard Moral Philosophy 1805–1861* (1970), which shows that Unitarianism was a religion of the heart as well as the mind.

The Transcendentalist period has been studied more than any other for obvious reasons. There are many fine biographies of the leaders, especially of Ralph Waldo Emerson, including *Emerson: The Mind on Fire* (1995) by Robert D. Richardson. A good introduction to the primary materials is the classic anthology, *The Transcendentalists* (1950), edited by Perry Miller. An excellent study on the relationship between Transcendentalism and the institutional church is William R. Hutchison's *The Transcendentalist Ministers: Church Reform in the New England Renaissance* (1959). Much biographical material about Unitarian ministers can be gleaned from Samuel A. Eliot's *Heralds of a Liberal Faith* (4 volumes, 1910–52), despite some inaccuracies and laudatory comments. The best modern biography of William Ellery Channing is *Channing, The Reluctant Radical* (1971) by Jack Mendelsohn. It especially chronicles Channing's struggle to become a reformer. In 1989 Conrad Edick Wright (son of C. Conrad) edited a group of essays that had been given at a conference on Unitarianism at the Massachusetts Historical Society. This work, *American Unitarianism: 1805–1865* (1989), is a treasure trove of recent scholarship. A good brief overview with an invaluable section of biographies is David Robinson's *The Unitarians and the Universalists* (1985), and the best introduction to the living religion is *A Chosen Faith: An Introduction to Unitarian Universalism* (revised 1998) by John A. Buehrens and Forrest Church.

Scholars of Unitarian or Universalist history must almost always first concentrate their primary research at the Andover Harvard Library of the Harvard Divinity School. Here one will find the library of the Universalist Historical Society, once housed at Tufts University, the collection of the American Unitarian Association, formerly archived at the 25 Beacon Street headquarters, along with the AUA Letter Books, an invaluable resource of correspondence between secretaries of the AUA and congregations all over the country. This library also houses records of many individual congregations, affiliate groups such as the Unitarian Universalist Service Committee, and important Unitarian and Universalist ministers and leaders. There are also materials at Harvard in the Hollis, Houghton, Pusey, and Schlesinger libraries. Certain congregations and some important individuals such as Charles Chauncy, William Ellery Channing, and Henry Ware have records or manuscript items at the Massachusetts Historical Society in Boston. The Unitarian Universalist Association has given most of its important records to Harvard Divinity School, but it still maintains an archive of church files, although the deceased minister files are now at Harvard. The two Unitarian Universalist seminaries, Meadville Lombard in Chicago and Starr King in Berkeley, both maintain collections. Meadville has material about the westward expansion of Unitarianism, and Starr King has a fascinating collection of Radical Reformation materials collected by Earle Morse Wilbur.

There are a number of important Web sites, and more are being created all the time. The most significant is the Dictionary of Unitarian Universalist Biography sponsored by the Unitarian Universalist Historical Society, edited by Peter Hughes, and found with a link through the UUA (uua.org/uuhs/duub). Current material on programs and literature of the UUA, including all of the UUA pamphlets, can be accessed through www.uua.org. Both the seminaries maintain Web sites that feature important pertinent sections. Starr King (www.sksm.edu) has a

Universalist site and also has Earle Morse Wilbur's book *Our Unitarian Heritage* available online. Meadville Lombard (meadville.edu) has it own online journal, *Journal of Liberal Religion*. Finally, the First Parish of Cambridge, Massachusetts, has developed a series of biographies of Notable American Unitarians and can be found at www.harvardsquarelibrary.org/unitarians. Other Web sites to note include the Unitarian Universalist Women's Heritage society (www.uuwhs.org) and the General Assembly of Unitarian and Free Christian Churches in the United Kingdom (www.unitarian.org.uk).

CONTENTS

I. PERIODICALS AND YEARBOOKS

American Journal of Theology and Philosophy
Journal of Liberal Religion—online from Meadville Lombard Theological School
Journal of the Liberal Ministry
Journal of Unitarian Universalist History
Journal of the Universalist Historical Society
Liberal Religious Education
Proceedings of the Unitarian Historical Society
Proceedings of the Unitarian Universalist Historical Society
Religious Humanism—published by Friends of Religious Humanism
Transactions of the Unitarian Historical Society (United Kingdom)
Unitarian Universalist Association Directory

Unitarian Universalism: Selected Essays
The Unitarian Universalist Christian
Unitarian Universalist World
Universalist Herald
Zygon: Journal of Religion and Science

II. PUBLISHED PRIMARY SOURCES

Adams, Henry. *The Education of Henry Adams: An Autobiography*. Vol. 1 Boston: Houghton Mifflin, 1946.

Ahlstrom, Sidney E. and Jonathan S. Carey, eds. *An American Reformation: A Documentary History of Unitarian Christianity.* Middletown, Conn.: Wesleyan University Press, 1985.

Albanese, Catherine L., ed. *The Spirituality of the American Transcendentalists: Selected Writings of Ralph Waldo Emerson, Amos Bronson Alcott, Theodore Parker, and Henry David Thoreau.* Macon, Ga.: Mercer University Press, 1988.

Alcott, Louisa May. *Transcendental Wild Oats*. Harvard, Mass.: Harvard Common, 1975. First published in 1873.

Ballou, Hosea. *A Treatise on Atonement*. Boston: Skinner House, 1986. Reprint of 1886 edition with a new introduction by Ernest Cassara. First published in 1805.

Butterfield, L. H., Marc Friedlaender, and Mary-Jo Kline, eds. *The Book of Abigail and John: Selected Letters of the Adams Family, 1762–1784.* Boston: Northeastern University Press, 2002.

Cassara, Ernest, ed. *Universalism in America: A Documentary History of a Liberal Faith*. Boston: Skinner House, 1997.

Channing, William Ellery. *The Works of William E. Channing, D.D.* Boston: American Unitarian Association, 1875.

Clarke, James Freeman. *Ten Great Religions: An Essay in Comparative Theology*. Boston: James R. Osgood, 1871.

Commager, Henry Steele, ed. *Theodore Parker, An Anthology.* Boston: Beacon, 1960.

De Benneville, George. "The Life and Trance of George De Benneville" in *The Annual Journal of the Universalist Historical Society* II (1960–61), 71–87.

Emerson, Ralph Waldo. *The Complete Works of Ralph Waldo Emerson, introduced by Edward Waldo Emerson.* 12 volumes. Boston and New York: Houghton Mifflin, 1876, 1883, 1884, 1903.

Fuller, S. Margaret. *Woman in the Nineteenth Century*. Columbia: University of South Carolina, 1980.

Greene, Dana, ed. *Suffrage and Religious Principle: Speeches and Writings of Olympia Brown.* Metuchen, N.J.: Scarecrow, 1983.

Hedge, Frederic Henry. *Reason in Religion*. Boston: American Unitarian Association, 1865.

Hochfield, George, ed. *Selected Writings of the American Transcendentalists*. New York: Signet Classic, 1966.

Howe, Charles, ed. *Clarence R. Skinner: Prophet of a New Universalism*. Boston: Skinner House, 1999.

Jefferson, Thomas. *The Jefferson Bible*. Boston: Beacon, 1989. First published in 1819. Introduced by Forrest Church.

Karcher, Carolyn L., ed. *A Lydia Maria Child Reader.* Durham, N.C.: Duke University Press, 1997.

Koch, Adrienne, and William Peden, eds. *The Life and Selected Writings of Thomas Jefferson.* New York: The Modern Library, 1944.

Livermore, Mary Ashton Rice. *The Story of My Life*. Hartford, Conn.: A.D. Worthington, 1899.

Meltzer, Milton, and Patricia G. Holland, eds. *Lydia Maria Child: Selected Letters, 1817–1880*. Amherst: University of Massachusetts Press, 1982.

Meyer, Howard N., ed. *The Magnificent Activist: The Writings of Thomas Wentworth Higginson, 1823–1911*. New York: Da Capo, 2000.

Miller, Perry, ed. *Margaret Fuller: American Romantic*. Ithaca, N.Y.: Cornell University Press, 1963.

———. *The Transcendentalists*. Cambridge, Mass.: Harvard University Press, 1950.

Murray, Judith Sargent. *Judith Sargent Murray: Her First 100 Letters*. Introduced and transcribed by Marianne Dunlop. Gloucester, Mass.: The Sargent House Museum, 1995.

Parke, David, ed. *The Epic of Unitarianism*. Boston: Beacon, 1957.

Passmore, John A., ed. *Priestley's Writings on Philosophy, Science and Politics*. New York: Collier, 1965.

Priestley, Joseph. *The Memoirs of Joseph Priestley* (abridged from 1806 edition). Washington, D.C.: Barcroft, 1964.

Reese, Curtis W. *The Meaning of Humanism*. Boston: Beacon, 1945.

Robinson, David, ed. *William Ellery Channing: Selected Writings*. New York: Paulist, 1985.

Skinner, Clarence Russell. *A Religion for Greatness.* Boston: Universalist Publishing House, 1945.

———. *The Social Implications of Universalism*. Boston: Universalist Publishing House, 1915.

Smith, Bonnie Hurd, ed. *From Gloucester to Philadelphia in 1790: Observations, Anecdotes, and Thoughts from the 18th Century Letters of Judith Sargent Murray*. Cambridge, Mass.: Judith Sargent Murray Society, 1998.

Stacy, Nathaniel. *Memoirs of the Life of Nathaniel Stacy: Preacher of the Gospel of Universal Grace.* Columbus, Pa.: Abner Vedder, 1850.

Stiernotte, Alfred P., ed. *Frederick May Eliot: An Anthology*. Boston: Beacon, 1959.

Voss, Carl Herman, ed. *A Summons unto Men: An Anthology of the Writings of John Haynes Holmes*. New York: Simon and Schuster, 1971.

Ware, Henry Jr. "On the Formation of the Christian Character" (orig. pub. 1831), in *The Unitarian Universalist Christian*, Vol. 43, No. 2 (Summer, 1988).

Willis, Gwendolen B., ed. "Olympia Brown, An Autobiography" in *Journal of the Universalist Historical Society*, Vol. IV (1963).

Wright, Conrad, ed. *Three Prophets of Religious Liberalism: Channing, Emerson, Parker.* Boston: Skinner House, 1996. 2nd edition.

III. BIOGRAPHY

Adams, James Luther. *Not without Dust and Heat: A Memoir*. Chicago: Exploration Press of the Chicago Theological Seminary, 1995.

Ahlstrom, Sidney and Robert Bruce Mullin. *The Scientific Theist: A Life of Francis Ellingwood Abbot*. Macon, Ga.: Mercer University Press, 1987.

Akers, Charles W. *Called unto Liberty: A Life of Jonathan Mayhew, 1720–1766*. Cambridge, Mass.: Harvard University Press, 1964.

Arvin, Newton. *Longfellow: His Life and Work*. Boston: Little, Brown and Company, 1963.

Axel, Larry E. and W. Creighton Peden, eds. "Biographies in Liberal Religious Scholarship" in *American Journal of Theology and Philosophy* VII, 2 (1986), 59–114.

Bainton, Roland H. *Hunted Heretic: The Life and Death of Michael Servetus, 1511–1553*. Boston: Beacon, 1960.

Baker, Carlos. *Emerson among the Eccentrics: A Group Portrait*. New York: Viking, 1996.

Baker, Liva. *The Justice from Beacon Hill: The Life and Times of Oliver Wendell Holmes*. New York: HarperCollins, 1991.

Barber-Braun, Sarah. "The Public Platform, Congregational Wisdom, and The Pulpit: Celia Burleigh's Call to Ordination, 1871" in *Unitarian Universalism: Unitarian Universalist Ministers Association Selected Essays 2000* (2000), 53–66.

Bedell, Madelon. *The Alcotts: Biography of a Family*. New York: Clarkson N. Potter, 1980.

Bemis, Samuel Flagg. *John Quincy Adams and the Union*. New York: Alfred A. Knopf, 1956.

Blanchard, Paula. *Margaret Fuller: From Transcendentalism to Revolution*. Reading, Mass.: Addison-Wesley, 1987.

Bolster, Arthur S. Jr. *James Freeman Clarke: Disciple to Advancing Truth*. Boston: Beacon, 1954.

Boorstin, Daniel. *The Lost World of Thomas Jefferson*. Boston: Beacon, 1960.

Brown, Thomas J. *Dorothea Dix: New England Reformer*. Cambridge, Mass.: Harvard University Press, 1998.

Capper, Charles. *Margaret Fuller: An American Romantic Life: The Private Years*. New York: Oxford University Press, 1992.

Caruthers, J. Wade. *Octavius Brooks Frothingham: Gentle Radical*. Montgomery: University of Alabama Press, 1977.

Cassara, Ernest. *Hosea Ballou: The Challenge to Orthodoxy*. Boston: Beacon, 1961.

Caswell, Jerry V. "A New Civilization Radically Higher than the Old: Adin Ballou's Search for Social Perfection" in *Journal of the Universalist Historical Society* VII (1967–1968), 70–96.

Clifford, Deborah Pickman. *Crusader for Freedom: A Life of Lydia Maria Child*. Boston: Beacon, 1992.

——. *Mine Eyes Have Seen the Glory: A Biography of Julia Ward Howe*. Boston: Little, Brown and Company, 1978.

Cole, Alfred S. *Clarence Skinner: Prophet of Twentieth Century Universalism*. Boston: Universalist Publishing House, 1956.

Cole, Phyllis. *Mary Moody Emerson and the Origins of Transcendentalism*. New York: Oxford University Press, 1998.

Commager, Henry Steele. *Theodore Parker*. Boston: Beacon, 1947.

Cory, David Munroe. *Faustus Socinus*. Boston: Beacon, 1932.

Cote, Charlotte. *Olympia Brown: The Battle for Equality*. Racine, Wis.: Mother Courage, 1988.

Crompton, Arnold. *Aurelia Henry Reinhardt: A Biographical Sketch*. Berkeley, Calif.: Starr King School, 1977.

——. *Thomas Starr King: Apostle of Liberty*. Boston: Beacon, 1950.

Crowe, Charles. *George Ripley, Transcendentalist and Utopian Socialist*. Athens: University of Georgia Press, 1967.

Davis, Allen F. *American Heroine: The Life and Legend of Jane Addams*. New York: Oxford University Press, 1973.

Delbanco, Andrew. *William Ellery Channing: An Essay on the Liberal Spirit in America*. Cambridge, Mass: Harvard University Press, 1981.

Dickerson, Dennis C. *Militant Mediator: Whitney M. Young, Jr*. Lexington: University of Kentucky, 1998.

Duberman, Martin. *James Russell Lowell*. Boston: Houghton Mifflin, 1966.

Edelstein, Tilden G. *Strange Enthusiasm: A Life of Thomas Wentworth Higginson*. New York: Atheneum, 1970.

Eliot, Samuel Atkins, ed. *Heralds of a Liberal Faith*. 4 volumes. Boston: American Unitarian Association, 1910–52.

Freeberg, Ernest. *The Education of Laura Bridgman*. Cambridge, Mass.: Harvard University Press, 2001.

Fritchman, Stephen H. *Heretic: A Partisan Autobiography*. Boston: Skinner House, 1977.

Frothingham, Richard. "John H. Dietrich: From Humanism to Theism" in *The Unitarian Universalist Christian* Vol. 42, no. 1 (1987), 25–34.

Gannett, William C., *Ezra Stiles Gannett: Unitarian Minister in Boston 1824–1871*. Boston: Roberts Brothers, 1875.

Gollaher, David. *Voice for the Mad: A Life of Dorothea Dix*. New York: Free Press, 1995.

Goodwin, Joan W. *The Remarkable Mrs. Ripley: The Life of Sarah Alden Bradford Ripley*. Boston: Northeastern University Press, 1998.

Grady, Charles W. "High Churchman in a Low Church: Frederic Henry Hedge's Vision of the Liberal Church" in *The Proceedings of the Unitarian Universalist Historical Society*, XXI, part I (1987–88), 1–12.

Graham, Thomas E. "Jenkin Lloyd Jones and the Western Unitarian Conference, 1880–1884" in *The Proceedings of the Unitarian Universalist Historical Society*, XXI, part II (1989), 49–70.

Griffin, Edward M. *Old Brick: Charles Chauncy of Boston, 1705–1787*. Minneapolis: University of Minnesota, 1980.

Grodzins, Dean. *American Heretic: Theodore Parker and Transcendentalism*. Chapel Hill: University of North Carolina Press, 2002.

Hale, Edward Everett Jr. *The Life and Letters of Edward Everett Hale*. 2 vols. Boston: Little, Brown, 1917.

Hathaway, Richard D. *Sylvester Judd's New England*. University Park: Pennsylvania State University, 1981.

Hawke, David Freeman. *Paine*. New York: Harper and Row, 1974.

Henry, Richard. *Norbert Fabian Capek: A Spiritual Journey*. Boston: Skinner House, Unitarian Universalist Association, 1999.

Hersey, Laura S. "By Their Works . . ." in *Biographical Sketches of Universalist Women*. Boston: The Association of Universalist Women, 1963.

Hitchings, Catherine F. "Universalist and Unitarian Women Ministers" in *Journal of the Universalist Historical Society* Vol. X, 1975.

Holst, Mary-Ella. "An Exploration of the Friendship of Elizabeth Cady Stanton and Susan B. Anthony." Boston: Unitarian Universalist Historical Society, 1987.

Holt, Earl. *William Greenleaf Eliot, Conservative Radical*. St. Louis, Mo.: First Unitarian Church, 1985. (Minns Lectures)

Howlett, Duncan. *No Greater Love: The James Reeb Story*. Boston: Skinner House, 1993.

Hoyt, Edwin P. *Horatio's Boys: The Life and Works of Horatio Alger, Jr*. New York: Stein and Day, 1974.

Hughes, Peter. "A Different Treatise on Atonement: The Theology of Paul Dean" in *The Unitarian Universalist Christian* 49, Nos. 1–2, 86–103.

Hunter, Edith F. *Sophia Lyon Fahs: A Biography*. Boston: Beacon, 1966.

Jacobs, Wilbur R. *Francis Parkman: Historian as Hero*. Austin: University of Texas Press, 1991.

Jellison, Charles. *Ethan Allen: Frontier Rebel*. Syracuse, N.Y.: Syracuse University Press, 1969.

Johnson, Edgar. *Charles Dickens: His Tragedy and Triumph*. New York: Simon and Schuster, 1952.

Johnston, Christine I. M. *Father of Canadian Psychiatry: Joseph Workman (1805–1894)*. Victoria, B.C.: Ogden Press, 2000.

Karcher, Carolyn L. *The First Woman in the Republic: A Cultural Biography of Lydia Maria Child*. Durham, N.C.: Duke University Press, 1994.

Kendrick, Stephen. *A Faith People Make: Illustrated Unitarian Universalist Lives*. Boston: Unitarian Universalist Denominational Grants Panel, 1988.

Kirker, Harold. *The Architecture of Charles Bulfinch*. Cambridge, Mass.: Harvard University Press, 1969.

Kring, Walter Donald. *Henry Whitney Bellows*. Boston: Skinner House, 1979.

——. *Herman Melville's Religious Journey*. Raleigh, N.C.: Pentland, 1997.

LaPorte, George H. "Francis Greenwood Peabody on the Individual, the Church, and Society" in *The Unitarian Universalist Christian* Vol. 28, No. 1 (1973), 50–59.

Levin, Phyllis Lee. *Abigail Adams: A Biography*. New York: St. Martin's, 1987.

Lippy, Charles H. *Seasonable Revolutionary: The Mind of Charles Chauncy*. Chicago: Nelson-Hall, 1981.

Lutz, Alma. *Susan B. Anthony: Rebel, Crusader, Humanitarian*. Boston: Beacon, 1959.

Malone, Dumas. *Jefferson and His Time*. 6 volumes. Boston: Little Brown, 1948.

Marshall, George N. *A. Powell Davies and His Times*. Boston: Skinner House, 1990.

McGehee, Charles White. "Elhanan Winchester: A Decision for Universal Restoration" in *Journal of the Universalist Historical Society* I (1959), 43–58.

——. "Minot Judson Savage: Rebuilder of Faith" in *The Proceedings of the Unitarian Historical Society*, XIII, part II (1961), 25–44.

McGiffert, Arthur Cushman Jr. *Pilot of a Liberal Faith: Samuel Atkins Eliot, 1862–1950*. Boston: Skinner House, 1976.

Mendelsohn, Jack. *Channing: The Reluctant Radical*. Boston: Little Brown, 1971.

Messerli, Jonathan. *Horace Mann: A Biography*. New York: Alfred A. Knopf, 1972.

Miller, Edwin Haviland. *Salem Is My Dwelling Place: A Life of Nathaniel Hawthorne*. Iowa City: University of Iowa Press, 1991.

Monzingo, Thomas. *Thomas Starr King: Eminent Californian, Civil War Statesman, Unitarian Minister*. Pacific Grove, Calif.: Boxwood, 1991.

Owen-Towle, Thomas. *O. Eugene Pickett: Borne on a Wintry Wind*. Boston: Skinner House, 1996.

Papa, Stephan. *The Last Man Jailed for Blasphemy*. Boston: Skinner House, 2000.

Pringle, Henry F. *The Life and Times of William Howard Taft*. 2 vols. New York: Farrar & Rinehart, 1939.

Pryor, Elizabeth Brown. *Clara Barton: Professional Angel*. Philadelphia: University of Pennsylvania Press, 1987.

Randall, Mercedes M. *Improper Bostonian: Emily Greene Balch*. New York: Twayne, 1964.

Richardson, Robert D. Jr. *Emerson: The Mind on Fire.* Berkeley: University of California Press, 1995.

——. *Henry David Thoreau: A Life of the Mind*. Berkeley: University of California Press, 1986.

Robinson, David. *Apostle of Culture: Emerson as Preacher and Lecturer*. Philadelphia: University of Pennsylvania Press, 1982.

——. "Thomas Lamb Eliot and the Unitarian Experience in Oregon" in *The Proceedings of the Unitarian Universalist Historical Society*, XXI, part II (1989), 71–79.

Robinson-Lorant, Laurie. *Melville: A Biography*. New York: Clarkson Potter, 1996.

Ronda, Bruce A. *Elizabeth Palmer Peabody: A Reformer on Her Own Terms*. Cambridge, Mass.: Harvard University Press, 1999.

Rowley, Charity, ed. "Fahs and MacLean: A Living Heritage" in *Liberal Religious Education* 4 (1990) 1–86.

Saxon, A. H. *P. T. Barnum: The Legend and the Man*. New York: Columbia University Press, 1989.

Saxton, Martha. *Louisa May: A Modern Biography of Louisa May Alcott*. New York: Avon, 1978.

Schlesinger, Arthur M. Jr. *A Pilgrim's Progress: Orestes A. Brownson*. Boston: Little Brown, 1966. (orig pub. 1939)

Schwartz, A. Truman and John G. McEvoy, eds. *Motion toward Perfection: The Achievement of Joseph Priestley*. Boston: Skinner House Books, 1990.

Schwartz, Harold. *Samuel Gridley Howe: Social Reformer, 1801–1876*. Cambridge, Mass.: Harvard University Press, 1956.

Sears, Stanley F. "The Contribution of John Haynes Holmes to Unitarian Universalism" in *Selected Essays: Unitarian Universalist Ministers Association* (1992).

Secrest, Meryle. *Frank Lloyd Wright*. New York: Alfred A. Knopf, 1992.

Seitz, Don C. *Horace Greeley: Founder of the* New York Tribune. Indianapolis, Ind.: Bobbs-Merrill, 1926.

Skinner, Clarence R. and Alfred S. Cole. *Hell's Ramparts Fell: The Life of John Murray*. Boston: Universalist Publishing House, 1941.

Smith, Ethel Sabin. *Aurelia Henry Reinhardt: She Turned Dreams into Reality*. Berkeley, Calif.: Starr King School, 1977.

Smith, Harmon. *My Friend, My Friend: The Story of Thoreau's Relationship with Emerson*. Amherst, Mass.: University of Massachusetts Press, 1999.

Smith, Page. *John Adams*. 2 vols. Garden City, N.Y.: Doubleday: 1962.

Sprague, William B. *Annals of the American Unitarian Pulpit*. New York: Robert Carter and Brothers, 1865.

Tharp, Louise Hall. *The Peabody Sisters of Salem*. Boston: Little Brown, 1950.

Tomalin, Claire. *The Life and Death of Mary Wollstonecraft*. New York: Harcourt, Brace, Jovanovich, 1974.

Tucker, Cynthia Grant. *A Woman's Ministry: Mary Collson's Search for Reform*. Philadelphia: Temple University Press, 1984.

Uglow, Jenny. *The Lunar Men: Five Friends Whose Curiosity Changed the World*. New York: Farrar, Straus & Giroux, 2002.

von Mehren, Joan. *Minerva and the Muse: A Life of Margaret Fuller.* Boston: University of Massachusetts Press, 1994.

Wach, Howard M. "A Boston Feminist in the Victorian Public Sphere: The Social Criticism of Caroline Healey Dall" in *New England Quarterly* 68 (September 1995): 429–450.

Warner, Samuel Bass Jr. *Province of Reason*. Cambridge and London: Harvard University Press, 1984.

Webb, Theodore. *Seven Sons: Millionaires and Vagabonds*. Victoria, B.C.: Trafford, 1999.

Wesley, Alice Blair, ed. *Odysseys: The Lives of Sixteen Unitarian Universalist Ministers*. Boston: Unitarian Universalist Ministers Association, 1992.

Whittemore, Thomas. *The Early Days of Thomas Whittemore: An Autobiography*. Boston: James M. Usher, 1859.

Wilder, Sarah. *Anna Tilden: Unitarian Culture and the Problem of Self Representation*. Athens, Ga.: University of Georgia Press, 1997.

Williams, George Huntston. *Rethinking the Unitarian Relationship with Protestantism: An Examination of the Thought of Frederic Henry Hedge*. Boston: Beacon, 1949.

——. "Wilbur's Vision: Freedom, Reason and Tolerance Reglimpsed" in *The Unitarian Universalist Christian* 51 and 52 (1996–1997), 178–197.

Willis, Gwendolen B., ed. "Olympia Brown: An Autobiography" in *Journal of the Universalist Historical Society* IV (1963), 1–92.

Wilson, Robert J. III. *The Benevolent Deity: Ebenezer Gay and the Rise of Rational Religion in New England, 1696–1787*. Philadelphia: University of Pennsylvania Press, 1984.

Yacovone, Donald. *Samuel Joseph May and the Dilemmas of the Liberal Persuasion, 1797–1871*. Philadelphia: Temple University Press, 1991.

IV. HISTORIES

A. General

Allen, Joseph Henry. *An Historical Sketch of the Unitarian Movement since the Reformation*. New York: The Christian Literature Co., 1894.

Bressler, Ann Lee. *The Universalist Movement in America, 1770–1880*. New York: Oxford University Press, 2001.

Bumbaugh, David. *Unitarian Universalism: A Narrative History*. Chicago: Meadville Lombard, 2000.

Comins, Sara. *In Unbroken Line: History of the Alliance, 1880–1955*. Boston: The General Alliance of Unitarian and Other Liberal Christian Women, 1955.

Conkin, Paul K. *American Originals: Homemade Varieties of Christianity*. Chapel Hill: University of North Carolina Press, 1997.

Cooke, George Willis. *Unitarianism in America*. New York: AMS Press, 1971 reprint of 1902 edition.

Eddy, Richard. *Universalism in America*. 2 vols. Boston: Universalist Publishing House, 1884–86.

Emerson, Dorothy May, ed. *Standing Before Us: Unitarian Universalist Women and Social Reform, 1776–1936*. Boston: Skinner House, 1999.

Folsom, Ida M. "Work of Universalist Women, 1869 to 1955." Boston: Association of Universalist Women, 1955.

Hill, Andrew. "A Liberal Religious Heritage: Unitarian & Universalist Foundations in Europe, America & Elsewhere." London: Unitarian Publications, n.d.

Howe, Charles A. *The Larger Faith: A Short History of American Universalism*. Boston: Skinner House, 1993.

Johnson, David. *Sixteen Unitarian and Universalist Issues*. Boston: Unitarian Universalist Association, 1975.

Kaufman, Peter Iver and Spencer Lavan, eds. *Along Together: Studies in the History of Liberal Religion*. Boston: Skinner House, 1978.

Lalone, Emerson Hugh. *And Thy Neighbor as Thyself: A Story of Universalist Social Action*. Boston: Universalist Publishing House, 1939.

Miller, Russell E. *The Larger Hope*. 2 vols. *The First Century of the Universalist Church in America*. Boston: Unitarian Universalist Association, 1979.

——. *The Second Century of the Universalist Church in America*. Boston: Unitarian Universalist Association, 1985.

Murdock, Virgil E. "The Institutional History of the American Unitarian Association." Boston: Minns Lectures, 1975–76.

Navias, Eugene B. *Singing Our History: Tales, Texts and Tunes from Two Centuries of Unitarian and Universalist Hymns*. Boston: Unitarian Universalist Association, 1975.

Richardson, Robert D. *125 Years of Unitarian Sunday Schools*. Boston: Unitarian Sunday School Society, 1952.

Robinson, David. *The Unitarians and the Universalists*. Westport, Conn.: Greenwood, 1985.

Robinson, Elmo Arnold. *American Universalism: Its Origins, Organization and Heritage*. New York: Exposition, 1970.

Scott, Clinton Lee. *The Universalist Church of America: A Short History*. Boston: Universalist Historical Society, 1957.

Whittemore, Thomas. *The Modern History of Universalism*. Boston: Thomas Whittemore, 1830.

Wilbur, Earle Morse. *A History of Unitarianism*. 2 volumes. *Socinianism and Its Antecedents*. Cambridge, Mass.: Harvard University Press, 1945. *In Transylvania, England, and America*. Cambridge, Mass.: Harvard University Press, 1952.

Wilbur, Earle Morse. *Our Unitarian Heritage*. Boston: Beacon, 1925.

Williams, George Huntston. *American Universalism*. Boston: Beacon, 1976. Reprint of Vol IX, *Journal of the Universalist Historical Society*, 1971.

——. ed. *Harvard Divinity School*. Boston: Beacon, 1954.

Wintersteen, Prescott B. *Christology in American Unitarianism*. Boston: Unitarian Universalist Christian Fellowship, 1977.

Wright, Conrad, ed. *A Stream of Light: A Sesquicentennial History of American Unitarianism*. Boston: Unitarian Universalist Association, 1975.

——. *Congregational Polity: A Historical Survey of Unitarian and Universalist Practice*. Boston: Skinner House, 1997.

——. *The Liberal Christians*. Boston: Beacon, 1970.

——. *Walking Together: Polity and Participation in UU Churches*. Boston: Unitarian Universalist Historical Society, 1998.

B. Canadian, European, and Asian

Barr, Margaret. *A Dream Come True: The Story of Kharang*. London: Lindsey, 1974.

Bolam, C. G., Jeremy Goring, H. L. Short, and Roger Thomas. *The English Presbyterians from Elizabethan Puritanism to Modern Unitarianism*. London: George Allen and Unwin, 1968.

Darling, Edward. *400 Years*. Minneapolis: First Unitarian Society, 1968.

Erdo, John (trans. by Judit Gellerd). *Transylvanian Unitarian Church*. Chico, Calif.: Center for Free Religion, 1990.

Ferencz, Joseph. *Hungarian Unitarianism in the Nineteenth and Twentieth Centuries*. Chico, Calif.: Center for Free Religion, 1990.

Gellerd, Judit, ed. *In Storm, Even Trees Lean on Each Other: UU Sermons on Transylvania*. Chico, Calif.: Center for Free Religion, 1993.

Gleadle, Kathryn. *The Early Feminists: Radical Unitarians and the Emergence of the Women's Rights Movement 1831–1851*. New York: St. Martin's, 1995.

Gordon, Alexander. *Heads of Unitarian History*. London: Redwood, 1970. First published in 1895.

Goring, Jeremy and Rosemary. *The Unitarians*. Oxford: Pergamon, 1984.

Hague, Graham and Judy (text). *The Unitarian Heritage: An Architectural Survey*. Sheffield, England: P. B. Godfrey, 1986.

Hewett, Philip. "A Faith Transplanted: The Unitarian Experience in Canada, Australia and New Zealand," in *Transactions of the Unitarian Historical Society*, XXII, No. 1, (April 1999).

——. *Racovia: The Unitarian Search for Community in Sixteenth Century Poland*. Boston: Minns Lectureship Committee, 1972.

——. *Unitarians in Canada*. Toronto: Fitzhenry and Whiteside, 1978.

Holt, Raymond V. *The Unitarian Contribution to Social Progress in England*. London: Lindsey, 1938. Rev. 1952.

Howe, Charles A. *For Faith and Freedom: A Short History of Unitarianism in Europe*. Boston: Skinner House Books, 1997.

Kot, Stanislas. *Socinianism in Poland*. Boston: Starr King, 1957.

Kucheman, Clark. "John Goodwin and John Biddle: Rational Theology and the Transformation of Puritanism" in *The Proceedings of the Unitarian Historical Society*, XIII, part II (1961), 62–74.

Lavan, Spencer. *Unitarians and India: A Study in Encounter and Response*. Boston: Beacon, 1977.

Muir, Frederic John. *Maglipay Universalist: A History of the Unitarian Universalist Church of the Philippines*. Annapolis, Md.: Unitarian Universalist Church of Annapolis, 2001.

Ruston, Alan, ed. "James Martineau: A Retrospect." *Transactions of the Unitarian Historical Society* XXII, No. 4 (2002), 321–408.

Schulman, Frank. *"Blasphemous and Wicked"* in *The Unitarian Struggle for Equality*. Oxford: Harris Manchester College, 1997.

Seaburg, Carl. *Dojin Means All People: The Universalist Mission to Japan, 1890-1942*. Boston: Universalist Historical Society, 1978.

Tarrant, W. G. *The Story and Significance of the Unitarian Movement*. London: Lindsey, 1910.

Varga, Bela. *Francis David: What Has Endured of His Life and Work?* Budapest: Hungarian Unitarian Church, 1981 (translated by Vilma Szantho Harrington)

Watts, Ruth. *Gender, Power and the Unitarians in England: 1760-1860*. Women and Men in History Series. New York: Addison Wesley Longman, 1998.

Williams, George H. *The Polish Brethren: Documentation of the History and Thought of Unitarianism in the Polish-Lithuanian Commonwealth and in the Diaspora, 1601-1685*. Missoula, Mont.: Scholars, 1980 (published as Vol. XVIII, parts 1 and 2, 1976–77 of the Proceedings of the Unitarian Historical Society).

Williams, George H. *The Radical Reformation.* Philadelphia: Westminster, 1962.

Zweig, Stefan. *The Right to Heresy: Castellio against Calvin*. Boston: Beacon, 1951.

C. Early American, Colonial, and Early Republic

Brooks, Van Wyck. *The Flowering of New England*. New York: E. P. Dutton, 1936, 1952.

Douglas, Ann. *The Feminization of American Culture*. New York: Alfred A. Knopf, 1977.

Frothingham, Octavius Brooks. *Boston Unitarianism 1820–1850: A Study of the Life and Work of Nathaniel Langdon Frothingham.* New York: G. P. Putnam's Sons, 1890.

Gausted, Edwin Scott. *The Great Awakening in New England*. Chicago: Quadrangle, 1968.

Haroutunian, Joseph. *Piety Versus Moralism: The Passing of the New England Theology*. New York: Harper Torchbook, 1970.

Harris, Mark W. *Among the Dry Bones: Liberal Religion in New Salem, Massachusetts*. Springfield, Mass.: Connecticut Valley District, Unitarian Universalist Association, 1981.

Heimert, Alan. *Religion and the American Mind: From the Great Awakening to the Revolution*. Cambridge, Mass.: Harvard University Press, 1966.

Howe, Charles, ed. *"Not Hell, But Hope"* (The John Murray Distinguished Lectures 1987–1991) Lanoka Harbor, N.J.: Murray Grove Association, 1991.

Howe, Daniel Walker. *The Unitarian Conscience: Harvard Moral Philosophy 1805–1861*. Cambridge, Mass.: Harvard University Press, 1970.

Koch, G. Adolf. *Religion of the American Enlightenment*. New York: Thomas Y. Crowell Co., 1968. First published in 1933 as *Republican Religion*.

Kring, Walter Donald. *Liberals among the Orthodox. Unitarian Beginnings in New York City, 1819–1839*. Boston: Beacon, 1974.

McLoughlin, William G. *New England Dissent, 1630-1833. The Baptists and the Separation of Church and State.* 2 vols. Cambridge, Mass.: Harvard University Press, 1971.

Marini, Stephen A. *Radical Sects of Revolutionary New England*. Cambridge, Mass.: Harvard University Press, 1982.

Stange, Douglas C. *Patterns of Antislavery among American Unitarians, 1831–1860*. Cranbury, N.J.: Associated University Presses, Inc., 1977.

Sykes, Richard Eddy. *Massachusetts Unitarianism and Social Change: A Religious Social System in Transition, 1780–1870*. Ann Arbor, Mich.: University Microfilms, 1968.

Wright, Conrad. *The Beginnings of Unitarianism in America*. Boston: Starr King, 1955.

——. *The Unitarian Controversy*. Boston: Skinner House Books, 1994.

Wright, Conrad Edick, ed. *American Unitarianism 1805–1865*. Boston: Massachusetts Historical Society and Northeastern University Press, 1989.

D. Transcendentalism

Boller, Paul F. Jr. *American Transcendentalism, 1830–1860: An Intellectual Inquiry*. New York: G. P. Putnam's Sons, 1974.

Brooks, Van Wyck. *The Flowering of New England*. New York: E. P. Dutton, 1936.

Buell, Lawrence. *New England Literary Culture*. Cambridge, Mass.: Cambridge University Press, 1986.

Capper, Charles and Conrad Edick Wright, eds. *Transient and Permanent: The Transcendentalist Movement and Its Contexts*. Boston: Massachusetts Historical Society and Northeastern University Press, 1999.

Francis, Richard. *Transcendental Utopias: Individual and Community at Brook Farm, Fruitlands, and Walden.* Ithaca, N.Y.: Cornell University Press, 1997.

Frothingham, Octavius Brooks. *Transcendentalism in New England*. Philadelphia: University of Pennsylvania Press, 1972. First published in 1876.

Grusin, Richard A. *Transcendentalist Hermeneutics: Institutional Authority and the Higher Criticism of the Bible*. Durham, N.C.: Duke University Press, 1991.

Gura, Philip F. *The Wisdom of Words: Language, Theology, and Literature in the New England Renaissance*. Middletown, Conn.: Wesleyan University Press, 1981.

Hutchison, William R. *The Transcendentalist Ministers*. Boston: Beacon, 1965.

Miller, Perry. *Nature's Nation*. Cambridge, Mass.: Harvard University Press, 1967.

Myerson, Joel. *New England Transcendentalists and the Dial*. Rutherford, N.J.: Farleigh Dickinson University Press, 1980.

Rose, Anne C. *Transcendentalism as a Social Movement, 1830–1850*. New Haven, Conn.: Yale University Press, 1981.

Smith, Timothy L. *Revivalism and Social Reform*. New York: Harper and Row, 1957.

Swift, Lindsay. *Brook Farm*. New York: Corinth, 1961.

E. Late 19th and 20th Centuries

Arnason, Wayne B. *Follow the Gleam: A History of the Liberal Religious Youth Movements*. Boston: Skinner House, 1980.

Bartlett, Laile E. *Bright Galaxy: Ten Years of Unitarian Fellowships*. Boston: Beacon, 1960.

Brooks, Van Wyck. *New England Indian Summer 1865–1915*. New York: E. P. Dutton, 1940.

Carpenter, Victor. "The Black Empowerment Controversy and the Unitarian Universalist Association, 1967–1970." Boston: Minns Lectures, 1983.

Cavicchio, Laura. "CLF, The Church of the Larger Fellowship: Unitarian Universalist Association" (unpublished paper, Andover Newton Theological School, 2002).

Commission of Appraisal. *Unitarians Face a New Age*. Boston: American Unitarian Association, 1936.

Commission on Appraisal. *Belonging: The Meaning of Membership*. Boston: Unitarian Universalist Association, 2001.

——. *A Brief Look at the History of Extension*. Boston: Unitarian Universalist Association, 1978.

——. *Empowerment: One Denomination's Quest for Racial Justice, 1967–1982*. Boston: Unitarian Universalist Association, 1984.

——. *Interdependence: Renewing Congregational Polity*. Boston: Unitarian Universalist Association, 1997.

——. *Our Professional Ministry: Structure, Support and Renewal*. Boston: Unitarian Universalist Association, 1992.

——. "The Unitarian Universalist Merger, 1961–1975." Boston: Unitarian Universalist Association, 1975.

Crompton, Arnold. *Unitarianism on the Pacific Coast: The First Sixty Years*. Boston: Starr King, 1957.

Cummins, Robert. *Excluded: The Story of the Federal Council of Churches and the Universalists*. Boston: Unitarian Universalist Association, 1966.

Di Figlia, Ghanda. *Roots and Visions: The First Fifty Years of the Unitarian Universalist Service Committee*. Boston: Unitarian Universalist Service Committee, 1990.

Free Church in a Changing World. Boston: Unitarian Universalist Association, 1963.

Fritchman, Stephen, ed. *Together We Advance*. Boston: Beacon, 1946.

Greeley, Dana McLean. *25 Beacon Street and Other Recollections*. Boston: Skinner House, 1971.

Hutchison, William R. *The Modernist Impulse in American Protestantism*. Oxford: Oxford University Press, 1982.

Leonard, Richard D. *Call to Selma*. Boston: Skinner House, 2001.

Lyttle, Charles H. *Freedom Moves West: A History of the Western Conference, 1852–1952*. Boston: Beacon, 1952.

Menand, Louis. *The Metaphysical Club: A Story of Ideas in America*. New York: Farrar, Straus & Giroux, 2001.

Morrison-Reed, Mark. *Black Pioneers in a White Denomination*. 3rd ed. Boston: Skinner House, 1994.

Olds, Mason. *American Religious Humanism*. Minneapolis, Minn.: Fellowship of Religious Humanists, 1996. Revised edition of *Three Pioneers of Religious Humanism: Dietrich, Reese and Potter*.

Persons, Stow. *Free Religion*. New Haven, Conn.: Yale University Press, 1947.

Pickett House and Eliot House. Boston: Skinner House, 1989.

Report of the Committee on Goals. Boston: Unitarian Universalist Association, 1967.

Ross, Warren R. *The Premise and the Promise: The Story of the Unitarian Universalist Association.* Boston: Skinner House, 2001.

Schulz, William F. *Making the Manifesto: The Birth of Religious Humanism*. Boston: Skinner House, 2002.

Tucker, Cynthia Grant. *Prophetic Sisterhood: Liberal Women Ministers of the Frontier*. Boston: Beacon, 1990.

Wilson, Edwin. H. *The Genesis of a Humanist Manifesto*. Amherst, N.Y.: Humanist, 1995.

Woods, Gretchen, ed. *Leaping from Our Spheres: The Impact of Women on Unitarian Universalist Ministry.* Boston: Unitarian Universalist Ministers Association Center Committee, 2001.

Zwerling, Philip. *Rituals of Repression*. Los Angeles: First Unitarian Church of Los Angeles (Minns Lectures), 1985.

F. Philosophy and Theology

Adams, James Luther. *On Being Human Religiously*, edited by Max L. Stackhouse. Boston: Beacon, 1976.

——. *Taking Time Seriously*. Glencoe, Ill.: Free Press, 1957.

——. *The Prophethood of All Believers*, edited by George K. Beach. Boston: Beacon, 1986.

——. *Voluntary Associations*, edited by J. Ronald Engel. Chicago: Exploration Press, 1986.

Beach, George K., ed. *The Essential James Luther Adams*. Boston: Skinner House, 1998.

Buehrens, John A., ed. *The Unitarian Universalist Pocket Guide.* 3rd ed. Boston: Skinner House, 1999.

Buehrens, John A. and Forrest Church. *A Chosen Faith*. Boston: Beacon, 1998.

Chryssides, George. *The Elements of Unitarianism*. Boston: Element Books Limited, 1998.

——, ed. *Unitarian Perspectives on Contemporary Religious Thought*. London: Lindsey, 1999.

Church, Forrest. *Bringing God Home*. New York: St. Martin's, 2002.

Davies, A. Powell. *America's Real Religion*. Boston: Beacon, 1949.

Dorrien, Gary. *The Making of American Liberal Theology: Imagining Progressive Religion, 1805–1900*. Louisville, KY: Westminster John Knox, 2001.

Gilbert, Richard S. *The Prophetic Imperative: Unitarian Universalist Foundations for a New Social Gospel*. Boston: Unitarian Universalist Association, 1980.

Greeley, Dana McLean. *Forward Through the Ages: The Writings of the Reverend Dana McLean Greeley, 1970 through 1986*. Concord, Mass.: The First Parish in Concord, 1986.

Hartshorne, Charles. *The Divine Relativity*. New Haven, Conn.: Yale University Press, 1964.

Hewett, Philip. *The Unitarian Way*. Toronto: Canadian Unitarian Council, 1985.

Howlett, Duncan. *The Fourth American Faith*. Boston: Beacon, 1964.

——. *The Critical Way in Religion*. Buffalo, N.Y.: Prometheus, 1980.

Kucheman, Clark, ed. *The Life of Choice: Some Liberal Religious Perspectives on Morality*. Boston: Skinner House, 1978.

Kurtz, Paul, ed. *Humanist Manifestos I and II*. Buffalo, N.Y.: Prometheus, 1973.

MacLean, Angus H. *The Wind in Both Ears*. 2nd ed. Boston: Unitarian Universalist Association, 1987.

McLennan, Scotty. *Finding Your Religion: When the Faith You Grew Up with Has Lost Its Meaning.* New York: Harper San Francisco, 1999.

Marshall, George. *Challenge of a Liberal Faith*. 3rd ed. Boston: Skinner House, 1988.

Mendelsohn, Jack. *Being Liberal in an Illiberal Age: Why I Am a Unitarian Universalist*. Boston: Skinner House, 1995.

Morgan, John C. *The Devotional Heart: Pietism and the Renewal of American Unitarian Universalism*. Boston: Skinner House, 1995.

Parke, David B, ed. *The Right Time: The Best of Kairos*. Boston: Skinner House, 1982.

Richardson, Peter Tufts. *Four Spiritualities: Expressions of Self, Expressions of Spirit*. Palo Alto, Calif.: Davies-Black, 1996.

Ross, Warren H., ed. *Regaining Historical Consciousness*. Berkeley, CA: Starr King School, 1994.

Schulz, William F. *Finding Time and Other Delicacies*. Boston: Skinner House, 1992.

Scott, Clinton Lee. *Religion Can Make Sense*. Boston: Universalist Publishing House, 1949.

Southworth, Bruce. *At Home in Creativity: The Naturalistic Theology of Henry Nelson Wieman*. Boston: Skinner House, 1995.

Turner, James. *Without God, Without Creed: The Origins of Unbelief in America*. Baltimore, Md.: Johns Hopkins University Press, 1985.

Wieman, Henry Nelson. *Man's Ultimate Commitment*. Carbondale, Ill.: University of Southern Illinois Press, 1958.

Wilson, Edwin H. *The Genesis of a Humanist Manifesto*. Amherst, N.Y.: Humanist, 1995.

V. WORSHIP

Commission on Common Worship. "Common Worship: Why and How?" Boston: Unitarian Universalist Association, 1981.

Davies, A Powell. *Without Apology: Collected Meditations on Liberal Religion*, ed. F. Forrester Church. Boston: Skinner House, 1998.

James, Jacqui. *Between the Lines: Sources for Singing the Living Tradition*. Boston: Skinner House, 1995.

Leavens, Robert French. *Great Companions*. 2 volumes. Boston: Beacon, 1941, 1944.

Navias, Eugene B. *Singing Our History*. Boston: Unitarian Universalist Association, 1975.

Pullman, M. *Hymns of the Spirit*. Boston: Beacon Press, 1937.

Rzepka, Jane and Ken Sawyer. *Thematic Preaching: An Introduction*. St. Louis, Mo.: Chalice, 2001.

Seaburg, Carl, ed. *Celebrating Christmas*. Boston: Unitarian Universalist Ministers Association, 1983.

——. *Great Occasions: Readings for the Celebration of Birth, Coming-of-Age, Marriage, and Death*. Boston: Beacon, 1968.

——. *The Communion Book*. Boston: Unitarian Universalist Ministers Association, 1993.

Seaburg, Carl and Mark Harris, eds. *Celebrating Easter and Spring*. Cambridge, Mass.: Anne Miniver, 2000.

Schulz, William F., ed. *Transforming Words: Six Essays on Preaching.* Boston: Skinner House, 1984.

Unitarian Universalist Association. *Hymns for the Celebration of Life*. Boston: Unitarian Universalist Association, 1964.

——. *Singing the Living Tradition*. Boston: Unitarian Universalist Association, 1993.

Vogt, Von Ogden. *Art and Religion*. Boston: Beacon, 1960.

Weston, Robert T. *Worship for a Free Church*. Boston: Minns Lectureship Committee, 1958.

About the Author

Mark W. Harris was born in Winchendon, Massachusetts, in 1951, and grew up in the nearby towns of Orange and New Salem. After graduating from Bates College (Maine) with a B.A. in 1973, he entered graduate school in history at the University of New Hampshire, where he earned an M.A. in 1975. He attended seminary at the Starr King School for the Ministry (California) and received his M.Div. in 1978. He has primarily been a parish minister during his career. His first pastorate was at St. Paul's Universalist Church in Palmer, Massachusetts (1979–1985). Always interested in history, Harris became the Unitarian Universalist Association's Director of Information, the denominational historian and archivist in 1985. After that he served the First Parish in Milton, Massachusetts, from 1989 to 1996, and he presently serves the First Parish of Watertown, Massachusetts, a congregation that dates from 1630. This is a position he first undertook as a copastorate with his wife Andrea Greenwood. Harris has also served brief ministries in Sheffield and London, England. He has taught in the summer at the Northeast Leadership School and has also taught courses in history and congregational polity at Andover Newton Theological School and Starr King School for the Ministry. The author of many denominational pamphlets, including *Unitarian Universalist Origins: Our Historic Faith*, he has also published *Among the Dry Bones* (1983), a history of rural Unitarianism, and coedited *Celebrating Easter: An Anthology of Unitarian Universalist Readings*, with Carl Seaburg. Harris is a past president of the Unitarian Universalist Historical Society. He is the father of four boys: Joel, Levi, Dana, and Asher.